Statistics Europe

Sources for social, economic and market research

Joan M. Harvey, MA, FLA

Edition 5

CBD Research Ltd
15 Wickham Rd, Beckenham, Kent, BR3 2JS, England
01-650 7745

First published 1968

Edition 5 1987

Published by

C.B.D. Research Ltd.
15 Wickham Rd, Beckenham, Kent BR3 2JS, England.
Telephone 01-650 7745.

Member: European Association of Directory Publishers
Adhérent: Association Européenne des Editeurs d'Annuaires
Mitglied: Europäischer Adressbuchverleger Verband

Members: Association of British Directory Publishers.

ISBN 0 900246 48 0

No payment is either solicited or accepted for the inclusion of entries in this publication. Every possible precaution has been taken to ensure that the information it contains is accurate at the time of going to press and the publishers cannot accept any liability for errors or omissions however caused.

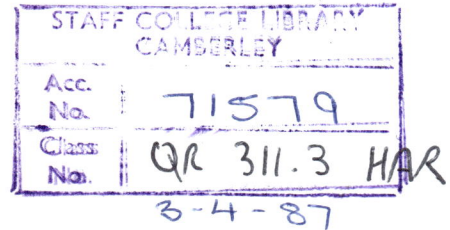

Printed in Great Britain by Unwin Brothers Limited
The Gresham Press, Old Woking, Surrey, England
a member of the Martins Printing Group

CONTENTS

INTRODUCTION

1. This fifth edition of "Statistics - Europe" is a complete revision of the fourth edition published five years ago. In those five years the economic climate has deteriorated in many European countries and this has meant that the governments of some individual countries have had to restrict the number of official documents published and the government departments have been able to offer less assistance than previously, and there appear to be fewer non-official publications issued at present. Many libraries in the United Kingdom have also found it necessary to limit their acquisitions so that locating copies of less-used material has become somewhat more difficult.

Obviously more information is available in some fields than in others; some countries still publish very little, whilst others publish statistics on every conceivable topic, and there may also be considerable duplication of information by two or more organisations. As had been stated before, not all the information collected is published, either because it has been supplied on the understanding that it will be treated as confidential or because it is not considered of sufficient general interest to make publications worth while. In the former case with regard to official publications of EEC countries, 'Confidentiality and business statistics in the European Community', published by the Statistical Office of the European Communities in 1977 (£3.20; $5.40; FrB 200) goes some way to explain the situation in each of the member countries; in the latter case it is frequently possible for enquirers to obtain the information from the organisation which collects it, often in the form of computer printout, although trade and other associations may restrict such a service to their members. The statistical information published by the United Nations, OECD, EEC and other international organisations is generally supplied by the governments of the countries concerned according to the classification of the international organisation and is, therefore, often in a form suitable for national comparisons to be made.

As in earlier editions it has been necessary for the compiler to do a certain amount of selection of items for inclusion. Although considerable effort has been made to examine up-to-date copies of each item included it has not always been possible to locate them; such items have been included, however, with as much information about them as possible, as the mere knowledge of their existence may be valuable to some users of the guide.

Cyprus has been omitted from this edition of "Statistics - Europe", being considered to be more suitable for inclusion in "Statistics - Asia and Australasia" in which it has also appeared.

2. ARRANGEMENT

The main body of the work is by countries arranged alphabetically by international code letters (United Nations Convention on Road Traffic 1968). Each entry, whether for the description of an organisation or of a publication, has been allocated a unique reference number. The list of countries (page xi) indicates the first page number for each country. A section for Europe as a whole precedes the individual countries. Each country section contains:

(1) the name, address and telephone number of the central statistical office of the country; this is followed by some information on the organisation and work of the agency and the facilities it provides;

(2) the principal libraries in the country where collections of statistical material may be consulted by the public;

(3) libraries and information services in other countries (particularly) English-speaking countries) where the country's statistical publications may be consulted;

(4) the principal bibliographies of statistics; only reasonably current bibliographies have been included, and sales lists are mentioned because of the general dearth of special bibliographies in this field; national bibliographies (e.g. the British National Bibliography) are not included, but should not be overlooked as a means of tracing statistical titles;

(5) the statistical publications are arranged in the following standard groups:

Δ A General

Δ B Production
- i. Mines and mining
- ii. Agriculture, fisheries, forestry, etc.
  - (a) Agriculture and horticulture
  - (b) Fisheries
  - (c) Forestry
  - (d) Hunting
- iii. Industry
  - (a) Food products, beverages, tobacco
  - (b) Textiles, paper, rubber, etc
  - (c) Chemicals, pharmaceuticals, etc.
  - (d) Metals, etc.
  - (e) Engineering
  - (f) Other industries
- iv. Construction
- v. Energy
- vi. Research and development

Δ C External trade

[continued next page]

Δ D Internal distribution and service trades
- i. Wholesale and retail trades
- ii. Service trades
- iii. Advertising
- iv. Tourism and travel

Δ E Population
- i. Vital statistics
- ii. Labour
- iii. Housing

Δ F Social and political
- i. Standard of living
- ii. Health and welfare
- iii. Education and leisure
- iv. Justice
- v. Religion
- vi. Elections

Δ G Finance
- i. Banking
- ii. Public finance
- iii. Railways and rail transport
- iv. Aviation and air transport
- v. Telecommunications and postal services

Δ I Environment

3. NOTES ON THE GROUPS

A Titles listed in Group A are useful only for general indications of overall patterns, and are often not sufficiently detailed for research into a particular or specific subject.

B Group B includes all production statistics. It includes reports of censuses, which are usually devoted more to the structure of the industry (finance, labour, machinery, power, etc) than to the quantity and value of goods produced. Research and development, including finance for R & D, is included in this section.

C The classification schemes used for the tabulation of foreign trade statistics follow closely similar patterns, as they are mainly based on the Customs Co-operation Council Nomenclature (CCCN), which superseded the Brussels Tariff Nomenclature (BTN), or on the United Nations Standard International Trade Classification (SITC), which are correlated. Many countries classify their imports and exports in more detail than the CCCN or SITC, and a useful key to the detailed classification of each country can be the International Customs Journal (Bulletin International des Douanes), which is obtainable from the International Customs Tariff Bureau, rue de l'Association 38, Bruxelles, Belgium; of from sales agents. It comprises about 200 volumes, each containing the customs tariff of a single country and kept up-to-date by supplements and new editions as required; it is available in several languages including English.

D Group D includes publications containing statistics of wholesale and retail trade, including prices, service trades, advertising, and tourism and travel.

E Censuses of population and housing, demography and population projections, vital statistics, housing statistics and labour statistics are included here.

F This group comprises social and political statistics. Fi cost of living and retail price indices, consumer prices, wages and salaries, household budget surveys, etc., Fii includes statistics on national health services, hospitals, national insurance schemes, social security, social insurance and social welfare; Fiii education and leisure statistics, includes all aspects of education from primary schools to universities, vocational and adult education; leisure includes entertainment, sport and recreation, libraries; arts, etc; Fiv includes both judicial and criminal statistics, also licensing. Fv has data on religion; and Fvi on elections.

G Group G includes all statistics of a financial nature. Gi includes publications by banks and other organisations which are devoted to banking statistics. Gii includes both national and local government financial statistics. Giii includes financial statistics for all types of companies and corporations, including building societies. Giv is concerned mainly with individual and industrial investment; Gv with the business of insurance companies; and Gvi with institutions and activities in the credit market.

H Group H covers transport and communications statistics generally. Hi includes statistics of ships and shipping, sea-borne transport, inland waterway transport, traffic at ports, and passenger and cargo traffic in ships. Hii includes statistics of roads and road construction, road traffic, road accidents, and passengers and goods conveyed by road. Hiii includes all types of railways, rolling stock, locomotives, passenger and goods traffic. Hiv includes statistics of airports, aircrafts, passenger and goods traffic. Hv includes statistics of telephones, telephone and telegraph services, other telecommunications services, post offices and postal services.

I This section is devoted to the increasing number of publications concerned with the environment which are not included elsewhere.

4. FORM OF ENTRY

The entry for each publication comprises:

(1) serial number;

(2) title, English translation of title if the original is not in English; name of responsible organisation (omitted if the responsible organisation is also the publisher);

(3) name and address of the publisher or of other agency or sales office from which the publication can be obtained (in many cases the publisher is indicated by an abbreviation, the full name and address being included in the list of abbreviations on page 0 unless it is the central statistical office, in which case reference is made to the entry for the organisation);

(4) date when first published if known; date of latest issue seen by the compiler (not necessarily the latest published) if published annually or less frequently; price (generally given in local currency and not including VAT or postage unless specifically mentioned); number of pages or volumes of the annual or less-frequently issued publications;

(5) (prefixed TF - time factor) indication of the lapse of time between the latest date included and the date of publication (as the actual date is seldom cited in the publication and seldom coincides with the normal date of an issue, part or edition, this information has been obtained mainly by observation of dates of receipt in libraries, and should be treated with caution); where the data contained in a publication coincide with date of the issue no TF is given;

(6) description of contents;

(7) ISSNs have been included, where known, for the first time.

5. REFERENCES

With the number of entries included it is not practicable to include references to the general section of each country group although some important references are given. Instead, the user is recommended to consult the subject index or to browse through the general section of the country concerned and/or the specific and general sections under Europe if no suitable item is listed in the specific section of the specific country.

6. CHANGES OF TITLE

In general, only the latest title of each publication is given. Many statistical publications have a long history of title variations, and it would be impossible to list all the changes. The librarian, sales agent, or publisher will be able to advise prospective users and purchasers of earlier issues if titles have changed.

7. INDEXES

Indexes to titles, organisations and subjects are included at the end of the volume. The subject index should enable the user to locate specialised source material more readily but it must be emphasised that the subject index is NOT a complete analytical index to all subjects covered by all statistical sources listed in the book.

8. ACKNOWLEDGEMENTS

The compiler would once again like to thank everyone who has helped in the preparation of this volume. As usual, she has had the utmost co-operation from most of the statistical offices, libraries, associations, and other organisations she has approached, and has appreciated the easy access she has been afforded to the many libraries she has used, particularly the Statistics and Market Intelligence Library of the Department of Trade and Industry, the Library of the Institute of Development Studies, the Library of the Office of Population Censuses and Surveys, the British Library Lending Division, the British Library of Political and Economic Science, and the Libraries of the Universities of Loughborough, Nottingham and Southampton, where much of the material has been examined.

Chichester,

June 1986

Directory of European Industrial & Trade Associations

Répertoire des Associations Européennes dans l'Industrie et le Commerce

Handbuch der Europäischen Verbände im Bereich der gewerblichen Wirtschaft

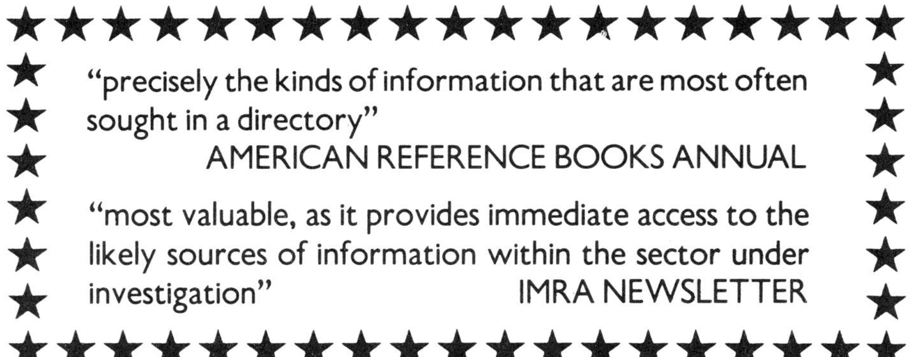

"precisely the kinds of information that are most often sought in a directory"
AMERICAN REFERENCE BOOKS ANNUAL
"most valuable, as it provides immediate access to the likely sources of information within the sector under investigation"
IMRA NEWSLETTER

C B D Research Ltd
Beckenham • Kent • England

Gale Research Co
Detroit • Michigan 48226 • USA

LIST OF COUNTRIES - TABLE DES PAYS - LÄNDVERZEICHNIS

* = Language(s) of text
Benelux - Economic Union of Belgium, the Netherlands & Luxembourg
BLEU - Belgo-Luxembourg Economic Union
BTN - Brussels Tariff Nomenclature
Bundesamt für Statistics - (see 635 for address)
c - circa
CBS, Vooburg - Centraal Bureau voor de Statistiek (see 1906 for address)
CCCN - Customs Co-operation Council for Nomenclature
CMEA - Council for Mutual Economic Assistance
COMECON - Council for Mutual Economci Assistance
COS, Malta - Central Office of Statistics (see 1789 for address)
CSO, Dublin - Central Statistical Office (see 1677 for address)
DCS Bucareşti - Direçtia Centrala de Statistica (see 2139 for address)
DIE, Ankara - Devlet Istatistik Enstitüsü (see 2327 for address)
Din - Dinar
DKr - Danish kroner
DM - Deutschemark
Dr - Drachma
DS, København - Danmarks Statistik (see 892 for address)
ed - edition
ECSC - European Coal and Steel Community
EEC - European Economic Community
EFTA - European Free Trade Association
ESA - European System of Integrated Economic Accounts
Eurostat - European Communities Statistical Office
eV - Eingetragener Verein
FAO - Food and Agriculture Organisation of the United Nations (see 004 for address)
Fl - Florin (Dutch Guilder)
FLux - Franc Luxembourg
Fmk - Finnish Mark
FrB - Belgian Franc
FrF - French Franc
FrS - Swiss Franc
FSU, Praha - Federalni Statistiký Úrad (see 692 for address)
Ft - Forint
GATT - General Agreement on Tariffs and Trade
GmbH - Gesellschaft mit beschränkter Haftung
Gr - Greek language
GUS, Warszawa - Glówny Urząd Statystyczny (see 2114 for address)
H I, Reykjavik - Hagstofa Islands (see 1757 for address)
HMSO, Belfast - H.M. Stationery Office, 80 Chichester Street, Belfast BT1 4JY
HMSO, London - H.M. Stationery Office, PO Box 276, London SW8 5DT
HMSO, Edinburgh - H.M. Stationery Office, 13a Castle Street, Edinburgh EH2 3AR
I£ - Irish pound
IFO - Institut für Wirtschaftsforschung
INE, Lisboa - Instituto Nacional de Estatística (see 2062 for address)
INE, Madrid - Instituto Nacional de Estadística (see 960 for address)
INS, Bruxelles - Institut National de Statistique (see 561 for address)
INSEE, Paris - Institut National de la Statistique et des Etudes Economiques (see 1026 for address)
ISSO - Internationale Selbstbedienungs - Organisation
ISTAT, Roma - istituto Centrale di Statistica (see 1614 for address)
Kcs - Koruna
Kohlhammer, Mainz - W. Kohlhammer GmbH, Philipp-Reis-Strasse 3, D-6500 Mainz 42
KSH, Budapest - Központi Statisztikai Hivatal (see 1553 for address)
L - Lira
NIMEXE - La Nomenclatura harmonisée pour les statistiques des pays de la CEE [Nomenclature used for classification of statistics of countries of the European Community]
NKr - Norwegian kroner
NSS, Athens - National Statistical Service of Greece (see 1516 for address)
NTIS - National Technical Information Service
OECD, Paris - Organisation for Economic Co-operation and Development (see 006 for address)
O.P. - out of print
OIE - Office of International Epizootics
OPCS - Office of Population Censuses and Surveys
öS - Austrian schilling
ÖSZ, Wien - Österreichisches Statistisches Zentralamt (see 478 for address)
Pts & Ptas - Pesetas
PTT - Postes, Télégraphes, Téléphones
RENFE - Red Nacional de los Ferrocarriles Españoles
SA - Société Anonyme
SB, Wiesbaden - Statistisches Bundesamt (see 713 for address)
SC, Stockholm - Statistika Centralbyrån (see 2155 for address)
SITC - Standard International Trade Classification
SKr - Swedish kroner
Staatsuitgeverij, Christoffel Plantijnstraat, Den Haag
STATEC, Luxembourg - Service Central de la Statistique et des Etudes Economiques (see 1770 for address)
SZS, Beograd - Savezni Zavod za Statistiku (see 2404 for address)
t - telephone number
tg - telegraphic address
tx - telex number
USS, San Marino - Ufficio Statale di Statistica (see 2145 for address)
UEBL - Union Economique Belgo-Luxembourgeoise
UNCTAD - United Nations Conference on Trade and Development
United Nations Publications, New York, NY 10017
UNDOX - United Nations Documents Index
UNESCO - United Nations Educational, Scientific and Cultural Organisation
Universitetsforlaget, Avdeling for offentlige publikasjoner, PO Box 8134 Dep, N-0033 Oslo 1
vol - volume
VP, Helsinki
WHO - World Health Organisation
yr - per annum (annual subscription)
Zly - Zloty

Cy, Moscow - see 2303
Cy, Budapest - see 615

ABBREVIATIONS AND SYMBOLS

Country & Language

A	Austria
AL	Albania
AND	Andorra
B	Belgium
BG	Bulgaria
Bg	Bulgarian
CH	Switzerland
CS	Czechoslovakia
Cs	Czechoslovakian
D	Federal Republic of Germany
Da	Danish
DDR	Deutsche Demokratische Republik
De	German
Din	Dinar
DK	Denmark
DKr	Danish Kroner
DM	Deutsche Mark
Dr or dr	Drachma
E	Spain
En	English
Es	Spanish
Esc	Escudo(s)
F	France
Fi	Finnish
FL	Liechtenstein
Fl	Florin (Dutch Guilder)
FLux	Franc Luxembourg
Fmk	Finnish Mark
Fr	French
FrB	Belgian Franc
GB	Great Britain
GIB	Gibraltar
GR	Greece
Gr	Greek
H	Hungary
Hu	Hungarian
I	Italy
IRL	Republic of Ireland
IS	Iceland
Is	Icelandic
It	Italian
Kcs	Koruna
L	Lira
L	Luxembourg
MAL	Malta
MC	Monaco
N	Norway
NI	Northern Ireland
NKr	Norwegian Kroner
NL	Netherlands
Nl	Dutch
No	Norwegian
öS	Austrian schilling
P	Portugal
PL	Poland
Pl	Polish
Pt	Portuguese
Ptas	Pesetas
R	Romania
Ro	Romanian
Ru	Russian
RSM	Republic of San Marino
S	Sweden
SF	Finland
SKr	Swedish Kronor
SU	Soviet Union
Sv	Swedish
TR	Turkey
Tr	Turkish
YU	Yugoslavia
Zl	Zloty

EUROPE
EUROPA

Some international organisations publishing statistics

001 United Nations.
New York, NY 100017, USA.
t 754 1234.
The Statistical Office of the United Nations collects and publishes data from as many countries as possible in periodic as well as ad hoc publications. On the basis of these statistics, the Statistical Office computes a large number of economic indicators in the form of global and regional aggregates and index numbers. It also publishes methodological studies, guides, manuals, and assists governments in implementing statistical practice recommended by the Statistical Commission. The Statistical Office is part of the United Nations Department of International Economic and Social Affairs.

002 United Nations Economic Commission for Europe.
Palais des Nations, CH-1211 Genève, Switzerland.
t 34 60 11. tx 28 96 96.
Created to initiate and participate in measures for facilitating concerted action for the reconstruction of Europe, to raise the level of European economic activity, and to maintain and strengthen the economic relations of European countries among themselves and throughout the world. The Commission is interested in the development of agriculture, coal, gas, electric power, housing, industry and its raw materials, steel, timber trade and transport. It carries out research and arranges conferences, including the Conference of European Statisticians.

003 United Nations Conference on Trade and Development (UNCTAD).
Palais des Nations, 1211 Genève 10, Switzerland.
t 34 60 11 & 31 02 11. tx 28 96 96.
UNCTAD was established in December 1964. Its permanent organ, the Trade and Development Board, meets twice a year and the four subsidiary organs (the Committees on Commodities, Manufactures, Shipping and Invisibles and Financing Relating to Trade) meet annually. It aims to evolve a co-ordinated set of policies to be adopted by all its member states, designed to accelerate the economic development of developing countries.

004 Food and Agriculture Organisations of the United Nations (FAO).
via delle Terme di Caracalla, 00100 Roma, Italy.
t (06) 5797. tx 61181 Foodagri.
Created to raise the levels of nutrition and standard of living, to secure improvements in the efficiency of production and distribution of all agricultural products, and to better the conditions of rural populations. To help achieve these aims, the FAO provides an intelligence service of facts and figures relating to nutrition, agriculture, forestry and fisheries, and also appraisals and forecasts of production, distribution and consumption in these industries.

005 UNESCO (United Nations Educational, Scientific and Cultural Organisation).
9 place de Fontenoy, 75707 Paris, France.
t 577 1610.
Established in 1946 'to contribute to peace and security by promoting collaboration among nations through education, science and culture, in order to further universal respect for justice, the rule of law, and for human rights and fundamental freedoms for all'. The organisation is concerned with education, natural science, social science, culture, mass communications, international exchanges, and technical assistance. It collects many statistics, some of which are included in its statistical yearbook and in other, mainly textual publications.

006 Organisation for Economic Co-operation and Development (OECD).
2 rue André-Pascal, 75775 Paris Cedex 16, France.
t 524 82 00. tx 62160 OCDE Paris. tg DEVELOPECONOMIE.
Twenty-four countries make up the OECD, a permanent co-operation designed to harmonise national policies. They include all Western European industrialised countries as well as certain others. In the course of its work OECD collects and publishes a considerable amount of information, supplied by member countries, taking care to make the figures as comparable as possible by adjusting, converting and reclassifying basic data. 'Activities of OECD ... report by the Secretary-General' is published annually.

007 European Communities. Communautés Européennes.
Bâtiment Berlaymont, 200 rue de la Loi, 1049 Bruxelles, Belgium.
t 735 80 40.
and
Bâtiment Jean Monnet, rue Alcide de Gasperi, Luxembourg - Kirchberg (Boite Postale 1907).
t 43011. tx COMEUR LU 3423.
The countries of the European Communities have bound themselves by three treaties (coal and steel, economic, and atomic energy) under which their future activities are to become more and more closely woven. The Statistical Office of the European Communities (Eurostat) compiles, analyses and publishes statistics of the member countries.

008 European Free Trade Association.
9-11 rue de Varembé, 1211 Genève 20, Switzerland.
t 34 90 00. tx 22660 EFTA-CH.
EFTA is an association of six countries: Austria, Iceland, Norway, Portugal, Sweden and Switzerland; Finland being a close associate. It aims to continue the expansion of economic activity, full employment, increased productivity, financial stability, and the improvement of the standard of living in the EFTA area, and to have fair competition in trade between member states.

International organisations, continued

009 Council for Mutual Economic Assistance (COMECON).
Kalinin Prospect 56, 121205 Moscow G - 205, USSR.
t 290 91 11 or 290 93 11. tx 141.
Founded in 1949, the member countries are Bulgaria, Cuba, Czechoslovakia, Germany (Democratic Republic), Hungary, Mongolia, Poland, Romania and the USSR. Aims are to promote the concerting and co-ordination of member countries' efforts, the planned development of their economies, continuous growth of labour productivity, steady rise in living standards, etc.

Libraries and information services

Many national, university and public libraries throughout the world are deposit libraries for United Nations publications (a 'List of depository libraries receiving United Nations material' is published as a separate booklet at intervals and it is also included annually in the Cumulative index to INDOC, the United Nations Documents Index); such libraries should have unrestricted documents and publications available for reference. United Nations Information Centres usually have the more recent UN publications available for reference.
It is usual for the official statistical offices of countries to exchange their publications with other national statistical offices and these publications are often, but not always, stored in the libraries of the statistical offices. These libraries are often accessible to those who wish to consult this type of material, even when generally closed to the public.

United Kingdom

The most accessible large collection of the publications referred to in this guide is at the Department of Trade and Industry's Statistics and Market Intelligence Library, 1 Victoria Street, London SW1H OET (t 01-215 5444/5445). Other large collections are in the Official Publications Library of the British Library, Great Russell Street, London EC1B 3DG (t 01-636 1544, Ext 487), Warwick University Library, Coventry (t (0203) 24011), and the British Library of Political and Economic Science, 10 Portugal Street, London WC2A 2HD (t 01-405 7686); a comprehensive collection of statistical publications of developing countries is in the library of the Institute of Development Studies at the University of Sussex, Andrew Cohen Building, Falmer, Brighton BN1 9RE (t (0273) 66261). Many of the larger public libraries are deposit libraries for United Nations publications, and one or two have collections of statistical yearbooks of overseas countries, but none take the more detailed statistical publications of individual countries listed in the following pages.

Australia

The two largest collections of statistical publications, including those of international organisations and of individual overseas countries, are in the National Library of Australia, Canberra A.C.T. 2600 (t (062) 631111) and the Australian Bureau of Statistics, Cameron Offices, Belconnen, A.C.T. 2617 (t (062) 527911). There are also collections of this type of material in the State libraries situated in each capital city, and in some university libraries, particularly the University of Sydney; the Universityof Melbourne, home of the Institute of Applied Economic and Social Research; and the Australian National University, where the library has a collection of statistical material to support the university's research in demography.
The United Nations Information Centre at 77 Kings Street, Sydney, N.S.W. 2000 (t (02) 292151) has a collection of United Nations publications available for reference, and the Library of the Department of Foreign Affairs, Administrative Building, Parkes, A.C.T. 2600 (t (062) 61911) holds a comprehensive collection of UN publications to which the public could be allowed access, also for reference only.

Canada

The Library of Statistics Canada, Ottawa K1A OT6 (t (613) 2365) has an extensive collection of statistical material, including publications of international organisations and of individual countries. The Library is open to the public and materials can be borrowed via interlibrary loan.
Many of the larger university, government department and provincial libraries in Canada are deposit libraries for United Nations publications but do not collect statistical publications of individual countries outside North America to any extent.

New Zealand

Both the Library of the Department of Statistics, Aorangi House, Molesworth Street, Wellington (Postal address: Private Bag, Wellington; t 729 119) and the National Library of New Zealand, 44 The Terrace, Wellington (Postal address: Private Bag, Wellington; t 722 101) have large collections of statistical material, including publications of international organisations and of individual overseas countries. Some material is also held in the university libraries, in the public libraries of main and secondary cities, and in the libraries of certain other government departments such as the Department of Trade and Industry. Much of the material available in New Zealand is accessible for loan through the country's library interloan system.

Libraries continued

U.S.A.

The Bureau of the Census Library of the U.S. Department of Commerce, Room 2451, Federal Office Building 3, Suitland, Maryland (mailing address: Washington DC 20233; t (301) 763-5042) maintains a collection of foreign censuses and statistical publications which may be consulted from 8.00 to 17.00 Monday through Friday.
The Library of Congress in Washington, the Joint International Monetary Fund and International Bank for Reconstruction and Development (World Bank) Library in Washington, and the United Nations Library in New York have extensive collections of publications of international organisations and of individual countries.
The United Nations Information Center, 2101 L Street N.W., Washington DC 20037 (t (202) 296-5370) has a collection of United Nations publications. And a large number of university and public libraries throughout the United States are deposit libraries for United Nations publications and also have some publications of other international organisations.

Bibliographies

010 UNDOC: current index: United Nations documents (Dag Hammerskjold Library).
A list published 10 times a year, of all unrestricted documents and publications of the United Nations arranged by the issuing departments of the UN. Series A is the subject index; series B the country index; and series C the list of documents issued. An annual cumulative checklist and cumulative subject index are included in the subscription. £114 yr; $120 yr. ISSN 0250-5584.

011 Catalogue of United Nations publications (United Nations Department of Conference Services, Publishing Division/Sales Section).
An official guide to United Nations publications in print. The issue for 1945-63 has been followed by annual volumes. Free.

012 Directory of international statistics (United Nations Statistical Office).
Issued as Statistical papers, series M, no. 56, Rev 1, the directory is to be in two volumes, Vol.I is in two parts, part 1 listing international statistical services, and part 2 listing data banks of economic and social statistics (published in 1982, £15 or $20). Vol II is to be published in 1986 and will have information on organisational responsibilities and functions of statistical services of the UN Statistical Office, regional commissions, special agencies, and other international organisations, and standards.

013 Bibliography of industrial and distributive-trade statistics (United Nations Statistical Office).
Issued as Statistical papers, series M, no. 36, Rev 5 in 1981, it lists the data being collected by each reporting country, mentioning the publications in which the data is published if it is published (£7.15 or $13).

014 Directory of environment statistics (United Nations Statistical Office).
Issued as Statistical papers, series M, no. 75 in 1983, contains facts and data, by country, on national authorities, sources and types of data collected by 150 member states, and a listing of environmental statistics publications published by other international organisations ($30).

015 World index of economic forecasts (George Cyriax, ed).
A guide to sources of economic forecasts, divided into four sections - forecast access tables, forecasts on principal OECD countries, forecasts/development plans for other countries, and a directory of forecasting organisations (2nd ed. published in 1981 by Gower Press, £75).

016 Catalogue of publications (OECD).
A sales list issued biennially with quarterly supplements. Free.

017 Published official sources of financial statistics (OECD).
Lists, by country, official institutions which publish financial statistics, with titles and frequency for all OECD countries and international organisations.
Also lists sources by subject, and includes a systematic classification of subjects. (Published in 1980 by OECD. £4.90; FrF 44 or $11).

018 Eurostat news (Eurostat).
A quarterly publications containing articles, news items and lists of new publications and forthcoming publications of the European Communities' Statistical Office. (Available free from the Office). ISSN 0378-4207.

019 A guide to current sources of wage statistics in the European Community (Eurostat)
Describes the principal statistical series in the field of statistics of earnings for the Community and member countries, covering average wages and incomes, wage rates, labour costs, structure of earnings, etc. (Published in 1984, in Fr & En eds. £6.50; $9; FrB 500).

020 Eurostat index: a detailed keyword subject index to the statistical series published by the Statistical Office of the European Communities, with notes on the series. 2nd ed. completely rev & enlarged. Available from Capital Planning Information, 6 Castle Street, Edinburgh EH2 3AT.

EUR

Statistical publications

Δ A General

021 Statistical yearbook. (United Nations Statistical Office).
UN, New York.
1947- 1982. cloth: $70 or £70. 1149p. *En, Fr.
TF: the 1982 edition, published in 1985, has data for many years up to 1982.
Main sections:
I: World summary. II: General socio-economic statistics - Population & manpower - National accounts - Wages & prices & consumption - Government sector statistics - Balance of payments - Finance - Health - Education - Culture - Cinemas - Housing - Science & technology - Development assistance - Industrial property. III: Statistics of basic economic activity - Agriculture - Forestry - Fishing - Industry - Mining & quarrying - Manufacturing - Energy - Construction - Wholesale & retail trade - External trade - International tourism - Transport - Communications.
Annex I: International comparisons of gross domestic product for selected countries, at average international prices, 1980.
Annex II: Country nomenclature.
Annex III: Conversion coefficients & factors.

022 World statistics in brief. (United Nations Statistical Office).
UN, New York.
1976- 9th, 1984. $3.50 or £2.70. 108p. *En.
TF: the 1984 edition, published late 1985, has data for 1975, 1980 & 1983.
Comparable statistics on demography and labour force; national accounts; agriculture and industry; trade, finance and tourism; transport and communications; education, health and nutrition.
Note: machine readable tape of country and regional tables is available (US$ 115).

023 Monthly bulletin of statistics. (United Nations Statistical Office).
UN, New York.
1947- £16, or £142.50 yr; $16, or $150 yr. *En, Fr.
TF: most tables include data for about 7 years and at least the last 12 months to two or three months prior to the date of the issue.
Special tables on industrial production, trade, transport, national accounts, etc., including retail price indexes relating to living expenditures of U.N. officials (published in the March and September issues) and schedule of daily subsistance allowance rates of U.N. officials (also in the March and September issues). Also regular tables on population, manpower, forestry, industrial production (index numbers), mining, manufacturing, construction, electricity and gas, internal trade, external trade, transport, wages and prices, and finance.

024 World economic outlook, 1985.
International Monetary Fund, 700 19th Street NW, Washington DC 2-431.
£9.95 or $12. 283p. ISSN 0251-6365. *En.
TF: published in 1985, with data for several years to 1984.
Includes a statistical appendix of tables on domestic economic activity and prices, international trade, balance of payments, external debt, country tables (principal projections and indicators.

025 World economic survey. (United Nations Department of International Economic and Social Affairs).
UN, New York.
1948- 1985. $14.50 or £14.50. 125p. ISSN 0084-1714. *En.
TF: the 1985 survey, published mid-1985, has data for 1984 and some earlier years.
Current trends in the world economy, particularly as they affect the progress of developing countries, by examining trade and prices.

026 Handbook of international trade and development statistics. (UNCTAD).
UN, New York.
1969- 1983. £56.25 or $62.50. 803p. *En, Fr.
1985 supplement £50 or $50. 604p.
TF: the 1983 edition, published in 1983, has data to 1980 or 1981; the 1985 supplement updates that information and was published in 1985. A new handbook is planned for 1987.
Intended to provide a complete basic collection of statistical data relevant to the analysis of problems of world trade and development, for the use of UNCTAD, etc. Contents are:
Part 1: Value of world trade by regions and countries; Part 2: Volume, unit value, and terms of trade index numbers by regions; commodity prices; consumer price indexes; Part 3: Network of world trade; summary by selected regions of origin and destination and structure of exports and imports by selected commodity groups; Part 4: Exports and imports for individual countries by commodity structure, and major exports of developing countries by leading exporters; Part 5: Balance of payments, financial resource flows and external indebtedness of developing countries; Part 6: Some basic indicators of development; Part 7: Special studies.
Annex A: Network of world exports by selected commodity classes and regions of origin and destination.

027 Statistical pocket book. (UNCTAD).
UN, New York.
$4 or £4. 111p. *En.
TF: issued in 1984 on the 20th anniversary of UNCTAD, with data mainly for 1982 and some for 1983 as well as earlier figures.
#Part 1: The developing countries in the world economy, income levels, population shares and gross domestic product, merchandise trade; Part 2: Basic development indicators for developing countries; Part 3: External sector of developing countries; Part 4: Illustrated data on sectoral issues; Part 5: Collective self-reliance.

Δ A, continued

028 UNESCO statistical yearbook ...
UNESCO, Paris.
1963- 1984. Fr 300 or £4.45. 106p. ISSN 0082-7541. *En, Fr, Es.
TF: the 1984 edition, published in 1984, has data for several years to 1982 or the latest available.
Reference tables - Education - Educational expenditure - Science and technology - Libraries - Book production - Newspapers & other periodicals - Cultural paper - Film & drama - Radio & television broadcasting.

029 UNESCO statistical digest.
UNESCO, Paris.
1981- 4th, 1984. Fr 36 or £5.50. 352p. *En, Fr.
TF: the 1984 edition, published in 1984, has data for several years to 1982.
Statistical summary of data on education, science & technology, culture & communication, by country. Covers 161 countries and provides a condensation of the 'UNESCO statistical yearbook' from which most of the data has been taken.

030 The world factbook. (Central Intelligence Agency).
Document Expediting (DOCEX) Project, Exchange and Gift Division, Library of Congress, Washington DC 20540.
(annual). 1985. not priced. 274p. *En.
TF: the 1985 edition has data for 1985.
Information for each country, arranged alphabetically, on land, people, government, economy, communications, and defence forces.

031 World development report. (World bank).
Oxford University Press, New York, for the World Bank.
1978- 1985. £17.50 (£8.95 paper). 300p. ISSN 0163-5085. *En.
TF: the 1985 edition, published in 1985, has data for 1983 and some earlier years in some tables.
Includes an annex on world development indicators, arranged by subject subdivided by countries, which includes basic indicators, growth and structure of production, growth of selected demand aggregates, structure of demand, growth and structure of merchandise trade, destination of merchandise exports, balance of payments, flows of external capital, external public debt, population and labour force growth, structure of population, demographic indicators, population projections, health-related indicators, and education.

032 World Bank atlas: population, per capita product and growth rates.
World Bank, 1818 H Street NW, Washington DC 20433.
1966- 1985. US$ 2.50. 29p. ISSN 0085-8293. *En.
TF: the 1985 edition, published in 1985, has data for 1982.
Tables, graphs, maps, etc. for 189 countries and territories, on population, gross national product, GNP per capita, life expectancy, infant mortality, and primary school enrolment.

033 World tables ... from the data files of the World Bank.
John Hopkins University Press, Baltimore & London, for the World Bank.
1971- 2nd, 1980. £16.50 (paper: £6.50); $27.50 (paper: $10). 474p. *En.
Economic and social time series for most developing and many industrialised countries. Nearly 250 tables covering more than 140 countries. Series I: Population, national accounts and prices; Series II: Balance of payments, external public debt, foreign trade indices, and central government finance; Series III: Comparative economic data; Series IV: Social indicators.

034 World in figures. (Economist Newspapers Ltd).
Economist Newspapers Ltd, 25 St James's Street, London SW1A 1HG.
1976- 4th rev. ed. 294p. *En.
TF: the 1984 edition, published in December 1984, contains the latest data available at time of publication.
Data for the world and for individual countries on population, gross domestic product, area, standard of living, world cities [population], world population ages, education, labour force, health, commodities equipment (radios, television, motor cars, commercial vehicles owned), production, transport, finance, economic aid, external service trades (tourism, banking, transport, invisible trade, etc), and foreign trade.

035 World military expenditure and arms transfers. (US Arms Control and Disarmament Agency).
GPO, Washington DC.
1964- 1985. $4.25; £21. 145. *En.
TF: the 1985 edition was published in 1986.
Data on military expenditure for about 120 countries, and the number of armed forces, as well as general economic information such as population, gross national product, foreign economic aid, and public expenditures on education and health.

036 Worldwide economic indicators: annual comparative statistics for 131 countries (with world and regional reports).
Business International Corporation, 1 Dag Hammerskjold Plaza, New York, NY 10017.
(annual). 1985. $180. 279p. *En.
TF: the 1985 edition, published in 1985, has data for 1980 to 1983 (estimates).
Key economic indicators, gross domestic product and net material product by activity, demographic and labour force data, wages and prices, foreign trade, miscellaneous production and consumption data.

Δ A, continued

037 Economic statistics, 1900–1983.
Economist Publications Ltd., 40 Duke Street, London W1A 1DW.
1985. £36. 152p. *En.
Historical series of economic indicators for six key industrial countries (GB, D, F, I, Japan, USA). Data on national output and expenditure, personal income and profits, trade, balance of payments, finance, prices and population.

038 Statistical indicators of short-term economic changes in ECE countries. (United Nations Economic Commission for Europe).
UN, New York.
1959– monthly. $45, or £42.75 yr. *En.
Statistics from 32 participating countries on the main indicators of the economic situation in Europe, the United States and Canada.

039 European historical statistics, 1750–1975 (B.R. Mitchell).
Macmillan, 4 Little Essex Street, London WC2.
1980. £45. 416p. *En.
Data from both Western and Eastern European countries on climate, population and vital statistics, labour force, agriculture, industry, external trade, transport and communications, finance, prices, education, and national accounts.
Note: First published in 1975 with data for 1750 to 1970.

040 Worldcasts.
Predicasts Inc., 200 University Circle Research Center, 11001 Cedar Avenue, Cleveland, Ohio 44106, USA.
(annual). $900 each part. 8 parts. ISSN 0163-6723. *En.
Worldcasts – products:
P-1 General, economic, utilities and services
P-2 Agriculture, mining, forestry, food, textiles, wood and paper
P-3 Chemicals, polymers, drugs, oil, rubber, stone, clay, glass
P-4 Primary markets, machinery, electronics, transportation equipment
Worldcasts – regional:
R-1 Common market
R-2 Other Europe (including USSR)
R-3 Americas (excluding USA)
R-4 Africa, Middle East, Japan, Asia and Oceania.
Data on population, general economic information, production and consumption including long range forecasts, for individual industries and regions.

041 World facts and figures (Victor Shower).
Wiley, Chichester, England.
1979. out of print. 269p. *En.
A revised & enlarged edition of 'The world in figures' issued in 1973. Data for 222 countries, over 2000 most important cities, over 2500 geographical and other features. Includes country and city comparisons, outstanding works of man, etc.

042 The new book of world rankings (G.T. Kurian).
Facts on File Publications, 460 Park Avenue South, New York, NY 10016.
1984. £9.95 or US$14.95. 915p. *En.
Ranks over 150 countries of the world according to their performance in about 340 key areas in the fields of geography and climate, vital statistics, population dynamics and the family, race and religion, politics and international relations, foreign aid, military power, economy, finance and banking, trade, agriculture, industry and mining, energy, labour, transportation and communications, consumption, housing, health and food, education, crime, media, the world's cities, and culture.

043 Statistics of world large cities.
Tokyo Metropolitan Government, Marunouchi, Chiyoda-ku, Tokyo.
1961– 1985. not priced. 91p. *En, Ja.
TF: the 1985 edition, published in 1985, has latest data available, usually for 1983 or 1984, together with some earlier figures.
Covers climate; land area; population by sex; population by age; vital statistics; deaths by age; deaths by major cause; medical facilities and personnel; theatres and cinemas; establishments (numbers and numbers of persons engaged); consumer price index; education; libraries and museums; electricity, gas and waterworks; post and telecommunication; transport; roads and parks; motor vehicles; water carriage; civil aviation; number of newly constructed dwellings; police and fire service.
Note: An 'international statistical yearbook of large towns' was published between 1927 and 1972 by the International Statistical Institute.

044 Handbook of economic statistics: a reference aid. (Central Intelligence Agency: US Office of Economic Research).
Document Expediting (DOCEX) Project, Exchange and Gift Division, Library of Congress, Washington DC 20540.
1975– 1985. not priced. 239p. *En.
TF: the 1985 edition, published in September 1985, has data for 1960, 1965, 1970, 1975, 1980 to 1984.
Data is for selected non-Communist countries and all Communist countries. Includes a graphic summary, economic profile, aggregative trends, Soviet economic performance, foreign trade and aid, energy, minerals and metals, chemicals and rubber, manufactured goods and forestry, agriculture, and transport.

Δ A, continued

045 International economic indicators. (Department of Commerce, International Trade Administration). GPO, Washington DC.
1975- quarterly. $4.95 ($6.19 abroad); or $18 ($22.50 abroad) yr. *En.
TF: each issue has data for several years and quarters to about three months prior to the date of the issue.
General, trade, price, financial, and labour indicators for the USA and seven other major industrial countries for comparison (D, F, GB, I, NL, Canada, Japan).

046 Economic and energy indicators (National Foreign Assessment Center, US Office of Economic Research). NTIS, PO Box 3, Newmans Lane, Alton, Hampshire GU34 2PG, England; and Document Expediting (DOCEX) Project, Exchange & Gift Division, Library of Congress, Washington DC 20540.
1981- bi-weekly. £105 yr (UK & Ireland). *En.
Information on changes in the domestic and external economic activities of the major non-Communist developed countries and selected developing countries. Economic indicators for industrial production, unemployment, and consumer price inflation; foreign trade and foreign trade prices; and monthly average prices for selected agricultural products and industrial materials.

047 World outlook.
Economist Intelligence Unit, 40 Duke Street, London W1A 1DW.
1978- 1986. not priced. 198p. *En.
Forecasts of political and economic trends for 1986 in over 165 countries on gross domestic product, consumer price inflation, population, foreign trade, finance, etc.

048 Quarterly review of country or region.
Economic Intelligence Unit, 40 Duke Street, London W1A 1DW.
1965- *En.
Statistical tables, using information drawn from official sources, covering economic trends and indicators of economic activity in industrial production, construction, employment, retail trade, wages and prices, money and banking, foreign trade and payments, exchange reserves, exchange rates, exports and imports (by broad commodity classification). There are separate reviews for most countries and regions of the world.

049 Quarterly economic reviews.
Economist Intelligence Unit, 40 Duke Street, London W1A 1DW.
1952- £16 or £53 yr (4 issues and annual supplement for one country). ISSN 0033-5495. *En.
92 separate review titles, each issued quarterly, covering political, economic and business conditions in over 165 countries, each issue containing a summary of the contents, a discussion of the main trends in the economy and forecasts for the year ahead, news analyses of the main issues, charts indicating main economic trends, and statistical appendices.

050 Allgemeine Auslandsstatistik: Vierteljahreshefte zur Auslandsstatistik [General foreign statistics: quarterly reports on foreign statistics] (SB, Wiesbaden).
Kohlhammer, Mainz.
1955- quarterly. DM 14.40 each issue. *De.
Inter-country comparisons as to selected facts which are of particular importance for the foreign trade relations of the FDR.
Note: to 1983 was 'Internationale Monatzahlen'.

051 Allgemeine Auslandsstatistik: Länderberichte [General foreign statistics: reports on foreign countries] (SB, Wiesbaden).
Kohlhammer, Mainz.
(irregular) DM 7.90 each issue. 60 reports a year. *De.
TF: published at varying intervals, and containing the latest available data for each country.
A series of reports, each on a particular country, on the climate, population, health, education, labour, agriculture, forestry, fisheries, production, foreign trade, transport, tourism, finance, prices, wages, etc. The reports were supported until 1983 by a series of briefer reports 'Allgemeine Auslandsstatistik: Länderkurzberichte'.

052 Fachserie 17: Preise. Reihe 11: Preise und Preisindizes im Ausland [Prices. Series 11: Prices and price indices in foreign countries] (SB, Wiesbaden).
Kohlhammer, Mainz.
(monthly and annual). DM 4.40 each monthly issue; 1983 annual DM 12.90. *De.

053 Compendium of human settlement statistics. (United Nations Statistical Office).
UN, New York.
1985. $50. *En.
Continues 'Compendium of housing statistics' (384).

054 Extebank monthly economic report.
Banco Exterior de España, Carrera de San Jerónimo 36, Madrid 14.
1977- monthly. free. ISSN 0014-5378. *En.
A series of economic reports on individual countries, with a few statistical tables.

055 Standard Chartered review.
Standard Chartered Bank Ltd, 38 Bishopsgate, London EC2N 4DE.
1919- monthly. free. ISSN 0305-9553. *En.
An economic report which includes features, area reports by geographical region subdivided by country. A few statistical tables in the text.

Δ A, continued

056 Lloyds Bank Group economic report.
Lloyds Bank Ltd, 6 Eastcheap, London EC3.
(irregular) free. *En.
A series of economic reports for each of the countries of the world, which include a few statistical tables.

057 ABECOR country reports. (Associated Banks of Europe Corporation).
Distributed by Barclays Bank plc, 54 Lombard Street, London EC3.
(irregular) free. *En.
A loose-leaf series of economic reports on over 100 individual countries, which contain a few statistical tables.

058 Economic survey of Europe. (United Nations Economic Commission for Europe).
UN, New York.
1947– 1984-85 (published late 1985). £35 or $35. 262p. ISSN 0070-8712. *En.
Analyses economic trends and records changing patterns of trade and output in Europe, Canada & USA.

059 European trends.
Economic Intelligence Unit, 40 Duke Street, London W1A 1DW.
1964– quarterly, with a supplement. £70 or $130 yr. ISSN 0014-3162. *En.
The European Communities' and related developments. An appendix has indicators of economic activity (industry, labour, finance, prices, and foreign trade) in leading industrialised countries, and foreign trade statistics for EEC and EFTA.

060 Main economic indicators. (OECD).
OECD, Paris.
1965– monthly. £3; Fr 30; DM 13; $7; or £30; Fr 300; DM 145; $62 yr. ISSN 0474-5523. *En, Fr.
TF: most tables contain figures for the last four complete years and quarterly or monthly figures for the last year to one or two months prior to the date of the issue.
Selected indicators for member countries on national accounts, industrial production, construction, retail sales, labour, wages, prices, finance, trade and payments, etc.
Note: also on magnetic tape (private sector: £2120; $4330; Fr 17315. timesharing bureaux: £8480; $17320; Fr 69260).

061 Main economic indicators: historical statistics. (OECD).
OECD, Paris.
1955/64– 1964-1983. Fr 175; £17.50; $35; DM 78. 656p. *En, Fr.
TF: the 1964-1983 edition, with data for those years, was published late 1984.
Similar subject coverage to 060 above.

062 OECD economic outlook.
OECD, Paris.
1968– 2 a year. £5.50; Fr 55; DM 24; $12; or £11; Fr 110; $22; DM 48 yr. ISSN 0474-5574. *En, Fr.
Projections of output, employment, prices and current balances over the next 18 months, based on a review of each member country and the feed-back effect on each of them of international developments.
Note: also available is 'OECD economic outlook historical statistics, 1960-1983' (published mid-1985. Fr 85; £8.50; $17; DM 37. 168p. *En, Fr). Magnetic tape of some 2000 macroeconomic series for the 24 member countries, as well as trade and payments data on non-OECD zones is available (private sector: £1380; Fr 16000; $2000. timesharing bureaux: £5520; Fr 64000; $8000).

063 OECD economic surveys.
OECD, Paris.
1962– 1984-1985. £2; $5; Fr 20; DM 9. ISSN 0376-6438. *En.
Detailed annual surveys of economic trends and prospects for each OECD country, including A, B, D, F, GB, I, IRL, IS L, N, NL, S, SF, TR, YU.

064 European marketing data and statistics.
Euromonitor Publications Ltd, 87-88 Turnmill Street, London EC1M 5QU.
1964– 1985. £75 or $113. 360p. ISSN 0071-2930. *En.
Covers 30 Western and Eastern European countries, and includes population, employment, production, trade, economy, living standards, consumption, market sizes, retailing, consumer expenditure, housing and households, health and education, culture and mass media, communications, travel and tourism.

065 State, economy, and society in Western Europe, 1815-1975: a data handbook in two volumes (Peter Flora and others).
Macmillan, 4 Little Essex Street, London EC2.
£40 or DM 296 for 2 vols. *En.
TF: Vol 1 was published in 1983, vol 2 in 1985.
Vol 1: The growth of mass democracies and welfare states (data on national states, mass democracies, personnel of the states, resources of the states, welfare states, population & families, urbanisation & housing, economic growth, division of labour & inequality, trade unions & strikes).
Vol 2: The growth of industrial societies and capitalist economies (data on major democratic developments, urbanisation & housing conditions, growth & composition of national product, occupational differentiation & income inequality, development of trade unions & industrial conflicts.
Each chapter is subdivided by country.

Δ A, continued

067 Basic statistics of the Community.
Eurostat, Luxembourg.
1960- 23rd, 1985. £3.20; $4.50; FrB 250. 289p. En, De, Fr, It, Nl, Da, Gr, Es, Pt.
TF: the 1985 edition, published early 1985, has data for several years to 1984 or the latest year available.
A selection of the Community's basic statistics and a comparison with a number of other European countries, USA, Canada, Japan, & USSR. General statistics; national accounts, finance & balance of payments; industry and services; agriculture, forestry, fisheries; and external trade.

068 Statistical panorama of Europe.
Eurostat, Luxembourg.
1984. free. 31p. *En, Fr, De, Nl, It, Da, Gr.
Graphical presentation of the statistics of the European Community, its member states, and the most important partners.

069 Yearbook of regional statistics.
Eurostat, Luxembourg.
1971- 1985. £14; $16; FrB 1000. *En, Fr, De, Nl, Da, It, Gr.
TF: the 1985 edition, published late 1985, has data for 1982 and some earlier years in some tables.
Statistics relating to economic and social factors in the regions of the European Community, including population and its structures; employment & unemployment; education, health & various social indicators; economic aggregates; main series on the different sectors of the economy: agriculture, industry, energy and the services sector; and the Community's financial participation in investments.

071 Social indicators for the European Community - selected series.
Eurostat, Luxembourg.
1960/75- 1984. FrB 750; Fr 113; £9.80; $14. 138p. *En/Fr, De/It, & Da/Nl eds.
TF: the 1984 edition has runs of figures usually to 1983, being data available mid-1984.
Part A: Indicators for specific social conditions: employment, unemployment, trend of employment in manufacturing industry, position of women, Community regional indicators. Part B: General social indicators.

072 European economy. (Commission of the European Community).
OOPEC, Luxembourg.
1978- 4 a year, plus supplements. £19.50 or $25 or FrB 1500 yr. ISSN 0379-2110. *En, Fr.
Each issue contains a statistical annex of main economic indicators on an annual basis. Supplements are: Series A: Recent economic trends (11 a year. £6.50; $9; FrB 500 yr. ISSN 0379-2056); Series B: Business and consumer survey results (11 a year. £8.50; $10.50; FrB 640 yr. ISSN 0379-2110).

073 Eurostat review.
Eurostat, Luxembourg.
1970/79- 1974-1983. FrB 600 or £7.50. 240p. *En/Fr/Nl or Da/De/It.
TF: the 1974-1983 edition, with data for those years, was published in 1985.
Time series of general statistics: national accounts, finance and balance of payments; population and social conditions; industry and services; agriculture, forestry and fisheries; and external trade.

074 Eurostatistics: data for short-term economic analysis.
Eurostat, Luxembourg.
1979- monthly. ECU 27.54; FrB 1250; £16.25; $20 yr. ISSN 0252-8266. *De, En, Fr.
TF: each issue has data for the last three years, six quarters and 12 or more months to between three and six months prior to the date of the issue.
Monthly report on short-term economic developments, designed to give an overview of the most important quantitative information available for the Community. Includes a brief article on latest trends, visual presentation of the most important economic series for the Community and member states, commodity tables and country tables.

075 Results of business surveys carried out among managements in the Community. (European Communities Commission, Directorate-General for Economic and Financial Affairs).
OOPEC, Luxembourg.
1962- 11 a year. £1.70; $3; FrB 150; or £15.75; $25; FrB 1350 yr. ISSN 0378-4479. *En, Fr, De, Nl, Da, It.
Results of the monthly and quarterly industry surveys, the half-yearly investment surveys, and the monthly or quarterly building surveys.

076 Yearbook of Nordic statistics. Nordisk statistisk arsbok (Nordic Council).
Nordiska Statistisken Sekretariat, Postbox 2550, DK-2100 København; or Nordiska Rådet, Box 19506, S-104 32, Stockholm 2.
1962- 1983. not priced. 404p. ISSN 0078-1088. *En, Sv.
TF: the 1983 edition, published early 1984, has data mainly for 1982 and some earlier years.
Comparable data for DK, N, S, SF, IS.
Main sections:
Climate & area; Population; labour market; Agriculture; Forestry; Fisheries; Mining & manufacturing; Energy; Housing & households; Internal trade; External trade; Transport & communications; Wages, prices & consumption; National accounts; Public finance; Official development assistance; Social welfare & public health; Statistics on crime & justice; Education; Research & experimental development activities; Cultural life & mass media; Elections; Regional statistics; Bibliography.

Δ A, continued

077 Nordic economic outlook.
Federation of Swedish Industries, Box 5501, S-114 85 Stockholm.
1975- ½-yearly. not priced. *En.
A joint product of experts in the federations of industries in the Nordic countries. Mainly text but includes some tables and graphs relating to the economic outlook of the five Nordic countries.

078 Nordisk statistik skriftserie [Statistical reports of the Nordic countries].
Nordiska Statistiska Sekretariatet, Postbox 2550, DK-2100 København Ø.
1954- irregular. not priced. ISSN 0332-6527. *each report is in one of the Nordic languages, some are also issued in a separate En translation.
A series of statistical reports of the Nordic countries concerning issues common to all five countries.

079 BENELUX: statistieken: statistiques [BENELUX: statistics].
Union Economique Benelux, rue de la Régence 39, 1000 Bruxelles.
1954- half-yearly. not separately priced. *Fr, Nl.
TF: varies with the subject and country; in general each issue covers a number of years and quarters up to about three months prior to the date of the issue.
Separate data for B, L, and NL, on population, vital statistics, employment, national product, agriculture and livestock, industrial production, foreign trade, transport, prices, wage increases in industry, and finance.
Note: issued as an annex to the quarterly review 'Benelux' (FrB 80 or FrB 250 yr; Fl 5.50 or Fl 17.25 yr).

080 BENELUX: statistieken: statistiques: tijdreeksen séries rétrospectives, 1948-1979 [BENELUX: statistics: retrospective series, 1948-1979].
Union Economic Benelux, 39 rue de la Régence, 1000 Bruxelles.
1981. FrB 80 or Fl 5.50. 138p. *Fr, Nl.
Separate data for each of the three countries (B, L, NL) on population, public health, housing, education, employment, agriculture, industry, internal trade, foreign trade, transport and communications, finance and credit, public finance, national accounts, balance of payments, prices and wages.

081 Comecon data. (Vienna Institute for Comparative Economic Studies).
Macmillan, 4 Little Essex Street, London WC2.
1979- 1983. £29.50. 491p. *En.
TF: published in alternate years, 'Comecon foreign trade data' being issued between. The 1983 edition was published mid-1984.
Detailed financial, economic and socio-economic statistics for the Soviet Union and Eastern Europe.

082 Comecon reports: quarterly Eastern Bloc survey.
Comecon Reports, World Reports (UK) Ltd., 108 Horseferry Road, London SW1P 2EF; or Christopher Story, Suite 1209, 280 Madison Avenue, New York.
1982- quarterly. £200 yr (UK & Ireland); $500 (USA & rest of world). ISSN 0142-0763. *En.
Economic and financial information, with statistical tables included in the text but no regular tables.

083 The East European and Soviet data handbook: political, social and development indicators, 1945-75 (Paul S. Shoup, ed).
Columbia University Press, 562 W 113th Street, New York, NY 10025.
1981. $52. 497p. *En.
Statistical tables on population and vital statistics, party membership, class structure, standard of living indicators, etc for the nine countries.

084 East European statistics service.
East-West, 10 blvd Saint-Lazare, 1210 Bruxelles.
(weekly) prices on application. *En.
Many statistical tables are included in the text, but there are no regular tables.

085 Yearbook of international commodity statistics. (UNCTAD).
UN, New York.
1984- 1984. $45 or £45. 573p. *En.
TF: the 1984 edition was published in 1985.
Statistical data at regional and country levels for trade in selected agricultural primary commodities, minerals, ores and metals.

086 Monthly commodity price bulletin. (Commodities Division, UNCTAD).
UN, New York.
1981- monthly. $4, or $36 yr including supplement published every two years. ISSN 0251-6438. *En, Fr, Es.
TF: each issue has data for the last five years in months to about three months prior to the date of the issue. The supplements have data for about 20 years.
Monthly and annual price series of food and tropical beverages; vegetable oils and oilseeds, agricultural raw materials, minerals, ores and metals.

087 Commodity trade and price trends ... (World Bank and International Development Association).
John Hopkins University Press, Baltimore and London.
1973- 1985. $25. 174p. ISSN 0251-401X. *En, Fr, Es.
TF: the 1985 edition, published in 1985, has long runs of figures to 1983.
Data on trade, price and freight rate indices; and prices of foods, non-foods, fuels, metals and minerals. Values are in US$ for comparison.

Δ A, continued

088 Commodity year book. (Commodity Research Bureau Inc).
Macmillan, 75 Montgomery Street, Jersey City, NY 07302.
1939- 1984. $39.95. 385p. ISSN 0069-6862. *En.
TF: the 1984 edition, published in 1984, has long runs of figures to the latest available.
Commodities are listed in alphabetical order, and charts and tables relate to prices, production, supply, distribution and consumption of the 110 main commodities traded throughout the world.

089 The Public Ledger commodity yearbook.
Turret-Wheatland Ltd, 12 Greycaine Road, Bushey Mill Lane, Watford, Herts WD2 4JP.
1980- 1986. not priced. 205p. *En.
TF: the 1986 edition, published in 1986, has data for several years to 1984 or 1984/85.
Data on grains and feeds, oilseeds and oils, produce markets, metals, and freight market.

Δ B Production

Δ B - i Mines and mining

090 World mineral statistics: production, exports, imports. (British Geological Survey: Natural Environmental Research Council).
HMSO, London.
1913/20- 1979-1983. £20. 279p. *En.
TF: the 1979-1983 edition, with data for those years, was published mid-1985.
Data on quantities produced, imported and exported of the following minerals for all countries so far as the information is available: aluminium and bauxite, antimony, arsenic, asbestos, barium, bentonite and fuller's earth, bismuth, bromine, cadmium, chromium, coal, cobalt, copper, diamond, diatomite, feldspar, fluorspar, gold, graphite, gypsum, iodine, iron ore, iron, steel and ferroalloys, kaolin, lead, lithium, magnesite, manganese, mercury, mica, molybdenum, nickel, petroleum and natural gas, phosphates, platinum, potash, rare earths, salt, sillimanite, silver, sulphur and pyrites, talc, tantalum and niobium, tin, titanium, tungsten, vanadium, zinc, zirconium, and other mineral commodities.

091 Minerals yearbook: volume 3 - area reports, international. (US Bureau of Mines).
GPO, Washington DC.
1932- 1982. $20. c 1100p. *En.
TF: the 1982 edition, published in 1984, has data for 1982 and earlier years. Sections available initially separately as preprints.
Detailed textual and statistical data on the mineral industry in each country of the world.

092 Minerals handbook. (Phillip Crowson, compiler).
Macmillan Publishers Ltd, for the Royal Institute for International Affairs.
1982/83- 1984-85. £40. 300p. *En.
TF: the 1984-85 edition, published late 1984, has data for 1980, 1981 or 1981/82, and earlier years in some tables.
Introductory summary tables, followed by separate sections on each of 37 minerals - world reserves, world production, secondary production, adequacy of reserves, consumption, end-use patterns, value of contained metal in annual production, substitutes and technical possibilities, prices, marketing arrangements, supply and demand by main market area.

093 Mineral commodity summaries. (US Bureau of Mines, with resource information by the Geological Survey).
US Bureau of Mines, 4800 Forbes Avenue, Pittsburgh, Pa 15213, USA.
1963- 1984. not priced. 183p. ISSN 0160-5151. *En.
TF: the 1984 edition, has data for 1983 and one or two earlier years.
Mainly US data, but also statistics on world resources for 86 mineral commodities.

094 EC raw materials balance sheets.
Eurostat, Luxembourg.
1975/78- 1979-1982. FrB 550. 238p. *En, De, Fr.
TF: the 1979-1982 edition, with data for those years, was published in 1985.
Supply balance sheets for 21 vital mineral raw materials.

095 Metal statistics.
Metallgesellschaft A.G., Reuterweg 14, Postfach 10 15 01, 6000 Frankfurt am Main, Germany.
1913- 1974-1984. not priced. 455p. ISSN 0076-6682 & ISSN 0170-9933. *En & De eds.
TF: the 1974-1984 edition, covering those years, was published in 1985.
A world survey of production and consumption of aluminium, lead, copper, zinc, tin, antimony, cadmium, magnesium, nickel, mercury and silver. There are comparisons by continent, and detailed surveys of the situation in producing countries.

096 Metal statistics. (American Metal Market).
Fairchild Publications, 7 East 12th Street, New York, NY 10003.
1908- 1985. $60. 314p. ISSN 0076-6658. *En.
TF: the 1985 edition, published in 1985, has data for 1983 and 1984.
Production, prices, consumption, shipments, foreign trade, and stocks for individual metals. Mainly USA but includes some world figures.

Δ B – i, continued

097 World metal statistics: yearbook.
World Bureau of Metal Statistics, 41 Doughty Street, London WC1N 2LF & 50 Broadway, New York, NY 10004.
1984– 1984. £50 or $100. 64p. *En.
TF: the 1984 edition, published in May 1984, has data for the years 1974 to 1983.
Annual data supplementing 098 for the major non-ferrous metals, with world mine or metal production data for chromium, cobalt, gold, manganese, mercury, titanium, tungsten and uranium. Also tables on annual prices for aluminium, copper, gold, lead, nickel, silver, tin and zinc.

098 World metal statistics.
World Bureau of Metal Statistics, 41 Doughty Street, London WC1N 2LF & 50 Broadway, New York, NY 10004.
1948– monthly. £570 or $1250 yr. ISSN 0043-8758. *En.
TF: each issue carries the latest monthly data available and data for about five earlier years.
Production, refining, consumption, scrap recovery, trade, stocks, etc., of metals (Aluminium & bauxite, antimony, cadmium, copper, lead, nickel, tin and zinc); US stock piles of principal non-ferrous metals; and metal prices.

099 World demand for raw materials in 1985 and 2000 (Wilfred Malenbaum).
McGraw-Hill Inc., 1221 Avenue of the Americas, New York, NY 10020.
$12.50; £26.95. 126p. *En.
TF: published in 1978, with data for 1951-55, 1961-65, 1971-75, 1985 and 2000.
Data for all metals and minerals.

100 'Metal bulletin' handbook.
Metal Bulletin Ltd., Park House, Park Terrace, Worcester Park, Surrey KY4 7HY.
1913– 1985. £24 for 2 vols. 2 vols. ISSN 0076-664X. *En.
TF: the 1985 edition, published late 1985, has data for several years to 1984.
Production, consumption, deliveries, exports and prices of non-ferrous metals and of iron and steel.
Vol 1: Prices; vol 2: Statistics and memoranda.

101 Iron ore statistics ...
Association of Iron Ore Exporting Countries, le Chateau, 2 bis chemin Auguste Vilbert, Grand-Saconnex 1218, Genève.
1975– 2 a year. not priced. *En, Fr, Es.
TF: issued in March and September, each issue has data for several years to the latest available.
Iron ore production, exports, consumption, etc., for the world and for the iron ore exporting countries; world production of crude steel; and world production of pig iron.

102 Lead and zinc statistics: monthly bulletin ...
International Lead and Zinc Study Group, 58 St James's Street, London SW1A 1LD.
1966– monthly. £80 yr or $120 yr. ISSN 0023-9577. *En, Fr.
TF: each issue has three or four years of annual figures and more recent quarterly and monthly figures to about three months prior to the date of the issue.
Current detailed statistics of zinc mine production, refined production, stocks, prices, foreign trade, and principal end-uses of lead and zinc.

103 Tin statistics.
International Tin Council, 1 Oxendon Street, London SW1Y 4EQ.
1959– 1972-1982. £15. 64p. *En.
TF: the 1972-1982 edition, with data for those years, was published late 1984.
Production, exports, imports, stocks, consumption, trade in manufactures, and labour for each country.

104 Quarterly statistical bulletin.
International Tin Council, 1 Oxendon Street, London SW1Y 4EQ.
1959– £12 each issue; £48 for 4 quarterly issues & 8 'Monthly statistical summary' issues. *En.
Up-dates the information in 103 above. 'Monthly statistical summary' is issued in the intervening months, and has data on the leading tables of the quarterly.
Note: prior to 1984 title was 'Monthly statistical bulletin'.

105 World copper statistics since 1950.
World Bureau of Metal Statistics, 41 Doughty Street, London WC1N 2LF.
£900 or $1900 inc. supplement; supplement only £100 or $300. c 75p. *En.
TF: the basic volume has data from 1950 to 1976 and the supplement updates the information to 1978.
Comprehensive statistics on a country basis world wide, with detailed figures on copper production and consumption from the mine through to end-use by markets.

106 Quarterly copper statistics.
World Bureau of Metal Statistics, 41 Doughty Street, London WC1N 2LF.
£150 or $350. *En.
TF: published in 1985 and covers the period 1961-1980 on a cumulative quarterly basis.
Copper mine production, refined copper production, refined copper consumption, consumption of copper in direct scrap, by country together with Western world area totals.

107 World wrought copper statistics.
World Bureau of Metal Statistics, 41 Doughty Street, London WC1N 2LF.
(annual) 1985. £150 or $350. *En.
TF: the 1985 edition, published in 1985, has data for 1984 and summary tables for 10 years to 1984.
Analysis by country of world trade in copper and copper alloy semi-manufactures by main types of shape.

A B - i, continued

108 World stainless steel statistics.
World Bureau of Metal Statistics, 41 Doughty Street, London WC1N 2LF.
1074- 1985. £150 or $350. *En.
TF: the 1985 edition, published in 1985, has data for 1984 and ten-year runs to 1984 in some tables.
World pattern of production, consumption and trade for stainless steel ingots and export and import figures by product form and country markets.

109 Statistical summary.
International Primary Aluminium Institute, New Zealand House (9th floor), Haymarket, London SW1Y 4TQ.
Vols 1 & 2, 1972-81. £8.24 or $15 each vol. Vol 3 (part), 1982, 1983 & 1984 free. *En.
Primary production, primary production capacity, receipts, inventory, and aluminium production; metallurgical and other uses. The parts of vol 3 include all the statistical series in vols 1 & 2.
Note: the volumes are further updated by single-sheet statistical releases: 'Primary aluminium production' and 'Primary & total aluminium inventories', both monthly; 'Aluminium production' and 'Movements of primary aluminium ...', both quarterly; 'Primary aluminium annual production capacity', half-yearly; and 'Aluminium annual production capacity', annually.

110 Aluminum statistical review.
The Aluminum Association, 818 Connecticut Avenue NW, Washington DC 20006.
1962- 1984. $25. 64p. *En.
TF: the 1984 edition, published in 1985, has data for 1974 to 1984.
Mainly US data, but includes a section of world statistics (pp.43-61) on primary aluminium production, supply and apparent consumption, per capita consumption, etc., by country.
Note: a historical supplement is also available.

111 Aluminium databook (Anthony Bird Associates).
Metal Bulletin Books Ltd, Park House, Park Terrace, Worcester Park, Surrey KT4 7HY.
1984- quarterly. £70 or £210 yr. *En.
TF: each issue has latest data available.
Primary aluminium production, stocks, stock-shipment ratios, capacity, utilisation, estimated consumption, intensity/competitiveness trends, price patterns, etc. Information is given for the world and for individual areas.

112 European aluminium statistics.
Aluminium-Zentrale eV, Königsallee 30, (Postfach 1207), D-4000 Düsseldorf, Germany.
1968- 1983. DM 40. 20p. *De, En, Fr.
TF: the 1983 edition, published mid-1984, has data for 1983 and some earlier years.
Includes production figures for primary and secondary aluminium, semis, castings and foil; foreign trade statistics; consumption of unwrought metal; per capita consumption and aluminium consumption by end uses.

113 Aluminium supplement in English.
Aluminium-Zentrale eV, Königsallee 30, Postfach 1207, D-4000, Dusseldorf 1, Germany.
1925- monthly. DM 26, DM 57.50; or DM 270, DM 690 yr. *De, contents pages & summaries also in En.
Includes a sectiion 'Wirtschaftnachrichten - economic news' which includes a statistical review with data on production, foreign trade, prices, etc., on aluminium and bauxite in particular countries and areas. No regular tables.

114 Annual review of the world silver industry. (The London Metal Research Unit).
Shearson Lehman Brothers Ltd, Peninsular House, 36 Monument Street, London EC3R 8LJ.
(annual). 1985. not priced. 111p. *En.
TF: the 1985 edition, published late 1985, has data to 1984 in the text.
Consumption, primary production, secondary production, stocks, investing in silver, and market highlights.

115 Tungsten statistics: quarterly bulletin of the UNCTAD Committee on Tungsten.
UN, New York.
1967- quarterly. £5 or $5 each issue. ISSN 0049-4828. *En & Fr eds.
TF: each issue has data for several years and includes the most recent annual and quarterly statistics available.
Prices, production, consumption, trade and stocks of tungsten for reporting countries.

116 Ferro alloy statistics: production, imports, exports and consumption of ferro alloys, 1978-1982. (Heinz H. Pariser, Alloy Metals & Steel-Market Research).
Metal Bulletin Books Ltd, Park House, Park Terrace, Worcester Park, Surrey KT4 7HY.
£52.50; $126 per title/volume. 14 vols. *En.
TF: published between 1983 and 1986.
Separate volumes on ferro manganese, ferro silicon, ferro chromium & ferro silicon chrome, nickel, titanium, tungsten, cobalt, molybdenum, silicon metal, silicon manganese, ferro aluminium, ferro titanium, ferro niobium, and ferro vanadium. Data is broken down, wherever possible, by country and grouped under the Americas, Western Europe (EEC and non-EEC countries), other Western/Third World countries and Eastern Bloc countries.

117 Non-ferrous metal data.
American Bureau of Metal Statistics Inc, 420 Lexington Avenue, New York, NY 10170.
1921- 1984. not priced. c 150p. ISSN 0360-9553. *En.
TF: the 1984 edition, published in 1985, has data to 1984 or the latest available.

Δ B – i, continued

118 Handbook of world salt resources (Stanley J. Lefond).
Plenum Press, 227 W 17th Street, New York, NY 10010.
1969. $25. 407p. *En.
Some statistics and statistical tables in the text.

Δ B – ii Agriculture, fisheries, forestry, etc.

119 State of food and agriculture ... world review ...
FAO, Roma.
1957- 1983. £16; $16. 237p. ISSN 0081-4539. En, Es & Fr eds.
TF: athe 1983 edition, published late 1984, has data for a number years to 1983 and some preliminary figures for 1984.
A world review of the factors affecting progress in food and agriculture in the developing countries.

120 World census of agriculture: analysis and international comparison of the results.
FAO, Roma.
1950- 3rd, 1970, published in 1981. not priced. 324p. *En.
Sections on holdings and holders; area of agricultural holdings; land use; land tenure, legal status and fragmentation; crops – area and production; livestock and poultry; wood and fishery products; employment in agriculture; farm population; agricultural power and machinery; fertilisers and dressings; irrigation and drainage; association of agricultural holdings with other industries; comparison of data for 1950, 1960 and 1970 world censuses of agriculture.
Note: a 'Report on the world census of agriculture' and a series of census bulletins have also been published.

121 FAO commodity review and outlook.
FAO, Roma.
1964- 1984-1985. £16. 137p. *En.
TF: the 1984-1985 edition, published in 1985, has data for 1982/83 and projections.
Reviews the general commodity situation and outlook, and the situation and outlook by commodities – sugar, beverages, and tropical crops; oilseeds, fats and oils, oilcakes and meals; cereals, cassava and livestock products; agricultural raw materials; other agricultural commodities; fishery products; forestry products; etc.

121A Commodity price charts.
Statistics Division, Overseas Development Administration, Eland House, Stag Place, London SW1E 5DH.
(quarterly). not priced. *En.
TF: each issue has long runs of monthly or quarterly figures to the latest available.
Charts showing prices for a selected number of internationally traded commodities.

122 World agricultural statistics: FAO statistical pocketbook.
FAO, Roma.
1983- 1984. £4. 94p. *En, Fr, Es.
TF: the 1984 edition, published in 1985, has data for 1971 to 1981.
Provides in internationally form the most important indicators relating to agriculture, fisheries, forestry and food for each country, economic class and region of the world.

Δ B – ii(a) Agriculture and horticulture

123 FAO production yearbook.
FAO, Roma.
1947- 1984. £15. 331p. *En, Fr, Es.
TF: the 1984 edition, published late 1985, has data for several years to 1984.
Data on land, population, index numbers of agricultural production, statistical summary of world and regional agricultural production, crops, livestock numbers and products, food supply, means of production (farm machinery, pesticides), and prices.
Note: the time series published in the yearbook are also available in computer-readable form.

124 FAO monthly bulletin of statistics.
FAO, Roma.
1952- monthly. £1.80 or £13.50 yr; $2 or $16 yr. *En, Es, Fr.
TF: each issue has data for about four years and several months or quarters up to between two and six months prior to publication.
Statistical tables on production, trade and prices for agricultural, fishery and forest products of reporting countries.

125 The world food book: A-Z, atlas and statistical source book (David Crabbe & Simon Lawson).
Kogan Page, 120 Pentonville Road, London N1 9JN; or Nichols Publishing Company, New York.
1981. £14.50. 240p. *En.
Includes 31 tables in the statistical appendix on world land; population engaged in agriculture; fertiliser usage; production and yield of cereals, starchy roots and tubers, grain legumes, by type, by region, by leading producers, by range of yields; trends in world production of various tropical products and meat; world food supply; and per capita consumption of above foods.

Δ B - ii(a), continued

126 World agricultural outlook and situation. (US Department of Agriculture; Economics, Statistics and Cooperatives Service).
GPO, Washington DC.
1953/54- quarterly. free. *En.
TF: each issue has long runs of figures to the latest available.
World economic conditions, commodity prices, world fertiliser situation, world commodity developments, regional agricultural developments.
Note: 'Foreign agriculture' (monthly $2.75 or $16 yr ($3.45 or $20 yr abroad) includes a few statistics in the text but carries no regular tables.

127 Review of the agricultural situation in Europe at the end of ... (Food and Agriculture Organisation of the United Nations <u>and</u> United Nations Economic Commission for Europe).
UN, New York.
1958- 1983. £27.35 or $25 for 2 vols. 2 vols. *En.
TF: the 1983 edition, published in 1984,shows the situation at the end of 1983.
All types of data on the dairy, meat, grain and produce industries.
Note: also titled 'Agricultural market review'.

128 Yearbook of agricultural statistics.
Eurostat, Luxembourg.
1961- 1984. FrB 600; £7.50; $11. 321p. *En, Fr, De, Da, Nl, It.
TF: the 1984 edition, published in 1984, has data for 4-5 years to 1982 or 1981/82.
Contains the most important items given in 'Agricultural statistics' in six sections - general, agricultural and forestry accounts, structure, production, supply balance sheets, and prices and price indices.

129 EC agricultural price indices (output and input).
Eurostat, Luxembourg.
(half-yearly) £14.50 or FrB 1100 yr. ISSN 0250-5967. *De, En, Fr, It.
Trends of monthly EC indices of producer prices of agricultural products and of purchase prices of the means of agricultural production during the latest 13 months for the European Communities and member states.

130 Community survey on the structure of agricultural holdings.
Eurostat, Luxembourg.
1950/76- 1979-80. 4 vols. *En, Fr, De, Da, Nl, It, Gr eds.
TF: the 1979/80 results were published in 1984 and 1985. Surveyed every 2 years.
Contents:
Vol I: Introduction and methodological basis.
Vol II: Main results: Part 1: Geographical division: Section A: Community by member states. Section 2: Division states by regions. Part 2: Division by size classes of holdings characteristics in following fields: (a) Legal personality and management of holding (b) Agriculture labour force, (c) Type of tenure, (d) Farm machinery and equipment, (e) Land use, (f) Livestock.
Vol III: Main results by member states.
Vol IV: Graphs.

131 The agricultural situation in the Community. (European Economic Comunity).
OOPEC, Luxembourg.
1975- 1985. FrB 1000; £13.20; $19. 439p. *En, Fr, De, Nl, It, Da, Gr.
TF: the 1985 edition, published in 1986, has data for 1982, 1983 and 1984.
Includes data on agricultural prices, structures, production and income, markets for agricultural products, consumption, and consumer and market prices. Statistical data and tables from p. 177-439.

132 Agricultural prices.
Eurostat, Luxembourg.
1969/75- 1973-1984. FrB 750; £9.50; $14. 340p. *En, Fr, De, It.
TF: the 1983-84 edition, with data for those years, was published in 1985.
Selling prices of main agricultural (crop and animals) products and purchase prices of the means of agricultural production. Prices given in national currencies and in ECUs.
Note: 'The rates of value-added tax in agriculture, 1968-84' (FrB 100. 25p. published in 1985) supplements the above). A quarterly 'Agricultural prices' is available on microfiche only (FrB 1200 for the complete series).

133 Prices on agricultural products and selected inputs in Europe and North America. (annual ECE/FAO (price review).
UN, New York.
1950- no 34, 1983-84 (published in 1985). $19. *En.

134 Prospects for agricultural production and trade in Eastern Europe, 1981-1982.
OECD, Paris.
2 vols. *En & Fr eds.
TF: includes long runs of statistics to 1979 or 1980.
Contents:
Vol 1: DDR, H, PL (£9.50; FrF 95; $21). Vol 2: BG, CS, R (£13; FrF 130; $26).

135 East Europe agriculture: a monthly review.
Agra Europe (London) Ltd, 25 Frant Road, Tunbridge Wells, Kent TN2 5JT.
1982- monthly. subscription rates on request. ISSN 0263-3205. *En.
Includes some statistics in the text, but no regular tables.

Δ B – ii(a), continued

136 Agricultural statistics of Eastern Europe and the Soviet Union, 1960-80. (US Department of Agriculture, Economic Research Service).
GPO, Washington DC.
1983. 125p. *En.

137 Crop production.
Eurostat, Luxembourg.
(quarterly) FrB 550; £7.20; $9 or FrB 1700; £22.25; $27.50 yr. ISSN 0378-3588. *En, De, Fr, It.
Data on land use, crop production of arable land (area, yield, production), fruit and vegetable production; meteorological reports; supply balances for crop products.

138 Cereals statistics.
Home-grown Cereals Authority, Hamlyn House, Highgate Hill, London N19 5PR.
1975- 1983. £6. 138p. *En.
TF: the 1983 edition, published early 1984, has data for several years to 1982/83 or 1983/84.
Section A: UK prices; section B: UK information; section C: EEC information; section D: world information; section E: quality; section F: miscellaneous. Information includes data on production (major producing countries), supplies and consumption, utilisation, trade, rice information, and futures prices.

139 World wheat statistics.
International Wheat Council, 28 Haymarket, London SW1Y 4SS.
1955- 1984. £25 or $40. 112p. ISSN 0512-3844. *En, Fr, Es, Ru.
TF: the 1984 edition, published in 1984, has long runs of figures to the 1982/83 season.
Note: data are updated in a press release 'Market report' (£20 or $40 yr).

140 Review of the world wheat situation.
International Wheat Council, 28 Haymarket, London SW1Y 4SS.
1958/59- 1984/85. £15 or $25. 44p. *En.
TF: the 1984/85 edition, published early 1986, has data for the 1983/84 crop year and estimates for 1984/85.
Reviews wheat production; world trade in wheat and wheat flour; carryover stocks; wheat prices and ocean freight rates; developments in national policies; course grains and rice; world wheat consumption.

141 Statistische informationen zum Getreide- und Futtermittelmarkt. Grain and feeding stuffs statistics.
Toepfer International, Ferdinandstrasse 12, 2000 Hamburg 1, Germany.
1980/81- 1981/82. not priced. 74p. *En, De.
TF: the 1981/82 edition, published early 1982, has data for several years to 1980, 1981 or 1980/81 season.
Production and trade in grain by countries, oilseeds, feeding stuffs, EC feeding stuffs market, prices, livestock, and meat consumption.

142 Annual review of oilseeds, oils, oilcakes, and other commodities.
Frank Fehr & Co Ltd, 64 Queen Street, London EC4R 1ER.
1918- 1984. £10. 72p. *En.
TF: the 1984 edition, published mid-1985, has data for several years to 1984.
A general review, then data for each of the commodities dealt with by the firm, including prices, production, imports, exports, etc.

143 World oils and fats statistics. (Economic and Statistics Department, Unilever Ltd., for the International Association of Seed Crushers).
Unilever Ltd, Unilever House, London EC4P 4BQ.
1966/67- 1985. £11. 16p. *En.
TF: the 1985 edition, published in 1985, has data for 1981/82 to 1984/85 (provisional).

144 International Association of Seed Crushers: [Annual report to Congress].
International Association of Seed Crushers, Salisbury Square House, Salisbury Square, London EC4P 4AN.
1924- 1985. £26. 119p. *En.
TF: the 1985 report, published in 1985, has data for 1981 to 1984.
Includes a statistical appendix on world oils and fats, including world summary, world production - types of oils and fats, world production of oilcake and meal, summary of world exports, and world exports in detail.

145 Fruit and tropical products.
Commonwealth Secretariat, Marlborough House, Pall Mall, London SW1.
1979- 2 a year, (December and June). £30 yr. ISSN 0142-1883. *En.
Annotated statistical data on fruit, cofee, cocoa, oilseeds and vegetable oils, and spices, including production, trade, prices and stocks.

146 Animal production.
Eurostat, Luxembourg.
(quarterly) FrB 550; £7.20; $9 or FrB 1700; £22.75; $27.50 yr. ISSN 0250-6580. *En, De, Fr, It.
Monthly statistics on meat: slaughterings, external trade and gross indigenous production; eggs and poultry: incubation, chicks hatched, and external trade; milk and dairy products.

147 Animal health yearbook.
FAO, Roma.
1957- 1984. £15; $15. 234p. ISSN 0066-1872. *En, Fr, Es.
TF: the 1984 edition, published in 1985, has data available at 31st December 1984.
Diseases of mammals, birds, bees, fish, by countries. Also numbers of inhabitants, livestock and veterinarians.

Δ B – ii(a), continued

148 International market review.
Meat and Livestock Commission, PO Box 44, Queensway House, Bletchley, MK2 2EF.
£14 yr. 3 a year. *En.
TF: each issue has data for that or the previous month and comparisons for the previous year.
Includes some statistical tables in the text on production, slaughter, prices, etc. of cattle, sheep, pigs, etc. in various countries.

149 Meat and dairy products.
Commonwealth Secretariat, Marlborough House, Pall Mall, London SW1.
1979– 2 a year, (November and May). £25 yr. *En.
Production, trade and stocks, and monthly averages of prices of selected products in major countries.

150 Meat balances in OECD countries.
OECD, Paris.
1963/77– 1977–83. £7.50; Fr 75; $15. 156p. *En, Fr.
TF: the 1977–83 edition, published early 1985, has data for the years 1977 to 1983.
In two parts: General tables, each dealing with a special subject, with data for each member country and totals by groups of countries; and Country tables.

151 International quarterly report of milk and dairy products (production, stocks, prices). (European Confederation of Agriculture).
Abteilung Statistik, Schweizerisches Bauernsekretariat, Brugg, Switzerland.
(quarterly) FrS 18 yr. *En, Fr, De.
TF: each issue has monthly data for two or more years to about six months prior to the date of the issue.
* Production of collected milk, butter and cheese, and whole and skim milk powder; stocks of skim milk powder and butter; prices for Western European countries, Canada, USA, Australia and New Zealand.

152 Milk and milk products balances in OECD countries.
OECD, Paris.
1957/70– 1975–1983. £9.50; Fr 95; $19. 178p. *En, Fr.
TF: the 1975–1983 edition, published mid-1985, has data for the years 1975 to 1983.
General and country tables on production, foreign trade and consumption.

153 World market for dairy products.
GATT, Centre William Rappard, rue de Lausanne 154, 1211 Genève 21.
1980– 1985. FrS 12. 76p. *En.
TF: the 1985 edition, published in 1985, has data for 1984 or 1985 and earlier years.
Includes statistical tables on quantities of production, exports, imports, consumption and stocks of skimmed milk powder, butter and cheese; production, exports and stocks of whole milk powder; and production and exports of anhydrous milk fat.

154 World statistical compendium for raw hides and skins, leather and leather footwear, 1961–1982.
FAO, Roma.
£8.80 or $11. 233p. *En, Fr, Es.
TF: published in 1983, updating earlier edition published in 1980.
Livestock population, raw hides and skins (production, trade, apparent availability), leather (production, trade, apparent availability), and footwear (production, trade, availability).
Note: issued as FAO statistics series no. 50.

155 Hides and skins.
Commonwealth Secretariat, Marlborough House, Pall Mall, London SW1.
1979– 2 a year, (December and June). £25 yr. ISSN 0142-1891. *En.
Livestock slaughterings, utilisation of hides and skins, and trade in various types of animal skins and leather. Also monthly average prices of hides and skins.

156 International egg statistics: bulletin.
International Egg Commission, 25/31 Knightsbridge, London SW1X 7NJ.
1968– 2 a year. not priced. *En.
TF: each issue has monthly data for two full years and the current year to one month prior to the date of the issue.
Data on 21 egg producing countries, with production, foreign trade, poultry numbers, chicken placements, egg prices, and prices of feeding-stuffs for layers.
Note: the Commission also issues six-monthly 'International chick placement bulletin' and 'International egg market review ...'.

157 La vigne dans la Communauté Européenne [Wine-growing in the European Community].
Eurostat, Luxembourg.
1985. FrB 250. 119p. *Fr, It; translation of text in En & De available on application.
A general overview of vineyards in Europe.

158 Jahrbuch der internationalen Gartenbaustatistik ... Yearbook of international horticultural statistics.
Internationaler Verband des Erwerbsgartenbaues, Bezuidenhoutseweg 153, Postbus 361, NL-2501 BE s'Gravenhage; or from member associations.
1951– 1985. Fl 40. 156p. *En, Fr, De.
TF: the 1985 edition, published in 1985, has data for several years to 1983 or 1984.
Non-edible horticultural products – area and production, sales and markets, external trade, consumption, prices and means of agricultural production.

Δ B – ii(a), continued

159 Community survey of orchard fruit trees.
Eurostat, Luxembourg.
1969/70– 1982. £4 or FrB 300. 92p. *En, De, Fr, It.
TF: the 1982 survey report, published in 1984, has data for 1982.
Data on the 590,000 hectares of commercial orchards under apples, pears, peaches and oranges in the EEC, including details of age of orchard and density of plantation for the main fruit varieties of each species in individual member states and production zones.

160 Spices: a survey of the world market.
UNCTAD/GATT, Genève.
1977. $40 each volume. 2 vols. *En.
A market study of 29 countries, reviewing overall international trade, market characteristics, consumption patterns, and spice trade structure. Contains data on supply and demand, prices and market access factors individually for the major spices and spice seeds. Vol I: Selected markets in Western Europe; Vol II: North America, Asia and the Pacific region, the Middle East, the Socialist countries of Eastern Europe.

161 Sugar yearbook.
International Sugar Organisation, 28 Haymarket, London SW1Y 4SP.
1947– 1984. £10. 345p. *En.
TF: the 1984 edition, published in 1985, has data for several years to 1984.
Data on production, exports, imports, consumption, stocks, and prices of sugar.

162 Annual report for the year.
International Sugar Organisation, 28 Haymarket, London SW1Y 4SP.
1947– 1984. not priced. 68p. *En.
TF: the 1984 report, published in 1985, has data for 1984 and some earlier years in some tables.
Includes statistical tables on the world sugar situation (production, consumption and stocks, trade, etc), and prices of sugar, as well as the accounts of the organisation.

163 Statistical bulletin.
International Sugar Organisation, 28 Haymarket, London SW1Y 4SP.
1947– monthly. £2.50, or £25 yr. *En.
Updates 162 above.

164 World sugar statistics.
F.O. Licht, Postfach 1220, 2418 Ratzeburg, Germany.
1938/39– 1984/85. not priced. 86p. *En & De eds.
TF: the 1984/85 issue, published late 1985, has data for the years 1983/84 and 1984/85 (provisional).
Sugar statistics for the world, and statistics of imports, exports, prices, consumption, and molasses by country.

165 Sugar review.
C. Czarnikow Ltd., 66 Mark Lane, London EC3P 3EA.
(weekly) not priced. *En.
A news bulletin which includes statistical tables on foreign trade, deliveries, futures markets, etc. for sugar.

166 Quarterly bulletin of cocoa statistics.
International Cocoa Organisation, 22 Berners Street, London W1P 3DB.
1975– £15 (£25 outside Europe) yr. *En, Fr, Es, Ru.
TF: each issue has latest available data to six months or more before the date of the issue.
World cocoa bean position, production, grindings, exports by country of cocoa beans and products, imports by country, prices, etc.

167 Cocoa price index and deflated cocoa prices.
International Cocoa Organisation, 22 Berners Street, London W1P 3DB.
1975– irregular. free. *En.
Note: the Organisation also issues a weekly 'Daily and indicator prices of cocoa beans ...'.

168 Cocoa statistics.
Gill & Duffus Ltd., St Dunstan's House, 201 Borough High Street, London SE1 1HW.
(annual) 1983. not priced. c 50p. *En.
TF: the 1983 edition, published in 1983, has long runs of figures to 1982.
Production and grindings of raw cocoa, imports and exports, supply and demand, and market prices. Also data on cocoa butter, cocoa powder and cocoa presscake.

169 Quarterly statistical bulletin ... (preliminary).
International Coffee Organisation, 22 Berners Street, London W1P 3DB.
1977– quarterly. free. *En.
TF: each issue has data up to about six months prior to the date of the issue.
Exports, imports, re-exports, supplies, prices. and selected background statistics.
Note: was a priced publication containing final figures until the issue for 1982, published in 1984.

170 Annual bulletin of statistics.
International Tea Committee, 5 High Timber Street, Upper Thames Street, London EC4V 3NH.
1946– 1985. £70. 163p. *En.
TF: the 1985 edition, published late 1985, has data for several years to 1984.
Area and production, exports, imports and consumption, stocks, auction prices, instant tea, etc.

Δ B ii(a), continued

171 Monthly statistical summary.
International Tea Committee, 5 High Timber Street, Upper Thames Street, London EC4V 3NH.
1946- £50 yr. *En.
TF: updates 170.
Planting, production, exports, imports, re-exports, stocks, monthly price quotations, consumption and import duties.

172 Edible nut statistics.
Gill & Duffus Ltd., 23 St Dunstan's Hill, London EC3R 8HR.
(quarterly) not priced. *En.
TF: each issue has long runs of annual and monthly figures to the date of the issue or the latest data available, and is published in the month of issue.
Crops, imports, exports, and edible nut kernel prices.
Note: there is also an 'Edible nut market report'.

173 Tobacco quarterly.
Commonwealth Secretariat, Marlborough House, Pall Mall, London SW1.
1979- £70 yr. ISSN 0142-1913. *En.
TF: each issue has data for three or four years and separate or cumulated data for months of the current and past year to about six months prior to the date of the issue.
Area and production of tobacco, exports and imports of manufactured tobacco, auction sales and prices of leaf tobacco and stock figures for certain countries; also production and consumption of tobacco products and trade in manufactured tobacco.

174 Food consumption statistics.
OECD, Paris.
1954/56- 1973-1982. £23; Fr 230; $56. 564p. *En, Fr.
TF: the 1973-1982 edition, with data for those years, was published early 1985.
A full statistical review of the flow of food products, including production, stocks, foreign trade, consumption, etc., and global food balances for each OECD member country.

175 Food balance sheets ... average.
FAO, Roma.
1964/66- 1979-81 (published in 1985). £11.60; $64. 290p. *En.
Average and per capita food supplies, by continent and by countries.

Δ B - ii(b) Fisheries

178 Yearbook of fishery statistics: catches and landings.
FAO, Roma.
1942- 1983. £24; $23.50. 402p. ISSN 0251-5679. *En, Fr, Es.
TF: the 1983 edition, published in 1985, has data for several years to 1983.
Annual statistics on nominal catches on a world-wide basis, with detailed breakdowns by countries, by species, and by major fishing areas.

179 Yearbook of fishery statistics: fishery commodities.
FAO, Roma.
1942- 1983. £18; $18. 211p. ISSN 0251-5687. *En, Fr, Es.
TF: the 1983 edition, published in 1985, has data for 1983 and some earlier years.
Production and international trade in fishery commodities.

180 Bulletin statistique des pêches maritimes [Statistical bulletin of sea fisheries].
Conseil International pour l'Exploration de la Mer, Palægade 2-4, DK-1261 København K.
1916- 1981. DKr 75. 103p. ISSN 0373-2045. *En; only title in Fr.
TF: the 1981 edition, published late 1983, has data for 1981.
Detailed statistics for member countries of catch, by fishing grounds and species.

181 Cooperative research report.
Conseil International pour l'Exploration de la Mer, Palægade, 2-4, DK-1261 København K.
1962- irregular. prices vary (1983 report DKr 110). ISSN 0105-3213. *En.
Some issues of the series contain statistical material, for example, the report of the Council's Advisory Committee on Fishing Management (No. 128 is the 1983 report, published in 1984. 298p). The many tables deal with the North-east Atlantic, including the Baltic

182 Review of fisheries in OECD member countries.
OECD, Paris.
1967- 1984. £11; Fr 110; $22. 318p. ISSN 0078-6241. *En.
TF: the 1984 edition, published late 1985, has data for 1984.
A general survey of the more important international developments, and statistical tables for each OECD member country on all aspects of the fisheries situation.

Δ B – ii(b), continued

183 European supplies bulletin.
Fishery Economics Research Unit, Sea Fish Industry Authority, 10 Young Street, Edinburgh EH2 4JQ.
(quarterly) £85 yr, £95 in Europe; £105 elsewhere). ISSN 0142-937X. *En.
Landings, values, marketing and trade in 16 European countries. Also commentary and profiles on the market for individual products.
Note: 'European supplies bulletin: six year review' has data for 1978 to 1983 and includes some production and consumption data not covered in the quarterly issues (1983. £25).

184 Yearbook of fishery statistics, 1985.
Eurostat, Luxembourg.
1985. FrB 400; £5.60. 119p. *En, Fr, De, It, Nl, Da, Gr.
Statistical data for member states and other countries on catches by fishing region, catches of principal species, fishing fleet, and foreign trade in fishery products.
Note: earlier publications were 'Fisheries: catches by fishery region, 1965-77'; 'Fisheries: products and fleet, 1974/75' and also 1976/77 issue; and a 'Quarterly bulletin of fisheries' from 1979-.

185 International whaling statistics (Norske Hvalraad) [Committee for Whaling].
Norske Hvalraad, Oslo.
1930- 1982/83. free. 61p. *En.
TF: the 1982/83 edition, published in 1984, has data for several years to 1982 or 1982/83 season.
Whaling results for various countries, including information on species, size, etc.

186 Statistical bulletin.
International Commission for the Conservation of Atlantic Tunas, Principe de Vergara 17, Madrid 1.
1971- 1983. not priced. 144p. *En, Fr, Es.
TF: the 1983 edition, published in 1984, has data from 1973 to 1983.
Contents:
I: Cumulative tuna catch by ocean and by country; II: Atlantic and Mediterranean cumulative tuna catch by species, by gear, be area and gear, and by country; III: Fishing power; IV: Statistics by country.

187 Tuna catch and effort, and size data for long-line fishery, collected at transhipment ports in the Atlantic.
International Commission for the Conservation of Atlantic Tunas, Principe de Vergara 17, Madrid 1.
1977- 1985. not priced. 130p. *En, Fr, Es.
TF: the 1985 edition, published mid-1985, has data for 1984.

Δ B – ii(c) Forestry

188 Yearbook of forest products statistics.
FAO, Roma.
1947- 1972-1983. £22. 408p. ISSN 0084-3768. *En, Fr, Es.
Production, trade and consumption of all kinds of round-woods, sawnwoods, wood-based panels, wood-pulp, paper and board, and forest products.
Note: Computer-readable data of time-series for production and trade are also available from Computer Systems Branch of FAO.

189 Forest products prices, 1961-1980.
FAO, Roma.
3rd ed, 1981. $7.50; £4. 113p. *En.

190 The forest resources of the ECE region (Europe, the USSR, North America). (United Nations Economic Commission for Europe and FAO).
UN, New York.
not priced. 228p. *En.
TF: published in 1985, the results of a survey taken in 1979.
General forest inventory data, volume and mass of tree and other woody biomass, role of forests, etc.
Note: FAO takes an inventory every five years, and previous results were published by FAO as 'World forest inventory'.

191 Forestry statistics.
Eurostat, Luxembourg.
1970/75- 1976-1980. £9.60; FrB 750. 188p. *En, Fr, De, Nl, Da, It, Gr.
TF: the 1976-1980 edition, with data for those years, was published in 1984.
The most important data on forestry for the member countries of the Community. In eight parts - Summary data on forestry in the EC; structure of forests; removals; supply balance sheets in raw wood; intra-EC trade in raw wood; supply balance sheets for the major wood products; pulpwood consumption by industrial products; and forest fires.

192 Timber bulletin for Europe. (United Nations Economic Commission for Europe and FAO).
UN, New York.
1948- half-yearly, with supplements. prices vary. *En, Fr.
TF: each issue contains data for several years and the last eight quarters up to about six months prior to publication. The half-yearly issues are up-dated by the supplements, which are usually devoted to one particular subject or aspect.

Δ B - iii Industry

193 Industrial statistics yearbook.
UN, New York.
1938/61- 1982. £50 or $50 each vol. 2 vols. *En.
TF: the volumes for 1982 were published in 1985. Vol I has data for 1982; vol II has data for 1973-1982.
Contents:
Vol I: 'General industrial statistics' has basic national data for each country.
Vol II: 'Commodity production data ...' has detailed information on world production of individual industrial commodities.
Note: Machine readable tapes are available of input to Vol I ($240) and Vol II ($230).

194 Indicators of industrial activity.
OECD, Paris.
1979- quarterly. £4 or £14 yr; Fr 40 or Fr 140 yr; $9 or $30 yr. ISSN 0252-4278. *En, Fr.
TF: each issue has runs of quarterly and monthly figures and is published about two months after the end of the period covered.
An overall view on the short term economic evolution in different branches of industry for all OECD member countries. Includes indices on production, deliveries, new orders, unfulfilled orders, produce and employment prices.
Note: Indexes of industrial production input in machine readable form are also available ($115).

195 Handbook of industrial statistics.
United Nations Industrial Development Organisation, International Centre, PO Box 300, A-1400 Vienna.
1982- 1984. £50 or $50. 578p. *En, Fr.
TF: published every two years, the 1984 handbook was issued in 1985 and has data for various periods to 1983.
Statistical indicators relevant to drawing international comparisons of the process of industrialisation. Detailed indicators for more than 70 countries on the manufacturing sector as a whole, its branches, and its products. Also indicators of trade in manufactures.
Note: the UNIDO Data Base of Industrial Statistics has data from 1963 and is updated annually. Covers approx. 80 countries and 28 industries in the manufacturing sector. Enquiries to the Statistics and Survey Unit, UNIDO, PO Box 300, A-1400 Vienna.

196 Industrial structure statistics, 1982.
OECD, Paris.
1984. Fr 70; $14. 128p. *En, Fr.
Information on the evolution of industrial structures in OECD member countries, including statistics of exports and imports by industry, disaggregated national accounts, etc.

197 Yearbook of industrial statistics.
Eurostat, Luxembourg.
1970- 1984. £8.10; $10; FrB 600. 171p. *En, Fr, De, Da, Nl, It, Gr.
TF: the 1984 edition, published in 1985, has data for 1983 or the latest available, and earlier comparative years.
A selection of data on industrial statistics covering the following domains: structure and activity, investments, data by size of enterprise, short-term trends, and external trade.
Note: earlier title was 'Industrial statistics: yearbook'.

198 Industrial production.
Eurostat, Luxembourg.
(quarterly) £8.50 or FrB 660 yr. ISSN 0254-0649. *En, Fr, De.
Annual and quarterly data on production in the EC member states of textiles, clothing, leather and footwear, paper and board, office machinery and electrical appliances.

199 Structure and activity of industry - annual enquiry - main results.
Eurostat, Luxembourg.
1972/73- 1981/82. FrB 900; £11.40; $16. 279p. *En, Fr, De, It, Da, Nl, Gr.
TF: the main results for 1981 and 1982 of the co-ordinated annual enquiry into industrial activity was published in 1985.
Enterprises, numbers of employees, labour costs, production value; data by kind-of-activity units; and tables presented by industries.

200 Industrial short-term trends.
Eurostat, Luxembourg.
1979- 11 a year. £15.75; FrB 1200; $20 yr. ISSN 0254-0231. *En, Fr, De.
Short-term indicators, comments and graphs; indices of industrial production for about 40 industrial branches and groups of branches, indices of turnover, new orders, employees, wages and salaries and hours worked.

201 Fachserie Auslandsstatistik. Reihe 2: Produzierendes Gewerbe im Ausland [Foreign statistics. Series 2: Production industries in foreign countries] (SB).
Kohlhammer, Mainz.
(irregular) *De.
Subseries are:
2.1. Local units, employment, turnover and production values of production industries in foreign countries (1978. DM 13.40).
2.2. Production of selected goods of production industries in foreign countries (1981. DM 20.30).

Δ B - iii, continued

202 The world's largest industrial enterprises, 1962-1983 (John M. Dunning & Robert D. Pearce).
Gower Publishing Co Ltd., Gower House, Croft Road, Aldershot, Hants GU11 3HR.
£45. 191p. *En.
TF: this 2nd ed. published in 1985. The 1st ed., covering 1962 to 1977, was published in 1981.
Divided into 19 industrial sectors, includes data on size of enterprises, degree of industrial concentration and diversification, profitability and growth performance, employment activities, and R & D performance.

203 Industrial property statistics ...
World Intellectual Property Organisation, 34 chemin des Colombettes, 1211 Genève 20.
1981- 1983. Publication A is free; 51p. Publication B FrS 75. c 400p. *En, Fr.
TF: the volumes for 1983 were published in 1984.
Publication A has statistics of major countries, presented in abridged form. Publication B has detailed statistics on application, grants, etc. of patents, utility models, inventor's certificates, varieties of plants, trademarks and service marks, industrial designs, international marks, international industrial designs, international patent applications, and European patent applications.

Δ B - iii(a) Food products, beverages, tobacco

204 Fedetab. (Fédération Belgo-Luxembourgeoise des Industries du Tabac).
Fedetab, avenue de Tervuren 270-272, Bte 20, B-1150 Bruxelles.
(annual) 1983. not priced. 52p. *Fr, Nl.
TF: the 1983 report has data for 1983 and also earlier years in some tables.
The annual report of the Federation, which includes statistical tables on production, number of enterprises, employment, consumption, sales, prices, taxes, etc. of tobacco, cigarettes, cigars and cigarillos for Belgium and the BLEU.
Note: Vademecum FEDETAB (2nd ed. 1978. FrB 1200. looseleaf) contained statistical and other reference data relating to the tobacco sector in Belgium, Western Europe, and other countries.

205 Statistiques ... statistics.
CAOBISCO. (Association for the Chocolate, Biscuit and Confectionery Industries if the EEC), 1 Defacqz (Bte 7), 1050 Bruxelles.
1960/61- 1983-1984. not priced. 72p. *Fr, En.
TF: the 1983-1984 edition, published in 1985, has data for 1983 and 1984 and also earlier years in some tables.
Data for the EEC member countries and some for non-member countries on production, trade (intra EEC and external trade), consumption, value of sales, VAT and other taxes, and raw materials.

Δ B - iii(b) Textiles, pulp and paper, rubber, etc

206 Quarterly statistical review.
Textile Statistics Bureau, 2nd floor, Royal Exchange, Manchester M2 7ER.
1946- £6 or £20 yr. *En.
TF: each issue includes long runs of figures to the latest available on each subject and country.
Apart from detailed United Kingdom statistics, the review contains international statistics on spun yarn production, woven cloth, exports of yarn and fabrics, imports of yarn and fabrics.

207 International textile review.
McGraw-Hill Publications, 457 National Press Building, Washington DC 20045.
1978- 2nd 1981. $117 in USA; $137 elsewhere. various pagings. *En.
Outlines current statistics of the textile industry in 26 countries, including production, consumption, prices, employment, foreign trade, and national trade policies. Mainly textual, but includes some statistics and statistical tables.

208 Textile organon.
Textile Economics Bureau Inc, 101 Eisenhower Parkway, Roseland, New Jersey NJ 07068.
1930- monthly. $25 or $140 yr; $35 or $210 yr abroad, except June & November issues ($40 each; $60 each abroad). ISSN 0040-5132. *En.
TF: each issue contains statistical data for about 10 years and monthly figures for 12 months up to one or two months prior to the date of the issue.
Mainly USA data but also includes statistics for the world for production, foreign trade, etc., of textiles of all types. The June & November issues include surveys on a world wide basis.

209 Textile industry in OECD countries.
OECD, Paris.
1953- 1982. £4.50; $9; Fr 45. 42p. ISSN 0474-6023. *En, Fr.
TF: the 1982 issue, published in December 1984, has data for 1982 and some earlier years in some tables. Final issue.
Production and consumption of textile goods and on the structure of the industry (labour force, investment, machinery) in OECD member countries.

210 Wool quarterly.
Commonwealth Secretariat, Marlborough House, Pall Mall, London SW1.
1979- £70 yr. ISSN 0142-1921. *En.
Production, demand and trade in wool and analytical tables on wool markets in a range of countries.

Δ B - iii(b), continued

211 Wool statistics.
Commonwealth Secretariat, Marlborough House, Pall Mall, London SW1.
1947/48- 1984-85. £16. 61p. ISSN 0260-216. *En.
The results of the 38th annual wool questionnaire on wool statistics, including data on the sheep population, supplies of raw wool, consumption, production, machinery installed, foreign trade, prices, etc., of wool, yarn, etc.

212 Wool facts.
International Wool Secretariat, 6-7 Carlton Gardens, London SW1Y 5AE.
1985. unpaged. *En.
TF: the 1985 edition, published in September 1985, has data for several years to 1984.
Brief statistical picture of the wool world. Summary charts are followed by data on raw fibres, raw material consumption in manufacturing, end-product consumption, etc.

213 Cotton.
International Cotton Advisory Committee, 1225 19th Street NW, Washington DC 20036.
1948- $78 (non-member countries); $28 (member countries) for annual review and monthly issues.
ISSN 0010-9754. *En, Fr, Es for the annual; separate eds for the monthly.
TF: the 1985 annual edition (169p) has data for 1980 to 1985 or the latest available.
Supply and distribution, production, acreage, yield, consumption, foreign trade, and stocks of cotton. Part 1 is titled 'Monthly review of the world situation'; Part 2 is 'World statistics: bulletin of the International Cotton Advisory Committee'.

214 International cotton industry statistics.
International Textile Manufacturers' Federation, Am Schanzengraben 29, Postfach CH-8039, Zürich.
1958- 1983. FrS 50. 46p. ISSN 0538-6829. *En.
TF: the 1983 edition, published in 1985, has data for several years to 1983.
Productive capacity (spindles and looms), machinery utilisation and raw material consumption in the short-staple section of the textile industries in virtually all countries of the world.

215 International cotton-system fibre consumption statistics.
International Textile Manufacturers' Federation, Am Schanzengraben 29, Postfach CH-8039, Zürich.
1974- quarterly. FrS 40. *En.
TF: each issue has data to the previous quarter.
Consumption and stocks of fibres (cotton and man-made) in the short-staple sector of the textile industries of the Federation's member countries.
Note: 'The Textile country reporter' (1979- FrS 50) contains monographs of the textile industry in various countries; reports published have included Greece and Hungary.

216 Information sur les textiles synthétiques et cellulosiques [Information on man-made fibres.].
Comité International de la Rayonne et des Fibres Synthétiques, 29 rue de Courcelles, 75008 Paris.
1969- 1984. not priced. 135p. *En, Fr, De
TF: the 1984 edition, published in 1984, has data for 1983 and also some earlier years in some tables.
Part 1: Production, consumption and employment; part 2: End-uses; part 3: Foreign trade in man-made-fibres

217 World statistics [and national statistics].
Association Internationale de la Soie, 55 montée de Choulans, 69323 Lyon Cedex 1, France.
1949- 1982. not priced. 14p. *En, Fr.
TF: the 1982 edition, published in 1983, has data for some years to 1981.
World output of fresh cocoons, production of raw silk, imports, exports, domestic consumption, closing stocks, silk waste and noils, combs, spun silk yarns, silk noil yarns, by country.
Note: the Association also issues single sheets of more detailed information for individual countries.

218 Jute, kenaf and allied fibres: quarterly statistics.
FAO, Roma.
1983- quarterly. not priced. *En, Fr, Es, & Ja.
A statistical information sheet issued to members of OECD and observers, with data on current supply and demand situation, prices, production, trade, manufacturing, and special information.

219 The footwear, raw hides and skins and leather industry in OECD countries.
OECD, Paris.
1955- 1982-1983. £4.50; $9; Fr 45. 60p. *En, Fr.
TF: the 1982-1983 edition, published mid-1985, is the final issue.
Trends in production, consumption, international trade, and prices for OECD member countries.

220 World footwear markets.
Shoe & Allied Trades Research Association, Rockingham Road, Kettering, Northants NN16 9JH.
1977- 1985. £30. c 100p. ISSN 0266-0709. *En.
TF: the 1985 edition, published in 1985, has data for several years to 1984.
Production and trade statistics from all major trading countries, including Western and Eastern Europe.

221 Wood pulp and fiber statistics.
American Paper Institute Inc., 260 Madison Avenue, New York, NY 10016.
1937- 47th, 1982-1983. Free to API members. 2 vols. *En.
TF: the 1982-83 edition, published late 1984, has long runs of figures to 1982 and 1983.
Book 1: USA, Canada, Finland, Norway & Sweden; book 2: other countries. Production imports and exports by type for each country.
Note: the 47th edition supplements the 42nd edition, 1950-1978.

Δ B - iii(b), continued

222 Pulp and paper industry.
OECD, Paris.
1954- 1982. £6.20; $12; Fr 62. 102p. ISSN 0474-5485. *En, Fr.
TF: the 1982 edition, published in 1984, has data for 1982.
Production, international trade (by origin and destination), and estimated consumption of the different grades of pulp, paper and board, together with some indications of utilisation of capacity, per capita consumption, and price trends.
Note: 'Pulp and paper: quarterly statistics', which updated the above with tables on stocks of paper pulp and waste paper, pulp and paper producation and trade, and shipments of market pulp, was discontinued from January 1985.

223 Pulp and paper capacities ...: survey.
FAO, Roma.
1976/81- 1984-1989 (published in 1985). £10. 247p. *En, Fr, Es.
An annex to the report has statistical data by countries.

224 L'Industrie des pâtes, papiers et cartons: statistics on pulp, paper and board industries: annual statistics.
European Confederation of Pulp, Paper and Board Industries, rue Washington 40, Boite 7, 1050 Bruxelles.
(annual). 1984. not priced. 82p. *En, Fr, De, Es.
TF: the 1984 edition, published late 1985, has data for 1984.
Data on pulpwood (receipts, consumption), other fibrous raw materials (imports, exports and consumption of waste paper; receipts and consumption of straw, textile rags and other fibrous raw materials), pulp and paper for textile manufacture (production, foreign trade, sales, consumption, pulp mills), and paper and board (production, foreign trade, structure of production).

225 Economic and structure development of the paper and board converting industry in the EC.
Internationales Komitee der Verarbeiter von Papier und Pappe in der Europäischen Gemeinschaft, Arndtstrasse 47, 6000 Frankfurt/Main 1, Germany.
not priced. 29p. *En, Fr, De.
Results of the business survey carried out among firms of the paper and board converting industry in the EC., 1983/84 (EC as a whole and individual member countries); structure and activity of industry processing of paper and board, 1979 and 1980; and enterprises employing ... to ... persons processing of paper and board, 1979.

226 Newsprint data - statistics of world demand and supply.
Canadian Pulp and Paper Association, 115 Metcalfe Street, Montreal, Que, H3B 2K9, Canada.
1935- 1984. free. 27p. ISSN 0068-9491. *En, Fr.
TF: the 1984 edition, published mid-1985, has the latest data available.
Note: 'Monthly newsprint statistics' is a 4-page update.

226A Rubber statistical bulletin.
International Rubber Study Group, 5-6 Lancaster Place, London WC2E 7ET.
1947- 6 a year. £57 or $60 yr. ISSN 0035-9548. *En.
TF: each issue has data for about 10 years and 12 months to three months prior to the date of the issue.
Production, consumption, stocks, exports and imports of natural, synthetic and reclaimer rubber, and end products.
Note: 'Statistical commentaries' (1980- irregular) supports the above publication with commentaries in readily digestible form (graphs). 'World rubber statistical handbook' is a historical base book for the bulletin (Vol 1: 1946-1970. £10 or $10. published 1974. Vol 2: 1965-1980. £10 or $10. published 1984).

226B Rubber trends.
Economist Intelligence Unit, 40 Duke Street, London W1M 5DG.
1959- quarterly. £160 yr. ISSN 0035-9564. *En.
World rubber trends and outlook, special reports on particular markets, and country statistics (supply, consumption, production, stocks, foreign trade, etc). Only a few countries are included in each issue.

Δ B - iii(c) Chemicals, pharmaceuticals, etc

227 Statistics on narcotic drugs ... (United Nations International Narcotics Control Board).
UN, New York.
1947- 1983. £12.50; $12.50. 150p. ISSN 0566-7658. *En, Fr & Es eds.
TF: the 1983 edition, published in 1984, has data for several years to 1983.
Drug manufacture, consumption, stocks, and seizure of illicit narcotics, by country.
Note: also 'Statistics on psychotropic substances' (1983. £12.50; $12.50).

228 Estimated world requirements of narcotic drugs ... (United Nations International Narcotics Control Board).
UN, New York.
1946- 1984 (one annual report plus 11 supplements). £42.75 or $45 yr. ISSN 0082-8335. *En, Fr, Es.
TF: the 1984 edition was published in 1984 and is up-dated during the year by the supplements as new information becomes available.
Estimates of requirements of narcotic drugs, opium production, the cultivation of opium poppy for purposes other than the harvesting of opium, and the manufacture of synthetic drugs.

Δ B - iii(c), continued

229 Comparative statement of estimates and statistics on narcotic drugs ... (United Nations International Narcotics Control Board).
UN, New York.
1972- 1983. £6 or $6. c 40p. *En, Fr, Es.
TF: the 1983 edition, published in 1985, has data for 1983.
Information on the movement of narcotic drugs and their production from raw materials to the consumption of the finished products, data being furnished by governments in accordance with international treaties.

230 Chemical industry year book.
Chemical Data Services, Room 905, Quadrant House, The Quadrant, Sutton, Surrey SM2 5AS.
1981- 2nd ed., 1984. £80. 187p. *En.
Reviews production of and trade in 50 chemicals (15 inorganics, 25 organics, 5 fertilisers and 5 polymers). In five sections - country by country production figures where available for the latest years published; imports and exports (volume and value) by country for the two latest available years; production figures by product subdivided by countries for 1978 to 1982; trade statistics by product subdivided by countries for the years 1980 to 1982; list of existing and planned plants for 47 of these chemicals in the countries covered.

231 Annual review of the chemical industry. (United Nations Economic Commission for Europe).
UN, New York.
1971- 1983. £30; $30. 217p. *En.
TF: the 1983 edition, published late 1985, has data for 1983.
Includes statistics on production, imports and exports of chemical products and employment in the industry in European countries, Japan, Canada & USA.

232 Chemfacts ...
Chemical Data Services, Room 905, Quadrant House, The Quadrant, Sutton, Surrey SM2 5AS.
1975- *En.
Product profiles, company information, and runs of statistical data on market trends, production and foreign trade. Recent editions are: Belgium (1981. £45); France (1978. £40); Federal Republic of Germany (1982. £60); Italy (1979. £40); Netherlands (1981. £45); Scandinavia (1981. £45); Spain (1982. £60); United Kingdom (1983. £60); Portugal (1983. £55).

233 World statistics - fertiliser products.
British Sulphur Corporation Ltd., 25 Wilton Road, London SW1V 1NH.
1983- 1985. £45 (£30 to subscribers to the organisation's journals). 48p. ISSN 0266-4054. *En.
TF: the 1985 edition, published mid-1984, has data for 1983/84 and some earlier years.
World production and consumption, trade and prices for finished fertiliser products for each region and major countries (production by product type; trade by product type, source and destination; trends).

234 Annual prospective medium-term supply/demand surveys for phosphate rock, sulphur, phosphoric acid and phosphate fertilisers.
International Phosphate Industry Association, 28 rue Marbeuf, 75008 Paris, France; & 57 Chiswell Street, London EC1Y 4SY.
Normally available only to member organisations, who may be provided also with detailed statistical data on such products on an annual, quarterly or monthly basis.

235 World statistics - fertilizer raw materials & intermediates.
British Sulphur Corporation Ltd., 25 Wilton Road, London SW1V 1NH.
1983- 1984. £45 (£30 to subscribers to the organisation). *En.
TF: the 1984 edition, published in December 1984, has data for 1983 and some earlier years.
Detailed data on world production, consumption and trade for fertiliser raw materials and intermediates for each region and major countries.

236 FAO fertiliser yearbook.
FAO, Roma.
1951/54- 1984. £9.60. 147p. ISSN 0251-1525. *En; table headings also in Fr & Es.
TF: the 1984 edition, published in 1985, has long runs of figures to 1983 or 1983/84.
Data on world production, consumption, trade, supply and prices of fertilisers (nitrogenous, phosphate, and potash).

237 Worldwide rubber statistics.
International Institute of Synthetic Rubber Producers Inc., 2077 S. Gessner Road, Suite 133, Houston, Texas 77063, USA.
1985- 1985. $60. 90p. *En.
TF: the 1985 edition, published in 1985, has data for 7 to 10 years to 1983 or 1984 or the latest available.
World rubber statistics (production, supply, tyres, etc), rubber consumption forecasts, and world production facilities.
Note: previously 'Synthetic rubber'.

Δ B – iii(d) Metals, etc

238 Statistisches Jahrbuch der Eisen- und Stahlindustrie [Statistical yearbook of the iron and steel industry] (Wirtschaftsvereinigung Eisen- und Stahlindustrie).
Verlag Stahleisen mbH, Breite Str. 27, Postfach 8229, 4000 Düsseldorf 1, Germany.
1922- 1985. not priced. 340p. ISSN 0081-5365. *De.
TF: the 1985 edition, published late 1985, has data for 1984 and several earlier years.
Data on production, consumption, stocks, prices, employment, wages, accidents and trade in the iron and steel industry. A section on German industry is followed by one for other countries.

239 International steel statistics.
United Kingdom Iron and Steel Statistics Bureau, 12 Addiscombe Road, Croydon CR9 6BS, England.
1959- 1984. Country books: £25 each; Summary tables: £75; complete series: £500. *En.
TF: the books are issued as and when the information for the relevant country becomes available.
24 annual books for separate countries or groups of countries show production, materials consumed. apparent consumption and detailed imports and exports of 130 iron and steel products by quality and market. The summary tables relate to iron ore, pig iron, scrap, crude steel, finished steel and trade.

240 Bulletin de la Chambre Syndicale de la Sidérurgie Française [Bulletin of the Association of French Iron & Steel Industry].
Chambre Syndicale de la Sidérurgie Française, 5 bis, rue de Madrid, 75008 Paris.
1946- monthly & annual. not priced. *Fr.
TF: each monthly issue has annual figures and monthly averages for the last ten years and monthly figures for the last 12-15 months up to two to six months prior to the date of publication. The annual issues cover the year of issue, and varying numbers of earlier years, and are published as and when the information for each country becomes available.
The monthly series contains statistical data on production and foreign trade of iron and steel and their products for the world, several European countries, USA and Japan. There are also separate annual issues of production and of foreign trade for each of those countries.

241 The iron and steel industry.
OECD, Paris.
1954- 1983. £5; $10; Fr 50. 50p. *En, Fr.
TF: the 1983 edition, published in 1985, has data for 1983.
Production, orders, consumption of raw materials for production of iron and steel, ores, raw and semi-finished products, finished products (rails, sleepers, bars, wire-road, etc), investment expenditure, prices, etc.

242 Annual bulletin of steel statistics for Europe. (United Nations Economic Commission for Europe).
UN, New York.
1973- 1983. £9.05; $9.50. 88p. *En, Fr, Ru.
TF: the 1983 edition was published in 1984, with data for 1979 to 1983.
Summary tables on production of specific irons and steels; detailed tables on production, consumption of raw materials, foreign trade, movement of scrap, consumption of energy in the steel industry, steel deliveries to consuming industries.

243 Quarterly bulletin of steel statistics for Europe. (United Nations Economic Commission for Europe).
UN, New York.
1950- quarterly. £8.50; $7 each issue. ISSN 0041-7378. *En, Fr, Ru.
Production of raw materials, finished stell, imports and exports.

244 The steel market. (United Nations Economic Commission for Europe).
UN, New York.
1953- 1983. £16.50; $16.50. 157p. *En.
TF: the 1983 edition, published in 1984, has data for 1979-1983.
Summary tables on production of specific irons and steels, followed by detailed tables on production, consumption of raw materials, foreign trade, movement of scrap, consumption of energy in the steel industry, steel deliveries to consuming industries.

245 The steel market ... and outlook ...
OECD, Paris.
(annual) 1984/85. £4.50; $9; Fr 45. 36p. *En.
TF: the 1984/85 edition, published in September 1985, has data for 1982 or 1983 to 1985.
Production, consumption and trade in steel.

246 Iron and steel yearbook.
Eurostat, Luxembourg.
1968- 1985. £12.70; FrB 1000; $18. 180p. *En, Fr, De, Da, It, Nl.
TF: the 1985 edition was published in 1985 and contains data for the years 1980 to 1984.
The structure and economic situation of the industry, including employment; size of enterprises; plants; crude steel, finished steel and end products; consumption of raw materials; work deliveries and receipts; external trade of scrap and ECSC products; indirect foreign trade; steel consumption; investments; prices; and levy.

Δ B - iii(d), continued

247 Iron and steel, 1952-1982.
Eurostat, Luxembourg.
£5.70 or FrB 450. 115p. *En, De, Fr, It.
TF: published in 1984.
Long-term series on the evolution of the structure and of the economic situation of the Community's iron and steel industry; employment; size of enterprise; plants; production of iron-ore, pig-iron, crude steel, finished steel and end products; consumption of raw materials; external trade in ECSC products; indirect foreign trade; steel consumption.

248 Quarterly iron and steel bulletin.
Eurostat, Luxembourg.
1953- quarterly. FrB 700; £9.20; $12 or FrB 2200; £28.75; $35 yr. ISSN 0378-3510. *E, Fr, De, It.
Annual, quarterly and monthly statistics of employment; consumption of raw materials; production of iron ore, pig-iron, crude steel, finished steel products and end-products; works deliveries and receipts; stocks; external and internal ECSC steel and scrap trade; and apparent steel consumption.

249 Monthly bulletin - iron and steel.
Eurostat, Luxembourg.
1953- monthly. FrB 150; £2; $3 or FrB 1100; £14.50; $21 yr. ISSN 0378-7559. *En, Fr, De, It.
Short-term economic statistics on production of pig-iron, crude steel, steel mill products; consumption and receipts of scrap; and number of short-term workers.

250 The non-ferrous metals industry.
OECD, Paris.
1954- 1982. £4.50; $9; Fr 45; DM 22. 50p. *En, Fr.
TF: the 1982 issue, published early 1984, has data for 1982 and some earlier years.
Production and consumption of aluminium, copper, lead, zinc, tin and nickel in OECD member countries; the use of the metals at the first processing stage; and despatches of aluminium in terms of end use.

251 World stainless steel statistics. (World Bureau of Metal Statistics).
Metal Bulletin Books Ltd, Park House, Park Terrace, Worcester Park, Surrey KT4 7HY, England.
1974- 1985. £152; $364. c 200p. *En.
TF: the 1985 edition, published mid-1985, has data for several years to 1984.
A comprehensive review of world stainless steel production and international trade (excluding Eastern Europe, China and USSR).

Δ B - iii(e) Engineering

252 The engineering industries in OECD member countries: basic statistics.
OECD, Paris.
1960- 1977-1980. £5; $10; Fr 50. 110p. *En, Fr.
TF: the 1977-1980 edition, with data for those years, was published in 1983.
Basic data on deliveries of 128 selected products; data on the principal factors of production (employment, added value, investments, wages and salaries, etc) of several important branches of the industry; and data on the product groupings at current and constant prices.

253 Annual review of engineering industries and automation. (United Nations Economic Commission for Europe).
UN, New York.
1979- 1982, (published in 1984). £11; $11. 91p. *En.
Analyses data on production, investments, manpower and price indices in Europe, Japan and North America.

254 Motor industry of Great Britain ... world automotive statistics.
Society of Motor Manufacturers and Traders, Forbes House, Halkin Street, London SW1X 7DS.
1947- 1985. £38 (£22 to members). ISSN 0077-1597. *En.
TF: the 1985 edition, published in 1985, has data for 1984.
Detailed statistics of production of motor cars, commercial vehicles, tractors, etc in the UK and overseas, and foreign trade of the UK and overseas countries.

255 World automotive market.
Automobile International, 386 Park Avenue South, New York, NY 10016.
1966- 1985. $22. 48p. *En.
TF: the 1985 edition, published in 1985, has data for several years to 1984.
Includes data on vehicle production, registration of motor cars and trucks and buses, and import statistics, by individual country.

256 World motor vehicle data.
Motor Vehicle Manufacturers Association of the United States Inc., 300 New Center Building, Detroit, Michigan 48202.
1964- 1983. $35 plus postage overseas. 346p. ISSN 0085-8307. *En.
TF: the 1983 edition, published in 1983, has data for 1981 or 1982 and many earlier years.

257 L'automobile dans le monde [The motor car in the world].
Fabrimetal, rue des Drapiers 21, 1050 Bruxelles.
(annual) 1983. not priced. 102p. *Fr, Nl.
TF: the 1983 edition, published in 1984, has data for 1982 and 1983.
Data on production, exports, registrations, people with cars, for the world, north America, Europe and Japan, etc.

Δ B - iii(e), continued

258 Das Auto - International - in Zahlen [Automobile - International - in figures].
Verband der Automobilindustrie eV, Westendstrasse 61, 6000 Frankfurt/Main, Germany.
(annual) 1984. DM 64.20. 326p. *De.
TF: the 1984 edition, published in 1984, has data for 1983 and for 1979 to 1983 in some tables.
Structure of the industry; production/assembly of the industry; foreign trade; data for individual countries.

259 Yearbook of West European electronics data.
Benn Electronics Publications Ltd, 146 Midland Road, Luton LU2 OBL.
1973- 12th ed., 1985. £150. 190p. ISSN 0306-5774. *En.
TF: the 1985 edition, published in 1984, has data for four years to 1985 (provisional).
Production data, market data, and foreign trade for electronic processing equipment, office equipment, control & instrumentation, medical & industrial electronics, communications, telecommunications, consumer electronics equipment, and components.

260 Economic handbook of the machine tool industry.
National Machine Tool Builders' Association, 7901 Westpark Drive, McLean, Va 22101, USA.
1969/70- 1985-86. $35 ($20 to members). c 300p. ISSN 0070-8550. *En.
TF: the 1985-86 edition, published late 1985, has data for several years to 1984.
Mainly data for the USA but also has a chapter on the world economy and one on the world machine tool industry, including production, trade and consumption, by country.

Δ B - iii(f) Other industries

261 The furniture industry in Western Europe: a statistical digest.
Furniture Industry Research Association, Maxwell Road, Stevenage, Herts SG1 2EW.
1961- 1984. £15 to members; £30 to non-members. 115p. *En.
TF: the 1984 edition, published late 1984, has data for 1983 and some earlier years in some tables.
Production, overseas trade, structure of the industry, working conditions, and trends in material usage for 15 countries. Also selected bar charts showing comparisons between the UK and European statistics.
Note: compiled by FIRA on behalf of the Union Européenne de l'Ameublement.

262 Boating industry reports ... statistics ...
International Council of Marine Industry Associations, Boating Industry House, Vale Road, Oatlands, Weybridge, Surrey KT13 9NS.
(annual) 1984. not priced. unpaged. *En.
TF: the 1984 edition, published in 1984, has data for 1982 and 1983.
Reports for each member country, including the majority of Western European countries, followed by sections of statistics for each country on boat parks (units); boat products (units); firms, employees, turnover; engine sales (units); and foreign trade.

263 World statistical review: production, trade, consumption.
CEMBUREAU, 2 rue Saint-Charles, 75740 Paris Cedex 15.
1976/77- No. 4, 1982. Fr 200. 25p. *En.
Includes a summary of the world cement market, and data on production, foreign trade and consumption for each country, arranged under regions.
Note: 'World cement market in figures, 1913-1977' was included in the price of the above.

264 An international survey of book production during the last decades.
UNESCO, Paris.
1982. Fr 14. 91p. *En.
Includes statistics of book production.

Δ B - iv Construction

265 Construction statistics yearbook.
UN, New York.
1963/72- 1982. £30; $30. 246p. *En.
TF: the 1982 edition, published in 1984, has data for 1982.
Sections on general indicators of activity, fixed assets, new building construction authorised, dwelling construction authorised, new buildings completed, and dwellings completed. Data is for all types of buildings.

266 Annual bulletin of housing and building statistics for Europe. (United Nations Economic Commission for Europe).
UN, New York.
1957- 1984. £12.50; $12.50. 102p. *En, Fr, Ru.
TF: the 1984 edition, published mid-1985, has data for the years 1980 to 1984.
General statistics and data on dwelling construction, materials used, and employment in the construction industry. Also includes wholesale price indices of building materials in Europe, Canada & USA.

Δ B – v Energy

267 Energy statistics yearbook.
UN, New York.
1952- 1983. £45 or $45. 474p. *En, Fr.
TF: the 1983 edition, published late 1985, has data for 1980 to 1983.
Statistics on production, trade and consumption of commercial energy, solid fuels, petroleum, petroleum products, and natural gas liquids, gaseous fuels, electrical energy, nuclear fuels, renewable energy sources, and energy prices, etc. for reporting countries.
Note: a machine-readable tape 'World energy supplies system' ($180) has time series from 1950 onwards.

268 Survey of energy resources.
World Energy Conference, 34 St James's Street, London SW1A 1HD.
1929- not priced. 2 vols. *En.
TF: a survey is taken every six or seven years and the results of the latest survey were published in 1980.
Part A: Text ...; part B: Appendices, including statistical data on solid fuels, crude oil, natural gas and natural gas liquids, oil shale and bituminous sands, hydraulic resources, nuclear resources, for each country.

269 International energy statistical review. (National Foreign Assessment Center).
NTIS, PO Box 3, Newman Lane, Alton, Hants GU34 2PG; or Document Expediting (DOCEX) Project, Exchange and Gift Division, Library of Congress, Washington DC 20540.
1978- monthly. £75 yr (UK & Ireland). ISSN 0160-1512. *En.
TF: includes data for the last 4-5 years in years, quarters and months to about four months prior to the date of the issue.
Deals mainly with the petroleum and natural gas industries, with charts on the total 'free world' and USSR oil production, inland oil production, and net oil imports.

270 Annual bulletin of general energy statistics for Europe. (United Nations Economic Commission for Europe).
UN, New York.
1968- 1983. £15 or $15. 122p. *En, Fr, Ru.
TF: the 1983 edition, published in 1985, has data for 1982 and 1983.
Basic data on the energy situation as a whole as well as details on the production of energy by form, overall energy balance sheets, deliveries of petroleum products for inland consumption, liquid fuels and nuclear, hydro and geothermal energy. Covers European countries, Canada and USA.

271 Energy statistics ... and main historical series.
OECD, Paris.
1950/64- 1982-1983. £10; $20; Fr 100. 180p. *En, Fr.
TF: the 1982-1983 edition, published in 1985, has data for 1982 and 1983.
Data on energy production, trade and consumption for each source of energy in all OECD member countries.
Note: OECD also has files on magnetic tape for basis energy statistics. Enquiries to Head of Division, Energy Statistics & Data Processing, OECD, 2 rue André-Pascal, 75775 Paris Cedex 16, France.

272 Energy balances of OECD countries.
OECD, Paris.
1969/74- 1982-1983. £10; $20; Fr 100. 186p. *En, Fr.
TF: the 1982-1983 edition, published in 1985, has data for 1982 and 1983.
General energy statistics (supply, demand and transformation, and end use) presented in a common unit (metric tons oil equivalent) for all OECD member countries.
Note: OECD also has files on magnetic tape for annual energy balances. Enquiries to Head of Division, Energy Statistics & Data Processing, OECD, 2 rue Andre-Pascal, 75775 Paris, Cedex 16, France.

273 Energy prices and taxes.
OECD, Paris.
3rd qtr, 1984- quarterly. £12 or £40 yr; $24 or $80 yr; Fr 120 or Fr 400 yr. *En, Fr.
TF: each issue, published some three or four months later, has the latest data available for each country and earlier figures.
Energy prices for all fuels, at every market stage – import prices, wholesale prices for industry, and retail prices for households.

274 Statistics review.
Energy Economics Research Ltd, 7/9 Queen Victoria Street, Reading, Berks RG1 1SY.
1980- 1985. £80 for subscribers to 'Oil and energy trends'; £115 for others. 93p. *En.
TF: the 1985 edition, published in May 1985, has data for 1984 and up to ten earlier years.
World data on crude oil reserves, natural gas reserves, crude oil production, natural gas production, coal and lignite production, primary electricity production, primary energy production; geophysical activity; number of rigs active; wells drilled; refining capacity; refining runs; production from refineries OECD area; oil demand (all products); demand by major product, OECD area; government crude oil sales prices; product prices; net imports of crude and products; principal international gas movement; value of net oil imports (15 countries); tanker fleet (by size and numbers); spot (dirty) freight rates (by major haul); dirty tonnage spot chartered (monthly); average freight rate assessments; capital exploration expenditures, etc.

275 Energy statistics yearbook.
Eurostat, Luxembourg.
1964- 1983. £10.10; $12; FrB 750. 218p. *En, Fr, It, De.
TF: the 1983 edition, published in 1985, has data for 1983 and earlier years in some tables.
Part 1: analyses characteristic data of the energy economy; part 2: deals with the 'energy supplied' balance sheets for the Community and each member state; and part 3: gives historical data for each energy source for the main aggregates that determine the structures of the energy economy.

Δ B – v, continued

276 Bulletin of energy prices: survey of consumer prices for oil, coal, gas and electricity in the Community...
Eurostat, Luxembourg.
No. 1, 1984– No. 1/2 1985 (published late 1985). FrB 200; £2.75; $3.50. 43p. *En, Fr.

277 Uranium: resources, production and demand.
OECD, Paris.
1967– 1983 (published in 1984). Fr 160; £16; $32; DM 71. 348p. *En.
Compilations of uranium resources and production data compared with the nuclear industry's future natural uranium requirements.

278 Annual oil and gas statistics and main historical series.
OECD, Paris.
1960– 1982–1983. £20; $40; Fr 200. 450p. *En, Fr.
TF: the 1982–1983 edition, published early 1985, has data for 1982 and 1983 and earlier historical figures.
Summary tables (crude oil, etc., finished products), consumption by end use sector, trade, natural gas.
Note: OECD also has files on magnetic tape. Enquiries to Head of Division, Energy Statistics & Data Processing, OECD, 2 rue André-Pascal, 75775 Paris Cedex 16.

279 Quarterly oil and gas statistics.
OECD, Paris.
1964– quarterly. £15 or £45 yr; $30 or $95 yr; Fr 150 or Fr 450 yr. ISSN 0378-6536. *En, Fr.
TF: each issue is published about four months after the end of the quarter to which it refers.
Detailed data on production, trade, refinery intake and output, as well as final consumption of nine product groups; trade data for 52 import origins and 32 export destinations; international marine bunkers; fuel deliveries to civil aviation; and natural gas product consumption.
Note: OECD also has files on magnetic tape. Enquiries to Head of Division, Energy Statistics & Processing, OECD, 2 rue André-Pascal, 75775 Paris Cedex 16.

280 Outlook for world oil into the 21st century. (Petroleum Industry Research Foundation Inc).
Electric Power Research Institute, 34i2 Hillview Avenue, Palo Alto, California 94304.
1978. not priced. various pagings. *En.
Attempts to forecast oil supply and demand in the non-Communist world for 1976 to 1990 and from 1990 to 2005. Statistical tables are included in the text.

281 Energy in profile.
Shell International Petroleum Co Ltd., Shell Centre, London SE1 7NA.
1974– quarterly. not priced. *En.
TF: each issue has data for several years to about 6 months prior to publication.
World energy supply and demand, energy consumption and costs, crude oil production and prices, refining capacity, natural gas trade and hard coal trade.
Note: issued in the 'Shell briefing service'.

282 Information handbook.
Shell International Petroleum Co Ltd., Shell Centre, London SE1 7NA.
1966– 1980–1981. free. 136p. *En.
TF: the 1980–1981 edition, published late 1980, has data for 1979 and some 1978 figures.
Facts and figures about the oil and natural gas, coal nuclear, petrochemicals and metals industries, as well as the activities of the Royal Dutch/Shell Group of companies.

283 Oil and gas and coal ... production, marine, crude oil movements, OPEC, refining, oil demand, natural gas, coal.
Shell International Petroleum Co Ltd., Shell Centre, London SE1 7NA.
1974– 1984 (published mid-1985) free. 9p. *En.
Note: issued in the 'Shell briefing service'.

284 Energi ed idrocarburi. Energy and hydrocarbons.
Ente Nazionale Idrocarburi, Piazzale E. Mattei 1, 00144 Roma.
1955/74– 1983. not priced. 204p. *It, En.
TF: the 1983 edition, published in 1983, has data for 1982 and long runs of annual figures to 1982 in some tables.
Includes, as well as Italian statistics, international statistics on economic indicators and energy; energy consumption; reserves of oil and gas; coal resources and reserves; production of oil and gas; crude oil production and reserves in OPEC countries; coal production and trade; geothermal power generation; refining; imports and consumption of oil and gas; transport of hydrocarbons; prices of crude oil and petroleum products; nuclear energy – reserves and production of uranium; nuclear energy – installed generating capacity; production, central stations on order.

285 Annual statistical bulletin.
OPEC, Obere Donau-strasse 93, A-1020 Wien.
1966– 1983. öS 350. 161p. ISSN 0475-0608. *En.
TF: the 1983 edition, published in 1984, has data from 1979 to 1983.
Summary and basic indicators are followed by sections on oil and gas data (exploration, crude oil and natural gas production, share of production by company, refining, consumption, exports, imports), transportation (tanker fleet, tanker freight rates, pipelines), prices (crude oil prices in OPEC member countries) and major oil companies (operations, finances, etc).
Note: OPEC has also issued a 41-page booklet 'Oil industry conversion factors' which is available on request; and 'OPEC annual report' includes statistical tables in the text and also an appendix 'OPEC statistical summary and indicators'.

B – v, continued

286 Facts and figures: a comparative analysis.
OPEC, Obere Donaustrasse 93, A-1020 Wien.
1980- 1984. free. 45p. *En.
TF: the 1984 edition, published late 1984, has data for 1983 and several earlier years.
A visual presentation of key statistics relating to the world energy industry. The booklet is divided into six sections, the first three providing a global overview of the industry, highlighting production, consumption and resource availabilities. Two sections relate to OPEC (oil flows and volumes, prices and values) and the last section contains national income, aid and trade comparisons between the industrialised and the developing countries.

287 Know more about oil: world statistics.
Institute of Petroleum, 61 New Cavendish Street, London W1M 8AR.
(annual) 1983. not priced. 8p. ISSN 0141-4305. *En.
TF: the 1983 issue, published mid-1984, has data for 1938, 1950, 1973, 1982 and 1983 (preliminary).
World commercial energy demand, estimated production, refining capacity, estimated consumption of petroleum products, tanker tonnage, and international trade.

288 Bulletin analytique pétrolier: supplement [Analytical bulletin of petroleum: supplement].
Comité Professionnel du Pétrole, 51 blvd de Courcelles, 75008 Paris.
1974- bi-monthly bulletin with about 50 supplements a year. Fr 675 yr, inc. supplements.
ISSN 0007-4101. *Fr.
The bulletin is an abstracting journal, in which some abstracts contain statistical data; the supplements are each devoted to a particular aspect of the petroleum industry and/or a particular country and are mainly statistical.

289 BP statistical review of world energy.
British Petroleum Company plc, Britannic House, Moor Lane, London EC2Y 9BU.
(annual) 1984. not priced. 32p. *En.
TF: the 1984 issue, published in 1984, has data for several years to 1983.
Reserves, production, consumption, trade, refining, tankers and energy.

290 Petroleum economist: the international energy journal.
Petroleum Press Bureau Ltd., PO Box 105, 25/31 Ironmonger Row, London EC1V 3PN.
1934- monthly. £72 or $122 yr. ISSN 0306-395X. *En & Ja eds.
Some statistical tables are included in the articles, and there are regular tables on world oil production, prices, and oil share quotations.

291 Twentieth century petroleum statistics.
DeGolyer & McNaughton, One Energy Square, Dallas, Texas 75206.
1945- 1982. $35. 105p. *En.
TF: the 1982 edition, published late 1982, has long runs of figures to 1981.
Statistics in graphs and tables on world-wide petroleum reserves, production, prices, imports, refinery capacity, consumption, drilling, etc.

292 Annual bulletin of electric energy statistics for Europe. (United Nations Economic Commission for Europe).
UN, New York.
1956- 1983. £12.50; $12.50. 101p. ISSN 0066-3816. *En, Fr, Ru.
TF: the 1983 edition, published in 1984, has data for 1983.
Basic data on developments and trends in the field of electric energy in European countries, Canada & USA. Also includes statistics on capacity of plants; production; imports, exports and consumption of electric energy; supplies of electric energy to consumers; consumption of fuels and corresponding production of electric energy; and international exchanges of electric energy.

293 Electrical energy - monthly bulletin.
Eurostat, Luxembourg.
1956- 11 a year. FrB 130; £1.70; $2.50 or FrB 700; £9.25; $12 yr. ISSN 0378-3561. *En, Fr, De.
TF: each issue has data to about two months prior to the publication date.
Monthly update of the principal statistical series characterising the short-term movements in the electrical economy in general and fuel consumption in power stations in particular.

294 Electricity prices.
Eurostat, Luxembourg.
1978/84- 1980-1985. FrB 450; £5.70; $7.50. 135p. *En, Fr, De & It eds.
TF: the 1980-1985 edition, with data for those years, was published late 1985.
Update of the annual enquiries on electricity prices in the countries of the Community, with time series back to 1980.

295 Annual bulletin of gas statistics for Europe. (United Nations Economic Commission for Europe).
UN, New York.
1955- 1983. £11 or $11. 107p. ISSN 0066-3824. *En, Fr, Ru.
TF: the 1983 edition, published in 1984, has data for 1970, 1980 to 1983.
Basic data on developments and trends in production, consumption, number of consumers of gas, natural gas and refined gas; and also on gas works.

Δ B – v, continued

296 Gas prices.
Eurostat, Luxembourg.
1970/76– 1978–1984. FrB 500; £6.60; $9. 180p. *En, Fr, De, & It eds.
TF: the 1978–1984 edition, with data for those years, was published in 1985.
Gas prices in approximately 30 locations for both domestic and industrial uses, with a breakdown by type of consumer. The statistical annex has tables and graphs on household and other industrial prices by country, conversion factors for price indices, and international comparisons.

297 Hydrocarbons: monthly bulletin.
Eurostat, Luxembourg.
1978– 11 a year. FrB 130; £1.70; $2.50 or FrB 1100; £14.50; $18 yr. ISSN 0378-3731. *En, Fr, De.
TF: each issue has data for two years, for each month available for the current year, and for the corresponding months of the previous year.
Monthly update of the principal statistical series characterising the short-term movements in the petroleum and gas industries.

298 Operation of nuclear power stations.
Eurostat, Luxembourg.
(annual) 1984. FrB 600; £7.50; $10. 200p. *En, Fr.
TF: the 1984 edition, published in 1985, has data for 1984.
Presents the main operating statistics; outlines the structure of the nuclear plant situation; and includes monthly operating data, yearly results, and annual local diagrams for each nuclear power station in the Community.

299 Annual bulletin of coal statistics for Europe. (United Nations Economic Commission for Europe).
UN, New York.
1947– 1983. £10.45; $11. *En, Fr, Ru.
TF: the 1983 edition, published in 1984, has data for several years to 1983.
Production, stocks, trade and availability of solid fuels and related products, subdivided by countries.
Note: Up-dated by 'Quarterly bulletin of coal statistics for Europe' (1947– £1.95 or $5 each issue. *En, Fr, Ru).

300 Coal information.
OECD, Paris.
1983– 1985. £40; $80; Fr 400. 438p. *En, Fr.
TF: the 1985 edition was published in August 1985.
Part I: provides an overview of the world coal market developments and prospects, forecasting trends in solid-fuel supply, demand and trade. Part II: gives more detailed and comprehensive picture of coal developments and future prospects.

301 International coal.
National Coal Association, 1130 17th Street NW, Washington DC 20036.
1976– 1983. $125 ($135 foreign mailing). 119p. *En.
TF: the 1983 edition, published in 1984, has data for 1983 and some earlier years.
World coal statistics (reserves, production, shipments, consumption, etc), the coal in world trade, and coal statistics for selected countries.

302 Coal – monthly bulletin.
Eurostat, Luxembourg.
11 a year. FrB 130; £1.70; $2.50 or FrB 700; £9.25; $11.20 yr. ISSN 0378-357X. *En, Fr, De.
TF: each issue has data to about two months prior to the date of publication.
Monthly update of the principal statistical series characterising short-term movements in the coal industry.

Δ B – vi Research and development

303 Government financing of research and development, 1975–1984.
Eurostat, Luxembourg.
1974/76– 1975–1983 (published late 1985). £5.90; $8.50; FrB 450. 290p. *En, Fr, De, It, Nl, Da, Gr.
An overall analysis of the public financing of R & D from 1975 to 1984 and a detailed analysis by objectives of this financing in 1984 in the member states.

304 OECD science and technology indicators. Resources devoted to R & D.
OECD, Paris.
1984. £13.50; $27; Fr 135. 378p. *En.
A report examining trends in the level and structure of national R & D efforts during the 1970s and prospects for the 1980s.

305 Current studies and research in statistics: series CSR-S.
UNESCO, 75700 Paris.
1970– irregular. free. * Fr, En.
A series of reports, some of which have a statistical content, for example:
CSR-S- 5 Development in human and financial resources for science and technology: basic statistical tables ...
CSR-S- 9 Participation of women in R & D: a statistical study.
CSR-S-11 Statistics on science and technology ...
CSR-S-16 Human and financial resources for research and experimental development in agriculture.
CSR-S-17 Estimated world resources for research in experimental development, 1970–1980.
CSR-S-18 Statistics on science and technology: latest available data.

Δ C External trade

306 International trade statistics yearbook.
UN, New York.
1950- 1983. £80 or $80 for 2 vols. 2 vols. ISSN 0084-3822. *En, Fr.
TF: the 1983 edition, published in 1985, has data for 1983.
Basic information for individual countries' external trade performance in terms of overall trends in current value as well as in volume and price, the importance of trading partners and the significance of individual commodities imports and exports. Vol I: Trade by country; vol II: Trade by commodity. Covers 163 countries or reporting areas.

307 World trade annual.
Walker & Company, 720 Fifth Avenue, New York, NY 10019.
1963- 1980 for main volumes. $100 each vol. 5 vols. ISSN 0512-3739. *En.
1979 for supplementary volumes. $125 each vol. 5 vols. ISSN 0512-3747.
TF: the 1980 edition has data for 1980 and was published in 1984; the 1979 edition has data for 1979 and was published in 1981.
The main volumes contain statistics of foreign trade for each of 1312 items of the SITC as reported by the 24 principal countries, the data being arranged in commodity order and subdivided by countries of origin and destination.
Vol 1: Food; beverages and tobacco; crude materials, edible, except fuels; animal and vegetable oils and fats.
Vol 2: Mineral fuels, lubricants and related materials; chemicals.
Vol 3: Manufactured goods classified chiefly by material.
Vol 4: Miscellaneous manufactured articles.
Vol 5: machinery and transport equipment; commodities and transactions not classified elsewhere.
Five supplementary volumes deal with the trade of Eastern Europe and the developing countries, the prime purpose of these volumes being to serve those who are interested in individual countries for which trade statistics are not easily available in internationally comparable form. Vol. 1 relates to Eastern Europe and the USSR. In all the volumes values are given in US$ and quantities in metric units.

308 Commodity trade statistics.
UN, New York.
1950- £95 or $100 yr. approx. 28 issues a year. *En.
Issued in fascicules of about 250 pages each as annual data for each reporting country becomes available. Each country's imports and exports are shown in the 625 sub-groups of the SITC, subdivided by countries of origin and destination. Values in each case are converted to US$ and quantities shown in metric units. In the front of each fascicule is an index showing in which issue appeared the latest data for each country.
Note: Machine readable tape of input is available. Prices and details on request to the UN Statistical Office.

309 Direction of trade statistics.
International Monetary Fund, Washington DC 20431.
1958/62- 11 monthly issue with annual summary ('Direction of trade yearbook'). £4 or £19.50 yr; $4 or $36 yr. ISSN 0252-306X. *En, Fr, Es.
TF: Up-to-dateness varies from country to country, but each issue has data for the two latest months available and comparative figures for the previous year. The yearbook has data for seven years for 157 countries.
Distribution by partner countries and by areas of countries' exports and imports. Monthly issues have data for some 135 countries.

310 International trade.
GATT, Palais des Nations, 1211 Genève 10.
(annual) 1983/84. £12; FrS 30. 216p. ISSN 0072-064X. *En.
TF: the 1983/84 edition, published early 1985, has data for several years to 1983.
An annual report concerned with main trends in international trade, trade in commodities, trade in industrial areas, trade in non-industrial areas, and trade of the eastern trading areas. Statistical tables are included in the text, as well as there being a statistical appendix.

311 World invisible trade.
British Invisible Exports Council, 14 Austin Friars, London EC2N 2HE.
1966- 1984. £6. 20p. *En.
TF: the 1984 edition, published mid-1984, has data for 1982 and some earlier years.

312 Monthly statistics of foreign trade (Series A).
OECD, Paris.
1950- monthly. £30 or $62 or Fr 300 yr. ISSN 0474-5388. *En, Fr.
TF: each issue has several years annual, quarterly and monthly data to three or four months prior to the date of the issue.
A detailed regional analysis of trade of the main country groupings in the OECD area, non-adjusted and seasonally adjusted.
Note: 'Historical statistics of foreign trade, series A, 1965-1980' was published in 1982 (£5.50; $11; Fr 55).

313 Trade by country (Series B).
OECD, Paris.
1977- 1983. £135 or $300 or Fr 1350 yr for about 140 microfiches. *En, Fr.
Available only on microfiches. Data is shown for each of the OECD member countries and Yugoslavia. Internationally comparative figures for imports and exports in $ and, where possible, metric tons, arranged by the SITC to five digits.

314 Foreign trade by commodities (Series C).
OECD, Paris.
1950- 1983. £8 or $16 or Fr 80 each vol. 2 vols. ISSN 0474-540X. *En, Fr.
TF: the 1983 edition, published in 1985, has data for 1983.
Vol I: Exports; vol II: Imports. Contains matrix tables showing trade between OECD countries and partner countries for commodity groups at the 1 and 2 digit levels of the SITC.
Note: more detailed data is available on microfiche (£80 or $160 or Fr 800 for c 110 microfiches).

315 EFTA trade.
EFTA Secretariat, 9-11 rue de Varembé, 1211 Genève 20.
1959/63- 1983. free. 112p. ISSN 0531-4119. *En; title & contents list also in Fr & De.
TF: the 1983 edition, published early 1985, has data for 1981/82 and 1982/83 or 1982 and 1983, with 1972 to 1983 in some tables.
Total trade of the EFTA countries; EFTA trade by area; EFTA trade by main product groups; Intra-EFTA trade; EFTA trade with the EC; EFTA trade with selected countries; EFTA trade with Eastern Europe; EFTA trade with developing countries; and EFTA trade in selected commodities. EFTA countries are A, CH, IS, N, S, SF.

316 Foreign trade by commodities: exports and imports.
OECD, Paris.
1950- 1983. £8 or $16 or Fr 80 each vol; £15 or $30 or Fr 150 for 2 vols. 2 vols. ISSN 0474-540X. *En, Fr.
TF: the 1983 edition, published in 1985, has data for 1983.
Matrix tables showing trade between OECD countries and partner countries for commodity groups defined to 1 and 2 digit levels of SITC. Vol I: Exports; vol II: Imports.
Note: more detailed data (ie., 3, 4 & 5 digit level of the SITC for quantities and values) are available in exactly the same format on microfiches (1983 data £80 or $160 or Fr 800 got 109 microfiches).

317 Analytical tables of foreign trade - SITC/CTCI, Rev.2 - exports.
Eurostat, Luxembourg.
(annual) 1983. £18.40; $26.50; FrB 1400 each vol. £93.90; $138; FrB 7200 for 6 vols. 6 vols. *En, Fr, De. Nl, It, Da, Gr.
TF: the 1983 edition, published in 1984, has data for 1983.
Vol I: Countries by products; Vols II-IV: Products by countries. Foreign trade of the European Community and the member states arranged by the SITC classification in order of 'product by country' to 3 and 5 digits and in order of 'country by product' to 5, 4, 3, 2 & 1 digits.

318 Analytical tables of foreign trade - SITC/CTCI, Rev. 2 - imports.
Eurostat, Luxembourg.
(Annual) 1983. £18.40; $26.60; FrB 1400 each vol. £93.90; $138; FrB 7200 for 6 vols. 6 vols. *En Fr, De, Nl, It, Da, Gr.
TF: the 1983 edition, published in 1984, has data for 1983. Contents as for 317.

319 Analytical tables of foreign trade - NIMEXE - imports.
Eurostat, Luxembourg.
(annual) 1983. £15.70; $22; FrB 1200 each vol. £157; $220; FrB 12000 for complete series of 13 vols. *En, De, Fr, Nl, Da, It, Gr, Es.
TF: the 1983 edition, published late 1984, has data for 1983.

320 Analytical tables of foreign trade - NIMEXE - exports.
Eurostat, Luxembourg.
(annual) 1983. £15.20; $20; FrB 1200 each vol. £152; $200; FrB 12000 for complete series of 13 vols. *En, De, Fr, Nl, Da, It, Gr, Es.
TF: the 1983 edition, published late 1984, has data for 1983.
Data on the foreign trade of the European Communities and member states broken down into 'products by country' for all 6-figure NIMEXE headings for 12 volumes, 'country by products' by NIMEXE chapter (2-figure code) for 13th volume. Volumes are A: Agricultural products; B: Mineral products; C: Chemical products; D: Artificial materials, leather; E: Wood, cork, paper; F: Textiles, footwear; G: Stone, plaster, glass, ceramics; H: Iron and steel; I: Other base metals; J: Machinery, appliances; K: Transport equipment; L: Optical precision instruments; Z: Countries - products.

321 External trade - statistical yearbook.
Eurostat, Luxembourg.
1985- 1985. £4.60; $6; FrB 350. 101p. *En, Fr, De, It, Nl, Da, Gr.
TF: the 1985 edition was published in 1985.
Main results of Community statistics on trends in the Community's external trade and in trade between member states from 1958 to 1984. Also summary of trends in the trade of Spain and Portugal between 1977 and 1984. Complements 'External trade monthly statistics'.

322 External trade monthly statistics.
Eurostat, Luxembourg.
1965- £4.60 or £40.75; $6.50 or $57 yr; FrB 350 or FrB 3100 yr. ISSN 0378-3723. *En, Fr, De, Nl, It, Da, Gr.
TF: each issue has long runs of quarterly and monthly figures to the latest available for each country.
Aims to provide rapid information on short-term development of Community foreign trade and trade between member states. Sections on general summary of trade by country; general summary of trade by commodities; indices of volume and value, etc; trends in trade, total, intra and extra-EC; trends in trade with major areas; and trade by partner countries.

Δ C, continued

323 NIMEXE - external trade statistics. Countries - products. SCE 2112.
Eurostat, Luxembourg.
(quarterly) on microfiche. prices on application.
Imports/exports of special trades under the nomenclature of goods for the trade statistics of the European Community and statistics of trade between member States (Nimexe).

324 NIMEXE - external trade statistics. Products/countries. SCE 1111/1112.
Eurostat, Luxembourg.
(quarterly) on microfiche. prices on application.
Imports/exports of special trade under the nomenclature of goods for the external trade statistics of the European Community and statistics of trade between member States (Nimexe).

325 SITC - external trade statistics. Countries - products. SCE 2311.
Eurostat, Luxembourg.
(quarterly) on microfiche. prices on application.
Imports/exports of special trade under the Standard International trade classification (SITC Rev.2)of the United Nations.

326 SITC - external trade statistics. Products - countries. SCE 1311/1312.
Eurostat, Luxembourg.
(quarterly) on microfiche. prices on application.
Imports/exports of special trade under the Standard International Trade Classification (SITC Rev.2) of the United Nations.

327 EC - ACP trade: a statistical analysis, 1970-1981.
Eurostat, Luxembourg.
1983. £3.90; $6; FrB 300. 510p. *En, Fr.
Analyses the development and structure of trade between the Community and the main industrialised countries on the one hand and the ACP states on the other. Part 1: The economy and external trade of the ACP countries; part 2: ACP(62) trade with the European Community and applicant states; part 3: Trade between the EC and ACP(62) by broad economic category; part 4: Main products imported by the EC from ACP(62); and part 5: Terms of trade of the EC with the ACP countries, 1970-1980.

328 COMECON foreign trade data. (Vienna Institute for Comparative Economic Studies).
Macmillan, 4 Essex Street, London WC2.
1980- biennial. 1984 (published in 1985). £30. 553p. *En.
Facts and figures of international trade flows, turnover in selected commodities traded between CMEA ('COMECON') and other supernational trading groups (OECD, EEC, EFTA) and on intra-CMEA trade. Yugoslavia, not a member of CMEA but associated with it, is treated similarly.

329 FAO trade yearbook.
FAO, Roma.
1947- 1983. £18. 373p. ISSN 0071-7126. *En, Fr, Es.
TF: the 1983 edition, published in 1985, has data for varying periods to 1983.
Imports and exports of agricultural commodities and agricultural requisites, classified by SITC, for each reporting country. Data is in US$ and metric quantities.
Note: computer-readable data of time-series also available from the Computer Systems Branch of FAO.

330 Agricultural trade in Europe. (United Nations Economic Commission for Europe).
UN, New York.
1960- 1983 (published in 1984). £10.45 or $11. 89p. *En.
Reviews and analyses recent developments in the import/export of agricultural products within Europe.

331 International textile machinery shipment statistics.
International Textile Manufacturers' Federation, Am Schanzengruben 29, Postfach CH-8039, Zürich.
1974- 1984 (Revised). FrS 50. 28p. *En.
TF: the 1984 revised report, published mid-1985, has data for 1984 and earlier years in some tables.
Results of an annual survey showing shipments, by country of destination, of different types of textile machinery; world spinning and weaving capacities, etc.

332 Foreign trade - products ECSC.
Eurostat, Luxembourg.
1978- quarterly. on microfiche only - complete series FrB 250; per microfiche FrB 50. *En.
Imports and exports of iron and steel products by country of origin & by geographical region destination.

333 Bulletin of statistics on world trade in engineering products. (United Nations Economic Commission for Europe).
UN, New York.
1963- 1983. £35; $35. 397p. *En, Fr, Ru.
TF: the 1983 edition, published late 1985, has data for 1983.
Exports of 37 countries, compiled from replies to questionnaires supplied by various countries or from official national services.

334 Annual bulletin of trade in chemical products. (United Nations Economic Commission for Europe).
UN, New York.
1974- 1983. £30; $30. 316p. *En, Fr, Ru.
TF: the 1983 edition, published early 1985, has data for 1983.
A detailed breakdown of trade in chemical products, arranged by commodities subdivided by countries of origin and destination.

Δ C, continued

335 Statistics of world trade in steel. (United Nations Economic Commission for Europe).
UN, New York.
1913/59- 1983. £8.10; $9.50. 71p. ISSN 0081-5195. *En, Fr, Ru.
TF: the 1983 edition, published in 1984, has data for 1983.
Basic data on exports of semi-finished and finished steel products by exporting countries of the world, subdivided by commodities, region and country of destination.

336 World trade: steel.
United Kingdom Iron and Stel Statistics Bureau, NLA Tower, 12 Addiscombe Road, Croydon CR9 6BS.
1970- quarterly. £125 yr (£140 yr abroad). *En.
TF: published about five months after the end of the quarter.
$ Export trade of 14 major steel producing countries in 28 product groups, covering 100 export markets. The annual issue covers value of trade.

337 World trade - stainless, high speed and other alloy.
United Kingdom Iron and Steel Statistics Bureau, NLA Tower, 12 Addiscombe Road, Croydon CR9 6BS.
(quarterly) £125 yr (£140 yr abroad). *En.
Export trade of major steel producing countries in selected alloy products.

338 MICOFEL: marché international des conserves de fruits et legumes: bulletin mensuel [MICOFEL: international trade in preserved fruit and vegetables: monthly bulletin] (Direction des Produits Agro-alimentaires).
Centre Français du Commerce Extérieur, 10 avenue d'Iéna, 75783 Paris Cedex 16.
(monthly) Fr 555 yr (Fr 585-Fr 663 yr abroad). ISSN 0397-9482. *Fr.

Δ D Internal distribution and service trades

Δ D - i Wholesale and retail trades

339 Retail trade international.
Euromonitor Publications Ltd, PO Box 26, 18 Doughty Street, London WC1.
1977/78- 1983. £96 each vol; £228 for 3 vols. 3 vols. *En.
TF: the 1983 edition was published in 1984, with data for various years to either 1980 or 1981.
Vol 1: United Kingdom; vol 2: Western and Eastern Europe; vol 3: the Americas, Asia, Africa & Australasia. Each volume generally covers broad trends in retailing; trends in consumer spending; breakdowns of consumer spending; total retail sales; retail sales by commodity; number of retail outlets; retail trade by organisation, department and variety stores; mail order, multiples, co-operatives, buying groups and voluntary chains; retail trade by type of outlet (supermarkets, hypermarkets, etc); food distribution; distribution of non-foods; outlook and projections. Vol 2: includes detailed surveys for France and West Germany and substantial sections on all other countries in Western Europe; Yugoslavia is included and there is a final section looking at the countries of the Eastern Bloc.

340 Retail sales - index numbers.
Eurostat, Luxembourg.
1985- monthly. £1.40 or £6 yr; $2 or $9 yr; FrB 100 or FrB 450 yr. ISSN 0256-2715. *En, Fr.
Volume indices (quantities) for retail trade sales in the European Community countries, USA and Japan. Intended to provide short-term indicators of trends in consumption of households and the activity of commercial enterprises.

341 Consumer Europe.
Euromonitor Publications Ltd, 18 Doughty Street, London WC1N 2PN.
1976- 8th, 1982. £87. 714p. ISSN 0308-4353. *En.
TF: the 1982 edition, published in 1982, has drata for the years 1975 to 1979 and estimates for 1980.
Sub-titled 'a statistical guide to Europe's consumer markets', the publication includes key marketing parameters, and data on production, trade, consumption, sales, consumer expenditures, etc.

342 ISSO report - self-service ...
Internationale Selbstbedienungs-Organisation, Burgmauer 53, D-5000 Köln 1, Germany.
1961- 10th, 1984. free. 36p. *De, En, Fr.
TF: the 1984 edition, published in 1985, has data to 1983.
A survey of self-service food stores, supermarkets and superstores/hypermarkets in Europe, giving details of establishments, etc.

Δ D - iii Advertising

343 The European advertising review & forecast. (Advertising Association).
Advertising Press, 22-24 Bell Street, Henley-on-Thames, Oxon RG9 2BG.
1984- 1984. £185.00. *En.
An overview of trends in advertising expenditure in Europe, including a section on advertising expenditure in Europe, 1970-1982, in local currency at current prices, in local currency at constant prices, in local currency at deflated by 'Index of Media' rates, as a % of GNP, by main media sector, and index of media rates, country by country.

Δ D - iii, continued

344 International journal of advertising: the quarterly review of marketing communications. (Advertising Association and CAM Foundation).
Holt Rinehart & Winston Ltd., 1 St Anne's Road, Eastbourne, East Sussex BN21 3UN.
1982- quarterly. £7 or £25 yr; $8.50 or $51 yr. *En.
Some issues include sections on advertising statistics (eg. v.3(3), 1984. Advertising expenditure in the UK: 1983 survey; c. 3(2), 1984. Trends in total advertising expenditure in 29 countries, 1970-1982).

Δ D - iv Tourism and travel

< see also 450a

345 World travel and tourism statistics: yearbook. (World Tourism Organisation).
Organizacion Mundial del Turismo, Capitán Haya 42, 28020 Madrid.
1947- v.38 (1983/84). $50. 491p. *En, Fr, Es.
TF: the 1983/84 edition, published in 1985, has data for 1983 and 1984.
Arranged by country, with data on visitors and tourists arriving, foreign visitors arriving, cruise passengers, by country of residence, length of stay, rooms and hotels available, receipts and expenditures.

346 Domestic tourism statistics. (World Tourism Organisation).
Organizacion Mundial del Turismo, Capitán Haya 42, E - Madrid 20.
1970/72- 1981-1982. not priced. 55p. *En, Fr, Es.
TF: the 1981-1982 edition, published in 1983, has data for 1981 and 1982. The survey is taken every three years.
Data by country on the percentage of the resident population travelling for tourism purposes, domestic tourist arrivals and nights in accommodation establishments, residents departures by mode of transport and purpose of visit, share of domestic tourism in total tourist movements, and total domestic tourist expenditure.

347 Economic review of world tourism. (International Union of Official Travel Organisations).
Organizacion Mundial del Turismo, Capitán Haya 42, E - Madrid 20.
1966- 1986. not priced. 91p. *En.
TF: the 1986 edition, published in 1985, has data for several years to 1984.
Analyses the position of travel and tourism within international trade and national economies. Statistical tables are included in the text.

348 Regional breakdown of world travel and tourism statistics. (World Tourism Organisation).
Organizacion Mundial del Turismo, Capitán Haya 42, E - Madrid 20.
1972/76- 1980-1984. not priced. 150p. *En, Fr, Es.
TF: the 1980-1984 edition, published in 1985, has data for 1981 or 1982 to 1984.
Arranged in four sections - 1: First results of 1985; 2: World summary; 3: Regional summary; 4: Annexes. Data includes international tourist arrivals at frontiers, excursionist arrivals, cruise passenger arrivals, average length of stay of international tourists, capacity of hotels and similar establishments, occupancy rates in hotels and similar establishments, international tourism receipts, international tourism expenditures, exchange rates. Arranged by continent, subdivided by countries.

349 International tourism quarterly.
Economist Intelligence Unit, 40 Duke Street, London W1A 1DW.
1971- quarterly. £27 or £95 yr; $50 or $180 yr. ISSN 0306-4336. *En.
Analyses and evaluates market and industrial trends for operators, carriers, hotels and official tourism organisations. No regular tables but many in the text, which is on particular countries or other subjects (ie. hotels) in each issue.

350 Worldwide lodging industry.
Horwath & Horwath International, 919 Third Avenue, New York, NY 10022.
1971- 14th report, 1984. not priced. 108p. ISSN 0361-218X. *En.
TF: the 1984 report, published in 1984, has data for 1982 or 1983.
Mainly international figures, but one or two tables subdivided into regions, including Europe.

351 Tourism policy and international tourism in OECD member countries.
OECD, Paris.
1970- 1983. £9.80; $19; Fr 98. 164p. *En & Fr eds.
TF: the 1983 edition, published in November 1984, has data for 1983.
Includes statistical data on government policy and action concerning tourism, international tourist flows in member countries, the economic importance of international tourism, transport, and tourist accommodation and catering.

352 Tourism compendium. (World Tourism Organisation).
Organizacion Mundial del Turismo, Capitán Haya 42, E - Madrid 20.
1975- 1981. $35. 224p. *En, Fr & Es eds.
TF: issued biennially, the 1981 edition, published in 1981, has data for several years to 1980.
A digest of the principal statistics published by WTO plus additional information of interest. Includes world and regional totals, then by country, A-Z, on arrivals, nights, length of stay, departures abroad, domestic tourism, tourism supply (beds, rooms, staff, etc), budget of NTAs, tourism and economy.

Δ D – iv, continued

353 The European tourist: a market profile (Esmond Devas).
Tourism Planning and Research Association, in association with Marketing Services (Travel and Tourism) Ltd, 52 High Holborn, London WC1V 6RL.
£20 or $30. unpaged. *En.
TF: published in 1985, with data for selected years to 1980, 1981 or 1982.
Holiday destination patterns in Europe, European long tern travel, and future prospects.

354 The BI guide to executive travel costs.
Business International S.A., 12–14 chemin Rieu, 1208 Genève.
1980– 1984. 204p. *En.
TF: the 1984 edition, published in 1984, has data as at January 1984.
Price data, typical daily expenditures, exchange rates and inflation, hotels.

Δ E Populatiion

355 Demographic yearbook.
UN, New York.
1948– 1983. £90 or $90. 1092. ISSN 0082-8041. *En, Fr.
TF: the 1983 edition, published in 1985, contains the latest data available for each country.
Includes annual tables on population, natality, foetal mortality, infant and maternal mortality, general mortality, nuptiality and divorce. Special topic tables on demographic and social characteristics, geographical characteristics, and educational characteristics.
Notes: machine-readable tape of input data ($290) is available. 'Demographic yearbook: historical tables' was issued in 1981 to commemorate the 30th anniversary of the yearbook.

356 Population and vital statistics report.
UN, New York.
(quarterly) £5.40 or £17.10 yr; $6 or $18 yr. *En.
Data from the latest census returns and births, deaths and infant mortality statistics for all reporting countries.
Note: a special supplement published in 1984 presented data on population estimates, crude birth and death rates, and infant mortality rates for the period since 1974. Also population by age, sex and urban/rural residence, age-specific birth and death rates for each country and area.

357 Concise report on the world population situation ... conditions, trends, prospects, policies.
UN, New York.
1970– 5th, 1983. $9. 521p. *En.
TF: the 1983 edition, published in 1983, has statistics for various years.
Includes some statistics in the text and also an annex 'Demographic indicators by country or area in the world, major areas and regions'.

358 World population prospects ... estimates and projections as assessed in... (United Nations Department of International and Economic Affairs).
UN, New York.
1963– 1982. £47 or $47. 532p. *En.
TF: the 1982 edition, published in 1985, has data for 1950 or 1980 to 2025.
Summary report assessing the prospects for major areas and regions and for individual countries.

359 Community censuses of population.
Eurostat, Luxembourg.
1968/71– 1981. *En, De, Fr, It, Nl, Da, Gr.
First results are being published in 'Population: statistical bulletin' for each member state.

360 Demographic indicators by countries: estimates and projections as assessed in 1980. (United Nations Department of International Economic and Social Affairs).
UN, New York.
1982. $40. *En.

361 Selected demographic iondicators by country, 1950–2000. (United Nations Department of International Economic and Social Affairs).
UN, New York.
1980. not priced. 208p. *En.
Trends and prospects of population, average annual growth rate, crude birth rate, crude death rate, etc. for the world and individual countries.

362 Statistical indicators of youth. (United Nations Department of International Economic and Social Affairs, Statistical Office, and Centre for Social Development and Humanitarian Affairs).
UN, New York.
To be published in 1986. *En, Fr.

363 International population dynamics, 1950–1979: demographic estimates for countries with a population of 5 million or more. (US Department of Commerce, Bureau of the Census).
GPO, Washington DC.
1980. $6.50. 262p. *En.

Δ E, continued

364 Estimates and projections of urban, rural and city populations, 1950-2025: the 1982 assessment. (United Nations Department of International Economic and Social Affairs).
UN, New York.
1985. not priced. 155p. (ST/ESA/SER.R/58). *En.

365 Demographic trends, 1950-1990.
OECD, Paris.
1980. £3.80; $8.50; Fr 34. 144p. *En.

366 Demographic statistics.
Eurostat, Luxembourg.
1960/76- 1985. £11.20; $13; FrB 800. 220p. *En, Fr, De, Nl, It, Da, Gr.
TF: the 1985 edition, published in 1985, has the latest data available, often with runs of earlier years.
Covers all the principal series of demographic statistics for each member state - population change, increase and migration, birth rate, births and deaths, population by sex and age-group, life expectancy, marriage and divorce, fertility rates and population projections.
Note: updated by OPCS, St. Catherine's House, 10 Kingsway, London WC2B 6JP.

367 World population ... recent demographic estimates for the countries and regions of the world. (US Department of Commerce, Bureau of the Census).
GPO, Washington DC.
1973- 1983. $13. c 500p. *En.
TF: issued biennially, the 1983 edition, published in 1984, has data for 1983.
Data on population growth, with countries ranked by population size.

368 Projections of the population of the Communist countries of Eastern Europe, by age and sex: 1975 to 2000. (Economic Analysis Bureau, Department of Commerce).
GPO, Washington DC.
1977. $1.15. 51p. *En.
Note: issued in the series 'International population reports P-91: 25'.

369 Demographic estimates for countries with a population of 10 million or more: 1981. (US Department of Commerce, Bureau of the Census).
GPO, Washington DC.
1981. $6.50. 173p. *En.

370 International mortality statistics (Michael Alderson).
Macmillan, 4 Essex Street, London WC2R 3LF.
£22.50. 533p. *En.
TF: published in 1981, with data for 1901 to 1970/75.
Aims to provide data on serial mortality of the 20th century for European and other selected countries in tabular form by sex, calendar period, cause of death and country.

Δ E - ii Labour

371 Yearbook of labour statistics. (International Labour Office).
Bureau International du Travail, CH-1211, Genève 22. or International Labour Office, 96/98 Marsham Street, London SW1P 4LY.
1935/36- 1985. £43.40; $74.10; FrS 130. 1007p. ISSN 0084-3857. *En, Fr, Es.
TF: the 1985 edition, published in 1985, has data for several years to 1983 or the latest available.
a comprehensive survey of annual data relating to economically active population, employment, unemployment, hours of work, wages, labour costs, consumer prices (indices), occupational injuries, and industrial disputes for 180 countries.
Note: Yearbook of labour statistics, 1935-36 to 1984' is a complete collection on microfiche (FrS 1580; £527.70; $900.60). Also available in separate years, 1935/36 to 1964; 1965-1984.

372 Bulletin of labour statistics. (International Labour Office).
Bureau International du Travail, CH-1211, Genève 22. or International Labour Office, 96/98 Marsham Street, London SW1P 4LY.
1965- quarterly, with 8 supplements. FrS 55 or $31.35 or £17 yr. ISSN 0007-4950. *En, Fr, Es.
TF: varies with each country; tables have monthly, quarterly and half-yearly data for the last three years.
Data on employment, unemployment, hours of work, wages, and consumer prices.

373 Labour force estimates and projections. (International Labour Office).
Bureau International du Travail, CH-1211, Genève 22.
1971- 2nd, 1977. FrS 80 for 6 vols. 6 vols. Vols I-V are in En, Es, Fr; vol. VI has separate eds in each language.
TF: the 2nd ed., published in 1977, has data from 1950 to 2000.
Prepared as a joint international effort of the United Nations and specialised agencies, and designed to produce a co-ordinated series of comprehensive demographic and related projections. Volumes are: I: Asia (FrS 15); II: Africa (FrS 15); III: Latin America (FrS 12.50); IV: North America, Europe, Oceania and USSR (FrS 15); V: World summary (FrS 12.50); VI: Methodological supplement (FrS 12.50).

Δ E – ii, continued

374 World labour report. (International Labour Office).
Bureau International du Travail, CH-1211 Genève 22. or International Labour Office, 96/98 Marsham Street, London SW1P 4LY.
£15.05 or FrS 45 each volume. 3 vols. *En.
TF: vols. 1 & 2 were published in 1984; vol. 3 to be published.
Volume 1 relates to employment, incomes, social protection, and new information technology. A statistical annex (p.196-215) has data on the structure of the economically active population, income distribution in selected countries, and social security. Volume 2 covers labour relations, workers' and employers' organisations, labour-management relations, international labour standards, freedom of association, abolition of forced labour, termination of employment, conditions of work, etc. Includes some tables in the text.

375 Economically active population, estimates and projections, 1950-2025. (International Labour Office).
Bureau International du Travail, CH-1211 Genève 22.
FrS 182.50 for complete set. 6 vols. *En, Fr, Es.
TF: this third edition published in 1986.
Data on population, economically active population and activity rates, by sex and age group for the period 1950-2025; economically active population in agriculture, industry and services, by sex, for the period 1950-80, for all countries, territories and regions of the world. Vol 1: Asia (FrS 37.50); II: Africa (FrS 40); III: Latin America (FrS 32.50); IV: Northern America, Europe, Oceania, USSR (FrS 37.50); V: World summary (FrS 32.50); VI: Methodological supplement (FrS 35).

376 Labour force statistics.
OECD, Paris.
1956/66- 1963-1983. £18.50; $37; Fr 185. 498p. *En, Fr.
TF: the 1963-1983 edition, published mid-1985, has data for the years 1963 to 1983.
Statistics on population, employment, labour force, and unemployment for member countries.

377 Quarterly labour force statistics.
OECD, Paris.
(quarterly) £8.50 or $17 or Fr 85 yr (not sold separately). ISSN 0304-3312. *En, Fr.
Statistics for both employed and unemployed sectors of the population in each of 13 industrialised countries; graphs and statistical tables of labour force trends over the preceding ten years, more recent figures being presented in more detail.

378 Labour costs.
Eurostat, Luxembourg.
1975- 2nd, 1981 (published in 1984). V.1: FrB 150; £1.90; $3; V.2: FrB 200; £2.50; $4. 2 vols. *En, Fr, De, It, Nl, Da, Gr.
Results of the 1981 survey of labour costs in industry, commerce, banking and insurance. Vol.1: Principal results; vol II: Results by size classes and regions.
Note: the complete edition is available on microfiches.

379 Labour force sample survey – results.
Eurostat, Luxembourg.
1973- 1983 (published in 1985). FrB 250; £3.30; $5. 145p. *En, Fr, De, It, Da, Nl, Gr.
TF: a survey is taken every two years.
The results are in tabular form in four sections – population and activity, employment, working time, search for work (unemployment).

380 Employment and unemployment.
Eurostat, Luxembourg.
1971/77- 1970-1983. FrB 800 or £8.80. 272p. *En, Fr, De, Nl, Da, It, Gr.
TF: the 1970-1983 edition, with data for those years, was issued in 1984.
Data on population; working population and employment according to sex, status and sector of activity; gainful employment in industry and the services; registered unemployment, vacancies and job placements; industrial disputes, and working hours. As far as available data relates to the 10 member states of the EC; the main data on Spain and Portugal are given in an annex.

381 Unemployment – monthly bulletin.
Eurostat, Luxembourg.
(monthly) FrB 600 or £6 yr. ISSN 0252-9220. *En, Fr, De & It eds.
Total of registered unemployed in each member state as at the end of the previous month; unemployed persons under 25 years subdivided by sex; unemployed foreigners; and numbers of vacancies and vacancies filled during the month.

382 Wages and total labour costs for workers: international survey ... (Svenska Arbetsgivareföreningen / Swedish Employers' Confederation).
Näringslivets Förlagsdistribution AB, Box 5157, S-102 44 Stockholm.
(annual) 1972-1982. SKr 55. 74p. ISSN 0280-4743. *En, Sv, Fr, De.
TF: the 1972-1982 edition, with data for those years, was published in November 1984.
Data on manufacturing (subdivided by industry), mining and quarrying and construction. Covers most Western European countries, Japan, USA and Canada.

Δ E – ii, continued

383 Earnings in industry and services.
Eurostat, Luxembourg.
1983- half-yearly. £7.60; FrB 600; $12 or £12; FrB 950; $18 yr. ISSN 0378-3596. *En, Fr, De, It, Nl, Da, Gr.
Harmonised data on manual workers' hourly earnings in industry, and non-manual workers' monthly earnings in industry, commerce, banking and insurance. Broken down by industrial groups, by sex and, for certain countries, by region.

Δ E – iii Housing

384 Compendium of housing statistics.
UN, New York.
1971- 3rd, 1975-1977. £17.05; $31. 362p. *En, Fr.
TF: the 3rd edition was published in 1980 and contains data received by the UN during the period 1975 to 1977.
Information derived from national housing censuses or from national sample surveys. Includes data on population growth, dwelling construction, cost of housing, and capital formation for housing in 176 countries. Continued by 'Compendium of human settlement statistics' (053).

Δ F Social

385 Compendium of social statistics.
UN, New York.
1963- 3rd, 1977 (published in 1980). £19.25; $35. 1345p. *En, Fr.
An international compendium presenting basic national social indicators required for describing the major aspects of the social situation in the world, as well as changes and trends in levels of living. Includes data on population; health; food consumption and nutrition; housing and community facilities; culture and communications; economic services; labour; agricultural population, resources and output; land use; refugees; education and literacy; social security; and energy.

386 Report on the world social situation. (United Nations Department of International Economic and Social Affairs).
UN, New York.
1952- 1984. $17.50. *En.
TF: the 1984 edition, published in 1985, has data for various periods to 1984. The report is published every two years. A supplement is to be issued in 1986.
Regional developments and sectoral developments (population, employment, wages and price trends, social security, food and agriculture, health, education, housing, women, youth, social welfare, crime prevention and criminal justice, children and adolescents, and environment. Tables are included in the text.

387 Social indicators for the European Community: selected series.
Eurostat, Luxembourg.
1960/75- 1984 (published in 1984). £9.80; $14; FrB 750. 1380p. *En/Fr; De/It; Da/Nl eds.
Devoted to illustrating, by means of easily understood indicators, some of the principal features of the social situation in the European Communities for which data was available mid-1984. Part A includes data on the position of women in the Community; part B has general social indicators.

Δ F – i Standard of living

388 Household income and expenditure statistics. (International Labour Office).
Bureau International du Travail, CH-1211, Genève 22.
1950/54- No.3, 1968-1976. FrS 40. 404p. *En.
TF: the 1968-1976 edition, with data for those years, was published in 1979.
Data for 87 countries on level, components and size distribution of household income and expenditure, is presented for urban and rural sectors, social and occupational groups, and households of different sizes.

389 Fachserie 17: Preise. Reihe 10: Internationaler Vergleich der Preise für die Lebenshaltung [Prices. Series 10: International comparison of consumer prices] (Statistisches Bundesamt, Wiesbaden).
Kohlhammer, Mainz.
(monthly & annual) DM 2.90 each monthly issue; DM 11.60 for 1983 annual issue. *De.

390 West European living costs.
Confederation of British Industry, Centre Point, 103 New Oxford Street, London WC1A 1DU.
1972- 1984 (published in 1984). £18. 95p. ISSN 0043-3136. *En.
General information and detailed data on accommodatiion, business accommodation, clothes and personal carem consumer goods, entertainment, indirect taxation, sports facilities, education, food, office services, transport, gross salaries, income taxation, social security, and utilities for individual countries. Values are given in local currency and UK£s.

391 Family budgets – comparative tables: Federal Republic of Germany, France, Italy, United Kingdom.
Eurostat, Luxembourg.
FrB 200; £2.70; $3.50. 197p. *En, Fr, De, It.
TF: published in 1984 with data for 1979.
First standardised results, derived from national family budget surveys. General data on households and accommodation; average annual expenditure of households; average annual quantitative consumption of certain selected items.

Δ F – i, continued

392 Family budgets – comparative tables: Netherlands, Belgium, Ireland, Denmark, Greece, Spain.
Eurostat, Luxembourg.
1985. FrB 250. *Da, En, Fr, Nl.
First standardised results, derived from national family budget surveys.

393 Structure of earnings ... principal results.
Eurostat, Luxembourg.
1974– 2nd 1978/79. FrB 1500 each volume. *En, Fr, De, Nl, It, Da, Gr.
TF: the volumes for the 1978/79 survey commenced publication in 1983.
34 tables, published separately for each member country, showing the main reults of the survey on the structure and distribution of earnings in industry, wholesale and retail distribution, banking and insurance. Published so far are Vols 2: France; 3: Luxembourg; 4: Belgium; 5: Denmark; 6: Netherlands; 7: Federal Republic of Germany.
Note: enlarged edition on microfiche (143 tables) is available.

394 Fachserie 16: Löhne und Gehälter. Reihe 5: Löhne und Gehälter im Ausland [...Wages and salaries abroad] (SB, Wiesbaden).
Kohlhammer, Mainz.
(annual) 2 sub-series. *De.
Sub-series are:
5.1. Earnings of employees in foreign countries (1984. DM 11.80. published 1985).
5.2. Agreed wages and salaries in foreign countries (1985. DM 8.90. published in 1985).

395 Executive living costs in major cities worldwide.
Business International S.A., 12–14 chemin Rieu, 1208 Genève.
1978– 2 a year (published in January & July). prices on application. loose-leaf. *En.
A comprehensive price survey in each of 93 cities; weighted index; exchange rates; local inflation index.

396 Level of living and inequality in the Nordic countries: a comparative analysis of the Nordic comprehensive surveys. (Nordic Council and Nordic Statistical Secretariat).
Nordiska Statistiska Sekretariatet, Postbox 2550, DK–2100 København Ø.
not priced. 226p. *En.
TF: published in 1984 with data for 1979 or 1980.
Data on population, the economy, education, working conditions, financial resources, consumer durables, housing, home environment, transport, leisure, social environment, health, social mobility, minorities, national standard of living – level and class differences, equality between the sexes.

397 Consumer prices in the EC 1980.
Eurostat, Luxembourg.
1983. FrB 300. £4.20; $6.50. 189p. *En/Fr, De/It & Da/Nl eds.
Main results of the survey of consumer prices in the European Community, Spain and Portugal in 1980 for the goods and services belonging to the final consumption of households. Average prices in national currencies for the capital cities of each country; and average annual prices in the form of indices for each country.

398 Consumer price indices.
Eurostat, Luxembourg.
1985– quarterly. FrB 1300 yr for 12 monthly issues & 4 quarterly issues. ISSN 0258-0861. *En, Fr.
TF: 1st issue to appear mid-March 1986, with monthly figures from 1981 to 1985.
Showing evolution of the consumer price indices for the eight main groups of consumption as well as for the 20 sub-groups on the basis of 1980=100. Data given for the 12 EC countries and USA.
Note: 'Consumer price indices, 1976-82' (77p. free) has long series of price indices base 1975=100; monthly and annual figures for the general index and for nine main groups as well as 18 detailed groups. Also a historical review for 1955–1982.

399 Prices and earnings around the globe: a comparison of purchasing power in 49 cities.
Union Bank of Switzerland, Zürich.
1971– 1985. not priced. 42p. *En, De, Fr, Es & It eds.
TF: the 1985 edition was published in 1985.

Δ F – ii Health and welfare

400 World health statistics quarterly.
World Health Organisation, 1211 Genève 27.
1948– (quarterly) £9.75 or £32 yr; FrS 27 or FrS 80 yr. ISSN 0043-8510. *En, Fr.
Includes detailed statistical analyses of selected health topics of current interest.

401 World health statistics annual.
World Health Organisation, 1211 Genève 27.
1939/46– 1984. £16. 401p. *En, Fr.
TF: the 1984 edition, published in 1985, has the latest data available to 1981 to 1982.
Provides data on vital statistics and causes of death (vital statistics, life tables, deaths according to cause, by country; morbidity; health resources (manpower, establishments); and a global overview.
Note: earlier editions were published in three volumes.

Δ F - ii, continued

402 The cost of social security. (International Labour Office).
Bureau International du Travail, CH-1211, Genève 22.
1949- 11th, 1978-1980. £16.70; $28.50; FrS 50. 122p. *En, Es, Fr.
TF: the 1978-1980 edition, published in 1985, has data for 1978 to 1980 or the latest available at time of publication.
Results of an enquiry aimed at establishing a consolidated statement of the financial operations of social security schemes existing in various countries, etc. Includes comparative tables of receipts and expenditures, benefits, etc. Also national accounts data, population data, and consumer price indices.

403 Health statistics in the Nordic countries. (Nordisk Medicinal-Statistisk Komitté.
NOMESKO, c/o Nordisk Statistisk Sekretariat, Postboks 2550, Sejrøgade 11, DK-2100 København Ø.
1978- 1982. free. 69p. *Da; title & table headings also in En.
TF: the 1982 edition, published in 1984, has data for several years to 1980 or 1981.
Data on population, fertility and births - infant mortality - contraception, health conditions - diseases, mortality - diseases accidents, health institutions - home nursing, primary care - use of drugs, health personnel, and health expenditures.

404 Comparative tables of the social security systems in Council of Europe member states not belonging to the European Communities Council of Europe, Strasbourg.
£4.70. 169p. *En.
TF: 2nd edition, published in 1985, has data as at July 1, 1984.

405 Social protection: statistical bulletin.
Eurostat, Luxembourg.
Irregular. not priced. *En.
Each issue has data on various subjects related to the European system of integrated social protection statistics (ESSPROS), including 'Social protection statistics (ESSROS) expenditure and receipts - results by schemes' which is issued annually (issue covering 1970-1983 published in 1985).

406 Family planning in five continents.
International Planned Parenthood Federation, 18/20 Lower Regent Street, London SW1Y 4PW.
1965- 1979. £1.25; $2.75. 68p. *En.
TF: the 1979 issue, published in 1979, has data for 1975 to 1980.
A quick reference source giving highlights of family planning situation all over the world, together with basic demographic statistics, by continent, then country A-Z (population, growth rate, births per 1000, deaths per 1000).

407 Nordisk läkemedelsstatistik [Nordic statistics on medicines] (Nordisk Läkemedelsnämnden [Nordic Council on Medicines]).
Nordiskstatistik Sekretariat, Postboks 2250, DK-2100 København Ø.
1975/77- 1978-1980 (published in 1983). not priced. 3 vols. ISSN 0332-6527. *Sv; title also in En.
Vol.1: Tables; vol.2: Medical register and classification of defined diagnoses; vol.3: Guidelines for ATC classification.

Δ F - iii Education and leisure

408 Current studies and research in statistics: series CSR-E.
UNESCO, place de Fontenoy, 75700 Paris.
No.1, 1970- irregular. free. *Fr; some are also in En & Es.
A series of reports, some of which have a statistical content, for example:
CSR-E-44 Statistics of educational attainment and illiteracy, 1970-1980.
CSR-E-46 Trends and projections of enrolment by level of education and by age, 1960-2000 (as assessed in 1982).
CSR-E-47 Technical and vocational education in the world, 1970-1980: a statistical report.
CSR-E-50 Female participation in higher education: enrolment trends, 1975-1982.

409 Education and training: statistical bulletin.
Eurostat, Luxembourg.
Irregular. not priced. *En.
Each issue is on a different subject in the field of education.

410 Educational statistics in OECD countries.
OECD, Paris.
1981. £4.80; $12. Fr 48. 231p. *En, Fr.
Brings together, on a comparable basis, a set of basic statistics tracing the recent development of educational systems in OECD member countries. Scope and duration of formal education, data on pupils and students undergoing education, new entrants, full-time enrolment rates by age and by level for the last year available, expenditure on education, etc.
Note: OECD also issued 'Education statistics yearbook' earlier, which covered 1974 and 1975.

411 Statistics of students abroad.
UNESCO, place de Fontenoy, 75700 Paris.
1962/68- 1974-1978. £4.80; Fr 32. 275p. *En, Fr.
TF: the 1974-1978 edition, with data for those years, was published in 1982.
Numbers of students enrolled abroad, by country of study.

Δ F – iii, continued

412 INTAMEL: International statistics of city libraries (compiled by Stadtbüchereien Hannover, for INTAMEL). Academic Press Inc., 111 5th Avenue, New York, NY 10003; and 24-28 Oval Road, London NW1 7DX.
1969- 1981. *En.
TF: the 1981 results were published in International Library Review, vol.15, no. 2, April 1983, p.165-172.
The results of a survey, including for each town, the numbers of inhabitants, book stock, periodicals, audio-visual media, loans, budgets, staff, libraries and branch libraries, opening hours, nominal lending period.

Δ F – iv Justice

413 International crime statistics. (International Criminal Police Organisation – INTERPOL).
Organisation Internationale de Police Criminelle – INTERPOL, 92210 Saint-Cloud, France.
1950/52- 1981-1982. not priced. 115p. *En, Fr, Es, Ar.
TF: the 1981-1982 edition, published in 1984, has data for 1981 and 1982.
Police statistics (not judicial) and quarterly crime figures, by type of crime, for each country affiliated to INTERPOL (50 countries).

414 Nordisk Kriminalstatistik 1950-1980. Nordic criminal statistics, 1950-1980.
Nordiska Statistiska Sekretariatet, Postbox 2550, DK-2100 København Ø.
3rd ed, 1982. not priced. 468p. ISSN 0280-7327.
Note: translated into English by Statistics Sweden, Unit of Justice and Social Statistics, Stockholm (text only. 33p. 1984) in the series 'RS promemoria'.

Δ F – v Religion

415 Annuarium statisticum ecclesiae ... Statistical yearbook of the Church ... (Central Statistics Office of the Church).
Segretaria di Stato, Ufficio Centrale di Statistica della Chiesa, Libreria Editrice Vaticana, Vatican City.
1970- 1979. L.16000. 345p. *Latin, En, Fr.
TF: the 1979 edition, published in 1981, has data for 1979.
Presents in summary form the principal data collected by means of questionnaire, etc., on area and population, workface for the apostolate, training centres and educational institutions, practice of religion, welfare institutions, papal-jurisdiction, religious institutes, and diocesan and regional tribunals.

Δ F – vi Elections

416 The international almanac of electoral history. (Thomas T Mackie & Richard Rose).
Macmillan, 4 Little Essex Street, London WC2.
1974- 2nd ed, 1982. £25. 430p. *En.
Numbers of votes and seats won, by parties, for most Western European countries, since the beginning of competitive national elections.

417 Europe votes ... European Parliamentary election results. (F.W.S. Craig & T.T. Mackie).
Parliamentary Research Service, 18 Lincoln Green, Chichester, West Sussex PO10 4DN.
1979- 2nd ed, 1979-1984. £12.50. 256p. *En.
TF: the 1979-1984 edition was published in 1985.
Detailed record of elections to the European Parliament from the first election in 1979. Contains results of elections in Belgium, Denmark, France, Germany, Greece, Ireland, Italy, Luxembourg, the Netherlands, and the United Kingdom.
Note: a loose-leaf updating service is available from the publishers (£15).

Δ G Finance

418 International financial statistics.
International Monetary Fund, Washington DC 20431.
1948- monthly. £48.75 or $100 yr for 12 monthly issues, & 2 supplements. *En, Fr & Es eds.
TF: varies with the country, but generally the last 8 quarters and the last 7 months are given up to about three months prior to the date of the issue.
General data on exchange rates and exchange rate arrangements, fund accounts, international liquidity, international banking, money and banking, interest rates, prices, production, etc., international transactions; government finances; national accounts and population for each country. Also world tables.
Note: also available on magnetic tape.

419 International financial statistics yearbook.
International Monetary Fund, Washington DC 20431.
1984- 1985. £25 or $25. 683p. ISSN 0251-6365. *En, Fr & Es eds.
TF: the 1985 edition, published in 1985, has data for 1950, 1955, and 1957 through 1984.
Similar subject content to the monthly (418).

Δ G, continued

420 OECD financial statistics.
OECD, Paris.
1969- subscription for all parts; £42; $90; Fr 420. ISSN 0304-3371. *En, Fr.
Issued in four parts:
Monthly financial statistics
Deals with international and domestic markets (in 2 sections. 24 issues a year).
Financial accounts ...
Flow of funds and balance sheet accounts for 20 countries (2 vols).
Non-financial enterprises financial statement
Data on enterprises in 12 countries (annual).
Methodological supplement (annual).
Provides a unique collection of statistical and descriptive data on the international financial market and on the domestic markets of OECD member countries.

421 Financial market trends.
OECD, Paris.
3 a year. £13; $26; Fr 130 yr. ISSN 0378-651X. *En.
Provides an assessment of trends and prospects in the international and major domestic financial markets of the OECD area. Includes statistics on current developments in euro-credits, euro-bonds, etc, and a review of monetary trends.

422 Currency trends.
Phillips & Drew, 120 Moorgate, London EC2M 6XP.
(quarterly) £70 or £250 yr. *En.
TF: each issue has data for a few past years and forecasts for two future years.
International capital flows, current accounts and basic balances, real exchange rates, government policy and interest rates, currency futures and options, and currency charts.

Δ G - ii Public finance

423 National accounts statistics.
UN, New York.
1957- 1982. 4 vols. *En.
TF: the volumes for 1982 were published in 1985. Vol.1 covers 1970 to 1982; vol.2 covers 1970 to 1982; and vol.3 covers 1981 and 1982. Vol.4 not published as yet.
Contents: Vol 1: Main aggregates and detailed tables (£85 or $85); Vol 2: Analyses of main aggregates... (£45 or $45); Vol 3: Government accounts and tables (£35 or $35).
Notes: machine readable tape for time series is available ($240). A supplement to the above 'National accounting practice in seventy countries' was published in 1979 in 3 vols.

424 Government finance statistics yearbook.
International Monetary Fund, Washington DC 30431.
1977- 1984. £20; $20. 889p. ISSN 0250-7374. *En; contents list & introduction also in Fr & Es.
TF: the 1984 edition, published in 1984, has data for 1974 to 1983 or the latest available.
Revenues, grants, expenditure, lending, financing, and debt of central governments for 129 countries. Also summary tables on state and local governments.

425 National accounts.
OECD, Paris.
1950/61- Vol I: 1960-1983. £8.80; $18; Fr 88. Vol II: 1971-1983. £29.50; $59; Fr 295. 2 vols. *En, Fr.
TF: Vol I: 1960-1983 was published in March 1985 and Vol II: 1970-1982 in September 1985.
Vol I: Main aggregates. Vol II: Detailed tables.
Data for each member country, including expenditure on GDP, value added by trend of economic activity, financing and composition of capital formation, income and outlay account of main sectors, etc.
Note: data is also available on magnetic tape, microfiche and diskette.

426 Quarterly national accounts.
OECD, Paris.
1976- £10 or $20 or Fr 100 yr (single issues £5; $10; Fr 50). ISSN 0304-3738. *En, Fr.
TF: each issue has the latest data available.
Quarterly statistics for OECD member countries covering final expenditures on GDP and its industrial origin, the composition of final consumption and capital formation.

427 Balance of payments of OECD countries.
OECD, Paris.
1960/77- 1963-1982. £11; $22; Fr 110. 164p. *En, Fr.
TF: the 1963-1982 edition, only the second issue of the title, was published in January 1985.

428 National accounts ESA - detailed tables by branches.
Eurostat, Luxembourg.
(annual). £1985. £5.90; $7.50; FrB 500. 173p. *En, Fr, De, Nl, Da, It, Gr.
TF: the 1985 edition, published in 1985, has data for 1984.
Main aggregates of economic accounts for the basic administrative units of the Community. Time series covering 1973-1984 for value-added by broad groups of branches (agriculture, industry, services), for population and for employment.

Δ G - ii, continued

429 Latest information on national accounts of developing countries.
OECD Development Centre, 94 rue Chardon Lagache, 75016 Paris.
1969- irregular. not priced. *En, Fr.
TF: No.17, with data available at the end of 1984, was published early 1985.
Aims to bring together in a readily accessible form the national accounts estimates of developing countries that are only available in widely scattered sources, and to provide whenever possible details on the actual meaning and quality of the estimates shown. Contents of each issue vary.

430 External debt of developing countries.
OECD, Paris.
(annual) 1983. £9; $18; Fr 90. 224p. *En.
TF: the 1983 edition, published in 1984, has data mainly for 1978 to 1982 and estimates for 1983.

431 Geographical distribution of financial flows to developing countries ... disbursements, commitments, external debt, economic indicators.
OECD, Paris.
1960/64- 1980-1983. £16; $32; Fr 160. 290p. ISSN 0474-5434. *En, Fr.
TF: the 1980-1983 edition, with data for those years, was published late 1984.
Data for over 110 selected developing countries. Also background economic and social data to provide perspective in interpreting the resource flow information for each country.

432 Money and finances.
Eurostat, Luxembourg.
1984- quarterly. £4.50 or £14 yr; $7 or $21 yr; FrB 350 or FrB 1200 yr. ISSN 0255-6510. *En, Fr.
Structural indicators referring to the evolution of certain financial aggregates in relation to GDP, the consolidated balance sheets of credit institutions, the money supply, exchange rates and foreign reserves. Annual, quarterly and monthly time-series data for the short-term economic analysis on money supply, capital markets, public finance, interest rates, exchange rates and official reserves. Also statistics related to the European Monetary System.

433 Revenue statistics of OECD member countries.
OECD, Paris.
1965/74- 1965-1984. £13.50; $27; Fr 135. 260p. *En, Fr.
TF: the 1965-1984 edition, with data for those years, was published mid-1985.
Data on tax levels and structures.

434 National accounts ESA - aggregates.
Eurostat, Luxembourg.
1955/65- 1960-1984. £6.60; $10; FrB 500. 137p. *En/Fr/Nl and Da/De/It eds.
TF: the 1960-1984 edition, with data for those years, was published late 1985.
Results of principal aggregates of national accounts drawn up according to ESA (European System of Integrated Economic Accounts), showing development and comparison between the Community as a whole, the 10 member states, the two prospective member countries (Spain and Portugal), the USA and Japan.

435 National accounts ESA - detailed tables by sector.
Eurostat, Luxembourg.
1955/65- 1970-1982. £16.10; $20; FrB 1200. 493p. *En/Fr/Nl and Da/De/It eds.
TF: the 1970-1982 edition, published early 1985, has data for the years 1970 to 1982.
Flows of income between institutional sectors (companies, households, governments, etc), and their financial transactions (change in assets and liabilities), compiled in accordance with ESA.

436 General government accounts and statistics.
Eurostat, Luxembourg.
1955/65- 1970-1982. £12.10; $15; FrB 900. 451p. *En, Fr, De, Nl, It, Da.
TF: the 1970-1982 edition, with data for those years, was published in 1984.
Accounts of the general government sectors of member countries, comparative summary tables, and detailed tables by country.

437 Balance of payments - global data.
Eurostat, Luxembourg.
1967- 1972-83. £4.80; $6; FrB 350. 89p. *En, Fr; translations into other languages available.
TF: the 1972-83 edition, with data for those years, was published in 1984.
Data for member countries, candidate member countries (Spain & Portugal) and the USA and Japan.

438 Balance of payments - geographical breakdown.
Eurostat, Luxembourg.
1967- 1979-1982. £9.20; $12; FrB 700. 229p. *En, Fr.
TF: the 1979-1982 edition, published in 1985, has data for 1979 to 1982.
The most recent available data on the geographical breakdown of balance of payments for each EEC country.

439 Balance of payments - quarterly data.
Eurostat, Luxembourg.
(quarterly) £4 or £10.50 yr; $5 or $13 yr; FrB 300 or FrB 800 yr. ISSN 0251-1800. *En, Fr.
Latest available quarterly and annual data on the global balance of payments (flows) of each European Community country, of the European Community as a whole, candidate countries (Spain and Portugal), and the USA and Japan.
Note: No.3 each year includes an annex with historical global data for 12 years.

Δ G – iii Company finance

440 Extel European companies service.
Extel Statistical Services Ltd., 37-45 Paul Street, London EC2A 4PB.
Prices on application. *En.
Card service providing information on some 750 major European companies, most of which are quoted on European stock exchanges, giving capital details, dividend & interest rates, debenture particulars, 5/12- year profit and loss accounts, 10-year quotation record, 3-year balance sheets, latest dividends etc.

Δ G – iv Investment

441 Annual investments in fixed assets.
Eurostat, Luxembourg.
1972/74- 1977-1982. £3.80; FrB 300; $5. 127p. *En, De, Fr.
TF: the 1977-1982 edition, with data for those years, was published in 1985.
Detailed results for each member state of the co-ordinated annual enquiry into capital investments industry. In two parts: Detailed results by national currency; Global results for the Community in ECUs.

442 World investment review: prospects for financial markets and economies.
Phillips & Drew, 120 Moorgate, London EC2M 6XP.
(quarterly, with monthly update). Monthly: £25; Quarterly: £100; £500 yr. *En.
International investment strategy, world economic summary, world economic forecasts, monetary analysis and interest rates, world trade and current accounts, international capital flows, exchange rates, commodity markets, gold, international rates of return, principal markets, and the economy of certain markets, including United Kingdom, Federal Republic of Germany, France, Netherlands, Switzerland, Scandiravia and Ireland.

443 Regional statistics: the Community's financial participation in investments.
Eurostat, Luxembourg.
1971- 1982. £3.20 or FrB 250. 88p. *En, Fr, De, Nl, Da, It, Gr.
TF: the 1982 edition, published in 1984, has data for 1982 and one or two earlier years in some tables.
Amounts of investment grants, numbers of projects, investments financed, loans granted, etc. by EAGGF, ERDF, ECSC and EIB.

444 Activités et statistiques [Activities and statistics] (Fédération Internationale des Bourses de Valeurs [International Federation of Stock Exchanges]).
FIBV, 22 blvd Courcelles, 75017 Paris.
1975- 1983/84. free. 39p. *En, Fr.
TF: the 1983/84- edition, published in 1985, has data for 1983 and 1984.
Includes a section of detailed stock market statistics (p.9-33) on member stock markets throughout the world.

445 International interest rate service.
Maxwell Stamp Associates Ltd., 55-63 Goswell Road, London EC1V 7PT.
1964- monthly, punched for folder. £35 yr (£40 yr abroad). *En.
Rates per annum in leading financial centres; and rates per annum in other countries.

Δ H Transport and communications

446 World transport data ...
Union Internationale des Transports Routiers, Centre Internationale, rue de Varembé 3, (B.P. 44), 1211 Genève 20.
1973- 4th, 1985. not priced. 376p. ISSN 0302-7902. *En, Fr.
TF: the 1985 edition, published in 1985, has data for several years to 1983 or the latest available.
Data for 166 countries on urban traffic, length of roads, length of railways, employment, road networks, number of motor vehicles, railway networks, rolling stock and traffic, sea traffic, passenger air traffic, goods air traffic, bus traffic, goods road traffic, inland waterways and traffic. Arranged by countries.

447 Commodity trade (by sea) statistics: results of the Maritime Transport Study ...
UN, New York.
1966/68- 1980. $38. 374p. *En.
TF: the 1980 edition, published in 1984, has data for 1977 to 1980.
A continuing survey on the analysis, by type of goods moved between regions of the world.

448 Annual bulletin of transport statistics for Europe. (United Nations Economic Commission for Europe).
UN, New York.
1949- 1983. £27 or $27. 271p. ISSN 0066-3859. *En, Fr, Ru.
TF: the 1983 edition, published in 1984, has data for 1982 and 1983 and also 1970 in some tables.
Basic data on transport and related trends in European countries, Canada & USA, including rail, road and inland waterway sectors, container transport, goods loaded and unloaded at seaports, transport by various modes of transport and commodity group. Includes data on length of networks; number, capacity and power of vehicles; internal and international traffic and transport; expenditure on roads and consumption of fuel by road motor vehicles.

449 ECMT – annual report. Volume II: Trends in transport investment and performance ... and statistical report on road accidents ... (European Conference of Ministers of Transport).
OECD, Paris.
1954- 1983. £5; $10; Fr 50. 56p. *En, Fr.
Note: Volume I is the annual report.

Δ H, continued

450 International statistical handbook of public transport.
Union Internationale des Transports Publics, avenue de l'Uruguay 19, B-1050 Bruxelles.
(annual) 1985-1986 (published in 1985). not priced. 3 vols. ISSN 0378-1968. *En, Fr, De.
Report of a study. Section I covers the technology of metropolitan railways/rapid transit and LRT - light rail transit; Section II is concerned with multi-mode surface transport; and Section III with surface public transport services using only one mode of vehicles plying on conventional highway and street surfaces. Data for more than 250 cities throughout the world.

450a Transport, communications, tourism statistical yearbook, 1970-1983.
Eurostat, Luxembourg.
1985. FrB 1200 or £16.20 or $ 20. 256p. *En, Fr, De, Nl, Da, It, Gr.
Statistics on the infrastructure, on the equipment and on the operations of the different modes of transport. Statistics on traffic accidents, on communications (post, telegraph, telex, telephone) and on tourism.

Δ H - i Ships and shipping

451 Statistical tables.
Lloyds Register of Shipping, 71 Fenchurch Street, London EC3M 4BS.
1955- 1985. not priced. 71p. ISSN 0076-0234. *En.
TF: the 1985 edition, published late 1985, has data for 1984 and earlier years in some tables.
Statistical data on ships registered at Lloyds, including country of registration, size and age, type, propulsion. Also numbers and tonnage of ships registered, launched and lost.

452 Maritime transport.
OECD, Paris.
1961- 1984. £7.50; $15; Fr 75. 187p. *En & Fr eds.
TF: the 1984 edition, published in 1985, has data for 1984.
International shipping developments, supply of shipping services, demand for shipping services, freight markets, taxation of shipping in OECD countries. Statistics are included in the text and there is a statistical annex.

453 Annual summary of merchant ships completed in the world during ...
Lloyds Register of Shipping, 71 Fenchurch Street, London EC3M 4BS.
1922- 1985. not priced. 16p. *En.
TF: the 1985 edition, published early 1986, has data for 1985 and some earlier years in some tables.
Also includes annual summary of merchant ships launched. Data includes type of ship, gross tonnage, countries of registration, when built, and where launched.
Note: Lloyds also publish other titles, including the annual 'Statistical summary of merchants ships totally lost, broken up, etc'. and the quarterly 'Merchant shipbuilding return' and 'Casualty return'.

454 Shipping statistics yearbook. (Institute of Shipping Economics).
Institut für Seeverkehrswirtschaft, Am Dom 5a, D-2800 Bremen 1, Germany.
1956- 1984. DM 69. 464p. ISSN 0721-3220. *En & De eds.
TF: issued biennially, the 1984 edition, published in 1984, has data to 1983.
Data on the world merchant fleet, shipping and seaborne trade, shipbuilding, ports and sea canals for the world, by region and by country.

455 Shipping statistics. (Institute of Shipping Economics and Logistics).
Institut für Seeverkehrswirtschaft, Am Dom 5a, D-2800 Bremen 1, Germany.
1956- monthly. DM 180 yr. ISSN 0721-3751. *En & De eds.
TF: each issue has data for several years and months up to one or two months prior to the date of the issue.
Data on the shipping market (supply of shipping services, demand for shipping services), shipbuilding, ports and sea canals.

456 Shipping statistics and economics.
H.P. Drewry (Shipping Consultants) Ltd., 34 Brook Street, London W1Y 2LL.
1970- monthly. £220; $375 yr. ISSN 0306-1817. *En.
TF: each issue has data for the previous month.
Data on the tanker market, combined carrier market, dry cargo market, world shipping, and reported fixtures.

457 Review of maritime transport: a report by the Secretariat of UNCTAD.
UN, New York.
1968- 1984. £9.50 or $9.50. 79p. ISSN 0085-560X. *En.
TF: the 1984 review, published in 1985, has data for several years to 1984.
A review of current and long-term aspects of maritime transport. Includes data on the development of international seaborne trade, development of the world fleet, productivity of the world fleet,-shipbuilding, and freight markets.
Note: machine readable tape of seaborne export data is available ($180 a year).

Δ H – i, continued

458 Statistique de la navigation maritime dans le Benelux. Benelux zeevaartstatistieken [Benelux maritime statistics] (INS, Bruxelles).
Benelux Secrétariat-General, 39 rue de la Regence, 1000 Bruxelles.
1979/81- 1979-1983. not priced. 111p. *Fr & Nl eds.
TF: the 1979-1983 edition, with data for those years, was published late in 1984.
Ships entering and leaving, by port and by class and tonnage; sea shipping by type; goods loaded and landed; sea shipping entering ports, by flag; goods unloaded by countries of origin; and goods loaded by countries of destination.

459 Fearnleys review.
Fearnley and Egers Chartering Co Ltd, Radhusgt 27, Oslo 1.
(annual) 1983. not priced. 44p. *En.
TF: the 1983 review, published early 1984, has data for several years to 1983.
Text and graphs on the world fleet, world seaborne trade, tonnage balance, dry cargo freight market, tanker freight market, new buildings, demolition, gas markets, second hand dry cargo, second hand tankers. Tables (p.23-38) on world seaborne trade, world fleet, world order book, tanker freight markets, dry cargo freight markets, Norwegian fleet representative sales.

460 Rapport annuel de la Commission Centrale pour la Navigation du Rhin [Annual report of the Central Commission for Navigation of the Rhine].
Commission Centrale pour la Navigation du Rhin, Palais du Rhin, F-67000 Strasbourg.
(annual) 1983. Fr 50. 128p. *Fr, De.
TF: the 1983 report, published in 1984, has data for 1983.
1. Administration; 2. Technical (navigable channels, ports); 3. Nautical (personnel, security, accidents); 4. Economics (composition of Rhine fleet, tugs, movement of merchandise); 5: Tribunals and jurisprudence. Note: 'Systeme d'observation du marche de la navigation Rhenane' [Trade carried on the Rhine] is also issued, quarterly in two volumes. Vol 1: Statistics (graphs and tables on Rhine traffic, movement of merchandise, Rhine ports, Rhine fleet, etc) and Vol 2: Conjuncture tests.

461 Registre international des bateaux du Rhin: Internationales Rheinschiffsregister ... [International register of ships on the Rhine] (Internationale Vereinigung des Rheinschiffsregisters (IVR)).
IVR, Koningin Emmaplein 6, 3016AA (Postbus 23210-3001 KE), Rotterdam, the Netherlands.
1981- 1984. Fl 400. *Nl, Fr, De.
Includes a 30-page chapter of statistics giving details of types, numbers, tonnage, etc. of ships of Switzerland, France, Federal Republic of Germany, Netherlands, Belgium and others plying the river Rhine.

Δ H – ii Roads and road transport

462 World road statistics.
International Road Federation, 525 School Street SW, Washington DC 200024; and Féderation Routière Internationale, rue de Lausanne 63, Genève, CH-1202.
1951- 1980-1984. $75; FrS 150. 217p. *En, Fr, De.
TF: the 1980-1984 edition, with data for those years, was published in 1985.
Data on road networks, production and export of motor vehicles, first registration and import of motor vehicles, vehicles in use, road traffic, motor fuels, road accidents, rates and basis of assessment of road user taxes, examples of average annual taxation, annual receipts from road user taxation, and road expenditure. Arranged alphabetically by country under continent.

463 Statistics of road traffic accidents in Europe. (United Nations Economic Commission for Europe).
UN, New York.
1954- 1983. £13.50 or $13.50. 108p. ISSN 0081-5160. *En, Fr, Ru.
TF: the 1983 edition, published in 1984, has data for 1983 or 1982 and 1970.
Accidents, including those involving injury, persons killed or injured, nature of the surroundings of the accident. Also, background data on road motor vehicles and mopeds, estimated vehicle-kilometres run, estimated population and distribution by age group.

464 Statistical report on road accidents. (European Conference of Ministers of Transport).
HMSO, London; or E.C.M.T. Paris.
(annual) 1983. £5. 55p. *En, Fr.
TF: the 1983 edition, published in 1985, has data for 1982.
Tables and charts showing trends in accidents for 19 ECMT countries (Western Europe and Yugoslavia) and four associated countries (USA, Canada, Australia and Japan).

Δ H – iii Railways and rail transport

465 Tableaux et graphiques indiquant l'évolution des principales données statistiques ferroviaires [Tables and graphs giving the principal statistics on railways] (International Union of Railways).
Union Internationale des Chemins de Fer, 14 rue Jean Rey, 75015 Paris.
1962- 1982. Fr 40. 48p. *Fr; table of contents also in En & De.
TF: the 1982 edition, published in 1982, has data for 1976 to 1980.
General data, followed by detailed data on traffic - fixed installations, rolling stock, wagons, personnel, passengers, goods, finances; traffic other than rail, roads and road vehicles, inland waterways.

Δ H – iii, continued

466 International railway statistics: statistics of individual railways. (International Union of Railways).
Union Internationale des Chemins de Fer, rue Jean Rey 14, 75015 Paris.
1925– 1983. not priced. 279p. *En, Fr, De.
TF: the 1983, edition, published late 1984, has data for 1983.
Data on the composition and resources of the railway systems, technical operating results, financial results, and miscellaneous information (fuel, motor fuel, electricity and lubricants for tractive vehicles, operating accidents, taxes, etc) for each railway.

Δ H – iv Aviation and air transport

467 Civil aviation statistics of the world. (International Civil Aviation Organisation).
ICAO, place de l'Aviation Internationale, 1000 Sherbrooke Street West, (PO Box 400), Montreal, Canada H3A 2R2.
1976– 10th, 1984. $12.50. 176p. *En, Es, Fr & Ru eds.
TF: the 1984 edition, published in 1985, has data for 1983 and 1984.
World statistics on aircraft, pilots, safety, fleets, traffic, and finance; aircraft, pilots and general statistics by region and state; statistics for commercial air carriers – traffic – by state; and airports. Mainly summarised and selected data from statistics provided to ICAO by contracting states.

468 World air transport statistics. (International Air Transport Association).
IATA, chemin de Joinville 26, (PO Box 160), 1216 Cointrin-Genève.
1957– 1984. $40. c 80p. ISSN 0084-1366. *En.
TF: the 1984 edition, published mid-1985, has data for 1984 and some earlier years in some tables.
Review of air transport developments, world air transport, IATA industry statistics (members, safety, finance, operations, fleet, etc), regional results and IATA members statistics (operations, employees, rankings, financial results).

469 Digest of statistics. (International Civil Aviation Organisation).
ICAO, place de l'Aviation Internationale, 1000 Sherbrooke Street West, (PO Box 400), Montreal, Canada H3A 2R2.
(irregular) various prices. *En.
Each issue of the digest is devoted to a particular topic, some titles being published regularly (eg. Series AT: Airport traffic (ISSN 0074-2422), Series F: Financial data (ISSN 0074-2430), Series FP: Fleet, personnel (ISSN 0074-2449), Series R: Civil aircraft on register (ISSN 0074-2457), and Series T: Traffic (ISSN 0074-2465)).

Δ H – v Telecommunications and postal services

470 Yearbook of common carrier telecommunications statistics ... and radiocommunication. (International Telecommunications Union).
Union Internationale des Télécommunications, place des Nations, CH-1211, Genève 20.
1964/73– 13th, 1975-1984. not priced. 417p. *En, Fr, Es.
TF: the 1975-1984 edition, with data for those years, was published in 1986.
In two sections – A: Size of telecommunications systems, traffic and staff, telephones, public telephones, telex, personnel; B: Demographic, economic and financial information (including investments).

471 The world's telephones: a statistical compilation.
A.T. & T. Long Lines, Room 220, 201 Littleton Road, Morris Plains, New Jersey 07950, USA.
1912– 1 January 1982 (published mid-1982). free. 144p. *En.
Includes numbers of telephones by world regions and by countries, indicating population ratio, type of telephone operation, PBX, subscriber lines, calls made. Total and main telephones in the world's principal cities.

472 Statistiques des services postaux [Statistics of postal services] (Union Postal Union).
Bureau International de l'Union Postale Universelle, CP 3000 Berne 15, Switzerland.
1975– 1984. not priced. loose-leaf. *Fr; contents list also in En, Ar, Es & Pt.
TF: the 1984 edition, published in 1985, has data for 1984.
Includes sections on staff, post offices, technical facilities; financial results; functioning of services; letter post; parcel post; air mail; and monetary articles. Data is arranged by country, subdivided by the sections listed below.
Note: the 'Annual report on the situation of the postal services' also includes statistical tables and charts in the text.

Δ I Environment

473 OECD environment data ... compendium 1985.
OECD, Paris.
£15; $30; Fr 150. 298p. *En, Fr.
TF: published mid-1985, with data on or to 1982, 1983 of 1984.
The state of the environment (air, inland waters, marine environment, land, forest, wild life resources, solid waste, noise, risks), pressures on the environment (agriculture, energy, transport), and managing the environment.

474 Water resources of the world: selected statistics. (Fritz van der Leeden).
Water Information Center Inc., 44 Sintsink Drive East, Port Washington, New York, NY 11050.
1975. $32.50. 568p. *En.
Data by continent and country on rivers, lakes, reservoirs, wells, dams, rain, etc. Also on hydroelectric and thermal power generating stations.

AUSTRIA
AUTRICHE
ÖSTERREICH

Central statistical office

478 Österreichisches Statistisches Zentralamt [Austrian Central Statistical Office].
Hintere Zollamtstrasse 2b, 1033 Wien.
t (0222) 6628-0.
Collects and edits statistical data for the use of the Austrian authorities. Publishes general statistical compilations, and statistics of housing, population, agriculture, production, industry, transport, foreign trade, justice, finance, elections, education and culture. More detailed data than is published can often be supplied on payment of a fee.
This office has been abbreviated to ÖSTZ, Wien in entries 479-560.

Libraries

Österreichisches Statistisches Zentralamt (see above) has a library and its collection includes Austrian statistical publications, those of other countries and of international organisations. The library is open to the public on weekdays from 9.00 to 15.00 and is closed on public holidays. The staff speak German and are able to communicate in English.
There are also libraries which can be consulted by the public in the Bundeskammer der Gewerblichen Wirtschaft [Federal Chamber of Commerce], Stubenring 12, 1010 Wien (t (0222) 52 15 11) and the nine Landeskammer [provincial chambers of commerce] throughout Austria.

Libraries and information services abroad

Copies of the more important Austrian statistical publications are available for reference in Austrian embassies and legations abroad, including:

United Kingdom	Austrian Embassy, 18 Belgrave Mews West, London SW1. t 01-235 3731.
Australia	Austrian Embassy, 107 Endeavour, Red Hill, Canberra. t 95 1533.
Canada	Austrian Embassy, 45 Wilbrod Street, Ottawa K1N 6M7. t 235 5521.
USA	Austrian Embassy, 2343 Massachusetts Avenue NW, Washington DC 20008. t (202) 483-4474.

Bibliographies

479 Publikationsverzeichnis, 1960-1979 [Publications, 1960-1979].
ÖSTZ, Wien.
This edition was published in 1980 and is available from the Office without charge.

480 Publikationsangebot... [Publications on offer...].
ÖSTZ, Wien.
Published twice a year and updates the above catalogue. Free from this Office.

481 Statistik in Österreich, 1918-1938: eine Bibliographie [Statistics in Austria, 1918-1938: a bibliography].
ÖSTZ, Wien.
1984. öS 350. 115p. *De.

Statistical publications

Δ A - General

482 Statistisches Handbuch für die Republik Österreich [Statistical handbook of the Austrian Republic].
ÖSTZ, Wien.
1950- 1984. öS 570. 664p. *De.
TF: the 1984 edition, published late 1984, contains the latest data available at the time and includes statistics for earlier years in many tables.
Main sections:
Geography and climate, administration - Population and demography - Health - Education - Culture - Employment, labour market - Social security - Social welfare, youth welfare - Personal income - Living standards - Standard of living, wages, prices - Housing - Other social questions - Environment - National accounts - Balance of payments - Structure, production and prices in agriculture - Plant production - Livestock - Forestry - Manufacturing - Energy - Mining - Construction - Internal and service trades - Foreign trade - Tourism - Transport - Gold and credit - Insurance - Joint stock companies anc co-operative societies - Budgets and balance sheets - Taxation - Justice - Elections - International sector.
Note: also available are 'Jahrbuch der Stadt Wien' [Yearbook of the city of Vienna] and 'Statistisches Taschenbuch der Stadt Wien [Statistical pocketbook of the city of Vienna] issued by the statistical office of the city.

483 Statistisches Jahrbuch Österreichischer Städte [Statistical yearbook of Austrian towns].
ÖSTZ, Wien.
1960- 1983. öS 180. c 80p. *De.
TF: the 1983 edition, published in 1984, has data for 1981 to 1983.
Statistical data for 67 towns and 120 large villages on local matters such as building, power, drainage, lighting, water supply, gas, buses, roads, etc.

484 Statistische Nachrichten [Statistical news].
ÖSTZ, Wien
1945- monthly. öS 110; or öS 1060 yr. *De.
TF: each issue is published soon after the end of the month, and contains annual statistics for the past five or more years and monthly statistics for at least 12 months up to one or two months prior to the month of issue.
Reports on the current work of the central statistical office and statistical data on national product, finance, budget, prices and wages, agriculture, industry, building, social security, transport, tourism, external trade, etc.

485 Monatsberichte [Monthly report].
Österreichisches Institut für Wirtschaftsforschung, Arsenal-Object 20, Wien 3 (Postfach 91, A-1103 Wien).
1928- monthly. öS 130; or öS 1300 yr. *De.
TF: each issue carries data for the past four complete years and monthly statistics for the current year to one or two months prior to the date of the issue.
Analytical and statistical essays as well as macroeconomic forecasts on a short term and medium term range. Each issue has a separate supplement, 'Statistische Übersichten' containing regular tables on the general economy, finance, prices and wages, agriculture and forestry, fuel and power, industrial production, retail trade, labour, transport, foreign trade, and also a section of international statistics.

486 Mitteilungen des Direktoriums der Österreichischen Nationalbank [Communications from the directors of the Austrian National Bank].
Österreichische Nationalbank, Otto-Wagner-Platz 3, Wien 9 (Postfach 61, 1011 Wien).
1956- monthly. öS 75; or öS 750 yr. *De.
Articles on the Austrian economy and a large number of regular statistical tables, mainly on banking and finance generally, but also including data on foreign trade, industrial production, prices and wages, labour market, internal trade and transport, agriculture and forestry. 'Austria's monetary situation' is an English translation of tables, explanations and sources of the German periodical and is published once or twice a year as necessary. 'Austria's monetary situation: survey' is a monthly abridgement in English of the textual part of the periodical. Both are issued with the original German version.

487 Austria: facts and figures.
Federal Press Service, Ballhausplatz 2, A-1014 Wien.
(annual) 1984. free. 239 + 20p supplement. *En.
TF: the 1984 edition, published in 1984, has data for 1983.
The supplement, titled 'Austria in figures', has statistics on population, government and politics, economy, social services, sport, schools - universities - research, culture, and the media.

488 Wirtschafts- und Sozialstatistisches Handbuch [Handbook of economic and social statistics].
Kammer für Arbeiter und angestellte für Wien, 1040 Wien.
1959- 1982. öS 100. 529p. *De.
International data, followed by statistics for Austria on population, housing and education; labour; economics; public finance; gold, money and credit market; prices, wages, cost of living; agriculture and forestry; mining, industry and energy; trade; transport and tourism; social statistics. Data is given for the country as a whole and for provinces.
Note: there is a retrospective edition covering 1945-1969.

489 Wirtschafts- und Sozialstatistisches Taschenbuch [Pocketbook of economic and social statistics].
Österreichischer Arbeiterkammertag, 1040 Wien.
1962- 1982 (published in 1982). öS 75. 511p. *De.
Includes statistical data on population and social affairs, the labour market, finance, prices, wages, cost of living, agriculture and forestry, mining and industry, trade, transport and tourism.

490 Jahrbuch der österreichischen Wirtschaft: Tätigkeitsbericht der Bundeskammer der gewerblichen Wirtschaft [Yearbook of Austrian economy: progress report of the Chamber of Trade].
Bundeskammer der gewerblichen Wirtschaft, Wiedner Hauptstrasse 63, 1045 Wien.
(annual) 1984. not priced. 339p. *De.
TF: the 1984 report, published in 1985, has data for 1984 and also 1983 and 1982 in some tables.
Includes a section of statistics (p.275-337) on the general economy, on particular industries, Chamber of Trade statistics, and international data.

491 CA quarterly: facts and figures on Austria's economy.
Creditanstalt-Bankverein, Schottengasse 6-8, 1010 Wien.
1982- quarterly. not priced. *En.
Contains articles, some of which include statistical tables.
Note: the Bank also issues 'The economic development - selected indicators', 4 pages of tables and graphs.

Δ B – ii Agriculture, fisheries, forestry, etc

492 Ergebnisse der landwirtschaftlichen Statistik [Agricultural statistics].
ÖSTZ, Wien.
1937/44– 1983. öS 210. 194p. ISSN 0067-2327. *De.
TF: the 1983 edition, published in 1985, has data for 1983.
Land under cultivation, cultivation and crops for each province and district; cultivation and crops on arable land, vine and fruit crops, livestock dairying and hunting.

493 Ergebnisse der land- u. forstwirtschaftlichen Betriebszählung... [Census of agriculture and forestry].
ÖSTZ, Wien.
1960– 1980. 11 vols. *De.
TF: the volumes for the provinces were published in 1982 and 1983.
Results of the census of agriculture, forestry and stock farming. The volumes are for Burgenland (öS 260), Salzburg (öS 220); Oberösterreich (öS 360), Kärnten (öS 290), Niederösterreich (öS 580), Steiermark (öS 400), Tirol (öS 290), Vorarlburg (öS 270), Wien (öS 180), Österreich Teil 1: Landwirtschaft (öS 220), Österreich Teil 2: Forstwirtschaft (öS 350); Landwirtschaftliche Maschinen und Geräte (öS 140).

Δ B – ii(a) Agriculture and horticulture

< see also 525

494 Die Buchführungsergebnisse aus der österreichischen Landwirtschaft [Book-keeping enquiry into the Austrian agricultural economy] (Bundesministerium für Land- und Forstwirtschaft).
Land- und Forstwirtschaftliche Landes-Buchführungs GmbH, Schauflergasse 6, 1014 Wien 1. (Postfach 98).
1961– 1984. öS 260. 149p. *De.
TF: the 1984 edition, published in 1985, has data for 1984.
A detailed breakdown of expenditure in agriculture, including agricultural machinery.

495 Landwirtschaftliche Maschinenzählung [Agricultural machinery statistics].
ÖSTZ, Wien.
1953– 1982. öS 190. 126p. *De.
TF: the results of the 1982 enquiry were published mid-1984. An enquiry of this nature is taken every four or six years.
Amounts of agricultural machinery and implements in use at the date of the enquiry.

496 Grunderwerb [Purchase of land].
ÖSTZ, Wien.
1977/80– 1982. öS 90. 40p. *De.
TF: the 1982 edition, published in 1984, has data for 1982.

497 Nutztierhaltung in Österreich [The livestock situation in Austria].
ÖSTZ, Wien.
1979– 1981. öS 360. 229p. *De.
TF: published every two years, the 1981 edition was issued in 1982.

498 Gartenbau- und Feldgemüseanbauerhebung [Development of horticulture and field vegetables].
ÖSTZ, Wien.
1964– 3rd, 1982. öS 350. 213p. *De.
TF: the results for 1982 were published in 1984. An enquiry is taken every ten years.
The results of an enquiry.

499 Der Weinbau in Österreich [Viticulture in Austria].
ÖSTZ, Wien.
1974– 1982. öS 160. 135p. *De.
TF: the results of the 1982 enquiry were published in 1984.

500 Der Intensivobstbau im Jahre... [Intensive fruit-growing...].
ÖSTZ, Wien.
1976– 1979. öS 220. 142p. *De.
TF: the results of the 1979 enquiry were published in 1981. An enquiry is made every five years.

501 Pferde- und Rinderrassenerhebung im Jahre... [Beef cattle and horses enquiry...].
ÖSTZ, Wien.
1959– 1978. öS 160. 67p. *De.
TF: the enquiry is held every five years, and the results of the 1978 enquiry were published in 1980.
Data for each breed of cattle and horses for each of the Austrian provinces.

Δ B – ii(c) Forestry

< see 525

A B – iii Industry

502 Industrie- und Gewerbestatistik [Industry and trade statistics].
ÖSTZ, Wien.
1959/60- Part 2: Industriestatistik 1982. öS 660. 410p. *De.
Part 2: Gewerbestatistik 1982. öS 580. 356p. *De.
TF: the 1982 editions, published in 1985, have data for 1982.
'Industriestatistik' has data on production, employment in the industries, orders, consumption of energy, wages and salaries, investment and depreciation, etc. 'Gewerbestatistik' has data on production, employees, salaries and wages, investment and depreciation in large, small and service industries.
Note: the publication is in transition from two separate publications.

A B – iii(b) Textiles, pulp & paper, rubber

503 Die Österreichische Textilindustrie [The Austrian textile industry].
Fachverband der Textilindustrie Österreichs, Rudolfsplatz 12, Wien 1013.
1969- 1983. not priced. [iii]67p. *De.
TF: the 1983 edition, published mid-1984, has data for 1983.
The annual report of the organisation, which includes statistics for foreign trade and production by fibre and end-use, number of employees, imports by fibre, and exports by commodity and country.

504 Statistischer Bericht [Statistical report].
Fachverband der Textilindustrie Österreichs, Rudolfsplatz 12, Wien.
1971- quarterly. not priced. *De.
TF: each issue has monthly, quarterly and cumulative data to the end of the period of the issue and is published about three months later.
Supplements 'Die Österreichische Textilindustrie' (503), with data on the economic situation, use of raw materials and production in the textile industry, employment situation in the Austrian textile industry, foreign trade, etc.

505 Verpackungsstatistik...Verpackungsproduktion, Aussenhandel, Verpackungsverbrauch [Packing statistics... production, foreign trade, internal trade].
Österreichisches Institut für Verpackungswesen an der Wirtschaftsuniversität Wien, Gumpendorfer Strasse 6, A-1060 Wien.
(annual) 1984. öS 210. 62p. *De.
TF: the 1984 edition, published in 1985, has data for 1983 and 1984.
Production, foreign trade and internal sales of packing materials.
Note: certain issues of their series 'Verpackungsforschung' also contain statistical information.

A B – iv Construction

506 Baustatistik [Construction statistics].
ÖSTZ, Wien.
1969- Part 1. 1983. öS 520. Part 2. 1982. öS 490. 2 vols. *De.
TF: the 1983 edition of Part 1 and the 1982 edition of Part 2 were both published in 1984.
Part 1 has the value of production, numbers employed, income and working hours, etc. Part 2 has salaries and wages, gross and net value of production, investment, and depreciation.

507 Baustatistik: Gerätesbestand im Hoch- und Tiefbau... [Construction statistics: apparatus for over and underground construction].
ÖSTZ, Wien.
1980- 31.12.1983. öS 160. 115p. *De.
TF: the issue with data as at 31.12.1983 was published in 1984.

508 Wohnungsdaten [House building activity and dwellings].
ÖSTZ, Wien.
1956- 1983/1984. öS 420. 256p. *De.
TF: the 1983/84 edition, published in 1985, has data for 1983/1984.
Data on housebuilding by regions, cost of house building, and dwellings.

A B – v Energy

509 Energieversorgung Österreichs [Energy supply].
ÖSTZ, Wien.
1975- monthly and annual. öS 55; or öS 570 yr (13 parts). *De.
General survey of consumption of energy, solid fuel, liquid fuel, gas, electric energy, etc.

510 Wirtschaftsstatistik...der Elektrizitätsversorgungsunternehmen [Economic statistics of electricity supply].
ÖSTZ, Wien.
1975- 1983. öS 90. 51p. *De.
TF: the 1983 edition, published in 1985, has data for 1983.
Data on employment, gross and net production, investment, etc.

Δ B – v, continued

511 Betriebstatistik erzeugung und verbrauch elektrischer Energie in Österreich. 1 Teil – Gesamtergebnisse [Statistics of production and sales of electric energy in Austria. part 1, general].
Bundesministerium für Handel, Gewerbe und Industrie, Am Hof 6A, 1011 Wien.
1946– 1984. not priced. 130p. *De.
TF: the 1984 edition, published mid-1985, has data for 1984 and earlier years in some tables.
Detailed statistical data on the production and sales of electric power.

512 Brennstoffstatistik...der Wärmekraftwerke für die öffentliche Elektrizitätsversorgung in Österreich [Fuel statistics...the heating industry for public electricity supply in Austria]
Bundesministerium für Handel, Gewerbe und Industrie; Bundeslastverteiler & Österreichischen Elektrizitätswirtschafts AG., Am Hof 6A, 1011 Wien.
(annual) 1983. not priced. 161p. *De.
TF: the 1983 edition, published in 1984, has data for 1982 and 1983 and also 1981 in some tables.
Includes data for Austria, Europe and the world.

513 Jahresbericht [Annual report of the Federation of Austrian Petroleum Industry].
Fachverband der Erdölindustrie Österreichs, Erdbergstrasse 72, 1031 Wien.
1947– 1983. free. 28p. *De.
TF: the 1983 report, published in 1984, has data for 1979 to 1983.
Includes a 6-page statistical section with data on Austrian crude oil production, number of wells, natural gas production and sales, petroleum derivitives production and sales, consumption and foreign trade.

Δ C External trade

514 Der Aussenhandel Österreichs. Series 1A: Spezialhandel nach handelsstatistischen Nummern; Gesamtübersichten [Austrian foreign trade. Series 1A: trade by commodity classification; summary].
ÖSTZ, Wien.
1947– quarterly. öS 390; or öS 1090 yr. ISSN 0004-816X. *De.
TF: each issue is published about one month after the end of the period covered and has data for the quarter of the issue and cumulative totals for the year to date.
Statistics of foreign trade arranged by the Austrian commodity classification (based on BTN), subdivided by countries of origin and destination. Also various summary statistical tables.

515 Der Aussenhandel Österreichs. Series 1B: Spezialhandel nach Ländern und Waren [Austrian foreign trade. Series 1B: trade by countries and commodities].
ÖSTZ, Wien.
1947– half-yearly. öS 250; or öS 400 yr. ISSN 0004-816X. *De.
TF: each issue is published about one month after the end of the period covered and has data for the half-year, the second issue each year also having annual figures.
Statistics of foreign trade by countries of origin and destination, subdivided by commodities.

516 Der Aussenhandel Österreichs. Serie 2: Gesamtübersichten und Spezialhandel nach dem internationalen Warenscheme (SITC-revised) [Austrian foreign trade. Series 2: summary and trade by the international commodity classification (SITC-revised)].
ÖSTZ, Wien.
1947– half-yearly. öS 210; or öS 340 yr. ISSN 0004-816X. *De.
TF: each issue is published about one month after the end of the period covered and has data for the half-year, the second issue also carrying annual figures.
Statistics of foreign trade arranged by the SITC-revised classification and summary tables.

Δ D Internal distribution and service trades

Δ D – i Wholesale and retail trades

517 Gross- und Einzelhandelsstatistik [Wholesale and retail trade statistics].
ÖSTZ, Wien.
1971– 1984. öS 210. 118p. *De.
TF: the 1984 edition, published in 1985, has data for 1984.
Wholesale and retail trade by type of commodity, and regional indexes of turnover for the wholesale and retail trade.

518 Konsumerhebung [Consumer situation].
ÖSTZ, Wien.
1964– 2nd, 1974. 2 vols. *De.
TF: the enquiry is made every ten years.
Vol 1: has data for Austria; vol 2: for the provinces.

Δ D – iv Tourism and travel

519 Der Fremdenverkehr in Österreich im Jahre... [Tourist trade in Austria...].
ÖSTZ, Wien.
1952/53– 1983. öS 440. 228p. *De.
TF: the 1983 edition, published in 1984, has data for each month and the full year of 1983.
Numbers of foreign visitors, by country of nationality and by resorts visited in Austria.

A

Δ E Population

521 Ergebnisse der Volkszählung [Census of population].
ÖSTZ, Wien.
1869- 1981. 28 vols. *De.
TF: a census is taken every ten years.
Vol 1A: results of the 1981 census and data on the population from 1869 onwards (öS 60).
Vol 2-11: demographic indications for individual provinces (Burgenland (öS 90); Kärnten (öS 90); Niederösterreich (öS 150); Oberösterreich (öS 140); Salzburg (öS 90); Steiermark (öS 150); Tirol (öS 100); Vorarlburg (öS 70); Wien (öS 90); Österreich (öS 90)).
Vol 12-21: data on non-Austrians, economic classifications, journey to work, occupations, languages, etc... (Burgenland (öS 110); Kärnten (öS 110); Niederösterreich (öS 290); Oberösterreich (öS 220); Salzburg (öS 100); Steiermark (öS 240); Tirol (öS 150); Vorarlburg (öS 100); Wien (öS 150); Österreich (öS 110)).
Vol 22: employed persons according to occupation and economic classification and journeys to work (öS 220).
Vol 23: education (öS 220).
Vol 24: schools and students (öS 220).
Vol 25: migration 1976-1981 (öS 100).
Vol 26: households and families (öS 110).
Vol 27: marriages and births (öS 240).
Vol 28: text (öS 380).

Δ E - i Vital statistics

522 Demographisches Jahrbuch Österreichs [Austrian demographic yearbook].
ÖSTZ, Wien.
1951- 1983. öS 410. 231p. *De.
TF: the 1983 edition, published in 1985, has data for 1983.

Δ E - ii Labour

< see also 521

523 Amtliche Nachrichten des Bundesministerium für Soziale Verwaltung und des Bundesministerium für Gesundheit und Umweltschutz [Official report of the Ministry of Social Affairs and the Ministry of Health and Environment].
Bundesministerium für Soziale Verwaltung, Stubenring 1, 1010 Wien.
1945- monthly. öS 860 yr (öS 990 yr abroad). *De.
TF: each issue has data for the previous month.
Includes labour market statistics and statistics of the activities of labour inspectors.

524 Arbeitsstättenzählung [Census on the labour situation].
ÖSTZ, Wien.
1973- 1981. 10 vols. *De.
TF: the 1981 census was the second to be taken.
The main reports of the census are for Austria as a whole (öS 490); Burgenland (öS 210); Kärnten (öS 230); Niederösterreich (öS 390); Oberösterreich (öS 360); Salzburg (öS 240); Steiermark (öS 330); Tirol (öS 280); Vorarlburg (öS 190); and Wien (öS 310).

525 Land- und forstwirtschaftliche Arbeitskräfte [Development of agricultural and forestry manpower].
ÖSTZ, Wien.
1973- 1983. öS 370. 181p. *De.
TF: an enquiry taken every three or four years. The 1983 results were published in 1985.

Δ E - iii Housing

< see also 508

526 Häuser- und Wohnungszählung [Census of housing and dwellings].
ÖSTZ, Wien.
1961- 1981. 10 vols. *De.
TF: a census is taken every ten years.
One volume for each of the provinces (Burgenland (öS 180); Kärnten (öS 340); Niederösterreich (öS 430); Oberösterreich (öS 380); Salzburg (öS 320); Steiermark (öS 380); Tirol (öS 330); Vorarlburg (öS 300); Wien (öS 430)) and one for Austria as a whole (öS 180).

Δ F Social and political

< see also 521

527 Sozialstatistische Daten [Social statistics].
ÖSTZ, Wien.
1977- 1980. öS 320. 467p. *De.
TF: issued every three years, the 1980 edition, published in 1981, has data for several years to 1979.
Population structure, vital statistics, health and medical service, education, culture, employment, labour, income, consumption, social security, welfare, social questions, housing, infrastructure and environment, leisure.

Δ F – ii Health and welfare

528 Bericht über das Gesundheitswesen in Österreich... [Report on public health in Austria] (Bundesministerium für Gesundheit und Umweltschutz & Österreichisches Statistisches Zentralamt).
ÖSTZ, Wien.
1960– 1983. öS 280. 263p. *De.
TF: the 1983 edition, published in 1985, has data for 1983.
Statistical data on diseases, accidents, hospitals, pharmacies, personnel, chemists, hygiene, health, cancer, social and vital statistics, and veterinary statistics.

529 Sozialhilfe [Social assistance].
ÖSTZ, Wien.
1965– 1983. öS 90. 39p. *De.
TF: the 1983 edition, published in 1984, has data for 1983.

530 Jugendwohlfahrtspflege [Child welfare].
ÖSTZ, Wien.
1965– 1983. öS 120. 51p. *De.
TF: the 1983 edition, published late 1984, has data for 1983.

Δ F – iii Education and leisure

‹ see also 521

531 Das Schulwesen in Österreich [The educational system in Austria].
ÖSTZ, Wien.
1971/72– 1983/84. öS 570. 344p. *De.
TF: the 1983/84 edition, published in 1985, refers to the 1983/84 school year.

532 Die Kindergärten (Kindertagesheime) [Nursery schools].
ÖSTZ, Wien.
1977/78– 1983/84. öS 500. 256p. *De.
TF: the 1983/84 edition, published in 1984, refers to the 1983/84 year.

533 Österreichische Hochschulstatistik. Studienjahr... [Austrian university statistics. Academic year...].
ÖSTZ, Wien.
1953/54– 1981/82. öS 510. 471p. *De.
TF: the 1981/82 edition, published in 1984, has data for 1981/82.
Universities, faculties, students, diplomas, teachers, etc.

534 Biblos.
Österreichische Zeitschrift für Buch- und Bibliothekswesen, Dokumentation, Bibliographie und Bibliophilie, Josefsplatz 1, A-1014 Wien 1.
1952– quarterly. öS 240 yr. *De.
Since 1957 issue no. 4 each year has contained 'Statistik der Österreichischen Bibliotheken' [Statistics of Austrian Libraries], compiled by Vereinigung Österr. Bibliothekare (VOB) [Association of Austrian Librarians], giving numbers of stock and personnel, use, etc. for 66 libraries.

Δ F – iv Justice

535 Statistik der Rechtspflege [Judicial statistics].
ÖSTZ, Wien.
1960– 1982. öS 380. 189p. *De.
TF: the 1982 edition, published in 1984, has data for 1982.

536 Kriminalstatistik [Criminal statistics].
ÖSTZ, Wien.
1960– 1982. öS 340. 171p. *De.
TF: the 1982 edition, published in 1984, has data for 1982.

Δ F – vi Elections

537 Die Nationalratswahlen [Elections].
ÖSTZ, Wien.
1962– 1983. öS 220. 100p. *De.
TF: the results of the elections held on 24th April 1983 were published late 1984.
Numbers of voters, parties, votes cast, results, etc. for provinces, towns and smaller areas.

538 Die Wahl des Bundespräsidenten [Election of the President of the State].
ÖSTZ, Wien.
1963– 1980. öS 170. 42p. *De.
TF: the results of the election held on 18th May 1980 were published later that year.

A

Δ G – i Banking

539 Jahresbericht... [Annual report...].
Verband Österreichischer Banken und Bankiers, Börsegasse 11, A-1013 Wien (Postfach 132).
(annual) 1984. not priced. 64p. *De.
TF: the 1984 report, published in 1985, has data for 1984 and some earlier years.
International money and banking, money and credit in Austria, etc., as well as financial data concerning the banks.

540 Bericht über das Gaschäftsjahr... [Annual report...].
Österreichische Nationalbank, Otto-Wagner-Platz 3, Wien 9 (Postfach 61, 1011 Wien).
1924- 1983. not priced. 173p. *De; an abridged ed. in English is also available.
TF: the 1983 report, published in 1984, has data for 1983.
General economic trends, money and credit, capital market, public finance, production and markets, balance of payments, and international settlements, as well as balance sheet, profit and loss accounts of the bank.

Δ G – ii Public finance

< see also 540

541 Gebarungsübersichten [Public finance].
ÖSTZ, Wien.
1955- 1982. öS 670. 374p. *De.
TF: the 1982 edition, published mid-1984, has data for 1982.
Public finance for the state, provinces and municipalities.

542 Österreichs Volkseinkommen... [Austria's national income].
ÖSTZ, Wien.
1950- 1983. öS 290. 248p. *De.
TF: the 1983 edition, published in 1985, has data for 1983 and from 1954 to 1983.
Detailed data on Austria's national income.

543 Einkommensteuerstatistik [Income tax statistics].
ÖSTZ, Wien.
1969- 1982. öS 350. 149p. *De.
TF: the 1982 edition, published in 1985, has data for 1982.

544 Lohnsteuerstatistik [Wage tax statistics].
ÖSTZ, Wien.
1976- 1979. öS 380. 206p. *De.
TF: the 1979 edition was issued in 1983. Published every three years.

545 Gewerbesteuerstatistik [Trade tax statistics].
ÖSTZ, Wien.
1976- 1981 (published in 1984). öS 230. 145p. *De.

546 Vermögensteuerstatistik [Property tax statistics].
ÖSTZ, Wien.
1974- 1980. öS 520. 281p. *De.
TF: published every three years, the 1980 edition was issued in 1984.

Δ G – iii Company finance

547 Statistik der Aktiengesellschaften in Österreich [Statistics of joint stock companies in Austria].
ÖSTZ, Wien.
1955/61- 1982. öS 250. 135p. ISSN 0081-5233. *De.
TF: the 1982 edition, published in 1984, has data for 1982.
Financial data on individual companies.

548 Umsatzsteuerstatistik [Turnover tax statistics].
ÖSTZ, Wien.
1968- 1981. öS 330. 163p. *De.
TF: the 1981 edition, published in 1984, has data for 1981.
Turnover tax by size of firms and by types of firms.
Note: a preliminary version 'Umsatzsteuerstatistik – Voranmeldungen' is issued about a year earlier (1983 ed. öS 270. 162p).

549 Bericht über das Geschäftsjahr [Report for the year of the Vienna Stock Exchange].
Wiener Börse Kammer, Wipplingerstrasse 34, A-1011 Wien.
1771- 1984. not priced. c 70p. *De.
TF: the 1984 report, published in March 1985, has data for 1984 and also for some earlier years in some tables.
Includes statistics in the text of the report and also a statistical section. Information includes number of members, number of securities traded, turnover, new listings, cancellations of listings, loans issued, bonds outstanding, average prices and yields of bonds, changes in listed capital, total nominal value and market value of listed shares, dividends and yields of listed shares, and share index.

Δ H Transport and communications

550 Österreichische Verkehrswirtschaft in Zahlen [Austrian transport economy in figures].
Bundeskammer der Gewerblichen Wirtschaft: Bundessektion Verkehr, Wiedner Hauptstrasse 63, Wien (Postfach 170, A-1045 Wien).
(annual) 1984. free. 48p. *De.
TF: the 1984 issue, published in 1984, has data for several years to 1983.
A brochure which includes data for each 'Fachverband' within the transport section of the Federal Chamber of Commerce, and also a section of general statistics relating to all types of transport.

Δ H - ii Roads and road transport

551 Strassenverkehrszählung (Bundesstrassen) [Traffic survey (State roads)].
ÖSTZ, Wien.
1962/63- 1980. öS 420. 289p. *De.
TF: the survey is usually taken at regular intervals of 5 years. The results of the 1980 survey were published in 1985.

552 Strassenverkehrszählung (Landesstrassen) [Traffic survey (provincial roads)].
ÖSTZ, Wien.
1962/63- 1980. öS 250. 151p. *De.
TF: the survey is taken 5-yearly. The results of the 1980 survey were published in 1985.

553 Fahrleistungen der Kraftfahrzeuge, Ergebnisse des Mikrozensus [Road traffic micro-census].
ÖSTZ, Wien.
1971- 2nd, 1977. öS 120. 86p. *De.
TF: the results of the 1977 census were published in 1979. A 3rd census was taken in 1983.

554 Strassenverkehrssicherheit im Jahre... [Traffic accidents involving damage to persons and property and driving licenses].
ÖSTZ, Wien.
1961- 1984. öS 420. 225p. *De.
TF: the 1984 edition, published in 1985, has data for 1984.

555 Bestandsstatistik der Kraftfahrzeuge in Österreich [Statistics of motor vehicles in Austria].
ÖSTZ, Wien.
1960- 1983. öS 560. 100p. *De.
TF: the 1983 edition, published in 1984, has data for 1983.
Motor vehicle registrations, by makes and by types of vehicles.

556 Monatliche Kraftfahrzeugzulassungsstatistik [Monthly motor vehicle licences in Austria].
ÖSTZ, Wien.
1960- monthly. öS 220; öS 2450 yr (öS 2650 yr abroad). *De.
TF: each issue has data for that month and is published two months later.
Motor vehicle licencing statistics by make of vehicle.

557 Kraftfahrzeugzulassungsstatistik. Neuzulassungen [Motor licence statistics. New licences].
ÖSTZ, Wien.
1979- monthly. öS 220; or öS 2450 yr. *De.

Δ H - iv Aviation and air transport

558 Zivilluftfahrt in Österreich [Civil aviation in Austria].
ÖSTZ, Wien.
1960- 1983. öS 200. 143p. *De.
TF: the 1983 edition, published in 1984, has data for 1983 and some earlier years.

Δ H - v Telecommunications and postal services

559 Geschäftsbericht [Report of the Austrian Post & Telegraph Administration].
Generaldirektion, Österreichische Post- und Telegraphenverwaltung, Wien.
(annual) 1984. free. c 200p. *De.
TF: the 1984 edition, published in 1985, has data for 1984.
Postal services, postal motorbus services, telecommunication services (telephone, telex, telegraph, television & broadcasting licences), and financial accounts of the organisation.

Δ I Environment

560 Umweltdaten [Environment statistics].
ÖSTZ, Wien.
1978- 1985. öS 190. *De.
TF: published every three or four years, the 1985 edition, published in 1985.
Soil and vegetation, water, air, refuse, noise.

AL

ALBANIA
ALBANIE
ALBANIEN
SHQIPERI

Central statistical office

560A Drejtoria e Përgithshme e Statistikes [Directorate-General of Statistics]
Tirana.

Libraries

Drejtoria e Përgithshme e Statistikes (see above) has a library which is not generally open to the public, although it is possible to apply for special permission to use the library for research. The statistical yearbook, however, is available in reference libraries throughout the country.

Statistical publications

Δ A General

560B 35 years of Socialist Albania: statistical data on the development of the economy and culture.
Drejtoria e Përgithshme e Statistikes, Tirana.
1958- lekë 13. 139p. *En & Albanian eds.
TF: the above edition was published in 1981.
A special issue of the Statistical yearbook of Albania [Vjetori statistikor i R P SH].
Main sections:
General information - Elections - Population - Workers & employees - Industry - Agriculture - Investments - Transport - Trade - National income & finance - Education & culture - Health services.

560C Albanian foreign trade. (Chamber of Commerce of the P S R of Albania).
Ndërmarrja e Shpërndarjes së Librit, Tirana.
every other month. not priced. *En.
Includes occasional statistics.

ANDORRA

No statistics are published. Foreign trade data is included with that of Spain.

B

BELGIUM
BELGIQUE
BELGIEN
BELGIE

Central statistical office

561 Institut National de Statistique. Nationaal Instituut voor de Statistiek [National Institute of Statistics]. rue de Louvain 44, 1000 Bruxelles/Leuvenseweg 44, 1000 Brussel.
t 02/513 96 50.
A department of the Ministry of Economic Affairs, the Institute is responsible for the collection, analysis and publication of Belgian official statistics in the fields of population, housing, public health, education, industry, foreign trade, internal trade, transport, tourism, salaries, family budgets, wholesale and retail prices, finance, justice, national accounts, etc.
Unpublished statistical information can often be supplied on request, at a charge based on the time involved, the main types of information being supplied being more detailed country breakdowns under particular customs headings of the foreign trade of BLEU, and specific detailed information from the censuses of population, industry and commerce. It is possible to pay an annual subscription for the regular supply of monthly, quarterly or annual detailed foreign trade statistics for particular commodity headings. Photocopying facilities are available for a fee.
Apart from the titles listed in the following pages, the Institute issues at irregular intervals a journal, 'Etudes statistiques. Statistische Studiën' with articles on various subjects of statistical interest, and an annual report on its activities.
The Institute has been abbreviated to INS, Bruxelles in entries between 563 and 613.

Libraries

All publications of the Institut National de Statistique (see above) may be consulted at the Institute, which is open to the public from 9.00 to 11.45 and from 13.00 to 16.00, except Saturdays, Sundays and holidays. Languages spoken are French, Dutch and English.
Statistical publications of Belgium, other countries and international organisations may be consulted at the Bibliothèque Centrale du Ministère des Affaires Economiques [the central library of the Ministry of Economic Affairs], Bibliothèque Fonds Quetelet, rue de l'Industrie 6, 1040 Bruxelles. The Institut Economique Agricole [Agricultural Economics Institute] also has a small library which is open to the public.

Libraries and information services abroad

Copies of the more general Belgian statistical publications are available for reference in Belgian embassies and legations abroad, including:

United Kingdom	Belgian Embassy, 103 Eaton Square, London SW1. t 01-235 5422.
Australia	Belgian Embassy, 19 Arkana Street, Yarralumla, Canberra. t 73 2501.
Canada	Belgian Embassy, 85 Range Road, Ottawa K1N 8J6. t 236 7267.
New Zealand	Belgian Legation, Robert Jones House, Jervois Quay, Wellington. t 729 558.
USA	Belgian Embassy, 3330 Garfield Street, Washington DC 20008. t (202) 333 6900.

Bibliographies

562 Catalogue des publications de l'Institut National de Statistique: situation à fin 1983. Catalogus van de publicaties uitgegeven door het Nationaal Instituut voor de Statistiek: toestand einde 1983. (Institut National de Statistique).
Available free from the Institut National de Statistique, rue de Louvain 44, 1000 Bruxelles, the catalogue lists all the publications of the Institute, including those which are out of print. It is updated by monthly supplements. In French and Dutch.

Statistical publications

Δ A General

< see also 079, 080

563 Annuaire statistique de la Belgique [Statistical yearbook of Belgium].
INS, Bruxelles.
1870- 1983. FrB 900 (FrB 1040 abroad). 788p. *Fr & Nl eds.
TF: the 1983 edition, published mid-1984, has data for 1983 generally, and earlier years in some tables.
Main sections:
Climate & territory - Population - Public health - Building & construction - Elections - Education & culture - Budget - Justice - Agriculture & forestry - Hunting & fisheries - Industry - Internal trade - Foreign trade - Transport - Tourism & hotel industry - Post, telegraph & telephones - Communications - Public finance - Exchange & stock market - Money market & monetary organisations - Capital market & non-monetary organisations - National income - Employment - Prices - Wages - Consumption - Social affairs - National accounts - International data.

Δ A, continued

564 Annuaire statistique de poche [Statistical pocketbook].
INS, Bruxelles.
1965- 1984 (published in January 1985). FrB 125 (FrB 160 abroad). 228p. ISSN 0067-5431. *Fr, Nl.
An abridged edition of 563.

565 Annuaire de statistiques régionales [Yearbook of regional statistics].
INS, Bruxelles.
1976- 1983. FrB 360 (FrB 480 abroad). 213p. *Fr & Nl eds.
TF: the 1983 edition, published in 1985, contains the latest data available at the time of publication.
Regional data on population, buildings and houses, public health, education, justice, agriculture and horticulture, energy and industry, transport and services, finance, credit, labour, social statistics, regional accounts, elections, etc.

566 Bulletin de statistique [Statistical bulletin].
INS, Bruxelles.
1909- monthly. FrB 180 (FrB 230 abroad); or FrB 900 yr (FrB 1200 yr abroad). ISSN 0045-1703. *Fr, Nl.
TF: each issue is published early the following month, with data for several years and the last 12 months up to one or two months prior to the date of the issue.
Statistical time series on population, housing, fishing, agriculture, industry, internal trade, foreign trade, service trades, transport, prices, wages, employment, finance and national accounts.
Note: prior to 1985 the bulletin also included articles on various subjects of statistical interest; articles are still published in 'Etudes statistiques'.

567 Communiqué hebdomadaire [Weekly report].
INS, Bruxelles.
1951- FrB 55 (FrB 70 abroad); or FrB 650 yr (FrB 870 yr abroad). *Fr, Nl.
Up-dates many of the tables included in 'Bulletin de statistique' such as production, finance, price indices, etc.
Note: free to subscribers to 'Bulletin de statistique' on special request.

568 Aperçu économique trimestriel [Quarterly economic account].
Ministère des Affaires Économiques, rue de l'Industrie 10, 1040 Bruxelles.
1984- quarterly. not priced. *Fr & Nl eds.
TF: each issue has data for several years, quarters and months to a month prior to the date of the issue, and is published a little later.
part III has tables and graphs on industrial production, exports, imports, commercial balance, employment, consumer prices, household consumption, etc.
Note: supersedes 'Aperçu de l'évolution économique' (1964- monthly).

569 Lettre de conjoncture [Economic letter].
Ministère des Affaires Économiques, rue de l'Industrie 10, 1040 Bruxelles.
1984- monthly. FrB 200 yr. ISSN 0772-0831. *Fr & Nl eds.
TF: includes quarterly and monthly data for the last year to the month prior to the month of publication.
A 6-page up-dating of 'Aperçu économique trimestriel' (568).

570 L'économie belge en... [The Belgian economy in...].
Direction Générale des Etudes et de la Documentation, Ministère des Affaires Economiques, Nijverheidsstraat, 1040 Bruxelles.
(annual) 1983. Vol.I FrB 200. Vol. II FrB 400. 2 vols. *Fr.
TF: the 1983 edition, publihsed in 1984, has data for several years to 1983.
Population, labour, agriculture and sea fisheries, industry, energy, transport, distribution, tourism, public finance, money and credit, insurance, prices, wages, investments, consumption, regional data, foreign economic relations (foreign trade of BLEU), international data. Vol.I is mainly text but includes tables in the text; Vol.II is devoted to statistical tables.

571 Notes memsuelles sur la situation économique [Monthy notes on the economic situation].
Conseil Central de l'Economie, 17-21 avenue de la Joyeuse Entrée, Bruxelles.
not priced. *Fr.
TF: each issue has monthly averages for the last three full years and monthly data for the last six months with comparative figures for the previous year, and is published one month later.
Mainly text, but including total monthly statistics for various economic subjects - industry, investment, internal trade, foreign trade, transport, employment, prices, wages, public finance, savings and credit etc.

572 Statistiques du commerce intérieur et des transports [Internal trade and transport statistics].
INS, Bruxelles.
1985- monthly. FrB 85 (FrB 135 abroad); or FrB 700 yr (FrB 1200 yr abroad). *Fr & Nl eds.
TF: each issue has long runs of annual and monthly figures in some tables, two or three months' figures in others to about six months prior to the date of the issue.
Internal trade and tourism, transport (ports, shipping, railways, air transport, motor vehicles, road accidents, modes of transport, goods in transit), half-yearly and annual statistics also.
Note: continues two separate publications relating to internal trade and to transport.

Δ A, continued

573 Bulletin de la Banque Nationale de Belgique [Bulletin of the National Bank of Belgium].
Banque Nationale de Belgique, blvd de Berlaimont 56, 1000 Bruxelles.
1926- monthly. FrB 40 (FrB 50 abroad); or FrB 400 yr (FrB 500 yr abroad). ISSN 0005-5611. *Fr.
TF: some tables have data for the month prior to the date of the issue, whilst others are up to six months earlier.
Most of each issue is devoted to statistical tables. Apart from financial and banking data, these include population, national accounts and economic enquiries, employment and unemployment, agriculture and fisheries, industry, services, wages, price indices, foreign trade of BLEU, balance of payments of BLEU, and public finance.
Note: a special issue is to be published in 1985 covering 1970 to 1980.

574 Rapports [Reports of the National Bank of Belgium].
Banque Nationale de Belgique, blvd de Berlaimont 56, 1000 Bruxelles.
1926- 1984. free. 373p. ISSN 0067-3978. *Fr & En eds.
TF: the 1984 report, published early 1985, has data for four or five years to 1984. The French edition is published about three months before the English edition.
Mainly on the operations of the bank, but also includes tables and graphs on economic and financial trends.

Δ B Production

Δ B – i Mines and mining

< see also 580

575 Statistiques...houille – cokes – agglomérés – métallurgie – carrières [Statistics...coal – coke – agglomerates – metals – quarries].
Administration des Mines, Ministère des Affaires Économiques et de l'Énergie, rue J.A. De Mot 30, 1040 Bruxelles.
quarterly not priced. *Fr, Nl.
TF: each issue has data for four months and is published about three months after the end of the period covered. Prior to January 1984 it was issued annually.
Sections on coal mines, coke plants, agglomerate manufacture, sale of solid fuels, metals (steel and non-ferrous), quarries and connected industries, and EEC statistics.
Note: provisional monthly statistics are also issued.

Δ B – ii Agriculture, fisheries, forestry, etc

576 Recensement général de l'agriculture et des forêts [General census of agriculture and forestry].
INS, Bruxelles.
1846- 1970. 10 vols. *Fr, Nl.
TF: a census is taken every ten years; the results of the 1970 census were published in 1976.
Vol 1: Methodology and some general statistics (FrB 500 (FrB 600 abroad))
Vol 2: Livestock (FrB 300 (FrB 360 abroad))
Vol 3: Machinery, implements, etc. (FrB 400 FrB 480 abroad))
Vol 4: Horticulture (FrB 350 (FrB 420 abroad))
Vol 5: Forestry (FrB 300 (FrB 360 abroad))
Vol 6: Methods of sales of products, co-operatives, employment, utilisation of machinery, contracts, etc (FrB 300 (FrB 360 abroad))
Vol 7: Results by administrative district and province (FrB 500 (FrB 600 abroad))
Vol 8: Crops and livestock (FrB 300 (FrB 360 abroad))
Vol 9: Implements and installations (FrB 500 (FrB 600 abroad))
Vol 10: Horticultural installations (FrB 700 (FrB 830 abroad)).

Δ B – ii(a) Agriculture and horticulture

577 Statistiques agricoles [Agricultural statistics].
INS, Bruxelles.
1969- monthly. FrB 85 (FrB 135 abroad; or FrB 700 yr (FrB 1200 yr abroad). *Fr, Nl.
TF: each issue is published early the following month, the tables containing data for several years and the last 14 months or three quarters up to one or three months prior to the date of the issue.
Monthly and quarterly figures on climate, the state of agriculture, milk industry, sea fishing, abbatoirs, contagious diseases, price indices, etc. Also the results of the annual censuses of agriculture and horticulture are included in certain issues.

578 L.E.I. statistieken. Statistiques de l'L.E.A. [Statistics of the IEA].
Institut Economique Agricole, blvd de Berlaimont 18, 1000 Bruxelles.
1960- 1984. not priced. 97p. *Nl, Fr.
TF: the 1984 edition, published in 1985, has data for 1965, 1980 to 1983.
Population, inventary of machinery, climate, structure data, areas (of crops), animal population, yields, production (tons), slaughtered animals, milk production, egg production, production/consumption of commercial fertilisers, production/consumption of compound feeding-stuffs, straight feeding-stuffs of own production, market prices, prices production means, hourly wages/manpower, fertilisers, sake of buildings/law, agricultural financing, foreign trade, etc.

Δ B – iii Industry

579 Recensement de l'industrie et du commerce [Census of industry and commerce].
INS, Bruxelles.
1846– 1970. 3 vols. *Fr, Nl.
Contents: Vol 1: Establishments and establishment divisions; vol 2: Principal results by municipality; vol 3: Results concerning enterprises.

580 Statistiques industrielles [Industrial statistics].
INS, Bruxelles.
1967– monthly FrB 85 (FrB 135 abroad); or FrB 700 yr (FrB 1200 yr abroad). *Fr & Nl eds.
TF: each issue has data for the past six years and the last 16 months up to two or three months prior to the date of the issue.
Monthly indices of industrial production, both general and for particular industries; monthly statistics showing the quantities of production, sales, imports and exports and stocks in each industry; employment in each industry. The second part of each issue contains annual statistics for each industry as they become available. Industries covered: coal and iron mining, quarrying, food, tobacco, textiles, hosiery, clothing, wood and wood production, paper, leather, rubber, chemicals, petroleum products, gas, non-ferrous metals, metal manufactures, plastics, electricity and water.
Note: extracts from the monthly issues giving data for single industries can be obtained separately (FrB 15 (FrB 30 abroad)).

581 Statistiques annuelles de la production [Annual production statistics].
INS, Bruxelles.
1953– 1979. FrB 200 (FrB 260 abroad). *Fr, Nl.
TF: the 1979 edition, published in 1984, has data for 1979.

Δ B – iii(b) Textiles, paper, rubber, etc

582 Bulletin statistique [Statistical bulletin].
Comité de l'Industrie Lainière Belge asbl, Montoyer 24, 1040 Bruxelles.
1930– 6 a year. not priced. *Fr.
Includes data on production, fibre consumption, deliveries, trade, etc. of the Belgian wool textile industry.
Note: the annual report of the Committee of the Belgian Wool Industry (available free) also includes statistical data.

583 Rapport [Report].
Comité Centrale de la Bonneterie Belge, Rode Beukendreef 14, 9831 Deurle.
1957– 1983. Free within Europe; mail expenses charged elsewhere. 2 vols. *Fr, Nl.
TF: the 1983 edition, published in 1984, has data for 1982 and 1983.
Includes a statistical section on production, sales, foreign trade and consumption of textiles and various types of clothing (hosiery, sportswear, underwear, pullovers, blouses, etc).

Δ B – iii(d) Metals, etc

584 L'industrie belge des métaux non-ferreux...recueil statistique... [The Belgian non-ferrous metals industry...statistical collection...].
Fédération des Entreprises de Métaux Non Ferreux, blvd de Berlaimont 12, 1000 Bruxelles.
(annual) 1983. not priced. 72p. *Fr, Nl.
TF: the 1983 edition, published in 1984, has data for 1983 and also some earlier years in some tables.
Detailed statistics of production, imports and exports of non-ferrous metals, both crude and semi-finished and also statistics of employment in the industry.

Δ B – iv Construction

585 Statistiques de la construction et du logement [Statistics of construction and housing].
INS, Bruxelles.
1971– 17/1985. FrB 375 (FrB 425 abroad). *Fr, Nl.
TF: the publication appears at irregular intervals, one or two a year. No. 17/1985 was published in 1985.
Data on population, licences to build, buildings commenced, buildings in course of construction, buildings demolished, employment and wages in the industry, production and prices, and the position of the building industry in the national economy.

Δ B – v Energy

< see also 580

586 Annuaire statistique [Statistical yearbook].
Fédération Professionnelle des Producteurs et Distributeurs d'Electricité de Belgique (FPE), avenue de Tervuren 34 bte 38, 1040 Bruxelles.
1952– 1983. FrB 300. 78p. *Fr & Nl eds.
TF: the 1983 edition, published in 1984, has data for 1983 and some earlier years.
Equipment, production of electricity, sales of electricity to neighbouring countries, consumption, etc.
Note: provisional statistics are also published annually at the end of December of the year under review (FrB 200).

Δ B – v, continued

587 Répertoire des centrales électriques [Power stations].
Fédération Professionnelle des Producteurs et Distributeurs d'Electricité de Belgique (FPE), avenue de Tervuren 34 bte 38, 1040 Bruxelles.
1959- 1983. FrB 200. 46p. *Fr & Nl eds.
TF: the 1983 edition, published in 1984, has data for 1983.
Installed capacity and production of all operating power stations in Belgium, both public and private enterprises. The information is given for the country as a whole and by enterprise and town.

588 Secteurs de distribution [Distribution].
Fédération Professionnelle des Producteurs et Distributeurs d'Electricité de Belgique (FPE), avenue de Tervuren 34 bte 38, 1040 Bruxelles.
1959- 1983. FrB 200. 29p. *Fr & Nl eds.
TF: the 1983 edition, published in 1984, has data as at 31.12.83.
Consumption of electricity by category of enterprise, in the public and private sectors, and by province. Summary tables also give certain earlier years for comparison.

589 Rapport annuel [Annual report].
Fédération Professionnelle des Producteurs et Distributeurs d'Electricité de Belgique (FPE), avenue de Tervuren 34 bte 38, 1040 Bruxelles.
1949- 1983. FrB 200. 87p. *Fr & Nl eds.
TF: the 1983 report, published in 1984, has data for 1983 and some 1982 figures for comparison.
The report itself includes a number of statistical tables and there is also a statistical section with tables showing production, consumption, exchanges with neighbouring foreign countries, primary energy, investments, and consumer and wholesale price indices of electricity.

590 Bulletin mensuel de l'énergie électrique [Monthly bulletin of electric energy].
Ministère des Affaires Economiques, Administration de l'Energie, Service de l'Énergie Électrique, rue J A De Mot 30, Bruxelles.
1955- not priced. *Fr, Nl.
TF: each issue has tables and graphs showing data for the last 12 or more months up to the date of the issue, and is published two or three months later.
Production and distribution of electric energy.

591 Annuaire statistique de l'industrie du gaz [Statistical yearbook of the gas industry] (Fédération de l'Industrie du Gaz).
FIGAZ, avenue Palmerston 4, 1040 Bruxelles,
TF: the 1984 edition, published September 1985, has data for 1984 and for some earlier years in some tables.
Equipment and investments, sales, prices, employment, etc. Data is given for Belgium and Western Europe.

Δ C External trade

592 Statistiques du commerce extérieur de l'Union Économique Belgo-Luxembourgeoise [Statistics of foreign trade of the Belgo-Luxembourgeoise Economic Union].
INS, Bruxelles.
1948- monthly. FrB 275 (FrB 310 abroad); or FrB 2800 yr (FrB 3250 yr abroad). ISSN 0072-6694. *Fr & Nl eds.
TF: each issue has data for the month and cumulations for the year to date, and is published two or three months later.
Includes principal results; trade by zones; and trade by country, subdivided by commodities, arranged both by CCCN and SITC.
Note: all information relates to BLEU, the figures for Belgian and Luxembourg foreign trade not being given separately.

Δ D Internal distribution and service trades

< see 572

Δ E Population

593 Recensement de la population et des logements [Census of population and housing].
INS, Bruxelles.
1846- 1981. *Fr, Nl.
TF: a census is taken every ten years. The results of the 1981 census are now being issued, from 1983.
Volumes published:
Vol 1: Population figures (FrB 350 (FrB 420 abroad))
Vol 4: Population by nationality.
A: The Kingdom, regions, provinces, arrondissements (FrB 250 (FrB 300 abroad))
B: Principal results by communes (FrB 250 (FrB 300 abroad))
Statistical atlas. Vol 1: Demographic data (FrB 200 (FrB 250 abroad))
General results: housing (FrB 350 (FrB 420 abroad)).

Δ E, continued

594 Perspective de population, 1981-2025 [Population projections].
INS, Bruxelles.
(irregular) 11 vols. *Fr, Nl.
TF: published in 1985.
Vol 1: Methodology & general results (FrB 250 (FrB 300 abroad))
Vol 2: Country and regions (FrB 250 (FrB 300 abroad))
Vol 3: Province of Antwerp (FrB 300 (FrB 350 abroad))
Vol 4: Province of Brabant (FrB 300 (FrB 350 abroad))
Vol 5: Province of Hainault (FrB 500 (FrB 550 abroad))
Vol 6: Province of Liege (FrB 300 (FrB 350 abroad))
Vol 7: Province of Limburg (FrB 300 (FrB 350 abroad))
Vol 8: Province of Luxembourg (FrB 300 (FrB 350 abroad))
Vol 9: Province of Namur (FrB 300 (FrB 350 abroad))
Vol 10: Province of East Flanders (FrB 500 (FrB 550 abroad))
Vol 11: Province of West Flanders (FrB 500 (FrB 550 abroad)).

595 Statistiques démographiques [Demographic statistics].
INS, Bruxelles.
1969- quarterly. FrB 85 (FrB 135 abroad); or FrB 250 yr (FrB 400 yr abroad). ISSN 0067-5490. *Fr, Nl.
TF: each issue has long runs of statistics to the latest available.
Distribution of population by area, growth rates, number of marriages and divorces, births and deaths.

596 Enquête socio-économique, 1977 [Socio-economic enquiry, 1977].
INS, Bruxelles.
1979. 3 vols. *Fr, Nl.
Content:
Vol 1: Population by marital status, and by age; aliens. Vol 2: Active population, geographical mobility of labour, etc. Vol 3: Housing, households.

Δ E - iii Housing

< see 585, 596

Δ F Social and political

597 Statistiques sociales [Social statistics].
INS, Bruxelles.
1970- irregular. FrB 85 (FrB 135 abroad); or FrB 250 yr (FrB 400 yr abroad). ISSN 0067-5563.
*Fr & Nl eds.
Price indices, wages, hours of work, employment, household budgets, accidents at work, industrial illnesses, etc. Not all subjects are covered in each issue.

Δ F - i Standard of living

< see also 392

598 Enquête sur les budgets des ménages, 1978-1979 [Enquiry on household budgets, 1978-1979].
INS, Bruxelles.
Published in 1983 and 1984. 5 vols. *Fr.
Contents:
Vol I: Income, consumption and savings of workers households (FrB 250 (FrB 300 abroad))
Vol II: Income, consumption and saving of independent households (FrB 250 (FrB 300 abroad))
Vol III: Income, consumption and savings of households of socio-professional groups and by regions (FrB 300 (FrB 350 abroad))
Vol IV: Income, consumption and savings by class of income (FrB 250 (FrB 300 abroad))
Vol V: Income, consumption and savings by region and by class of income (FrB 250 (FrB 300 abroad)).

599 Nombre de détenteurs d'appareils de radio et de télévision: situation au 31 décembre... [Numbers of holders of radio and television apparatus: situation as at 31st December...].
INS, Bruxelles.
1964- 1983. FrB 185 (FrB 235 abroad). *Fr, Nl.
TF: the issue with data as at 31st December 1983 was published in February 1984.
Numbers of radio and television apparatus (black and white and colour) by province, town, etc., and by home and office.

Δ F - ii Health and welfare

600 Annuaire statistique de la santé publique [Statistical yearbook of public health].
Ministère de la Santé Publique et de la Famille, Cité Administrative de l'Etat, Quartier Vésale, 1010 Bruxelles.
1969- 1981. not priced. 429p. *Fr, Nl.
TF: the 1981 edition, published in 1982, has data for many years to 1981.
Demographic indicators and statistical data on morbidity, medical and social services, capacity and utilisation of medical infrastructure, medical personnel, paramedical personnel, technical and other personnel, public hygiene and environmental hygiene, education, and cost of health services and of scientific research.

Δ F – iv Justice

601 Statistiques judiciaires [Judicial statistics].
INS, Bruxelles.
1931– quarterly. FrB 85 (FrB 235 abroad); or FrB 250 yr (FrB 450 yr abroad). *Fr, Nl.
Each issue is devoted to a particular subject within the field of judicial statistics.

Δ G Finance

602 Statistiques financières [Financial statistics].
INS, Bruxelles.
1972– irregular – 2-3 issues a year. FrB 125 (FrB 175 abroad); or FrB 375 yr (FrB 525 yr abroad).
*Fr, Nl.
Each issue deals with a particular subject within the field of financial statistics.

603 Association Belge des Banques: rapport annuel [Belgian Association of Banks: annual report].
Association Belge des Banques, rue Ravenstein 36 (Boîte 5), 1000 Bruxelles.
1936– 1984. not priced. 122p. *Fr.
TF: the 1984 report, published in 1984, has data for several years to 1983.
Includes a section of statistical tables on banking and finance generally (p.92–114 in the 1984 report).

604 Aspects et documents.
Association Belge des Banques, rue Ravenstein 36 (Boîte 5), 1000 Bruxelles.
1979– irregular. separately priced. ISSN 0771-4092. *Fr.
A series of booklets relating to the structure, activities, services and problems of the banking sector. Many include a few statistics, including:
No. 29. Les banques au sein du secteur financier depuis 1975. 1. Analyse comparative (FrB 50)
No. 30. Les banques au sein du secteur financier depuis 1975. 2. Statistiques (FrB 50)
No. 32. Vade-mecum statistique du secteur bancaire (FrB 200)
No. 33. Les banques au sein du secteur financier en 1983 (FrB 50).
The above were issued in 1984.

Δ G – ii Public finance

605 Les comptes nationaux de la Belgique [National accounts of Belgium].
INS, Bruxelles.
1952/62– 1953/62-1970-83. FrB 150 (FrB 200 abroad). *Fr, Nl.
TF: the 1953/62-1970-83 edition, with data for those years, was published in 1984 in the series 'Études statistiques. Statistische studien'.
National production, national accounts, etc.

Δ G – v Insurance

606 Rapport sur les activités et sur la situation des entreprises d'assurances en Belgique [Report on the activities and situation of insurance companies in Belgium].
Office de Contrôle des Assurances, square de Meeus 1, 1040 Bruxelles.
1965– 1984. FrB 480. 276p. *Fr.
TF: the 1984 report, published in 1985, has data for 1979 or earlier to 1983.
The second part of the report contains statistics relative to finance, life insurance, motor insurance, various risks, etc.

Δ H Transport and communications

< see also 572

607 Statistique du trafic international (BLEU) des ports [Statistics of international traffic (BLEU) at ports].
INS, Bruxelles.
1959– quarterly. FrB 85 (FrB 135 abroad); or FrB 600 yr (FrB 800 yr abroad). *Fr, Nl.
TF: each issue has cumulative data to the end of the period of the issue and is published about 10 months later.
Commodity trade carried by canal, river, rail and road to the ports. Part 1: port of Antwerp; part 2: other Belgian ports.

Δ H – i Ships and shipping

608 La navigation intérieure [Inland navigation].
INS, Bruxelles.
1949– 1982 (issued in 1985). FrB 200 (FrB 250 abroad). *Fr, Nl.
Note: prior to the 1982 issue title was 'Statistique de la navigation du Rhin. Statistiek der Rijnvaart'.

Δ H – ii Roads and road transport

609 Recensement de la circulation [Census of traffic].
INS, Bruxelles.
1952– 1980. FrB 150 (FrB 200 abroad). *Fr, Nl.
TF: the results of the 1980 census were published in 1984. A census is taken every five years.

Δ H – ii, continued

610 Véhicules à moteur neuf mis en circulation [New registered motor vehicles].
INS, Bruxelles.
1953– 1983. FrB 250 (FrB 300 abroad). ISSN 0067-5555. *Fr, Nl.
TF: the 1983 edition, published mid-1984, has data for 1983.

611 Statistique mensuelle des véhicules neufs immatriculés en Belgique: bulletin d'information [Monthly statistics of new vehicles registered in Belgium: information bulletin] (Fédération Belge des Industries de l'Automobile et du Cycle 'reunis' (FEBIAC)).
FEBIAC, blvd de la Woluwe 46, B-1200 Bruxelles.
not priced. *Fr, Nl.
TF: data is for the month of issue, published about three months later.
Countries of manufacture and makes of cars, coaches, goods vehicles, tractors, etc. registered.

612 Parc des véhicules à moteur: situation au 1er août...[Motor vehicle registrations: situation as at 1st August...].
INS, Bruxelles.
1953– 1984. FrB 250 (FrB 300 abroad). *Fr, Nl.
TF: the 1984 edition, published in 1984, has data for 1st August 1984.

613 Accidents de la circulation sur la voie publique avec tués ou blessés [Accidents on the public roads resulting in death or injury].
INS, Bruxelles.
1927– 1983. FrB 250 (FrB 300 abroad). ISSN 0067-5504. *Fr, Nl.
TF: the 1983 edition, published in 1985, has data for 1983.

Δ H – iii Railways and railway transport

614 Annuaire statistique... [Statistical yearbook].
Société Nationale des Chemins de Fer Belges, rue de France 85, 1070 Bruxelles.
1952– 1978. not priced. 32p. *Fr, Nl.
TF: the 1978 edition, published in 1979, has data for 1978 and some earlier years.
Data on railway track and installations, rolling stock, locomotives, passenger and goods traffic, personnel, receipts and expenditures, and accidents.

BG

BULGARIA
BULGARIE
BULGARIEN

Central statistical office

615 Централно Статистическо Управление при Министерския Съвет, София.
[Central Statistical Office at the Council of Ministers, Sofia].
10, 6th September Street, Sofia.
t 7 87 11.
The Office is the only institution in Bulgaria authorised to compile and tabulate statistical information. It also issues certain statistical publications. Unpublished statistical information is not supplied. This Office has been abbreviated to ЦСУ, София for entries between 607-627.

Libraries

The library of Централно Статистическо Управление has many statistical publications, which may be consulted by the public.

Statistical publications

Δ A General

616 Статистически годишник на Народна Република България [Statistical yearbook of Bulgaria].
ЦСУ, София.
1956- 1984. Leva 18.83. 711p. ISSN 0204-4838. *Bg.
TF: the 1984 edition, published late 1985, has data for 1983 and most tables include 1939 and typical years in the period 1948 to 1982.
Main sections:
Area and climate - Basic data on socio-economic development of the country - Population - Living standards - Labour - Production funds and capital investment - Social product and national income - Scientific and technical progress - Industry - Construction - Agriculture - Mining - Transport - Communications - Internal trade and prices - Tourism - Foreign trade - Public utilities - Education - Culture and art - Public health - Finance, credit and insurance.

617 Статистически справочник [Statistical handbook].
ЦСУ, София.
1958- 1985. Leva 1.32. 311p. *Bg.
TF: the 1985 edition, published in 1985, has data for 1975, 1980, 1983 and 1984.
An abridged version of (616).

618 Statistical reference book P.R. Bulgaria. (Committee for Unified System of Social Information & Bulgarian Chamber of Commerce and Industry).
Foreign Language Press, 1 Levski Street, Sofia.
Leva 1.32. 94p. *En, Ru, Fr & De eds.
TF: published in 1984, the reference book has data for the years 1975 to 1983. An earlier edition was published in 1976 with data for 1956 to 1975.
Basic data on the national economy development, labour, fixed assets and capital investments, gross national product and national income, science and technical progress, industry, construction, agriculture, transport, communications, foreign trade, population and living standards, and a section on Bulgaria and other countries of the world during 1981.

619 Статистически известия [Statistical news].
ЦСУ, София.
monthly. not priced. *Bg; table of contents also in En & Ru.
Statistical data on the various branches of economic activity of Bulgaria, including industry, capital investment and construction, agriculture, transport, trade and prices, and also surveys by districts

620 Bulgarian foreign trade. (Bulgarian Chamber of Commerce and Industry).
Bulgarreklama Agency, 42 Parchevich Street, Sofia.
1947- every two months. not priced. ISSN 0204-8892. *En, Fr, De, Es, & Ru eds.
Includes a few statistics in the articles, but no regular tables.

621 P.R. Bulgaria economic outlook. (Bulgarian Chamber of Commerce and Industry).
Bulgarreklama Agency, 42 Parchevich Street, Sofia.
(annual) 1985. not priced. 43p. *En.
TF: the 1985 edition, published in 1985, has data for several years to 1984.
Includes sections of general data, socio-economic development, capital investments and production assets, gross national product and national income, science and technological progress, industry, agriculture, transport and communications, foreign trade and foreign economic relations, international tourism, and general living standards.

Δ A, continued

622 Economic bulletin: facts and figures.
Sofia Press Agency, Levski Street, Sofia.
(monthly) not priced. *En.
Press notices, with a very few figures in the text.

Δ B - ii(a) Agriculture and horticulture

623 Селско стопанство 1973 [Agriculture in Bulgaria, 1973].
[Ministry of Information and Communications].
Leva 7.50. 550p. *Bg.
TF: published in 1973, the volume has data for the years 1964 to 1971.
A statistical collection on the development and structure of Bulgarian agriculture, including general characteristics, agricultural organisation and enterprises, capital investment, stocks of machines, mechanisation, cultivation, stock raising, purchasing, and a review by district.

624 Cotton production in the People's Republic of Bulgaria. (Ministry of Agriculture and Food Industry & National Centre for Scientific and Technical Information on Agriculture, Food Industry and Forestry).
National Centre for Scientific and Technical Information on Agriculture, Food Industry and Forestry, 6 Dragon Tsankor blvd, Sofia.
1976. Leva 2. 72p. *En.
Mainly text, but includes some statistics and statistical tables.

Δ B - ii(c) Forestry

625 Горско стопанистворо [Forestry].
ЦСУ, София.
Leva 3.80. 299p. *Bg.
TF: published in 1972, the data is for 1970.
The area of forest reserves, by type of forest; afforested areas by type of timber and age; timber stock; wood pulp obtained; forest cultivation; machines in forestry, etc.

Δ B - iii Industry

626 Промишленост [Industry].
ЦСУ, София.
1958- 1970. Leva 4.00. 314p. *Bg.
TF: not published every year, the 1970 edition appeared in 1970 and contains data for 1969 and selected earlier years.
Data on production, fixed assets, labour, etc, for state and co-operative enterprises for the whole country and for the administrative sub-divisions separately.

Δ B - iv Construction

627 Жилищно строителство [Housing construction].
Министерство на Информацията и Съобщенията, София.
[Ministry of Information and Communications].
1975. Leva 1.46. 113p. *Bg.
Housing construction of state and co-operative enterprises, organisations and institutions, as well as co-operative groups and individual housing construction. The first part gives data for the whole country and the second part for districts.

Δ C External trade

628 Вьшна търговия на Народна Република България: Статистически данни
[Foreign trade of the People's Republic of Bulgaria: statistical survey].
ЦСУ, София.
1950/67- 1970-1984. Leva 4.71. 310p. *Bg, Ru.
TF: the 1970-1984 edition, with data for those years, was published in 1985.
Detailed tables of foreign trade by commodity and by country; and also for some goods arranged by commodity and subdivided by countries of origin and destination, and by countries subdivided by commodities.

629 Foreign trade of the People's Republic of Bulgaria: statistical survey, 1939-1968.
State Information Office of the Council of Ministers & Ministry of Foreign Trade.
Leva 3.20. 294p. *En.
TF: published in 1970, the data is for 1939, 1950, 1955, 1960, 1965, 1967 and 1968.
Main tables show imports and export statistics arranged by country of origin and destination and subdivided by commodities.
Note: cover title is '25 years of the foreign trade of the People's Republic of Bulgaria'.

Δ D – i Wholesale and retail trades

630 Вътрешна търговия [Internal trade].
Министерство на Информацията и Съобщенията, София.
[Ministry of Information & Communications].
(annual) 1973. Leva 1.80. 141p. *Bg.
TF: the 1973 edition has data for 1972 and long runs of earlier years in summary tables.
Contents are 1 - general review, 1952-1972; 2 - country as a whole; 3 - review by districts. Data includes type of outlets, density, public establishments; workers and employees, pay and productivity; finances; retail trade by commodities; retail trade indices; retail trade in food and non-food commodities; and profitability.

Δ D – iv Tourism and travel

631 Туризъм [Tourism] (Комитет за Социална Информаця при Министерския Съвет)
[Committee for Social Information at the Council of Ministers].
ЦСУ, София.
1971– 1985. Leva 1.13. 83p. ISSN 0324-0681. *Bg, En.
TF: the 1985 edition, published in 1985, has data for the years 1965, 1970, 1975 and 1980 to 1984.
A: General review (international tourks, domestic tourism, accommodation establishments; B: District review (domestic tourism, accommodation establishments).

Δ E Population

632 Население [Population].
ЦСУ, София.
1968– 1974. Leva 4.40. 346p. *Bg; tables & diagram headings also in Fr & Ru.
TF: the 1974 edition, published in 1975, has data for 1973.
Population, growth (national increase) births, deaths, marriages, divorces, mechanical movement of population, review by districts, and an international survey.

Δ F Social and political

Δ F – i Standard of living

633 Доходи, разходи и потребление на наблюдаваните домакнства 1962/1970г
[Incomes, expenditure and consumption of households].
ЦСУ, София.
1962/1970– 1962-1972. Leva 2.50. 197p. *Bg.
The composition, occupation, expenditure and consumption of 2,510 households selected at random. Basic data; household budgets generally, by number of persons in household, by number of children, number of incomes, etc.

Δ G Finance

634 Капитални вложения и строителство 1975 [Capital investment and construction, 1975].
Министерство на Информацията и Съобщенията, София.
[Ministry of Information & Communications].
Leva 1.55. 110p. *Bg.
TF: published in 1975, the volume contains data for 1973 and earlier years in some tables.

SWITZERLAND
SUISSE
SCHWEIZ

Central statistical office

635 Bundesamt für Statistik: Office Fédéral de la Statistique [Federal Statistical Office].
Hallwylstrasse 15, CH-3003 Bern.
t (031) 61 86 60. tx 32526 Answerback SLBBE CH.
Founded in 1860, the Office is one of the oldest offices of the central administration. It is responsible for most Swiss economic statistics, except foreign trade. Unpublished information can be supplied for a fee to cover working time.
The Office has been abbreviated to BS, Bern in entries 638-689.

Libraries

The library of Bundesamt für Statistik (see above) has a large collection of statistical material which may be consulted by the public.
Other libraries with this type of material are those belonging to Bundesamt für Industrie [Federal Office for Industry], Bundesgasse 8, 3000 Bern (t 62 21 22); Statistisches Amt des Kantons Basel-Stadt [Statistical Office of Basle], Rheinsprung 24, 4000 Basel (t 23 66 80); and Statistisches Amt der Stadt Zürich [Statistical Office of Zurich], Hirschengraben 56, 8001 Zürich (t 47 49 00).

Libraries and information services abroad

Swiss statistical publications are available for reference in Swiss embassies abroad, including:

United Kingdom	Swiss Embassy, Montague Place, London W1. t 01-723 0701
Australia	Swiss Embassy, 7 Melbourne Avenue, Forest, Canberra ACT. t 73 3977
Canada	Swiss Embassy, 5 Marlborough Avenue, Ottawa K1N 8E6. t 235 1837
New Zealand	Swiss Embassy, Panama House, 22-24 Panama Street, Wellington CI. t 721 593
USA	Swiss Embassy, 2900 Cathedral Avenue NW, Washington DC 20008. t (202) 745-7900.

Bibliographies

636 Veröffentlichungen [Publications].
A list of publications issued by Bundesamt für Statistik [Federal Statistical Office], arranged in subject order. A new edition is published every two years and is available on request to the Office.
*Fr, De.

637 Schweizerische Bibliographie für Statistik und Volkswirtschaft [Swiss bibliography of statistics and political economy].
Published annually by Bundesamt für Statistik since 1937, it includes statistical publications, although the larger part of the material included is not statistical.

Statistical publications

Δ A General

638 Statistisches Jahrbuch der Schweiz: Annuaire statistique de la Suisse [Statistical yearbook of Switzerland].
BS, Bern.
1891- 1984. FrS 74. 658p. ISSN 0081-5330. *De, Fr.
TF: the 1984 edition, published late 1984, has data for 1983 and 10 to 15 earlier years in many tables.
Main sections:
Geography - Population - Demography - Agriculture, forestry, fishing & hunting - Industrial production, arts & crafts - Energy - Trade (foreign & internal) - Tourism - Transport & communications - Road accidents - Money & credit - Insurance - Price indexes - Household budgets - National accounts - Employment, labour, wages - Company information - Public finance - Arts (radio & TV, theatre, cinemas, publications, journals, newspapers, public libraries) - Education - Research & development - Public health - Sports, gymnastics - Justice - International co-operation & development - Public assistance - Intellectual property - Political (elections, etc) - International statistics.
Note: statistical yearbooks are available for all Swiss cantons and many Swiss cities, and are issued by the relevant local statistical office.

639 La vie économique: rapports économiques et de statistique sociale [Economic reports and social statistics] (Départment Fédéral de l'Economie Publique).
La Feuille Officielle Suisse du Commerce, C.P. 2170, 3001 Bern.
1928- FrS 8 or FrS 77 yr (FrS 88 yr abroad). *Fr & De eds.
TF: issued at the end of the month, the data is usually for the previous month and some earlier months and years.
A monthly review, with quarterly supplements containing reports by the Commission for Economic Research. Contains regular statistics of wholesale and retail price indices, production, employment, wages, transport, tourism, finance, social insurance, and demography.

Δ A, continued

640 Monatsbericht: Bulletin mensuel [Monthly bulletin of the National Bank of Switzerland] (Schweizerische Nationalbank, Banque National Suisse).
Orell Füssli Arts Graphiques SA, 8036 Zürich 3.
1926- FrS 30 yr (FrS 42 yr abroad). ISSN 0036-7729. *De, Fr.
TF: each issue has data for four or five years and 12 or more months to about three months prior to publication.
Includes statistical tables on banking, finance, foreign trade, prices (wholesale, consumer, agricultural and world market price indices), wages, gross national product, production, trade, transport, etc.

641 UBS business facts and figures.
Union Bank of Switzerland, Bahnhofstrasse 45, 8021 Zürich (PO Box 8021).
10 a year. Free. *En, De, Fr & Es eds.
TF: indications are given for the previous year (annual figures) and for the last four months to two months prior to the date of the issue.
Includes a page of Swiss business indicators (economy, National Bank, banks, interest rates in %), and articles which include statistical tables and graphs.

642 Economic survey of Switzerland.
Union de Banques Suisses, Bahnhofstrasse 45, 8021 Zürich.
1863- 1984. not priced. *En, Fr, It, Es & Pt eds.
TF: the 1984 edition, published in 1985, has data for a number of years to 1984.
A review of economic developments and selected industries, trades and professions. Statistical tables are included in the text.

643 Rapport annuel du Vorort: Vorort/Jahresbericht [Annual report of the Headquarters of the Swiss Union of Commerce and Industry] (Union Suisse du Commerce et de l'Industrie, Schweizerischer Handels- und Industrie-Verein).
Union Suisse du Commerce et de l'Industrie, Börsenstrasse 26, 8001 Zürich.
1965- 1984/85. not priced. 200p. *De, Fr.
TF: the 1984/85 edition, published in 1985, has data for four or five years to 1984.
Includes a section of statistical data on population, vital statistics, industrial production and construction indices, energy, retail trade index, finance and banking, insurance, tourism, transport and communication, labour, wages, price indices, foreign trade, balance of payments, gross national product, etc.

644 Statistik der Schweizer Städt: Statistiques des villes suisses [Statistics of Swiss towns].
Schweiz. Städteverbande: Union des Villes Suisses, Junkerngasse 56 (Postfach 225), CH-3010 Bern 8.
1939- 1984. not priced. 78p. *De, Fr.
TF: the 1984 edition, published late 1984, has the latest data available, and earlier years also in some tables.
Area of towns, arranged by size; population; active population, employment; transport and communications, tourism; housing; service industries (water, gas, electricity); prices and price indexes; finance, taxes; political (national and local government).

Δ B Production

Δ B - ii Agriculture, fisheries, forestry, etc.

Δ B - ii(a) Agriculture and horticulture

645 Eidgenössische Landwirtschaft- und Gartenbauzählung: Recensement féderal de l'agriculture et de l'horticulture [Federal census of agriculture and horticulture].
BS, Bern.
1905- 1980. 6 vols. *De, Fr.
TF: the results of the 1980 census were published between 1981 and 1983.
Contents:
Vol 1: principal results by communes (FrS 47)
Vol 2: Agricultural exploitation (FrS 28)
Vol 3: Agricultural exploitation by systems of soil utilisation and by types of enterprise (FrS 34)
Vol 4: Horticultural exploitation (FrS 19)
Vol 5: Soil utilisation (FrS 23)
Vol 6: Texts and retrospective comparisons (FrS 35).

646 Landwirtschaftliches Jahrbuch der Schweiz: Annuaire agricole de la Suisse [Agricultural yearbook of Switzerland].
Eidgenössische Volkswirtschaftsdepartement, Bern.
1887- 1982. FrS 39 yr (FrS 69 yr abroad). *De, Fr.
TF: each annual issue is published in four quarterly parts, the parts for 1982 being published in 1982, with annual or monthly data for several years or months to the latest available.
Includes a number of tables on a variety of agricultural subjects.

Δ B - ii(a), continued

647 Statistische Erhebungen und Schätzungen über Landwirtschaft und Ernährung... [Statistics and evaluations concerning agriculture and food].
Schweizerischen Bauernsekretariat, Brugg.
1924- 1983. not priced. 188p. *Fr, De.
TF: the 1983 edition, published early 1984, has long runs of figures to 1982 or 1982/83.
Production, foreign trade, food balances, consumption, prices and price indices, wages, agricultural credit, agricultural insurance, measures of encouragement, agricultural population, agricultural education, etc.

648 Milchstatistik der Schweiz... Statistique laitière de la Suisse [Milk statistics in Switzerland].
Schweizerisches Bauernsekretariat, Brugg.
1946/50- 1983. FrS 15. p 75-98. *De, Fr.
TF: the 1983 edition, published in 1984, has long runs of figures to 1982/83 or 1983.
Production, utilisation, machinery used, foreign trade, stocks, consumption, and prices of milk, cheese, butter and cream.
Note: an offprint from 'Landwirtschaftlichen Jahrbuch der Schweiz'.

649 Der Schweizerische Obstbaumbestand, 1981. Les arbres fruitiers en Suisse, 1981 [Fruit trees in Switzerland, 1981].
BS, Bern.
1983. FrS 30. *De, Fr.
The general results of a census of fruit trees.

Δ B - ii(c) Forestry

650 Jahrbuch der schweizerischen Wald- und Holzwirtschaft: Forststatistik. Annuaire suisse de l'économie forestière et de l'industrie du bois: statistique forestière [Swiss yearbook of forest economy and the wood industry: forest statistics].
BS, Bern.
1930- 1981. Vol 1: FrS 24; vol 2: FrS 25. 2 vols. *De, Fr.
TF: the 1981 edition, published in 1983, has data for 1981.
Vol.1 has data on forest fires, wages and labour; vol.2 on the economy of forestry, the forestry industry, foreign trade, and hunting.

Δ B - iii Industry

651 Betriebszählung: Industrie, Gewerbe, Dienstleistungen: Recensement fédéral des entreprises: industrie, arts et métiers, services [Federal census of enterprises: industry, arts and professions, services].
BS, Bern.
1905- 1975. 5 vols. *De, Fr.
TF: a census is taken every ten years.
Contents:
Vol 1: Establishments, principal figures for Switzerland.
Vol 2: Enterprises, principal figures for Switzerland
Vol 3: Establishments, principal figures for cantons
Vol 4: Establishments, principal figures for municipalities
Vol 5: Proprietary establishments, wholesale trade, retail trade, hotels and restaurants, etc.

Δ B - vi Research and development

652 Forschung und Entwicklung des Bundes, 1978-1981. Recherche et développement de la Confédération, 1978-1981 [Research and development in the Confederation].
BS, Bern.
1983. FrS 11. *De, Fr.
The results of two enquiries effected in four years on the expense in money and in personnel of the Confederation of Switzerland in the field of R & D.

Δ C External trade

653 Jahresstatistik des Aussenhandels der Schweiz: Statistique annuelle du commerce extérieur de la Suisse [Statistical yearbook of the foreign trade of Switzerland].
Eidgenössische Oberzolldirektion, Monbijoustrasse 40, 3003 Bern.
1885- 1983 Vol.1 FrS 50 (FrS 62 abroad); 1984 Vol.2 FrS 50 (FrS 62 abroad); 1984 Vol.3 FrS 37 (FrS 41 abroad). 3 vols. ISSN 0081-525X. *Fr, De.
TF: Vol.1 has data for 1983, vol.2 & 3 for 1984. Published in 1985.
Contents:
Vol 1: has imports and exports by commodities arranged by the Swiss customs tariff subdivided by countries of origin and destination
Vol 2: has imports and exports arranged by countries subdivided by commodities
Vol 3: has data on other traffic, e.g., foreign trade according to means of transport, transit according to means of transport, traffic of processed commodities, border traffic, customs revenue, etc.

Δ C, continued

654 Monatsstatistik des Aussenhandels der Schweiz: Statistique mensuelle du commerce extérieur de la Suisse [Monthly statistics of the foreign trade of Switzerland].
Eidgenössische Oberzolldirektion, Monbijoustrasse 40, 3003 Bern.
1885- FrS 18 (FrS 22 abroad); or FrS 156 yr (FrS 185 yr abroad). ISSN 0049-2183. *Fr, De.
TF: each issue contains data for one month, and is published four weeks after the end of that month.
Totals of foreign trade by countries of origin and destination, also data on imports and exports arranged by the Swiss customs tariff classification subdivided by countries, and indices of volume and average values.

655 Schweizerische Aussenhandelsstatistik: Jahresbericht. Statistique du commerce extérieur de la Suisse: commentaires annuels [Foreign trade of Switzerland: annual commentaries].
Eidgenössische Oberzolldirektion, Montbijoustrasse 40, 3003 Bern.
(annual) 1983. FrS 19 (FrS 23 abroad) each volume; both volumes FrS 31 (FrS 40 abroad). 2 vols. *De, Fr.
TF: the 1983 volumes, published in 1984, have data for several years to 1983.
Part 1 relates to suppliers and outlets; part 2 to economic branches.

656 Eingeführte Motorfahrzeuge: Vehicules à moteur importés [Motor vehicles imported].
BS, Bern.
1929- 1984. FrS 7.50. *De, Fr.
TF: the 1984 edition, published in 1985, has data for 1984.
General view of the number and value of imports of private cars, motor cycles and commercial vehicles, by makes.

657 Eingeführte Motorfahrzeuge. Véhicules à moteur importés [Motor vehicles imported].
BS, Bern.
(monthly) FrS 4 or FrS 39 yr. *De, Fr.

Δ D - iv Tourism and travel

658 Tourismus in der Schweiz. Tourisme en Suisse [Tourism in Switzerland].
BS, Bern.
1975- 1984. FrS 18. 124p. *De, Fr.
TF: the 1984 edition, published in 1985, has data for 1983 and 1984.
Commentaries and statistical data on tourism in hotels and curative establishments, including numbers of rooms, demand, arrivals, etc. for the country and by canton.
Note: also published are special reports relating to cantons, hotels, special hotels, types of tourists, etc.

659 Tourismus in der Schweiz. Tourisme en Suisse [Tourism in Switzerland].
BS, Bern.
1975- monthly. FrS 6.50 or FrS 90 yr. *De, Fr.
TF: each monthly issue has data for the month of the issue and is published about three months later.
Number of visitors by regions, by nights, by categories, etc. Special issues are devoted to a particular aspect of tourism or a particular canton.

Δ E Population

660 Volkzählung. Recensement... [Census of population].
BS, Bern.
1860- 1980. 41 vols. *De, Fr.
TF: the results of the 1980 census are being published from 1981 to 1985.
Contents:
Vol 1: Population resident in municipalities (FrS 13)
Vol 2: Municipalities; sex, origin, religion, maternal language, marital status, place of birth, domicile in 1975, households (FrS 38)
Vol 3: Municipalities; ages (FrS 31)
Vol 4: Municipalities; economic activity (FrS 46)
Vol 5: Municipalities; property (FrS 50)
Vol 6: Housing. Part I: Conditions (FrS 41)
Vol 7: Housing. Part II: Numbers, occupation, etc. (FrS 45)
Vol 8: Switzerland; sex, nationality, religion, language, age, civil status, place of birth, and domicile (FrS 21)
Vol 9: Economic activity (FrS 45)
Vol 10: Switzerland; education (FrS 46)
Vol 11: Switzerland; commuting to work (FrS 31)
Vol 12: Switzerland; households, families (FrS 36)
Vol 13: Switzerland; property, housing (FrS 30)
Vol 14: Switzerland; Fertility (FrS 15)
Vol 15-40: Data for 26 cantons, numbered alphabetically
Vol 41: Switzerland; totals (FrS 28).
Note: 'Wohnbevölkerung der Gemeinden. Population résidente des communes' [Population resident in towns] is a 49-page booklet published in 1981 (FrS 4).

Δ E, continued

661 Bericht zur demographischen Entwicklung in der Schweiz seit 1971. L'évolution démographique en Suisse depuis 1971 [Demographic evolution in Switzerland since 1971].
BS, Bern.
1984- FrS 11. 65p. *Fr, De.

662 Bilanz der Wohnbevölkerung in den Gemeinden der Schweiz. Bilan démographique des communes suisses [Demographique balance in Swiss municipalities].
BS, Bern.
1981- 1983. FrS 22. 122p. *De, Fr.
TF: the 1983 edition, published in 1984, has data for 1983.
Population resident in municipalities, districts, cantons and built-up areas. Principal results.

663 Die kurzfristige Entwicklung der Fruchtbarkeit in der Schweiz seit 1946. L'évolution à court terme de la fécondité en Suisse depuis 1946 [Fertility in Switzerland since 1946].
BS, Bern.
1984. FrS 7. 35p. *Fr, De.

664 Die Scheidungen in der Schweiz seit 1967. Les divorces en Suisse depuis 1967 [Divorce in Switzerland since 1967].
BS, Bern.
FrS 6. 20p. *Fr, De.
TF: published in 1985, in the series 'Cahiers statistiques'.

Δ E - i Vital statistics

665 Bevölkerungsbewegung in der Schweiz. Mouvement de la population en Suisse [Vital statistics in Switzerland].
BS, Bern.
1867- 1983. FrS 19. 90p. *De, Fr.
TF: the 1983 edition, published in 1985, has data for 1983.
Vital statistics (marriages, divorces, births, deaths, and causes of death).

666 Heiraten, Lebendgeborene und Gestorbene in den Gemeinden. Marriages, naissances et décès dans les communes [Marriages, births and deaths in the municipalities].
BS, Bern.
1971- 1980. FrS 12. *De, Fr.
TF: the 1980 edition, published in 1982, has data for 1980.

667 Schweizerische Sterbetafel, 1978/1983. Table de mortalité pour la Suisse, 1978/1983 [Swiss mortality tables].
BS, Bern.
1985. FrS 19. 89p. *De, Fr.

Δ F Social and political

668 Sozialindikatoren. Indicateurs sociaux [Social indicators].
BS, Bern.
FrS 12 each volume. 12 vols. *Fr, De.
TF: the volumes are being published from 1982 onwards.
Chronological tables and graphs comparing regions and groups of the population. 186 indicators measuring the quality of life. Contents: 1: Health; 2: Education; 3: Labour; 4: Condition of work; 5: not yet issued; 6: Social security; 7: Housing; 8: Transport; 9: Natural environment; 10: Family and social environment; 11a: Politics of the State; 11b: Criminality; 12: Energy.

669 La consommation des boissons alcooliques en Suisse de 1976 à 1980 et durant les périodes antérieures [Consumption of alcoholic beverages in Switzerland from 1976 to 1980 and earlier periods] (E Schmid).
Régie Fédérale des Alcools, Länggassstrasse 31, 3000 Berne 9.
1981. not priced. 33p. *Fr.
Data on 100 years of consumption of alcohol.

Δ F - ii Health and welfare

670 Das Schweizer Spital; L'Hôpital suisse: [The Swiss hospital].
Vereinigung Schweizerischer Krankenhäuser (VESKA), Rain 32, CH-5001 Aarau.
1947- monthly. FrS 6 or FrS 75 yr. *De.
TF: the November 1984 issue, published then, has data for the year 1983.
A review which includes some statistics in the text and also, in the November issue, a section of tables on numbers of hospitals, beds, patients journeys to hospital, occupation of beds, personnel, duration of stay; numbers of beds by medical discipline and by type of hospital; finances; etc.

671 Jahresbericht. Rapport annuel [Annual report. Swiss Association of Hospital Establishments].
Vereinigung Schweizerischer Krankenhäuser (VESKA), Rain 32, 5001 Aarau.
1940- 1983. FrS 5. 42p. *De, Fr.
TF: the 1983 report, published in 1984, has data for 1982 and some earlier years.
part 1: Swiss hospitals in figures (number of establishments, beds and admissions; hospitalisation journeys; occupation of beds; personnel; income and expenditure; diagnoses and operations); part 2: Activities of VESKA; part 3: Appendices (membership).

Δ F – iii Education and leisure

672 Schülerstatistik. Statistique des élèves [Schoolchildren statistics].
BS, Bern.
1976/77- 1982/83. 4 vols. *De, Fr.
TF: the 1982/83 volumes, published in 1983, have data for the 1982/83 school year, generally.
Volumes are:
Schweiz [Switzerland]. Has principal data, both current and retrospective for five earlier years, by type of school (FrS 18).
Schuljahr [School year]. National and cantonal results (FrS 18).
Schuljahr: Berufsausbildung (Sekundarstufe II) [School year: professional education] (FrS 15)
Schuljahr: Kantone (übertrittsmatrix) [Cantons] (FrS 13).

673 Studenten en den schweizerischen Hochschulen. Etudients des hautes écoles suisses [Students in Swiss universities].
BS, Bern.
1890/1935- 1982/83. FrS 16. *De, Fr.
TF: the 1982/83 edition, published in 1984, has data for the academic year 1983/83.
Numbers of students in Spring semester 1982 and Winter semester 1983, subdivided by courses of study, etc.

674 Hochschulpersonalstatistik. Statistique du personnel des hautes écoles [Academic and administrative staff in universities].
BS, Bern.
1981- 31 December 1982. FrS 9. *De, Fr.
Statistics of professors and assistants and administrative staff.

675 Schweizerische Bibliotheken. Bibliothèques suisses [Swiss libraries].
BS, Bern.
1950- 1982. FrS 4. *De, Fr.
TF: the 1982 edition, published in 1983, has data for 1982.
Data on receipts, expenses, personnel, increases, collection, borrowings, etc.

Δ F – iv Justice

676 Die Strafurteile in der Schweiz. Les condamnations pénales en Suisse [Penal sentences in Switzerland].
BS, Bern.
1980- 1981. FrS 16. *Fr, De.
Statistics of sentences pronounced by Swiss 'tribunaux'.

Δ F – vi Elections

677 Nationalratswahlen: Elections au Conseil National [Elections to the National Council].
BS, Bern.
1919/28- 1983. not priced. 29p. *Fr, De.
TF: the results of the 1983 election were published in 1984.
Numbers of candidates, votes recorded, and results.

Δ G Finance

Δ G – ii Public finance

678 Öffentliche Finanzen der Schweiz. Finances publiques en Suisse [Public finance of Switzerland].
BS, Bern.
1938/71- 1981. FrS 23. 157p. *De, Fr.
TF: the 1981 edition, published in 1983, has data for 1981 and several retrospective years.

679 Steuerbelastung in der Schweiz. Charge fiscal en Suisse [Taxation].
BS, Bern.
1919- 1984. FrS 18. 97p. *De, Fr.
TF: the 1983 edition, published in 1985, has data for 1984.
Revenue received from taxation, compiled by the Federal Administration for Taxation.

Δ G – iii Company finance

680 Aktiengesellschaften in der Schweiz. Sociétés anonymes en Suisse [Companies in Switzerland].
BS, Bern.
(annual) 1982. FrS 8. *De, Fr.
TF: the 1982 edition, published in 1983, has data for 1982.
Financial data on Swiss companies, by canton.

681 Buchhaltungsergebnisse schweizerischer Unternehmungen. les résultats comptables des entreprises suisses [Financial results of Swiss enterprises].
BS, Bern.
1980/81- 1981/82. FrS 15. *De, Fr.
Data on 7500 Swiss industrial and commercial enterprises, arranged by industry or activity. Tables of macroeconomic figures, ratios and structural data.

Δ G - iii, continued

682 Switzerland's largest companies.
Union de Banques Suisses, Bahnhofstrasse 45 (Postfach 8021), 8021 Zürich.
1968- 1985. free. 23p. *En, De & Fr eds.
TF: the 1985 edition, published in 1985, has data for 1984.
Financial data on individual industrial, commercial and service companies, banks, and insurance companies. Originally published in German by the Schweizerische Handelszeitung in more detail.
Note: the organisation also issues annually the 'Swiss stock guide' with company studies, including financial statistics, on Swiss banks, insurance companies, financial and industrial companies, and investment trusts.

Δ G - v Insurance

683 Die privaten Versicherungsunternehmungen in der Schweiz: Les enterprises d'assurances privées en Suisse [Private insurance enterprises in Switzerland].
Eidgenössisches Versicherungsamt, Bundesrain 20, 3003 Bern.
(annual) 1978. FrS 17.40. c 200p. *De, Fr.
TF: the 1978 edition, published in 1980, has data for 1978.
Life insurance business, accidents and damage, etc.

Δ H Transport and communications

684 Schweizerische verkehrsstatistik. Statistique suisse des transports [Swiss statistics of transport].
BS, Bern.
1948- 1982. FrS 39. 246p. *De, Fr.
TF: the 1982 edition, published in 1983, has data for 1982.
Describes the material, infrastructure and activities of transport enterprises - railways, rack-railways, funicular railways, lake transport, oil and petroleum used, air traffic, international transport of goods, etc.

Δ H - ii Roads and road transport

685 Schweizerische Strassenverkehrszählung. Recensement suisse de la circulation routière [Census of Swiss road traffic].
BS, Bern.
1970- 1980. FrS 11. *De, Fr.
TF: a census is taken every five years. The results of the 1980 census were published in 1983.
Numbers of motor vehicles, journeys by type of vehicle and by provenance of vehicle, for Switzerland, cantons and towns.

686 Strassenverkehrsunfälle in der Schweiz. Accidents de la circulation routière en Suisse [Road accidents in Switzerland].
1930- 1984. FrS 24. 124p. *De, Fr.
TF: the 1984 edition, published in 1985, has data for 1984 and some earlier years.
Types of accidents, persons involved, localities, causes, licences revoked, etc.

687 In Verkehr gesetzte neue Motorfahrzeuge. Véhicules à moteur neufs mis en circulation [new vehicles on the road].
BS, Bern.
1929- monthly & annual. Monthly: FrS 7 or FrS 95 yr; 1983 annual: FrS 16. *De, Fr.
Includes data on cars, minibuses, buses, coaches, delivery vehicles (lorries, etc), tractors, motorcycles & scooters, by type and model and by cantons.

688 Motorfahrzeugbestand in der Schweiz. Effectif des Véhicules à moteur en Suisse [Numbers of motor vehicles in Switzerland].
BS, Bern.
1958- 1983. FrS 49. 381p. *De, Fr.
TF: the 1983 edition, published in 1984, has data as at 30 September, 1983.
Data by model, total for the country and for each canton.

689 Motorfahrzeugbestand in der Schweiz nach Kantonen, Bezirken und Gemeinden. Effectif des véhicules à moteur en Suisse par canton, district et commune [Numbers of motor vehicles in Switzerland by canton, district and municipality].
BS, Bern.
1958- 1982. FrS 17. 93p. *De, Fr.
TF: published every two years, the 1982 edition was issued in 1983, with data as at 30 September 1982.

Δ H - iii Railways and railway transport

690 Statistisches Jahrbuch. Annuaire statistique [Statistical yearbook].
Schweizerische Bundesbahnen, Bollwerk 10, 3030 Bern.
1922- 1983. not priced. 198p. *De, Fr.
TF: the 1983 edition, published in June 1984, has data for 1983 and many earlier years.
Fixed installations, rolling stock, personnel, passenger and goods traffic, stations, lines, electricity consumption, lubricants used, accidents, etc.

CH

Δ H – v Telecommunications and postal services

691 Statistisches Jahrbuch. Annuaire statistique PTT [Statistical yearbook PTT].
Generaldirektion PTT, 3030 Bern.
1971- 1983. not priced. 124p. *Fr, De.
TF: the 1983 edition, published in 1984, has data for several years to 1983.
Post, telephone and telecommunications economy, traffic (post and telecommunications), installations, personnel, finances, an international review, and data for the Principality of Liechtenstein.

CZECHOSLOVAKIA
TCHECOSLOVAQUIE
TSCHECHOSLOWEKEI
CESKOSLOVENSKO

Central statistical office

692 Federální Statistický Úřad [Federal Statistical Office].
Sokolovská 142, Praha 8 - Karlin.
t 814.
Set up in January 1969, the responsibilities of the Office include the collection, analysis and publication of social and economic statistics for the whole of the Czechoslovak Socialist Repub'ic, the undertaking of statistical surveys, and the co-ordination of the work of the Czech, Slovak and regional statistical offices.
The office has been abbreviated to FSU, Praha in entries which follow.

Libraries

The library of Výzkumný Ústav Sociálně Ekonomických Informací a Automatizace v Ríseni [Institute of Socio-Economic Information and Automation in Management], Sokolovská 142, Praha 8 - Karlin (t 814) has a collection which includes all statistical publications of Czechoslovakia and a wide choice of the important publications of other countries and of international organisations. The library is open to the public from 8.15 to 15.30 daily and the staff speaks Russian and English as well as Czech.

Bibliographies

693 Průvodce statistickou literatúrou, by Jaroslav Podzimek.
This guide to the statistical literature was published in 1970 and is available from the library referred to above, price Kcs 25.

694 Bibliografie československé statistiky a demografie.
This bibliography of Czechoslovak statistics and demography is issued annually from 1945/68 and is available from the Institute referred to above.

Statistical publications

Δ A General

695 Statistická rocenka Ceskoslovenské Socialistické Republiky [Statistical yearbook of the Czechoslovak Socialist Republic].
FSU, Praha.
1934-38; 1957- 1984. Kcs 78. 704p. ISSN 0070-248X. *Cs; an English translation of the text is available separately.
TF: the 1984 edition, published late 1984, has data for 1983 and for several earlier years.
Main sections:
Basic indicators - Geography & climate - Living environment - Population - Labour - Social product & national income - Public finance - Prices - Capital construcion & stock tangible capital assets - Industry - Building & construction - Agriculture - Forestry - Transport - Communications - Communal & housing economy - Tourism - Internal trade - External trade - Living standard - Education - Culture - Public health-Social security - Physical training - Scientific & technical development - International statistics.
Note: 'Historická statistická ročenka CSSR [Historical statistical yearbook of Czechoslovakia: summary sheets] (910p) was published by FSU in 1985.

696 Statistické přehledy [Statistical surveys].
FSU, Praha.
1967- monthly. Kcs 6 each issue. *Cs; brief indication of the contents also in En & Ru.
TF: many tables contain data for the last six years and at least 12 months, the latest information being for about two months prior to publication.
Population, employment and wages, production and distribution, investment, housing construction, industrial production, agriculture, transport, retail turnover, wholesale and retail price indices, credit, savings, foreign trade by groups of countries, and an international comparison of the industrial production index and the cost of living index.

697 Ekonomický vývoj [Economic development].
FSU, Praha.
1964- 1983. not priced. 213p. *Cs.
TF: the 1983 edition, published in 1985, has data for 1983 and several earlier years.
Economic data for the Federal Republic, the Czech Socialist Republic, and the Slovak Socialist Republic.

698 Bulletin.
Státní Banka Československá, Praha 1.
(annual) 1984. not priced. 30p. ISSN 0081-539X. *En.
TF: the 1984 edition, published in 1984, has data for the years 1980 to 1983.
A report on the economic and monetary development in the Czechoslovak Socialist Republic, including statistical tables and charts on industrial production, building work, foreign trade, prices, agricultural production, and finance.

Δ A, continued

699 ČSSR 25 let od Února 1948 [Czechoslovak Socialist Republic. 25 years from February 1948].
FSU, Praha.
not priced. *Cs.
Statistics, facts and graphs concerning the economic, social and cultural development of the Czech Socialist Republic from 1948 to 1972.

Δ B Production

Δ B – ii Agriculture, fisheries, forestry, etc

700 Statistická rocenka aború zemedelské zásobování a nákup [Statistical yearbook of agricultural supply and purchase].
FSU, Praha.
(annual) 1983 (published in 1984). not priced. 139p. *Cs.

Δ B – iii Industry

701 Statistická ročenka průmyslů [Statistical yearbook of industry].
FSU, Praha.
(annual) 1983 (published in 1984). not priced. 667p. *Cs.

Δ B – iii(a) Food products, beverages, tobacco

702 Statistická ročenka potravinarskeho průmyslů [Statistical yearbook of the food industry].
FSU, Praha.
(annual) 1981. not priced. 153p. *Cs.
TF: the 1981 edition was published in 1982 and is the latest available in 1985.

Δ B – iii(c) Chemicals, pharmaceuticals, etc

703 Statistická ročenka chemického průmyslů [Statistical yearbook of the chemical industry].
FSU, Praha.
(annual) 1982. not priced. 267p. *Cs.
TF: the 1982 edition was published in 1983, and is the latest available in 1985.

Δ B – iii(d) Metals, etc. and (e) Engineering

704 Statistická ročenka hutnictví a strojírenství [Statistical yearbook of metallurgy and engineering].
FSU, Praha,
(annual) 1983 (published in 1984). not priced. 431p. *Cs.

Δ B – v Energy

705 Statistická ročenka energetiký [Statistical yearbook of energy].
FSU, Praha.
(annual) 1983 (published in 1984). not priced. 183p. *Cs.

Δ C External trade

706 Facts on Czechoslovak foreign trade (Czechoslovak Chamber of Commerce and Industry).
Československá Obchodní a Průmyslova komora, Argentinská 38 (PO Box 30), 17005 Praha 7.
1962- 1984. not priced. 186p. *En; also available in De, Ru & Fr.
TF: the 1984 edition, published in 1984, has data for 1975, 1980, 1982 and 1983.
Includes data on foreign trade, arranged by commodities and by countries.
Note: the Chamber also issues 'Economic digest' monthly, which has no regular tables but includes statistics in articles, and 'Czechoslovak foreign trade', also monthly and having no regular tables.

Δ D Internal distribution and service trades

707 Statistická ročenka spotřebního průmyslů [Statistical yearbook of the consumer industry].
FSU, Praha.
(annual) 1980. not priced. 217p. *Cs.
TF: the 1980 edition was published in 1981, and is the latest available in 1985.

Δ E Population

708 Sčítání lidu, domů a bytů v Československé Socialistické Republike [Population and housing census of Czechoslovakia].
FSU, Praha.
1961- 1980. not priced. *Cs.
TF: the results were published in 1982. The previous census was taken in 1970.
a 2% sample of the census returns.

709 Demosta [Bulletin for demography and statistics].
FSU, Praha.
1968- quarterly. not priced. *Cs; separate translations of contents available in En, Ru, Fr & Es.
Articles on population and demography and the results of surveys, etc.

Δ E - i Vital statistics

710 Pohyb abyvatelstva v Československé Socialistické Republike v roce... [Vital statistics yearbook].
FSU, Praha.
(annual) 1981. not priced. *Cs.
TF: the 1981 edition, published in 1982, has data for 1981, and is the latest available in 1985.

Δ E - iii Housing

Δ F Social and political

Δ F - ii Health and welfare

711 ČSSR zdravotnictví [Health services in Czechoslovakia] (Ústav pro Zdravotnickou Statistiku) [Institute for Health Statistics].
Ústav pro Zdravotnickou Statistiku, Tr. W Piecka 98, Praha 10.
1948/58- 1983. not priced. 515p. *Cs; separate translation of text in En.
TF: the 1983 edition, published in 1985, has data for several years to 1982.
Population and vital statistics, health statistics of the population, network of health institutions, activities of health institutions, health care; health costs, doctors, dentists, pharmacists, other health workers, and medical schools. Data is given for both the Czech and Slovak republics.

Δ F - iii Education and leisure

712 Śtatistika Školství...Česká Socialistická Republika [Education statistics...Czech Socialist Republic].
Ústav Skolských Informaci, Praha.
(annual) 1983 (published in 1984). not priced. 513p. *Cs.

D

GERMANY (FEDERAL REPUBLIC)
ALLEMAGNE (REPUBLIQUE FEDERALE)
BUNDESREPUBLIK DEUTSCHLAND

Central statistical office

713 Statistische Bundesamt [Federal Statistical Office].
Gustave-Stresemann-Ring 11, (Postfach 5528), 6200 Wiesbaden.
t (06121) 751. tx 4 186511 stb d.
An independent central federal authority, within the department of the Federal Ministry of the Interior, the functions of the office are to collect, compile and publish statistics for general as well as federal purposes. The office deals with all economic and social statistics for the Bundesrepublik as a whole, and with international statistics, whilst the statistical offices of the regions collect and process regional statistics. Unpublished statistical information can often be supplied. An annual report 'Die Arbeiten des Statistischen Bundesamt' describes the activities of the organisation. Most of the publications of the Statistisches Bundesamt are available on microfiche from Chadwyck-Healey Ltd. Most of the publications of the Statistisches Bundesamt (SB, Wiesbaden in the text) are published by W Kohlhammer GmbH, Postfach 42 11 20, 6500 Mainz 42. This is abbreviated to Kohlhammer, Mainz in the entries.

Libraries

The library of the Statistisches Bundesamt (see above) has a collection of statistical publications which may be consulted by the public. The library is open from 8.00 to 13.00, Monday to Friday, except on public holidays. The regional statistical offices in Kiel, Hamburg, Bremen, Düsseldorf, Wiesbaden, Bad Ems, Stuttgart, München, Saarbrücken and Berlin also have libraries containing German statistical publications. There are also many German statistical publications in the libraries of universities, research institutes, etc.

Libraries and information services abroad

The more general German statistical publications are available in German embassies abroad, including:

United Kingdom	Embassy of the German Federal Republic, 23 Belgrave Square, London SW1X 8PZ. t 01-235 5033.
Australia	Embassy of the German Federal Republic, 119 Empire Circuit, Yarralumla, Canberra. t 73 3177.
Canada	Embassy of the German Federal Republic, 1 Waverley Street, Ottawa K2P 0T8.
New Zealand	Embassy of the German Federal Republic, Hobson Street, Wellington C1. t 736 063.
USA	Embassy of the German Federal Republic, 4645 Reservoir Road, NW, Washington DC 20007. t (202) 298 4000.

Bibliographies

714 Das Arbeitsgebiet der Bundesstatistik.
This survey of German Federal statistics was last compiled and published by Statistisches Bundesamt in 1981 (unabridged version in German DM 29.40; abridged versions in English, French and Spanish DM 15.80 each).

715 Veröffentlichungs-verzeichnis [List of publications].
A sales catalogue issued annually by Statistisches Bundesamt in German. An English version is issued in alternate years.

The periodical 'Wirtschaft und Statistik' (717) includes, each month in the centre pages of the issue, a list of new publications of the Federal Statistical Office.

Statistical publications

Δ A General

716 Statistisches Jahrbuch für die Bundesrepublik Deutschland [Statistical yearbook for the Federal Republic of Germany] (SB, Wiesbaden).
Kohlhammer, Mainz.
1952- 1985. DM 98. 776p. *De.
TF: the 1985 edition, published mid-1985, has data for 1984, 1983 and earlier years.
Main sections:
Geography & meteorology - Summary data - Population - Elections - Religion - Industry - Labour - Agriculture, forestry, fisheries - Production - Construction & housing - Trade, services, tourism - Foreign trade - Transport - Money & credit, insurance - Justice - Education & culture - Health - Social - Finance & taxation - Economic accounts - Wages & salaries - Prices - Balance of payments - Environment - Economic organisations & professions - Appendices with data on DDR & East Berlin - International statistics.

Δ A, continued

717 Wirtschaft und Statistik [Economics and statistics] (SB, Wiesbaden).
Kohlhammer, Mainz.
1921- monthly. DM 13.20; or DM 150 yr. *De; contents list of articles also in En.
TF: tables usually include data for about the last five years and the last 12 months up to two months prior to the date of the issue.
The first part of each issue consists of articles on basic methodological questions and comments on the results of new and current statistics. In the centre of each issue is a cumulative subject index for the year to date and a list of new publications issued during the month. The latter half of the review is 'Statistische Monatszahlen' - statistical tables on population, health, education, justice, elections, employment, agriculture and forestry, fisheries, industrial enterprises and handicrafts, building construction and housing, wholesale and retail trade, hotels, tourism, foreign trade, transport, money and credit, social statistics, finance and taxation, prices and price indices, wages and salaries, provision and consumption, and national accounts.
Note: selected methodological articles from this review appear in English translation in a series ' 'Studies on statistics' which is published at irregular intervals and is included in the subscription to 'Wirtschaft und Statistik' for subscribers outside Germany.

718 Statistischer Wochendienst [Weekly statistical service] (SB, Wiesbaden).
Kohlhammer, Mainz.
1950- weekly. DM 2.20. *De.
Contains all results of short-term statistics having become available during the week, and comparative figures.

719 Indikatoren zur Wirtschaftsentwicklung: Zeitreihen mit Saisonbereinigung [Indicators of economic development: seasonally adjusted time series] (SB, Wiesbaden).
Kohlhammer, Mainz.
monthly. DM 13.20. *De.
major economic indicators and the last 13 months original figures as well as seasonaly and calendar-adjusted figures, concerning the labour market, manufacturing industry, mining industry, construction industry, productivity and wages costs in industry, taxation, transport, foreign trade, companies, prices, turnover of wholesale trade, and turnover of retail trade.

720 Die Lage der Weltwirtschaft und der westdeutschen Wirtschaft [Economic situation for the world and West Germany].
Arbeitsgemeinschaft Deutscher Wirtschaftswissenschaftlicher Forschungsinstitute, Hamburg.
2 a year (issued in Spring and Autumn). not priced. *De.
An assessment of the situation by the five member institutes of the association.

721 Lange Reihen zur Wirtschaftsentwicklung [Long-term series on economic development] (SB, Wiesbaden).
Kohlhammer, Mainz.
(biennial) 1984. DM 18.70. 231p. *De.
TF: the 1984 edition, published in 1984, has data for 1983 and some earlier years.
Time series for the assessment of economic development since 1950. Contains basic data of medium material detail on population and employment and the most important results of continuous economic statistics.

722 Economic bulletin (Deutsches Institut für Wirtschaftsforschung).
Gower Publishing Co Ltd., Gower House, Croft Road, Aldershot, Hants GU11 3HR, England.
1965- monthly. £70.00 yr. *En.
Published by the Gower Press for the German Institute for Economic Research, the monthly issues contain articles which include statistical tables and graphs. Economic forecasts are also included.

723 Vierteljahrshefte zur Wirtschaftsforschung [Quarterly bulletin for economic research] (Deutsches Institut für Wirtschaftsforschung).
Duncker & Humblot, Dietrich-Schäfer-Weg 9, D-1000 Berlin 41.
(quarterly) not priced. *De.
Mainly text, but includes a few regular tables on economic accounts, employment, etc.

724 Arbeits- und Sozialstatistik: Hauptergebnisse [Labour and social statistics: principal results].
Bundesminister für Arbeit und Sozialordning, Postfach 5300 Bonn 1.
1975- 1984. not priced. 197p. ISSN 0341-7840. *De.
TF: the 1984 edition, published in 1984, has data for 1982 or 1983 and earlier years.
In four sections: Population and occupations; Living standards, income, working hours; Social security; Work and social jurisdiction, disputes.

725 Statistisches Taschenbuch...Arbeits- und Sozialstatistik [Statistical pocketbook...Labour and social statistics].
Bundesminister für Arbeit und Sozialordnung, Postfach 5300 Bonn 1.
(annual) 1984. not priced. 135p. *De.
TF: the 1984 edition, published mid-1984, has long runs of figures to 1982 and 1983.
Contents: General data; Population and labour market; Production, productivity, strikes; Employment; Wages and salaries; Consumption and prices; Social security; International tables.

726 IFO Spiegel der Wirtschaft: economic indicators: Struktur und Konjunktur in Bild und Zahl (IFO).
Campus Verlag GmbH, Myliustrasse 15, 6000 Frankfurt/Main 1.
(annual) 1984/85. not priced. various pagings. ISSN 0170-3617. *De; main headings & contents list also in En.
TF: the 1984/85 edition, published in 1985, has data for 1983 and earlier years.
Statistical tables, charts and graphs on national product and its components, the labour market and wages, prices, foreign trade, public finance, money, interest rates, capital, net financial position of the market, manufacturing industry, electricity and water supply, construction industry, transport, wholesale and retail trade, agriculture, international surveys, forecasts and plans.

727 Bevölkerungsstruktur und Wirtschaftskraft der Bundesländer [Population structures and economic resources of the Federal provinces] (SB, Wiesbaden).
Kohlhammer, Mainz.
1950- 1984. DM 19.10. 214p. *De.
TF: the 1984 edition, published in 1985, has data for several years to 1983.
Major demographic and economic data available for each of the Länder [provinces].

728 Statistical compass (SB, Wiesbaden).
Kohlhammer, Mainz.
1977- 1985. DM 3. 48p. *En, Es, Fr & De eds.
TF: the 1985 edition, published in 1985, has data for 1984 or 1983 and earlier years.
A booklet containing summary tables on subjects similar to those in the statistical yearbook (716).

729 The economic situation in the Federal Republic of Germany: monthly review (Federal Minister of Economics).
BMWI, Villemomblerstrasse 76, 5300 Bonn-Duisdorf.
(monthly not priced. *En & De eds.
TF: each issue has data for about four months to two or three months prior to the date of the issue.
Includes a statistical annex with key data on overall economic developments (national accounts), new orders in manufacturing, turnover in manufacturing, output of goods - production sector, situation in the construction industry, employment and labour market, trade and payments, money and credit, interest rates, wages and salaries, prices, tax revenue of Federal Government and Länder, and economic data relating to Berlin.

730 Leistung in Zahlen [Results in figures].
BMWI, Villemomblerstrasse 76, 65 Bonn-Duisdorf (Postfach 5300 Bonn).
(annual) 1983. free. 132p. *De.
TF: the 1983 edition, published in 1984, has data for several years to 1983.
Annual official government statistics on population, earnings, labour; revenues and expenditure, gross social product, economy (production, shipping, energy, construction, agriculture, crafts, trade (turnover), transport), foreign trade, Germany in the Common Market, social budget, finance, etc.

731 Wirtschaft in Zahlen [The economy in figures] (SB, Wiesbaden).
Kohlhammer, Mainz.
(irregular) 1983 (published in 1984). DM 28. *De.
An overview of economic development in the Federal Republic of Germany, primary consideration being given to the individual branches of economic activity and their respective contribution to the economy as a whole.

732 IFO - Schnelldienst [IFO - fast service].
IFO, München.
(weekly) DM 220 yr. ISSN 0018-974X. *De.
Contains up-to-date information on the subjects covered in 726 above.

733 Städte in Zahlen: ein Strukturbericht zum Thema finanzen (bzw. Wirtschaft, Bevölkerung, Bauen und Wohnen, Kultur) [Cities in figures...].
Verband Deutscher Städtestatistiker [Union of German Municipal Statisticians], Steckelhorn 12, 2000 Hamburg 11.
(annual) 1984 (published in 1984). DM 17. 144p. *De.
A statistical abstract comparing and analysing the performance of German cities - population 50,000 or more inhabitants - on finance, economics, population structure and development, construction and housing, culture. Topics alternate every year.

734 Zahlen und Fakten der genossenschaftlichen Banken, Waren-, Verwertungs- und Dienstleistungsgenossenschaften [Facts and figures relating to the co-operative banks, commodity and service co-operatives].
Deutscher Genossenschafts- und Raiffeisenverband eV (DGRV), Adenauerallee 127, (Postfach 19 01 41) 5300 Bonn 1.
(annual) 1984. free. 31p. *De & En eds.
TF: the 1984 edition, published in 1984, has data as at 1.1.84.
Tables in text include important figures relating to the overall organisation, balance sheet of the banks, important figures on the Raiffeisen Co-operations, important figures relating to the small-scale industry and service co-operatives, regional data.

Δ B Production

735 Zensus im Produzierenden Gewerbe [Census of production industries] (SB, Wiesbaden).
Kohlhammer, Mainz.
1962– 1979. 7 vols. *De.
TF: the results of the 1979 census were published between 1981 and 1984. A later census was taken for 1983.
Contents:
Vol 1: Mining & manufacturing. Employment turnover, gross & net production values of enterprises and local units by branches of economic activity (DM 12.20)
Vol 2: Mining & manufacturing. Investments & stocks on hand of enterprises & local units by branches of economic activity & size classes (DM 11.60)
Vol 3: Mining & manufacturing. Employment, turnover, gross & net production values of enterprises & local units by branches of economic activity & size classes (DM 12.20)
Vol 4: Mining & manufacturing. Regional interaction of enterpriese & local units (DM 11)
Vol 5: Mining & manufacturing. Enterprises and their local units by main economic activity (DM 10.30)
Vol 6: Building industry. Employment, turnover, investments, gross & net production values of enterprises by branches of economic activity & size classes (DM 10.40)
Vol 7: Power & water supply. Employment, turnover, investments, gross & net production values of enterprises by branches of economic activity and size classes (DM 9.20).

736 Fachserie 4: Produzierendes Gewerbe. Reihe 4: Bergbau und Verarbeitendes Gewerbe. 1. Beschäftigung. Umsatz u.ä. der Unternehmen und Betriebe im Bergbau und im Verarbeitenden Gewerbe [Series 4: production industries. Sub-series 4: mining and manufacturing. 1: Employment, turnover and the like of enterprises and local units in mining and manufacturing] (SB, Wiesbaden).
Kohlhammer, Mainz. *De.
4.1.1. Employment, turnover and power supply... (monthly DM 10.30 yr; 1983 annual issue; DM 8.60)
4.1.2. Local units, persons engaged and turnover, by size classes of persons engaged (annual. 1983. DM 8.40)
4.1.3. Regional distribution (4-yearly. 1982. DM 18.70)
4.1.4. Employment and turnover by federal Länder (annual. 1983. DM 10.30).

737 Fachserie 4: Produzierendes Gewerbe. Reihe 4: Bergbau und Verarbeitendes Gewerbe. 2: Beschäftigte, Umsatz und Investitionen der Unternehmen und Betriebe im Bergbau und im Verarbeitenden Gewerbe [Production industries. Series 4: mining and manufacturing industries. 2: employment, turnover and investment in undertakings and enterprises] (SB, Wiesbaden).
Kohlhammer, Mainz.
(annual) 1982 (published in 1984). 2 vols. *De.
Vol 1: Undertakings (DM 11.60). Vol 2: Enterprises (DM 8.60).

738 Fachserie 4: Produzierendes Gewerbe. Reihe 4: Bergbau und Verarbeitendes Gewerbe. 3: Kostenstruktur der Unternehmen im Bergbau und im Verarbeitended Gewerbe [Production industries. Series 4: mining and manufacturing industries. 3 Cost structure of enterprises in mining and manufacturing] (SB, Wiesbaden).
Kohlhammer, Mainz.
(annual) 1982 (published in 1984). 3 vols. *De.
Vol 1: In mining, primary and producers' goods industries (DM 12.90)
Vol 2: In industries producing investment goods (DM 12.90)
Vol 3: In industries producing consumer goods, food, beverages and tobacco (DM 14.40).

739 Fachserie 17: Preise. Reihe 3: Index der Grundstoffpreise [Prices. Series 3: Price indexes for selected basic materials] (SB, Wiesbaden).
Kohlhammer, Mainz.
monthly & annual. DM 4.40 each monthly issue; 1983 annual issue DM 10.30. *De.

Δ B – i Mines and mining

740 Jahresbericht und Statistik [Annual report and statistics].
Fachvereiningung Metallerzbergbau eV, Tersteegenstrasse 28, (Postfach 8706) 4 Düsseldorf 2.
(annual) 1983. free. 46p. *De.
TF: the 1984 report, published in 1984, has data for 1983 and some earlier years.
Includes a section of statistical tables in metallic ore mines, production, sales, wages, prices, etc. Mainly for the Federal Republic of Germany, but also some data for Europe and the world.

741 Der Kohlenbergbau in der Energiewirtschaft der Bundesrepublik Deutschland... [The coal-mining industry and other energy industries in the Federal Republic of Germany].
Statistik der Kohlenwirtschaft eV, Glückaufhaus, Friedrichstrasse 1, 4300 Essen.
(annual) 1983. free. 88p. *De.
TF: the 1983 edition, published late 1984, has data for 1983 and long runs of earlier years.
The energy and coal market, coal mining (sales and turnover, demand, coal refining, stocks, productivity, investment, employees, etc). Data is on hard coal and lignite and some data on other kinds of energy are also included.

742 Zahlen zur Kohlenwirtschaft [Figures for the coal industry].
Statistik der Kohlenwirtschaft eV, Glückaufhaus, Friedrichstrasse 1, 4300 Essen.
2 or 3 a year. free. *De.
TF: each issue has several years of annual figures for most tables and several months of monthly figures to about three months prior to the date of publication.
Detailed statistical tables of the coal-mining industry (hard coal and lignite) including stocks, sales, foreign trade, transport, coal and the electricity industry, etc.

Δ B – i, continued

743 Statistisches Jahrbuch der Eisen- und Stahlindustrie [Statistical yearbook of the iron and steel industry] (Wirtschaftsvereinigung Eisen- und Stahlindustrie).
Verlag Stahleisen GmbH, Breite Strase 27, 4000 Düsseldorf.
1929- 1984. DM 42.50. c 350p. *De.
TF: the 1984 edition, published in 1984, has data several years to 1983.
Production, consumption, stocks, prices, employment, wages, accidents, and trade in the industry.

744 Fachserie 4. Produzierendes Gewerbe. Reihe 8: Fachstatistiken. 1: Eisen und Stahl (Eisenerzbergbau, Eisenschaffende Industrie, Eisen-, Stahl- und Tempergiesserei) [Production industries. Series 8. 1: Iron and steel (iron-ore mining; iron and steel industry; iron steel and malleable iron foundries)] (SB, Wiesbaden).
Kohlhammer, Mainz.
monthly & quarterly. DM 4.70 each for monthly issues; DM 15 each for quarterly issues. *De.

Δ B – ii Agriclture, fisheries, forestry, etc

745 Statistisches Jahrbuch über Ernährung, Landwirtschaft und Forsten der Bundesrepublik Deutschland [Statistical yearbook of food, agriculture and forestry in the Federal Republic of Germany] (Bundesministerium für Ernährung und Forsten).
Landwirtschaftsverlag GmbH, Münster-Hiltrup.
1956- 1984. For price, enquire of publisher. 441p. ISSN 0072-1581. *De.
TF: the 1984 edition, published in 1984, has data for 1983, 1982/83 and some earlier years in some tables.
The general economy, including population, employment, social product and income, and industrial production, followed by detailed data on agriculture (including land use, labour, education, machinery and mechanical techniques, the use of fertilisers and other products, crops, horticulture and viticulture, livestock, co-operatives, financing, marketing, prices and wages, foreign trade, forestry including wood products, hunting, etc). Also includes a section on agriculture, etc., in the EEC.

746 Statistischer Monatsbericht [Monthly bulletin of statistics].
Bundesministerium für Ernährung, Landwirtschaft und Forsten, Postfach 18 02 03, 6000 Frankfurt/Main.
1948- DM 16; or DM 170 yr. *De.
TF: each issue has the latest figures available for particular tables, in some cases up to two months prior to the date of the issue.
Contains more up to date information on subjects covered by (745).

747 Agrarbericht der Bundesregierung [Agricultural report of the Federal Government].
Bundesministerium für Ernährung, Landwirtschaft und Forsten, Postfach 18 02 03, 6000 Frankfurt/Main.
1956- 1985. free. 410p. ISSN 0072-1565. *De.
TF: the 1985 report, published in 1985, has data for 1983/84 and earlier runs for some tables.
Content: Part A: Situation of the agricultural economy (agriculture, forestry and timber, fisheries); part B: Aims/target and programme for agriculture and food policy; part C: Programme overlap aspects and activity.

748 Landwirtschaftszählung [Census of agriculture] (SB, Wiesbaden).
Kohlhammer, Mainz.
1971- 1979. 6 vols. *De.
Content:
Vol 1: Working conditions in agriculture and forestry holdings (DM 16.80)
Vol 2: Holdings according to the main emphasis of their livestock keeping (DM 14.20)
Vol 3: Land tenure, letting of rooms, equipment of residential houses (DM 9.20)
Vol 4: Agricultural and non-agricultural training, household structure, social security (DM 10.40)
Vol 5: Methodological foundations, processing and presentation programme
Vol 6: Non-administrative territorial units.

749 Fachserie 3: Land- und Forstwirtschaft, Fischerei. Reihe 1: Ausgewählte Zahlen für die Agrarwirtschaft [Agriculture and forestry, fisheries. Series 1: selected figures on agriculture] (SB, Wiesbaden).
Kohlhammer, Mainz.
(annual) 1983 (published in 1984). DM 18.70. *De.
Employment, machinery, land-use, fertilisers, horticulture, viticulture, animal production, fisheries, food consumption, prices, wages and weather. Data is included for the country as a whole and for the provinces.

750 Fachserie 17: Preise. Reihe 1: Preise und Preisindizes für Land- und Forstwirtschaft [Prices. Series 1: prices and price indices for agriculture and forestry] (SB, Wiesbaden).
Kohlhammer, Mainz.
monthly & annual. DM 4.40; the 1983 annual issue is DM 11.60. *De.
Purchaser and producer indices for agricultural products, raw materials, equipment, and forestry products. Also producer prices for agriculture and forestry, and purchase prices for fresh fish at auctions and agricultural products.

Δ B – ii(a) Agriculture and horticulture

751 ZMP - Bilanzen... [ZMP - balances] (Zentrale Markt- und Preisberichtstelle für Erzeugnisse der Land-, Forst- und Ernärungswirtschaft).
ZMP, Godesburger Allee 142-148, Bonn-Bad Godesburg (Postfach 25 69), 5300 Bonn 1.
(annual) 1983/84- 8 parts. *De.
TF: the 1983/84 edition has data for the crop year 1983/84.
Contents:
Agrarmarkte in Zahlen [Agricultural market in figures] (DM 2.30)
Vieh; Fleisch [Livestock; meat] (DM 17)
Eier; Geflüge [Eggs; poultry] (DM 15)
Milch; Milcherzeugnisse [Milk] (DM 15)
Getreide; Futtermittel [Grain; feeding stuffs] (DM 17)
Kartoffeln [Potatoes] (DM 15)
Obst [Fruit] (DM 17)
Gemüse [Vegetables] (DM 17).

752 Fachserie 3: Land- und Forstwirtschaft, Fischerei. Reihe 2: Betriebs-, Arbeits- und Einkommensverhältnisse [Agriculture and forestry, fisheries. Series 2: Operating and working conditions, income situation] (SB, Wiesbaden).
Kohlhammer, Mainz.
1978- annual. 10 vols. *De.
Contents:
Part 1.1: Size structure of holdings (1983. DM 8.60)
Part 1.2: Land utilisation of holdings (1983. DM 21.50)
Part 1.3: Livestock on holdings (1983. DM 18.70)
Part 1.4: Holdings systems and incomes (biennial. 1981. DM 11.60)
Part 1.5: Socio-economic conditions (biennial. 1981. DM 12.90)
Part 1.6: Land tenure and transactions of real property (biennial. 1983. DM 12.90)
Part 1.7: Outside income and operating conditions, selected groups of holdings (biennial. 1981. DM 15.80)
Part 2: Labour force (1983. DM 10.30)
Part 3: Technical equipment (3-yearly. 1984. DM 2.90)
Part 4: Purchasing values of agricultural property (1983. DM 2.90).

753 Fachserie 3: Land- und Forstwirtschaft, Fischerie. Reihe 3: Bodennutzung und Pflanzliche Erzeugung [Agriculture and forestry, fisheries. Series 3: Land utilisation and vegetable production] (SB, Wiesbaden).
Kohlhammer, Mainz.
1978- annual. 10 titles. *De.
Contents:
3: Land utilisation and vegetable production (1983. DM 12.90)
3.1: Land utilisation:
3.1.1: Classification of total areas (4-yearly. 1981. DM 4)
3.1.2: Agriculturally used areas (1984. DM2.90)
3.1.3: Areas of vegetable cultivation (1984. DM 2.90)
3.1.4: Areas of fruit trees (5-yearly. 1982. DM 12.20)
3.1.5: Vine acreage (1983. DM 5.70)
3.1.6: Cultivation of ornamental plants (3-yearly. 1984. DM 2.90)
3.1.7: Tree nurseries, areas and plants in tree nurseries (1984. DM 4.40)
3.2: Vegetable production:
3.2.1: Growth and yields - field crops, vegetables, fruit, grapes (14 issues a year. DM 2.90)
3.2.2. Production and stocks of wine (2 a year. DM 4.40).

754 Fachserie 3: Land- und Forstwirtschaft, Fischerei. Reihe 4: Viehbestand und tierische Erzeugung [Agriculture, forestry, fisheries. Series 4: Livestock and animal production] (SB, Wiesbaden).
Kohlhammer, Mainz.
1978- 1983 (published in 1984). DM 8.60. 64p. *De.
Contains data on total numbers of cattle, sheep, pigs, poultry, horses, goats by administrative areas; milk production and utilisation; slaughtering; and laying and slaughtering of poultry.
Note: more specialised titles in this series are:
4.1: Livestock (quarterly. DM 1.60 each issue)
4.2.1: Slaughterings and meat production (quarterly. DM 4.40)
4.2.2: Milk production and utilisation (1983. DM 2.90)
4.2.3: Poultry production (half-yearly. DM 2.90)
4.3: Meat inspection, including poultry (1983. DM 10.30).

755 Weinbauerhebung [Census of viticulture] (SB, Wiesbaden).
Kohlhammer, Mainz.
1972/73- 1979/80. DM 18.20. *De.

756 Deutsche Weinbauwirtschaft: Zahlen und Fakten [German winegrowing industry: figures and facts].
Deutscher Weinbauverband eV, Haussallee 26, Bonn.
not priced. 21p. *De.
TF: published in 1983, the booklet has data for several years to 1982.
Includes statistical tables on wine and wine-growing in the Federal Republic of Germany.

757 Gartenbauerhebung [Census of horticulture] (SB, Wiesbaden).
Kohlhammer, Mainz.
1972/73- 1981/82. DM 18.70. *De.
Data on the cultivation of horticultural produce for sale, and on fruit orchards.

D

Δ B – ii(b) Finance

758 Binnenfischereierhebung [Census of inland fisheries] (SB, Wiesbaden).
Kohlhammer, Mainz.
1972- 2nd, 1981/82 (published in 1984). DM 5.70. 23p. *De.

759 Fachserie 3: Land- und Forstwirtschaft, Fischerei. Reihe 4: Viehbestand und tierische Erzeugung. 5: Hochsee- und Küstenfischerie; Bodensee fischerei [Agriculture and forestry, fisheries. Series 4: Livestock and animal production. 5: Sea and inshore fisheries; Lake Constance fisheries] (SB, Wiesbaden).
Kohlhammer, Mainz.
monthly & annual. DM 2.90 each monthly issue; 1983 annual is DM 7.40. *De.
Weight and value of catches, landings, types of fish, and processing, by different fishing grounds, type of ship, length of voyage, and ship's nationality.

760 Jahresbericht über die Deutsche Fischwirtschaft... [Annual report on German fisheries...] (Bundesministerium für Ernährung und Forsten).
Gebr. Mann u. Heenemann Verlags-GmbH, Bessemerstra. 83, 1000 Berlin 42.
1924- 1982/83- Enquire of publisher for price. 185p. ISSN 0075-2851. *De; contents table & summaries also in En.
TF: the 1982/83 edition, published in December 1983, has data for 1982.
Mainly textual, with c 30 pages of statistics on deep sea trawler fishery, lugger herring fishery, cutter deep sea and coastal fisheries, industrial fish, landings in foreign ports, catches of foreign fishing vessels landed in the Federal Republic of Germany, etc. Part 1 has current data in detail and part 2 has basic tables on same subjects.

Δ B – ii(c) Forestry

761 Forsterhebung, 1972 [Census of forestry, 1972] (SB, Wiesbaden).
Kohlhammer, Mainz.
DM 14.60. 265p. *De.
Only one volume published – the structural conditions of the forest industry.

Δ B – iii Industry

762 Handwerkszählung [Census of the craft industry] (SB, Wiesbaden).
Kohlhammer, Mainz.
1968- 2nd, 1977 (published in 1979). 3 vols. *De.
Heft 1: Methodology; undertakings accordance to economic sector (DM 7.90)
Heft 2: Undertakings according to economic sector and size category (DM 12.80)
Heft 3: Undertakings according to trade sector; subsidiary concerns (DM 15).
There is also a special number (Sonderbericht) on regional distribution of handicrafts (DM 18.20).

763 Fachserie 2. Unternehmen und Arbeitsstätten. Reihe 1: Kostenstruktur in ausgewählten Wirtschaftszweigen. 1.1. Kostenstruktur im Handwerk [Enterprises and local units. Series 1. Cost structure in industry. 1.1. Cost structure in handicrafts] (SB, Wiesbaden).
Kohlhammer, Mainz.
4-yearly. 1982. DM 18.70. *De.

764 Fachserie 4. Produzierendes Gewerbe. Reihe 2: Indizes für das Produzierende Gewerbe [Production industries. Series 2: Indices for the production industries] (SB, Wiesbaden).
Kohlhammer, Mainz.
monthly. *De.
In two parts:
part 1: Indices of production and of labour productivity, production of selected commodities in production industries (DM 8.90. Provisional monthly indices are also published, DM 1.60 each)
part 2: Indices of orders received, turnover and unfilled orders for manufacturing and building industry proper (DM 7.40).

765 Fachserie 4. Produzierendes Gewerbe. Reihe 3: Produktion im Produzierenden Gewerbe [Production industries. Series 3: Output in production industries] (SB, Wiesbaden).
Kohlhammer, Mainz.
(quarterly & annual. *De.
In two parts:
3.1. Output of production industries within the country and abroad (quarterly. DM 19.10, and annual, 1983. DM 18.70).
3.2. Output of production industries by branches of economic activity and groups of products (1982. DM 15.90).

766 Fachserie 4. Produzierendes Gewerbe. Reihe 7. Handwerk. 1: Beschäftigte und Umsatz im Handwerk [Production industries. Series 7. Handicrafts. 1: Employment and turnover in the craft industries] (SB, Wiesbaden).
Kohlhammer, Mainz.
quarterly. DM 2.30 each issue. *De.
Note: the 4th issue each year now has annual figures.

767 Fachserie 17. Preise. Reihe 2: Preise und Preiseindices für gewerbliche Produkte (Erzeugerpreise) [Prices. Series 2: Prices and price indices for industrial products (Producers' prices)] (SB Wiesbaden).
Kohlhammer, Mainz.
monthly & annually. DM 5.90 each month; 1983 annual issue DM 14.40. *De.

Δ B – iii(b) Textiles, paper, rubber, etc

768 HPV – Statistik [Statistics (of the Central Association of the Paper, Paperboard & Plastics Converting Industry)].
Hauptverband der Papier, Pappe und Kunststoffe Verarbeitenden Industrie eV, Arndtstrasse 47, 6000 Frankfurt/Main 1.
(annual) 1983/84. not priced. 40p. *De.
TF: the 1983/84 edition, published in 1984, has data for several years to 1983.
For paper & paperboard manufacture – turnover, production, orders received, capacity utilisation, investment, price indices, employment, productivity, wages, foreign trade, sales, etc. For plastics manufacture – production, price indices and foreign trade.
Note: the organisation also issues an 8-page folder 'Die Papier, Pappe und Kunststoffe verarbeitende Industrie in Zahlen', annually.

769 Textil-Fakten: Markt- und Strukturdaten der Textil- und Bekleidungswirtschaft [Textile facts: market and structure data on the textile and clothing industry].
Deutscher Fachverlag GmbH, Schumannstrasse 27, 6000 Frankfurt/Main 1.
(annual) 1983/84. DM 180. 734p. ISSN 0344-032X. *De.
TF: the 1983/84 edition, published early 1984, has data for several years to 1981 or 1982.
Data, compiled by this marketing service, on developments in the textile industry, the clothing industry, the shoe-making industry, wholesale trade, retail trade, foreign trade, and some international data.

Δ B – iii(c) Chemicals, pharmaceuticals, etc

770 Chemiewirtschaft in Zahlen [The chemical industry in figures].
Verband der Chemischen Industrie eV, Karlstrasse 21, D-6000 Frankfurt/Main 1.
1959- 1984. free. 119p. *De.
TF: the 1984 edition, published in 1984, has data for about ten years, including the last 12 months or three years in quarters, to 1983.
Detailed statistical tables on turnover, production, wages, foreign trade, energy used, price indices, investment, etc., in the Federal Republic and West Berlin, and some international statistics for comparison.
Note: a very few statistics are included in the organisation's annual report [Jahresbericht] (1877- 1983/84. free. 146p. *De).

771 Fachserie 4. Produzierendes Gewerbe. Reihe 8: Fachstatistiken 2: Düngemittelversorgung [Production industries. Series 8. 2: Fertiliser supply] (SB, Wiesbaden).
Kohlhammer, Mainz.
monthly & annual. DM 1.60 each monthly issue; 1984 annual DM 4.40. *De.

Δ B – iii(e) Engineering

772 Statistisches Handbuch für den Maschinenbau [Statistical handbook for mechanical engineering].
Verband Deutscher Maschinen- und Anlagenbau eV, Lyoner Strasse 18, 6000 Frankfurt/Main.
1930- 1982. not priced. 279p. *De.
TF: the 1982 edition, published late 1982, has data for 1981 or 1980 and earlier years in some tables.
General economic data and statistics of the whole mechanical engineering industry; production, employment, exports and imports in the various branches of engineering industry; and international comparative tables.

773 Tatsachen und Zahlen aus der Kraftverkehrswirtschaft [Facts and figures of the motor transport industry].
Verband der Automobilindustrie eV, Westendstrasse 61, 6000 Frankfurt/Main.
1936/37- 1984. DM 79.50. 458p. *De.
TF: the 1984 edition, published in 1984, has data for 1983 and several earlier years.
Detailed statistics of production, shipments from works, imports, exports, stocks, licences issued, etc. Information on the motor industry in general, on fuels, on roads, and on transport in general. Data is for the whole country, provinces and towns.

774 Deutscher Schiffbau [German shipbuilding industry].
Verband der Deutschen Schiffbauindustrie eV, An der Alster 1, 2000 Hamburg 1.
(annual) 1983. free. 44p. *De; table headings also in En.
TF: the 1983 edition, published in 1984, has data for 1983 and some earlier years.
Includes a statistical section on German shipbuilding and repairing, and on developments in world shipbuilding, trade and merchant fleets.

Δ B – iii(f) Other industries

775 Buch und Buchhandel in Zahlen [Books and the book trade in figures].
Börsenverein des Deutschen Buchhandels eV., Grosser Hirschgraben 17, 6000 Frankfurt/Main.
1952- 1985. not priced. 112p. *De.
TF: the 1985 edition, published in 1985, has data for from 1980 or 1981 to 1984.
Includes data on production, trade, foreign trade, exhibitions, libraries, taxes, etc.

D

Δ B – iv Construction

776 Gebäude- und Wohnungszählung. 1% Wohnungsstichprobe [Census of buildings and dwellings. 1% housing statistics] (SB, Wiesbaden).
Kohlhammer, Mainz.
1972- 1978. 6 vols. *De.
Contents:
Part 1: Bases of the survey (DM 9.50)
Part 2: Selected structure data (DM 6.o.p)
Part 3: Buildings and dwelling units - structure, occupancy, modernisation (DM 9.50)
Part 4: Rents and rental burden of households (DM 7.20)
Part 5: Housing supply of households and families (DM 9.80)
Part 6: Residential surroundings - available infrastructure and environmental conditions (DM 7.20).
Note: the last full census was taken in 1968, the results published in 8 vols and one special number.

777 Ausgewählte Zahlen für die Bauwirtschaft [Selected figures for the construction industry] (SB, Wiesbaden).
Kohlhammer, Mainz.
monthly. DM 10.30 each issue. ISSN 0072-1719. *De.
Compilation of data from building reports, the statistics of building activity and various other sources. Presents an outline of the entire construction industry, from the use of the production factors to the completed building project.

778 Fachserie 5: Bautätigkeit und Wohnungen [Building activity and dwellings] (SB, Wiesbaden).
Kohlhammer, Mainz.
(annual) *De.
There are three annual reports issued under this overall title:
Series 1: Building activity (1982. DM 9.70.o.p)
Series 2: Grants made in social residential construction promoted by public authorities (1983. DM 8.60)
Series 3: Housing stock (1983. DM 7.40).
Note: Special reports include 'Series S.I. Construction statistics, 1960-1980' (DM 12.90.o.p).

779 Baustatistische Jahrbuch [Building statistics yearbook].
Hauptverband der Deutschen Bauindustrie eV, Abraham-Lincoln-Strasse 30, (Postfach 2966), D-6200 Wiesbaden.
(annual) 1984 (published in September 1984). DM 20. *De.

780 Fachserie 4: Produzierendes Gewerbe. Reihe 5: Baugewerbe [Production industries. Series 5: Building industry] (SB, Wiesbaden).
Kohlhammer, Mainz.
(annual) 3 vols. *De.
Contents:
1: Employment, turnover, machinery and equipment of local units in building industry (1983. DM 10.30)
2: Employment, turnover and investments of enterprises in building industry (1982. DM 7.40)
3: Cost structure of enterprises in the building industry (1982. DM 10.30).

781 Fachserie 17: Preise. Reihe 4: Messzählen für Bauleistungspreise und Preisindizes für Bauwerke [Prices. Series 4: Comparative figures for building costs and price indexes for building work] (SB, Wiesbaden).
Kohlhammer, Mainz.
quarterly. DM 7.40. *De.
Note: there is also a preliminary version (DM 2.90 each issue).

782 Fachserie 17: Preise. Reihe 5: Kaufwerte für Bauland [Prices. Series 5: Cost of building land] (SB, Wiesbaden).
Kohlhammer, Mainz.
quarterly & annual. DM 4.40 each issue; 1983 annual issue DM 8.60. *De.

Δ B – v Energy

783 Statistik der Energiewirtschaft [Statistics of the energy industry] (Vereinigung Industrielle Kraftwirtschaft (VIK)).
Energieberatung GmbH, Richard-Wagner-Strasse 41, D-4300 Essen 1.
(annual) 1983/84. DM 102 (DM 66 abroad) 188p. *De; contents list & table headings also in En & Fr.
TF: the 1983/84 edition, published in 1984, has long runs of figures to 1983.
Data on production, foreign trade, consumption, sales, prices, reserves, etc. of energy generally, and of coal, mineral oil, gas, electricity relating to West Germany, and energy in the world economy.

784 VIK - Mitteilungen [VIK - review] (Vereinigung Industrielle Kraftwirtschaft (VIK)).
Energieberatung GmbH, Richard-Wagner-Strasse 41, D-4300 Essen 1.
6 a year. DM 20 (DM 13.50 abroad;) DM 117 yr (DM 78 yr abroad). *De.
Mainly concerned with industrial energy consumption and production. Includes statistical tables, graphs, etc. in the text.
Note: there is also an annual report of the association, free to subscribers to either of the other two titles.

785 Ausgewählte Zahlen zur Energiewirtschaft [Selected figures on energy production] (SB, Wiesbaden).
Kohlhammer, Mainz
monthly & annual. DM 8.90 each issue; 1983 annual DM 10.30. *De.
Abstracts of production and consumption in the entire field of power supply.

Δ B – v, continued

786 Fachserie 4: Produzierendes Gewerbe. Reihe 6: Energie- und Wasserversorgung [Production industries. Series 6: Energy and water supply] (SB, Wiesbaden).
Kohlhammer, Mainz.
(annual) 2 vols. *De.
Contents:
1: Employment, turnover, investments and cost structure of enterprises of power and water supply (1982, published 1984. DM 11.60)
4: Power generating plants of local units in mining and manufacturing (1983, published 1984. DM 4.40).

787 Jahresbericht [Annual report].
Wirtschaftsverband Erdöl- und Erdgasgewinnung eV [Petroleum and Natural Gas Production Trade Association], Brühlstrasse 9, 3000 Hannover 1.
1945- 1983. free. 56p. *De.
TF: the 1983 report, published in 1984, has data for 1981, 1982 & 1983.
Production, drilling, etc. in the various German fields by the various companies. Also some statistics on other countries.
Note: the association also issues a small statistical brochure 'Erdgas und Erdöl in Zahlen' annually.

788 Gasstatistik, Berichtsjahr [Gas statistics, year under review].
Bundesverband der Deutschen Gas- und Wasserwirtschaft eV, Euskirchener Strasse 80, 5300 Bonn 1.
(annual) 1983. DM 82.50. 398p. *De.
TF: the 1983 edition, published late 1984, has data for 1983 and some earlier years in some tables.
Includes data on the structure of the industry, production, finances, deliveries and customers payments, storage, distribution, investment, operations, etc.
Note: Lände volumes are also available, DM 59.75 each.

789 Die Öffentliche Elektrizitätsversorgung [Public electricity provision] (Vereinigung Deutscher Elektrizitätswerke eV).
Verlags- und Wirtschaftsgesellschaft der Elektrizitätswerke mbH, Stresemannallee 23, 6000 Frankfurt/Main 70.
(annual) 1984. not priced. 56p. *De.
TF: the 1984 edition, published in 1985, has data for 1984 and one or two earlier years in some tables.
A general summary on public electricity provision, including some statistical tables in the text and also a section of statistical tables.

790 Die Elektrizitätswirtschaft in der Bundesrepublik Deutschland [The electricity industry in the Federal Republic of Germany] (Bundesministerium für Wirtschaft: Elektrizitätswirtschaft).
BMWI, Langsdorf Strasse, 5300 Bonn.
1956- 1984. not priced. 45p. *De.
TF: the 1984 edition, published late 1985, has data for 1984.
Data on the total electricity industry, public electricity supply, electricity for industry, and electricity for railways.
Note: the monthly 'Elektrizitätswirtschaft' includes more up-to-date figures.

Δ C External trade

791 Fachserie 7: Aussenhandel. Reihe 1: Zusammenfassende Übersichten für den Aussenhandel [Foreign trade. Series 1: General summary of foreign trade] (SB, Wiesbaden).
Kohlhammer, Mainz.
monthly & annual. DM 8.90 for monthly issues; 1983 annual DM 15.90. *De.
TF: each issue is published four or five weeks after the end of the period covered.
Summary statistical tables on foreign trade in goods, trade in improved goods, foreign trade including invisible trade, warehousing in bond, etc.

792 Fachserie 7: Aussenhandel. Reihe 2: Aussenhandel nach Waren und Ländern (Spezialhandel) [Foreign trade. Series 2: Foreign trade by commodities and countries (special trade)] (SB, Wiesbaden).
Kohlhammer, Mainz.
monthly. DM 24.90 each issue.
TF: each issue has data for the month and cumulated figures for the year to date, and is published about two months after the period covered.
Statistics of imports and exports arranged by commodities subdivided by countries of origin and destination.
Note: an annual supplement, 'Ergänzungheft 1: Lagerverkehr, Ubergang von Waren aus dem Veredelungsverkehr in den freien Verkehr, Zollerträge, Ausfuhr (Spezialhandel) von Waren ausländischen Ursprungs [Supplement 1: Foreign trade by commodities and countries (special trade). Customs storage trade, transfer of goods from improvement trade to free circulation, customs revenue, exports (special trade) of goods of foreign origin] (1983, published 1984. DM 24.50).

793 Fachserie 7: Aussenhandel. Reihe 3: Aussenhandel nach Ländern und Warengruppen (Spezialhandel) [Foreign trade. Series 3: Foreign trade by countries and commodity groups (special trade)] (SB, Wiesbaden).
Kohlhammer, Mainz.
half-yearly. DM 24.90 each issue. *De.
TF: each issue has data for the half-year and the second issue each year has annual figures also; each issue is published about two months after the end of the period covered.
Statistics of imports and exports are arranged by countries of origin and destination subdivided by commodity groups.
Note: there are also annual supplementary volumes; Supplement 1: imports by countries of production and of purchase and by commodity groups (1983. DM 18.70) and Supplement 2: exports by countries of consumption and of sale and by commodity groups (1983. DM 21.50).

Δ C, continued

794 Fachserie 7: Aussenhandel. Reihe 4: Aussenhandel mit ausgewählten Waren. 1: Ein- und Ausfuhr von Mineralöl (Generalhandel) [Foreign trade. Series 4: Foreign trade with selected commodities. 1: Imports and exports of mineral oil (general trade)] (SB, Wiesbaden).
Kohlhammer, Mainz.
monthly. DM 7.40. *De.
TF: each issue has data for the month of the issue and cumulated figures for the year to date, the December issue containing annual figures.

795 Fachserie 7: Aussenhandel. Reihe 5: Aussenhandel mit ausgewählten Ländern [Foreign trade. Series 5: Foreign trade with selected foreign countries] (SB, Wiesbaden).
Kohlhammer, Mainz.
1978- 2 titles. *De.
Contents:
5.1: Foreign trade with the developing countries - special trade (annual. 1983. DM 15.90).
5.2: Trade with the state trading countries (2-yearly. 1982. DM 8.10).

796 Fachserie 7: Aussenhandel. Reihe 6: Durchfuhr im Seeverkehr und Seeumschlag [Foreign trade. Series 6: Transit trade in sea-borne transport and transhipment] (SB, Wiesbaden).
Kohlhammer, Mainz.
(annual) 1984. DM 8.90. 49p. *De.
TF: the 1984 edition, published in 1985, has data for 1984.
Trade by ports, by commodity groups, by the EEC transport classification, by countries, etc.

797 Fachserie 7: Aussenhandel. Reihe 7: Aussenhandel nach Ländern und Warengruppen der Industriestatistik (Spezialhandel) [Foreign trade. Series 7: Foreign trade by countries and commodity groups of industry statistics (special trade)] (SB, Wiesbaden).
Kohlhammer, Mainz.
(annual) 1983. DM 8.60. *De.
TF: the 1983 edition, published in 1984, has data for 1983.
Main tables show statistics of imports and exports arranged by countries of origin and destination subdivided by commodity groups of the classification for industrial statistics.

798 Foreign trade according to the Standard International Trade Classification (SITC-Rev II) - special trade (SB, Wiesbaden).
Kohlhammer, Mainz.
(annual) 1983. DM 21.50. 323p. *En.
TF: the 1983 edition, published in 1984, has data for 1983.
An English language summary of the foreign trade of the Federal Republic, arranged by commodities subdivided by countries of origin and destination. Data is given in both quantities and values, DM & US$. The German version is published as Fachserie 7, Reihe 8: Aussenhandel nach dem Internationalen Warenverzeichnis für den Aussenhandel (SITC-Rev II) und Ländern (Spezialhandel) (1983 edition: DM 24.50).

799 Fachserie 6: Handel, Gastgewerbe, Reiseverkehr. Reihe 6: Warenverkehr mit der Deutschen Demokratischen Republik und Berlin (Ost) [Commerce, hotel and restaurant trade, tourism. Series 6: Trade in goods with the German Democratic Republic and East Berlin] (SB, Wiesbaden).
Kohlhammer, Mainz.
monthly & annual. DM 8.80 each monthly issue; 1983 annual DM 11.60. *De.
Statistics of trade arranged by commodity groups, type of transport and border crossing points used.

800 Fachserie 17: Preise. Reihe 8: Preise und Preisindizes für die Ein- und Ausfuhr [Prices and price indices for imports and exports] (SB, Wiesbaden).
Kohlhammer, Mainz.
monthly & annual. DM 5.90 each monthly issue; 1983 annual is DM 18.70. *De.

Δ D Internal distribution and service trades

801 Handels- und Gaststättenzählung [Census of distribution] (SB, Wiesbaden).
Kohlhammer, Mainz.
1968- 2nd, 1979. 9 vols. *De.
Contents:
Grosshandel [Wholesale trade]
1. Enterprises of wholesale trade (DM 13.40.o.p)
2. Multi-unit enterprises of wholesale trade (DM 10.40)
3. Local units of wholesale trade (DM 14.20)
Handelsvermittlung [Agents and brokers business]
1. Enterprises of agents and brokers business (DM 11.60)
2. Multi-unit enterprises... (DM 9.20)
3. Local units of agents... (DM 12.90)
Einzelhandel [Retail trade]
1. Enterprises of retail trade (DM 10.90.o.p)
2. Multi-unit enterprises as well as enterprises by type of operation of retail trade (DM 10.40)
3. Local units of retail trade (DM 14.20)
4. Stores of retail trade (DM 14.20)
Gastegewerbe [Hotel and restaurant industry]
1. Enterprises of the hotel and restaurant industry (DM 7.20)
2. Multi-unit enterprises and local units of the hotel and restaurant trade (DM 10.40).

Δ D – i Wholesale and retail trades

802 Hauptgemeinschaft des Deutschen Einzelhandels...Arbeitsbericht [Federation of German Retail T^ade...Work report].
Hauptgemeinschaft des Deutschen Einzelhandels, Sachsenring 89, 5000 Köln 1.
1948– 1983. not priced. 163p. *De.
TF: the 1983 report, published in 1984, has data for three or four years to 1983.
Includes statistical tables on taxation, enterprises and turnover in retail trade.

803 Fachserie 6: Handel, Gastgewerbe, Reiseverkehr. Reihe 1: Grosshandel [Commerce, hotel & restaurant trade, tourism. Series 1: Wholesale trade] (SB, Wiesbaden).
Kohlhammer, Mainz.
1978– 3 titles. *De.
Contents:
1: Persons engaged and turnover in wholesale trade – index numbers (monthly. DM 4.40 each issue)
2: Employment, turnover, purchases of goods, stocks and investments in wholesale trade (annual. 1981. DM 15.90)
3: Range of goods sold as well as supply and marketing channels in wholesale trade (irregular. 1980. DM 24.50).

804 Fachserie 6: Handel, Gastgewerbe, Reiseverkehr. Reihe 3: Einzelhandel [Commerce, hotel and restaurant trade, tourism. Series 2: Retail trade] (SB, Wiesbaden).
Kohlhammer, Mainz.
3 titles. *De.
1. Persons engaged and turnover in retail trade – index numbers (monthly. DM 4.40 each issue)
2. Employment, turnover, purchase of goods, stocks and investments in retail trade (1983. DM 10.30)
3. Range of goods sold, as well as supply channels in retail trade (irregular. 1979. DM 2‾.50).

805 Fachserie 6: Handel, Gastgewerbe, Reiseverkehr. Reihe 5: Warenverkehr mit Berlin (West) [Commerce, hotel and restaurant trade, tourism. Series 5: trade in goods with Berlin (West)] (SB, Wiesbaden).
Kohlhammer, Mainz.
(annual) 1984 (published in 1985). DM 2.90. *De.
Arranged by commodity groups, methods of transport and border control posts, etc.

806 Fachserie 17: Preise. Reihe 6: Index der Grosshandelsverkaufspreise [Prices. Series 6: Index of wholesale prices] (SB, Wiesbaden).
Kohlhammer, Mainz.
monthly & annual. DM 4.40 each monthly issue; 1983 annual DM 10.30. *De.

807 Fachserie 2: Unternehmen und Arbeitsstätten. Reihe 1: Konstruktur in ausgewählten Wirtschaftszweigen. 3: Kostenstruktur im Einzelhandel [Enterprises and local units. Series 1: Cost structure in selected branches of economic activity. 3: Cost structure in retail trade] (SB, Wiesbaden).
Kohlhammer, Mainz.
(4-yearly) 1981. DM 13.60. *De.

808 Fachserie 2. Unternehmen und Arbeitsstätten. Reihe 1: Kostenstruktur in ausgewählten Wirtschaftszweigen. 2: Grosshandel...[Enterprises and local units. Series 1: Cost structure in selected branches of economic activity. 2: Wholesale trade, commercial representatives and agents, publishing trade] (SB, Wiesbaden).
Kohlhammer, Mainz.
(4-yearly) 1980 (published in 1982). 2 vols. *De.
Contents:
Vol 1: Cost structure in wholesale trade, publishing etc. (DM 14.20)
Vol 2: Cost structure of commercial representatives and agents (DM 13.60).

809 SB in Zahlen [SB in figures] (Institut für Selbstbedienung und Warenwirtschaft).
Verlag Gesellschaft für Selbstbedienung GmbH, Burgmauer 53, 5000 Köln 1.
(annual) 1984. DM 34.10. 320p. *De.
TF: the 1984 edition, published late 1984, has data for 1983.
Development and structure of department stores, compares the management and activities of stores, and includes data on sales, etc.

810 SB-Warenhaus-report (SB-department store-report] (Institut für Selbstbedienung und Warenwirtschaft).
Verlag Gesellschaft für Selbstbedienung GmbH, Burgmauer 53, 5000 Köln 1.
(biennial) 1984. DM 288. 492p. *De.
TF: the 1984 edition, published late 1984, has data for 1983.
Structure, range, performance, costs, etc. of department stores.

Δ D – ii Service trades

811 Fachserie 2: Unternehmen und Arbeitsstätten. Reihe 1: Kostenstruktur in ausgewählten Wirtschaftzweigen. 4: Kostenstruktur im Gastegewerbe [Enterprises and local units. Series 1: Cost structure in selected branches of economic activity. 4: Cost structure of the hotel and catering industry] (SB, Wiesbaden).
Kohlhammer, Mainz.
(4-yearly) 1981. DM 7. 35p. *De.
TF: the 1981 edition, published in 1983, has data for 1981.

Δ D – ii, continued

812 Fachserie 2: Unternehmen und Arbeitsstätten. Reihe 1: Kostenstruktur in ausgewählten Wirtschaftszweigen. 6: Freie Berufe [Enterprises and local units. Series 1: Cost structure in selected branches of economic activity. 6: Liberal professions] (SB, Wiesbaden).
Kohlhammer, Mainz.
(4-yearly) 1979. 2 vols. *De.
Contents:
Vol 1: Cost structure of physicians, dentists, veterinarians (DM 7.20)
Vol 2: Cost structure of lawyers and notaries public, of auditors and tax consultants, of architects and consulting engineers (DM 8.60).

813 Wasserstatistik, Berichtsjähr... [Water statistics...].
Bundesverband der Deutschen Gas- und Wasserwirtschaft eV, Euskirschener Strasse 80, D-5300 Bonn 1.
1889- 1983. DM 88. 469p. *De.
TF: the 1983 edition, published late 1984, has data for 1983 and some earlier years in some tables.
Includes data on demand and supply, deliveries, distribution, investment, operations, etc.
Note: Lände volumes are also available, DM 52 each.

814 Fachserie 6: Handel, Gastgewerbe, Reiseverkehr. Reihe 2: Handelsvermittlung... [Commerce, hotel and restaurant industry, tourism. Series 2: Agents and brokers business] (SB, Wiesbaden).
Kohlhammer, Mainz.
(annual) 1981. DM 14.40. *De.
Employment, turnover, purchases of goods, stocks and investments in the agents and brokers business.

815 Fachserie 6: Handel, Gastgewerbe, Reiseverkehr. Reihe 4: Gastgewerbe [Commerce, hotel and restaurant trade, tourism. Reihe 4: Hotel and restaurant industry] (SB, Wiesbaden).
Kohlhammer, Mainz.
3 titles. *De.
Contents:
1. Persons engaged and turnover in hotel and restaurant industry – index numbers (monthly. DM 1.60 each issue)
2. Employment, turnover, purchase of goods, stocks and investments in the hotel and restaurant industry (1983 edition published early 1986. DM 7.50)
3. Range of goods available in the hotel and restaurant industry (irregular. 1980. DM 4.40).

Δ D – iv Tourism and travel

816 Fachserie 6: Handel, Gastgewerbe, Reiseverkehr. Reihe 7: Reiseverkehr [Commerce, hotel and restaurant trade, tourism. Series 7: Tourism] (SB, Wiesbaden).
Kohlhammer, Mainz.
4 titles. *De.
Contents:
1. Overnights in accommodation units (monthly. DM 8.80 each issue).
2. Accommodation capacity (6-yearly. 1981. DM 15.90)
3. Holiday and recreation trips (annual. 1982. DM 8.10)
4. Frontier crossing tourism (annual. 1983. DM 4.40).

Δ E Population

817 Volks- und Berufszählung [Population and occupational census] (SB, Wiesbaden).
Kohlhammer, Mainz.
1950- 1970. 26 vols. *De.
TF: a census is usually taken about every ten years; however, the next census is to be taken in 1987.
Contents:
Vol 1: Basic methodology for country and provinces (DM 3)
Vol 2: Basic methodology for districts (DM 13)
Vol 3: General results by country and provinces (DM 3)
Vol 4: General results by district (DM 11)
Vol 5: Age and family status (DM 15)
Vol 6: Population by regions (DM 8)
Vol 7: Births (DM 4)
Vol 8: Population by households (DM 9)
Vol 9: Population by families (DM 6)
Vol 10: Children and young people in families (DM 7)
Vol 11: Population in institutions (DM 6)
Vol 12: Older citizens (DM 13)
Vol 13: Economic development and demographic characteristics of the population (DM 6)
Vol 14: Development of the population by income groups (DM 15)
Vol 15: Population by livelihood (DM 11)
Vol 16: Occupational activities of women and mothers (DM 9)
Vol 17: Population gainfully employed in regular work (DM 11)
Vol 18: Population gainfully employed and their net wages (DM 6)
Vol 19: The gainfully employed in social, socio-economic and professional groups (DM 15)
Vol 20: Gainfully employed professional and senior people (DM 15)
Vol 21: Commuters (DM 10)
Vol 22: Expellees and Germans from the DDR (DM 8)
Vol 23: Foreigners (DM 7)
Vol 24: Statistical survey of international comparisons (DM 13)
Vol 25 & 26: Survey of the method & accurancy of the census (DM 16.90 & DM 11.20).

Δ E, continued

818 Fachserie 1: Bevölkerung und Erwerbstätigkeit. Reihe 2: Ausländer [Population and employment. Series 2:- Foreigners] (SB, Wiesbaden).
Kohlhammer, Mainz.
(annual) 1983. DM 10 30. 64p. *De.
TF: the 1983 edition, published in 1984, has data as at 30 September 1983.
Numbers of aliens by country of origin, age, marital status, sex, length of stay, for the country as a whole, by provinces and cities.

819 Fachserie 1: Bevölkerung und Erwerbstätigkeit. Reihe 3: Haushalte und Familien (Ergebnisse des Microzensus) [Population and employment. Series 3: Households and families (results of the microcensus)] (SB Wiesbaden).
Kohlhammer, Mainz.
(annual) 1982 (published in 1983). DM 15. 164p. *De.
Detailed data on private households, members of households, families, women and mothers, foreigners, children and young people.

820 Fachserie 1: Bevölkerung und Erwerbstätigkeit. Reihe 1: Gebiet und Bevölkerung [Population and employment. Series 1: area and population] (SB, Wiesbaden).
Kohlhammer, Mainz.
quarterly & annual. DM 4.40 each quarterly issue; 1983 annual issue DM 19.10. *De.
The average population and registered population of the country and of the provinces, and trends in migration and population movement.

Δ E - ii Labour

821 Fachserie 1: Bevölkerung und Erwerbstätigkeit. Reihe 4: Erwerbstätigkeit [Population and employment. Series 4: Employment] (SB, Wiesbaden).
Kohlhammer, Mainz.
1978- *De.
Contents:
4.1.1: State and development of employment (annual. 1983. DM 14.40)
4.1.2: Occupation, training and working conditions of economically active persons (2-yearly. 1982. DM 12.20)
2: Persons engaged subject to social insurance contributions (quarterly and annual. DM 4.40 each quarterly; 1983 annual DM 11.60)
3: Strikes and lock-outs (1982. DM 2.70. Later issues to be issued by the Ministry of Labour).

822 Amtliche Nachrichten der Bundesanstalt für Arbeit [Official news of the Federal Institute for Labour].
Bundesanstalt für Arbeit, Regensburger Strasse 104, 8500 Nürnberg 1.
1953- monthly. DM 9; DM 100 including special issues eg., 'Arbeitsstatistik - Jahreszalen' (DM 15 alone).
ISSN 0007-585X. *De.
TF: each issue has long runs of figures to the latest available.
Includes detailed statistical tables on the labour market, unemployment insurance and assistance, and budget and finance in West Germany. All tables subdivided by industry and by province, city, etc.

Δ E - iii Housing

< see 778

Δ F Social and political

< see also 819

Δ F - i Standard of living

< see also 391

823 Fachserie 16: Löhne und Gehälter. Reihe 1: Arbeiterverdienste in der Landwirtschaft [Wages and salaries. Series 1: earnings of agricultural workers] (SB, Wiesbaden).
Kohlhammer, Mainz.
(annual) 1983. DM 1.60. 4p. *De.
TF: the 1983 edition, published in 1983, has data for 1981, 1982 & 1983.

824 Fachserie 16: Löhne und Gehälter. Reihe 2: Arbeitnehmerverdienste in Industrie und Handel [Wages and salaries. Series 2: Earnings of employees in industry and trade] (SB, Wiesbaden).
Kohlhammer, Mainz.
(quarterly) 2 vols each quarter. *De.
Contents:
1: Earnings of wage earners in industry (DM 7.40 each issue)
2: Earnings of salaried employees in industry and commerce (DM 10.30 each issue).
Note: quarterlies with preliminary figures are also published (DM 1.60 each issue).

825 Fachserie 16: Löhne und Gehälter. Reihe 3: Arbeiterverdienste im Handwerk [Wages and salaries. Series Earnings of wage earners in handicrafts] (SB, Wiesbaden).
Kohlhammer, Mainz.
(half-yearly) DM 2.90 each issue. *De.

Δ F - i, continued

826 Fachserie 16: Löhne und Gehälter. Reihe 4: Tariflöhne und Tarifgehälter [Wages and salaries. Series 4:Agreed wages and salaries] (SB, Wiesbaden).
Kohlhammer, Mainz.
4 parts. *De.
Contents:
1: Agreed wages (half-yearly. DM 18.70 each issue)
2: Agreed salaries (half-yearly DM 11.60 each issue)
3: Index of agreed wages and salaries (quarterly. DM 4.40 each issue)
4: Salaries of Federal government officials (irregular. 1983. DM 1.50).

827 Gehalts- und Lohnstrukturerhebung [Survey of salary and wage structure] (SB, Wiesbaden).
Kohlhammer, Mainz.
1972- 2nd, 1978. DM 9.80. *De.
Earnings of wage earners and salaried employees in production industries, wholesale and retail trade, credit institutions and insurance.

828 Fachserie 17: Preise. Reihe 7: Preise und Preisindizes für die Lebenshaltung [Prices. Series 7: Consumer prices and price indices] (SB, Wiesbaden).
Kohlhammer, Mainz.
monthly & annual. DM 8.80 each monthly issue; 1983 annual issue DM 15.90. *De.
Note: a monthly with preliminary figures is also issued (DM 1.60 each issue).

829 Fachserie 15: Wirtschaftsrechnungen. Reihe 1: Einnahmen und Ausgaben ausgewählter privater Haushalte [Family budget surveys. 1: Income and expenditure of selected private households] (SB, Wiesbaden).
Kohlhammer, Mainz.
quarterly & annual. DM 2.90 each quarterly issue; 1983 annual DM 14.40. *De.
TF: the quarterly issues appear about four months after the end of the period covered and contain data for the quarter, with data for the corresponding period the previous for comparison.
Income and expenditure of selected types of private households - 2-person household of recipients of pensions and welfare benefits with little income; 4-person households of wage earners and salaried employees with medium income; and 4-person households of officials and salaried employees within the upper income group.

Δ F - ii Health and welfare

830 Fachserie 12: Gesundheitswesen. Reihe 1: Ausgewählte Zahlen für das Gesundheitswesen [Public health. Series 1: selected figures on public health] (SB, Wiesbaden).
Kohlhammer, Mainz.
(annual) 1983. DM 11.80. 89p. *De.
TF: the 1983 edition published late 1985, has data for 1983.
Population, health insurance, occupational diseases, notifiable diseases, causes of death, public health service employment, hospitals, accidents, etc.

831 Fachserie 12: Gesundheitswesen. Reihe 2: Meldepflichtige [Public health. Series 2: Notifiable diseases] (SB, Wiesbaden).
Kohlhammer, Mainz.
(annual) 1983 (published in 1984). DM 10.30. *De.

832 Fachserie 12: Gesundheitswesen. Reihe 3: Schwangerschaftsabbrüche [Public health. Series 3: abortions] (SB, Wiesbaden).
Kohlhammer, Mainz.
(annual) 1983 (published in 1984. DM 2.90. *De.

833 Fachserie 12: Gesundheitswesen. Reihe 4: Todesursachen [Public health. Series 4: Causes of death] (SB, Wiesbaden).
Kohlhammer, Mainz.
quarterly & annual. DM 1.40 each quarterly issue; 1982 annual issue DM 11.60. *De.

834 Fachserie 12: Gesundheitswesen. Reihe 5: Berufe des Gesundheitswesen [Public health. Series 5: Public health occupations] (SB, Wiesbaden).
Kohlhammer, Mainz.
(annual) 1982 (published in 1984). DM 4.40. 24p. *De.
Doctors and dentists by specialisation, province and sex; doctors who have qualified during the year; public health offices and personel; chemists; and numbers of employed in public health by province, occupation and sex.

835 Fachserie 2: Gesundheitswesen. Reihe 6: Krankenhäuser [Public health. Series 6: Hospitals] (SB, Wiesbaden).
Kohlhammer, Mainz.
(annual) 1983. DM 5.90. 36p. *De.
TF: the 1983 edition was published late 1985, with data for 1983.
Numbers of hospitals, beds, ailments treated, patients, staff, births and deaths.

Δ F – ii, continued

836 Fachserie 13: Sozialleistungen [Social security schemes] (SB, Wiesbaden).
Kohlhammer, Mainz.
(annual) 7 titles. *De.
Contents:
1: Persons insured in health and pension insurance (irregular. 1982. DM 9.70 published in 1984)
2: Public assistance (1982. DM 10.30 published in 1984)
3: Additional aid to war victims (1983. DM 5.70 published in 1984)
4: Housing allowances (1983. DM 10.30 published in 1984)
5: Handicapped persons and rehabilitation measures:
5.1: Handicapped persons (2-yearly. 1981. DM 10.40)
5.2: Rehabilitation measures (1980. DM 10.40)
6: Youth welfare:
6.1: Educational assistance and expenditure on youth welfare (1982. DM 10.30)
6.2: Provision of youth work in the framework of youth welfare (4-yearly. 1982. DM 5.90)
6.3: Established and active people in youth welfare (annual. 1982. DM 14.70).

Δ F – iii Education and leisure

837 Fachserie 11: Bildung und Kultur. Reihe 1: Allgemeines Schulwesen [Education and culture. Series 1: general education] (SB, Wiesbaden).
Kohlhammer, Mainz.
(annual) 1984 (published late 1985). DM 14.70. 122p. *De.
A general analysis of numbers of pupils, classes, teachers, foreign pupils, schools, school leavers, etc.

838 Bildung im Zahlenspiegel [Education in figures] (SB, Wiesbaden).
Kohlhammer, Mainz.
(annual) 1984 (published in 1985). DM 15.90. *De.
Summary of statistical data from a large number of surveys, classified by spheres of education. Useful for educational planning.

839 Fachserie 11: Bildung und Kultur. Reihe 2: Berufliches Schulwesen [Education and culture. Series 2: Vocational education] (SB, Wiesbaden).
Kohlhammer, Mainz.
(annual) 1983 (published in 1984). DM 18.70. *De.
Students, courses, technical schools, etc.

840 Fachserie 11: Bildung und Kultur. Reihe 3: Berufliche Bildung [Education and culture. Series 2: Vocational training] (SB, Wiesbaden).
Kohlhammer, Mainz.
(annual) 1984 (published in 1984). DM 14.40. *De.
Numbers of institutions offering training, numbers receiving training, occupations for which training is given, examinations, etc.

841 Fachserie 11: Bildung und Kultur. Reihe 4: Hochschulen [Education and culture. Series 4: Universities] (SB, Wiesbaden).
Kohlhammer, Mainz.
In four parts. *De.
Contents:
4.1: Students at university (Winter & Summer semesters. Winter semester, 1983/84. DM 15; Summer semester, 1984. DM 15.90; Preliminary issues DM 5.70 each)
4.2: Examinations at universities (annual. 1982. DM 18.70)
4.4: Personnel at universities (annual. 1982. DM 15)
4.5: Finances of universities (annual. 1982. DM 8.60).

842 Fachserie 11: Bildung und Kultur. Reihe 5: Presse [Education and culture. Series 5: The press] (SB, Wiesbaden).
Kohlhammer, Mainz.
1975- 1982. DM 11.60. *De.
TF: the 1982 edition, published in 1984, has data for 1982.
Book, newspaper and magazine publishing, including editorial policy, turnover, employees, prices,

843 Fachserie 11: Bildung und Kultur. Reihe 6: Filmwirtschaft [Education and culture. Series 5: The film industry] (SB, Wiesbaden).
Kohlhammer, Mainz.
2-yearly. 1981. DM 8.10. *De.
TF: the 1981 edition, published in 1983, has data for 1981. Prior to 1981 it was issued annually.
Companies in and connected with the film industry; production of films; employment; distribution; numbers of cinemas, including number of seats, performances, turnover, etc.

844 Fachserie 11: Bildung und Kultur. Reihe 7: Ausbildungsförerung [Education and culture. Series 7: Government-sponsored promotion of education] (SB, Wiesbaden).
Kohlhammer, Mainz.
1982- 1983 (published in 1984). DM 8.90. *De.

Δ F – iii, continued

845 Filmstatistisches Taschenbuch [Film statistics pocketbook].
Spitzenorganisation der Filmwirtschaft eV, Langenbeckstrasse 9, (Postfach 5129) 6200 Wiesbaden 1.
(annual) 1984. DM 18.50. 55p. ISSN 0071-4941. *De.
TF: the 1984 edition, published in September 1984, has data for 1983 and long runs of earlier figures.
Mainly statistical tables on film production, film hire, film theatres, film attendance, types of film shown, etc. Also international data and films/videos shown on television, etc.

Δ F – iv Justice

846 Fachserie 10: Rechtspflege [Justice] (SB, Wiesbaden).
Kohlhammer, Mainz.
(annual) 5 parts. *De.
Contents:
1: Selected figures on the administration of justice (1982, published 1983. (DM 8.60)
2: Civil courts and criminal courts (1981, published 1982. DM 14.20)
3: Criminal statistics of the courts (1983, published 1984. DM 12.90)
4: Execution of sentences (1983, published 1984. DM 7.40)
5: Probation service (1983, published 1984. DM 11.60).

Δ F – vi Elections

847 Wahl zum Deutschen Bundestag [Elections to the German Parliament] (SB, Wiesbaden).
Kohlhammer, Mainz.
1948- 10th, 1983. 5 vols. *De.
TF: an election is held every four years.
Contents:
Vol 1: Results and comparative figures of previous elections to the Bundestag and to the Landtage, as well as structural data for the 1983 Bundestag constituencies (DM 11)
Vol 2: Preliminary results by constituency (DM 9.70)
Vol 3: Final results by constituency (DM 11)
Vol 4: Electoral participation of and votes cast by men and women, according to age (DM 9.70)
Vol 5: Textual evaluation of the election results (DM 18.70).
Note: also a special report on candidates for election to the 10th Bundestag (DM 17.70).

848 Wahl und Abgeordneten des Europäischen Parlaments aus der Bundesrepublik Deutschland [Elections of the members from the Federal Republic of Germany for the European Parliament] (SB Wiesbaden).
Kohlhammer, Mainz.
1979- 1984. 5 vols. *De.
TF: elections are five-yearly, the results of the 1984 elections were published in 1984.
Contents:
1: Results and comparative figures of the 1979 election to the European Parliament and earlier elections to the Bundestag and the Landtage, as well as structural data for the towns not attached to a 'Landkreis' and the 'Landkreise'. (DM 14.40)
2: Provisional results... (DM 7.40)
3: Final results... (DM 10.30)
4: Voting... (DM 8.60)
5: Textual evaluation... (DM 16.20).

Δ G Finance

849 Monthly report of the Deutsche Bundesbank.
Deutsche Bundesbank, Wilhelm-Epstein-Strasse 14, (Postfach 100602), D-6000 Frankfurt/Main 1.
1949- not priced. ISSN 0418-8292. *En & De eds.
TF: each issue has data for three or more years and 12 or more months to about two months prior to the date of the issue.
Includes an overall monetary survey and statistical sections on the activities of the bank and other banks, minimum reserves, interest rates, reserves, capital market, public finance, general economic conditions, foreign trade and payments.
Note: the English version is not so detailed as the German version; and the bank's annual report, in En & De, contains a few financial statistics in the text as well as the accounts of the bank.

Δ G – i Banking

850 Verband der Privaten Bauspartassen: Bericht... [Association of Private Savings-Banks: report...].
Verband der Privaten Bausparkassen eV, Dottendorfer Strasse 82, 5300 Bonn 1.
1948- 1983. free. 69p. *De.
TF: the 1983 report, published in 1984, has data for 1983 and some earlier years.
Includes some statistics in the text of the report and a statistical section with a variety of statistics on the finances, etc. of private savings banks, for the Federal Republic as a whole and for the provinces.

Δ G - ii Public finance

851 Fachserie 18: Volkswirtschaftliche Gesamtrechnungen. Reihe 1: Konten und Standardtabellen [National accounts. Series 1: Accounts and standard tables] (SB Wiesbaden).
Kohlhammer, Mainz.
(annual) 1983. DM 21.50. 396p. *De.
TF: the 1983 edition, published in 1984, has data for 1983 and many earlier years.
Note: a preliminary annual issue is also published (1983. DM 12.90), and revised results for 1960 to 1981 were published as a special report, Reihe S.5, in 1981.

852 Fachserie 18: Volkswirtschaftliche Gesamtrechnungen. Reihe 2: Input-Output-Tabellen [National accounts. Series 2: Input-output tables] (SB, Wiesbaden).
Kohlhammer, Mainz.
(irregular) 1980. DM 18.70. *De.

853 Fachserie 14: Finanzen und Steuern. Reihe 2: Vierteljährliche Kassenergebnisse der öffentlichen Haushalte [Finance and taxes: Series 2: quarterly accounts of public housekeeping] (SB, Wiesbaden).
Kohlhammer, Mainz.
(quarterly) DM 7.40 each issue. *De.
Income and expenditure of federal and local authorities.

854 Fachserie 14: Finanzen und Steuern. Reihe 3: Rechnungsergebnisse [Finance and taxes. Series 3: Accounting results] (SB, Wiesbaden).
Kohlhammer, Mainz.
(annual) 1982. 4 vols. *De.
Contents:
3.1: Accounting results of the public overall budget (DM 21.50)
3.3: Accounting results of communal budgets (DM 21.50)
3.4: Accounting results of public budgets in education, science and culture (DM 18.70)
3.5: Accounting results relating to social security and for public health, sports and recreation (DM 15.90).

855 Fachserie 14: Finanzen und Steuern. Reihe 4: Steuerhaushalt [Finance and taxes. Series 4: Tax budget] (SB, Wiesbaden).
quarterly. DM 4.40 each issue. *De.
Note: prior to 1981 there was also an annual issue.

856 Fachserie 14: Finanzen und Steuern. Reihe 5: Schulden der öffentlichen Haushalte [Finance and taxes. Series 5: Liabilities of public budgets] (SB, Wiesbaden).
Kohlhammer, Mainz.
(annual) 1983 (published in 1984). DM 10.30. *De.

857 Fachserie 14: Finanzen und Steuern. Reihe 6: Personal des öffentlichen Dienstes [Finance and taxes. Series 6: Public service personnel] (SB, Wiesbaden).
Kohlhammer, Mainz.
(annual) 1983 (published in 1984). DM 10.30. *De.

858 Fachserie 14: Finanzen und Steuern. Reihe 7: Einkommen- und Vermögensteuern [Finance and taxes. Series 7: Income and property tax] (SB, Wiesbaden).
Kohlhammer, Mainz.
(triennial) 4 vols. *De.
Contents:
7.1: Income tax (1980. DM 14.40) 7.2: Corporation tax (1977. DM 9.20)
7.3: Wages tax (1980. DM 7) 7.4: Property tax (1980. DM 11.60).
Each volume has detailed statistics.

859 Fachserie 14: Finanzen und Steuern. Reihe 8: Umsatzsteuer [Finance and taxes. Series 8: Turnover tax] (SB, Wiesbaden).
Kohlhammer, Mainz.
(biennial) 1982 (published in 1984). DM 15.90. 176p. *De.
Businesses liable for turnover tax according to economic sector, according to legal form of company, and turnover tax prior to deduction of tax previously charged.

860 Fachserie 14: Finanzen und Steuern. Reihe 9: Verbrauchsteuern [Finance and taxes. Series 9: Excise duties] (SB, Wiesbaden).
Kohlhammer, Mainz.
9 vols. *De.
Contents:
1: Beer tax
  9.1.1. Sales of tobacco & cigarette paper (quarterly. DM 2.90 each issue)
  9.1.2. Tobacco industry (annual. 1983. DM 2.90)
2: Beer tax
  9.2.1. Sales of beer (monthly. DM 1.60 each issue)
  9.2.2. Brewing industry (annual. 1983. DM 4.40)
3: Mineral oil tax (annual. 1983. DM 4.40)
4: Spirits monopoly (annual. 1983. DM 4.40)
5: Sparkling wine tax (annual. 1983. DM 1.60)
6: Petty excise duties
  6.3. Salt tax (annual. 1983. DM 1.60)
  6.5 Sugar tax (annual. 1984. DM 2.90).

Δ G – ii, continued

861 Fachserie 14: Finanzen und Steuern. Reihe 10: Realsteuern. 1: Realsteuern vergleich [Finance and taxes. Series 10.1: Comparison of taxation on real estate, commercial tax and payroll tax] (SB, Wiesbaden).
Kohlhammer, Mainz.
(annual) 1983 (published in 1984). DM 10.30. *De.

Δ G – iii Company finance

< see also 859

862 Fachserie 2: Unternehmen und arbeitsstätten. Reihe 2: Kapitalgesellschaften. 1: Abschlüsse der Aktiengesellschaften [Enterprises and local units. Series 2: Joint stock companies. 1: Accounts...] (SB, Wiesbaden).
Kohlhammer, Mainz.
(annual) 1980 (published in 1981). DM 13.60. 127p. *De.

863 Fachserie 2: Unternehmen und Arbeitsstätten. Reihe 4: Zahlungsschwierigkeiten [Enterprises and local units. Series 4: Insolvencies] (SB, Wiesbaden).
Kohlhammer, Mainz.
2 vols. *De.
Contents:
4.1. Bankruptcy proceedings (monthly. DM 2.90 each issue)
4.2. Financial settlement of bankruptcy proceedings (annual. 1982. DM 4.40).

Δ G – iv Investment

864 Fachserie 9: Geld und Kredit. Reihe 2: Aktienmärkte [Money and credit. Series 2: Share markets] (SB, Wiesbaden).
Kohlhammer, Mainz.
monthly. DM 2.90 each issue. *De.
Stock exchange index, the quotations, dividends, etc. of companies.

865 Börsenstatistik [Stock exchange statistics].
Frankfurter Wertpapierbörse, Postfach 2913, 6000 Frankfurt/Main 1.
monthly. free (not usually sent by mail, but collected from the exchange). *De.
TF: each issue has data for several months and one or two half-year figures to the month of issue, and is published about a month later.
Turnover of stock of German and foreign companies, options, etc.

866 Frankfurter Wertpapierbörse: Jahresbericht [Frankfurt Stock Exchange: annual report].
Frankfurter Wertpaperbörse, Börsenplatz 6, (Postfach 2913, 6000 Frankfurt/Main 1.
(annual) 1983. free. 74p. *En & De eds.
TF: the 1983 report, published in 1984, has data for 1983 and for three or four earlier years.
Mainly concerned with the activities of the Stock Exchange, but includes statistical tables in the text and has a statistical section with details of trade done in shares, bonds, securities, etc. on the Frankfurt Stock Exchange, and some international data on securities admitted to trading and turnover.

867 Personal- und Personalnebenkostenerhebungen [Surveys of personal expenditure and incidental wage expenses] (SB, Wiesbaden).
Kohlhammer, Mainz.
1970- 1981. 2 vols. *De.
TF: issued three-yearly. The 1981 volumes were issued in 1982 and 1983.
Contents:
Aufwendungen der Arbeitgeber im Produzierenden Gewerbe [Expenditure of employers in production industries] (DM 20.30).
Aufwendungen der Arbeitgeber im Gross- und Einzelhandel sowie im Bank- und Versicherungsgewerbe [Expenditure of employers in wholesale and retail trade, as well as in banking and insurance] (DM 14.40).

Δ H Transport and communications

868 Fachserie 8: Verkehr. Reihe 1: Güterverkehr der Verkehrszweige [Transport. Series 1: Good transport by branches of transport] (SB, Wiesbaden).
Kohlhammer, Mainz.
quarterly & annual. DM 7.40 each quarterly issue; 1983 annual DM 11.60. *De.

869 Fachserie 2: Unternehmen und Arbeitsstätten. Reihe 1: Kostenstruktur in ausgewählten Wirtschaftszweigen. 5: Verkehrsgewerbe [Enterprises and local units. Series 1: Cost structure in selected branches of economic activity. 5: Transport industry] (SB, Wiesbaden).
Kohlhammer, Mainz.
(4-yearly) 1979. DM 7.20 each vol. 2 vols. *De.
Contents:
1.5.1. Cost structure of other than Federally owned railways, public road traffic, and travel business (travel agencies)
1.5.2. Cost structure of commercial goods transport by motor vehicles, forwarding trade and warehousing, inland waterways transport (goods transport), sea-borne and coastal shipping.

Δ H, continued

870 Fachserie 17: Preise. Reihe 9: Preise für Verkehrsleistungen [Prices. Series 9: Transport prices] (SB, Wiesbaden).
Kohlhammer, Mainz.
(annual) 1984. DM 7.40. 55p. *De.
TF: the 1984 edition, published December 1985, has long runs of figures to 1984.
Prices for passengers and goods by rail, freight by road, forwarding by rail or road, freight by inland shipping, passengers and freight by air. Price indices of freight by sea, and posts and telecommunications.

Δ H – i Ships and shipping

871 Fachserie 8: Verkehr. Reihe 4: Binnenschiffahrt [Transport. Series 4: Inland shipping] (SB, Wiesbaden).
Kohlhammer, Mainz.
monthly & annual. DM 4.40 each monthyly issue; 1983 annual DM 18.70. *De.
Number of ships, shipping traffic, goods traffic, accidents, and enterprises in inland shipping.

872 Fachserie 8: Verkehr. Reihe 5: Seeschiffahrt [Transport. Series 5: Sea-borne shipping] (SB, Wiesbaden).
Kohlhammer, Mainz.
monthly & annual. DM 4.40 each monthly issue; 1983 annual issue DM 18.70. *De.
Number of flags of ships, destination of goods by product group, types of ship, trade through ports, domestic trade, containerisation, crews, etc.

873 Die Deutscher Küstenschiffahrt...Jahresbericht... [German coastal shipping...annual report... of the German Coastal Shipowners Association].
Verband Deutscher Küstenschiffseigner, Grosse Elbstrasse 36 II, Hamburg 50.
1896- 1983. not priced. 24p. *De.
TF: the 1983 report, published in 1984, has data for 1983.
Includes a statistical section showing shipping tonnage by size of ship, ships built, etc.

Δ H – ii Roads and road transport

874 Fachserie 8: Verkehr. Reihe 3: Strassenverkehr. 1: Strassen, Brücken, parkeinrichtungen [Transport. Series 3: Road transport. 1: Roads, bridges, parking facilities] (SB, Wiesbaden).
Kohlhammer, Mainz.
(irregular) 1976. DM 14.60. *De.
TF: the 1976 edition was published in 1978.
The length of public streets and types of construction; bridges by type of design and construction; and parking places by size, type and number of spaces.

875 Fachserie 8: Verkehr. Reihe 3: Strassenverkehr. 2: Personenverkehr der Strassenverkehrsunternehmen [Transport. Series 3: Road transport. 2: Passenger transport by road carriers] (SB, Wiesbaden).
Kohlhammer, Mainz.
monthly & annual. DM 4.40 each monthly issue; 1983 annual DM 14.40. *De.
Number of carriers, their employees, turnover, types of service, numbers of passengers, fares, and numbers and types of buses and trams.

876 Fachserie 8: Verkehr. Reihe 3: Strassenverkehr. 3: Strassenverkehrsunfälle [Transport. Series 3: Road transport. 3: Road accidents] (SB, Wiesbaden).
Kohlhammer, Mainz.
monthly & annual. DM 4.40 each monthly issue; 1983 annual DM 14.40. *De.

877 Bestand an Kraftfahrzeugen und Kraftfahrzeuganhängern... [Inventory of motor vehicles and trailers] (Kraftfahrt-Bundesamt).
Kirschbaum Verlag, Siegfriedstrasse 28, 5300 Bonn 2.
1955- 1983. not priced. 490p. *De.
TF: the results of the survey taken on 1 July 1983 were published late 1983.
Numbers of private cars, commercial vehicles, motor cycles, etc., by type of vehicle and by region of Germany.

878 Statistische Mitteilungen des Kraftfahrt-Bundesamtes und der Bundesanstalt für den Güterfernverkehr [Statistical information from the Federal Office of Motor Transport and the Federal Institute for Long-distance Raod Haulage] (Kraftfahrt-Bundesamtes und Bundesanstalt für den Güterfernverkehr).
Kirschbaum Verlag, Siegfriedstrasse 28, 5300 Bonn 2.
1955- monthly. DM 14 or DM 144 yr. ISSN 0341-468X. *De.
TF: each issue has data for the month which is two months earlier that the date of the issue.
Up-dates the information in 877 above.

Δ H – iii Railways and rail transport

879 Fachserie 8: Verkehr. Reihe 2: Eisenbahnverkehr [Transport. Series 2: Railway transport] (SB, Wiesbaden).
Kohlhammer, Mainz.
monthly & annual. DM 2.90 each monthly issue; 1983 annual DM 19.10. *De.
Operating performance, including passenger numbers, quantities of goods carried, miles covered; income from services; and a breakdown of goods carried by province.

Δ H – iii, continued

880 V.W.Z: Verkehrswirtschaftliche Zahlen [Railway industry figures].
Bundesverband des Deutschen Güterfernverkehrs (BDF) eV., Haus des Strassenverkehrs, 6000 Frankfurt/Main 93.
(annual) 1983 (published in 1984). *De.

881 BDE-Mitgliederhandbuch [BDE-organisation handbook].
Bundesverband Deutscher Eisenbahnen, Volksgartenstrasse 54a, 5000 Köln 1.
(triennial) 1984/85. DM 40. 278p. *De.
TF: the 1984/85 edition, published in 1985, has data for 1984/85 and some earlier years.
Detailed statistics of railway traffic, rolling stock, lines, track, employment, passenger and goods traffic, etc.
Note: BDE also issues free an annual 'BDE-Faltblatt' and a four-page brochure 'Statistiche Zahlen'.

Δ H – iv Aviation and air transport

882 Fachserie 8: Verkehr. Reihe 6: Luftverkehr [Transport. Series 8: Air transport] (SB, Wiesbaden).
monthly & annual. DM 5.90 each monthly issue; 1983 annual DM 15.90. *De.
Transport of passengers and freight in the Federal Republic and overseas, including numbers of passengers by destination, goods by type of product, traffic at individual airports, employees, number of aircraft, and turnover of airlines.

Δ I Environment, etc

883 Fachserie 19: Umweltschutz. Reihe 1: Abfallbeseitigung [Environment protection. Series 1: Waste removal] (SB Wiesbaden).
Kohlhammer, Mainz.
1975- 1982. 2 vols. *De.
TF: published every two years, the 1982 edition was issued in 1983.
Contents:
1.1. Public waste removal (DM 9.30)
1.2. Waste removal in production industries and hospitals (DM 14.40).

884 Fachserie 19: Umweltschutz. Reihe 2: Wasserversorgung und Abwasserbeseitigung [Environmental protection. Series 2: Water supply and waste-water disposal] (SB, Wiesbaden).
Kohlhammer, Mainz.
1975- 2 vols. *De.
TF: Part 1 is published 4-yearly and part 2 biennially.
Contents:
2.1. Public water supply and waste water disposal (1979. DM 8.10)
2.2. Water supply and waste water disposal in the economy (1981. DM 11).

885 Fachserie 19: Umweltschutz. Reihe 3: Investitionen für Umweltschutz im Produzierenden Gewerbe [Environmental protection. Series 3: Investments for environmental protection in production industries] (SB, Wiesbaden).
Kohlhammer, Mainz.
1975- 1982 (published in 1984). DM 14.40. *De.

GERMAN DEMOCRATIC REPUBLIC
REPUBLIQUE DEMOCRATIQUE ALLEMANDE
DEUTSCHE DEMOKRATISCHE REPUBLIK

Central statistical office

886 Staatliche Zentralverwaltung für Statistik [State Central Administration for Statistics].
Hans-Beimler-Strasse 70/72, 1026 Berlin.
t 230. tx 114872 or 114876 Answerback ZVST DD.
A central organ of the Cabinet Council, the Administration is responsible for accountancy and statistics, and collects and compiles most of the official statistics of the country, both for the use of the government and for publication.

Libraries

The libraries of the Hochschule für Ökonomie [College of Economics], Hermann Duncker Strasse 8, 1157 Berlin-Karlshorst, and of the Deutsche Wirtschaftsinstitut [German Institute of Economics], Clara Zetkin Strasse 112, 108 Berlin, have collections of statistical publications which may be consulted by the public.

Statistical publications

Δ A General

887 Statistisches Jahrbuch der Deutschen Demokratischen Republik [Statistical yearbook of the German Democratic Republic] (Staatliche Zentralverwaltung für Statistik).
Staatsverlag der DDR, Otto-Grotewohl-Strasse 17, 108 Berlin.
1956- 1985. not priced. 552p. ISSN 0323-4258. *De.
TF: the 1985 edition, published mid-1985, has data for 1984 and also 1960, 1970, 1980, 1982-83 in some tables.
Main sections:
Summary - Economics - Finance, prices, consumption - Cultural and social sphere - Population - Representation of the people, national front, political organisation - Geography and meteorology - Appendix includes international data.

888 Statistical pocketbook of the German Democratic Republic (Staatliche Zentralverwaltung für Statistik).
Staatsverlag der DDR, Otto-Grotewohl-Strasse 17, 108 Berlin.
1960- 1984. not priced. 160p. ISSN 0585-1785. *En; also available in DE, Ru, Fr, Es, SV & Arabic.
TF: the 1984 edition, published in 1984, has long runs of figures to 1983.
Territory & population; economic survey; followed by statistical data on industry, construction, crafts, agriculture and forestry, transport, domestic trade, foreign trade, finance, earnings, prices, consumption, culture (education, libraries, publishing, radio & TV, sport, & tourism), public health system, population, geographical and meteorological data, and an international survey.

889 Statistische Praxis [Statistical application] (Staatliche Zentralverwaltung für Statistik).
Staatsverlag der DDR, Otto-Grotewohl-Strasse 17, 108 Berlin.
(monthly) not priced. *De.
Mainly economic and statistical articles, but a 4-page supplement 'Statistische monatszahlen' in each issue contains statistical data on production, retail trade, building, investment, transport, agriculture, etc.

Δ E Population

890 Volks-, Berufs-, Wohnraum- und Gebäudezählung am 31.12.1981 in der Deutschen Demokratischen Republik: ausgewählte Ergebnisse [Population, occupations, housing and building census: selected results at 31.12.1981 in the German Democratic Republic].
Staatliche Zentralverwaltung für Statistik, Hans-Beimler-Strasse 70/72, 1026 Berlin.
1985. not priced. 200p. *De.

Δ E - i Vital statistics

891 Demographic surveys of the German Democratic Republic (State Central Statistical Office).
Staatliche Zentralverwaltung für Statistik, Hans-Beimler-Strasse 70/72, 1026 Berlin.
1983. not priced. 173p. *En.

DK

DENMARK
DANEMARK
DÄNEMARK
DANMARK

Central statistical office

892 Danmarks Statistik [Statistics Denmark].
Sejrøgade 11, Postboks 2550, 2100 København Ø.
t (01) 29 82 22. tx 1 62 36.
Danmarks Statistik is an independent statistical authority, supervised by a Board consisting of the Government Statistician and six persons familiar with social and economic conditions, and is responsible for the preparation of the major part of Denmark's official statistics. It is also the central and co-ordinating body in the production of statistics. Regular monthly statistics of imports and exports of specified commodities or groups of commodities can be supplied on payment of a subscription. Other unpublished information can often be supplied for a fee. Photocopies can also be supplied.
This office has been abbreviated to DS København in entries below.

Libraries

The library of Danmarks Statistik (see above) has all the publications of that organisation, publications of other countries and of international organisations. It is open to the public from 12.00 to 16.00, Monday to Thursday, and 12.00 to 15.00 on Friday. The staff speaks English, German and Danish.
Danish statistical publications are also available for reference in Det Kongelige Bibliotek [the Royal Library], Christians Brygge 8, 1219 København K (t 15 01 11) and in the central libraries, university libraries and commercial libraries in Denmark.

Libraries and information services abroad

The most important statistical publications of Denmark are available in Danish embassies abroad, including:

United Kingdom	Royal Danish Embassy, 55 Sloane Street, London SW1. t 01-235 1255
Canada	Royal Danish Embassy, 85 Range Road, Ottawa K1N 8J6. t 234 0704
USA	Royal Danish Embassy, 3200 Whitehaven Street NW, Washington DC 20008. t (202) 234 4300.

Bibliographies

893 Vejviser i statistikken [Guide to the statistics].
This guide to the publications issued by Danmarks Statistik indicates the individual publications issued as a result of surveys, enquiries and censuses; contents and frequency of serial publications; the existence of unpublished archive data; and information on the methods of collection and processing. It is in Danish and the latest issue, published in 1984, costs DKr 30.33. ISSN 0109-8314.
A complete list of publications of Danmarks Statistik is published in 'Statistisk årbog' (894).

Statistical publications

Δ A General

< see also 076, 077, 078

894 Statistisk årbog [Statistik yearbook].
DS, København.
1887- 1984. DKr 73.77. 28+667p. ISSN 0070-3567. *Da, En.
TF: the 1984 edition, published in 1984, has data for 1983 with figures for earlier years also in some tables.
Mains sections:
Area & population (inc. health) - Environment - Housing - Real property - Agriculture, etc. (forests & plantations, shipping, fur farms) - Manufacturing, construction and commerce - External trade - Transport & communications - Consumption & prices - Insurance - Social security - Earnings & labour market - Justice - Education & culture - Elections - Public finance - Taxes & duties - Assessments of income & property - National accounts - Faroe Islands - Greenland - International tables.

895 Statistisk månedsoversigt [Monthly review of statistics].
DS, København
1984- monthly. DKr 13.93; DKr 139.34 yr including supplement. ISSN 0108-5603. *Da, En.
TF: each issue has data for 5 years and 24 months to about three months prior to the date of the issue.
Essential short-term statistics - population, justice, labour market, incomes, consumption, prices, agriculture, manufacturing industry, energy, construction industry, transport, tourism, general economic statistics, internal trade, external trade, money and credit market, public finance, balance of payments, and international statistics.
Note: replaces 'Konjunkturoversigt' [Economic trends] published from 1936.

Δ A, continued

896 Nyt fra Danmarks Statistik [News from Danmarks Statistik].
DS, København.
approx. 260 issues a year. DKr 586.07 yr. *Da.
A rapid-release service, primarily intended for the news media. It presents summary results of the most important monthly, quarterly and annual enquiries and surveys.

897 Statistisk tiårs-oversigt [Ten-year statistical survey].
DS, København.
1950- 1984. DKr 37.70. 181p. ISSN 0070-3583. *Da.
TF: published annually with data for the past ten years, the 1984 edition, published mid-1984, has data for the years 1974 to 1983.
Data on similar subjects to 'Statistisk årbog' but in less detail. Aims to serve two purposes:- to present comparable annual statistics for the past ten years, and to facilitate the use of statistical information in the educational sector with standard tabulations, percentage distributions and charts.

898 Statistiske efterretninger [Statistical news].
DS, København.
1909- approx 80 issues a year. *Da.
See individual subject entries.

899 Indkomst og erhvervsforholdene i Grønland ved hjemmestyrels indførelse [Income and business conditions in Greenland at the introduction of home rule].
DS, København.
1944. DKr 33.61. 137p. *Da.

900 General erhvervsstatistik og handel [General economic statistics and internal trade].
DS, København.
1983- monthly. DKr 4.92; DKr 31.97 yr. ISSN 0108-5573. *Da.
Accounts, joint-stock companies, business units registered for VAT settlement, sales by non-agricultural industries, employers' labour cost aggregates, index of retail sales.
Note: issued in the series 'Statistiske efterretninger' [Statistical news].

901 Statistikservice [Statistics service].
DS, København.
1983- *Da.
Individual series, normally containing time series covering several years and/or distribution by industry categories or regions, at a higher level of disaggregation than the corresponding breakdowns given in 'Statistiske efterretninger'. Titles are:-
Arbejdsløshedsstatistik. Månedlig registreret ledighed [Unemployment statistics. Monthly registered unemployment] monthly.
Arbejdsmarked statistik, kvartalsvis [Labour market statistics, quarterly].
Konjunkturtendenser i udvalgte lande [Economic trends in selected countries] 24 a year.
Løn- og indkomststatistik [Statistics of earnings and incomes] 4-6 a year.
Månedlig beskæftigelses- og lønstatistik for industri [Monthly statistics of industrial employment and labour costs].
Månedlig ordre- og omsætningsstatistik for industri [Monthly statistics of industrial sales and order books].
Prisstatistik [Price statistics] monthly.
Socialstatistik [Social statistics] 6-8 a year.
Udenrigshandelen fordelt på varer og lande [External trade by commodities and countries] quarterly.
Varestatistik for industri [Manufacturers' sales of commodities] quarterly, in four series (Series A: Animal and vegetable products, food, beverages and tobacco; B: Mineral and chemical products, wood, paper and articles thereof; C: Textile articles, footwear, sports equipment, etc.; D: Metals, metal goods, machinery, appliances and transport equipment).

902 Årbog for Færøerne [Faroe Islands yearbook].
Færøerne landsstyre, Rigsombudsmanden på Færøerne.
(annual) 1981 (published in 1982). not priced. 305p. *Da.
Includes tables in the text on population, agriculture and fisheries, trade, transport, economy, social conditions, education, politics, religion, and culture.

903 Færøerne og Grønland [Faroe Islands and Greenland].
DS, København.
1983- c 9 a year. DKr 4.92; DKr 20.49 yr. ISSN 0108-5557. *Da.
Population, external trade, prices and incomes.
Note: issued in the series 'Statistiske efterretninger' [Statistical news].

904 Danish economic survey (Ministry for Economic Affairs: The Economic Secretariat).
Ministry for Economic Affairs: The Economic Secretariat, Slotsholmsgade 12, DK-1216 København K.
(annual) October 1985. free. 42p. ISSN 0109-6370. *En.
TF: the 1985 edition, published in 1985, has data for 1983 to 1986.
Part I: The Danish economy in 1985 and 1986; II Public finance; III: Selected tables (central government finance, local government finance, employment, gross fixed investments, and personal income).
Note: a translation of parts of 'Økonomisk oversigt'.

Δ A, continued

905 Denmark quarterly review.
Kjøbenhavns Handelsbank, 2 Holmens Kanal, DK-1091 København.
1950- quarterly. not priced. *En.
TF: includes data from two to six months earlier than the date of the issue.
Includes Danish economic indicators for foreign trade, balance of payments, etc; manufacturing industries; agriculture; building and construction; labour, prices and consumption; money and capital market; as well as articles dealing with economic developments and with the Danish economy in general.

Δ B Production

Δ B - ii Agriculture, fisheries, forestry, etc

Δ B - ii(a) Agriculture and horticulture

906 Landbrugsstatistik [Agricultural statistics].
DS, København.
1936- 1983. DKr 30.33. 311p. ISSN 0070-3559. *Da; table of contents and headings also in En.
TF: the 1983 edition, published in 1984, has data for 1983 usually compared with statistics for earlier years.
Data on agriculture (farms by size and type of farming, tenancies and manager-operated farms, manpower, capital formation, machinery, raw material consumption, total area & agricultural area, crop products, livestock, livestock production, human consumption of food, agricultural accounts, agricultural statistics for municipalities), forestry (forest area, felling), agriculture and horticulture census, 1984, and greenhouse census, 1984.

907 Landbrug [Agriculture].
DS, København.
1983- c 16 a year. DKr 4.92; DKr 50.82 yr. ISSN 0108-5522. *Da.
Production and prices, crops, cereal stocks, feeding stuff consumption, stocks of pigs and cattle, factor incomes, capital formation, volume and price indexes.
Note: issued in the series 'Statistiske efterretninger' [Statistical news].

908 Statistics (Danske Slagterier [Association of Danish Slaughterhouses]).
Danske Slagterier, Axeltorv 3, DK-1609 København V.
(annual) 1984. not priced. 40p. *En & Da eds.
TF: the 1984 edition, published early 1985, has data for 1983 and 1984 and some earlier years in some tables.
Data on production, slaughtering, grading, prices, export, consumption, storage, etc. of pigs, pigmeat, bacon, etc.

Δ B - ii(b) Fisheries

909 Fiskeriberetning [Annual report on fisheries].
Fiskeriministeriet, Stormgade 2, DK-1470 København K.
1921- 1977. DKr 16.85. c 100p. *Da; summary in En.
TF: the 1977 edition, published in 1978, has data for 1977 and also for earlier years in some tables.
Data on the number of fishermen, equipment (fishing vessels, gear and nets), catch of fish and crustaceans, fishery commodities (canned and cured fish), exports of fish and fish products.

910 Faroe sea food.
L/F Föroya Fiskasöla, 3800 Tórshavn, (PO Box 68) Faroe Islands.
(annual) 1983. not priced. 34p. *Da; with summary in En.
TF: the 1983 report, published in 1984, has data for 1983 and some earlier years.
The annual report and accounts of the organisation, which also includes statistical data on catches, exports, prices, etc.

Δ B - iii Industry

911 Industri og energi [Manufacturing industry and energy].
DS, København.
1983- c 17 a year. DKr 4.92; DKr 43.44 yr. ISSN 0108-5468. *Da.
Employment and labour costs, sales and order books, accounts, tendancy surveys; energy balance sheet, energy supplies, manufacturers' energy consumption.
Note: issued in the series 'Statistiske efterretninger' [Statistical news].

912 Varestatistik for industri [Manufacturers' sales of commodities].
DS, København.
1966/67- 1983. DKr 47.54. 236p. ISSN 0107-7131. *Da.
TF: previously quarterly, from 1983 issued annually. 1983 edition published in 1984, has data for 1983.
Sales of manufacturing industries' own products, distributed by NIMEXE and subdivisions of it. Sales of manufacturing industries' by ISIC divisions.

Δ B – iii, continued

913 Beretning om foreningens virksomhed [Report on the Textile Industry Society's activities].
Textilindustrien, Bredgade 41, Postboks 300, 7400 Herning.
(annual) 1984-1985. not priced. 44p. *Da.
TF: the 1984-1985 report was published in 1985, with data for 1984.
Includes a few statistical tables and graphs in the text on manufacturing, trade, technology, labour etc. in the Danish textile industry.

914 Danish shipbuilding...annual report of the Association of Danish Shipbuilders.
Skibsvarftsforeningen, Store Kongensgade 128, DK-1264 København K.
(annual) 1984. not priced. *En & Da eds.
Includes statistical data of ships on order, tonnage launched, tonnage completed, etc. for Denmark and by individual shipyards.

Δ B – iv Construction

915 Bygge- og anlægsvirksomhed [Construction industry].
DS, København.
1983- c 20 a year. DKr 4.92 or DKr 49.18 yr. ISSN 0108-5549. *Da.
Employment, labour costs, building cost indexes, housing construction; tendancy surveys, accounts statistics; sales and assessments of real property.
Note: issued in the series 'Statistiske efterretninger' [Statistical news].

Δ B – v Energy

916 Dansk elforsyning, statistik [Danish electricity supply, statistics].
Danske Elværkers Forening [Association of Danish Electric Utilities], Rosenørns Allé 9, DK-1970 København V.
1976- 1984. DKr 35. 45p. ISSN 0106-4711. *Da; summary in En.
TF: the 1984 edition, published in May 1985, has data for 1984.
Tables, figures and text concerning production, distribution and consumption of electricity, technical installations, economy and prices of the supply industry.

917 Oversigt over tariffer og investeringsbidrag pr.1 Januar... [Survey of electricity tariffs and connection charges...]
Danske Elværkers Forening, Rosenørns Allé 9, DK-1970 København V.
(annual) 1984 (published in May 1984). DKr 80.00. *Da.
Survey of the tariffs of the individual electricity supply companies and the connection charges for new consumers and for reinforcement of existing consumers.

Δ C External trade

918 Danmarks vareingførsel og -udførsel [Foreign trade of Denmark].
DS, København.
1883- 1982. DKr 55.74 each vol. 3 vols. ISSN 0070-2781. *Da, En.
TF: the 1982 edition, published in 1984, has data for 1982.
Content:
V. I: Summary of Danish imports and exports. Distribution by commodities (SITC) and countries, etc. Separate sections for Faroe Islands and Greenland.
V. II: Distribution by commodities (CCCN).
V.III: Distribution by commodities and countries.

919 Kvartalsstatistik over udenrigshandelen [Quarterly bulletin of external trade].
DS, København.
1983- quarterly. DKr 43.44 each issue. ISSN 0106-9780. *Da, En.
TF: each issue has data for that quarter and cumulated figures for the year to the end of that quarter.
Main table gives detailed foreign trade statistics arranged by commodities subdivided by countries of origin and destination.

920 Udenrigshandelen fordelt på varer og lande [External trade by commodities and countries].
DS, København.
quarterly & annual. DKr 205.74 quarterly; DKr 59.02 annual; DKr 676.23 yr for quarterly & annual. *Da.
TF: each annual has data for the year of the issue; each quarterly has cumulated data for the quarter to the end of the period of the issue.
Detailed foreign trade by commodities subdivided by countries of origin and destination.
Note: issued in the series 'Statistikservice'.

921 Udenrigshandel [External trade].
DS, København.
1983- c 20 yr. DKr 4.92 or DKr 81.15 yr. ISSN 0108-5506. *Da, En.
Imports, exports, current-value indexes, quantity indexes, terms of trade, distributions by countries and by commodity groups and by modes of transport.
Note: issued in the series 'Statistiske efterretninger' [Statistical news].

Δ C, continued

922 Føroysk hagtídindi [Faroes statistical bulletin].
Hagdeildin, Box 355, Tinganes, Faroe Islands.
1983- monthly. not priced. *Da.
TF: each issue has data for one month and is published a few weeks later.
Data on the foreign trade of the Faroe Islands.

Δ D Internal distribution and service trades

< see also 915

923 Detailpriser [Retail prices].
DS, København.
1921- quarterly. DKr 5.33 yr or DKr 21.31 yr. ISSN 0417-0164. *Da.
Average prices of the most commonly consumed food products in selected municipalities.

924 Ejendomssalg [Sales of real property].
DS, København.
1983- 1983. DKr 20.00. 74p. ISSN 0070-3508. *Da; contents list and main headings also in En.
TF: the 1983 edition, published in 1984, has data for 1982 and some earlier years in some tables.
Total sales; agricultural holdings; residential, commercial and industrial properties; building sites.

Δ E Population

925 Folke- og boligtællingen [Census of population and housing].
DS, København.
1801- 1981. DKr 33.61 each vol. *Da; contents tables and headings also in En.
TF: a census is taken every five or ten years.
Contents:
L 1: Landstabelværk [National tables]
A 1: København, Frederiksberg, Hovedstadsregionen [Regional tables...]
A 2: Københavns, amtskommune
A 3: Frederiksborg amtskommune
A 4: Roskilde amtskommune
A 5: Vestsjællands amtskommune
A 6: Storstrøms amtskommune
A 7: Barnholms amtskommune
A 8: Fyns amtskommune
A 9: Sønderjyllands amtskommune
A10: Ribe amtskommune
A11: Vejle amtskommune
A12: Ringkøbing amtskommune
A13: Arhus amtskommune
A14: Viborg amtskommune
A15: Nordjyllands amtskommune.

926 Befolkning og valg [Population and elections].
DS, København.
1983- 20-24 yr. DKr 4.92; DKr 48.36 yr. ISSN 0108-5530. *Da.
Population size, births, deaths, internal and external migration, population forecasts, national elections, local government elections.
Note: issued in the series 'Statistiske efterretninger'.

927 Befolkningen i kommunerne, 1 Januar... [The population in municipalities on January 1... distributed by sex, age and marital status].
DS, København.
1970- 1984. DKr 39.34. 173p. ISSN 0108-8076. *Da.
TF: the results for 1 January 1984 were published a few months later.

Δ E - i Vital statistics

928 Befolkningens bevægelser [Vital statistics].
DS, København.
1931/33- 1982. DKr 30.33. 251p. ISSN 0070-3478. *Da, En.
TF: the 1982 edition, published in 1983, has data for 1982.
Births, marriages, deaths, divorces and migration.

929 Dødsarsagerne [Causes of death].
Sundhedsstyrelsen [National Board of Health], Store Kongensgade 1, 1264 København K.
1875- 1982. DKr 35. 205p. ISSN 0108-5646. *Da; table headings & summaries also in En.
TF: the 1982 edition, published in 1984, has data for 1982.

Δ E – ii Labour

930 Arbejdløsheden [Unemployment].
DS, København.
1910/14- 1983. DKr 33.61. 132p. *Da, En.
TF: the 1983 edition, published in 1984, has data for 1983.
A summary of data on unemployment for the past ten years, and the rate of employment by age, etc., for the year under review.

931 Arbejdsmarkedsstatistik. Kvartalsvis regionalstatistik [Labour market statistics. Quarterly regional statistics].
DS, København.
(quarterly) not priced. ISSN 0105-0788. *Da.

932 Arbejdsmarked [Labour market].
DS, København.
1983- c 15 a year. DKr 4.92 or DKr 32.25 yr. ISSN 0108-5514. *Da.
Employment, unemployment, notified employment vacancies, industrial accidents, government employees.
Note: issued in the series 'Statistiske efterretninger' [Statistical news].

Δ F Social and political

933 Social sikring og retsvæsen [Social security and justice].
DS, København.
1983- monthly. DKr 4.92 or DKr 34.43 yr. ISSN 0108-5441. *Da.
Social resources, social security benefits, public health insurance, Social Assistance Act benefits, housing subsidies, child allowances; civil justice, reported crimes.
Note: issued in the series 'Statistiske efterretninger' [Statistical news].

Δ F – i Standard of living

< see also 396, 392

934 Indkomst, forbrug og priser [incomes, consumption and prices].
DS, København.
1983- c 20 a year. DKr 4.92 or DKr 44.26 yr. ISSN 0108-5565. *Da.
Incomes, earnings; consumer expectation surveys, consumer price index, index of net retail prices, wages regulating price index, wholesale price index, price index for imported raw materials.
Note: issued in the series 'Statistiske Efterretninger' [Statistical news].

935 Indkomster og formuer [Incomes and property assessments].
DS, København.
(annual) 1982. DKr 47.54. 247p. ISSN 0107-105X. *Da; contents list also in En.
TF: the 1982 edition, published in 1984, has data for 1982.
Demography, employment classification, income data, income deductions and tax relief, wealth, and regional tables.

936 Levevilkar i Danmark [Living conditions in Denmark] (Danmarks Statistik and the National Institute of Social Research).
DS, København.
1976- 1984. not priced. *Da, En.
TF: published every four years, the 1984 edition was issued in 1985.
A compendium of social statistics concerning the main aspects of the Danish population's living conditions. Chapters on health, education, work, income, wealth and consumption, family circumstances, housing, leisure and political activity.

Δ F – ii Health and welfare

< see also 403, 407

937 Medicinsk fødselsstatistik [Medical birth statistics].
Sundhedsstyrelsen [National Health Service], Store Kongensgade 1, 1264 København K.
1970- 1979 (published in 1982). DKr 25.00. *Da; summary also in En.

938 Personale- og økonomistatistik for sygehusvæsenet [Personnel and economic statistics for hospitals].
Sundhedsstyrelsen, Store Kongensgade 1, 1264 København K.
1976- 1984. DKr 25. *Da; headings of tables also in En.
TF: the 1984 edition, published in 1984, has data for 1983.

939 Ahlimilen sygehusvæsenet [Performance statistics of hospitals].
Sundhedsstyrelsen, Store Kongensgade 1, 1264 København K.
1975/76- 1983 (published in 1984). DKr 40. *Da.

940 Statistik om prevention og aborter [Statistics of prevention and abortion].
Sundhedsstyrelsen, Store Kongensgade 1, 1264 København K.
1974- 1981 (published in 1982). DKr 25. *Da.

Δ F - ii, continued

941 Tiårs-oversigt for sundhedsvæsenet, 1973-82 [Ten-year overview of the health system].
Sundhedsstyrelsen, Store Kongensgade 1, 1264 København K.
DKr 45. 107p. *Da.
TF: published in 1985.
Data on births, deaths, abortions, primary and secondary health care, education of health personnel, etc.

Δ F - iii Education and leisure

942 Educational statistics: statistical material 1977/78 relating to courses (mainly under the Ministry of Education).
Undervisningsministeriet, Frederiksholms Kanal 21, 1220 København K.
not priced. 15p. *En.
Data on educational institutions, pupils, students, graduates and school leavers, classes, teachers, and operational expenditure.

943 Uddannelse og kultur [Education and culture].
DS, København.
1983- monthly. DKr 4.92 or DKr 46.72 yr. ISSN 0108-5492. *Da.
Vocational secondary education, further education, primary and secondary school education/apprenticeship training; cinemas, theatres, museums; the national church.
Note: issued in the series 'Statistiske efterretninger' [Statistical news].

Δ F - iv Justice

< see also 414

944 Kriminalstatistik [Crime statistics].
DS, København.
1940- 1979 & 1980. DKr 39.34. 163p. ISSN 0070-3540. *Da; table headings also in En.
TF: the 1979 & 1980 edition, published in 1983, has data for 1979 and 1980.
Offences, convictions, charges, remands, appeals, etc.

Δ F - vi

see also < 925, 926

945 Folketingsvalget [National elections].
DS, København.
1854- 1984. DKr 16.39. 100p. *Da.
TF: date related to the 10 January 1984 election were published in 1984.

Δ G Finance

946 Danmarks Nationalbank monetary review.
Danmarks Nationalbank, Havnegade 5, 1093 København K.
1962- quarterly. free. *En.
TF: each table covers several years and has monthly or quarterly figures for the last 18 months to about three months prior to the date of the issue.
Assets and liabilities of the bank, Denmark's international liquidity, recorded capital payments to and from foreign countries, balance of payments, terms of trade, prices and wages, government finance, government lending and borrowing, commercial bank liquidity, lending and investments by commercial banks and major savings banks, principal assets of insurance companies and pension funds, yield of selected bonds quoted on the stock exchange.
Note: an edition in Danish 'Danmarks Nationalbank kvartalsoversigt' has been issued from 1963 onwards.

947 Penge- og kapitalmarked [Money and credit market].
DS, København.
1983- 15-20 a year. DKr 4.92 or DKr 56.56 yr. ISSN 0108-5476. *Da.
Liquidity, bank balances, mortgage registrations, bond issues; insurance, pension funds; fire damages; forced sales of real property, etc.
Note: issued in the series 'Statistiske efterretninger' [Statistical news].

948 Report and accounts for the year...
Danmarks Nationalbank, Havnegade 5, 1093 København K.
(annual) 1983. free. 80p+36 tables. *En & Da eds.
TF: the 1983 report, published mid-1984, has long runs of annual, monthly and quarterly figures to the end of 1983.
As well as the report and accounts of the bank, includes an appendix of tables of financial data relating to Denmark.

Δ G – ii Public finance

949 Nationalregnskab, offentlige finanser og betalingsbalance [National accounts, public finance and balance of payments].
DS, København.
1983- c 20 a year. DKr 4.92 or DKr 45.08 yr. ISSN 0108-545X. *Da.
National accounts, local government budgets and accounts, personal taxation, advance assessment of incomes, real property taxation, taxes and duties, customs and excise duties, balance of payments, and foreign debt.
Note: issued in the series 'Statistiske efterretninger' [Statistical news].

950 Nationalregnskabsstatistik... [National accounts statistics...].
DS, København.
1966/81- 1982. DKr 39.34. 220p. ISSN 0108-8173. *Da, En.
TF: the 1982 edition, published in 1984, has data for 1982.

951 Skatter og afgifter - oversigt [Taxes and duties - summary].
DS, København.
1976- 1984. DKr 33.61. 137p. ISSN 0105-1164. *Da; table of contents, main headings & summary also [in En.
TF: the 1984 edition, published in 1985, has data for 1984.
Total taxation, payments of taxes and duties, overdue tax, personal taxation, taxation of corporations, taxation of real property, customs and excise duties, international comparisons.
Note: incorporates 'Personbeskatninger i indkomstoret... [Taxes on personal incomes], 1970-.

952 Kommunale finanser [Local government finance].
DS, København.
1915- 1982. DKr 33.61. 133p. ISSN 0106-9802. *Da; contents list and headings also in En.
TF: the 1982 edition, published in 1984, has data for 1982.
Current expenditure, current receipts, capital expenditure, and financing.

Δ G – iii Company finance

953 Regnskabsstatistik for industrien [Industrial accounts statistics].
DS, København.
(annual) 1982. not priced. 174p. ISSN 0108-738X. *Da; contents list also in En.
TF: the 1982 edition, published in 1983, has data for 1982.
Accounts statistics for industrial enterprises.

Δ H Transport and communications

954 Samfærdsel og turisme [Transport and tourism].
DS, København.
1983- c 20 a year. DKr 4.92 or DKr 54.92 yr. ISSN 0108-5484. *Da.
Motor vehicle stock and registrations, goods transport by road, vehicle inspections, road traffic accidents; ships, sea transport, shipping; air transport; holidays and travel, nights spent in hotels, travellers' currency.
Note: issued in the series 'Statistiske efterretninger' [Statistical news].

Δ H – i Ships and shipping

955 Danmarks skibe og skibsfart [Danish ships and shipping].
DS, København.
1883- 1982. DKr 20.49. 122p. ISSN 0070-3486. *Da, En.
TF: the 1982 edition, published in 1984, has data for 1982.
Number of Danish ships, shipping at Danish ports by Danish and foreign ships, Danish shipping in foreign trade, and statistics of shipowners' accounting.

956 Skibsfartsberetning [Annual report on Danish shipping].
Danmarks Rederiforening, Ammaliegade 33, DK-1256 København K.
(annual) 1984/85. not priced. 44p. *Da.
TF: the 1984/85 report, published in 1985, has data for several years to 1983.
Includes data on freight markets, prices of fuel-oil, world tonnage, and the Danish merchant fleet at 1 January 1985.
Note: a 15-page booklet in English, 'Danish shipping 85', includes some of the data from the report.

Δ H – ii Roads and road transport

957 Statistik over registrering of nye automobiler i Danmark [Statistics of motor vehicle registrations in Denmark].
Automobil-Importørernes Sammenslutning, Ryvangs Allé 68, 2900 Hellerup.
1949- monthly. not priced. *Da.
Registrations by make and mark of vehicle.

Δ H – ii, continued

958 Færdselsuheld [Road traffic accidents].
DS, København.
1940– 1983. DKr 27. 136p. ISSN 0070-3516. *Da; table of contents & main headings also in En.
TF: the 1983 edition, published in 1985, has data for 1983.

Δ H – iii Railways and railway transport

959 Årsberetning [Annual report of the Danish State Railways].
Danske Statsbaner, Sølvgade 40, DK-1349 København K.
1978– 1983. not priced. 40p. *Da; with summaries in En, Fr & De.
TF: the 1983 report, published in 1984, has data for 1983 and 1982.
Mainly text but includes some statistical tables and graphs on passenger traffic, goods traffic, ferry traffic, bus traffic, production, and personnel, as well as the accounts of the organisation.

SPAIN
ESPAGNE
SPANIEN
ESPAÑA

Central statistical office

960 Instituto Nacional de Estadística [National Institute of Statistics].
Paseo de la Castellana 183, 28046 Madrid.
t 279 93 00/234. tx 42086 PLDES E
The Institute is divided into five main divisions - Coordination (national, international, publications, documentation and information, data processing, administration), Population (demographic, social, justice and administrative, public health, cultural), Enterprise (agriculture, mining, building and electricity, manufacturing, trade and transport, services, financial, salaries and cost of living), Economic analyses (methodology, national accounts, conjectural and economic and investment analysis), and Censuses and surveys (sample design, evaluation of results, programming of field work, training, data collection and supervision, studies of censuses and surveys).
The Institute has been abbreviated to INE, Madrid in the entries which follow.

Libraries

The library of the Instituto Nacional de Estadística (see above) has all the Spanish statistical publications and also those of other countries and of international organisations. It is open to the public daily from 9.30 to 13.30 and from 15.45 to 17.45, except for the month of August when it is closed. The staff speaks English, French, Italian, Portuguese, Russian and German as well as Spanish.

Bibliographies

961 Catalogo descriptivo de publicaciones estadísticas (Administración Pública Central y Organización Sindical).
A descriptive catalogue of statistical publications of central government and the sindical organisation; a comprehensive listing of items. The original volume was published at the end of 1970 and this has been supplemented by two or more volumes - Vol I: Apéndice 1976-1982; Vol II: lists of publications of civil ministries. *Es.

962 Publicaciones en existencia (Instituto Nacional de Estadística).
An annual sales list, available free on request.

Statistical publications

Δ A General

963 Anuario estadístico de España (edición normal) [Statistical yearbook of Spain].
INE, Madrid.
1912- 1984. Ptas 3575 (microfiche Ptas 650). 860p. ISSN 0066-5177. *Es.
TF: the 1984 edition, published in 1985, has data for about ten years up to 1983 or the latest available.
Main sections:
Geography & climate - Demography - Agriculture, forestry, cattle & fisheries - Industry - Transport & communications - Foreign trade - Finance - Prices & wages - Employment, social security & action - Health & benefits - Education & cultural expansion - Tourism & other services (entertainment, etc) - Justice & culture (including religion) - Housing & buildings - International statistics - Provincial statistics.

964 Anuario estadístico de España (edición manual) [Statistical yearbook of Spain (pocket edition)].
INE, Madrid.
1912- 1985 (published in 1985). Ptas 1425. *Es.
An abridged version of 963.

965 Reseñas estadísticas provinciales [Review of provincial statistics].
INE, Madrid.
1943- Ptas 525 each volume. 28 vols. *Es.
TF: the volumes are published at irregular intervals and may be recent or up to 15 years old. Each volume has data for six or seven years for most tables.
Subject coverage is similar to that of 'Anuario estadística de España' with separate volumes for each Spanish province.

966 Así es España en cifras [Spain in figures].
INE, Madrid.
(annual) 1985. free. 25p. *Es.
TF: the 1985 edition, published in 1985, has data from the statistical yearbook for 1984 and other publications of INE.

Δ A, continued

967 Boletin de estadística [Monthly bulletin of statistics].
INE, Madrid.
1918- Ptas 525; or Ptas 3100 yr (microfiche Ptas 1200 yr). ISSN 0038-6391. *Es.
TF: tables usually include data for the last three to five years and the last twelve months, the latest figures available varying from three to six months prior to the date of the issue.
Population, labour and social action, health, justice, production, transport, communications, financial services, tourism, editorial production, consumption, wages, industrial prices, consumer prices, foreign trade, and international statistics.

968 Indicadores de coyuntura [Economic indicators].
INE, Madrid.
1963- monthly. Ptas 275, or Ptas 2375 yr. *Es.
Includes indices of cost of living, wholesale prices, foreign trade, tourism, reserves in foreign currency, rate of exchange, industrial production, housing, investment, sales in department stores, receipts and expenditures of the central administration, monetary system, finance and stock exchange, unemployment and salaries.

969 Indicadores estadísticos regionales (una aproximación a la contabilidad regional [Regional statistical indicators].
INE, Madrid.
1984. 2nd ed. 103p. Ptas 1200. *Es.

970 Informe economico [Economic report].
Banco de Bilbao, Alcalá 16, Madrid 14.
(annual) 1982 (published in 1983). not priced. 303p. *Es.
Includes data on the national economy, national accounts, employment, industry, money and finance, etc.
Note: an abridged English version is also available.

971 Boletin economico de información comercial España [Economic bulletin of Spanish commercial information].
Ministerio de Economic y Hacienda, Paseo de la Castellana 162, Madrid.
1949- weekly. Ptas 150 each issue. ISSN 0019-1971. *Es.
Includes a statistical section on economics and finance, food, prices, etc.

972 Censo de locales de España, 1980 [Census of premises in Spain].
INE, Madrid.
58 fascicules in 3 vols. *Es.
TF: being published from 1982 onwards.
Content:
Vol 1: National results (Ptas 1050)
Vol 2: Results for autonomous communities (Ptas 525)
Vol 3: Provincial results (51 vols, one for each province plus Ceuta-Melilla (Ptas 525 to Ptas 2075 each).

Δ B Production

Δ B – ii Agriculture, fisheries, forestry, etc

973 Manual de estadística agraria [Pocketbook of agricultural statistics].
Ministerio de Agricultura, Paseo Infanta Isabel 1, Madrid 7.
(annual) 1981. Ptas 200. 102p. *Es.
TF: the 1981 edition, published in 1981, has data for several years to 1980.
Data on demography; distribution of land; agricultural, animal and forestry production; media production (fertilisers, agricultural machinery, etc); economic data (price indices, wages, accounts, etc); food balances; and international information.

Δ B – ii(a) Agriculture and horticulture

974 Censo agrario de España [Census of agriculture].
INE, Madrid.
1962- 1982. *Es.
TF: a census is taken every ten years. The results of the 1982 census were published from 1985.
Contents:
Vol I: National results (Ptas 1050)
Vol II: Autonomous communities (Ptas 1050 each vol)
Vol III: Provincial results (Ptas 1050 each volume)
Vol IV: Results for cities and towns (Ptas 525/900 each volume).

975 Anuario de estadística agraria [Statistical yearbook of agriculture].
Ministerio de Agricultura, Pesca y Alimentacion, Paseo de Isabel 1, Madrid 7.
1928- 1982. not priced. 682p. *Es.
TF: the 1982 edition, published in 1984, has data for 1982.
Data on area & climate, demography, distribution of land, agricultural production, livestock production, forestry, methods of production (fertilisers, tractors, agricultural machinery, energy, etc), economic information (prices, rents, finances, foreign trade, etc), and other (agricultural balance).

Δ B – ii(a), continued

976 Censo de maquinaria agricola [Census of agricultural machinery].
Ministerio de Agricultura, Paseo Infanta Isabel 1, Madrid 7.
1961– 1969 (published in 1970). free. 45p. *Es.
Data on agricultural machinery in existence by provinces; increases in the amount of machinery used; and graphs and maps.

Δ B – iii Industry

977 Encuesta industrial [Industrial enquiry].
INE, Madrid.
1978/81– 1978/1981 (published in 1984). Ptas 1750. 412p. *Es.
Data on number of establishments, by types of business; employment, hours worked, wages, consumption and cost of power used, raw materials, etc.
Note: supersedes 'Estadística industrial de España'.

978 Censo industrial de España, 1978 [Industrial census of Spain].
INE, Madrid.
TF: the reports were published from 1982 onwards. *Es.
Resumen national [National summary] (Ptas 775)
Cuadernos provinciales [Provincial tables] (Ptas 375)
Cuadernos regionales [Regional tables] (Ptas 525)
Empresas industriales [Industrial firms] (Ptas 650)
Empresas de electricidad y construcción [Electrical and construction firms] (Ptas 650).
Note: continues the annual 'Estadística industrial de España'.

979 Numeros indices de la producción industrial: boletin informativo trimestrial [Index numbers of industrial production: quarterly information bulletin].
INE, Madrid.
Ptas 275 each issue.
Note: there is also a monthly 'Hoja informativo mensuel' (Ptas 50 each issue).

980 Indices de precios industriales: boletin informativo [Index of industrial prices: information bulletin].
INE, Madrid.
(quarterly) Ptas 275 each issue. *Es.
Note: there is also a monthly 'Hoja informativo mensuel' [Monthly information sheet] (Ptas 50 each issue).

Δ B – iii(a) Food products, beverages, tobacco

981 Estadística de las industrias derivadas de la pesca [Statistics of fish processing industries].
INE, Madrid.
1933– 1978. Ptas 375. c 100p. *Es.
TF: the 1978 edition has data for 1978 and 1977.
Data on factories, employment, wages, installations, production, consumption of raw materials and auxiliary materials, power, etc.

Δ B – iii(d) Metals, etc.

982 UNESID información siderúrgica [UNESID metal information] (Unión de Empresas Siderúrgicas [Unior of Metal Companies].
UNESID, Castello 128, 28006 Madrid.
1969– monthly. Ptas 500 (US$ 10 abroad) or Ptas 5000 yr (US$ 80 yr abroad). *Es; tables of ccntents also in En.
TF: each issue has the latest data available and also figures for some earlier years.
Includes statistical tables in the text, and regular tables of steel industry in the world (production by countries) and foreign trade (detailed statistics of Spanish imports and exports by commodities, and imports and exports by commodities subdivided by countries).

Δ B – iii(f) Other industries

983 Estadística de la producción editorial: libros y publicaciones periódicas [Statistics of publishing: books and periodical publications].
INE, Madrid.
1965– 1983. Ptas 275. *Es.
TF: the 1983 edition, published in 1985, has data for 1983.

Δ B – iv Construction

984 Censo de edifícios, 1980 [Census of buildings].
INE, Madrid.
57 fascicules in 4 vols. *Es.
TF: published between 1982 and 1983.
Vol I: National results (Ptas 775).
Vol II: Results for autonomous communities (Ptas 275).
Vol III: Results for provinces (Ptas 275 each fascicule).
Vol IV: Results for municipalities (Ptas 1425).

E

Δ B – v Energy

985 Anuario de energia [Energy annual] (Ingenieria Quimica S.A.).
Energia: revista de Ingenieria Energética, Triana 51, Madrid 16.
(annual) 1980. not priced. 752p. *Es.
TF: the 1980 edition has data for 1980 and some earlier years.
Includes tables on various aspects of energy production, consumption and trade.

986 Memoria estadística eléctrica [Report on electricity statistics].
UNESA, Francisco Gervás 3, Madrid.
(annual) 1982. not priced. 109p. *Es.
TF: the 1982 edition, published in 1983, has data for 1982 and some earlier years.
There is a statistical section and statistics are included in the text on the electricity economy, installations and lines, production and consumption, etc.

Δ B – vi Research and development

987 Estadística sobre actividades en investigación cientifica y desarrollo technologico [Statistics of activities of scientific investigation and technological development].
INE, Madrid.
1969– 1973–74. Ptas 375. *Es.
TF: the 1973–74 edition, published in 1978, has data for 1973 and 1974.

Δ C External trade

988 Estadística del comercio exterior de España: comercio por productos: comercio por países en Nomenclatura de Bruselas [Statistics of foreign trade of Spain: trade by commodities: trade by countries (BTN)].
Dirección General de Aduanas, Guzmán el Bueno 137, Madrid 3.
1922– 1983. Ptas 2000 for 2 vols. 2 vols. *Es.
TF: the 1983 edition, published in 1984, has data for 1983.
Imports and exports arranged by commodities subdivided by countries of origin and destination; and imports and exports arranged by countries subdivided by commodities.

989 Estadística del comercio exterior de España: comercio con la C.E.E. en nomenclatura Bruselas [Statistics of foreign trade of Spain: trade with EEC arranged by the Brussels Nomenclature].
Dirección General de Aduanas, Guzmán el Bueno 137, Madrid 3.
1970– 1983. Ptas 1000. 699p. *Es.
TF: the 1983 edition, published in 1984, has data for 1983.
Trade by commodities subdivided by EEC countries, and trade with EEC countries subdivided by commodities.

990 Estadística del comercio exterior de España: comercio por zonas [Statistics of foreign trade of Spain: trade by zones].
Dirección General de Aduanas, Guzmán el Bueno 137, Madrid 3.
(annual) 1982. Ptas 1000. 504p. *Es.
TF: the 1982 edition, published in 1984, has data for 1982.
Trade by commodities subdivided by zones within Spanish possessions (Peninsula, Las Palmas, Santa Cruz de Tenerife, Ceuta & Melilla) and trade by zones subdivided by commodities.

Δ D Internal distribution and service trade

Δ D – iv Tourism and travel

991 Movimiento de viajeros en establecimientos turisticos [Movement of travellers in tourist establishments].
INE, Madrid.
1965– quarterly. Ptas 375 each issue. *Es.
TF: each issue has quarterly and monthly figures up to the date of the issue and is published some months later.
National and provincial data is given.
Note: there is also an annual summary volume, 'Resumen anual' (1982, published 1983. Ptas 775. 150p) and a monthly information sheet, 'Hoja informativo mensual' (Ptas 50 each issue).

Δ E Population

992 Censo de la población [Census of population].
INE, Madrid.
1957– 1981. prices vary. *Es.
TF: a census is taken every ten years; the 1981 census results are being published from 1984 onwards.
Contents published:
Vol I: part 1: National results: characteristics of the population
Vol II: part 1: Results for autonomous communities: characteristics...
Vol III: part 1: Provincial results: characteristics...
Vol IV: 2° municipal results (districts and municipalities of more than 100,000 inhabitants).

Δ E, continued

993 Poblaciónes de derecho y hecho de los municipios españoles... [Total population of Spanish townships].
INE, Madrid.
1975- 1981 (published in 1982). Ptas 800. 153p. *Es.

994 Población de los actuales terminos municipales, 1900-1981: poblaciónes de hecho segun los censos [Population of townships according to the census results].
INE, Madrid.
1985. Ptas 1050. 243p. *Es.

995 Proyección de la población española para el periodo 1978-1995 [Projections of the population for the period 1978-1995].
INE, Madrid.
1985. Ptas 650. *Es.

996 Encuesta de migraciones interiores, 1980-81-82 [Enquiry on internal migration].
INE, Madrid.
1984. Ptas 375. *Es.

997 Migraciones: resultados por comunidades autónomes año 1983 [Migration: results for autonomous communities, 1983].
INE, Madrid.
1985. not priced. 31p. *Es.

Δ E - i Vital statistics

998 Movimiento natural de la población española [Vital statistics of Spain].
INE, Madrid.
1858- 1978-79. 11 vols. *Es.
Contents:
Vol I: National and provincial data (Ptas 650)
Vol II: Provincial and municipal data (Ptas 775 each for 9 vols)
Vol III: Deaths according to cause of death (Ptas 1300).

Δ E - ii Labour

999 Encuesta de población activa: principales resultados [Enquiry on the active population: main results].
INE, Madrid.
1964- quarterly. Ptas 650 each issue. *Es.
TF: previously annual and then half-yearly, now quarterly.
Note: also available are 'Resultados por comunidades autónomas' (quarterly. Ptas 900 each issue) and 'Hoja informativa mensuel' (Ptas 50 each issue).

1000 Boletin de estadísticas laborales [Bulletin of labour statistics].
Ministerio de Trabajo y Seguridad Social, Secretaria General Texnica, Madrid.
1983- annual. not priced. ISSN 0212-7180. *Es.
TF: the first issue was published in December 1983.
Note: 'Anuario de estadísticas laborales, 1982-83' was published in 1984.

Δ E - iii Housing

1001 Censo de Viviendas [Census of housing].
INE, Madrid.
1970- 1981. *Es.
TF: results of the 1981 census are being published from 1983 onwards.
Contents include: Vol 4: Results by municipal level (Ptas 900).

Δ F Social and political

Δ F - i Standard of living

< see also 392

1002 Encuesta de equipamiento y nicel cultural de la familias [Enquiry relating to families].
INE, Madrid.
1968- 1985. 4 vols. *Es.
TF: published between 1975 and 1977.
Contents: Vol 1: Living conditions of families. Methodology and national and regional results (Ptas 600); Vol 2: Living conditions of families. Provincial results (Ptas 600); Vol 3: Social mobility between generations. Methodology and results (Ptas 600); Vol 4: Internal migration, 1970-1975. Methodology and results (Ptas 800).

Δ F – i, continued

1003 Indices de precios de consumo: boletín informativo [Consumer price indices: information bulletin].
INE, Madrid.
(monthly) Ptas 175 or Ptas 2075 yr. *En.
Note: also issued are 'Cifras provisionales (hoja informativo' [Provisional figures...] (Ptas 50) and 'Resumen anual' [Annual summary] (Ptas 1200).

1004 Encuesta permanente de consumo [Permanent enquiry on consumption].
INE, Madrid.
1977/80– quarterly. Ptas 275 each issue. *Es.

1005 Encuesta de presupuestos familiares [Enquiry into family budgets].
INE, Madrid.
1958– 1980/81– 4 vols. *Es.
TF: the survey is taken at irregular intervals. The results of the 1980/81 survey were published in 1983 and 1984.
Contents:
Vol 1: Income and expenditure of homes: national data (Ptas 2375)
Vol 2: Appliances and conditions in family homes: national data (Ptas 1050)
Vol 3: Consumption of food, drink and tobacco, by values (Ptas 1050)
Vol 4: Results by autonomous communities (Ptas 650 each community).

Δ F – ii Health and welfare

1006 Estadística de establecimientos sanitarios con regimen de internado [Statistics of medical establishments...].
INE, Madrid.
1972– 1979. Ptas 775. 181p. *Es.
TF: the 1979 edition, published in 1983, has data for 1979.

1007 Encuesta de morbilidad hospitalaria [Enquiry into hospital morbidity].
INE, Madrid.
1979– 1980. Ptas 1750. 407p. *Es.
TF: the 1980 edition, published in 1983, has data for 1980.

1008 Estadística del suicidio en España [Statistics of suicides in Spain].
INE, Madrid.
1966/70– 1976–1980. Ptas 650. *Es.
TF: the 1976–1980 edition, with data for those years, was published in 1982.

1009 Boletin epidemiologico semanal: vigilancia epidemologica [Weekly epidemiological bulletin...].
Ministerio de Sanidad y Consumo, Dirección General de Salud Publica España, Paseo del Prado, 18–20 Madrid 14.
(weekly) not priced. *Es.
Each issue has four pages of staistical data.

Δ F – iii Education and leisure

1010 Estadística de la enseñanza en España [Statistics of education in Spain].
INE, Madrid.
1956/57– 1981–82. Ptas 2375. *Es.
TF: the 1981–82 edition was published in 1984.
Data on primary, secondary and higher education.

Δ F – iv Justice

1011 Estadísticas juridiciales de España [Judicial statistics of Spain].
INE, Madrid.
1962/63– 1979 (published in 1983). Ptas 525. *Es.

1012 Suspensiones de pagos y declaraciones de quiebra [Suspensions of payments and declarations of bankruptcy].
INE, Madrid.
(annual) 1984 (issued in 1985). Ptas 525. *Es.
Note: also available is a monthly information sheet, 'Hoja informativo mensual' (Ptas 50 each issue).

Δ G – ii Public finance

1013 Contabilidad nacional de España [National accounts of Spain].
INE, Madrid.
1954/56– 1970–1980. Ptas 1300. c 100p. *Es.
TF: the 1970–1980 edition, with data for those years, was published in 1984.
Data on the general economic situation, gross national product, national accounts, etc.

Δ G – ii, continued

1014 La renta nacional y su distribución [National income and its distribution].
INE, Madrid.
1968– 1978/1979. Ptas 1300. *Es.
TF: the 1978 and 1979 edition, with data for those years, was published in 1982.

1015 Estadísticas presupuestarias y fiscales [Budget and fiscal statistics].
Ministerio de Economia y Hacienda, Almagro 34, Madrid.
(annual) 1982. not priced. 195p. *Es.
TF: the 1982 edition, published in 1984, has data for 1982 and 1981 for comparison in some tables.

Δ G – iii Company finance

< see also 1011

1016 Estadística de sociedades mercantiles [Statistics of mercantile companies].
INE, Madrid.
1965/66– 1983. Ptas 525. *Es.
TF: the 1983 edition, published in 1985, has data for 1982.

Δ G – iv Investment

1017 Estadística de efectos protestados [Statistics on securities].
INE, Madrid.
(annual) 1984. not priced. 259p. *Es.
TF: the 1984 edition, published in 1985, has data for 1984.

Δ G – vi Credit market

1018 Prestamos hipotecarios [Mortgage loans].
INE, Madrid.
1962– 1982. Ptas 375. *Es.
TF: the 1982 edition, published in 1984, has data for 1982.

1019 Estadística de ventes a plazos [Statistics of sales by instalments].
INE, Madrid.
1967/68– 1977. Ptas 650. 110p. *Es.
TF: the 1977 edition, published in 1978, has data for 1977.

1020 Memoria del credito oficial [Report on official credit].
Instituto de Credito Oficial, Ministerio de Economia y Hacienda, Paseo del Prado 4, 28014 Madrid.
(annual) 1984. not priced. 289p. *Es.
TF: the 1984 edition, published in 1985, has long runs of figures to 1984.
Includes a section of statistical tables relating to credit.

Δ H Transport and communications

Δ H – i Ships and shipping

1021 Tráfico marítimo y comercio por vías de transporte [Shipping and trade by transport routes].
Dirección General de Aduanas, Guzmán el Bueno 137, Madrid 3.
1957– 1980. Ptas 500. 954p. *Es.
TF: the 1980 edition, published in 1982, has data for 1980.

Δ H – ii Roads and road transport

1022 Boletín informativo: anuario estadístico general [Information bulletin: annual general statistics].
Dirección General de Trafico, Ministerio del Interior, Josefa Valcarcer 28, 28027 Madrid.
1960– 1984. Ptas 1000. 180p. ISSN 0085-6568. *Es.
TF: the 1984 edition, published in 1985, has data for 1984.
Data on road traffic, including accidents, licenses, transfers, foreign vehicles, etc.

1023 Encuesta nacional sobre transporte de mercancios por carretera: resultados nacionales y provinciales [National enquiry on the transport of goods by road: national and provincial results].
INE, Madrid.
1969– 2nd, 1977. Ptas 800 each vol. 2 vols. *Es.
TF: the results of the 1977 enquiry were published in 1978 & 1979.
Volume 1 has national data, vol. 2 provincial data.

E

Δ H – iii Railways and rail transport

1024 Memoria correspondiente al ejercicio... [Report... (of the Spanish State Railways)] (RENFE).
RENFE, avenida Pío XII s/n, Nuevos Pabellones Chanmartín, Madrid 28036.
(annual) 1984. not priced. *Es.
TF: the 1984 report, published in 1985, has data for 1984 and some earlier years.
Includes statistical tables and graphs on passenger and goods transport services, consumption of power, traffic, finances, etc.

Δ H – v Telecommunications and postal services

1025 Anuario de las comunicaciones [Communications yearbook].
Ministerio de Transportes, Turismo y Comunicaciones, Pl. San Juan de la Cruz 3, Madrid.
1982- 1982. not priced. 113p. *Es.
TF: the 1982 edition, published in 1984, has data for 1981.
Data for post offices, telegraph offices and telephone service, including centres and buildings, equipment, services, employment, economic and financial information and tariffs. Also monthly data on equipment and services, provincial data, historical data and international data.

FRANCE
FRANKREICH

Central statistical office

1026 Institut National de la Statistique et des Etudes Economiques (INSEE) [National Institute for Statistics and Economic Studies].
18 blvd Adolphe Pinard, 75675 Paris Cedex 14.
t 539 22 77. tx 200655 Answerback INSEELEC.
INSEE is the central official organisation for economic information in France. It is concerred with social and economic demography, consumption, prices, income, national accounts, and national ard regional economic plans.
In the entries which follow, the Institut is abbreviated to INSEE, Paris.

Libraries

The library of INSEE (see above) includes all publications of INSEE and those of foreign governments and international organisations. It is open to the public for reference from 9.15 to 12.30 and from 13.45 to 17.30 from Monday to Friday. Regional offices of INSEE in the main cities of France all have INSEE publications available for reference in their libraries.

Libraries and information services abroad

Copies of certain French statistical publications are available for reference in French embassies abroad, including:

United Kingdom	French Embassy, 12 Stanhope Gate, London W1. t 01-493 5021.
Australia	French Embassy, 6 Darwin Place, Yarralumla, Canberra. t 95 1000.
Canada	French Embassy, 42 Sussex Drive, Ottawa K1M 2C9. t 233 5681.
New Zealand	French Embassy, 1-3 Willeston Street, Wellington. t 720 200.
USA	French Embassy, 2535 Belmont Road NW, Washington DC 20008. t (202) 328 2600.

Bibliographies

1027 Courrier des statistiques (information sur le système statistique publique) [News of statistics (information on the system of national statistics)].
A quarterly bulletin (Fr 78 yr or Fr 100 yr abroad). ISSN 0151-9514.

1028 Catalogue (INSEE).
An annual sales list of publications of INSEE. Free from INSEE.
Note: many French government departments, including Direction Générale des Douanes et Droits Indirects [Customs Department]; Ministère de l'Agriculture: Service Central des Enquêtes et Etudes Statistiques [Ministry of Agriculture: Central Service of Statistical Enquiries and Studies]; and Ministère des Transports [Ministry of Transport]) also issue annual sales catalogues of their statistical publications.

1029 Répertoire des sources statistiques [Repertory of statistical sources] (INSEE).
Vol.1 has information on demographic and social statistics; vol.2 on production statistics, monetary and financial statistics. (Published in 1983. Fr 75 each volume).

Statistical publications

Δ A General

1030 Annuaire statistique de la France [Statistical yearbook of France].
INSEE, Paris.
1885- 1983. Fr 360. 919p. *Fr.
TF: the 1983 edition, published in 1983, has data for 1982 and long runs of earlier years in many tables.
Main sections:
Geography and demography - Population and condition life - General economic data (national accounts, enterprises & establishments, industrial production, energy balances, production & wholesale price indices, retail price indices, productivity, economic movements) - Activities of production (by industry) - Service trades (tourism, transport, posts & telecommunications, etc) - Consumption, etc (household consumption, prices, wages, social services, insurance, foreign trade, internal trade) - Finance.

1031 Tableaux de l'économie française [Pictures of the French economy].
INSEE, Paris.
1958- 1984. Fr 32. 182p. *Fr.
An abridged version of 1030 above.

Δ A, continued

1032 Bulletin mensuel de statistique [Monthly bulletin of statistics].
INSEE, Paris.
1950- Fr 23 (Fr 28 abroad); or Fr 240 yr (Fr 275 yr abroad). ISSN 0007-4713. *Fr.
TF: each issue contains two years annual figures and at least 12 months up to one or two months prior to the date of the issue for most tables.
Weekly and/or monthly (& some quarterly) data on climate, demography, employment, health, agriculture, fisheries, industry, transport, internal trade, bankruptcy of firms, foreign trade, agriculture and food price indexes, energy and industry prices and price indexes, consumer price indexes, retail prices in Paris region, wages, social security, finance, etc.
Note: also available on microfiche Fr 15; or Fr 125 yr (Fr 155 yr abroad).

1033 Information rapides [Rapid information].
INSEE, Paris.
approx 250 issues a year. Fr 8 or Fr 1030 yr (Fr 1260 abroad). ISSN 0151-1475. *Fr.
Complements ′Tendances de la conjoncture′ (820), giving more up to date figures. The issues are two types: ′Notes′ contains the latest results of enquiries, etc. ′Cahiers′ gives more detailed data. There are 12 subject areas covered including industry, construction, labour, labour market, prices, and trade.

1034 Economie et statistique: revue mensuelle [Economics and statistics: monthly review].
INSEE, Paris.
1969- 11 issues a year. Fr 31 (Fr 37 abroad) or Fr 295 yr (Fr 350 yr abroad). Microfiche Fr 15 or Fr 125 yr (Fr 155 yr abroad). ISSN 0336-1454. *Fr.
A review of information work of INSEE and other statistical work. The studies are presented in easily comprehensible form and limited to essential statistical tables.

1035 Statistiques et indicateurs des régions françaises [French regional statistics and indicators].
INSEE, Paris.
1975- 1984. Fr 135 (Fr 63 on microfiche). 644p. *Fr.
TF: the 1984 edition, published in 1985, has data for several years to 1984.
Population, employment, agriculture & fisheries, industry & energy, services and tertiary activities (posts & telecommunications, health, tourism, information dissemination), foreign trade & transport, education, conditions of life in households, credit & fiscality, etc.
Note: issed in the series ′Les collections de l′INSEE, Série R′.

1036 Indicateur statistique [Statistical indicators].
Caisse Nationale de l′Assurance Maladie des Travailleurs Salariés, 66 avenue du Maine, 75682 Paris Cedex 14.
TF: the 1984 edition, published in 1984, has data for 1982 and/or 1983 or the latest available.
Detailed statistical tables on economic and social statistics (economy, households, labour and employment, vital statistics), health statistics, social security statistics, and administrative data.

1037 Guide statistique de la BNP [Statistical guide of the National Bank of Paris].
Banque Nationale de Paris, 6 blvd des Capucines, 75009 Paris.
1965- 1983. not priced. 304p. *Fr.
TF: the 1983 edition, published in 1983, has data for varying periods.
Sections on France and the state of the world; ′agents′ (population, vital statistics, town and country, households, employment, enterprises); world economy (national accounts, investments, productivity); economic cycle (research, energy, raw materials, agriculture, manufacturing industry, housing and construction, transport and telecommunications, consumption, distribution, finances, foreign exchange, labour, social data). Information is for France compared with other countries.
Note: the Bank has also issued ′Guide statistique des 22 régions de France′ (1980. 285p).

1038 Tendances de la conjoncture [Economic trends].
INSEE, Paris.
1968- monthly 8 issues plus supplements). Fr 46 or Fr 470 yr (Fr 52 or Fr 570 yr abroad). *Fr.
TF: each issue is in 2 parts. Part 1 has data for 10 years, part 2 for 20 years.
Graphs and indices of trends in industrial production, employment, consumption, internal trade, investment in industry, housing, construction and public works, foreign demand and foreign trade, agriculture, wholesale and retail prices, cost of living, money and credit, national accounts, etc.

1038a La zone franc... [The franc area].
Comité Monétaire de la Zone Franc, 39 rue Croix-des-Petits-Champs, 75049 Paris Cedex 01.
1967- 1983. not priced. 408p. *Fr.
TF: the 1983 edition, published in 1984, has data for 1981 to 1983.
Trends in production, foreign trade, finance and investment, money and credit, balance of payments, currency reserves, etc. in the French-speaking and franc CFA countries, including France and Monaco. Tables are included in the text.

Δ A, continued

1039 Les collections de l'INSEE [The collections of INSEE].
INSEE, Paris.
1969- prices vary for single issues; Fr 1795 (Fr 2170 abroad) for complete collection of 36 vols a year (Microfiches: Fr 810 (Fr 1050 abroad). ISSN 0533-0815. *Fr.
The results of studies carried out by INSEE, the series do not include some annuals which are referred to elsewhere in this guide. The subjects of the 5 series are:
Série C Accounts and plans. 8 a year. Fr 435 yr (Fr 540 yr abroad)
Série D Demography. 10 a year. Fr 570 yr (Fr 670 yr abroad)
Série E Enterprises. 8 a year. Fr 460 yr (Fr 540 yr abroad)
Série M Households. 10 a year. Fr 570 yr (Fr 670 yr abroad)
Série R Regions. 4 a year. Fr 245 yr (Fr 290 yr abroad).
A new series 'Premiers résultats' [First results] is monthly & free to subscribers to 'Les collections...'.
Note: the series are also available on microfiche.
Note 2: the series 'Archives et documents' (1980- irregular. separately priced) is intended for a more limited, specialist audience, covering the subjects of the issues in more detail.

Δ B Production

1040 Enquête annuelle d'entreprise [Annual survey of enterprises].
Ministère du Redéploiement Industriel et du Commerce Extérieur, Le Service d'Etude des Strategies et des Statistiques Industrielles (SESSI), 85 blvd du Montparnasse, 75270 Paris Cedex 06.
1968- 1982 (published in 1984). Fr 64 each vol. 4 vols. *Fr.
Contents:
Vol 1: Energy, water, urban heating, various minerals and metals, metallurgy.
Vol 2: Mechanical, construction, electrical and electronic industries.
Vol 3: Chemicals and associated industries.
Vol 4: Textiles, clothing, leather, paper, wood and other industries.
Note: First results were published mid-1983 (Fr 34) and provisional results late 1983 (Fr 64). More detailed data is available on microfiche (Fr 5 each fiche).

Δ B - ii Agriculture, fisheries, forestry, etc

1041 Annuaire de statistique agricole [Yearbook of agricultural statistics].
Ministère de l'Agriculture, Service Central des Enquêtes et Etudes Statistiques, 4 avenue de Saint-Mandé, 75570 Paris Cedex 12.
1903- 1982. Vol 1: Fr 350 (microfiche Fr 80); Vol 2: Fr 200 (microfiche Fr 40). ISSN 0243-6825. *Fr.
TF: the 1982 edition, published late 1984, has data for 1982.
Vol. 1 has national data on climate, agricultural structure & organisation of production, education, labour, social, detailed production, forests, agriculture & food industries, prices, foreign trade, etc. Vol. 2 has regional and departmental data.

Δ B - ii(a) Agriculture and horticulture

< see also 1104

1042 Recensement général de l'agriculture [General census of agriculture].
Ministère de l'Agriculture, Service Central des Enquêtes et Etudes Statistiques, 4 avenue de Saint-Mandé, 75570 Paris Cedex 12 and INSEE.
1955- 1979-1980. *Fr.
TF: main results of the 1979-1980 census were published in 1981; others from 1981-
Contents:
Résultats nationaux: (Fr 50 each vol)
Vol 1: Inventaries. Vol 2: Population
Vol 3: Cultivation. Vol 4: Livestock
Vol 5: Mountainous zone. Vol 6: Exploitation
Résultats par départements:
Communes (Fr 35) Agricultural regions.

1043 Bulletin de statistique agricole [Bulletin of agricultural statistics].
Ministère de l'Agriculture, SCEES, Paris.
1962- 6 a year. Fr 50 (Microfiche Fr 10) or Fr 250 yr (Microfiche Fr 60 yr). ISSN 0336-9919. *Fr.
Presents monthly series for three years on agriculture and the agriculture and food industries.

1044 Collections de statistiques agricoles [Collections of agricultural statistics].
Ministère de l'Agriculture, Service Central des Enquêtes et Etudes Statistiques, 4 avenue de Saint-Mandé, 75570 Paris Cedex 12.
(irregular - about 10 a year). Fr 80 or Fr 700 yr (Fr 90 or Fr 810 yr abroad). ISSN 0336-5638. *Fr.
A collection of statistical studies and commentaries on various themes, including 'Enquête annuelle d'entreprise...principaux résultats'.

1045 Les comptes de l'agriculture française... [Accounts of French agriculture].
INSEE, Paris.
1968- 1983. Fr 110 (Microfiche Fr 30). 268p. *Fr.
TF: the 1983 edition, published in 1984, has data for 1980 to 1983.
A report is followed by statistical data on production and social matters (salaries, security, etc).
Note: issued in the series 'Collections de l'INSEE, series C'.

Δ B – ii(a), continued

1046 Réseau d'information comptable agricole (System of agricultural accounts information].
INSEE, Paris.
1974- 1980-1981. Fr 67 (Microfiche Fr 39). 358p. *Fr.
TF: the results of the 1980-1981 enquiry were published in 1984.
Principal results of the enquiry for France as a whole and by regions.
Note: issued in the series 'Collections de l'INSEE, series E'.

1047 Graph-agri: annuaire de graphiques agricoles [Graph-agri: yearbook of agricultural graphs].
Ministère de l'Agriculture, Service Central des Enquêtes et Etudes Statistiques, 4 avenue de Saint-Mandé, 75570 Paris Cedex 12.
1979- 1983. Fr 95. ISSN 242-2085. *Fr.
Recent information in the form of tables, charts and graphs, with brief comments, on the agricultural world and its evolution in the last 10 years.
Note: also 'Graph-agri régions' [Graph-agri regions] is published at irregular intervals (Fr 90).

1048 L'économie laitière en chiffres [Milk economy in figures] (Centre National Interprofessionnel de l'Economie Laitère (CNIEL).
CNIEL, 8 rue Danielle Casanova, 75002 Paris.
(annual) 1983. Fr 21. 167p. *Fr.
TF: the 1983 edition, published May 1983, has data for 1982 and for one or two earlier years for comparison in some tables.
The structure of the milk industry, production, manufacturing, prices, foreign trade, consumption, etc., for France, the EEC and the world.

Δ B – ii(b) Fisheries

1049 Statistiques des pêches maritimes [Statistics of sea fisheries].
Direction des Pêches Maritimes, 3 place de Fontenoy, 75700 Paris.
1921- 1980 et 1981. not priced. 163p. *Fr.
TF: the 1980 & 1981 edition, published in 1983, has data for 1980 and 1981. A 1982-1983-1984 edition was due to be published in 1985.
Detailed tables of fish landed at French ports, the fishing fleet, related industries, equipment for fishing, foreign trade, etc.

1050 Germes.
Union des Armateurs à la Pêche de France, 59 rue des Mathurins, 75008 Paris.
(annual) 1986 (published early 1986). not priced. *Fr.
Data on the state of the French fishing fleet on the 1st January.

Δ B – iii Industry

1051 Annuaire de statistique industrielle [Yearbook of industrial statistics].
Ministère du Redéploiement Industriel et du Commerce Extérieur, Le Service d'Etude des Strategies et des Statistiques Industrielles (SESSI), 85 blvd du Montparnasse, 75270 Paris Cedex 06.
1947- 1984. Fr 270. 454p. *Fr.
TF: the 1984 edition, published late 1984, has data for 1983 and five earlier years.
3000 statistical series; annual results on production, deliveries, stocks, & foreign trade. Includes data on energy; minerals & ferrous metals - first manufacture; minerals, metals & semi-finished products; construction materials; glass; chemicals; foundries; metalwork; mechanical construction; electric & electronic construction; motor vehicles & other land transport; naval & aeronautic construction; precision instruments & machines; agriculture & food; tobacco; textiles & skins; woodwork; furniture; paper & board; rubber; plastics.

1052 Bulletin mensuel de statistique industrielle [Monthly bulletin of industrial statistics].
Ministère du Redéploiement Industriel et du Commerce Extérieur, Le Service d'Etude des Strategies et des Statistiques Industrielles (SESSI), 85 blvd du Montparnasse, 75270 Paris Cedex 06.
1945- 11 issues a year. Fr 290 yr. ISSN 0151-0770. *Fr.
TF: each issue has data for five quarters, previous year, year of reference, and the last few months to the latest data available.
Up-dates the information contained in 1051 above.

1053 Les chiffres clés de l'industrie [Key figures of industry].
Ministere du Redeploiement Industriel et du Commerce Exterieur, 85 blvd du Montparnasse, 75270 Paris Cedex 06.
(annual) 1985. Fr 62. 83p. *Fr.
TF: the 1985 edition was published in 1985.
Data on the place of French industry in the world, the role of industry in the French economy, international exchanges, the fabric of French industry, and the main sectors of industry, including investments, production, etc.

1054 Comptes régionaux des branches industrielles... [Regional accounts by industries].
INSEE, Paris.
1970- 1979 & 1980. Fr 58 (Microfiche Fr 27). 256p. *Fr.
TF: the 1979 & 1980 edition, with data for those years, was published in 1984.
Note: issued in the series 'Collections de l'INSEE, series R'.

Δ B – iii, continued

1055 Les consommations d'énergie dans l'industrie [Consumption of energy in industry].
Ministère du Redéploiement Industriel et du Commerce Extérieur, Le Service d'Etude des Strategies et des Statistiques Industrielles (SESSI), 85 blvd du Montparnasse, 75270 Paris Cedex 06.
(annual) 1982. Fr 64. *Fr.
Data on industrial establishments with 20 employees or more, including purchases, stocks, consumption by type of product assembled, sectoral data, regional data, etc.

Δ B – iii(a) Food products, beverages, tobacco

< see also 1090

1056 La conserve agricole...rapport économique [Canned agricultural produce...economic report].
Confédération Française de la Conserve, rue d'Alésia 44, 75682 Paris Cedex 14.
(annual) 1983. Fr 150 (Fr 190 abroad). c 60p. *Fr.
TF: the 1983 report, published in 1984, has data for several years to 1982 or 1983.
Includes tables in the text and a section of statistical tables at the end of the report on production, sales, etc. of canned vegetables.

1057 Données statistiques sur l'industrie sucrière [Statistics of the sugar industry].
Syndicat National des Fabricants de Sucre de France, 23 avenue d'Iéna, 75783 Paris Cedex 16.
(annual) 1983 (published in 1984). not priced. *Fr.

1058 Rapport annuel... [Annual report on the cognac market].
Bureau National Interprofessionnel du Cognac, 3 Allées de la Corderie, (B.P. 18), 16101 Cognac Cedex.
(annual) 1984/85. not priced. c 250p. *Fr.
TF: the 1984/85 report, published late 1985, has data for the period 1st September 1984 to 31st August 1985. Data is also published at the end of the calandar year and monthly.
General information regarding the production and shipments of cognac.

1059 Statistiques... [Statistics...].
Société Nationale d'Exploitation Industrielle des Tabacs et Allumettes (SEITA), quai d'Orsay 53, 75340 Paris Cedex 07.
(annual) 1982 (published in 1983). not priced. *Fr.
Data on production, consumption, foreign trade, etc. of tobacco and matches.

Δ B – iii(b) Textiles, paper, rubber, etc

< see also 1091

1060 Statistiques de l'industrie française des pâtes, papiers et cartons [Statistics of the French pulp, paper and board industry].
Centre d'Etudes et de Productivité des Industries des Papiers, Cartons et Celluloses, 154 blvd Haussmann, 75008 Paris.
(annual) 1983. not priced. 34p. *Fr.
TF: the 1983 edition, published in 1984, has data for several years to 1983.
Statistical tables and graphs on the pulp industry (reception of wood, consumption of wood, etc., production of pulp and paper); paper and board industry (reception and stock of primary materials, production, production by regions, exports, imports, apparent consumption, energy consumption); and foreign data (EEC and other countries production and export of pulp, paper and board).

1061 Statistiques annuelles [Annual statistics].
Fédération Nationale des Transformateurs de Papier, 90 rue d'Amsterdam, 75009 Paris.
(annual) 1983. not priced. 1p. *Fr.
TF: the 1983 edition, published in 1984, has data for 1982 and 1983.
Production of converted papers, numbers of establishments involved, number of employees, hours worked, etc.

1062 Statistiques générale de l'industrie textile française [General statistics of the French textile industry].
Union des Industries Textiles, 10 rue d'Anjou, 75008 Paris.
(annual) 1981. not priced. c 50p. *Fr.
TF: the 1981 edition, published mid-1982, has data for 1981 and earlier years in some tables.
Number of enterprises and factories, wages, machinery imported, index numbers and also quantities of production, consumption, wholesale and retail price index numbers, and foreign trade.

1063 Industrie lainière française: statistiques de production [French wool industry: production statistics].
Comité Central de la Laine et des Fibres Associées, 12 rue d'Anjou, 75008 Paris.
(annual) 1983 (published in 1984). not priced. *Fr.

1064 Industrie lainière française: main-d'oeuvre, materiel et investissements... [French wool industry: labour, raw materials, and investments...].
Comité Central de la Laine et des Fibres Associées, 12 rue d'Anjou, 75008 Paris.
(annual) 1983 (published in 1984). not priced. *Fr.

Δ B – iii(b), continued

1065 L'industrie cotonnière française [The French cotton industry].
Syndicat Général de l'Industrie Cotonnière Française, B.P. 724.08, 75367 Paris.
(annual) 1981. not priced. c 50p. *Fr.
TF: the 1981 edition, published in 1982, has data for 1981 and some earlier years.
Includes data on production, consumption, investment, stocks, structure of establishments, manufacturers' exports, etc.

1066 Industrie française des textiles chimiques [French synthetic textile industry].
Syndicat Français des Textiles Artificiels et Synthétiques, 55 rue la Boétie, 75008 Paris.
(annual) 1984. free. 16p. *Fr.
TF: the 1984 edition, published in 1985, has data for 1984 compared with 1983 and earlier data in some charts.
Data on internal trade, foreign trade, production, prices, employment, etc.

Δ B – iii(c) Chemicals, pharmaceuticals, etc

1067 Exercice: Union des Industries Chimiques [annual report: Union of the Chemical Industry].
Union des Industries Chimiques, 64 avenue Marceau, 75008 Paris.
(annual) 1983. not priced. 51p. *Fr.
TF: the 1983 edition, published in 1984, has data for 1983 and also some figures for 1982.
The statistical section (p 45-51) has data on the French chemical industry (wholesale price index, turnover, investment, labour, production of principal products, foreign trade arranged by commodity groups and by countries of destination and origin).

Δ B – iii(d) Metals, etc

1068 Le fer blanc en France et dans le monde [Tin-plate in France and in the world].
Chambre Syndicale des Producteurs de Fer-blanc et de Fer-noir, 5 rue Paul Cézanne, 75008 Paris.
(annual) 1983. not priced. 24p. *Fr.
TF: the 1983 edition, published in 1984, has data for 1983 and some earlier years, and estimates for 1984.
Production, deliveries, apparent and real consumption, imports and exports, and utilisation of tin-plate.

Δ B – iii(e) Engineering

1069 Les industries mécaniques [Mechanical industries].
Fédération des Industries Mécaniques et Tranformatrices des Métaux, 10 Avenue Hoche, 75008 Paris Cedex 08.
1955- bi-monthly. Fr 35 or Fr 630 yr (Fr 735 yr abroad). *Fr.
Includes some tables and graphs on the industry.

1070 Les industries électriques, électroniques et informatiques: statistiques [Electric, electronic and informatics industries: statistics].
Fédération des Industries Electriques et Electroniques, 11 rue Hamelin, 75783 Paris Cedex 16.
1974- 1982. not priced. c 30p. *Fr.
TF: the 1982 edition, published in 1983, has data for 1982.
Data on the structure of the industries, geographical location, foreign trade, production and assembly, wages and employment, internal trade, investments, and input and output.

1071 Le froid – la climatisation, cuisines professionnelles [Refrigeration – air-conditioning, professional kitchens].
FCC, 17 blvd Poissonnière, 75002 Paris.
1954- monthly. Fr 30 or Fr 240 yr (Fr 300 yr abroad). *Fr.
Includes a few statistical tables in the text, but no regular tables.

Δ B – iii(f) Other industries

1072 Les chiffres clés de la plaisance [Key figures of pleasure boating].
Fédération des Industries Nautiques, Port de la Bourdonnais, 75007 Paris.
1977- 1984. Fr 26. c 30p. *Fr.
TF: the 1984 edition, published in 1984, has data for several years to 1983.
Data on the industrial and commercial sector dealing with pleasure boats (construction of boats, equipment, foreign trade, education, number of boats registered) and some international statistics.

Δ B – iv Construction

1073 Statistiques de la construction [Construction statistics] (Ministère de l'Urbanisme, du Logement et des Transports).
La Documentation Française, 29-31, quai Voltaire, 75340 Paris Cedex 07.
(monthly) Fr 21 or Fr 210 yr. *Fr.
TF: each issue has data for several months & quarters to about three months prior to the date of the issue.
Monthly & quarterly data on housing, demand, building authorised, started, finished; constructions authorised & started for buildings other than habitations.
Note: a retrospective volume, 'Statistiques rétrospectives des constructions authorisées à usage autre qu'habitation' was issued in 1982.

Δ B – v Energy

< see also 1055

1074 Résultats techniques d'exploitation.
Electricité de France, 2 rue Louis-Murat, 75008 Paris.
1960- 1984. not priced. c 30p. *Fr.
TF: the 1984 edition, published in 1985, has data for 1984 and some earlier years.
Data on production, distribution and consumption of all types of electric energy in France.

1075 Les chiffres clés énergie.
Ministère Recherche Industrie Energie, 101 rue de Grenelle, 75700 Paris.
(annual) 1982-1983. not priced. 153p. *Fr.
TF: the 1982-1983 edition, published in 1984, has data for several years to 1980, 1981 or 1982.
Production and reserves, consumption, foreign trade for world energy, energy in France, and petrol in the world.

1076 Bulletin mensuel [Monthly bulletin].
Comité Professionnel du Pétrol, 51 blvd de Courcelles, 75008 Paris.
1962- monthly. Fr 545 yr. *Fr.
TF: each issue has data for that month and the previous month, and some earlier figures. It is published about three weeks after the month of the issue.
The French petroleum market (demand, stocks, sales, prices, etc); the activities of the French petroleum industry (production, foreign trade, refining, transport, cost of crude oil, etc); the French economy (economic indicators, statistics of energy other than petroleum, statistics of energy, statistics of transport, etc), and international data.

1077 Pétrole... [Petroleum].
Comité Professionnel du Pétrole, 51 blvd de Courcelles, 75008 Paris.
1974- 1984. Fr 585. c 400p. *Fr.
TF: the 1984 edition, published mid-1985, has data for several years to 1984.
A statistical yearbook with sections on petroleum in the French economy, French petroleum industry (including research, production, foreign trade, transport of crude oil, refining, stocks, transport of refined petroleum products, sales, labour, petrochemicals, investments), French market for petroleum products (by product), prices and taxes on petroleum products, and world petroleum.

1078 L'industrie française du pétrole [The French petroleum industry].
Union des Chambres Syndicales de l'Industrie du Pétrole, 16 avenue Kléber, 75116 Paris.
(annual) 1984. not priced. 72p. *Fr.
TF: the 1984 edition, published late 1984, has long runs of figures to 1984.
Petroleum energy & stocks, petroleum & natural gas in the world, and petroleum in the French economy (exploration and production , transport of crude oil - fleet and pipelines, refining, petrochemicals, consumption, distribution, protection of the environment, security, employees). Statistical tables are included in the text.

1079 Le marché pétrolier français: statistiques mensuelles par département et par région [The French petroleum market: monthly statistics by departments and regions].
Comité Professionnel du Pétrole, 51 blvd de Courselles, 75008 Paris.
(monthly) not priced. *Fr.
TF: each issue has data for about 12 months and is published about three months after the end of the period covered.

1080 Lubrifiants: statistiques [Lubricants: statistics].
Centre Professionnel des Lubrifiants, 4 avenue Hoch, 75008 Paris.
(annual) 1984. not priced. 115p. *Fr.
TF: the 1984 edition, published mid-1985, has data for 1984 and some earlier years.
Resources & stocks, distribution, additives, etc. Also resources and distribution of lubricarts in several European countries, USA, Canada & Japan.

1081 Production [et] distribution de l'énergie électrique en France: statistiques... [Production & distribution of electric energy in France: statistics] (Direction du Gaz, de l'Electricité et du Charbon, Ministère du Redéploiement Industriel et du Commerce Extérieur).
Electricité de France, 2 rue Louis-Murat, 75008 Paris.
1963- 1983. 93p. *Fr.
TF: the 1983 edition, published in 1985, has data for 1983.
Electricity production, consumption, balance of production & consumption, and data on the network of transport of electric energy in each region of France.

1082 Statistiques de l'industrie gazière en France [Statistics of the gas industry in France].
Direction du Gaz, de l'Electricité et du Charbon, Ministère du Redéploiement Industriel et du Commerce Extérieur, 24 rue de l'Université, 75007 Paris.
1948- 1982. not priced. 31p. *Fr.
TF: the 1983 edition, published in 1984, has data for 1983.
Production, distribution, transport, supply & utilisation of gas in France. There is also an annex of retrospective statistics.

Δ B – v, continued

1083 Statistiques...production, transport, distribution [Statistics...].
Gaz de France, 23 rue Philibert-Delorme, 75840 Paris Cedex 17.
1947– 1983. not priced. 100p. *Fr.
TF: the 1983 edition, published in 1984, has data for 1983.
Detailed data on the production, transport & distribution of Gas.
Note: Gaz de France also issue 'Statistiques provisionales' [provisional statistics] (1984 published early 1985).

Δ C External trade

1084 Statistiques du commerce extérieur de la France: importations, exportations en N G P [Statistics of foreign trade of France: imports, exports by a general nomenclature of products].
Direction Générale des Douanes et Droits Indirects, 8 rue de la Tour-des-Dames, 75436 Paris Cedex 09.
1960– 1984. 4 vols. *Fr.
TF: the 1984 edition, published in 1985, has data for 1984.
Contents:
Vol I: General observations and results (Free with vols 2-4).
Vol II: Detailed tables of imports and exports for classes 01 to 71 of N G P subdivided by countries of origin and destination (Fr 130).
Vol III: ...for classes 72 to 99 of N G P (Fr 130).
Vol IV: Data arranged by countries (Fr 60).

1085 Statistiques du commerce extérieur de la France: annuaire abrégé... [Statistics of the foreign trade of France: abridged yearbook...].
Direction Général des Douanes et Droits Indirects, 8 rue de la Tour-des-Dames, 75436 Paris Cedex 09.
1963– 1984. Fr 120. c 200p. *Fr.
TF: the 1984 edition, published in 1985, has data for 1984.
A condensed version of 1084.

1086 Statistiques du commerce extérieur de la France: résultats annuels: Commentaires [Statistics of foreign trade of France: annual results: commentaries].
Direction Générale des Douanes et Droits Indirects, 8 rue de la Tour-des-Dames, 75436 Paris Cedex 09.
1955– 1983. Fr 120. *Fr.
TF: the 1983 edition, published in 1984, has data for 1983.
General data on foreign trade, with graphs, diagrams and tables showing trends.

1087 Statistiques du commerce extérieur: résultats trimestriels [Foreign trade statistics: quarterly results].
Direction Générale des Douanes et Droits Indirects, 8 rue de la Tour-des-Dames, 75436 Paris Cedex 09.
(quarterly) Fr 45 or Fr 130 yr. *Fr.
TF: each issue has data for five separate quarters and is published about two months after the end of the latest quarter covered.
Main tables show statistics of imports and exports arranged by countries of origin and destination and subdivided by commodities. Increase or decrease in values over the same period in the previous year is shown.

1088 Statistiques du commerce extérieur de la France: tableau général des transports [Statistics of the foreign trade of France: general tables of transport].
Direction Générale des Douanes et Droits Indirects, 8 rue de la Tour-des-Dames, 75436 Paris Cedex 09.
1960– 1982. Fr 320. 2 vols. *Fr.
TF: the 1982 edition, published in 1983, has data for 1982.
Data on the mode of transport of goods from countries of origin and to countries of destination, including the tonnage of goods. Vol. I has data arranged by commodities subdivided by countries; Vol. II has data by countries subdivided by commodities.

1089 Statistiques du commerce extérieur de la France: le transport du commerce extérieur [Statistics of the foreign trade of France: transport of foreign trade].
Direction Générale des Douanes et Droits Indirects, 8 rue de la Tour-des-Dames, 75436 Paris Cedex 09.
1964/65– 1981. Fr 160. c 55p. *Fr.
TF: the 1981 edition, published in 1982, has data for 1981.
Data on the foreign trade of France, its mode of transport in France and abroad, and traffic at French ports by the fleets of the principal nationalities.

1090 Statistiques des exportations de vins et spiritueux [Statistics of exports of wines and spirits].
Compagnie Française de Contrôle et d'Expertise Comptables (CFCE), 6 avenue de Messine, 75008 Paris.
(annual) 1982 (published in 1984). not priced. *Fr.

1091 Industrie lainière française: statistiques du commerce extèrieur de produits lainiers... [The French wool industry: foreign trade statistics of woollen products...].
Comité Central de la Laine et des Fibres Associées, 12 rue d'
(annual) 1983 (published in 1984). not priced. *Fr.

1092 Industrie du cuir: commerce extérieur [Leather industry: foreign trade].
Conseil National du Cuir, 109 rue du Faubourg-Sainte Honoré, 75008 Paris.
(annual) 1983 (published in 1984). not priced. *Fr.

Δ D Internal distribution and service trade

Δ D – i Wholesale and retail trade

1093 Le commerce... [Trade].
INSEE, Paris.
1969/71- 1983. Fr 60 (Microfiche Fr 18). 136p. *Fr.
TF: the 1983 edition, published in 1984, has data for 1982 or 1983 and some earlier years.
Data on wholesale and retail trade, enterprises, etc.
Note: issued in the series 'Collections de l'INSEE, series C'.

1094 Enquete annuelle d'entreprise dans le commerce [Annual enquiry on commercial enterprises].
INSEE, Paris.
1971- 1982 (published in 1984). Fr 55 (Microfiche Fr 24). 228p. *Fr.
Note: issued in the series 'Collections de l'INSEE, series E'.

Δ D – ii Service trades

1095 Enquête annuelle d'entreprise dans les services: principaux résultats... [Annual enquiry on service enterprises: principal results].
INSEE, Paris.
1982- 1982 (published in 1984). Fr 55. 180p. *Fr.
Notes: issued as 'Collections de l'INSEE, series E. Other titles in the series include 'Enquête annuelle d'entreprise dans les services: publicité: (résultats détaillés...)' and 'Enquête annuelle d'entreprise dans les services: activités cinématographiques (résultats...)'.

Δ D – iii Advertising

1096 Proscop média: géographie du marché français [Proscop media: geography of the French market].
Institut Proscop, 25 rue Marbeuf, 75008 Paris.
1973/74- 1985. not priced. 311p. *Fr.
TF: the 1985 edition, published mid-1985, includes estimates for 1984 & many other figures without dates.
Socio-economic data concerning the advertising audience, by Departement.

Δ D – iv Tourism and travel

1097 Annuaire statistique du tourisme [Statistical yearbook of tourism]. (Ministère du Commerce Extérieur et du Tourisme, Direction du Tourisme).
La Documentation Française, 29-31 quai Voltaire, 75340 Paris Cedex 07.
1983- 1983. Fr 250. 510p. *Fr.
TF: the 1983 edition, published in 1983, has data for 1981 and earlier years.
National data on hotels, camping, lodgings for the young, rural lodgings, other lodgings, sports & tourist equipment, education and employment. Also regional data by area.
Note: statistical tables, but no regular tables, are also included in 'L'économie du tourisme' (1982- quarterly. Fr 51 or Fr 181 yr (Fr 193 yr abroad)) and 'Regards sur l'économie du tourisme' (1974- quarterly. Fr 38 each issue.

Δ E Population

1098 Recensement général de la population [Census of population].
INSEE, Paris.
1861- 1982. *Fr.
Published volumes are:
Population de la France (Métropole et départements d'outre-mer), régions, départements, arrondissements, cantons, communes [Numbers of inhabitants of France by regions, departments, etc] (Fr 220).
Principaux résultats – sondage au 1/20 – France métropolitaine [Principal results – 1/20 sample – metropolitan France] (Fr 50).
Les étrangers [Foreigners] (Fr 70).
Population de la France (départements, arrondissements, cantons, communes de la Métropole). Fascicules for departments (Fr 7 each); Collection of 96 fascicules (Fr 440); volume for all France (Fr 220).
Tableaux statistiques de population légale: population légale des communes de plus de 2000 habitants [Population of communes with over 2000 inhabitants] (Fr 30).
Guide d'utilisation du RP82 [Guide to the 1982 publication census] (Vol.1 Fr30, Vol. 2 Fr 90).
Population légale et statistiques communales complémentaires: évolutions démographiques, 1975-1982 et 1968-1975:
Le fascicule départmental (orange) (Fr 28).
Le volume régional (various prices).
La collection des 96 fascicules départementaux (22 vols. Fr 1900).
Villes et agglomérations urbaines Towns and urban areas] (Fr 70).
Resultats du sondage au $\frac{1}{4}$ [Results of $\frac{1}{4}$ sample].
Le fascicule départmental (vert) (various prices).
Le fascicule régional (various prices).
La collection des 96 fascicules départementaux (Fr 2700).
La collection des 22 volumes régionaux (Fr 1000).
Zones de peoplement industriel et urbain [Industrial & urban zones] (Fr 140).
Composition communale des zones de peuplement industriel (Fr 110).
Note: there are also issues on the census of population in 'Collections de l'INSEE'.

Δ E – i Vital statistics

1099 La situation démographique... [The demographic situation].
INSEE, Paris.
1968/69- 1981. Fr 40 (Microfiche Fr 12). 90p. *Fr.
TF: the 1981 edition was published in 1983, with data for 1983 and earlier years.
Principal information about the movement of population, external migration, marriage, divorce, births and deaths for France and by regions, departments and large urban communities.
Note: issued as 'Collections de l'INSEE, series D'.

Δ E – ii Labour

1100 Statistiques du travail: bulletin mensuel [Employment statistics: monthly bulletin] (Ministère du Travail, de l'Emploi et de la Formation Professionnelle).
La Documentation Française, 29-31 quai Voltaire, 75340 Paris Cedex 07.
(monthly) Fr 22 or Fr 280 yr. *Fr.
TF: each issue has data for several years, quarters and months to the month prior to the date of the issue, and is published three months later.
Detailed data on employment & wages, registration for employment, public assistance, foreign labour, etc.

1101 Structure des emplois... [Structure of employment].
INSEE, Paris.
1968- 1981 (published in 1984). Fr 45 (Microfiche Fr 18). 160p. *Fr.
Results of an annual enquiry in establishments with 10 or more employees.
Note: issued as 'Collections de l'INSEE, series D'.

1102 Enquête sur l'emploi...résultats détaillés [Enquiry on employment...detailed results].
INSEE, Paris.
1971- 1983 (published in 1984). Fr 55 (Microfiche Fr 24). 208p. *Fr.
Data on the population, the active population, occupations, employment, etc.
Note: issued in the series 'Collections de l'INSEE, series D'.

1103 L'apprentissage de 1977 à 1983 [Apprenticeship, 1977 to 1983] (Ministère des Affaires Sociales et de la Solidarité Nationale, Service des Etudes et de la Statistiques, Travail-Emploi).
Documentation Française, 29-31 quai Voltaire, 75340 Paris Cedex 07.
1984. not priced. 71p. *Fr.
Note: issued in the series 'Dossiers statistiques du travail et de l'emploi', no. 2.

1104 Accidents du travail et des maladies professionnelles des salaires agricoles: statistiques [Accidents at work...statistics].
Caisse Nationale de l'Assurance Maladie des Travailleurs Salariés, 66 avenue du Maine, 75682 Paris Cedex 14.
(annual) 1982. not priced. *Fr.
TF: the 1982 edition, published in 1983, has data for 1982.
Data on the frequency of accidents, gravity and incapacity, risks, finance, assurances, etc.
Note: previously issued triennially with the title 'Statistiques nationale d'accidents du travail'.

Δ F Social and political

1105 Données sociales [Social statistics].
INSEE, Paris.
1973- 4th, 1984. Fr 160. 580p. *Fr.
TF: the 1984 edition, published in 1984, has data mainly to 1980 or the latest figures available.
Population, health, education, employment, conditions of work, income, consumption, social and cultural practices, social security, unemployment compensation, education and health care, etc.

Δ F – i Standard of living

< see also 391

1106 La consommation des ménages... [Consumption of households].
INSEE, Paris.
1959/68- 1983. Fr 40 (Microfiche Fr 18). 104p. *Fr.
TF: the 1983 edition, published in 1984, has data for 1976 to 1983.
Data is given by product, by function and by durability.
Note: issued in the series 'Collections de l'INSEE, series M'.

1107 Consommation et lieux d'achat des produits alimentaires... [Consumption by place of purchase of food products].
INSEE, Paris.
1969- 1981 (published in 1984). Fr 60 (Microfiche Fr 30). 280p. *Fr.
Note: issued in the series 'Collections de l'INSEE, series M'.

1108 L'équipement des ménages en biens durables au début de... [Durable household goods...].
INSEE, Paris.
1973- 1983 (published in 1983). Fr 38 (Microfiche Fr 12). 60p. *Fr.
Note: issued in the series 'Collections de l'INSEE, series M'.

Δ F – ii Health and welfare

1109 Annuaire des statistiques sanitaires et sociales [Yearbook of medical and social statistics].
Ministère de la Santé et de la Sécurité Sociale, 14 avenue Duquesne, 75700 Paris.
(annual) 1980. Fr 30. 194p. *Fr.
TF: the 1980 edition, published in 1980, has data to 1977 or 1978.
Demographic indicators, morbidity and mortality by cause, medical and paramedical professions, hospitals, maternal and infant protection, social aid, social establishments, and finances.

1110 Statistique des causes médicales de décès [Statistics of medical causes of death] (Institut National de la Santé et de la Recherche Médicale [National Institute of Health and Medical Research]).
INSERM, 44 chemin de Ronde, 78110 Le Vésinet.
1968- 1978 (published in 1982). Fr 64.20 each vol. 2 vols. *Fr.
Vol I: The results for France; vol II: The regions.

1111 Causes médicales de décès...résultats définitifs: France [Medical causes of death...final results] (Institut National de la Santé et de la Recherche Médicale [Nationale Institute of Health and Medical Research]).
INSERM, 44 chemin de Ronde, 78110 Le Vésinet.
1979- 1982. not priced. *Fr.
Data is given by age, by sex, and by age group.
Note: monthly and annual provisional results are also issued.

Δ F – iii Education and leisure

< see also 1072

1112 Statistiques des enseignements [Statistics of education].
Ministère de l'Education Nationale, Service de l'Informatique de Gestion et des Statistiques (SIGES), Vanves.
1967/68- 19 fascicules a year. Fr 168 yr (Fr 13 each fascicule). *Fr.
TF: the fascicules relating to an academic year are published during the following calendar year and include some data for earlier years also.
Each fascicule, as listed below, is concerned with a particular aspect of education, including finance, educational establishments, personnel, students, pupils, examinations and diplomas.
Chapter 1 – Fascicule 1: the budget relative to national education; burseries and State aid.
Chapter 2 – Fascicule 1: primary education.
2: secondary school education.
Chapter 3 – Fascicule 1: personnel in public and private education.
2: recruitment.
Chapter 4 – School children
Fascicule 1: world comparisons.
2: pre-school and primary school children.
3: secondary school children.
Chapter 5 – Students
Fascicule 1: public education.
2: universities.
3: non-university higher education.
4: continuing education.
Chapter 6 – Examinations and diplomas
Fascicule 1: elementary & secondary education; technical & professional education.
2: the Baccalauréat.
3: universities.
4: non-university higher education.

1113 Repères et references statistiques sur les enseignements et la formation...année scolaire et universitaire... [Landmarks and references in education...school and university year].
Ministère de l'Education Nationale, Service de l'Informatique de Gestion et des Statistiques (SIGES), Vanves.
1984- 1984. Fr 50. 215p. ISSN 0761-3423. *Fr.
TF: the 1984 edition, published in 1984, relates to the school and university year 1982/83.
Data on the educational system, budget, costs and financing, educational aids (burseries, transport, etc), establishments, personnel, pupils in schools, pupils in colleges and lycées, apprentices, students (university), further education – 16-18 year olds, examinations and certificates, etc.
Note: 'Tableaux des enseignements et de la formation' was issued annually between 1969 and 1982, and two special retrospective vols for 1958/59- 1967/68 and 1967/68 to 1976/77 are also available (Fr 110 each vol).

1114 Bulletin des bibliothèques de France [Bulletin of French libraries].
BBF, 17-21 blvd du 11 Novembre 1918, 69100 Villeurbanne.
1956- 6 a year. Fr 70 or Fr 340 yr (Fr 390 yr abroad). *Fr.
Many issues include a section of statistics relating to a particular aspect of library services, e.g. 'Bibliothèques municipales: statistiques, 1982' [Municipal libraries: statistics] (v 30. no.1. 1985. p. 105-112); 'Bibliothèques centrales de prêt: statistiques, 1983' [Central lending libraries, statistics] (v 30. nos.3-4. 1985. p. 312-314); and 'Enquête statistique générale auprès des bibliothèques universitaires (ESGBU)', '1983 et 1984' [General statistical enquiry on university libraries] (v 30. nos.4-5. 1984. p. 349-), which is taken annually.

Δ F - iii, continued

1115 Données statistiques sur l'édition de livres en France [Statistics of book publication in France] (Syndicat National de l'Édition).
Cercle de la Librairie, 35 rue Grégoire-de-Tours, 75279 Paris Cedex 06.
1979- 1983. not priced. 28p. *Fr.
TF: the 1983 edition, published in 1984, has data for 1983 and 1982 also in some tables.
Production, sales, stocks, etc. of books by category (new, new editions, new impressions, etc).

1116 Presse & statistiques [Publishing & statistics] (Bureau de la Statistique du Service Juridique et Technique de l'Information).
S.J.T.I., 69 rue de Varenne, 75700 Paris.
1972- 1982. not priced. 123p. *Fr.
TF: the 1982 edition, published in 1984, has data for 1982 and earlier years in some tables.
Includes statistical tables and graphs on periodical titles published by frequency and by principal subject; national, local and specialised titles, etc.

Δ F - iv Justice

1117 Annuaire statistique de la justice [Statistical yearbook of justice] (Ministère de la Justice, Service de l'Administration Générale et de l'Equipement, Division de la Statistique de la Justice).
Documentation Française, 29-31 quai Voltaire, 75340 Paris Cedex 17.
1981- 1983. Fr 180. c 190p. *Fr.
TF: the 1983 edition, published in 1985, has data for several years to 1983.
General statistics; law; administrative justice; judicial institutions; civil and penal; education of offenders; prisons; judicial profession; personnel; institutions; court decisions; etc.

Δ G Finance

< see also 1038a

1118 Statistiques & études financières [Financial statistics and studies] (Ministère de l'Economie, des Finances et du Budget, Direction de la Prévision).
Imprimerie Nationale, 27/29 rue de la Convention, 75015 Paris.
1949- quarterly. Fr 30 or Fr 100 yr (Fr 130 yr abroad). *Fr.
Contains articles on varying subjects within the financial field, some of which include statistical tables.

1119 Compte rendu... [Report...]
Banque de France, 43 rue de Valois, 75001 Paris.
1910- 1984. free. 124p. *Fr.
TF: the 1984 report, published in 1985, has data for 1984 and some earlier years.
Data on the French economy, money and credit, foreign relations, and the finances and activities of the Bank.

1120 Bulletin trimestriel de la Banque de France [Quarterly bulletin...].
Banque de France, 43 rue de Valois, 75001 Paris.
1971- quarterly. Fr 36 or Fr 90 yr. *Fr.
TF: published in the last month of each quarter.

1121 La monnaie... [Money...] (Banque de France & Conseil National du Credit).
Banque de France, 43 rue de Valois, 75001 Paris.
1970- 1984. free. 55p. *Fr.
TF: the 1984 edition, published mid-1985, has data for 1984 and some earlier years.
Brief commentaries, tables and charts relating to the principal monetary statistics.
Note: 'Bulletin trimestriel de la Banque de France' also includes a section of statistical tables (1971- quarterly. Fr 36 or Fr 90 yr).

Δ G - i Banking

1122 Situation financière des régions en...opérations des guichets bancaires [Financial situation in the regions...transactions at bank counters].
Banque de France, 43 rue de Valois, 75001 Paris.
(annual) 1984. free. c 70p. *Fr.
TF: the 1984 edition, published in 1985, has data for 1984.

1123 Situation financière des régions de province en...opérations des résidents [Financial situation of provinces...transactions of residents].
Banque de France, 43 rue de Valois, 75001 Paris.
(annual) 1984. free. c 30p. *Fr.
TF: the 1984 edition, published in 1985, has data for 1984.

Δ G – ii Public finance

1124 Rapport sur les comptes de la nation [Report on national accounts].
INSEE, Paris.
1949/59– 1983. Fr 210 (Fr 118 on microfiche). 710p (in 4 vols). *Fr.
TF; the 1983 report, published in 1984, has data for one or two years to 1983.
The volumes are Report; Aggregate accounts; Comments and tables; Documents, guides and T.E.S. Coverage is wide, including population and employment, production, consumption, investment, prices, revenue, financial problems, wages and social services.
Note: issued in the series 'Collections de l'INSEE, series C'.

Δ G – v Insurance

1125 Recueil de données statistiques sur l'assurance automobile en France [Collection of statistical data on motor vehicle insurance in France].
Association Générale des Sociétés d'Assurance contre les Accidents, 118 rue de Tocqueville, 75850 Paris Cedex 17.
(annual) 1982 (published in 1984). not priced. *Fr.

Δ H Transport and communications

1126 Annuaire statistique des transports [Statistical yearbook of transport].
Ministère des Transports, Département des Statistiques des Transport, 55–57 rue Brillat Savarin, 75658 Paris Cedex 13.
1955/59– 1984. Fr 100. c 250p. *Fr.
TF: the 1984 edition, published in 1985, has data for 1984.
Principal statistics relative to the activities of transport enterprises, employment of vehicles; covers airports, sea ports, waterways, railways and roads.
Note: a monthly 'Bulletin mensuel de statistique' up-dates the information given in the annual, and there is also a pocketbook version of the annual 'Mémento de statistique des transports'.

1127 Note de conjoncture.
Ministère des Transports, Département des Statistiques des Transport, 55–57 rue Brillat Savarin, 75658 Paris Cedex 13.
(monthly) not priced. *Fr.
Statistics, graphs and commentary on the economy generally, and the transport sector in particular (wage rates, licences, failure of companies, goods and passenger traffic).

1128 Les transports en France [Transport in France].
INSEE, Paris.
1963/68– 1983–1984. Fr 60. 158p. *Fr.
TF: the 1983–1984 issue, with data for those years, was published late 1985.
Part 1: Report; part 2: Tables. Data is for all kinds of transport (road, rail, sea, air).
Note: issued in the series 'Collections de l'INSEE, series C'.

Δ H – i Ships and shipping

1129 Annuaire de la marine marchande [Yearbook of the merchant fleet].
Comité Central des Armateurs de France, 73 blvd haussmann, 75008 Paris.
1904– 1985. Fr 115. 276p. *Fr.
TF: the 1985 edition, published in 1985, has data for the position as at january 1985 and some retrospective years.
Includes a 6-page section of statistics on the French merchant fleet, including new registrations, tonnages by type of ship, etc.
Note: the organisation also issues an annual 'Le transport maritime: études et statistiques' (1983 ed. Fr 30) which includes some statistical tables in the text.

1130 Résultats de l'exploitation des ports maritimes: statistiques [Results of the operations of the maritime ports: statistics].
Direcion des Ports et de la Navigation Maritimes, 244 blvd Saint-Germain, 75007 Paris.
1966– 1983. not priced. 279p. ISSN 0396-5406. *Fr.
TF: the 1983 edition, published in 1984, has data for 1983 and also 1981 & 1982 in some tables.
Statistics on traffic at French ports by nationality (flag), movement of commercial shipping, passengers, cargoes, victualling, and coastal trade.

1131 Statistique mensuelles des ports maritimes: principaux résultats provisoires [Monthly statistics of the maritime ports: principal provisional results].
Direction des Ports Maritimes et des Voies Navigables, 244 blvd Saint-Germain, 75007 Paris.
(monthly) not priced. *Fr.
Up-dates the information in 1130 above.

1132 Statistiques annuelles de la navigation intérieure par sections de voies navigables... [Annual statistics of interior navigation by sections of navigable waterways].
Office National de la Navigation, 2 blvd de Latour Maubourg, 75007 Paris.
1950/69– 1984. Fr 204. *En.
Traffic, foreign trade carried by the Rhine and Moselle, other river traffic, traffic by sea.

Δ H – ii Roads and road transport

1133 Fichier central des automobiles: parc et immatriculations... [Central index of motor vehicles: numbers and registrations].
Ministère des Transports, Département des Statistiques des Transport, 55–57 rue Brillat Savarin, 75658 Paris Cedex 13.
(annual) 1983–84 (published late 1984). not priced. *Fr.

Δ H – iii Railways and rail transport

1134 La SNCF en... (Société Nationale des Chemins de Fer Français [French National Railways].
SNCF, 88 rue Saint-Lazare, 75436 Paris Cedex 09.
1951– 1984 (provisional). free. 8p. *Fr.
TF: the 1984 report, published in January 1985, has data for 1984.
Includes a statistical section on passenger traffic, goods carried, tonnage carried, personnel and productivity, motor engines of the SNCF, consumption of energy, employment, and quality of service, etc.

1135 Mémento de statistiques [Statistical memoranda].
SNCF, 88 rue Saint-Lazare, 75436 Paris Cedex 09.
(annual) 1984. not priced. 80p. *Fr.
TF: the 1984 edition, published in 1985, has data for 1984 compared with 1983.
Lines and installations, financial results, passenger and baggage traffic, goods traffic, personnel and rolling stock, consumption of energy, etc.
Note: 'Rapport: exercice', the report and accounts of the French National Railways, includes a variety of graphical presentations on passenger and goods traffic, productivity, consumption of energy, etc.

Δ H – iv Aviation and air transport

1136 Bulletin statistique de la DGAC [Statistical bulletin of the DGAC – Direction Générale de l'Aviation Civile – General Direction of Civil Aviation].
DGAC, 246 rue Lecourbe, 75732 Paris Cedex 15.
(monthly with annual supplement). not priced. *Fr.
The traffic of French air transport companies; traffic between France and other countries, traffic between the principal French towns, traffic at aerodromes, and movements of machines, passengers, freight and post.

Δ H – v Telecommunications and postal services

1137 Statistique annuelle du service des telecommunications [Annual statistics of telecommunication services].
Direction Générale des Télécommunications, Paris.
(annual) 1982. *Fr.

1138 Statistiques [Statistics].
Direction Générale des Postes, Paris.
(annual) 1982. *Fr.

Δ I Environment

1139 Dossier statistique de l'environnement [Environmental statistics] (Ministère de l'Environnement).
Le Documentation Française, 29–31 quai Voltaire, 75340 Paris Cedex 07.
1975– 3rd, 1982. Fr 100. 446p. *Fr.
TF: the 1982 edition was published in 1982, and contain data for various years.
Chapters are: 1: Space and territory; 2: Physical environment (water, sea, air, earth and waste); 3: Living environment; 4: Quality of life; 5: The environment and the economy.

LIECHTENSTEIN

Central statistical office

1140 Amt für Volkswirtschaft [Office of Economics].
FL-4940 Vaduz.
t 075-66111. tx 77855.
The Office is responsible for the collection, analysis and publication of statistical data relating to the Principality of Liechtenstein.

Libraries

As complete as possible a collection of publications about Liechtenstein is to be found in the Liechtenstein National Library at Vaduz.

Bibliographies

1141 Statistische publikationen.
Published by Amt für Volkswirtschaft (see above), the latest issue of this catalogue of publications is dated 1984.

Statistical publications

Δ A General

1142 Statistisches Jahrbuch [Statistical yearbook].
Amt für Volkswirtschaft, FL-9490 Vaduz.
1960- 1984. free. 392p. *De.
TF: the 1984 edition, published in 1984, has data for 1983 and many earlier years.
Main sections:
Geography - Climate - Population - Demography, occupations, labour market - National product, income - Agriculture & forestry - Industry, trade, building - Trade, foreign trade - Tourism - Transport, communications - Energy - Banking - Insurances - Price indexes - National finance - Education, culture, art - Health & environment - Clubs, sport, relief work - Judiciary - Elections.

1143 The Principality of Liechtenstein: a documentary handbook (Walter Kranz ed, Presse- und Informationsstelle).
Landesverwaltung des Fürstentums Liechtenstein, Vaduz.
1966- 5th, 1981. free. 302p. ISSN 0048-5306. *En, De & Fr eds.
A general handbook about the country and its history, with a few tables and statistics in the text, on public finance, taxation, banking, national income and product, population, employment, exports, tourism, etc.
Note: also available is 'The Liechtenstein economy' published in 1982, which has articles about the country and a few statistics in the articles.

1144 Liechtensteinische industriekammer: Jahresbericht [Liechtenstein Chamber of Industry: annual report].
Liechtensteinische Industriekammer, AHV-Gebäude, Vaduz.
1947- 1983. free. 21p. *De.
TF: the 1983 report, published in April 1984, has data for ten years up to and including 1983.

Δ B Production

Δ B - ii Agriculture, fisheries, forestry, etc

Δ B - ii(a) Agriculture and horticulture

1145 Landwirtschaftszählung [Agricultural census].
Amt für Volkswirtschaft, FL-9490 Vaduz.
1929- 1980. free. 140p. *De.
TF: the results of the 1980 census were published in 1982.
Agricultural land, labour, crops, etc.

1146 Viehzählung [Census of cattle].
Amt für Volkswirtschaft, FL-9490 Vaduz.
1950- 2nd, 1972. free. 530p. *De.
TF: the results of the 1972 census were published in 1973.

1147 Obstbaumzählung [Census of fruit trees].
Amt für Volkswirtschaft, FL-9490 Vaduz.
1951- 1971. free. 31p. *De.

FL

Δ B – iv Construction

1148 Baustatistik [Construction statistics].
Amt für Volkswirtschaft, FL-9490 Vaduz.
1962- 1984. free. 20p. *De.
TF: the 1984 edition, published in 1985, has data for 1984.
Data on building and construction.
Note: issued in the series 'Statistische information'.

Δ B – v Energy

1149 Energiestatistik [Energy statistics].
Amt für Volkswirtschaft, FL-9490 Vaduz.
1959- 1984. free. 13p. *De.
TF: the 1984 edition, published in 1985, has data for 1984 and many earlier years.
Data on production, imports and exports, and internal trade of electricity, coke, coal, heating oil, diesel oil, petrol and natural gas.
Note: issued in the series 'Statistisches information'.

Δ C External trade

Note: The Treaty of 1923 between Switzerland and the Principality of Liechtenstein made the two states one customs territory as from 1 January 1924. The foreign trade statistics of Switzerland therefore includes those of Liechtenstein. No statistics of imports into Liechtenstein alone are collected, and only rough totals of exports.

Δ D Internal distribution and service trades

Δ D – iv Tourism and travel

1150 Fremdenverkehrsstatistik [Tourist statistics].
Amt für Volkswirtschaft, FL-9490 Vaduz.
1960- 1983. free. 79p. *De.
TF: the 1983 edition, published early 1984, has data for 1983.
Monthly figures and totals for the year, winter and summer seasons, for each resort & town, of the numbers of the various types of accommodation & numbers of visitors by nationality.

Δ E Population

1151 Liechtensteinische Volkszählung [Census of population of Liechtenstein].
Amt für Volkswirtschaft, FL-9490 Vaduz.
1812- 1980. *De.
TF: the results of the census are being published from 1980 onwards.
Vol 1: Demographic characteristics and households in communities
Vol 2: Family names, employment
Vol 3: Building and housing
Vol 4: Socio-economic groups, communities, migration
Vol 5: Nationality, place of birth, place of residence, education, marriage, etc
Vol 6: Occupations
Vol 7: Building and housing
Vol 8: Households.

1152 Wohnbevölkerungsstatistik [Housing and population statistics].
Amt für Volkswirtschaft, FL-9490 Vaduz.
1976- 31 December 1983. not priced. 58p. *De.
TF: the edition with data for 31 December 1983 was published in 1984.
Data on housing and population, age structure, religion, and comparative tables.

1153 Ausländerstatistik [Statistics of foreigners].
Amt für Volkswirtschaft, FL-9490 Vaduz.
1970- 3 a year. free. *De.
TF: published in April, August and December each year, each issue has data for the position during that month; there are long runs of annual figures for summary data.
Foreigners in Liechtenstein by sex, occupation, place of residence, nationality, etc.

1154 Einbürgerunsstatistik [Naturalisation statistics].
Amt für Volkswirtschaft, FL-9490 Vaduz.
1970/81- 1970-1982. *De.

Δ E – i Vital statistics

1155 Zivilstandsstatistik [Demography].
Amt für Volkswirtschaft, FL-9490 Vaduz.
1954- 1983. free. 58p. *De.
TF: the 1983 edition, published in 1984, has data for 1983.

Δ E – iii Housing

< see 1152

Δ F Social and political

Δ F – ii Health and welfare

1156 Krankenassenstatistik [Health cost statistics].
Amt für Volkswirtschaft, FL-9490 Vaduz.
1944/51- 1983. free. *De.
TF: the 1983 edition, published in 1984, has data for 1983 and some earlier years in some tables.
Patients, costs, etc.

1157 Unfallversicherungsstatistik [Accident insurance statistics].
Amt für Volkswirtschaft, FL-9490 Vaduz.
1970- 1980. free. 2p. *De.
TF: the 1980 edition, published in 1981, has data for 1980 and earlier years. Publication has been temporarily suspended.
Note: issued in the series 'Statistisches information'.

Δ G Finance

1158 Rechenschaftsbericht der Regierung des Fürstentums Liechtenstein an den hohen Landtag für das Jahr...
[Statement of accounts of the Government of the Principality of Liechtenstein].
Regierungskanzlei der Regierung des Fürstentums Liechtenstein [Government Office], Vaduz.
1922- 1984. free. 236p. *De.
TF: the 1984 edition, published in 1985, has data for 1984.

1159 Bankenstatistik [Banking statistics].
Amt für Volkswirtschaft, FL-9490 Vaduz.
1980- 1984. free. 5p. *De.
TF: the 1984 edition, published in 1985, has data for 1984.
Data on the activities of the three Liechtenstein banks.
Note: issued in the series 'Statistisches information', earlier data being published in the annual reports of the three banks.

Δ H Transport and communications

Δ H – ii Roads and road vehicles

1160 Motorfahrzeugbestand [Motor vehicles on the road].
Amt für Volkswirtschaft, FL-9490 Vaduz.
1961- 1984. free. 30p. *De.
TF: the 1984 edition, published in 1984, has data as at 1st July 1984 and some earlier years.
The makes of motor vehicles in Liechtenstein, new registrations, road statistics, etc.

GB

UNITED KINGDOM
ROYAUME UNI
VEREINIGTE KÖNIGREICH

Central statistical office

1161 Central Statistical Office
Great George Street, London SW1P 3AQ.
t 01-944 5422.
Established in January 1941, within the Cabinet Office, which is under the general responsibility of the Prime Minister. Its main functions are to assist the central organs of government on all questions involving the use of statistics, to prepare statistical reports, etc. needed for the Cabinet and its committees, to maintain general liaison with departments on statistical questions, to undertake the preparation of some original statistical series, to prepare statistics derived from official sources for publication, and to keep in touch with international organisations on statistical matters. Unpublished information can often be supplied by the Office or by the government departments which are the primary source for the published statistcs.

Libraries

The Department of Trade and Industry's Statistics and Market Intelligence Library at 1-19 Victoria Street, London SW1H OET (01-215 3520) has a large collection of the publications referred to in this guide, including those of the United Kingdom and the international organisations and those of individual European countries. The Library is open to the public from 9.30 to 17.30, Mondays to Fridays, except on official holidays.
Large collections of the material referred to in the previous paragraph are also held by the Library of the University of Warwick, Coventry CV4 7AL (t 0203 24011); the Official Publications Library of the British Library Reference Division, Great Russell Street, London WC1B 3DG (t 01-636 1544); and the British Library of Political and Economic Science, London School of Economics, 10 Portugal Street, London WC2A 2HD (t 01-405 7686).
United Kingdom publications, including statistical material, are taken by the larger public libraries, and many such libraries are deposit libraries for United Nations publications and European Community publications, as well as taking a selection of the publications of other international organisations.
A few of the larger public libraries have collections of the statistical yearbooks of individual European countries.
The United Nations Information Centre at 14-15 Stratford Place, London W1 (t 01-629 3916) has a collection of United Nations publications available for reference; the European Communities Information Office, 8 Storey's Gate, London SW1P 4LY (t 01-222 8122) has a collection of publications of that organisation available for reference; and the International Labour Office, 96/98 Marsham Street, London SW1P 4LY (t 01-828 6401) has publications of that Office available for reference and sale.

Libraries and information services abroad

The more important statistical publications of the United Kingdom are available for reference in British embassies abroad, including:

Australia	British High Commission, Commonwealth Avenue, Canberra, ACT 2600. t 73 0422. United Kingdom Information Library, Gold Fields House, Sydney Cove, Sydney, NSW. t 27 7521.
Canada	British High Commission, 80 Elgin Street, Ottawa K1P 5K7. t 237 1530.
New Zealand	British High Commission, Reserve Bank of New Zealand Building, 9th floor, 2 The Terrace, Wellington 1. t 726 049.
USA	British Embassy, 3100 Massachusetts Avenue NW, Washington DC 20008. t (202) 462 1340. British Trade Development Office, 150 East 58th Street, 19th & 20th floors, New York, NY 10022. t 593 2258.

Note: a complete list of British Commercial Representatives overseas is published quarterly in 'British business' (see1180).

Bibliographies

1162 Guide to official statistics. No. 5, 1986.
Compiled by the Central Statistical Office and available from HMSO, London (price £21.95). ISSN 0261-1791.

1163 Government statistics: a brief guide to sources.
Published annually by the Central Statistical Office and available free from Information Services Division, Cabinet Offices, Great George Street, London SW1P 3AQ. Contains information on the most important Uk government publications containing statistics, and also a list of departmental responsibilities and contact points for further information.

1164 Statistical news: developments in British official statistics.
A quarterly compiled by the Central Statistical Office and published by HMSO, London (£14 a year). Includes details of new official statistical publications as well as articles and information about current developments in official statistics. ISSN 0017-3630.

Bibliographies, continued

1165 Reviews of United Kingdom statistical sources (W.F. Maunder, ed).
Pergamon Press, Oxford (early vols published by Heinemann Educational Books).
A continuous series of books on what published data are available on particular topics and in which publications. A quick reference list of individual series is given as well as a subject index to the text of each review. The volumes published so far are:
Vol 1 - 1: Personal social services, and
2: Voluntary organisations in the personal social service field
Vol 2 - 3: Central government routine health statistics, and
4: Social security statistics
Vol 3 - 5: Housing in Great Britain, and
6: Housing in Northern Ireland
Vol 4 - 7: Leisure and Tourism
Vol 5 General sources of statistics
Vol 6 - Wealth and Personal income
Vol 7 - Road passenger transport and Road goods transport
Vol 8 - Land use and Town and country planning
Vol 9 - Health surveys and related studies
Vol 10 - Port and inland waterways and Civil aviation
Vol 11 - Coal industry, Gas industry and Electricity industry
Vol 12 - Construction and the related professions
Vol 13 - Wages and earnings
Vol 14 - Rail and sea transport
Vol 15 - Crime.

1166 Sources of unofficial UK statistics.
Compiled by David Mort & Leona Siddall, Warwick Statistics Service, and published by Gower Publishing Company Ltd in 1986 (£45. 467p), the volume comprises 1059 entries arranged alphabetically by publishing organisation, supported by a general subject index.

Statistical publications

Δ A General

1167 Annual abstract of statistics (Central Statistical Office).
HMSO, London
1840/53- 1985. £17.50. 353p. ISSN 0072-5730. *En.
TF: the 1985 edition, published early 1985, has data for 1983 or earlier, and also for about ten previous years in many tables.
Main sections:
Area & climate - Population & vital statistics - Social conditions - Justice & crime - Education - Labour - Defence - Production (energy, iron & steel, industrial materials, building & construction, manufactured goods) - Agriculture, fisheries & food - Transport & communications - Distributive trades, research & development - External trade - Balance of payments - National income & expenditure - Personal income, expenditure & wealth - Home finance - Banking, insurance, etc - Prices.
Note: many local authorities also publish statistical yearbooks for their areas, including 'Annual abstract of Greater London statistics' of the GLC, 'South Yorkshire statistics' by the South Yorkshire County Council, 'Shetland in statistics' by the Shetlands Islands Council, 'Facts and figures' by the Corporation of the city of Glasgow 'Humberside statistical bulletin' by the University of Hull, 'Statistics '84' by West Midlands County Council, etc.

1168 Monthly digest of statistics (Central Statistical Office).
HMSO, London.
1946- £5.95 or £65 yr. ISSN 0308-6666. *En.
TF: each issue contains data for about six years, with monthly and quarterly figures for the last two years, up to one, two or three months prior to the date of the issue.
National income and expenditure; population and vital statistics; employment; social services; law and enforcement; agriculture and food; production, output and costs; energy; chemicals; metals, engineering and vehicles; textiles and other manufactures; construction; transport; retailing; external trade; overseas finance; home finance; prices and wages; entertainment; and weather.

1169 Economic trends (Central Statistical Office, in collaboration with the statistical divisions of government departments and the Bank of England).
HMSO, London.
1953- (supplement 1975-) monthly. £9.95 or £115 yr (including supplement). ISSN 0015-203X. *En.
Latest developments in the economy, data on current economic events, and a table of monthly indicators. key indicators on a variety of topics, including production, distribution, employment and finance are arranged in tabular form and there are also charts. Also included are reference cycles which identify leading indicators in the business cycle. The supplement provides notes and definitions for economic trends and long runs of up to 30 years data for some of the main economic indicators.

Δ A, continued

1170 Regional trends (Central Statistical Office).
HMSO, London.
1965- 1985. £17.50. 160p. ISSN 0261-1783. *En.
TF: the 1985 edition, published in May 1985, has data for several years to 1983.
Brings together the official statistics of the UK which are available on a regional basis, a regional profile being followed by population and vital statistics; housing; health; land enforcement; education; employment; personal income and expenditure; regional accounts; production, investment and energy; agriculture and forestry; transport and environment; EC comparisons.

1171 Digest of Welsh statistics (Welsh Office, in collaboration with statistical divisions of other government departments).
E & SS Division, Welsh Office, Crown Building, Cathays Park, Cardiff CF1 3NQ.
1954- 1984. £4. 208p. ISSN 0262-8295. *En; title page & introduction also in Welsh.
TF: the 1984 edition, published late 1984, has data for several years to 1983 or 1983/84.
Data on various aspects concerning Wales, including population; vital statistics; social conditions (health and personal social services); social security; law, order and protection services; housing and planning (new towns, Welsh language, electorate, recreation); education (schools, higher and further education); labour; production and distribution (industrial production, energy, construction, investment, agriculture, forestry and fishing); transport and communications; finance, incomes and expenditure; and environment.

1172 Welsh economic trends (Welsh Office, in collaboration with the statistical divisions of other government departments).
E & SS Division, Welsh Office, Crown Building, Cathays Park, Cardiff CF1 3NQ.
1974- No. 9, 1984. £7.50. 112p. ISSN 0262-8309. *En, title page & introduction also in Welsh.
TF: issued at irregular intervals. The 1984 edition, published early 1984, has data for 1983 and several earlier years.
Population, regional income and expenditure, the working population, earnings and hours, household income and expenditure, industrial activity, capital expenditure, and public expenditure.

1173 Local government trends.
Chartered Institute of Public Finance and Accountancy, 3 Robert Street, London WC2N 6BH.
1973- 1984. £18. ISSN 0307-0441. *En.
TF: the 1984 edition, published in 1985, has data for several years to 1984.
A review of local government in England and Wales drawing on published statistics and covering demographic features, employment and earnings, local authority expenditure, and statistical trends in each of the main service areas of local authorities.
Note: 'Local government comparative statistics' (1984 ed. £18. 76p) is a compendium of data used by local authorities to compile their annual reports.

1174 The Scottish abstract of statistics
The Librarian, Scottish Office, Room 2/65, New St Andrews House, Edinburgh EH1 3TG.
1971- 1984. £24.50. 170p. *En.
TF: the 1984 edition, published in 1984, has data to 1982.
Tables, graphs and commentary on a wide variety of subjects, including education, leisure, housing, population and vital statistics, social security, health, social work, labour, industrial activity, personal income and expenditure, law enforcement, transport and communications, trade through Scottish ports, finance, weather and water. Data is for Scotland.

1175 Scottish economic bulletin (Industry Department for Scotland: Economic and Statistical Unit).
HMSO, Edinburgh.
(quarterly) £6 each issue. *En.
Contains an economic review, articles and a series of charts and statistics, including data on oil related activity, personal income and consumption, investment and output in manufacturing industry, investment and employment in assisted areas, assistance to industry and employment, etc. The main quarterly series covers employment, unemployment, index of industrial production, etc. and the main annual series shows population, employment by industry, average weekly earnings, trade, tourism, etc.

1176 Northern Ireland annual abstract of statistics (Statistics Branch, Department of Economic Development).
HMSO, Belfast.
1954- No. 3, 1984. £11.50. 184p. ISSN 0267-6044. *En.
TF: the 1984 edition, published in 1985, has data for 1983 and runs of earlier years in many tables. Prior to 1982 it was published twice a year.
Northern Ireland population and vital statistics; households and individuals; social services and health; law and order; education; housing; environment and climate; transport and communications; tourism; labour; earnings and income; production output and energy; agriculture, forestry and fishing; regional accounts; public finance; banking, insurance and other financial institutions.

1177 Isle of Man digest of economic and social statistics (Economics Section, Treasury, Isle of Man).
Isle of Man Government Offices, Buck's Road, Douglas, Isle of Man.
1975- 1985. £4. 226p. *En.
TF: the 1985 edition, published early 1985, has latest data available and figures for earlier years for comparison.
Intended to give a comprehensive statistical picture of recent social, demographic and economic trends. General information; national income; population and vital statistics; employment; prices; agriculture; fisheries; construction, housing and rates; industry; travel and tourism; transport and communications; energy; external trade; government finance; health and social services; education; miscellaneous (criminal data, company registration, meteorology, etc).

Δ A, continued

1178 Co-operative statistics.
Co-operative Union Ltd., Holyoake House, Hanover Street, Manchester M60 OAS.
1938- 1983. not priced. 64p. *En.
TF: the 1983 edition, published in 1984, has data for 1983.
Numbers and sizes of societies, their activities, membership, share capital, reserves, employees and wages, trade, etc.

1179 British historical facts (Chris Cook and Brendan Keith).
Macmillan, 4 Little Essex Street, London WC2.
2 vols. £25 each vol. *En.
TF: the volume for 1760-1830 was published in 1980; that for 1830-1900 in 1975.
Mainly textual, but includes election results as well as a few other statistics.

1180 British business: weekly export and industrial news from the Department of Trade and Industry.
British Business, Oakfield House, Perrymount Road, Haywards Heath RH16 3DH.
1886- weekly. £1.25 or £75 yr. *En.
Includes many monthly, quarterly and annual statistical tables on industrial production, foreign trade, distribution, employment, prices, etc. Each issue includes an index to the tables which are published regularly.
Note: change of name from 1980, previously 'Trade and industry' and 'Board of Trade journal'.

1181 National Institute economic review (National Institute for Economic and Social Research).
NIESR, Dean Trench Street, Smith Square, London SW1.
1959- quarterly. £12.50 (£18 abroad) or £45 yr (£60 yr abroad). ISSN 0027-9501. *En.
Economic articles often including statistical tables, and a statistical appendix with data on gross domestic product; production in industry; production of coal, oil, steel and cars; industry survey results; orders; labour market: productivity; prices; incomes; consumers' expenditure: retail sales; fixed investment changes in volume stocks; credit; financial indicators; UK foreign trade; and UK balance of payments.

1182 Economic progress report (Treasury).
Publications Division, Central Office of Information, Hercules Road, London SE1 7DU.
1970- monthly. free. *En.
Includes a regular page of economic indicators.

1183 UK economic prospects.
Economist Intelligence Unit, 40 Duke Street, London W1A 1DW.
(quarterly) £75 or $150 yr. *En.
A quarterly assessment of current trends in the UK economy.

1184 Economic outlook (London Business School: Centre for Economic Forecasting).
Gower Publishing Co Ltd., Gower House, Croft Road, Aldershot, Hants GU11 3HR.
1976- monthly (3 major forecasts & 9 intermediate forecast releases). £90 yr ($170 yr Europe to $210 yr elsewhere). *En.
A rolling four-year business forecast of the UK economy. Major forecast issues include a forecast summary (highlights of the economic forecast for the next four years), key activity indicators (projections of key business activities such as consumer expenditure, investment, production, money, stock, prices, unemployment and savings), an economic policy review, a major feature article, and the forecast in detail. The forecast releases are 4-page summaries reviewing the previous month's economic indicators.

1185 LCCI economic report and survey.
Economic Research Unit, London Chamber of Commerce and Industry, 69 Cannon Street, London EC4N 5AB.
(quarterly) £5 or £17.50 yr. *En.
Contains an economic commentary by the LCCI's economic adviser and results of the LCCI London and South-east manufacturing trend surveys, covering all standard economic indicators (production levels, domestic and export orders, new investment, prices, profit performance, etc).

1186 Economic forecasts: the background for business and investment.
Phillips & Drew, 120 Moorgate, London EC2M 6XP.
(monthly) £40 or £400 yr. *En.
TF: annual and quarterly forecasts are for two years ahead.
Short-term signals, policy assessment, international prospect, followed by summary of UK forecasts; wages, costs and prices; consumption; investment; components of demand; balance of payments; money supply and flow of funds; company profits; company sector liquidity; personal sector liquidity; UK medium-term outlook; and North Sea oil.

1187 Home Office statistical bulletin (Home Office Statistical Department, Tolworth Tower, Surbiton, Surrey KT6 7DS).
Home Office Library, Room 1003, 50 Queen Anne's Gate, London SW1H 9AT.
1975- irregular (c 25 a year). Prices vary between £1 & £2 each (prices for supplementary tables are higher (eg. £4, £35). ISSN 0143-6384. *En.
Each issue on a different subject, some titles appearing regularly, either quarterly or annual, and these are included separately in this guide.

1188 Public bodies (Cabinet Office, Management and Personnel Office).
HMSO, London.
(annual) 1985. £11. 89p. *En.
TF: the 1985 edition, published in 1985, has data for 1984 or 1984/85.
Lists nationalised industries and non-departmental public bodies, and gives some basic facts about them, including number of bodies, staff, expenditure, etc.

Δ B Production

1189 Commercial and industrial floor space statistics, England (Department of the Environment).
HMSO, London.
1967- 1981-1984. £5.85. 46p. *En.
TF: the 1981-1984 edition, published May 1985, has changes from April 1981 to March 1984, and estimated stock as at 1st April 1984.
Estimated floor space stock for each region, country and local authority in seven categories - industries, warehouses (covered), warehouses (open land storage), shops with living accommodation, shops and restaurants, commercial offices and central government offices.

1190 Commercial and industrial floorspace statistics: Wales (Welsh Office, Crown Buildings, Cathays Park, Cardiff CF1 3NQ.
1980- 1984. £4. 74p. ISSN 0262-5334. *En, title page & introduction also in Welsh.
TF: the 1984 edition, published late 1984, has data for 1983 or 1983/84 and earlier years for comparison. Data for 1974 to 1979 was included in the general title compiled jointly by the Department of the Environment and the Welsh Office.
Numbers of hereditaments and floorspace, gross and net changes by county and by sub-division.

Δ B - i Mines and mining

1191 United Kingdom mineral statistics (Natural Environment Research Council).
HMSO, London.
1973- 1984. £20. 169p. *En.
TF: the 1984 edition, published May 1985, has data for 1983 and earlier years in most tables.
Minerals in the economy, mineral production, UK overseas trade in minerals and mineral-based products, commodity summaries and commodity reviews, and UK production, consumption and trade.

Δ B - ii(a) Agriculture and horticulture

1192 Agricultural statistics: United Kingdom... (Ministry of Agriculture, Fisheries and Food, Department of Agriculture and Fisheries for Scotland, and Ministry of Agriculture, Northern Ireland).
HMSO, London.
1939/44- 1983. £9.75. 93p. *En.
TF: the 1983 edition, published in 1984, has data for 1983.
Details of the United Kingdom area of agricultural land and the distribution of holdings, crop production and yields, livestock, labour force, and machinery. Also includes horticultural statistics, county statistics and prices.

1193 Welsh agricultural statistics.
E & SS Division, Welsh Office, Crown Buildings, Cathays Park, Cardiff CF1 3NQ.
1979- 1984. £3. 90p. ISSN 0262-8325. *En, title page & introduction also in Welsh.
TF: the 1984 edition, published late 1984, has data for 1983 and earlier years in some tables.
Data on agricultural area, livestock, agricultural holdings, labour & machinery, production & marketing, livestock prices, land prices & rents, grants & subsidies, farm structure, less-favoured areas, and UK country comparisons.
Note: 'Welsh agricultural statistics supplement' has been replaced by 'Farm accounts in Wales' (1982/83 ed. published May 1984. £4. 67p. ISSN 0265-0967).

1194 Agricultural statistics: Scotland (Department of Agriculture and Fisheries for Scotland).
HMSO, Edinburgh.
1912- 1984. £4.90. 58p. *En.
TF: the 1984 edition, published mid-1985, has data for 1984.
Contains similar information to 1192 but solely for Scotland.

1195 Economic report on Scottish agriculture (Department of Agriculture and Fisheries for Scotland).
HMSO, Edinburgh.
1980- 1983. £7.80. 100p. *En.
TF: the 1983 edition, published in 1985, has data for 1983 or 1982/83.
Physical and financial statistics on Scottish agriculture: cropping, livestock, labour, prices, output, input and net income in aggregate and by farm type.

1196 Statistical review of Northern Ireland agriculture.
Economics and Statistics Division, Department of Agriculture for Northern Ireland, Dundonald House, Upper Newtownards Road, Belfast BT4 3SB.
(annual) 1983. free. 85p. *En.
TF: the 1983 edition, published id-1984, has data for 1983 and long runs of earlier figures in some tables.
Data on production, output, input and income; prices; exports; livestock numbers and area of crops; fixed assets and equipment; distribution of farms and livestock (by crops) by number of livestock (or area of crop) and by area of farm; forestry and fishing.

1197 Northern Ireland agriculture (Department of Agriculture for Northern Ireland).
HMSO, Belfast.
1941/42- 1984/85. £8.25. 156p. *En.
TF: the 1984/85 edition, published in 1985, has data for crop years to 1983 or 1984.
A statistical appendix includes data on policy developments; output, input and income of agriculture; marketing (including export) livestock and crops; agricultural education and training; agricultural research and development training; finance, etc. Also includes data on horticulture, forest service and fisheries.

Δ B – ii(a), continued

1198 Farm incomes in England (Ministry of Agriculture, Fisheries and Food).
HMSO, London.
1944/45-1947/48- 1982-83 including comparisons with 1981-82 & some reference to earlier years.
£7.25. 67p. *En.
TF: the 1982-83 edition was published in 1984.
A report based on the Farm Management Survey, being collected economic and financial information about farming at the farm level as shown by records from a sample of farmers.
Note: earlier editions included Wales.

1199 Output and utilisation of farm produce in the United Kingdom (Ministry of Agriculture, Fisheries and Food, & the Agricultural Departments for Scotland, Northern Ireland and Wales).
Ministry of Agriculture, Fisheries and Food, Tolcarne Drive, Pinner, Middlesex HA5 2DT.
1946/47- 1977 to 1983. £6. 35p. *En.
TF: the 1977 to 1983 edition, with data for those years, was published in 1984.
Agricultural output, main farm crops, horticulture, fatstock, poultry, milk and milk products, eggs, wool, and concentrated feeding stuffs.

1200 Smallholdings statistics (Society of County Treasurers).
County Treasurer, Berkshire County Council, PO Box 12, Shire Hall, Shinfield Park, Reading RG2 9XB.
(annual) Actural 1984/85. not priced. 16p. ISSN 0307-8299. *En.
TF: the 1984/85 issue, published in November 1985, has data for 1984/85.
Data on number, size and average size of non-commercial, intermediate and commercial holdings for all English and Welsh counties. Also capital and revenue expenditure, etc.

1201 Farmland market.
Published jointly by The Estates Gazette Ltd., 151 Wardour Street, London W1V 4BN & Farmers Weekly, 1 Throwley Way, Sutton, Surrey SM1 4QQ, in collaboration with the Institute of Agricultural Economics, Oxford University.
1974- 2 a year. £24 yr. *En.
Includes statistical tables on Ministry of Agriculture land prices, current agricultural land prices, rents, finances, market prices, etc.

1202 Statistics of agricultural co-operation in the United Kingdom.
The Plunkett Foundation for Co-operative Studies, 31 St Giles, Oxford OX1 3LF, on behalf of the Co-operative Development Board of Food from Britain and the Federation of Agricultural Co-operatives (UK) Ltd.
(annual) 1983-84. not priced. 42p. ISSN 0266-0091. *En.
TF: the 1983-84 edition was published in April 1985.
Data on numbers of co-operatives, members, staff; turnover of UK agriculture & horticultural cc-operatives

1203 Statistical handbook of UK agriculture (Alison Burrell, Berkeley Hill, John Redland of Wye College).
Macmillan Publishers Ltd (Distributed by Globe Book Services Ltd)., Brunel Road, Houndmills, Basingstoke, Hants RG21 2XS.
£40. 184p. *En.
TF: published in 1984 with data to 1983.
Data on production and trade, food, product prices, land tenure, crops, economic indicators, expenditure, prices, income, land used, labour, economy, the European Communities, land prices, cereals.

1204 Statistical record.
Weatherby & Sons, Sanders Road, Wellingborough, Northants.
1971- quarterly. not priced. *En.
Computer-compiled statistics of horse racing and breeding.

1205 United Kingdom dairy facts and figures.
Federation of United Kingdom Milk Marketing Boards, Thames Ditton, Surrey KT7 0EL.
1963- 1983. £5. 234p. *En.
TF: the 1983 edition, published late 1983, has data for 1982 or 1982/83.
Producers, dairy farming, milk supplies, milk utilisation, prices, returns and marketing allowances, advertising and sales promotion, milk transport, bulk collection, UK trade in milk products, etc.

1206 Potato statistics in Great Britain.
Potato Marketing Board, 50 Hans Crescent, London SW1X 0NB.
(annual) 1979-83. £5. *En.
TF: the 1979-83 edition, with data for those years, was published in 1984.
Data on producers, consumption, area planted by variety, yields, imports, etc.
Note: up-dated by an 8-page leaflet 'Potato statistics bulletin'. Other leaflets are also available, including 'Potato processing in Great Britain, 1983'.

1207 Hop report.
Wigan Richardson International Ltd., 3 Church Road, Paddock Wood, Kent TN12 6ES.
(annual) 1985 season. not priced. 19p. *En.
TF: the report for the 1985 season, published in 1986, has data for 1984/85, 1984 or 1985.
Data on crop, market demand, imports and exports, etc.

Δ B – ii(a), continued

1208 Animal health (Ministry of Agriculture, Fisheries and Food & Department of Agriculture and Fisheries for Scotland).
HMSO, London.
1974– 1984. £9.30. 158p. *En.
TF: the 1984 edition, published mid-1985, has data for 1984.
The annual report of the Chief Veterinary Officer. Includes statistical tables on diseases, imports, exports, veterinary public health, preventive veterinary medicine, and improved livestock production, etc.

1209 Basic horticultural statistics for the United Kingdom.
Ministry of Agriculture, Fisheries and Food, Great Westminster House, Horseferry Road, London SW1P 2AE.
(annual) 1975–1984. free. unpaged, 39 tables. *En.
TF: the 1975–1984 edition, with data for calendar and crop years for 1975 to 1984, was published in April 1985.
A summary of cropped area and value of total horticultural output, is followed by data on area, gross yield, production, market patterns, etc. of fruit, vegetables, non-edible horticultural produce, hops, and potatoes. Also foreign trade statistics.

Δ B – ii(b) Fisheries

< see also 1196, 1197

1210 Sea fisheries statistical tables (Ministry of Agriculture, Fisheries and Food).
HMSO, London.
1888– 1983. £10. 46p. *En.
TF: the 1983 edition, published September 1985, has data for 1983 & earlier years in some tables.
Data for the UK on total supplies of fresh chilled and frozen fish; landings by vessels, main varieties, major ports, foreign fishing vessels, regions of capture, etc; consumption level estimates; fishermen and fishing vessels; and international trade of the UK with EEC, EFTA and all other countries.

1211 Monthly return of sea fisheries statistics, England and Wales.
Fisheries Statistics Unit, Ministry of Agriculture, Fisheries and Food, Horseferry Road, London SW1P 2AE.
(monthly) not priced. *En.
TF: each issue has data for the month of the issue and is published some three or four months later.
Data on species caught, in tonnes & value, in British vessels & in foreign vessels, & landed at ports.

1212 Scottish sea fisheries statistical tables.
Department of Agriculture and Fisheries for Scotland, 500 Gorgie Road, Edinburgh EH11 3AW.
1922– 1984. £6. 52p. *En.
TF: the 1984 edition, published in 1985, has data for 1984 and also earlier in some tables.
Data on fish landings in Scotland by UK vessels, Scottish vessels, foreign vessels; Scottish fishing vessels; disposal and processing of fish.
Note: the Department's 'Monthly summary of sea fisheries statistics, Scotland: month of...final figures' is also available.

1213 The Scottish fishing fleet...
Department of Agriculture and Fisheries for Scotland, 500 Gorgie Road, Edinburgh EH11 3AW.
(annual) 1984. £6. 62p. *En.
TF: published in 1985, data is mainly for the position as at 31 December 1984 but summary tables have long runs of figures.
Detailed data on numbers of vessels by length, year built, tonnage, horsepower, base district, method, etc. Also a list of individual vessels.
Note: the Department also issues 'Scottish inshore fishing fleet – cost and earnings survey' annually (1981, published 1983. £2.25p).

1214 Report on the sea and inland fisheries of Northern Ireland (Department of Agriculture, Northern Ireland).
HMSO, Belfast.
1931– 1984 (published in 1985). £3.70. 25p. *En.
Data on sea fisheries, salmon and inland fisheries, public expenditure on fisheries, legislation.

1215 Supplies bulletin (Fishery Economics Research Unit).
FERU, Sea Fishery Industry Authority, 10 Young Street, Edinburgh EH2 4JQ.
(approx quarterly) not priced. ISSN 0309-5517. *En.
Up-to-date statistics on catches by UK vessels, UK supplies of Demersal food fish available for consumption; UK imports and exports of fish and fish products; and auction, wholesale and retail prices.

1216 Household fish consumption in Great Britain (Fishery Economics Research Unit).
FERU, Sea Fish Industry Authority, 10 Young Street, Edinburgh EH2 4JQ.
(quarterly) £55 yr. *En.
An analysis of sales of fresh/chilled and frozen fish by species for household consumption in Britain and in each of the major television regions.

Δ B – ii(c) Forestry

< see also 1196, 1197

Δ B – ii(c), continued

1217 Report and accounts of the Forestry Commission...
HMSO, London.
1920/21- 1984/85 (published late 1985). £10. 115p. *En.
Includes statistical tables on the forest authority (schemes, planting, etc), forestry enterprises (land use, forest land acquired, planting, area of plantations, sales of timber, properties managed, public recreational facilities), and land use, planting and timber production by forests for England, Wales and Scotland separately.

1218 Census of woodlands and trees, 1979-82.
Forestry Commission, 231 Corstorphine Road, Edinburgh EH12 7AT.
£3. 66p. *En.
TF: published in 1983.
Census of woodland and non-woodland trees in England.

Δ B – iii Industry

1219 Report on the census of production (Business Statistics Office).
HMSO, London.
1907- 1983. each part separately priced. *En.
TF: the reports on the 1983 census are being published from 1985 onwards. The census has been taken annually since 1970.
Published annually in the 'Business monitor PA series' in separate parts for each industry, following a similar pattern to the 'Business monitor: production series (1220), with a separate volume of summary tables. Include data on total purchases, total sales, stocks, work in progress, capital expenditure, employment, and wages and salaries.
Note: A 'Historical record of the census of production 1907 to 1970' was published in 1979 (£10. 467p).

1220 Business monitor: production series (Business Statistics Office).
HMSO, London.
1962- Monthly series £15.75 yr, except MM17 (£16.75 yr); quarterly series £8.50 yr; complete set £575 yr. *En.
TF: titles are issued quarterly except where there is an indication to the contrary. Delay in publication varies considerably, some titles appearing about two months after the end of the period covered and others up to six months. Earlier and comparative figures are usually included.
Data varies in each title and may include orders in hand, new orders, production, deliveries, exports, raw materials used, and stocks. The titles in the series include:
Energy industries: Coal mining; Extraction of mineral oil & natural gas; Mineral oil refining; Lubricating oils & greases; Electricity; Gas.
Extraction of minerals & ores other than fuels: manufacture of metals & mineral products & chemicals: Extraction & preparation of metalliferous ores/Salt/Miscellaneous minerals; Steel wire & steel wire products; Aluminium & aluminium alloys; Copper, brass & other copper alloys; Miscellaneous non-ferrous metals & their alloys; Extraction of stone, clay, sand & gravel/Working of stone & miscellaneous non-metallic materials; Structural clay products; Cement, lime & plaster; Ready mixed concrete/ Miscellaneous building products of concrete, cement or plaster; Asbestos; Abrasives; Flat glass/Glass containers/Miscellaneous glass products; Refractory goods; Ceramic goods; Inorganic chemicals (except industrial gases); Basic organic chemicals (except specialised pharmaceutical chemicals); Fertilizers; Synthetic resins & plastics materials/Synthetic rubber; Dyestuffs & pigments; Paints, varnishes & painters' fillings; Printing ink; Formulated adhesive & sealants/Adhesive film, cloth & foil; Chemical treatment of oils & fats/Essential oils & flavouring materials; Miscellaneous chemical products for industrial use; Formulated pesticides; Pharmaceutical products; Soap & synthetic detergents; Perfumes, cosmetics & toilet preparations; Photographic materials & chemicals/Polishes & miscellaneous specialised products mainly for household & office use; Production of man-made fibre.
Metal goods, engineering & vehicle industries: Iron castings; Non-ferrous metal foundries; Forging, pressing & stamping; Bolts, nuts, washers, rivets, springs & non-precision chains; Heat & surface treatment of metals (including sintering); Metal doors, windows, etc; Hand tools & implements; Cutlery, spoons, forks & similar tableware; razors; Metal storage vessels (mainly non-industrial)/Packaging products of metal; Domestic heating & cooking appliances (non-electrical); Metal furniture & safes; Domestic utensils of metal; Miscellaneous finished metal products; Fabricated construction steelwork; Boilers & process plant fabrications; Agricultural machinery; Wheeled tractors; Metal-working machine tools; Engineers' small tools; Textile machinery; Food, drink & tobacco processing machinery; packaging & bottling machinery; Chemical industry machinery; furnaces & kilns; gas, water & waste treatment plant; Mining machinery; Construction & earth-moving equipment; Mechanical lifting & handling equipment; Precision chains & other mechanical power transmission equipment; Ball, needle & roller bearings; Machinery for working wood, rubber, plastics, leather, & making paper, glass, bricks & similar materials; laundry & dry-cleaning machinery; Printing, bookbinding & paper goods machinery; Industrial (including marine) engines; Compressors & fluid power equipment; Refrigerating, space heating, ventilatirg & air-conditioning equipment; Scales, weighing machinery & portable power tools; Miscellaneous industrial & commercial machinery; Pumps; Industrial valves; Miscellaneous mechanical marine & precision engineering; Ordnance, small arms & ammunitions; Office machinery/Electronic data processing equipment; Insulated wires & cables; Basic electrical equipment; Batteries & accumulators; Alarms & signalling equipment; Electrical equipment for motor vehicles, cycles & aircraft; Miscellaneous electrical equipment for industrial use; Telegraph & telephone equipment; Electrical instruments & control systems; Radio & electronic capital goods; Components other than active components, mainly for electronic equipment; Gramophone records & pre-recorded tapes; Electronic consumer goods & miscellaneous

[continued next page]

Δ B – iii, continued

1220, continued

equipment; Domestic electrical appliances; Electric lamps & lighting equipment; Car & commercial vehicle production (monthly); Motor vehicles & engines/Motor vehicle bodies; Trailers & semi-trailers/ Caravans; Motor vehicle parts; Shipbuilding & repairing; Railway & tramway vehicles; Motor cycles, cycles & miscellaneous vehicles; Aerospace equipment manufacturing & repairing; Measuring, checking & precision instruments & apparatus; Medical & surgical equipment & orthopaedic appliances; Spectacles & unmounted lenses/Optical precision instruments; Photographic & cinematographic equipment; Clocks, watches & other timing devices.

Other manufacturing industries: Margarine & compound cooking fats; Organic oils & fats; Bacon curing & meat products; Poultry & poultry products; Animal by-products; Fruit & vegetable products; Fish products; Starch; Bread & flour confectionery; Biscuits & crispbread; Ice-cream; Miscellaneous foods; Spirit distilling & compounding; Wines, cider & perry; Brewing & malting; Soft drinks; Tobacco; Woollen & worsted; Spinning & doubling of cotton etc./Throwing, texturing, etc., of continuous filament yarn; Weaving of cotton, silk & man-made fibres; Spinning & weaving of flax, hemp & ramie; Jute & polypropylene yarns & fabrics; Hoisery & other weft knitted goods; Warp knitted goods; Textile finishing; Carpets & other textile floor coverings; Lace; Rope, twine & net; Narrow fabrics; Miscellaneous textiles; Leather & fellmongery/Leather goods; Footwear; Weatherproof outerwear; Men's & boy's tailored outerwear; Women's & girl's tailored outerwear; Work clothing & men's & boy's jeans; Men's & boy's shirts, underwear & nightwear; Women's & girl's light outerwear lingerie & infant's wear; Hats, caps & millinery/Gloves; Miscellaneous dress industries; Soft furnishings; Canvas goods, sacks & miscellaneous made-up textiles; Household textiles; Fur goods; Sawmilling, planing, etc of wood; Semi-finished wood products; preservation & treatment of wood; Wood chipboard (monthly); Builders' carpentry & joinery; Wooden containers; Miscellaneous wooden articles; Articles of cork & plaiting materials, brushes & brooms; Wooden & upholstered furniture; Shop & office fitting; Pulp, paper & board (monthly); Pulp, paper & board; Wallcoverings; Household & personal hygiene paper products; Stationery; Packaging products of paper & pulp; Packaging products of board/Miscellaneous paper & board products; Printing & publishing of newspapers; Printing & publishing periodicals; Printing & publishing of books; Miscellaneous printing & publishing; Rubber tyres & inner tubes/Retreading & specialist repairing of rubber tyres; Miscellaneous rubber products; Plastic-coated textile fabrics/Plastic floor coverings; Plastics semi-manufactures; Plastics building products; Plastics packaging products; Miscellaneous plastics products; Jewellery & coins; Musical instruments; Toys & games; Sports goods; Miscellaneous stationers' goods; Miscellaneous manufacturing industries.

Monitors covering a number of industries: Index of commodities; Guide to short-term statistics of manufacturers' sales; Manufacturing industries.

1221 Annual census of production: report on the census of production and construction in Northern Ireland (Statistics Branch Department of Economic Development).
HMSO, Belfast.
1949- 1981 (published in 1984). £6.80. 70p. *En.
Covers manufacturing, energy, water supply, minerals, construction, etc. Relating to establishments with 20 or more employees data includes number of establishments, work done, output, material costs, net output, value added, employment, wages & capital expenditure.

1222 Index of production press release [Northern Ireland].
Statistics Branch, Department of Economic Development, Netherleigh, Massey Avenue, Belfast BT4 2JP.
(quarterly) free. *En.
Index numbers of production arranged by industrial sector.

1223 Industrial trends survey.
Confederation of British Industry, Centre Point, 103 Oxford Street, London WC1A 1DU.
(quarterly) £106 yr to members; £170 yr to non-members. *En.
Survey results providing information about trends in demand and activity, costs and prices, etc. Data is given by industries and relates to the general business situation, export prospects, seasonal variations, stocks, new orders, output, cists, capital expenditure, etc.
Note: since 1975 an abbreviated enquiry has been carried out in intervening months using five questions from the quarterly questionnaire (monthly issues £106 yr (£170 yr to non-members; combined subscription £180 yr to members, £260 yr to non-members).

1224 Industrial performance analysis.
ICC Information Group Ltd., 28/42 Banner Street, London EC1Y 8QE.
1976- 10th, 1985/86 (published in 1985). £44. *En.
Guide to profitability and performance in British industry, based on an analysis of over 12000 British companies over a three-year period, 1981-1984. Data on 140 industries in 25 major industrial groupings.

Δ B – iii(a) Food products, beverages, tobacco

1225 Annual report.
The Cocoa, Chocolate and Confectionery Alliance, 11 Green Street, London W1Y 3RF.
(annual) 1983. not priced. 48p. *En.
TF: the 1983 report, published in 1984, has data for 1983 and also earlier years in some tables.
Includes a statistical appendix (p 22-32) on sales by manufacturers, imports, consumer and trade values of home trade despatched (totals and by type), labour employed, top 20 markets for chocolate confectionery and sugar confectionery, exports, imports of cocoa materials, ingredients purchased, chocolate and sugar confectionery in the EEC. Appendix II is the financial report of the Alliance.
Note: more detailed 4-weekly summaries issued to members can be made available to non-members (£200 yr).

Δ B – iii(a), continued

1226 Annual report.
The Cake and Biscuit Alliance Ltd., 11 Green Street, London W1Y 3RF.
(annual) 1983. not priced. 39p. *En.
TF: the 1983 edition, published in 1984, has data for 1979 or 1980 to 1983.
Includes a section of statistics (deliveries of cakes and biscuits to home market and to export markets, imports, ingredients purchased. Also annual accounts of the Alliance.
Note: more detailed 4-weekly summaries issued to members can be made available (£100 yr).

1227 Statistical report.
Scotch Whisky Association, 20 Atholl Crescent, Edinburgh EH3 8HF.
(annual) 1984. not priced. 12p. *En.
TF: the 1984 edition, published in 1985, has data for 1983 and 1984, and earlier figures in some tables.
Production, warehoused and exported, stocks, excise duty paid, and exports by country. Also exports and sales of Northern Irish Whiskey.

1228 UK statistical handbook (The Brewers' Society).
Brewing Publications Ltd, 42 Portman Square, London W1H 0BB.
1973- 1982. £14.50. 103p. *En.
TF: the 1982 edition, published in 1984, has data to 1981 or 1982.
Data on beer production and consumption; brewery markets; wines, spirits, cider and soft drinks; prices, income, expenditure; excise and customs duties; licensing statistics; drunkenness statistics; other UK statistics; international statistics; and structure of the industry.

1229 Brewing review.
The Brewers' Society, 42 Portman Square, London W1H 0BB.
1977- quarterly. not priced. *En.
TF: each issue has monthly and quarterly data for several years.
Each issue includes a 'Statistical review' with data on UK beer production, UK beer imports and exports, home beer production adjusted for overseas trade, the lager market, beer packaging sales, wine consumption, spirit consumption, consumers' expenditure and government revenue, general index of retail prices (all items), and weather statistics for England and Wales.

Δ B – iii(b) Textiles, paper, rubber, etc

1230 Quarterly statistical review.
Textile Statistics Bureau, 2nd floor, Royal Exchange, Manchester M2 7ER.
1946- £6 or £20 yr. *En.
TF: each issue includes long runs of figures to the latest available on each subject. Includes detailed United Kingdom statistics on employment, foreign trade, etc. in the textile and clothing industries.

1231 Monthly bulletin of statistics.
Statistical Bureau of the Confederation of British Wool Textiles Ltd and the National Wool Textile Export Corporation, 60 Toller Lane, Bradford BD8 9BZ.
1950- £30 yr. *En.
TF: data is for the month of the issue, published early the following month.
Data on production, consumption, deliveries of wool, yarn, woollen fabrics, and products, and production personnel.

1232 Statistics.
Silk Association of Great Britain, c/o Rheinbergs Ltd., Morley Road, Tonbridge, Kent TN9 1RN.
(quarterly) price negotiable. *En.
Detailed statistics of imports and exports of silk, by type and by country. Figures are based on HM Customs & Excise statistics.

1233 Paper facts and figures.
Benn Business Information Services Ltd., PO Box 20, Sovereign Way, Tonbridge, Kent TN9 1RQ.
1961- 6 a year. £36 yr. *En.
Factual information on over 1000 mill and merchant branded printing and writing papers and boards, including stocks and up to date prices.

1234 B.P.B.I.F. grey book.
British Paper and Board Industry Federation, Plough Place, Fetter Lane, London EC4A 1AL.
(monthly) £750 yr. *En.
Monthly key indicators; and statistical tables on waste paper key figures; paper and board production, sales, imports, exports and apparent consumption; waste paper consumption; intake, stocks, imports and exports; pulp imports; and price indices. Also quarterly pulp consumption and stocks.
Note: B.P.B.I.F. green book (monthly. £500 yr) has similar data but excludes foreign trade. B.P.B.I.F. reference tables (annual. £60) has statistical tables on paper and board apparent consumption, production, imports and exports; pulp, waste paper; finance; industrial relations; energy; and an international section.

Δ B - iii(b), continued

1235 Statistical review of packaging (economic edition)...United Kingdom.
Pira, Randalls Road, Leatherhead, Surrey KT22 7RU.
1969- 1978-1982, published in July 1983. £120 (£100 to pira members). 250p. *En.
Data on all packaging materials (plastics, paper, paper sacks, fibreboard, folding cartons and rigid boxes, cellulose film, glass, closures, metal cans, aerosols, steel drums, aluminium foil, collapsible tubes, wooden containers, jute, laminates, etc.
Note: also available is 'Statistical review of packaging, update 1979-1983 - United Kingdom' (£85; £65 to Pira members) published in July 1984.

1236 Hollings apparel industry review.
Manchester Polytechnic, Hollings Faculty, Department of Clothing Design and Technology, Old Hall Lane, Manchester M14 6HR.
(3 a year) £15 yr. *En.
Each issue contains discussion papers, the Spring and Autumn issues also having a range of statistical tables and charts relating to the clothing industry including production, productivity, consumers' expenditure, price indices, employment, earnings, hours worked, foreign trade, capital expenditure, etc.-
Note: title until January 1984 was 'The Hollings statistical bulletin for the clothing industry'.

1237 Footwear industry statistical review.
British Footwear Manufacturers' Federation, 72 Dean Street, London W1V 5HB.
1969- 1984. £3.50. 28p. ISSN 0308-9398. *En.
TF: the 1984 edition, published late 1985, has data for several years to 1984.
Data on the long-term view, structure, materials, production and profitability, employment and earnings, producer and retail prices, supplies to the home market and expenditure, retail distribution, overseas trade, and EEC statistics. Brings together in one publication the more important statistics for the industry.
Note: updated by the Federation's 'Quarterly review' and 'Monthly statistics' which provide the main short-term indicators for the industry, together with a short commentary. A 'Quarterly statistical supplement' gives detailed production, foreign trade, and consumption statistics by sectors of the industry every quarter as they become available from official sources.

Δ B - iii(c) Chemicals, pharmaceuticals, etc

1237A Fertiliser statistics.
Fertiliser Manufacturers' Association Ltd., 90-93 Cowcross Street, London EC1M 6BH.
1959- 1982. £2. 6p. *En.
TF: the 1982 edition, published in 1983, has data for several years to 1981/82.
Data on cropping and fertiliser consumption for the UK, England and Wales, Scotland and Northern Ireland.
Note: the Association also publishes 'Fertiliser review' (1986. £3. 20p) which includes some statistics in the text.

Δ B - iii(d) Metals, etc

1238 Iron and steel industry: annual statistics.
United Kingdom Iron and Steel Statistics Bureau, NLA Tower, 12 Addiscombe Road, Croydon CR9 6BS.
1959- 1984. £40. 66p. *En.
TF: the 1984 edition, published in 1984, has data for several years to 1984.
50 detailed statistical tables relating to the UK iron and steel industry, with historical comparisons and detailed trade information. Includes a general summary and data on raw materials, energy, cokemaking, ironmaking, steelmaking, steel products, iron foundries, prices, manpower, general industrial data, and UK foreign trade.

Δ B - iii(e) Engineering

1239 Machine tool statistics.
The Machine Tool Trades Association, 62 Bayswater Road, London W2 3PH.
(annual) 1984. £15. 26p. *En.
TF: the 1984 edition, published mid-1984, has long runs of figures to 1983.
Includes details of machine tool production, order intake, exports and imports, population, prices, employment, costs, earnings, and some international comparisons.

1240 British Aerosol Manufacturers' Association annual report.
BAMA, 93 Albert Embankment, London SE1 7TU.
1961- 1983. free. 29p. *En.
TF: the 1983 edition, published in 1984, has data for the years from 1979 to 1983.
Includes two pages of statistics - Appendix 'B': Total number of containers filled by companies in their own plants (by type of product) and Appendix 'C': BAMA estimate of total UK aerosol filling (by type of product).

1241 Quarterly review (Association of Manufacturers of Domestic Electrical Appliances).
AMDEA, 593 Hitchin Road, Stopsley, Luton LU2 7UN.
1980- quarterly. £500 yr (including yearbook). *En.
Provides a commentary & month by month UK delivery & export data on at least 30 UK manufactured product headings; quarterly data on total UK trade availability, import penetration & the origin of imports, etc.

Δ B – iii(e), continued

1242 Annual report (British Radio and Electronic Equipment Manufacturers' Association).
BREMA, 19 Charing Cross Road, London WC2H OES.
1945- 1984. free to members. c 40p. *En.
TF: the 1984 report, published mid-1985, has data for several years to 1984.
Includes a statistical supplement with data on market development, distribution and installations, foreign trade, etc.

1243 Monthly statistical review (Society of Motor Manufacturers and Traders).
SMMT, Forbes House, Halkin Street, London SW1X 7DS.
1947- £42 yr (£50 yr overseas) non-members; £21 yr (£30 yr overseas) members; single issue £4.50. *En.
A monthly summary of the latest statistical data on the motor industry, including production of cars and commercial vehicles by manufacturer, registration of motor vehicles (new registrations of cars, top twenty, commercial vehicles; data by taxation class), overseas trade in products of the motor industry.
Note: other statistical services of the SMMT include 'Motorstat' and 'Motorstat express'.

Δ B – iii(f) Other industries

1244 Statistical digest for the furniture industry (Furniture Industry Research Association).
FIRA, Maxwell Road, Stevenage, Herts SG1 2EW.
1951/52- 1983 (published in April 1984). £28 (£12 to members). 76p. ISSN 0142-9957. *En.
Industry turnover; distribution of firms and turnover; employment and earnings in Great Britain; consumption, sources and price indices of timber and timber substitutes; manufacturers deliveries of domestic furniture; overseas trade; price indices; total market size and annual changes in deliveries; retail sales; sales of other durables; total UK consumer expenditure; household expenditure; housing; and advertising expenditure.
Note: there is also 'Statistical digest...synopsis' (1983. £1) available to members only.

1245 Quarterly bulletin of statistics (Furniture Industry Research Association).
FIRA, Maxwell Road, Stevenage, Herts SG1 2EW.
(quarterly) £10 (£5 members) or £25 (£12 members) yr. *En.
Monthly manufacturers' deliveries by value and volume, monthly index of manufacturers' orders on hand, quarterly value figures on manufacturers' deliveries by product group, overseas trade figures, indices of retail and credit sales through furniture shops, and short-term (3 months) forecasts.

1246 British shipbuilders: report and accounts.
HMSO, London.
1977/78- 1984-85. £1.50. 63p. *En.
TF: the 1984-85 report, published mid-1985, has data for about eight years to 1984/85 financial year.
Includes a section of statistical data on five year financial record, production, world merchant shipbuilding (new orders), regional output, British Shipbuilders market share, world tonnage laid up, employment, price increase).

1247 Quarterly statistics.
The Publishers Association, 19 Bedford Square, London WC1B 3HJ.
(quarterly) not priced. ISSN 0260-5198. *En.
Contents include a review summary and data on total sales, hardback and paperback sales: home and export, export markets, book prices, and relevant indices.

Δ B – iv Construction

1248 Housing and construction statistics: Great Britain (Department of the Environment, Welsh Office & Scottish Development Department).
HMSO, London.
1947- quarterly. £3.50 or £27.50 for 8 issues. ISSN 0308-9819. *En.
TF: each issue has data for 3 to 5 years and the last eight quarters to the date of the issue, and is published about three months later.
Part 1: buildings under construction, house purchase and finance, rents, and information on production and delivery of building materials. Part 2: details of special housing, renovations, local authority loans, employments and vacancies in the industry, and production costs.

1249 Housing and construction statistics, 1974-1984: Great Britain (Department of the Environment, Welsh Office & Scottish Development Department).
HMSO, London.
1969/79- 1985. £25. 179p. *En.
Designed to provide a broad perspective on developments over the past decade. Data on construction includes orders, output, labour, structure, materials and investment. Data on housing includes housebuilding, renovations, slum clearance, stock of dwellings, finance, rents and rent regulations.

1250 Monthly statistics of building materials and components.
Statistics Construction Divn, Department of the Environment, 43 Marsham Street, London SW1P 3PY.
not priced. monthly. ISSN 0264-6188. *En.
TF: each issue has data for several years, quarters and months to about three months prior to the date of publication.
Indices of construction materials; production, sales, deliveries, stocks, etc. of sand & gravel, bricks, cement, concrete products, metals, timber, etc, & foreign trade of selected materials & component materials.

Δ B – iv, continued

1251 BSRIA statistics bulletin.
Building Services Research and Information Association, Old Bracknell Lane, Bracknell, Berks RG12 4AH.
1976- quarterly. £35 yr (£40 yr in Europe; £45 yr elsewhere); free to members of BSRIA. ISSN 0308-6224.
TF: each issue has data for two or more years and cumulations of quarterly data for the last two years to date, being published about six months after the end of the period covered. *En
Information on the building services market, including a survey of market trends, production, overseas trade, and home demand data, etc.

1252 Construction forecasts (NEDO Building EDC, Sector Working Group).
NEDO Books, Millbank Tower, Millbank, London SW1P 4QX.
2 a year (mid & end). £10 each issue. *En.
A detailed presentation of the short-term prospects for the construction industry.

1253 BMP statistical bulletin.
National Council of Building Material Producers, 33 Alfred Place, London WC1E 7EN.
1974- monthly. £24 yr. ISSN 0144-9036. *En.
TF: each issue has data for three years and five or more quarters or months to about six months prior to the date of publication.
House building – starts – under construction – completions – time lag, renovations, indices of house prices, building societies, private architects' workload and commissions, fixed capital expenditure, new orders and output – current and constant prices, production (sand & gravel, cement, concrete building blocks, bricks, ready-mixed concrete, plaster and plasterboard), building material prices, sales, wholesale prices, imports and exports of selected building materials, BMP forecasts.
Note: also published are 'BMP forecasts' (3 a year. 4p. ISSN 0144-9060) and 'The BMP guide to construction,' 1984/85, a 28-page guide with some statistics.

1254 BCIS quarterly review of building prices.
Building Cost Information Service, Royal Institution of Chartered Surveyors, 85-87 Clarence Street, Kingston upon Thames KT1 1RB.
1981- quarterly. £70 yr. ISSN 0260-6216. *En.
Commentary and forecast, followed by indices of tender prices and building costs, average building prices (by type of buildings), location factors, general applications, insurance valuations, current cost accounting, and building regulations prescribed fees.
Note: also a loose-leaf information service issued in 12 bulletins each year (£126 yr).

1255 RIBA quarterly statistical bulletin.
Statistics Section, Royal Institute of British Architects, 66 Portland Place, London W1N 4AD.
1959- quarterly. £4 or £15 yr (free to architects & various official & semi-official bodies. *En.
TF: each issue has data for nine years and 20 quarters to three months priot to publication.
Quarterly enquiry into private architects' workload (total figures, sub-totals by building type, sub-totals by region, employment, and rehabilitation work.
Note: also available are 'Education statistics' (annual. £2.50) with information on the numbers of students in schools of architecture, examination pass rates, etc; 'Architects employment and earnings survey' (annual. £11.50 plus 50p postage); 'Census of private architectural practices' (every 4 years. 1984. £2); and reports of other surveys not taken on a regular basis.

Δ B – v Energy

1256 Digest of United Kingdom energy statistics (Department of Energy).
HMSO, London.
1938/43- 1985. £12.50. 110p. *En.
TF: the 1985 edition, published mid-1985, has data for the years 1980 to 1984.
Tables and charts of UK energy production and consumption. Separate sections deal with production and consumption of individual fuels, oil and gas reserves, fuel prices and foreign trade in fuels.
Note: further statistical information can be obtained from the annual reports and accounts of each of the nationalised industries.

1257 Energy trends: a statistical bulletin (Department of Energy & Central Office of Information).
Information Division, Department of Energy, Thames House South, Millbank, London SW1P 4QJ.
1975- monthly. £7 yr in UK; £10 yr in Europe. ISSN 0308-1222. *En.
TF: each issue has data for two to four years and three months, to two or three months prior to the date of publication.
Monthly and quarterly tables for production and consumption of fuels, aggregated energy consumption, and fuel prices.

1258 CEGB statistical yearbook.
Central Electricity Generating Board, Press & Publicity Office, 15 Newgate Street, London EC1A 7AU.
1963/64- 1984/85. not priced. 13p. *En.
Operations and plant, power stations, transmission, etc., supplementing the information included in the Board's 'Annual report and accounts'.
Note: the annual reports of the regional electricity boards also include some statistics, mainly financial.

Δ B – v, continued

1259 Energy for industry and commerce: quarterly bulletin.
The Energy Information Centre, Cambridge Information and Research Services Ltd., PO Box 147, Grosvenor House, High Street, Newmarket CB8 9AL.
£47.50 yr (free to members). *En.
TF: each issue has long monthly runs of figures to about three months prior to the date of the issue.
Statistical tables and graphs are included in most of the sections, which are Fuel pricing survey, market trends and prospects, oil news, gas news, coal news, electricity news.
Note: updated by a 2-page 'Monthly fuel price monitor'.

1260 Handbook of electricity supply statistics.
Electricity Council, 30 Millbank, London SW1P 4RD.
1970– 1984. free. 155p. ISSN 0440-1905. *En.
TF: the 1984 edition, published late 1984, has data for 1983 or 1983/84 and several earlier years.
The power stations, the national grid system, distribution systems, transmission and distribution, generation, finance, commerce, CEGB bulk supply tariff, appliances and contracting, employment and earnings, electricity supply in GB, Scotland and Northern Ireland, energy in the EEC, world electricity production, miscellaneous (prices, etc).
Note: the Electricity Council's 'Statement of accounts and statistics' contains data on electricity supplies and sales, generation, transmission, industrial sales, and accidents as well as the financial accounts of the Council (1984/85 report, published mid-1985. £2.50).

1261 Report and accounts... (British Gas Corporation).
HMSO, London.
1973– 1984/85. £2. 63p. ISSN 0072-0216. *En.
Includes some statistics on the production and consumption of gas.
Note: the annual reports of the regional boards also contain some statistics.

1262 Development of the oil and gas resources of the United Kingdom (Department of Energy).
HMSO, London.
1973– 1984. £8.50. 53p. *En.
Department of Energy estimates of oil and gas reserves on the UK continental shelf; statistics on oil and gas exploration, development and production, etc.

1263 UK petroleum industry statistics: consumption and refinery production.
(Institute of Petroleum, 61 New Cavendish Street, London W1M 8AR.
(annual) 1982 & 1983 (published in May 1984. not priced. 9p. ISSN 0141-4305. *En.
Deliveries, estimated end-use analyses, production, etc.

Δ B – vi Research and development

1264 Industrial research and development expenditure and employment (Business Statistics Office).
HMSO, London.
1975– 1981 (issued early 1985). £7.50. 40p. *En.

1265 Annual review of government funded R & D (Cabinet Office).
HMSO, London.
1983– 1985 (published 1985). £9.50. 149p. *En.
Reviews departments' plans & projections for R & D expenditure over the period covered by the last Public Expenditure Survey; also summary accounts of government R & D expenditure and industry; international comparisons; R & D financed by the European Communities; related government activities, etc.

Δ C External trade

1266 Overseas trade statistics of the United Kingdom (Department of Trade and Industry).
HMSO, London.
1848– monthly. £15.95 or £201 yr. ISSN 0436-3574. *En.
TF: each issue contains data for that month, cumulated figures for the year to date, and is published about three weeks after the end of the period covered.
The main tables contain statistics of imports, exports and exports of imported merchandise, classified by commodities and subdivided by principal countries of origin and destination.

1267 Overseas trade analysed in terms of industries (Business Statistics Office).
HMSO, London.
(quarterly) £7.70 yr. *En.
An analysis of commodities imported and exported, according to the industries of which they are the principal products.
Note: issued as Business Monitor MO 10.

1268 Overseas transactions (Business Statistics Office).
HMSO, London.
(annual) 1983. £10. 88p. *En.
TF: the 1983 edition, published in 1985, has data for 1979 to 1983.
Summaries and detailed tables of UK outward direct investment overseas and inward direct investment in the UK; overseas royalties and similar transactions; and overseas transactions in films and TV material.
Note: issued as Business Monitor MA 4.

Δ C, continued

1269 Monthly review of external trade statistics.
Department of Trade and Industry, S2I1, Room 255, 1 Victoria Street, London SW1H OET.
1975- £3 or £36 yr (including annual supplement). *En.
TF: each issue has data for several years, quarters and months and is published about two months after the end of the period covered.
Data on visible trade with a short commentary section, a section of graphs and key statistical series, and a main section of tables (UK balance of payments, exports and imports by main commodity groups and by area, derived statistics of UK trade, international statistics, etc). The annual supplement gives longer runs of data.

1270 Import penetration and export sales ratios for manuacturing industry (Business Statistics Office).
HMSO, London.
(quarterly) £1.95 or £8.50 yr. *En.
TF: each issue has data for seven quarters to the date of the issue and is published four or five months later.
Presents four ratios relating to overseas trade in practically every sector of manufactured goods to domestic production and apparent consumption of those goods.
Note: issued as 'Business Monitor MQ 12'.

1271 Annual report.
British Invisible Exports Council, 14 Austin Friars, London EC2N 2HE.
1967- 1983/84 (published mid-1984). not priced. 38p. *En.
Mainly text, but also includes some statistics on world invisible trade, Britain's invisible trade, employment in services, etc.
Note: previously Committee on Invisible Exports.

1272 Trade bulletin (Fishery Economics Research Unit).
F.E.R.U., Sea Fish Industry Authority, 10 Young Street, Edinburgh EH2 4JQ.
(monthly) not priced. ISSN 0144-9303. *En.
TF: each issue has data for the latest month and year to date, and corresponding data for the previous year for comparison.
Quantity and value of imports and exports of fish intended for human consumption.

1273 UK yearbook of timber statistics.
Timber Trade Federation of the United Kingdom, Clareville House, Whitcomb Street, London WC2H 7DL.
1955- 1980-82. not priced. 35p. *En.
TF: the 1980-82 edition, published in 1983, has data for 1980 to 1982 and earlier years in some tables.
UK imports and exports of all types of timber and timber products, such as telegraph poles, railway sleepers, etc., subdivided by countries of origin and destination.

1274 Quarterly review of UK trade statistics.
Statistical Bureau of the Confederation of British Wool Textiles Ltd and the National Wool Textile Export Corporation, 60 Toller Lane, Bradford BD8 9BZ.
1950- £17 yr. *En.
TF: each issue contains cumulated figures for the year to the date of the issue and also data for two previous years, and is issued about three months later.
UK exports of wool, yarn, wool fabrics and products, etc., subdivided by area and country of destination.

1275 UK exports of iron and steel.
Iron and Steel Statistics Bureau, PO Box 230, 12 Addiscombe Road, Croydon CR9 6BS.
1970- monthly. £50 yr. *En.
TF: published about seven weeks after the end of the month.
Cumulative export statistics for the year to date covering 150 products and 100 countries of destination.

1276 UK imports of iron and steel.
Iron and Steel Statistics Bureau, PO Box 230, 12 Addiscombe Road, Croydon CR9 6BS.
1970- monthly. £50 yr each title. *En.
TF: published about seven weeks after the end of the month.
There are two separate publications under this title, each detailing import statistics for over 150 iron and steel products from over 50 countries: 'Current month' identifies actual imports for each individua month; 'Calendar month to date' contains cumulative data for the year to the date of the issue.

1277 Total exports of new and used machine tools.
The Machine Tool Trades Association, 62 Bayswater Road, London W2 3PH.
(quarterly) not priced. *En.
TF: each issue has cumulated figures for the current year.
Summary data by area and country; detailed data by commodity subdivided by countries of destination.

Δ D Internal distribution and service trades

1278 The A-Z of UK marketing data, 1980.
Euromonitor Publications Ltd, 87-88 Turnmill Street, London EC1M 5QU.
1980 (data to 1977 or 1978). 529p. *En.
A dictionery of UK market facts and figures for the world of business and commerce, arranged alphabetically by 350 subjects/products.

Δ D, continued

1279 Market intelligence.
MINTEL Publications Ltd., 7 Arundel Street, London WC2R 3DR.
(monthly) £55; or £325 yr. *En.
Five market reports on consumer goods markets and services each month, each including statistical data.

1280 Marketing pocket book.
The Advertising Association, 15 Wilton Road, London SW1V 1NJ.
(annual) 1984. £7.50. 116p. *En.
TF: the 1984 edition, published in November 1983, has data to 1982 or the latest available.
Sections on economic and demographic data, the consumer, distribution, advertising expenditure, media, international, maps.

Δ D – i Wholesale and retail trades

1281 Wholesaling and dealing (Business Statistics Office).
HMSO, London.
1950- 4th, 1974. £3. 148p. *En.
TF: the 1974 report, published in 1979, refers to 1974 and is the latest to be published.
The results of a large scale enquiry covering businessmen in Great Britain engaged in wholesale distribution,merchanting and factoring, dealing in coal, oil, builders' materials, grain and agricultural supplies, industrial materials and machinery, scrap and waste materials, and the leasing of industrial and office machinery. Data includes the numbers of businesses, turnover, purchase for resale, stocks, persons engaged (working proprietors and employees), wages and salaries, net capital expenditure, etc.
Note: issued as 'Business Monitor SDO 26'.

1282 Retailing (Business Statistics Office).
HMSO, London.
1976- 1982. £12.50. 110p. *En.
TF: published every two years, the 1982 report was issued in 1984.
Detailed statistics on types and numbers of businesses, turnover, gross margins, numbers employed, etc.
Note: issues as 'Business Monitor SDO 25'. Replaces the 'Census of distribution and other services'.

1283 Retail trade (Business Statistics Office).
HMSO, London.
(monthly) £14.50 yr. *En.
Summary of figures for retail trade and detailed index numbers of sales in various kinds of shops.
Note: issued as Business Monitor SDM 28.

1284 Retail business.
Economist Intelligence Unit, 40 Duke Street, London W1A 1DW.
(monthly) £20 or £165 yr. ISSN 0034-012. *En.
A research journal covering consumer goods markets, marketing and distribution. Includes statistical tables in the text.

1285 Retail prices indexes, 1914-1984 (Department of Employment).
HMSO, London.
£4.50 (published May 1985). 47p. *En.
Detailed statistics for various groups, sub-groups and sections, covering more than 600 separate goods and services for which price movements are regularly measured.

1286 Report on the census of retail distribution and other services of Northern Ireland...main results (Department of Commerce, Northern Ireland).
HMSO, 80 Chichester Street, Belfast BT1 4JY.
1965- 1975. not priced. 67p. *En.
TF: a census is taken every ten years, and the results of the 1975 census were published in 1979.
Contains data on all sectors of retail distribution and service trades.

1287 Economic survey (The Booksellers Association Charter Group).
Booksellers Association Service House Ltd., 154 Buckingham Palace Road, London SW1W 9TZ.
(annual) 1982-83 (published 1984). not priced. 13p. ISSN 0141-917X. *En.
Data on business, trade, profits, book prices, consumer expenditure, etc.

1288 Average prices of British academic books.
Centre for Library and Information Management, Loughborough University, Loughborough, Leics LE11 3TU.
1974- 1984/85. £7.50 (£8 abroad). 17p. *En.
TF: the 1984/85 edition, published early 1986, has data for July-December 1984, January-June 1985 and July-December 1985.

1289 The Bookseller.
J Whitaker & Sons Ltd., 12 Dyott Street, London WC1A 1DF.
1858- weekly. £0.65 or £40 yr. *En.
Data on books published, totals and by individual publishers monthly; book prices six-monthly.

Δ D – i, continued

1290 Library Association record.
The Library Association, 7 Ridgmount Street, London WC1E 7AE.
1899- monthly. £46 yr or $99 yr. *En.
Includes tables of periodical prices in the May issue.

Δ D – ii Service trades

1291 Equipment leasing.
Equipment Leasing Association Ltd., 18 Upper Grosvenor Street, London W1X 9PB.
1973- 1980. free. *En.
Includes a statistical appendix, 'ELA statistics: summary of the leasing business of ELA members' which is included as a 4-page separate supplement at the back of the booklet, the latest covering several years to 1983.
Note: the annual report of the Association also includes a section of statistical data, including assets acquired by type of asset and by type of lessee.

1292 Computer services (Business Statistics Office).
HMSO, London.
(quarterly) £8.50 yr. *En.
TF: each issue has data for the last two years and five quarters to the quarter of the issue, and is published two or three months after the end of the period covered.
The business of computer services or bureaux, including statistics of billings to clients, personnel employed, etc.
Note: issued as 'Business Monitor: SDQ 9'.

1293 Cinemas (Business Statistics Office).
HMSO, London.
(annual) 1983 (published 1984). £4.20. c 15p. *En.
Numbers of cinemas, admissions, etc.
Note: issued as 'Business Monitor MA2'.

1294 Fire statistics, United Kingdom.
Home Office, Library (Room 1001), 50 Queen Anne's Gate, London SW1H 9AT.
(annual) 1983. £3.50. 77p. *En.
TF: the 1983 edition, published late 1984, has historical data for 1973 to 1983 and detailed data for 1983.
Data on casualties & rescues, fires in occupied buildings, outdoor fires & fires in derelict buildings.

1295 Fire service statistics...actuals.
Chartered Institute of Public Finance and Accountancy, 3 Robert Street, London WC2N 6BH.
(annual) 1984-85 (published late 1985) £11. 23p. ISSN 0309-622X. *En.
Final figures of expenditure and income per 1000 population. Also figures for fire stations, training, appliances, return of calls, inspections, and manpower.
Note: also 'Fire service statistics...estimates' (1985-86. £11. 16p. published mid-1986. ISSN 0307-0573).

Δ D – iii Advertising

1296 Quarterly digest of advertising expenditure.
Media Expenditure Analysis Ltd., 63 St Martin's Lane, London WC2N 4JT.
£480 yr. *En.
Advertising expenditure of individual brands, by product groups and brands.
Note: MEAL also offers a variety of services, including standard monthly product group reports, a microfilmed advertisement service, and quarterly agency reports (press and TV).

1297 Advertising statistics yearbook: advertising industry facts, figures & trends (The Advertising Association).
Advertising Press, 22-24 Bell Street, Henley-on-Thames, Oxon RG9 2BG.
1983- No.2, June 1984. £15. 143p. ISSN 0266-0024. *En.
TF: the 1984 edition, published in 1984, has data for a number of years to 1981, 1982 or 1983.
Includes media statistics (by media), advertisers' statistics, advertising agency statistics, and miscellaneous statistics (complaints, attitudes, international advertising expenditure statistics).

1298 Quarterly review of advertising statistics (The Advertising Association).
Advertising Press, 22-24 Bell Street, Henley-on-Thames, Oxon RG9 2BG.
1984- quarterly. £45 yr (£50 yr abroad). *En.
TF: data at current prices, at constant 1980 prices, and in % change terms.
Based on the Association's quarterly survey of advertising expenditure in the press and poster media, plus data on TV and radio advertising expenditure. Sections on national newspaper advertising, regional newspaper advertising, consumer magazines, business and professional magazines, poster advertising expenditure, radio advertising expenditure, television advertising expenditure, total advertising expenditure, etc.

Δ D – iii, continued

1299 ABC circulation review.
Audit Bureau of Circulations Ltd., 13 Wimpole Street, London W1M 7AB.
(twice yearly). free to members. *En.
TF: each issue has data for four quarters and six months, and is published two weeks later.
Gives the certified average net sales and net circulation figures for some 2000 publications in the UK and certain overseas countries. Includes newspapers, journals, magazines and annual publications.

Δ D – iv Tourism and travel

1300 Digest of tourist statistics.
British Tourist Authority, Finance Department, Thames Tower, Black's Road, London W6 9EL.
1969- No.11, 1983. £10. 70p. *En.
TF: the 1983 edition, published in 1983, has data for 1982 and some earlier years in some tables.
Includes data on international travel, UK travel costs, tourism, data from the international passenger survey and other reports and surveys relating to travel and tourism.

1301 Overseas travel and tourism (Business Statistics Office).
HMSO, London.
(quarterly) £8.50 yr. *En.
TF: each issue has data for several years and quarters to the period of the issue and is published about six months later.
Data on foreign visitors to the United Kingdom and visits abroad by UK residents.

1302 Tourism intelligence quarterly.
British Tourist Authority, Queen's House, 64 St James's Street, London SW1A 1NF.
1978- quarterly. £8.50 yr. *En.
Collates and interprets current statistical data relating to international tourism and tourism in the United Kingdom. Areas regularly monitored include overseas visitors to the UK, UK residents travelling abroad and within Britain, UK travel account, hotel occupancy, traffic at UK airports and seaports, etc.

1303 National travel survey (Department of Transport).
HMSO, London.
1965- 4th, 1978/79 (published in 1983). £13.95. 140p. *En.
This occasional survey was part of a series designed to provide a national data bank of the travel patterns of the population of Great Britain for use in the overall planning of national transport facilities
Note: there is also a supplementary report 'Cycling: an analysis of the 1978/79 national travel survey' (available from the Department of Transport. £5).

1304 English heritage monitor.
English Tourist Board, Socio-economic Research Unit, Research Services Branch, 4 Grosvenor Gardens, London SW1W ODU.
1983- 1984. £5.50. 68p. *En.
TF: the 1984 edition, published in 1985, has data for 1982/83, 1983 or 1984.
A yearly analysis of trends affecting England's architectural heritage, including 20 tables or listed buildings, ancient monuments, local authority expenditure on conversation and tourism, by-passes, visitor trends, etc.

1305 Isle of Man tourist survey, 1981, passenger survey 1982/83.
Isle of Man Treasury, Government Offices, Buck's Road, Douglas, Isle of Man.
£1. 41p. *En.
A tourist survey referring to staying tourists to the island and the report includes statistics of length of stay, previous visits, holiday planning time, package holidays, holiday activities, area of residence, type of transport, expenditure by tourists. The passenger report is mainly financial and includes all types of visitors to the island, not just tourists.
Note: a previous report was 'Manx tourist 77'.

1306 Passenger arrivals statistics 1971-1984.
Isle of Man Treasury, Government Offices, Buck's Road, Douglas, Isle of Man.
not priced. 7 sheets of computer printout. *En.
TF: monthly data for 1971 to 1984, published in January 1985.
Passenger arrivals to the Isle of Man by air and by sea; air passenger arrivals; sea passenger arrivals; air arrivals by routes; sea arrivals by routes; countries from which passengers arrived; carriage of motor cars to the Isle of Man; distribution between day and other passenger arrivals.

Δ E Population

1307 Census (Office of Population Censuses and Surveys).
HMSO, London.
1801- 1981 (published between 1981 and 1984). *En.
National report, Great Britain: Part. 1 [demographic characteristics, economic characteristics, housing and amenities and household composition] (£11.70). Part. 2 [answers by householders on social class, travel to work, family structure, country of birth, etc] (£6.80).

[continued next page]

Δ E, continued

1307, continued

County reports, England and Wales [2 parts for each county. Part 1 relates to demographic characteristics, economic characteristics, housing and amenities and household composition; part 2 gives information on the counties and their administrative districts] (separately priced).
Communal establishments, Great Britain (£7.40).
Country of birth, Great Britain (£9.10).
Historical tables, 1801-1981, England and Wales (£3.50).
Household and family composition, England and Wales (£10).
Housing and households, England and Wales (£18.40).
Key statistics for local authorities (£9.10).
Key statistics for urban areas (6 reports, separately priced).
National migration, Great Britain (2 parts. £11.70 & £7.40).
Workplace and transport to work, England and Wales (£16.90).
Regional migration reports, England and Wales (each in 2 parts, 9 vols. in each part, separately priced.
New towns report, England and Wales (2 parts. £10.80 & £6.80).
Qualified manpower, England and Wales (2 parts. £10.80 & £6.80).
Persons of pensionable age, Great Britain (£14.40).
Report for Wales (£9.10 also available in Welsh).
Sex, age and marital status, Great Britain (£5).
Usual residence, Great Britain (£11.80).
Welsh language in Wales (£5 also available in Welsh).
Economic activity [companion volumes to County reports presenting data for economic activity of the population in each county, including information on employment status, economic position and socio-economic groups by area of residence and sex] (separate vols. for each county, individually priced).
The following volumes are available from OPCS, St Catherine's House, 10 Kingsway, London WC2B 6JP:
Census 1981, ward and civil paris monitors: England and Wales [54 vols, one per county. £40 the set. ISSN 0144-5537].
Census, 1981, county monitors [giving key county results].
Census, 1981, Parliamentary constituency monitors (12 vols. £6 the set).

1308 Census, Scotland (Registrar-General for Scotland).
HMSO, Edinburgh.
1801- 1981 (published between 1981 and 1984). *En.
Economic activity (10% sample) (£10) [also reports for each region on microfiche, £4 each].
Household and family composition (10% sample) (£8.40).
Housing and households report (£7.80).
Key statistics for urban areas, Scotland. Localities (£6.30).
Country of birth (£4.40).
New towns (2 vols. £5.80 & £4.10).
Workplace and transport to work (10% sample) (£12.50).
Scottish summary (2 vols. £6.80 & £6.30).
Migration (Vol. 1 & 2. 100% £13.30 & £10).
(Vol. 3 & 4. 10% sample. £8.40 & £6.70).
Gaelic report (£6.80).
Historic tables, 1801-1981 (£3).

1309 The Northern Ireland census,(Department of Health and Social Services, Registrar General, Northern Ireland).
HMSO, Belfast.
1801- 1981 (published between 1982 and 1984). 9 vols. *En.
Summary report (£6.75).
Preliminary report (£4.10).
Migration report (£3.45).
Workplace and transport to work report (£3.45).
Housing and household composition report (£8.50).
Economic activity report (£8.50).
Education report (£6.25).
Religion report (£7.75).
Report for Belfast local government districts (£7.90).
Note: 'Northern Ireland: a census atlas', by Paul A. Compton and others was published in 1978 by Gill and Macmillan, 15/17 Eden Quay, Dublin 1.

1310 Isle of Man...census report.
Chief Registrar, General Registry, Douglas, Isle of Man.
1821- 1981. Part I: £1; part II: £5; part 3: £9. 3 vols. *En.
TF: a census is taken every ten years, the results of the 1981 census being published in 1982 & 1983.
A sample census was taken in 1976.
Part I contains such information as will be of immediate general interest (population by sex, visitors, etc); part II has data on population, households, residence, persons not borne in the Isle of Man, private households, etc; part III has data on economically active and employment status, employed population by industry, etc.

Δ E, continued

1311 Report of the census [of the Island of Jersey].
Greffier to the States of Jersey, Jersey.
1801- 1981. £5. 90p. *En.
TF: the report of the 1981 census was published in 1982.
Data on population; acreage and population; age and marital condition; length of residence, by parish, sex, age, etc; dwellings by rooms and household spaces, amenities, use of motor vehicles, employment status; occupations and industry, etc.

1312 Census [of the Bailiwick of Guernsey] (Census Office, Guernsey).
States of Guernsey, Board of Administration, Guernsey.
1801- 1981 (published early 1982). not priced. 58p. *En.
Covers Guernsey, Alderney and Sark, and contains data on population; usual residence; sex, age and marital status; birthplace and residence; terminal educational age; occupation and industry; houses and households; non-private households; use of vehicles; sewerage arrangements, etc.

1313 Population trends (Office of Population Censuses and Surveys).
HMSO, London.
(quarterly) c £4.50 each issue. ISSN 0307-4463. *En.
TF: each issue has long runs of annual and quarterly figures to about three months prior to the date of the issue.
Data on population, components of population change, vital statistics, live births, marriages, divorces, migration, deaths and abortions for England and Wales.

1314 Population projections (Office of Population Censuses and Surveys).
HMSO, London.
1970/2010- 1983-2023. £8.20. 53p. *En.
TF: the projections for 1983 to 2023 were published in 1985.
Population projections by sex and age for the United Kingdom and constituent counties.
Note: prepared by the Government Actuary in consultation with the Registrar General, and published in the OPCS Monitor series PP2, and on microfiche.

1315 Population projections: area (Office of Population Censuses and Surveys).
HMSO, London.
1974/91- 1981-1993 (published 1984). £5.20. 41p. *En.
Population projections by sex and age for standard regions, counties, London boroughs and metropolitan districts of England.
Note: issued in the OPCS Monitor series PP3.

1316 Based home population projections for the counties of Wales.
Welsh Office, Crown Building, Cathays Park, Cardiff CF1 3NQ.
(biennial) 1981 (published 1983). £2. 22p. ISSN 0262-5180. *En; title page & introduction also in Welsh.

1317 The Registrar-General's annual report for Scotland.
HMSO, Edinburgh.
1855- 1983 (published 1984). £11.50. *En.
Population, vital and mortality statistics.

1318 Annual report of the Registrar-General (General Register Office, Department of Health and Social Services, Northern Ireland).
HMSO, Belfast.
1922- 1982. £12.40. 196p. *En.
TF: the 1982 report, published in 1985, has data for 1982 and long runs of earlier years in some tables.
Data for Northern Ireland on population, marriages, live births - fertility, illegitimate births, still births, deaths, certificates of deaths, life tables, migration, administration, and meteorology. Also a page of comparative statistics for Northern Ireland, England and Wales, Scotland and the Irish Republic. 'Abstracts' (p 51-191) are in fact much more detailed data by district council areas, by age, sex, etc.
Note: 'The Registrar-General's quarterly return for Northern Ireland' (£3.10 each issue) updates some of the above data.

1319 Chief Registrar's annual report and statistical review.
General Registry, Government Office, Isle of Man.
1877- 1984 (published late 1985). £2. 46p. *En.
Data on births, marriages and deaths in the Isle of Man.

1320 Population estimates, Scotland (General Register Office for Scotland).
HMSO, Edinburgh.
(annual) 1984 (published 1985). £1.20. 11p. *En.
Annual mid-year estimates of population data to local authority level.

1321 International migration (Office of Population Censuses and Surveys).
HMSO, London.
1971/74- 1984 (published 1985). £5.20. 43p. *En.
TF:has data for some earlier years in some tables.
Presents analyses of population change and detailed statistics of migration, including citizenship, country of birth, country of last or next residence, occupation, age, sex and marital status. Also includes some census data and Home Office statistics on acceptances for settlement and citizenship.

Δ E, continued

1322 Control of immigration statistics, United Kingdom (Home Office).
HMSO, London.
1962- 1984 (published 1985). £6.75. c 70p. *En.
Numbers of Commonwealth citizens and foreign nationals subject to immigration control, entering and leaving the United Kingdom.
Note: issued as a Command paper. There is also a quarterly statistical bulletin available from the Home Office (£2 each).

1323 Tables of persons acquiring citizenship (Home Office).
HMSO, London.
(annual) 1983 (published 1984). £3. 14p. *En.
Note: issued as a Command paper.

Δ E - i Vital statistics

1324 Birth statistics: review of the Registrar General on births and patterns of family building in England and Wales (Office of Population Censuses and Surveys).
HMSO, London.
1974- 1984 (published late 1985). £8. 105p. ISSN 0140-2587. *En.
Note: issued in the OPCS reference series FM1.

1325 Marriage and divorce statistics: review of the Registrar General on marriages and divorce in England and Wales (Office of Population Censuses and Surveys).
HMSO, London.
1974- 1983 (published 1986). £8. 99p. ISSN 0140-8992. *En.
TF: has data for several years to 1983.
Annual and serial tables on marriages and divorces for England and Wales, classified by many background variables, eg., age at and order of marriage.
Note: issued in the OPCS reference series FM2.

1326 Vital statistics: local and health areas: vital statistics for administrative and health areas in England and Wales (Office of Population Censuses and Surveys).
HMSO, London.
1974- 1983 (published 1985). £5.20. 46p. *En.
Births by legitimacy and sex of child, deaths, infant deaths and stillbirths for each local government district and health authority.
Note: issued in the OPCS reference series VS.

1327 Statistics of deaths reported to coroners: England and Wales.
Home Office Statistical Department, Room 1813, Tolworth Tower, Surbiton, Surrey KT6 7DS.
(annual) 1983 (published April 1984). £1.50. 9p. *En.
Deaths reported to coroners during the year using total figures to show verdicts returned at inquests, deaths registered, inquests held, post-mortems held and types of inquests.
Note: issued as a 'Home Office statistical bulletin'.

1328 Mortality statistics (Office of Population Censuses and Surveys).
HMSO, London.
1974- *En.
Titles within the series are:
DH1. Mortality statistics (1980, published 1984. £4.70)
DH2. Mortality statistics: cause (1982, published 1983. £6.80)
DH3. Mortality statistics: childhood and maternity (1982, published 1984. £6.80).
DH4. Mortality statistics: accidents and violence (1983, published 1984. £6.50).
DH5. Mortality statistics: area (1983, published 1984. £6.50).
DH6. Mortality statistics: perinatal and infant (1980, published 1983. £6.20).

1329 Mortality statistics: series tables: review of the Registrar General on deaths in England and Wales, 1841-1980 (Office of Population Censuses and Surveys).
HMSO, London.
£4.10. (published 1985). 29p. *En.
Note: issued in the series DH1.

1330 Immigrant mortality in England and Wales, 1970-1978: causes of death by country of birth.
Office of Population Censuses and Surveys, St Catherine's House, 10 Kingsway, London WC2B 6JP.
£13. (published 1984). 144p. *En.
Note: issued in the series 'Studies on medical and population subjects' SMPS 47.

Δ E - ii Labour

1331 British labour statistics: yearbook (Department of Employment).
HMSO, London.
1969- 1976 (published 1979). £20. 372p. *En.
Data on wage rates and normal hours of work of manual workers; earnings and hours worked; retail prices; employment; unemployment, vacancies and placings; family expenditure; membership of trade unions; stoppages of work due to industrial disputes; accidents at work.
Note: 'British labour statistics: historical abstract, 1886-1968' was issued in 1971 (out of print).

Δ E – ii, continued

1332 Employment gazette (Department of Employment).
HMSO, London.
1893– monthly. £2.95 or £34.50 yr. ISSN 0309-5045. *En.
TF: each issue includes monthly averages for ten years and monthly index numbers for the last five years up to the month prior to the date of the issue.
Includes index of retail prices, and tables and charts on employment, unemployment, wage rates, hours of work, manpower, earnings and stoppages of work. Also special articles, news and notes.

1333 Unemployment press release.
Department of Economic Development, Netherleigh, Massey Avenue, Belfast BT4 2JP.
(monthly) free. *En.
Provides counts of unemployed claimants in Northern Ireland by sex and district council, separate figures being given for school leavers and persons under age 25. Also information on vacancies, placings, employment and training measures.

1334 Quarterly employment enquiry results.
Department of Economic Development, Netherleigh, Massey Avenue, Belfast BT4 2JP.
(quarterly) free. *En.
Data on employees in employment, arranged by industrial classification.

1335 Civil service statistics (Treasury).
HMSO, London.
1970– 1985. £7. 32p. *En.
TF: the 1985 edition, published mid-1985, has data for three or more years to 1984 or 1985.
Part 1 contains a broad historical picture of the Civil Service; part 2 has statistical tables on staff in post, new entrants and leavers, voluntary resignations, salary bands, etc.

1336 ...Survey of professional engineers.
Engineering Council, 10-16 Maltravers Street, London WC2R 3ER.
1966– 1983. not priced. 60p. *En.
TF: the 1983 report has data for 1983 and some earlier years in some tables. The survey is taken every two or three years.
Data on employment, incomes, fringe benefits, overtime, field of work, trade unions, qualifications, further training, current occupations, location, and responsibility.

1337 Census of staff in librarianship and information work in the UK.
Department of Education and Science, Publications Despatch, Honeypot Lane, Stanmore, Middx DA7 1AZ.
1972– 1981. not priced. *En.
TF: the census is taken every five years. The results of the 1981 census were published in 1983.

1338 Women and employment: a lifetime perspective (Office of Population Censuses and Surveys & Department of Employment).
HMSO, London.
£9.50. (published 1984). 216p. *En.
Based on a 1980 Department of Employment national survey of women of working age. Includes information on occupational segregation, pay, employment conditions, trade union activity, the share of domestic work between husbands and wives, etc.

1339 New earnings survey (Department of Employment).
HMSO, London.
1968– 1985. £8.50 each or £48 yr for 6 issues. 6 parts. ISSN 0262-0553. *En.
TF: the results of the 1985 survey were published in 1985/6.
Earnings from employment in industry, occupation, region, etc in April.
Part A: Streamlined analyses and key analyses by agreement.
Part B: Report, summary analyses and other analyses by agreement
Part C: Analyses by industry
Part D: Analyses by occupation
Part E: Analyses by region and age group
Part F: Hours, earnings of part-time women, employees, types of collective agreement.

1340 British journal of industrial relations.
London School of Economics and Political Science, Houghton Street, Aldwych, London WC2A 2AE.
1963– 3 a year. £10 or £17 yr; $19 or $38 yr. ISSN 0007-1080. *En.
Each issue includes a 3-page 'Statistical background to the industrial relations scene' with data from government sources on the labour market, wages and earnings, industrial production, and industrial disputes.

Δ E – iii Housing

< see also 1248, 1249

1341 Local housing statistics, England and Wales (Department of Employment & Welsh Office).
SPPG4, Department of the Environment, Kingsgate House, Victoria Street, London SW1E 6SJ.
1946– quarterly. (No.73. April 1985. £8) each issue individually priced. *En.
Data on housing programme, slum clearance, renovations, completions, improvement grants, sales by local authorities, etc.

Δ E - iii, continued

1342 Welsh housing statistics.
Welsh Office, E & SS Division, Crown Building, Cathays Park, Cardiff CF1 3NQ.
1980- 1984. £3. 75p. ISSN 0262-8333. *En; title page & introduction also in Welsh.
TF: has data for 1983 and earlier years in some tables.
Dwelling stock; new house building; rehabilitation of dwellings; sales and lettings of local authority dwellings; housing corporations; private sector housing; homelessness; finance; rent, rates and rating survey, 1981. Appendix 1: Welsh house condition.

1343 Scottish housing statistics (Scottish Development Department).
HMSO, Edinburgh.
1978- 1983-84. £8. 46p. *En.
TF: the 1983-84 edition, published in 1985, has data to 1984, with long runs of figures in some tables.
Housebuilding, public sector house sales, improvements, finance, rents, capital payments and allocations for housing, special needs housing, homelessness.
Note: early issues were published quarterly and the current edition includes annual information previously included in the quarterly. 'Statistical bulletins, Scotland', available from the Scottish Office Library, New St Andrew's House, Edinburgh EH1 3TD) has data on housing trends and a variety of housing topics.

1344 Northern Ireland housing statistics (Housing Division, Department of the Environment for Northern Ireland).
HMSO, Belfast.
1946- 1984 (published 1985). £3.90. 27p. *En.
Contains similar data to (1343) above, but for Northern Ireland.

1345 Housing revenue account statistics...actuals.
Chartered Institute of Public Finance and Accountancy, 3 Robert Street, London WC2N 6BH.
1949/50- 1983/84 (published 1985). £14. 31p. ISSN 0260-4078. *En.
Final figures and details of rents, rent arrears, sales of council houses, etc.
Note: also 'Housing revenue account statistics...estimates' (1984/85. £14); 'Housing rents statistics at April of each year' (1983-84. £14); and 'Housing management and maintenance statistics...actuals' (1983-84. £14).

Δ F Social and political

1346 Social trends (Central Statistical Office).
HMSO, London.
1970- No.15, 1985. £19.95. 208p. ISSN 0306-7742. *En.
TF: the 1985 edition, published January 1985, has data for several years to 1983.
Contents of each annual issue vary. The 1985 issue includes tables drawn from a variety of sources on population trends; households and families; education; employment; income and wealth; resources and expenditure; health and personal social services; housing; transport, communications and the environment; participation (voluntary and charitable activities, trade unions, political participation and administration); and law enforcement.

1347 Welsh social trends (Welsh Office, in collaboration with statistical divisions of other government departments).
Welsh Office, E & SS Division, Crown Building, Cathays Park, Cardiff CF1 3NQ.
1974- No.6, 1985. £4.75. 87p. ISSN 0140-9018. *En; title page & introduction also in Welsh.
TF: issued biennially. The 1985 edition, published in 1985, has data for 983 and earlier years in some tables.
Population, vital statistics, social characteristics, economic characteristics, social security, health and personal social service, housing, justice and crime, and finance.

1348 Statistical bulletin (Scottish Education Department: Social Work Services Group).
Scottish Office Library, New St Andrew's House, Edinburgh EH1 3TD.
(irregular) £0.50 each; £5 yr per topic. ISSN 0144-5081. *En.
Sub-series: Residential accommodation; Further education; School leavers; Schools, pupils and teachers; Universities and student awards; Children in care; Children's hearing; Homecare services; Staff of social work departments; Community service; Housing trends; Housing (various topics).

Δ F - i Standard of living

< see also 391, 1339

1349 Household food consumption and expenditure: National food survey (Ministry of Agriculture, Fisheries and Food: National Food Survey Committee).
HMSO, London.
1950- 1983 (published January 1985). £16.95. 216p. *En.
Data relating to all households in the National Food Survey sample, including average consumption, expenditure and prices; regional and type of area averages of consumption, expenditure and related food price levels; income group averages of consumption, expenditure and related food price levels; household consumption group average for consumption, expenditure and related food price levels; age of housewife group averages; housing tenure; and freezer-owning and other household group averages.
Note: unpublished data and analyses may also be purchased.

Δ F - i, continued

1350 General household survey (Office of Population Censuses and Surveys: Social Survey Division).
HMSO, London.
1971- 1983 (published 1985). £13.70. 303p. *En.
A continuing household survey, with chapters on population (households, families, ethnic groups); marriage and fertility; contraception, sterilisation and infertility; housing; employment; education; health; and leisure.
Note: sub-titled 'an inter-departmental survey sponsored by the Central Statistical Office'.

1351 Family expenditure survey (Department of Employment).
HMSO, London.
1957/59- 1983 (published January 1985). £14.25. 117p. *En.
Shows in great detail income and expenditure by type of household for the UK as a whole and for regions.
Note: preliminary results of the survey are published in the 'Employment gazette' (1332).

1352 Northern Ireland family expenditure survey: report (Ministry of Finance, Northern Ireland).
HMSO, Belfast.
1967- 1978 (published 1980). £4. 60p. *En.
Data on household expenditure (by composition of groups of households, by occupation of head of household, by occupation of head of household and income of household); expenditure on commodity or service as % of total weekly household expenditure; household income; characteristics of households; characteristics of persons in households; distribution of households with certain durable goods.

1353 Isle of Man family expenditure survey.
Isle of Man Treasury, Government Offices, Buck's Road, Douglas, Isle of Man.
1976/77- 3rd, 1981/82. £0.60. 30p. *En.
TF: the 1981/82 edition has data for 1981/82, and for 1976/77 for comparison in some tables.
Sections on family expenditure survey, distribution of households, and retail price index, 1976-83.

1354 IDS report.
Income Data Services Ltd., 193 St John Street, London EC1V 4LS.
1966- 2 a month. price varies according to type of subscriber. *En.
Each issue has a feature on a particular subject and regular retail price and average earnings indexes.

1355 Survey of personal incomes (Board of Inland Revenue).
HMSO, London.
1937/38- 1982-83. £4.95. c 100p. *En.
TF: the 1982-83 edition, published in 1985, has data for the fiscal years 1981/82 and 1983.
Analysis of taxable incomes and income tax range, source, sex and marital status.

1356 Reward: salary and living costs report.
Reward Regional Surveys, 1 Mill Street, Stone, Staffs ST15 8BA.
1975- 2 a year. £48 or £80 yr. *En.
Salaries and trends for professional and executive staff, based on information provided by over 600 companies in the UK representing a wide range of industry and company size.

1357 CSU statistical package.
Central Services Unit, Crawford House, Precinct Centre, Manchester M13 9EP.
(annual) £85 yr. *En.
Includes 'CSU statistical quarterly' with data on graduate employment market and salary survey reflecting current rates for new and recent graduates; 'Grey' books, one for universities and one for polytechnics, describing in summary form what recent graduates did after graduating and in what numbers; 'Statistical supplements to the 'Grey' books; etc.

Δ F - ii Health and welfare

1358 Compendium of health statistics.
Office of Health Economics, 12 Whitehall, London SW1A 2DY.
1975- 5th, 1984. £15. various pagings. *En.
TF: has data for several years.
Data on the National Health Service, NHS staff, hospital services, family practitioners, mortality and morbidity.

1359 Health and personal social services statistics for England (with summary tables for Great Britain) (Department of Health and Social Security).
HMSO, London.
1969- 1985. £7.75. 157p. *En.
TF: issued at irregular intervals. The 1985 edition has data for 1983 and some earlier comparative years.
Includes data on finance; manpower; NHS hospital administration; family practitioner committee services; community health services; homes, hostels and sheltered housing; maternity care; preventive medicine; abortions and morbidity.

1360 Health and personal social services statistics for Wales.
Welsh Office, E & SS Division, Crown Building, Cathays Park, Cardiff CF1 3NQ.
1969- 1984. £3. 124p. ISSN 0307-0840. *En; title page & introduction also in Welsh.
TF: the 1984 edition, published in December 1984, has data for 1982 or 1982/83 and some earlier years in some tables.
Population and vital statistics, finance, manpower, NHS hospital administration, family practitioner committee services, community health services, personal social services, mental illness and mental handicap, preventive medicine, morbidity, abortions, and miscellaneous health statistics.
Note: also issued by the Welsh Office are 'Welsh hospital waiting list bulletin' (1984- 2 a year. £2 each. ISSN 0266-0776); 'Mental health statistics for Wales' (1981- 1984. £3. 106p. ISSN 0260-5252); and 'Staff of social services departments' (annual. 1983. £2. 40p. ISSN 0262-5172).

1361 Scottish health statistics (Common Services Agency for the Scottish Health Service).
HMSO, Edinburgh.
1958- 1983. £15.50. 140p. *En.
TF: the 1983 edition, published mid-1985, has data for 1983 and earlier years in some tables.
Population and vital statistics; mortality for selected causes; morbidity; hospital diagnostic statistics; family planning, abortion and maternity; hospital and associated services non-diagnostic statistics; general medical and dental and ophthalmic and pharmaceutical services; community health; manpower; and cost of health services.

1362 Annual report (Northern Ireland Department of Health and Social Services).
Central Services Agency, 27 Adelaide Street, Belfast BT2 8FH.
1973- 1983 (published late 1984). not priced. 76p. *En.
Data on all services - general practitioner, general medical, general dental, pharmaceutical, general ophthalmic, hospital appointments, catering, domestic, laundry, and finance.
Note: the Department also issues 'Analyses of running costs, related income and statistics of hospitals, other residential facilities and ambulance services administered by Health and Social Service Boards (1978/79- 1984/85 published early 1986. 94p).

1363 Health and safety statistics (Health and Safety Executive).
HMSO, London.
1975- 1981/82 (published 1985). £7.50. 74p. ISSN 0140-5934. *En.
TF: has data for earlier years in some tables.
Statistics on industrial accidents and occupational diseases in specific industries, including railways, mines, quarries and agriculture. Figures for compensation and some international comparisons of fatal accident rates.

1364 Hospital in-patient enquiry, main tables (Department of Health and Social Security, Office of Population Censuses and Surveys, and Welsh Office).
HMSO, London.
1969- 1981. £9 (on microfiche only). 32p. *En.
TF: the results of the 1981 enquiry were issued in 1984.
Based on a one in ten sample of NHS patients in hospitals in England and Wales.
Note: Summary tables are also available, in printed form (price on application to HMSO).

1365 Key statistical indicators for National Health Service management in Wales (Welsh Office/NHS Working Party).
Welsh Office, Crown Building, Cathays Park, Cardiff CF1 3NQ.
1982- 1983. £2. 37p. ISSN 0264-6714. *En; title page & introduction also in Welsh.
TF: the 1983 edition, published in 1984, has data for 1982/83 and earlier years.
Data on hospital costs; community health service costs; catering costs; estate management service; staff; bed utilisation - general surgery and urology; hospital waiting lists; ambulance services; community nursing, health visiting & midwifery staff; mental illness services; and mental handicap services.

1366 Teaching hospital statistics...actuals.
Chartered Institute of Public Finance and Accountancy, 3 Robert Street, London WC2N 6BH.
(annual) 1983-84. £8. *En.
A detailed breakdown of the operating costs of teaching hospitals in England and Wales showing 'in-patient' and 'out-patient' unit costs under various medical, care and general headings.
Note: also 'Non-teaching hospital statistics' (1983-84. £8), a sample survey publication summarising, in standardised form, the revenue consequences of capital schemes.

1367 Birth counts: statistics of pregnancy and childbirth (Alison Macfarlane & Miranda Mugford of the National Perinatal Epidemiology Unit, in collaboration with OPCS).
HMSO, London.
Text £9.95; tables £19.95. 2 vols. *En.
TF: published in 1984, data is for various years with long runs of figures in some tables.
The volume of tables has 310 pages of statistical data on pregnancy, childbirth and new born babies, the health services provided for them and the social, economic and environmental factors which can affect the outcome of pregnancy.

1368 Abortion statistics...England and Wales (Office of Population Censuses and Surveys).
HMSO, London.
1977- 1982 (published 1984). £6.20. 58p. *En.
A comprehensive collection of statistics relating to legally induced abortions, taking accounts of such factors as the age and marital status of the women, areas in which they live, complications, deaths, medical grounds and medical or surgical methods used.

Δ F – ii, continued

1369 Communicable disease statistics (Office of Population Censuses and Surveys).
HMSO, London.
(annual) 1982 (published 1983). £6.80. 65p. *En.
Statistics on notifiable and infectious diseases recorded in England and Wales, including notifications and death rates for specific diseases such as tuberculosis, tetanus, and meningitis, defined by sex, age group and area.

1370 Personal social services statistics...actuals.
Chartered Institute of Public Finance and Accountancy, 3 Robert Street, London WC2N 6BH.
1949/50- 1984-85 (published March 1986). £15. 71p. ISSN 0309-653X. *En.
A detailed analysis of residential, day and community care provision, showing gross and net expenditure and the number of clients. Also expenditure on field work, administration and joint financing, etc.
Note: also 'Personal social services statistics...estimates' (1985-86 published August 1985. £15. 51p. ISSN 0144-610X).

1371 Homelessness statistics...actuals.
Chartered Institute of Public Finance and Accountancy, 3 Robert Street, London WC2N 6BH.
(annual) 1984-85 (published October 1985). £11. 27p. ISSN 0144-4514. *En.
A financial survey of the operation of the Housing (Homeless Persons) Act 1977.

1372 Homelessness statistics, England and Wales.
Department of the Environment, SPPG4, Rm 2140, 43 Marsham Street, London SW1P 3PY.
(6-monthly) free. *En.

1373 Residential accommodation for the elderly, younger physically handicapped and blind.
Welsh Office, Crown Building, Cathays Park, Cardiff CF1 3NQ.
(annual) 1983/84. £2. 54p. ISSN 0262-8031. *En; title page & introduction also in Welsh.
TF: the 1983/84 edition, published in December 1984, has data for the year ended 31.3.84.
National summary tables, followed by local authority tables subdivided by county. Data includes numbers of homes; places; residents; sex, type and age of residents.

1374 Social security statistics (Department of Health and Social Security).
HMSO, London.
1972- 1984. £17.25. 286p. *En.
TF: the 1984 edition, published in 1984, has data for 1982 or 1983 and some earlier years.
Unemployment benefit, sickness benefit, invalidity benefit, non-contributory invalidity pensions, attendance allowances, maternity benefits, death grant guardian's allowances and child's special allowances, widow's benefit, retirement pension, injury benefit, family income supplement, war pensions, contributions, finance, etc. for Great Britain.

1375 Northern Ireland social security statistics (Department of Health and Social Services for Northern Ireland).
HMSO, Belfast.
(annual) 1984. £8.50. 211p. *En.
TF: the 1984 edition, published mid-1984, has data for 1979 to 1983.
Data on various allowances and benefits, invalidity pension, workmen's compensation scheme.

1376 Charity statistics.
Charities Aid Foundation, 48 Pembury Road, Tonbridge, Kent TN9 2JD.
1977/78- 8th, 1984/85. £11. 131p. *En.
Data on the top 200 charities, grant-making trusts & corporate donors (donations, profits, employees, etc.

Δ F – iii Education and leisure

1377 Education statistics for the United Kingdom (Department of Education and Science, in collaboration with the Scottish Education Department, the Northern Ireland Department of Education, and the University Grants Committee, in consultation with the Welsh Office).
HMSO, London.
1967- 1984 (published January 1985). £7.95. 61p. *En.
TF: has data for 1965/66, 1970/71, 1975/76, 1980/82 to 1982/83 academic years.
A detailed overview of the educational system of the United Kingdom, bringing together the main statistics to give a general picture. Includes data on population, schools, further and higher education, finance, teaching staff, qualifications and destinations of students.

1378 Statistics of education.
Department of Education and Science, Room 337, Mowden Hall, Staindrop Road, Darlington DL3 9DG.
(annual) 5 sets. £12 per set (individual tables £0.25, minimum charge £1.50 for 6 pages or less). *En.
The five sets of statistical tables refer to schools; school-leavers and examinations; further education; teachers in service; finance and awards.
Note: from 1961 to 1977 'Statistics of education' was issued in 6 volumes annually (£10-£12 each volume) on schools; school-leavers, CSE & GCE (England); further education (England); teachers in service (England and Wales); finance and awards (England and Wales); universities: United Kingdom.

Δ F - iii, continued

1379 Digest of statistics: England.
Statistics Branch, Dept of Education and Science, Room 337, Mowden Hall, Staindrop Road, Darlington DL3 9DG.
(annual) 1983. £2. unpaged; 30 tables. ISSN 0265-6531. *En.
TF: has data for 1970/71, 1973/76, 1979/80 to 1981/82.
Data on finance & awards, schools, school leavers, 16-19 year olds, further education, higher education, overseas students, and teachers.

1380 Statistics of education in Wales.
Welsh Office, Crown Buildings, Cathays Park, Cardiff CF1 3NQ.
1976- No.8, 1983. £3. 168p. ISSN 0262-8317. *En; title page & introduction also in Welsh.
TF: the 1983 edition, published in 1984, has data for 1982/83 or 1981/82 and some earlier years in some tables.
General statistics, provision for the under 5s, primary education, secondary education, Welsh, school leavers, special education, school services, higher and further education provided by the non-university sector, teachers, teacher training, higher education provided by the universities, adult education, finance, and unit costs.

1381 Education in Northern Ireland (Department of Education, Northern Ireland).
HMSO, Belfast.
(annual) 1983. £3.60. 38p. *En.
TF: the 1983 edition, published in 1984, has data for 1982/83 academic year and earlier years in some tables.
Includes a section of statistical tables on School pupils and teachers; further education - vocational courses, teacher training - number of full-time students; and higher education - number of full-time students.
Note: to be published every three years in future. 'Basic education statistics (Northern Ireland)' (free) is an annual information card available from the Department of Education, Northern Ireland.

1382 University statistics (University Grants Committee).
Universities' Statistical Record, Central Record Office, PO Box 40, Cheltenham GL50 1JY.
1980- 1983/84 (published 1984 and 1985). 3 vols. *En.
Contents:
Vol 1: Students and staff (£8.25).
Vol 2: Graduates' first destination (c £10).
Vol 3: Finance (c £8).

1383 Statistical bulletin.
Department of Education and Science, Elizabeth House, York Road, London SE1 7PH.
(irregular) not priced. ISSN 0142-5013. *En.
Each issue is on a separate educational subject, eg., education statistics, student awards, enrolments, schools, etc. Data is for the United Kingdom.

1384 Statistical bulletin.
Department of Education for Northern Ireland, Rathgael House, Balloo Road, Bangor, Co Down BT19 2PR.
(irregular) free. *En.
Each issue is on a separate subject: First destination of primary degree graduates (annual); School leavers (biennial); Enrolments on non-advanced courses of further education (annual); Qualifications of Northern Ireland school leavers; Pupils and teachers in grant-aided schools (annual); School population projections; Adult and continuing education and non-vocational further education.

1385 Statistics of overseas students in the UK.
British Council, 65 Davies Street, London W1Y 2AA.
(annual) 1982/83 (published 1984). £6.75. 26p. *En.
A reference guide to the numbers, countries of origin, subject groups of study, and location of overseas students in Britain.

1386 Graduates and jobs (Department of Education and Science).
HMSO, London.
£2.20. (published 1984). 40p. *En.
Data based on surveys by careers services at higher education establishments into jobs obtained by 1982 graduates in the six months after graduation. Information given separately for men and women, and for universities and polytechnics. Further tables examine the academic qualifications of recent entrants to degree courses.

1387 First destinations of polytechnic students qualifying in 1983 (AGCAS Polytechnic Statistics Working Group).
Committee of Directors of Polytechnics, 309 Regent Street, London W1R 7PE.
not priced. (published 1984). 249p. *En.
A statistical report on those obtaining first degrees and higher diplomas by full-time and sandwich course study.

1388 Statistical supplement [to the annual report].
Universities' Central Council on Admissions, PO Box 28, Cheltenham, Glos GL50 1HY.
61/63- 1982-83. £3. 28p. *En.
TF: the 1982-83 edition, published in 1984, has data for 1982/83 and 1983.

Δ F - iii, continued

1389 Digest of sports statistics.
Sports Council, 16 Upper Woburn Place, London WC1H OGP.
£6. 112p. *En.
TF: published in 1983. Data for several years to 1980.
Information, including statistical tables, on all sports.
Note: Information series no.7.

1390 Digest of countryside recreation statistics.
Countryside Commission, John Dower House, Crescent Place, Cheltenham, Glos GL50 3RA.
1969- 1979. out of print. unpaged. *En.
TF: the 1979 edition, published in 1980, has data for several years to 1978.
Social, economic and demographic information, and data on outdoor recreation activities, holidaymaking, land resources, water resources, financial resources, and national parks.

1391 National countryside recreation survey, 1984.
Countryside Commission, 19/23 Albert Road, Manchester M19 2EQ.
£4.25. *En.
TF: published in 1985.
A summary of the main findings of a comprehensive review of people's recreation behaviour.

1392 Leisure and recreation statistics...estimates.
Chartered Institute of Public Finance and Accountancy, 3 Robert Street, London WC2N 6BH.
1976/77- 1984/85 (published 1984). £14. 107p. ISSN 0260-7603. *En.
Analyses of estimated expenditure and income on sport and recreation (indoor and outdoor), cultural and other facilities (country parks, allotments, etc). Also numbers of facilities and staff employed.
Note: other publications include 'Leisure and recreation statistics... actuals', 'Leisure changes', and 'Leisure usage...actuals'.

1393 Facts about the arts: a summary of available statistics (Muriel Nissel, ed).
Policy Studies Institute, 100 Park Village East, London NW1 3SR.
£12.50. 191p. *En.
TF: published in 1983 as PSI No.615, and giving the latest data available with short runs for comparisons in some tables.
Sections on finance, the artist, artistic activities (theatre, music, visual arts, community arts, literature, film, broadcasting), audience profile, buildings.

1394 Public library statistics...actuals.
Chartered Institute of Public Finance and Accountancy, 3 Robert Street, London WC2N 6BH.
1961/62- 1984-85 (published early 1986). £15. 47p. ISSN 0309-6629. *En.
Final outturn figures for expenditure and income, manpower, agency services, books and other stocks, and service points. Summary tables included for annual issues and inter-library loans. Covers Great Britain and Northern Ireland'.
Note: also 'Public library statistics...estimates' (1985/86 (published mid-1985). £11. 11p. ISSN 0309-6629).

Δ F - iv Justice

1395 Judicial statistics, England and Wales (Lord Chancellor's Department).
HMSO, London.
1927- 1984. £9.10. 118p. *En.
TF: the 1984 edition, published mid-1985, has data for 1984 compared with 1983 and earlier years in some tables.
Includes statistics relating to the Judicial Committee of the Privy Council, the House of Lords, the Court of Appeal, the High Court, the Crown Court, the Offices of the Supreme Court, county courts, other civil courts and tribunals, the Judiciary and Taxation of costs and legal aid.
Note: issued as a Command paper.

1396 Civil judicial statistics, Scotland (Scottish Courts Administration).
HMSO, Edinburgh.
1935- 1983 (published late 1985). £6.35. 50p. *En.
Statistics relating to the civil business of civil courts, and legal and public departments.
Note: previously titled 'Judicial statistics, Scotland'.

1397 Criminal statistics, England and Wales (Home Office).
HMSO, London.
1893- 1983 (published late 1984). £12.30. 210p. *En.
Offences recorded by the police (including separate figures on those in which firearms were reported to have been involved), homicide, cautioning by the police, court proceedings and sentencing, use of remand, previous convictions, legal aid, mentally disordered offenders, appeals, the prerogative of mercy, proceedings brought by the Director of Public Prosecutions.
Note: four volumes of supplementary tables (1983 editions published in 1984, price £6-£11 each) are available from the Publications Officer, Home Office Library, Room 1001, 50 Queen Anne's Gate, London SW1H 9AT. Vol 1: Proceedings in magistrates' courts; v 2: Proceedings in the Crown Court; v 3: Tables by police force areas and some court areas; v 4: Convictions, cautions, DPP prosecutions, mentally disordered offenders, appeals, prerogative of mercy, legal aid.

Δ F - iv, continued

1398 Criminal statistics (Scotland) (Scottish Home and Health Department).
Scottish Office Library, Room 2/65, New St Andrew's House, Regent Road, Edinburgh EH1 3TD.
1925- 1980-1982. £6.60. 62p. *En.
TF: the 1980-82 edition, with data for those years, was published late 1984.
Contains similar information to 1397 above but for Scotland.

1399 Administration of justice statistics...estimates.
Chartered Institute of Public Finance and Accountancy, 3 Robert Street, London WC2N 6BH.
(annual) 1985/86. £11. 12p. *En.
TF: the 1985/86 estimates were published mid-1985.
Estimated expenditure and income figures for both magistrates' and coroners' courts per thousand population. Also numbers of defendents proceeded against and details reported to coroner.

1400 Prison statistics, England and Wales (Home Office).
HMSO, London.
1962- 1983 (published late 1984). £10.85. 170p. *En.
The prison population, remand prisoners, sentenced young offenders, adult male and female prisoners under sentence, non-criminal prisoners, fine defaulters, reconvictions, offences and punishments, and miscellaneous tables (health and medical services, means of restraint, etc).
Note: previously included in 'Report on the work of the Prison Department: statisticsl tables', which still includes some statistical data.

1401 Prisons in Scotland: report... (Scottish Home and Health Department).
HMSO, Edinburgh.
1927- 1984 (published 1985). £2.75. 151p. *En.
Includes statistical data on prisons in Scotland.

1402 Probation statistics, England and Wales.
Home Office Statistical Department, Room 844/5, 50 Queen Anne's Gate, London SW1H 9AT.
1973- 1984 (published 1985). £4. 118p. ISSN 0265-573X. *En.
Tables and commentary on the world of the Probation Service, including probation, supervision under the Children and young persons act, 1969, suspended sentence supervision, money payment supervision, community service, after-care, domestic supervision, reports and conciliation work, manpower, average caseloads and numbers of reports completed, and expenditure and costs.

1403 Probation statistics...actuals.
Chartered Institute of Public Finance and Accountancy, 3 Robert Street, London WC2N 6BH.
(annual) 1984-85 (published late 1985). £11. 13p. ISSN 0140-8291. *En.
Final outturn figures for expenditure and income per 1000 population aged 15-29, and manpower for the probation service in England and Wales.
Note: also 'Probation statistics...estimates' (1985-86. £11. 15p. ISSN 0264-6544).

1404 Police statistics...actuals.
Chartered Institute of Public Finance and Accountancy, 3 Robert Street, London WC2N 6BH.
(annual) 1984/85 (published late 1985). £11. 25p. ISSN 0144-9915. *En.
Final outturn figures for expenditure and income, and manpower for all police forces and regional crime squads.
Note: also 'Police statistics...estimates' (1985/86 (published mid-1985). £15. 51p. ISSN 0144-9885).

1405 Offences of drunkenness, England and Wales.
Home Office Statistical Department, Room 1813, Tolworth Tower, Surbiton, Surrey KT6 7DS.
(annual) 1983 (published mid-1984). £2.50. 16p. *En.
Offences, persons proceeded against, findings of guilt, sentences and treatment centres.
Note: issued as a 'Home Office statistical bulletin'.

1406 Offences relating to motor vehicles, England and Wales.
Home Office Statistical Department, Room 1813, Tolworth Tower, Surbiton, Surrey KT6 7DS.
1928- 1983 (published late 1984). £2.50. 20p. *En.
A commentary on trends over the last ten years and detailed tables for the current year, including data on written warnings, fixed penalty notices, court proceedings and sentences, licence disqualifications and endorsements. Supplementary tables are also available (£5).
Note: issued as a 'Home Office statistical bulletin'.

1407 Statistics of breath tests.
Home Office Statistical Department, Room 1813, Tolworth Tower, Surbiton, Surrey KT6 7DS.
(annual) 1983 (published mid-1984). £2.50. 20p. *En.
A commentary on trends in breath tests and blood or urine tests on drivers suspected or having consumed alcohol.
Note: issued as a 'Home Office statistical bulletin'.

1408 Statistics on the prevention of terrorism.
Home Office Statistical Department, Room 1813, Tolworth Tower, Surbiton, Surrey KT6 7DS.
1979- quarterly. £2.50 each quarter. *En.
TF: each issue contains data referring to the previous quarter.
Quarterly data on detentions, charges, exclusion orders and deportations made under the Prevention of Terrorism Acts.
Note: issued as a 'Home Office statistical bulletin'.

Δ F – iv, continued

1409 Liquor licensing statistics, England and Wales...
Home Office Statistical Department, Room 1813, Tolworth Tower, Surbiton, Surrey KT6 7DS.
(triennial) 1982/83 (published late 1983). £1. 9p. *En.
Using the total number of licences in force the tables show the types of premises licensed to sell liquor, the numbers of licences applied for and granted and reasons for removal from the register. Supplementary tables are also available (£25) which show the total number of licences by type and Petty Sessional Division.
Note: issued as a 'Home Office statistical bulletin'.

1410 Betting licensing statistics, Great Britain...
Home Office Statistical Department, Room 1813, Tolworth Tower, Surbiton, Surrey KT6 7DS.
1974- 1983/84 (published late 1984). £1.50. 9p. *En.
Using the total number of licences in force the tables show the total applications for grants, renewals and cessations, the results of any proceedings and the number of licences in force in Licensing Areas for Bookmakers' Permits, Betting Office Licences and Betting Agency Permits. Supplementary tables are also available showing all the above details, excluding the results of proceedings, by petty sessional divisions, for England, Scotland and Wales.
Note: issued as a 'Home Office statistical bulletin'.

1411 Notifiable offences recorded by the police.
Home Office Statistical Department, Room 1813, Tolworth Tower, Surbiton, Surrey KT6 7DS.
1975- quarterly. £1.50 each issue. *En.
TF: each issue contains data referring to the previous quarter.
Quarterly data on notifiable offences recorded by the police by offence group; and annual data on offences cleared up.
Note: issued as a 'Home Office statistical bulletin'.

1412 Statistics of the misuse of drugs in the United Kingdom.
Home Office Statistical Department, Room 1813, Tolworth Tower, Surbiton, Surrey KT6 7DS.
1974- 1983. £2.50. 27p. *En.
TF: the 1983 edition, published mid-1984, has data from 1973 to 1983.
Seizures of drugs, offenders and addicts.
Note: issued as a 'Home Office statistical bulletin'. Also available are supplementary tables. £6).

1413 Statistics of experiments on living animals: Great Britain (Home Office).
HMSO, London.
1956- 1984 (published mid-1985). £4.70. 30p. *En.
The major characteristics (numbers, type, hazards, safety, relation of pain to experiment); licensees and registered places; historical data; and general system of control.
Note: published as a Command paper.

1414 Bankruptcy: general annual report... (Department of Trade).
HMSO, London.
1883- 1984 (published 1985). £3.50. 22p. *En.
Includes a section of statistical tables on the amount of insolvencies; numbers of receiving orders; failures, liabilities and assets; numbers of proceedings, etc.

Δ F – v Religion

1415 Church statistics.
Central Board of Finance of the Church of England, Church House, Dean's Yard, London SW1P 3NZ.
1885- 1985. £1.25. *En.
Membership and financial figures for 1983, and clergy and other statistics as at end of 1984.
Note: now a separate publication, was previously included as a statistical supplement to the 'Church of England year book'.

Δ F – vi Elections

1416 Electoral statistics: parliamentary and local government electors in constituencies and local government areas of England and Wales, Scotland and Northern Ireland (Office of Population Censuses and Surveys).
HMSO, London.
1974- 1985 (published 1986). £4.10. 27p. *En.
The number of electors on the register.
Note: there is also an OPCS Monitor 'Electoral statistics – parliamentary' available free from OPCS, St Catherine's House, 10 Kingsway, London WC2B 6JP.

1417 Election expenses (Home Office).
HMSO, London.
1945- 1983. £9.55. 111p. *En.
TF: the 1983 edition, published in December 1983, has details of expenses for the June 1983 election.
Election expenses for each candidate, by constituency, postal voting and spoilt ballot paper, by constituency for England, Wales, Scotland and Northern Ireland. Tables also give details of electorate, votes polled and the legal maximums for each candidate/constituency.

Δ F – vi, continued

1418 European Assembly election expenses, United Kingdom...
Home Office Statistical Department, Room 1813, Tolworth Tower, Surbiton, Surrey KT6 7DS.
1979– 1984. £2.50. 24p. *En.
TF: the 1984 edition, published in November 1984, has data for the June 1984 election.
European Assembly election expenses for each candidate, postal voting and spoiled ballot papers, all by constituency, for England, Wales, Scotland and Northern Ireland. Tables also give details of electorate, votes polled and the legal maximums for each candidate/constituency.
Note: issued as a 'Home Office statistical bulletin'.

1419 British parliamentary election results (F.W.S. Craig).
Parliamentary Research Services, 18 Lincoln Green, Chichester, West Sussex PO19 4DN (early editions were published by Macmillan Press).
Contents:
Vol 1: 1832–1885 (2nd ed., 1986. £25)
Vol 2: 1885–1918 (2nd ed., 1986. £25)
Vol 3: 1918–1949 (3rd ed., £25)
Vol 4: 1950–1973 (2nd ed., 1983. £25)
Vol 5: 1974–1983 (1st ed., 1984. £15).

1420 Britain votes...the General Election...and by-elections... (F.W.S. Craig).
Parliamentary Research Service, 18 Lincoln Green, Chichester, West Sussex PO19 4DN.
1974/77– 1983. £8.50. 256p. *En.
TF: the issue covering the General Election of 1983 and by-elections to December 1983 was published in 1984.
Supplements 'British parliamentary election results'.
Note: a loose-leaf updating service is available from the publisher (£15).

1421 British electoral facts, 1832–1980 (F.W.S. Craig).
Parliamentary Research Service, 18 Lincoln Green, Chichester, West Sussex PO19 4DN.
4th ed, 1981. £8.50. 224p. *En.
Facts and statistics on all of the 38 General Elections and some by-elections that have taken place in the UK since the Reform Act of 1832. Also records local government elections from 1945, the European elections of 1979, and the referendums of the 1970s.

1422 British parliamentary constituencies: a statistical compendium (Ivor Crewe & Anthony Fox).
Faber & Faber Ltd., 3 Queen Square, London WC1N 3AU.
£25. 397p. *En.
TF: published in 1984 with 1979 and 1983 election figures.
Has a standard entry for each of the 650 parliamentary constituencies, including size, election results, electoral statistics (turnout, % and ranking of each party) and standard social and demographic characteristics.

1423 British political facts... (David Butler and Anne Sloman).
Macmillan, 4 Little Essex Street, London WC2.
1963– 8th, 1900–1979 (published 1980). £15. 492p. *En.
Includes a chapter on 'Elections: general election statistics', which has election results from 1900 to 1979.

Δ G Finance

1424 Financial statistics (Central Statistical Office).
HMSO, London.
1962– monthly. £8.25 or £100 yr. ISSN 0015-203X. *En.
TF: each issue has data for several years, quarters and months up to the date of the issue and is published some four to six weeks later.
Aims to bring together the key financial and monetary statistics of the United Kingdom, including financial accounts, general government and public sector finance, central government, local authorities, public corporations, monetary sector, other financial institutions, companies, personal sector, overseas sector, money, credit and liquidity, capital issues and stock exchange transactions, exchange rates, interest rates and security prices, and sectoral balance sheets.
Note: 'Financial statistics: explanatory handbook' (1986 ed. (was published early 1986) £6.95).

1425 Bank of England quarterly bulletin.
Economics Division, Bank of England, London EC2R 8AH.
1960– £7.50 or £27 yr (£9–13 or £33–44 yr abroad, depending on area). ISSN 0005-5166. *En.
TF: each issue contains data for several years up to the latest available.
Sections on recent economioc and financial developments, articles and speeches, short notes, banking, and a statistical annex with data on central government, banking, capital markets, external finance, etc.

1426 Quarterly economic review.
Trade Indemnity plc, 12 Great Eastern Street, London EC2A 3AX.
(quarterly) not priced. *En.
Text, plus some tables and charts, on the UK economy, industrial performance, bad debts and business failures.
Note: Updated in part by a monthly 2-page 'News release'.

Δ G – i Banking

1427 Clearing statistics.
Committee of London Clearing Bankers, 10 Lombard Street, London EC3V 9AP.
(monthly) free. *En.
TF: each issue has data for the month of issue, corresponding figures for the previous year, and cumulations for the years to date, and % changes.
Note: the Committee also issues 'Balances of the London clearing banks' (monthly), 'Analyses of advances to UK residents by the London clearing banks' groups' (quarterly), and a one-page 'Annual summary of clearing statistics'.

1428 Abstract of banking statistics.
Statistical Unit, The Committee of London Clearing Bankers, 10 Lombard Street, London EC3V 9AP.
1984- 1984. free. 71p. *En.
TF: the 1984 edition, published in April 1984, has data for several years to 1983.
Brings together a wide range of annual statistics covering the London and Scottish clearing banks, paper and automated clearings and the use of credit cards.

Δ G – ii Public finance

1429 United Kingdom national accounts (Central Statistical Office).
HMSO, London.
1938/40- 1985. £12.95. 129p. *En.
TF: the 1985 edition, published in September 1985, has data for 1974 to 1984.
Detailed estimates of national product, income and expenditure, covering industry, the personal sector, public corporations, central and local government, capital formation and financial accounts.
Note: known as the 'Blue book'. Prior to the 1984 edition the title was 'National income and expenditure'.

1430 Isle of Man national income estimates.
Isle of Man Treasury, Government Offices, Buck's Road, Douglas, Isle of Man.
(annual) 1982/83. not priced. 14p. *En.
TF: the 1982/83 edition, published mid-1984, has data for 1971/72 to 1982/83.

1431 United Kingdom balance of payments (Central Statistical Office).
HMSO, London.
1946/57- 1985. £8.95. 78p. *En.
TF: the 1985 edition, published in September 1985, has data from 1974 to 1984.
Note: known as the 'Pink book'.

1432 Local government financial statistics, England and Wales (Department of the Environment and Welsh Office).
HMSO, London.
1934/35- 1982/83 (published 1984). £4.60. 42p. *En.
Data on local authority income and expenditure; rate fund services account; housing revenue account; trading services accounts; special fund; rate fund revenue account, net expenditure and income; expenditure in the context of public and national expenditure, etc.
Note: also 'Welsh local government financial statistics' (1978- No.8, 1984. £3. 116p. ISSN 0140-4482) issued by the Welsh Office, and published late 1984 with data for 1982/83.

1433 Scottish local government financial statistics.
Scottish Office, New St Andrew's House, Regent Road, Edinburgh EH1 3SX.
1961- 1979-80 (published 1983). £6.25. 33p. *En.
Similar in content to 1432 above, but for Scotland.

1434 Finance accounts of Northern Ireland for the financial year... (Department of Finance and Personnel for Northern Ireland).
HMSO, Belfast.
1932/33- 1983/84 (published late 1985). £4.30. 33p. *En.
Contains the main financial statistics for Northern Ireland, including consolidated fund accounts, public income, public expenditure, capital receipts and issue, etc.

1435 District councils summary of statements of accounts (Department of the Environment for Northern Ireland).
HMSO, Belfast.
1968/69- 1983/84 (published 1985). £1.85. 7p. *En.
Similar in content to 1432, but for Northern Ireland.

1436 Finance and general statistics.
Chartered Institute of Public Finance and Accountancy, 3 Robert Street, London WC2N 6BH.
(annual) 1985-86. £19. 100p. ISSN 0263-2276. *En.
TF: the 1985-86 edition, published mid-1985, has estimates for 1985-86.
Summary information on local authority budgets average rate payments and rate increases. Estimated net expenditure figures, analysed over services are shown for each local authority in England and Wales.
Note: there is also a 15-page supplementary report.

Δ G - ii, continued

1437 Finance and general statistics of county councils.
Society of County Treasurers, Shire hall, Shinfield Park, Reading RG2 9XB.
(annual) Actuals 1983/84. £4.50. *En.
TF: the 1983/84 issue was published in March 1985.
Data for all metropolitan and non-metropolitan English and Welsh counties. An analysis of the financing of expenditure by rates, government grants, etc., plus salient fiancial and non-financial statistics expressed per head of population for all services.

1438 Inland revenue statistics (Board of Inland Revenue).
HMSO, London.
1970- 1985. £10.50. 108p. *En.
TF: the 1985 edition, published in 1985, has the latest data available to 1982, 1982/83 or 1984/85.
Data on all taxes administered by the Inland Revenue, including income tax, corporation tax, petroleum revenue tax, capital transfer tax, capital gains tax, development land tax and stamp duties. Also tables on numbers of taxpayers, rateable values, agricultural land transactions, and estimates of distribution of personal wealth.
Note: the annual 'Report of the Commissioners of H.M. Inland Revenue' also includes statistics of all taxes administered by the Inland Revenue, in particular tax collected, tax recovered as a result of investigative activities, tax remitted or written off, and costs of collection.

1439 Taxation: the leading authority on the law, practice and administration of taxation.
Tolley Publishing Co Ltd., 17 Scarbrook Road, Croydon, Surrey CRO 1SQ.
1927- weekly. £0.70 each issue. ISSN 0040-0149. *En.
Includes a section on 'Some useful statistics', with all stocks index, retail price index, indexation allowance - indexed rise.

1440 British aid statistics (Overseas Development Administration).
HMSO, London.
1965- 1978-1982 (published 1983). £5. 80p. ISSN 0068-1210. *En.
Statistics of UK economic aid to developing countries, including summary of UK contribution to world flows, summary of the british programme, multilateral aid, project aid by economic sector, technical co-operation, and country programmes.

1441 British overseas aid (Overseas Development Administration).
HMSO, London.
(annual) 1984 (published 1985). £6.95. 65p. *En.
A commentary on the activities of the Overseas Development Administration during the year. Includes statistical tables in the text and a statistical appendix.

1442 Capital expenditure and debt financing statistics.
Chartered Institute of Public Finance and Accounting, 3 Robert Street, London WC2N 6BH.
1981/82- 1984/85 (published 1985). £19. 67p. ISSN 0263-2985. *En.
Note: earlier title was 'Return of outstanding debt'.

1443 Rate collections statistics...actuals.
Chartered Institute of Public Finance and Accountancy, 3 Robert Street, London WC2N 6BH.
(annual) 1984-85 (published early 1986). £19. 77p. ISSN 0210-5546. *En.

1444 Rating review, actual income and expenditure...summary volume (Chartered Institute of Public Finance and Accountancy, Scottish Branch).
Strathclyde Regional Council, Finance Department, Strathclyde House, 20 India Street, Glasgow G2 4PF.
(annual) 1984-85 (published December 1985). £4. 35p. *En.
Data relates to Scotland.

1445 Report of the Commissioners of H.M. Customs and Excise.
HMSO, London.
1909/10- 1983/84. £7.55. 100p. *En.
TF: the 1983/84 report, published in 1984, has data for the financial year 1983/84 and some earlier years in some tables.
Customs and excise duties collected, including those on hydrocarbon oil, power alcohol and petrol substitutes, spirits, beer, wine, matches, mechanical lighters; the number of distilleries, betting and gaming duties; value added tax; car tax; protective duties; etc. Indicates production, foreign trade of some of the commodities listed above.
Note: the Bill of Entry Service also issues some monthly bulletins, eg., 'Spirits bulletin', 'Wine bulletin', 'Betting and gaming bulletin', with information on duties paid.

1446 Input-output tables for the UK (Central Statistical Office).
HMSO, London.
1954- 1979 (published 1983). £9.95. 108p. *En.
Note: issued as 'Business monitor PA 1004'. Earlier issues were published in the series 'Studies in official statistics'.

Δ G – iii Company finance

1447 Companies in...annual report... (Department of Trade and Industry).
HMSO, London.
1891- 1984. £4.95. 28p. *En.
TF: the 1984 report, published in 1985, has data for 1983 and 1984 and earlier years in some tables.
Summary of changes in number of companies on register, new company registrations, new registrations analysed by classes and by share capital, public companies, liquidations, winding-ups, removals from register, investigations, prosecutions, etc.

1448 Companies general annual report (Department of Commerce, Northern Ireland).
HMSO, Belfast.
1932- 1983 (published 1984). £2. 13p. *En.
Data on number of companies registered, liquidations and dissolutions, numbers on register, classification of companies (public limited by shares, private limited by shares, etc), documents registered and files inspected.

1449 Company finance (Business Statistics Office).
HMSO, London.
1969- 15th, 1984. £8.95. 78p. *En.
TF: the 1984 edition, published in 1984, has data for 1980, 1981 and 1982 or the latest available.
Analyses of the accounts of listed and unlisted companies.
Note: issued as Business Monitor MA3 series.

1450 Stock Exchange quarterly.
The Stock Exchange, St Alphage House, Fore Street, London EC2.
1984- quarterly. for price see Note. ISSN 0267-1530. *En.
TF: data is given as at the date of the issue and is published about six weeks later.
Includes a section of 'Statistical highlights' with nominal and market values of listed securities and listed companies, turnover, price indices, etc; new issues, unlisted securities market, etc.
Note: incorporates the Stock Exchange fact book. Updated by the Stock Exchange fact sheet (monthly). Subscription of £40 yr (£50 abroad) comprises the Stock Exchange quarterly, the Stock Exchange fact sheet, and Stock Exchange companies (bi-annual shareholder analysis).

1451 Acquisitions & mergers of companies (Business Statistics Office).
HMSO, London.
(quarterly) £7.70 yr. *En.
Note: issued as Business Monitor MQ7.

1452 Extel UK listed companies service.
Extel Statistical Services Ltd., 37-45 Paul Street, London EC2A 4PB.
1922- prices on application. *En.
Details of some 3,100 companies quoted on the stock exchanges of the British Isles, including data on capital balance sheet, profit and loss account, dividends, share prices, etc. Annual cards are issued for each company and new cards when dividends are announced or other events justify the issue.

1453 Extel unquoted companies service.
Extel Statistical Services Ltd., 37-45 Paul Street, London EC2A 4PB.
Prices on application. *En.
Details on cards of some 2,100 British companies whose shares are not quoted on the stock exchanges, including data on capital, profit and loss account, turnover, exports, number employed and pay-roll, balance sheet, etc. New cards are issued as and when data becomes available.

1454 Extel unlisted securities market service.
Extel Statistical Services Ltd., 37-45 Paul Street, London EC2A 4PB.
Prices on application. *En.
Details of all companies traded on the Stock Exchange's Unlisted Securities Market, including data on capital, profit and loss accounts, dividends, share prices, etc. Annual cards are issued for each company, and new cards are issued as and when new data becomes available.
Note: Extel publishes twice-yearly an Unlisted Securities Market handbook containing abridged information on the U.S.M. companies.

1455 Extel over the counter service.
Extel Statistical Services Ltd, 37-45 Paul Street, London EC2A 4PB.
Prices on application. *En.
Details of all companies traded on the Over the Counter Markets, including data on capital, profit and loss accounts, dividends, market makers, etc. Annual cards are issued for each company and new cards when events justify the issue.

1456 Extel analyst's card service.
Extel Statistical Services Ltd., 37-45 Paul Street, London EC2A 4PB.
Prices on application. *En.
Complements (1452) above, covering some 1,300 major British companies and giving a 10-year record (analysed and adjusted) of capital changes, balance sheets, profit and loss accounts, share prices, dividends, etc. Updated weekly.
Note: Extel provides other card services and also various reference books.

Δ G - iii, continued

1457 Building society fact book.
Building Societies' Association, 3 Savile Row, London W1X 1AF.
1980- 1984. £2. 31p. ISSN 0266-4828. *En.
TF: the 1984 edition, published mid-1984, has data for 1983.
The annual report of the Association, covering the financial and economic environment, the structure of the industry, building societies and the savings market, building societies and the housing market, building societies' operations, etc. Statistical tables complement the descriptive text.

1458 A compendium of building society statistics.
Building Societies' Association, 3 Savile Row, London W1X 1AF.
1978- 5th ed, (published Oct 1984). £4. 159p. *En.
TF: the 5th edition has data for several years to 1983.
Comprehensive source of statistics on building society activity and other related variables. In 7 parts (A: Building society financial statistics, 1956-1983; B: Registry of Friendly Society's statistics on building societies 1890-1983; C: Rates of interest; D: House prices; E: 5% sample survey of building society mortgages; F: Miscellaneous building society statistics: G: Miscellaneous economic statistics, 1948-1983).

1459 BSA bulletin.
Building Societies' Association, 3 Savile Row, London W1X 1AF.
1962- quarterly. £2 or £8 yr. ISSN 0261-6394. *En.
TF: each issue has annual and quarterly or monthly figures for several years to about one quarter or one month prior to the date of the issue.
Includes a commentary on building societies and the housing market in the preceding quarter, and 18 statistical tables on trends in building society activity and the housing market, as well as articles, etc.

Δ G - iv Investment

1460 News from Unit Trust Association Information Unit.
Unit Trust Association, 16 Finsbury Circus, London EC2M 7JP.
1959- monthly. free. *En.
A press notice which includes 'Monthly unit trust statistics' (sales, repurchases, net new investments, value of funds, accounts, etc) and 'Quarterly performance statistics' (by sector, type of unit trust, etc).

1461 Investor's chronicle.
Investor's Chronicle, Greystoke Place, Fetter Lane, London EC4A 1ND.
1860- weekly. £0.95 or £49 yr. *En.
Includes a statistical section with economic and market indicators and data on sector performance.

1462 Money management and unit holder.
Financial Times Business Publications Ltd., Greystoke Place, Fetter Lane, London EC4A 1ND.
1963- monthly. £33 yr. *En.
Includes 'Money management statistics' on buff paper, with data on unit trusts, insurance funds, building society rates, and insurance rates.

1463 Statistical handbook, 1983/84.
Department of National Savings, Statistics Branch, 375 Kensington High Street, London W14 8SD.not priced.
93p loose-leaf. *En.
TF: published December 1984 and regularly updated.
Tables relating to the Department generally, National savings certificates, income bonds, deposit bonds, National Savings Bank investment account, National Savings Bank ordinary account, premium savings bonds, save as you earn, British savings bonds, National savings stock register, interest rates/RPI, etc.

1464 The savings market.
Wootten Publications Ltd., 150-152 Caledonian Road, London N1 9RD.
1976- quarterly. £5 or £17.50 yr. *En.
TF: each issue carries the latest available data.
A tabular guide of facts and figures for different types of savings; lump sum investment (including unit trusts, unit linked bonds and growth and income bonds) and regular savings (life assurance, pension schemes).

Δ G - v Insurance

1465 The British insurance industry: a statistical review (R.L. Carter & A.H. Godden).
Insurance Week, Kluwer Publishing Ltd., 1 Harlequin Avenue, Brentford, Middx TW8 8EW.
1982- 3rd, 1984/85. £45. 272p. *En.
TF: the 1984/85 edition, published in 1984, has data for 1983.
occasionally 1984, and some earlier figures in some tables.
Sections are: A: Company performance; B: UK business per DTI returns; C: Business written overseas; D: Insurance Association's statistics; E: Lloyds; F: Overseas earnings of the UK insurance industry; G: British insurance as an investment; H: Companies in the British insurance market; I: Foreign insurance companies in the UK market.
Note: data was formerly published in the weekly 'Policy holder insurance news'.

Δ G – v, continued

1466 Report of the Chief Registrar...incorporating his report as the Industrial Assurance Commissioner (Registry of Friendly Societies).
HMSO, London.
(annual) 1983-1984. £10. 138p. *En.
TF: the 1983-1984 report, published in 1985, has data for 1983 and earlier years in some tables.
Data on building societies, friendly societies, industrial assurance, industrial and provident societies, superannuation and other trust funds, etc.

1467 Insurance companies' and private pension funds' investments (Business Statistics Office).
HMSO, London.
(quarterly) £7.70. *En.
TF: each issue has data for several years and quarters up to the quarter of the issue and is published about three months later
Note: issued as Business Monitor MQ5.

1468 Insurance business statistics (Business Statistics Office).
HMSO, London.
1964/66- 5th, 1981 (published 1985). £9.40. 77p. *En.
General information about all insurers, a summary insurer-by-insurer of the accounts and statements and general statistics of insurance business.
Note: issued as Business Monitor MA16.

1469 Life assurance in the United Kingdom (Life Offices' Association; Associated Scottish Life Offices; and Industrial Life Offices' Association, in collaboration with the Linked Life Assurance Group).
Life Offices' Association, Aldermanbury House, Queen Street, London EC4N 1TP.
1962/66- 1979-1983 (published 1984). free. 20p. ISSN 0265-7341. *En.
A commentary and statistical data on new individual business, individual business in force, permanent health insurances, pension and life insurance schemes, income and outgo, and life insurance funds.

1470 Insurance facts and figures.
British Insurance Association, Aldermanbury House, Queen Street, London EC4N 1TU.
1969- 1983. free. 27p. ISSN 0308-8308. *En.
TF: the 1983 edition, published late 1984, has data for 1983 and some earlier years.
A review of statistics, followed by more detailed data on premium income; fire and accident (non-motor) & motor underwriting results; marine, aviation and transport; specialist re-insurance and 3-year account business; overall trading profit; UK general business statistics; life assurance; investments and investment income; invisible earnings; and family expenditure.
Note: more specific are the annual 'BIA members' statistics' (1983 (published November 1984). 19p), 'UK market statistics' (1982 ed (published March 1984) 10p), and 'Insurance premiums in the UK, 1960-1982' (published March 1984. 25p).

Δ G – vi Credit market

1471 Credit business of finance houses and other specialist consumer credit grantors (Business Statistics Office).
HMSO, London.
(monthly) £15.75 yr. *En.
TF: each issue contains four years monthly and annual figures to the date of the issue, and is published two or three months later.
Note: issued as Business Monitor SDM6.

1472 Assets and liabilities of finance houses and other consumer credit companies (Business Statistics Office).
HMSO, London.
(quarterly) £8.50 yr. *En.
TF: each issue has data for three years in quarterly figures to the quarter of the issue, and is published two or three months after the end of the quarter of the issue. Data is selective.
Note: issued as Business monitor SDQ7.

1473 Credit quarterly review.
Finance Houses Association, 18 Upper Grosvenor Street, London W1X 9PB.
1960- quarterly. free. *En.
TF: each issue has four quarters figures to the date of the issue and is published one or two months later.
Includes a section of statistical data on outstanding instalment credit to FHA members, new outstanding instalment credit extended to FHA members, outstanding instalment credit unearned, and new instalment credit extended and repaid

1474 Consumer credit business of retailers (Business Statistics Office).
HMSO, London.
(monthly) £15.75 yr. *En.
TF: each issue has monthly figures for four years or more to the date of the issue, and is published two or three months later.
Note: issued as Business monitor SDM8.

Δ H Transport and communications

1475 Transport statistics, Great Britain (Department of Transport, Scottish Development Department and Welsh Office).
HMSO, London.
1964/74- 1974-1984 (published September 1985). £17.50. 213p. *En.
Contains four articles, followed by statistical data on transport, an overall view; road transport; rail transport; water transport; air transport; international comparisons; and selected historical series.

1476 Department of Transport statistics bulletin.
Department of Transport, 43 Marsham Street, London SW1P 3PY.
Includes several sub-series:
Traffic in Great Britain (quarterly. £6 each issue)
Road accident statistics: English regions (annual. 1983 is £5.50)
Road accidents and casualties in Great Britain (quarterly. £4 each issue)
International road haulage by UK registered vehicles: provisional results of International Road Haulage survey.

1477 Inland transport statistics, Great Britain, 1900-1970: volume 1. Railways, public road passenger transport, London's transport (D.L. Munby and A.H. Watson).
Oxford University Press, Walton Street, Oxford OX1 6DP.
£40. 705p. *En.
TF: published in 1979.
Accurate quantitive data covering the history of transport between the years 1900 and 1970.
Note: a second volume (in progress) will cover private vehicles and roads, road haulage, and other sectors.

Δ H - i Ships and shipping

1478 Port statistics (Department of Transport & British Ports Association).
British Ports Association, 1-19 New Oxford Street, London WC1A 1DZ.
1980- 1984. £21. 129p. ISSN 0263-9149. *En.
TF: the 1984 edition, published in 1985, has data for 1984 and earlier years in some tables.
Data for all ports of Great Britain, by mode of appearance; selected ports by mode of appearance and bulk commodity; container and roll-on traffic; other port statistics (international passenger movement, accompanies passenger vehicles); landing of fish, oil rig traffic, manpower and finance.
Note: previously 'Annual digest of port statistics'(National Ports Council. 1964-).

1479 Port statistics bulletin.
Department of the Environment, SPPG4, Kingsgate House, Victoria Street, London SW1E 6SJ.
(occasional) No.1, £7.50. *En.
Different titles and prices are given to each issue. No.1 is titled 'Traffic through Great Britain seaports'.

1480 General trends in shipping (Business Statistics Office, on behalf of the Department of Transport).
HMSO, London.
1978- No.8, November 1985. £8.50. 58p. *En.
TF: the 1985 issue, published late 1985, has data for 1984 and some earlier years.
Detailed statistics on the United Kingdom merchant fleet, world fleets, and international trade.
Note: issued as Business monitor MR15.

1481 Annual statistical abstract of the UK ports industry.
British Ports Association, Commonwealth House, 1-19 New Oxford Street, London WC1A 1DZ.
1961/62- 1983 (published 1985). 2 vols. not priced. *En.
Vol.1 contains information primarily relating to the mode of transport, vol.2 has emphasis more on commodity detail.

1482 Quarterly statistical abstract of the UK ports industry.
British Ports Association, 1-19 New Oxford Street, London WC1A 1DZ.
1961/62- £10.50 each issue. ISSN 0264-1070. *En.
TF: each issue has cumulative data for the year to date and is published some six months after the end of the period covered.
Data on UK trade by port and commodity groups, by trading areas and mode (type of transport). Also trade by port and mode for non-fuel tonnage.

1483 Nationality of vessels in United Kingdom sea-borne trade (Business Statistics Office).
HMSO, London.
(annual) 1980-82 (published 1984). £9.50. *En.
Note: issued as Business monitor MA8.

1484 UK unitised trade statistics.
Transmodel Industries Research, 88-90 Grays Inn Road, London WC1X 8AA.
1983- 2nd, 1984 (published 1985). £75. 111p. ISSN 0267-0550. *En.
UK seaport trade, UK container trade, UK trailer trade, each given by customs port and overseas area.

Δ H – i, continued

1485 Lloyd's shipping economist.
Lloyd's of London Press Ltd., Sheepen Place, Colchester, Essex CO3 3LP.
1979– monthly. £274 yr (by airmail to Europe: £319, North America: $590, other areas: £366).
ISSN 0144-6673. *En.
TF: each issue has the latest data available and also earlier figures in many tables.
Includes statistical tables in the text on world shipping, costs, market sectors (new buildings, sale and purchase, casualties, general cargo carriers/unitised, dry bulk carriers, tankers, gas carriers).

1486 Casualties to vessels and accidents to men: vessels registered in the United Kingdom. Return for... (Department of Transport).
HMSO, London.
(annual) 1984. £5.50. 28p. *En.
TF: the 1984 issue, published in 1985, has data for 1984 and earlier years in some tables.

1487 British Waterways Board: report and accounts.
HMSO, London.
(annual) 15 months to March 31, 1985. £3.50. 89p. *En.
TF: the 1984/85 report, with data for the 15 months, was published in July 1985.
Includes a 2-page statistical appendix with data on traffic in waterways, fleets, warehouses, docks, and fuels used.

Δ H – ii Roads and road transport

1488 Basic road statistics.
British Road Federation, 6 Portugal Street, London WC2A 2HG.
1949– 1984. £6. 32p. *En.
TF: the 1984 edition, published in 1984, has data for several years to 1983.
Data on motor vehicles, road networks, road traffic, energy and transport, public expenditure on transport taxation, road accidents, regional statistics, and international comparisons.

1489 Transport of goods by road in Great Britain: annual report on the continuing survey of road goods transport (Department of the Environment).
Department of Transport, Publications Sales Unit, Building 1, Victoria Road, South Ruislip, Middx HA4 0NZ.
1952– 1984 (published 1985). £8. 41p. *En.
Analyses freight activity and vehicle kilometres done on public roads in the UK by goods vehicles greater than 3½ tonnes gross vehicle weight and 1525 kgs unladen, registered in Great Britain.
Note: issued as Department of Transport statistics bulletin 85 (23).

1490 Highways and transportation statistics...actuals.
Chartered Institute of Public Finance and Accountancy, 3 Robert Street, London WC2N 6BH.
(annual) 1984-85 (published early 1986). £11. 15p. *En.
Final outturn figures for highways and transportation expenditure by county councils in England and Wales.
Note: also 'Highways and transportation statistics...estimates' (1985-86 (published late 1985). £15. 27p. ISSN 0260-9894).

1491 International road haulage by UK registered vehicles: annual report on...survey results.
Department of Transport, Publications Sales Unit, Building 1, Victoria Road, South Ruislip, Middx HA4 0NZ.
(annual) 1983 (published 1984). £10. *En.
Note: provisional results are published in the Department of Transport statistical bulletin.

1492 Motor vehicle registrations (Business Statistics Office).
HMSO, London.
(monthly) £13.75 yr. *En.
Numbers of road vehicles and new registrations.
Note: issued as Business monitor MM1.

1493 Road accidents, Great Britain (Department of Transport & Scottish Office).
HMSO, London.
1951– 1984 (published late 1985). £6.90. 99p. *En.
Accident and casualty rates for each class of road user.
Note: 'Road accidents: Wales' is issued by the Welsh Office (1980-1983 (published mid-1984). £2. 38p. ISSN 0263-9653).

Δ H – iii Railways and rail transport

1494 British Railways Board annual report and accounts.
British Railways Board, Euston Square, PO Box 100, London NW1 2DZ.
1963– 1984/85 (published mid-1985). £4. 48p. ISSN 0305-1420. *En.
Passenger receipts and traffic, freight receipts and traffic, operations (mileage, loads, etc), assets (rolling stock, etc., yards, track), ships and hovercraft owned and passenger and freight receipts and traffic, length of quays in harbours, number of hotels and refreshment rooms in operation, numbers of staff, etc.

1495 Railway safety...report...on the safety record of the railways of Great Britain (Department of Transport).
HMSO, London.
(annual) 1984. £4.90. 46p. *En.
TF: the 1984 report, published in 1985, has data for 1984 and 1983.

Δ H – iv Aviation and air transport

1496 UK airlines: annual operating, traffic and financial statistics.
Civil Aviation Authority, 37 Gratton Road, Cheltenham, Glos GL50 2BN.
1983– 1983. £8. 93p. *En.
TF: the 1983 edition, published in 1984, has data for 1983 and earlier years in some tables.
Size of UK airlines, main outputs, scheduled services, non-scheduled services, operations (by licence class), exempt operations, sub-charter operations, aircraft type and utilisation.
Note: up-dated by 'UK airlines: monthly operating and traffic statistics' (1983– £2.50 or £25 yr), formerly part of 'CAA monthly statistics'.

1497 UK airports: annual statements of movements, passengers and cargo.
Civil Aviation Authority, 37 Gratton Road, Cheltenham, Glos GL50 2BN.
1983– 1983. £8. 61p. *En.
TF: the 1983 edition, published in 1984, has data for 1983 and earlier years in some tables.
Size of UK airports, main outputs, use, movements, airport activity, air passengers, and air cargo.
Note: up-dated by 'UK airports: monthly statements of movements, passengers and cargo' (1983– £2.50 or £25. ISSN 0265-0258), previously part of 'CAA monthly statistics'.

1498 Local authority airports financial statistics...actuals.
Chartered Institute of Public Finance and Accountancy, 3 Robert Street, London WC2N 6BH.
1978/79– 1984-85 (published early 1986). £11. 21p. ISSN 0260-9967. *En.
Analyses of revenue accounts and balance sheets of local authority airports, plus a comprehensive range of non-financial information (passenger and cargo usage, aircraft and air transport movements, employees, etc).
Note: also 'Local authority airports financial statistics...estimates' (1984-85 estimates published May 1984. £10. 23p. ISSN 0260-9975).

1499 Accidents to aircraft on the British Register.
The Library, Civil Aviation Authority, 45-49 Kingsway, London WC2B 6TE.
1972– 1984 (published 1985). £7. 91p. ISSN 0306-3556. *En.

Δ H – v Telecommunications and postal services

1500 Statistics.
British Telecom Headquarters, 47/57 Gresham Street, London EC2V 7JL.
1969– 1983. not priced. 107p. *En.
TF: the 1983 edition, published in 1984, has data for several years to 1983 or the latest available.
Data on telephones (stations, exchange connections, equipment and line plant, traffic), telegraphs (equipment, traffic), telex, datel, manpower, motor transport, finances, and a historical section.

1501 Post Office report and accounts.
Post Office Headquarters, 33 Grosvenor Place, London SW1X 1PX.
(annual) 1984/85. £1.50. 72p. *En.
TF: the 1984/85 report, published mid-1985, has data for the financial year 1984/85.
As well as the accounts of the Post Office and National Girobank, the report includes graphs of performance indicators and a ten-year operational summary, with statistics on the Royal Mail, motor transport, counters, personnel, etc.
Note: a quarterly leaflet 'Quality of the inland letter service' (free) is also available.

Δ I Environment

1502 Digest of environmental protection and water statistics (Department of the Environment).
HMSO, London.
1978– No.7, 1984. £7.85. 61p. *En.
TF: the 1984 edition, published May 1985, includes the latest data available and some earlier figures.
A compendium of statistics on air pollution, freshwater and marine pollution, radioactivity, noise, derelict land and mineral workings, solid waste, water supply and use, landscape and conservation.

GIBRALTAR

Central statistical office

1503 Economic Planning and Statistics Office.
Cathedral Square, Gibraltar,
t 70071. tx 2223 ADM SEC GK. tg SECRETARY GIBRALTAR.

Statistical publications

Δ A General

1504 Abstract of statistics.
Economic Planning and Statistics Office, Cathedral Square, Gibraltar.
1972- 1984. £2. 84p. *En.
TF: the 1984 edition, published early 1985, has data for 1984 and several earlier years.
Main sections:
Population - Housing - Education - Health - Public safety - Civil administration - Employment - Income and expenditure - Trade - Tourism - Public finance - Banking statistics - Transport and communications - Public utilities - Meteorological data.

Δ C External trade

1505 Imports & exports statistics.
Economic Planning and Statistics Office, Cathedral Square, Gibraltar.
(annual) 1984 (published 1985). not priced. 23p. *En.
Imports and exports by main commodities subdivided by main countries of destination, by main countries of origin and destination, by main commodities, imports from EEC countries, etc.

Δ D - iv Tourism and travel

1506 Tourist survey report.
Economic Planning and Statistics Office, Cathedral Square, Gibraltar.
1972- 1984. not priced. 15p. *En.
TF: the 1984 report, published in 1985, has data for 1984 and earlier years in some tables.
Percentages of visitors by country of residence, areas of residence, type and size of party, number of children, number of previous visits, by number of days spent in Gibraltar, type of accommodation, and tourist expenditure.

1507 Hotel occupancy survey.
Economic Planning and Statistics Office, Cathedral Square, Gibraltar.
1972- 1984. not priced. 15p. *En.
TF: the 1984 edition, published in 1985, has data from 1972 to 1984.
Numbers of arrivals, tourist arrivals, guest nights sold/offered to all arrivals and tourist arrivals, and average length of stay of all arrivals and tourist arrivals.

Δ E Population

1508 Census of Gibraltar (Census Office).
Government Secretariat, Gibraltar.
1871- 1981. not priced. 169p. *En.
TF: a census is taken about every ten years. The results of the 1981 census were published in 1982.
Nationality, age and sex; permanent residents; religion; demographic data; manpower; education and qualifications; and housing.

Δ E - ii Labour

1509 Department of Labour and Social Security: report for the year...
Government Secretariat, Gibraltar.
1965/66- 1980-81 (published 1982). £0.65. 63p. *En.
A general view of the labour field, wages and conditions of employment, industrial relations, safety, health and welfare, living conditions, social insurance, social welfare, and industrial training.

1510 Employment survey report.
Economic Planning and Statistics Office, Cathedral Square, Gibraltar.
1972- 1985. not priced. 27p. *En.
TF: the 1985 report, published in 1985, has data for 1985 and long runs of earlier years in some tables.
Number of employees by sex, sector and nationality; average earnings, hours worked and overtime; employees in the public and private sectors by industry; movements of employees; etc.

Δ F Social and political

< see also 1509

Δ F – ii Health and welfare

1511 Department of Medical and Health Services: annual report.
Government Secretariat, Gibraltar.
1951– 1980 (published 1982). £0.75. 62p. *En.
Includes data on hospitals and institutions, vital statistics, infectious diseases, school medical and dental services, child welfare clinic, environmental health (vaccination & immunisation, animal control), etc.

Δ F – iii Education and leisure

1512 Department of Education biennial report for the period...
Government Secretariat, Gibraltar.
(biennial) 1978–1980. £0.75. 42p. *En.
TF: the 1978–1980 report, published in 1982, has data from September 1978 to August 1980.
Data on all types of education, staffing, finance, buildings, etc.

Δ G Finance

1513 Annual accounts... (Principal Auditor).
Government Secretariat, Gibraltar.
1975/76– 1981–1982. not priced. 157p. *En.
TF: the 1982–1983 report, published in 1983, has data for the 1981/82 fiscal year.
Revenues and expenditure, and departmental accounts.

Δ H Transport and communications

Δ H – i Ships and shipping

1514 Port Department: annual report.
Government Secretariat, Gibraltar.
1963– 1981. £0.50. 25p. *En.
TF: the 1981 report, published in 1982, has data for 1981 and also a few earlier years in some tables.
Includes a statistical appendix on net tonnage entering Gibraltar, main imports, deep-sea merchant shipping operations, berthing dues, vessels licensed, revenue & expenditure of the Pilotage Authority, etc.

Δ H – iv Aviation and air transport

1515 Air traffic survey.
Economic Planning and Statistics Office, Cathedral Square, Gibraltar.
1972– 1984. not priced. 19p. *En.
TF: the 1984 edition, published in 1985, has long runs of figures to 1984 or the latest data available.
Statistical data on air traffic operations between Gibraltar and the United Kingdom for both scheduled and charter airlines. It also includes some general data on commercial freight.

GREECE
GRECE
GRIECHENLAND
HELLENIC REPUBLIC

Central statistical office

1516 National Statistical Service of Greece.
14-16 Lycourgou Street, Athens 12.
t 3249-302. tx 21674. Answerback ESYE GR.
An independent public authority under the Ministry of National Economy, composed of the Central Statistical Survey, statistical services of each ministry, and 50 field offices. It is the function of the Service (i) to compile and analyse the country's basic statistical data of general interest, including the various census results; (ii) to collect and analyse statistical data of special interest, compiled either specifically or as a by-product of other administrative functions, provided that the collection and processing of such data can be treated according to methods of mass-production, involving mechanisation, personal specifications, etc., and (iii) to co-ordinate the statistical work carried out by the various statistical organisations with a view to preparing and carrying out an adequate statistical programme for the country. Unpublished statistical information can be provided, if available, for a fee. Statistical field offices are in the capital towns of each department of Greece.
This service has been abbreviated to NSS, Athens in entries between 1516-1553.

Libraries

The Library of the National Statistical Service of Greece (see above) contains all the publications of the Service and many of its predecessor, as well as several statistical publications of other Greek public services and organisations. It also has many statistical publications of other countries and of international organisations. The library is open to the public daily from 8.00 to 14.00 in winter and 8.00 to 13.00 in summer, and the staff speaks Greek, English and French.

Libraries and information services abroad

Greek statistical publications are available for reference in Greek embassies abroad including:

United Kingdom	Greek Embassy, 1a Holland Park, London W11. t 01-727 8040.
Australia	Greek Embassy, Stonehaven Crs., Redhill, Canberra. t 73 3011.
Canada	Greek Embassy, 76080 Maclaren Street, Ottawa K2P 0K6. t 238 6271.
USA	Greek Embassy, 2211 Massachusetts Avenue NW, Washington DC 20008. t 667 3168.

Bibliographies

A price-list of statistical publications is issued by the National Statistical Service of Greece at intervals and is available on request.

Statistical publications

Δ A General

1517 Statistical yearbook of Greece.
NSS, Athens.
1955- 1983. Dr 300 ($10 abroad). 494p. ISSN 0081-5071. *Gr, En.
TF: the 1983 edition, published in 1984, has data for 1983 and many tables also have data for earlier years.
Main sections:
Territory & climate - Population - Employment & unemployment - Public health - Social welfare & insurance - Education - Justice - Agriculture, livestock, forestry, fishing - Mines (quarries & salterns) - Manufacturing - Energy: electricity & gas - Construction & municipal, communal works - Trade - Transport & communication - Travelling & tourist movement - Mineral springs, balneal stations - Museums & archaeological sites - Press & public shows - Public finance - Money & banking - Prices & household expenditure - Balance of payments - International tables.

1518 Concise statistical yearbook.
NSS, Athens.
1962- 1983-84. Dr 150 ($5 abroad). 235p. ISSN 0069-8245. *Gr, En.
TF: the 1983-84 edition, published in 1984, has data for 1982 and some earlier years.
An abridged version of (1517) containing the principal data for population and economic and social information, summary tables and diagrams.

Δ A, continued

1519 Monthly statistical bulletin.
NSS, Athens.
1956- Dr 50 ($2 abroad); or Dr 600 yr ($24 yr abroad). *Gr, En.
TF: tables usually include data for several years and the last 12 months, the latest figures being about three months prior to the date of the issue.
Climate - environment; population; employment - unemployment - labour - wages, public health; agriculture - livestock - forestry - fishing; industry - electricity - gas; construction; trade; transport - communications; tourism; public finance; prices; money & banking; & quarterly national accounts.

1520 Monthly statistical bulletin.
Bank of Greece, Athens.
1936- $25 yr ($45 yr by air). ISSN 0005-5190. *Gr, En.
TF: each issue has data for several years and months to about two or three months prior to the date of the issue.
Money and banking, public finance, balance of payments, production, and prices.

1521 Commercial Bank of Greece: economic bulletin.
Commercial Bank of Greece, 11 Sophocleous Street, Athens 122.
(quarterly) free. *En & Gr eds.
Includes a feature on developments in the Greek economy which has statistical tables.

1522 Greece: a portrait.
Research and Publicity Center Kede Ltd., Amerikis 10, Athens.
TF: published in 1979. 191p.

Δ B Production

1523 Résultats du recensement des industries manufacturières-artisanat, du commerce et autres services [Results of the census of manufacturing, handicraft industries, commerce and other services].
NSS, Athens.
1958- 4th, 1978 (published 1981). Dr 200 ($10 abroad) each volume. 2 vols. *Gr, Fr.
Vol I: number of establishments, employees, and machinery by branches of economic activity. Vol II: number of establishments, employees by sex, status in the professions, and branches of economic activity. Both volumes have data for Greece, each industrial centre, and other parts of Greece.

Δ B - i Mines and mining

1524 Annual statistical survey on mines, quarries and salterns.
NSS, Athens.
1959- 1982 (published 1984). Dr 50 ($2.50 abroad). 39p. ISSN 0071-7415. *Gr, En.
Production and employment in the mines, quarries and salterns.

1525 Bulletin on the mining activities of Greece.
General Directorate of Mines, Ministry of Industry and Energy, Athens.
(annual) 1976. not priced. 69p. *Gr, En.
TF: the 1976 edition, published in 1979, has data for 1976 and also for some earlier years in some tables.
Includes a section of statistical tables (p 25-41) on production of crude ores, concentrated ores and metallurgical products, employment and accidents, accomplished researches, consumption of timber and explosives, domestic consumption of certain mining and metallurgical products, exports of mining and metallurgical products, and similar data for quarry products.
Note: It is understood that publication is to be resumed shortly by the Ministry of Energy and Natural Resources.

Δ B - ii Agriculture, fisheries, forestry, etc

1526 Agricultural statistics of Greece.
NSS, Athens.
1961- 1981 (published 1984). Dr 100 ($4 abroad). c 100p. ISSN 0065-4574. *Gr, En.
Cultivated areas, irrigated crops by categories, number of trees, agricultural machinery, crop and livestock production, number of domestic animals, production of certain forest products, inner waters fishing and inshore fishing by boats and motor propelled vessels of 19 h.p. or less.

Δ B - ii(a) Agriculture and horticulture

1527 Résultats du recensement de l'agriculture-élevage [Results of the agricultural and livestock census].
NSS, Athens.
1950- 1971. $5. *Gr, Fr.
Number, size and fragmentation of agricultural holdings,crop areas and irrigated land, livestock holdings and the number of animals by kind, agricultural machinery by kind. £% sample elaboration.
Note: a general elaboration of the census has also been published in Gr & En in two volumes (Dr 150 ($7)) each volume.

Δ B – ii(b) Finance

1528 Results of sea fishery by motor vessels.
NSS, Athens.
1964/65- 1981 (published 1984). Dr 30 ($9 abroad). 31p. *Gr, En.
Numbers of motor fishing vessels by categories and hp group; overseas and open sea fishing vessels by tonnage groups, quantity and value of catch by category, kind of fishing, kind of fishing tools, and species of fish, and employment.

Δ B – iii Industry

1529 Annual industrial survey.
NSS, Athens.
1958- 1977 (published 1982). Dr 100 ($7 abroad). 144p. ISSN 0071-7393. *Gr, En.
Establishments of large scale industry, with industrial activity, number of establishments, wages, production, value of materials consumed, value added, asset information by manufacturing branch, for the manufacturing industries, electricity and gas enterprises in Greece as a whole and in Greater Athens.

Δ B – iv Construction

1530 [Results of the census of buildings, 1 December 1970].
NSS, Athens.
Volumes are:
Provisional summary results... ($1.50 abroad. *Gr only)
Provisional summary results...(urban, semi-urban, rural areas) 177p. Dr 30 or $1.50. *Gr only.
Provisional summary results...(by principal category of use & number of floors) $1 abroad. *Gr only.
Results... (data by municipality and commune) 344p. Dr 150 or $8. *Gr only.
Note: also published 'Provisional summary results of the general census of dwellings, 1971' $1.50. *Gr only.

Δ C External trade

1531 Commerce extérieur de la Grèce [Foreign trade of Greece].
NSS, Athens.
1953- 1979-1980 (published 1982). Dr 300 ($12 abroad). 544p. *Gr, Fr.
Detailed tables of imports and exports arranged by commodities, subdivided by countries of origin and destination, and by countries subdivided by commodity groups. Summary tables.

1532 Bulletin de statistique du commerce extérieur (cumulativement) [Bulletin of foreign trade statistics (cumulative)].
NSS, Athens.
1953- 1983. Dr 300 or $10. 354p. ISSN 0256-3614. *Gr, Fr.
TF: the 1983 edition, published late 1984, has data for the four quarters and annual figures for 1983.
Main tables shows detailed statistics of imports and exports arranged by commodities subdivided by countries of origin and destination.
Note: prior to 1979 the publication was issued quarterly (monthly until 1975).

Δ D Internal distribution and service trades

Δ D – iv Tourism and travel

1533 [Tourist statistics].
NSS, Athens.
1981- 1981. $4 abroad. *Gr.

Δ E Population

1534 Results of the population and housing census.
NSS, Athens.
1940- 1981. *Gr; En or Fr.
TF: a census is taken every ten years. The results of the 1981 census are being published from 1982 onwards.
Results published so far include:
Vol III: Demographic and social characteristics of the population 10% sample elaboration of the census questionnaire) (Dr 300; $10. 167p. Gr, Fr. published in 1984).
De facto population of Greece...by departments, eparchies, municipalities, communes and localities (Dr 200; $10. 189p. *Gr; (preface & contents list also in Fr).

1535 The population of Greece in the second half of the 20th century.
NSS, Athens.
1980. $10 abroad. 143p. *Gr, En.
Original population, marriages and reproduction, mortality, migration, population projections.

Δ E – i Vital statistics

1536 Mouvement naturel de la population de la Grèce [Vital statistics of Greece].
NSS, Athens.
1956- 1981 (published 1984). Dr 150 ($7 abroad). 175p. ISSN 0077-6114. *Gr, Fr.

Δ E – ii Labour

1537 [Labour force survey (employment)].
NSS, Athens.
1981- 1983 (published 1984). Dr 80 ($3 abroad). 103p. *Gr.
Note: replaces 'Employment survey conducted in urban and semi-urban areas', published from 1969/72 to 1980.

Δ E – iii Housing

< see 1530

Δ F Social and political

Δ F – i Standard of living

< see also 392

1538 Household expenditure survey.
NSS, Athens.
1963/64- 1974. Dr 50 ($2.50 abroad). 216p.
TF: first published in Gr in 1975; the above edition in Gr & En also in 1975; a third publication in Gr & En of 64p in 1978.
Data for the whole country, for urban areas, and for semi-urban and rural areas. Includes size of communities, size of households, occupational status and age of head of household, purchases, quantities of food consumed by households, etc.

Δ F – i Health and welfare

1539 Social welfare and health statistics.
NSS, Athens.
1967- 1981 (published 1983). Dr 100 ($4 abroad). 95p. *Gr, En.
Numbers of hospitals, beds and doctors by region and department, patients by categories of diseases and days of treatment.

1540 Enquête annuelle sur l'activité des organismes de sécurité sociale [Annual enquiry on the activities of social security organisations].
NSS, Athens.
1962- 1980 (published 1983). Dr 50 ($2.50 abroad). *Gr; contents list & summary also in Fr.
Persons insured: state pensioners; receipts and expenditures of the social insurance organisations; work accidents by kind, cause and branch of economic activity.

Δ F – iii Education and leisure

1541 Statistique de l'enseignement [Education statistics].
NSS, Athens.
1954/55- 1979/80. Dr 200 ($7 abroad). 416p. *Gr; contents list & summary also in Fr.
TF: published 1983, has data for the academic year 1979/80.
Number of schools, teachers & pupils by region and department in elementary, secondary, technical and professional education; and numbers of students, graduates, teaching staff by educational institution in higher education.

1542 [Cultural statistics].
NSS, Athens.
1975- 1979-80 (published 1982). Dr 50 ($2.50 abroad). 60p. *Gr.

Δ F – iv Justice

1543 [Statistics on civil, criminal and reformatory justice].
NSS, Athens.
1956- 1981. Dr 100 ($5 abroad). 134p. *Gr.

Δ G Finance

Δ G – ii Public finance

1544 National accounts of Greece.
Ministry of Coordination, National Accounts Service, Syntagma Square, Athens.
1946/53– 1970-1979 (published 1981). free. 127p. *Gr; contents list & main table headings also in
Gross national product and expenditure account, national income account, consolidated appropriation account for households and private non-profit institutions, consolidated gross capital formation & saving account, plus international comparative tables.

1545 Provisional national accounts of Greece.
Ministry of National Economy, Athens.
(annual) 1982. free. 119p. *Gr; contents list & main table headings also in En.
TF: the 1982 edition, published in 1983, has data for 1970, 1975 to 1982.

1546 Quarterly national accounts of Greece.
Ministry of National Economy, Athens.
quarterly. free. *Gr; contents list & main headings also in En.
TF: each issue has data for each quarter of the year to date and is published about four months later.

1547 Public finance statistics.
NSS, Athens.
1962– 1980-1981. Dr 100 ($4 abroad). 148p. ISSN 0256-3568. *Gr, En.
TF: the 1980-81 edition, published in 1985, has data for five years to 1980 or 1981.
Taxation of the state and legal entities, revenue – expenditure, revenue, income taxation, property taxation, import duties, consumption and transaction taxes, other revenue, expenditures, investments, public credit, revenue and expenditure of public legal entities, and personnel movement.

1548 Statistical bulletin of public finance.
NSS, Athens.
1959– quarterly. Dr 100 ($4 abroad); or Dr 240 yr ($12 yr abroad). *Gr, En.
State revenue by principal sources, import duties and taxes, receipts from advertisements of National Radio TV Foundation, expenditure of state budget, current expenditure of ministries and branches of economic activity, public debt, etc.
Note: issued monthly until June 1973.

1549 [Statistics of declared income of physical persons and its taxation].
NSS, Athens.
1960– 1982 (published 1983). Dr 100 ($4 abroad). 54p. *Gr.

1550 [Statistics of the declared income of legal entities and its taxation].
NSS, Athens.
1959– 1982 (published 1984). Dr 50 ($2.50 abroad). 46p. *Gr.

Δ H Transport and communications

1551 [Transport and communication statistics].
NSS, Athens.
1967– 1980 (published 1983). Dr 100 ($5 abroad). 121p. *Gr.
State railways, including network, rolling stock, passenger and goods transported, receipts and expenditures; motor vehicles registered, by category and use; analytical tables of road traffic accidents; activities at the country's airports, and domestic and international traffic of 'Olympic Airways'; telecommunications, including installed capacity telephone connections, telephone calls, traffic in telegrams and radiotelegrams.

Δ H – i Ships and shipping

1552 Shipping statistics.
NSS, Athens.
1967– 1981 (published 1985). Dr 100 ($4 abroad). 163p. ISSN 0072-7423. *Gr, En.
Greek merchant fleet, by category and tonnage; Greek merchant ships mortgaged for loans; laid up merchant ships; employment of Greek and foreign seamen; total shipping traffic; international shipping; coastal traffic; traffic of ferry-boats and passenger car ferries; traffic of merchant ships in the Corinthian and Suez canals and in principal foreign ports; and casualties to ships and persons at sea. An appendix has tables of Greek-owned and world merchant fleet, Greek seamen, economic magnitude of merchant shipping, shipbuilding and repairing activity, and general tables.

Δ H – iii Railways and railway transport

1553 Annual report.
Hellenic Railways Organisation, 1 Karolou Street, Athens 107.
(annual) 1984. not priced. c 60p. *Gr; summary in En.
TF: the 1984 report, published in 1985, has data for 1984 and 1983.
Includes data on passenger traffic on the railway and buses owned or rented by the Organisation, goods traffic, rolling stock, financial results, etc.

HUNGARY
HONGRIE
UNGARN

Central statistical office

1554 Központi Statisztikai Hivatal [Central Statistical Office].
Keleti Károly u. 5-7, 1525 Budapest 11.
t 358-530. tx 22 4308. STATI H.
The President of the Office, by the authority of the Council of Ministers, is responsible for providing guidance and directions for the coordination, development and supervision of statistical activities, supervising all the statistical activities in the framework of national professional management of statistical activities; giving orders for the collection and implementation of the central state statistical system; organising and directing the operations of the national census; developing and improving methods of statistical activities; and maintaining a library authorised for copyright deposit, reference archives and a statistical documentation service, etc. The Office issues a journal. 'Statisztikai szemle' [Statistical review] monthly in Hungarian, with contents list also in En, Fr, De & Ru (Ft 13 yr) as well as the other periodicals listed below. More detailed statistics than those published may be available and can be supplied on request.
This office has been abbreviated to KSH, Budapest, for entries between 1554-1613.

Libraries

The library of Központi Statisztikai Hivatel (see above) is a copyright deposit library for Hungarian publications, and is the primary source of published statistics in Hungary. The library is open to the public from 8.30 to 20.00 on Tuesdays, Wednesdays, Thursdays and Fridays; from 13.00 to 20.00 on Mondays. In summer it is closed for one month. The staff of the library speak English, German, French and Russian, as well as Hungarian.
Other libraries having collections of statistical publications are the Library of Parliament, Kossuth Lajor tér., Budapest V, and the library of the Karl Marx University of Economic Sciences, Dimitrov tér 8, Budapest IX.

Libraries and information services abroad

The more general Hungarian statistical publications are available for reference in the Hungarian embassies and legations abroad, including:

United Kingdom	Hungarian Embassy, 46 Eaton Place, London SW1X 8BY. t 01-235 8767.
Canada	Hungarian Embassy, 7 Delaware Avenue, Ottawa K2P 0Z2. t 232 1711.
USA	Hungarian Embassy, 3910 Shoemaker Street NW, Washington DC. t (202) 362-6730.
	Hungarian Legation, 8 East 75th Street, New York, NY 10021. t (212) 879-4125.

Bibliographies

1555 Statisztikai adatforrások. Bibliográfia 1975-1984 [Sources of statistical data. Bibliography, 1975-1984] (Központi Statisztikai Hivatal).
Compiled by the Library and Documentation Service of the Central Statistical Office and including only publications of the Office. In Hu, Ru, En & De.
Earlier volumes were issued for 1867-1967 and 1945-1974, the latter in Hu only.

1556 Magyar kozgazdasági és statisztikai irodalom: bibliográfia [Hungarian bibliography of economics and statistics] (Központi Statisztikai Hivatal) 1957-59-.
Compiled annually by the library of the Central Statistical Office, in cooperation with the libraries of the Karl Marx University of Economic Sciences and the Institute of Economics of the Hungarian Academy of Sciences.
Titles of entries are translated into En & Ru.

1557 A Statisztikai Kiadó Vállalat katalógusa [Catalogue of the Statistical Publishing House].
A sales list issued at intervals by the Statistical Publishing House (Statisztikai Kiadó Vállalat, Kaszásdülö u. 10-12, Budapest II.1033). Titles of entries are translated into En, De & Ru.

Statistical publications

Δ A General

1558 Statisztikai évkönyv [Statistical yearbook].
KSH, Budapest.
1871- 1983 (published 1984). Ft 214. 418p. ISSN 0073-4039. *Hu.
TF: contains data for 1983 and also figures for five or ten earlier years in some tables.
Main sections:
Long-range time series - Social and economic structure - Population - Vital statistics - Labour - National product, national income - Accumulated assets of national economy - Investments - Industry - Construction industry - Agriculture, forestry - Water works and supply - Transport, post & telecommunications - Energy - Material consumption - Internal trade - Tourism - External trade - Income & consumption of the population - Social welfare - Public health - Housing - public utilities - Environmental statistics - Education - Scientific research - Culture, sports - Justice - Accidents - fire loss - Computer techniques - Small organisations - Meteorological - County data - International data - Exchange rates.
Note: the Central Statistical Office also publishes 'Budapest statisztikai évkönyve' [Statistical yearbook of Budapest] and Budapest statisztikai zseblönyve' [Budapest statistical pocketbook].

1559 Statistical yearbook.
KSH, Budapest.
1965- 1982 (published 1984). Ft 192. 380p. *En, Ru.
An English/Russian version of the above.

1560 Magyarország [Hungary].
KSH, Budapest.
1980- 1984. Fl 7. 40p. *Hu; also eds in En, Ru, De, Fr & Es (Ft 15 each).
Contains principal data on Hungary.

1561 Területi statisztikai évkönyv [Regional statistical yearbook].
KSH, Budapest.
1964- 1982. Ft 124. 212p. ISSN 0303-5344. *Hu.
TF: the 1982 edition, published in 1983, has data for 1982.
Similar data to 1558, but regionally.
Note: the monthly 'Területi statisztikai' has no regular statistical tables, but some statistics are included in the articles, mainly analyses.

1562 Megyei évkönyv-sorozat [County yearbooks].
KSH, Budapest.
1956- 1983 (published 1984). each volume separately priced. 19 vols. *Hu.
Each volume has data for one county, covering much the same subjects as 1558.

1563 Népessé- és társadalomstatisztikai zsebkönyv [Population- and socio-statistical pocketbook].
KSH, Budapest.
1982- 1983 (published 1984 (English ed 1985)). Ft 63. 315p. *Hu & En eds.
Population, main data on vital events (marriages, divorces, births, abortions, deaths, internal migration) international data, mobility, housing conditions - housing management, environmental protection, civil security, public health, social provision, education, research and experimental development, culture - sport, accidents at work, damage by fire, jurisdication, and time budget.

1564 Hungary '82: a yearbook (Univ. Press).
'Kultura', PO Box 149, 1389 Budapest 62.
1966- 1982 (published 1983). not priced. c 250p. *En.
Mainly text, but includes tables on population, industry, agriculture, education, etc.

1565 Magyar statisztikai zsebkönyv [Statistical pocketbook of Hungary].
KSH, Budapest.
TF: the 1984 edition, published in 1985, has data for several years to 1984 (preliminary figures).
Population - vital statistics; employment; income - consumption, housing - environment, social welfare, public health, education, scientific research, culture, sports, accidents - fire loss, insurance, justice, national income, investments, industry, energy, construction industry, agriculture, water works and supply, transport, posts and telecommunications, internal trade, external trade, tourism, services rendered to the population, computer techniques, small organisations. Appendix on state administration, geographical data, climate and exchange rates.

1566 Statistical pocketbook of Hungary.
KSH, Budapest.
1958- 1983. Ft 60. 215p. *En; also available in Ru & De.
TF: the 1983 edition, published in 1984, has data for several years to 1983 (provisional figures).
An English version of 1565.

Δ A, continued

1567 Statisztikai havi közlemények [Monthly statistical bulletin].
KSH, Budapest.
1957- Ft 35; or Ft 420 yr. ISSN 0018-781X. *Hu; En, Ru & De translations of headings and concepts used are published every three years.
TF: each issue is published about the 10th of the month, containing data for the previous month and usually for the last 18 months and several years.
Summary, population, vital statistics, industry, production and external trade of industrial products, investments, construction industry, sales of agirucltural products, transport, external trade, internatl trade, main data of money circulation, prices, tourism, public health, accidents, meteorological data, international data. The first part of each issue shows detailed monthly statistics; the second has quarterly, half-quarterly, half-yearly and annual statistics for the more important subjects; the thirs part is a subject index to current Hungarian statistical publications.

1568 Hungary...
Hungarian News Agency MTI. Publishing Office, PO Box 3, 11-1426 Budapest.
Twice a year. $5.00 yr. *En, Fr, Es, Ru & De eds.
Each issue is a survey on topical issues about Hungary, with tables in the text.

1569 Economic bulletin.
Magyar Nemzeti Bank, Szabadság tér 8/11, Budapest V.
1958- quarterly. not priced. *En.
TF: each issue has data for several years and months up to about six months prior to the end of the quarter of the issue.
Includes a section of statistical tables on industry, employment, wages, sales, production of principal articles, crop results, livestock, sales of farm produce, passenger and goods transport, foreign trade, balance of payments, retail trade turnover, price index numbers, international tourism, etc.

1570 The Hungarian economy: a quarterly economic and business review.
'Kultura', PO Box 149, 1389 Budapest.
1972- quarterly. not priced. *En.
A special quarterly edition in English of the weekly 'FIGTELO', published in Hungarian. Contains no regular tables, but statistics are included in the articles and features.

1571 Hungaropress (Hungarian Chamber of Commerce: Information Service).
Hungaropress, PO Box 106, 1389 Budapest.
fortnightly. free. *En.
A news bulletin which includes some statistics in the text.

1572 Marketing in Hungary (Hungarian Chamber of Commerce).
'Kultura', PO Box 149, 1389 Budapest.
1970- quarterly. not priced. ISSN 0025-3731. *En & De eds.
A market research review, with some statistics in the text, but no regular tables.

1573 Hungary in figures.
Magyar Kereskedelmi Kamara [Hungarian Chamber of Commerce] PO Box 106, H-1389 Budapest.
(annual) [1984]. free. *En, Fr, De, Ru, It & Es eds.
TF: the 1984 edition, published in 1984, has data for 1983 and 1982/83 and earlier years in some tables.
A six-page folder with general statistical data on geography, tourism, infrastructure, manpower, public health, social insurance, consumption, education, culture, structure of the economy, production results, and foreign trade.

1574 The Hungarian co-operative movement in figures.
National Co-operative Council, Alkotmany u. 25, Budapest V.
1970- not priced. 120p. *En.
TF: published in 1979, with data for several years to 1977 or 1978.
Data on co-operative agriculture, industry, and consumption and marketing.
Note: the first two surveys were titled 'Statistical survey of the Hungarian Co-operative movement.

1575 Beruházási, épitöipari, lakásstatisztikai zsebkönyv [Pocketbook of investment, housing and construction statistics].
KSH, Budapest.
1979- 1983 (published 1984). Ft 22. 169p. ISSN 0139-3510. *Hu.
Note: there is also an edition of 169 141 pages, with translations of contents in En & Ru.

Δ B Production

Δ B - ii Agriculture, fisheries, forestry, etc

< see also 1574

1576 Mezögazdasági statisztikai zsebkönyv [Statistical pocketbook of agriculture].
KSH, Budapest.
1958- 1983. Ft 44. 308p. ISSN 0441-4683. *Hu.
TF: the 1983 edition, published in 1984, has data for 1980 to 1983 generally.
Main sections: Summarising data, human and material preconditions for production - technical preconditions for production - production output - enterprises' economy - sale of agricultural products - forestry - water economy - county-level data - international data.

Δ B – ii, continued

1577 Mezögazdasagi statisztikai évkönyv [Statistical yearbook of agriculture].
KSH, Budapest.
1980– 1983. Ft 155. 276p. *Hu.
TF: the 1983 edition, published in 1984, has data for 1983 and some earlier years.
Main sections: Summarizing data – staff number, employment, earnings – land area – fixed assets – investments – agrotechnics – research and development – product value – plant cultivation – stockbreeding – prices, price indices – forestry – county level data – international data.

Δ B – iii Industry

1578 Iparstatisztikai évkönyv [Statistical yearbook of industry].
KSH, Budapest.
1961– 1983 (published 1984). Ft 225. 400p. *Hu.
Main sections: Summarizing data – structure of the socialist state industry – concentration of industrial organisations – production, sales, changes in prices – technical level – labour – materials and energy consumption – financial data – industrial activities of non-industrial branches – data of new-type ecoromic units – data of certain manufacturing branches.
Note: a version with 111 extra pages containing En & Ru explanations of the tables is also available.

1579 Ipari zsebkönyv. Pocket book of industry...
KSH, Budapest.
(annual) 1984. not priced. 157p. ISSN 0230-919X. *Hu, En, Ru.
TF: the 1984 edition, published in 1985, has data for 1984 and also earlier years in some tables.
Chapters are: Main figures of the People's economy and the industry; Structure of industry; Production, productivity, changes in prices; Utilisation of materials and energy; Technical level; Labour; Data of finance and rentability; Regional data; International data.

1580 A kisipar... [Private industry].
KSH, Budapest.
1970/78– 1982 (published 1983). not priced. 59p. *Hu.
Data on private industry.

1581 Kohászati és gépipari adattár [Data on the metallurgical and machine industry].
KSH, Budapest.
not priced. (published 1979). 507p. *Hu.

1582 Könnyüipari adattár [Data on light industry].
KSH, Budapest.
1967– 3rd [1978]. Ft 311. 757p. *Hu.
TF: the 1978 edition, published in 1978, has data for 1970-1975.
Light industry in the national economy, geographical location, centralisation of enterprises and concentration of settlements, branch structure, investments, fixed equipment, production, productivity, labour, energy carriers, sales, profits, profitability, sales indices of material prices, etc. Also state industry, co-operative industry, and private industry covering the same subjects; and data on various industries.

1583 Vegyipari adattár [Data on chemical industry].
KSH, Budapest.
1971– 2nd, 1970-1975 (published 1979). Ft 100. 205p. *Hu.
Summarising data – geographical situation – sectoral structure, concentration – oridyction, productivity – sales turnover – price index – material consumption – labour – stock of fixed assets – investments – machinery – financial data – data on manufacturing branches – chemical industry of co-operatives – professional data – international data.

1584 Számítástechnikai statisztikai évkönyv... [Statistical yearbook of computing].
KSH, Budapest.
1970– 1983 (published 1984). Ft 62. 176p. *Hu.

1585 Számítástechnikai statisztikai zsebkönyv [Pocketbook of computing statistics].
KSH, Budapest.
1983– 1984. Ft 20. 64p. *Hu.

Δ B – iv Construction

< see also 1575

1586 Epítöipari statisztikai évkönyv [Statistical yearbook of construction].
KSH, Budapest.
1981– 1983 (published 1984). Ft 198. 393p. *Hu.
Note: earlier titles were 'Epítöanyagipari adattár 1974-1975' [Data on the building industry] issued for 1969-1971 and 1973 and for 1976-1980 in 1981.

1587 Lakásstatisztikai évkönyv [yearbook of housing statistics].
KSH, Budapest.
1961/75– 1983 (published 1984). Ft 140. 279p. ISSN 0209-5513. *Hu; separate translations of text in En & Ru also available.

H

Δ C External trade

1588 Külkereskedelmi statisztikao évkönyv [Statistical yearbook of foreign trade].
KSH, Budapest.
1971- 1983 (published 1984). Ft 222. 442p. ISSN 0133-9133. *Hu.
Main tables show detailed statistics of imports and exports arranged by commodities subdivided by countries of origin and destination, and by countries of origin and destination subdivided by commodities.
Note: a version with 80 extra pages containing En & Ru explanations of the tables is also available.

1589 Hungarian foreign trade (Hungarian Chamber of Commerce).
'Kultura', PO Box 149, 1389 Budapest.
1959- quarterly. Ft 9 yr. ISSN 0018-7747. *En, Fr, De, Es & Ru eds.
A few foreign trade statistics are included in the text.

1590 Directory of Hungarian foreign trade companies (Hungarian Chamber of Commerce).
Magyar Kereskedelmi Kamara, PO Box 106, H-1389 Budapest.
1969- 1983/84. not priced. 382p. *En.
TF: the 1983/84 edition, published in 1983, has data for 1982.
Mainly directory information, but with tables on Hungary's imports and exports arranged by main supplier and buyer countries.

Δ D Internal distribution and service trades

< see also 1574

1591 Belkereskedelmi és idegenforgalmi adatok [Internal trade and tourism data].
KSH, Budapest.
1950- quarterly. not priced. ISSN 0139-4533. *Hu.
Quarterly data on internal distribution, tourism, etc.

1592 Belkereskedelmi statisztikai évkönyv [Statistical yearbook of internal trade and tourism].
KSH, Budapest.
1968- 1983. Ft 130. 258p. ISSN 0134-1138. *Hu.
TF: the 1983 edition, published in 1984, has data for 1983 and several earlier years.
Sales and stocks, by quantity and value, for each region of Hungary; also includes prices of food, clothing, durables, fuel and building materials.
Note: a version with 69 extra pages containing En & Ru explanations of the tables is also available.

Δ D - iv Tourism and travel

1593 Idegenforgalmi évkönyv [Yearbook of tourism statistics].
KSH, Budapest.
1969- 1983 (published 1984). Ft 158. 280p. *Hu.
Results of an annual tourist traffic survey, and data on international tourist traffic, internal tourist traffic, excursions and transit traffic, tourists, hikers, accommodation, travel bureaux, etc.
Note: a version with 86 extra pages containing En & Ru explanations of the tables is also available.

Δ E Population

1594 Evi népazámlálás [Census of population].
KSH, Budapest.
1870- 1980. prices of the volumes vary. 37 vols in 76 parts. *Hu.
TF: the results of the 1980 census were published between 1980 and 1984.
Contents:
1. Preliminary data (7 vols).
2. Data for Budapest (3 vols)
3. Data for county Baranya (3 vols).
4. Data for county Bács-Kiskun (3 vols)
5. Data for county Békés (3 vols).
6. Data for county Borsod-Abauj-Zemplén (3 vols)
7. Data for county Csongrád (3 vols).
8. Data for county Fejér (3 vols)
9. Data for county Gyor-Sopron (3 vols).
10. Data for county Hajdu-Bihar (3 vols)
11. Data for county Heves (2 vols).
12. Data for county Komárom (2 vols)
13. Data for county Nógrád (2 vols).
14. Data for county Pest (2 vols)
15. Data for county Somogy (3 vols).
16. Data for county Szabolcs-Szatmár (2 vols)
17. Data for county Szolnok (3 vols).
18. Data for county Tolna (3 vols)
19. Data for county Vas (2 vols).
20. Data for county Veszprém (2 vols).
21. Data for county Zala (3 vols).
22. Demographic data.
23. Occupational data (2 vols).
24. Household and family data I.
25. Data on dwellings I.
26. Occupational data II.
27. Household and family data II.
28. Data on dwellings II.
29. Main data for cities.
30. Main data for villages.
31. Data on population and dwellings by size of settlement.
32. Data on qualified active earners (2 vols).
33. Fertility data.
34. Working place and residence of active earners.
35. Data on the population having third level education.
36. Main data on building estates.
37. Recapitulation of the data collection and processing.

Note: a 'microcensus' was taken in 1984 and publications include 'Az 1984 évi mikrocenzus adatai' (Ft 250. 572p. Hu only. published in 1985) and 'Az 1984 évi mikrozenzus föbb eredményei' (published in 1985. 75p).

Δ E, continued

1595 1980 Hungarian census of population: summary data...
KSH, Budapest.
1984. not priced. 217p. *Hu, En & Ru eds.
Contains the most important results of 15 subject volumes and seven working papers connected with the population census.

1596 Demográfiai évkönyv [Demographic yearbook].
KSH, Budapest.
1957- 1983 (published 1984). Ft 252. 447p. ISSN 0073-4020. *Hu.
Note: a version with 153 extra pages containing En & Ru explanations of the tables is also available.

1597 Magyarország népességének, 1980-2021 [Population projections for Hungary, 1980-2021].
KSH, Budapest.
1980. not priced. 309p. *Hu.

1598 Main results of the 1977 Hungarian fertility, family planning and birth control study.
KSH, Budapest.
1979. not priced. 147p. *En & Hu eds.

1599 Longitudinal marriage surveys in Hungary, 1966-1980.
KSH, Budapest.
1984. not priced. 153p. *En.
Data on family planning, fertility and birth control attitudes of couples married in 1966 and 1974 up to 1977; marriage and family in the 1970s.

Δ E - i Vital statistics

1600 Area life tables of the population of Hungary (Central Statistical Office, in co-operation with the World Health Organisation, Regional Office for Europe).
KSH, Budapest.
1984/85- not priced. 8 vols. *En.
Vol I: (complete life tables) 1970-1973
Vol II: (complete life tables) 1974-1977
Vol III: (complete life tables) 1978-1981
Vol IV: (complete & abridged life tables) 1982
Vol V: Abridged life tables of the population of Hungary 1949-1981
Vol VI: Abridged area life tables of the population of Hungary 1970-1981
Vol VII: Life tables of the population of Hungary by the population size of settlements (completed and abridged life tables) 1980-1982
Vol VIII: Life tables of urban and rural population by countries...

1601 Magyarorszag halandosagi [Mortality tables].
KSH, Budapest.
1900/01-1967/68- 1949-1978 (published 1980). not priced. *Hu.

Δ E - iii Housing

< see 1575

Δ F Social and political

Δ F - i Standard of living

1602 Háztartásstatisztika [Household statistics].
KSH, Budapest.
1959- 1983 (published 1984). Ft 74. 145p. *Hu.
Budgets and income tax of intellectuals, workers and retired people in cities, towns and villages.

1603 A lakosság jövedelme és fogyasztása [The income and consumption of the population].
KSH, Budapest.
1960/63- 1960-1983 (published 1984). Ft 67. 118p. *Hu.
Consumption of food, clothing and consumer durables, and also the relation between consumption and production, foreign trade, stocks, etc.

1604 A fogyasztói árak változása a lakosság rétegeinél [Changes in consumers' prices for the major strata of the population].
KSH, Budapest.
1968- quarterly. prices vary with each issue. *Hu.
Consumer prices and cost and standard of living.

H

Δ F – ii Health and welfare

1605 Egészségügyi helyzet [Public health].
KSH, Budapest.
(annual) 1981 (published 1983). Ft 102. 203p. *Hu.

1606 Társadalmi szolgáltatások, 1960–1971 [Social services, 1960–1971].
KSH, Budapest.
1974. Ft 49. *Hu.

Δ F – iii Education and leisure

1607 Education and cultural conditions in Hungary.
KSH, Budapest.
1950/1980– 1960/1984 (published 1985). 302p. Ft 190. *En, Hu & Ru eds.
Aims to give a comprehensive picture of the cultural developments during the past two decades through the use of statistical data.

Δ G Finance

1608 Ágazati kapcsolatok mérlege... [Input–output tables].
KSH, Budapest.
1972– 1970–1979 (published 1982). Ft 200. 426p. *Hu; separate translations available in En, Ru, De, Fr.

Δ G – iv Investment

< see also 1575

1609 Beruhazasi statisztikai évkönyv. Yearbook of investment statistics.
KSH, Budapest.
1980– 1983 (published 1984). not priced. 195p. ISSN 0230-418. * Hu; En & Ru explanations of the tables.
Note: there is also an edition in Hungarian only (Ft 72. 141p). Earlier information is given in 'Beruházúsi adattár [Investment data], 1950–1977 (Ft 190. 330p. in Hungarian only).

Δ H Transport and communications

1610 Közlekedési, posta és távközlési évkönyv [Transport and communications yearbook].
KSH, Budapest.
1971– 1983. Ft 116. 228p. *Hu.
TF: the 1983 edition, published in 1984, has data for 1983 and also earlier years in some tables.
Summary tables and detailed statistical data on transport of goods, passenger ships, motor vehicle traffic, international vehicle traffic & transport mileage, operating mileage of agricultural vehicles, etc.
Note: a version with 142 extra pages containing En & Ru explanations of the tables is also available.

Δ I Environment

1611 Környezetstatististzikai adatgyüjtemény [Environmental statistics].
KSH, Budapest.
1978. not priced. 209p. *Hu.
TF: with data from 1975.
A data collection of environmental statistics.

1612 Environmental statistics, 1975–1980 (Central Statistical Office).
KSH, Budapest.
1981. not priced. 67p. *En.
A collection of data on land use; the state of soil and the major factors affecting soil; forests and parks; and nature conservation.

1613 Vizgazdálkodási statisztikai zsebkönyv [Pocketbook on water economy].
KSH, Budapest.
1984. Ft 35. 280p. *Hu.

ITALY
ITALIE
ITALIEN
ITALIA

Central statistical office

1614 Istituto Centrale di Statistica [Central Institute of Statistics].
via Cesare Balbo 16, 00184 Roma.
t (06) 46 73. tg ISTAT. tx 610338 Answerback ISTAT.
The Institute is an independent body although, to all intents and purposes, a government institution. Its functions are to collect, compile and publish the general and special statistical data required by the government, to carry out statistical enquiries, to advise on programmes of statistical work, to co-ordinate statistical work of government departments and agencies, to sponsor and encourage statistical studies, etc. Statistical information too detailed for publication, information available prior to publication, and special tabulations can often be supplied on reimbursement of the expense incurred in preparing them. The Institute has been abbreviated to ISTAT, Roma, for entries between 1614-1676.

Libraries

The Istituto Centrale di Statistica (see above) has a library which has a collection of Italian statistical publications, those of other countries, and those of the principal international organisations. The library is open to the public from 9.00 to 12.00, Mondays to Fridays, but is closed on public holidays and during the month of August. The Institute also has a bookshop where its publications are sold.

Libraries and information services abroad

Italian statistical publications are available for reference in Italian embassies abroad, including:
United Kingdom Italian Embassy, 14 Three Kings Yard, London W1. t 01-629 8200.
Australia Italian Embassy, 12 Grey Street, Deakin, Canberra. t 73 3333.
Canada Italian Embassy, 275 Slater Street, Ottawa K1P 5H9. t 232 2153.
New Zealand Italian Legation, 38 Grant Road, Thorndon, Wellington. t 735 339.
USA Italian Embassy, 1601 Fuller Street NW, Washington DC 20009. t (202) 328-5500.

Bibliographies

1615 Catalogo delle pubblicazioni [Catalogue of publications].
An annual sales list issued by the Istituto Centrale di Statistica (see above). Current publications of ISTAT are arranged in subject order with a description of the contents of each title, and a good subject index.

Statistical publications

Δ A General

1616 Annuario statistico italiano [Italian statistical yearbook].
ISTAT, Roma.
1927- 1984. L 15,000. 439p. ISSN 0066-4545. *It.
TF: the 1984 edition, published late 1984, has data for 1983 and runs of earlier years.
Main sections:
Geography & climate - Population - Health & social assistance and security - Education & cultural & various social statistics - Justice - Agriculture, forestry, hunting & fishing - Industry - Building & public works - Transport & communications - Foreign trade - Internal trade - Credit & insurance, money market & finance - Prices - Employment & wages - Consumption - Balance of payments - Public finance - National economic accounts - International statistics.

1617 Sommario di statistiche storiche dell'Italia [Summary of Italian historical statistics].
ISTAT, Roma.
1861/1965- 1861-1975 (published 1978). L 70,000. 226p. *It.
Climate, population, health & assistance, education, culture, social statistics, justice, agriculture and forestry, industry, construction and public works, transport & communications, foreign trade, internal trade, credit and insurance, prices, labour & wages, consumption & sale of foodstuffs, public finance, and national economic accounts.

1618 Bollettino mensile di statistica [Monthly bulletin of statistics].
ISTAT, Roma.
1926- L 7,000 or L 55,000 yr (L 65,000 yr abroad). ISSN 0021-3136. *It.
TF: each issue includes data for the last two complete years, monthly data for the current year to date and the corresponding period for the previous year. Published about two months after the date of the issue.
Climate, population, health & social assistance, education, justice, agriculture & forestry, industry, internal trade, transport & communications, credit, foreign trade, banking, prices & cost of living, labour, public finance, national accounts, & some international statistics. Provincial & municipal statistics for many subjects listed above are given in an appendix. Supplements on particular topics, separately priced, are issued from time to time.

Δ A, continued

1619 Compendio statistico italiano [Italian statistical abstract].
ISTAT, Roma.
1927- 1984. L 10,000. 432p. ISSN 0069-7958. *It.
TF: the 1984 edition was published late 1984.
An abridged version of 1616.

1620 Indicatori mensili [Monthly indicators].
ISTAT, Roma.
(monthly) L 2,000 or 18,000 yr (L25,000 yr abroad). ISSN 0390-6620. *It.
Supplies (in anticipation of normal publications) summary data in the form of tables and graphs on the principal trends relative to the Italian economy, including population, production, foreign trade, prices and wages.

1621 Notiziario ISTAT [ISTAT news].
ISTAT, Roma.
(frequency varies). All 4 series: L 75,000 yr (L 106,000 yr abroad). Subscriptions for single series given below. *It.
Up-to-date statistical information in advance of publication in 'Bollettino mensile di statistica' (1618).
Series 1: Demography and social (L 800 or L 13,000 yr (L 20,000 yr abroad)).
Series 2: Production activity, including foreign trade. (L 800 or L 44,000 yr (L 60,000 yr abroad)).
Series 3: Labour, wages and prices. (L 800 or L 15,000 yr (L 20,000 yr abroad)).
Series 4: Various subjects (L 800 or L 8,000 yr (L 12,000 yr abroad)).

1622 Index: bollettino mensile del Centro Statistica Aziendale [Index: monthly bulletin of the Business Statistics Centre].
Centro Statistica Aziendale, via A. Baldesi 18, 50131 Firenze.
1935- monthly. L 190,000 yr, including supplements. *It.
TF: each issue has data for several months to one month prior to the date of publication.
Tables of index numbers of wholesale prices, consumer prices, labour costs in various types of industry, and construction costs of housing, roads, railways, etc.
Note: Subscription to 'Index' includes monthly 'Lettere d'Affari', 'Previsioni a breve termine' and 'Circolari di aggiornamento'. 'Serie storiche 1928-1977' (L 15,000) provides a time series for 1928 to 1977 of the same data as covered by 'Index'.

1623 Statistiche sul Mezzogiorno d'Italia, 1861-1953 [Statistics on southern Italy, 1861-1953] (Associazioni per lo Sviluppo dell'Industria nel Mezzogiorno).
SVIMEZ, via Porta Pinciana 6, 00187 Roma.
1954. L 7,000. 1100p. *It; summary edition in English.
Territory & climate, population, housing, agriculture & forestry, industry, transport & communications, trade & tourism, credit & capital market, labour & co-operatives, income, consumption, standard of living, finance, education, culture, entertainment, health, relief & welfare, justice, elections, etc.

1624 Rapporto...sul'economia del Mezzogiorno [Report on the economy of Southern Italy] (Associazione per lo Sviluppo dell'Industria nel Mezzogiorno).
SVIMEZ, via di Porta Pinciana 6, 00187 Roma.
1974- 1984. L 14,000. 220p. *It.
TF: has data for 1983 and several earlier years in many tables.
Includes statistical tables in the text and a statistical appendix on economic accounts for Southern Italy, Central-Northern Italy and Italy as a whole; finances of Southern Italy; and socio-economic indicator for Southern Italy.

1625 The Italian economy facts and figures.
Banco di Roma, 307 via del Corso, Roma.
(quarterly) free. *En.
TF: each issue has data for five years and six or seven quarters to the quarter prior to the date of publication.
Includes statistical tables in the text and a section of economic indicators on gross domestic product, industrial production, plant utilisation, employment, consumer and wholesale prices, foreign trade and balance of payments, and financial and money markets.
Note: taken from the Italian publication 'Notizie economiche'.

1626 Congiuntura italiana: rassegna mensile [Monthly review of the Italian economy].
Istituto Nazionale per lo Studio della Congiuntura, via Palermo 20, 00184 Roma.
1958- 11 a year. L 7,000 (L 8,000 abroad) or L 70,000 yr (L 80,000 yr abroad). ISSN 0010-5759. *It.
TF: each issue contains monthly figures and graphs for up to five years to about three months prior to publication.
National accounts, industrial production, internal trade, foreign trade, prices, money and financial market, public finance, employment. Includes detailed graphs as well as statistical tables.
Note: 'Congiuntura estera: rassegna mensile' (1959- L 7,000 (L 8,000 abroad) or L 70,000 yr (L 80,000 yr abroad). ISSN 0010-5740) is a monthly review of other countries compared with Italy.

1627 Quaderni analitici [Analytical notebook].
Istituto Nazionale per lo Studio delle Congiuntura, via Palermo 20, 00184 Roma.
1965- 1984. L 4,000 (L 4,500 abroad) or L 200,000 yr (L 220,000 yr abroad). 8 vols. ISSN 0075-1987. *It
Data on industrial production, internal and international prices, foreign trade, labour force, economic enquiry on industry, quarterly economic accounts, monthly enquiry on the family, etc.

Δ A, continued

1628 Rapporto semestrale [Bi-annual report on the Italian economic situation].
Istituto Nazionale per lo Studio della Congiuntura, via Palermo 20, 00184 Roma.
1961– 2 a year. L 15,000 each issue (English version L 8,000 each issue). ISSN 0392-6761. *It; English version of summary & appraisal (inc. statistical appendix) available separately.
TF: each issue has data for five years, three or four quarters, and 24 months for some tables to two or more months prior to the date of the report.
An analysis of the current Italian economic situation, as well as a forecast of the next 12-18 months' developments. Includes a statistical appendix on use and supply of goods and services, industrial production, exports and imports, balance of payments, retail prices, and labour market.

Δ B Production

Δ B – i Mines and mining

1629 L'industria mineraria: trimestrale di tecnica, economia et diretto a cure della Associazione Mineraria Italiana [The mineral industry: quarterly...of the Italian Mining Association].
Associazione Mineraria Italiana, via Cola di Rienzo 297, 00192 Roma.
1950– quarterly. L 8,000 or L 50,000 yr (L 60,000 yr abroad). *It.
Includes a one-page section of statistics of production of the principal minerals and metals.

Δ B – ii Agriculture, fisheries, forestry, etc

1630 Annuario statistico della zootecnia, pesca e caccio [Statistical yearbook of animal husbandry, fishing and hunting].
ISTAT, Roma.
1949/50– 1983. L 7,000. ISSN 0390-6426. *It.
TF: the 1983 edition, published in 1985, has data for 1983 and some earlier years.
Production of animals and animal husbandry, the fishing fleet, production and sales of fish, and the protection of animals and wild birds.

Δ B – ii(a) Agriculture and horticulture

1631 Censimento generale dell'agricoltura [General census of agriculture].
ISTAT, Roma.
1961– 3rd, 1982. *It.
TF: results of the 1982 census are being published from 1983–. A census is taken every ten years.
Volumes published:
Vol I: Provisional results, by province and communes (L 8,000)
Vol II: Structural characteristics of agricultural business. Part 1: Provinces (separately priced for each province).

1632 Annuario dell'agricoltura italiana [Yearbook of Italian agriculture].
Istituto Nazionale di Economia Agraria, via Barberini 36, 00187 Roma.
1947– 1982. L 40,000. 538p. *It; contents list & summaries also in En.
TF: the 1982 edition, published in 1984, has data for 1982 or 1982/83 and some earlier years.
Includes statistical tables on agriculture and the national economy; public policy and financing in agriculture; agricultural credit; factors of production in agriculture (employment and co-operatives), investments and technical resources, land markets and values); production, processing and marketing of agricultural products (by type of product); Appendix I: statistical data by regions; Appendix II: INEA farm accounting data; Subject index.

1633 Annuario di statistica agraria [Yearbook of agricultural statistics].
ISTAT, Roma.
1954– 1983 (published 1984). L 11,000. c 350p. ISSN 0075-1669. *It.
Data on crop cultivation, food produced, prices, wages, finances, machinery used, consumption of fertilisers, oil, petrol, electricity, etc.

Δ B – ii(c) Forestry

1634 Annuario di statistica forestale [Yearbook of forestry statistics].
ISTAT, Roma.
1948/49– 1983 (published 1985). L 5,000. c 200p. ISSN 0075-1707. *It.
Area & climate, forest area, wood hewn, utilisation of wood, employment in forestry, firewood, wood products. The economic data of forestry, including foreign trade, production and prices, and international comparisons.

Δ B – iii Industry

1635 Censimento generale dell'industria, del commercio, dei servizi e dell'artigianato [General census of industry, trade, services and crafts].
ISTAT, Roma.
6th, 1981. *It.
TF: a census is taken every ten years, the results of the 1981 census are being published from 1983-
Contents:
Vol 1: (in two parts) with provisional data for regions and provinces and for towns (L 20,000 for 2 vols).
Vol 2: 95 fascicules for provinces, 20 for regions, and one of national data on the structural characteristics of industry, commerce, etc. (prices vary; volume for Italy is L 14,000).
Vol 3: Papers on the census (L 11,000).

1636 Annuario di statistiche industriali [Yearbook of industrial statistics].
ISTAT, Roma.
1956- 1982. L 11,000. c 350p. ISSN 0075-1723. *It.
TF: the 1982 edition, published in 1984, has data in most tables to 1982, but sometimes 1980 is the latest, for several earlier years.
A summary of the principal data; and statistical data on industrial production and consumption, machinery installed, prices and salaries, foreign trade, and retrospective data and estimates for the future in the international field.

1637 Le prospettive dell'industria italiana [Prospects for Italian industry].
Confederazione Generale dell'Industria Italiana, viale dell'Astronomia 30, 00144 Roma.
1964/66- 1982/83. L 18,000. 173p. *It.
TF: the 1982/83 edition, published in 1983, has factual data for 1979/1980 and projections for 1982 and 1983.
General consideration; prospective industrial activity, by industry; and indicators of industrial production, investment, etc, for Italy as a whole and for north and south Italy.

Δ B – iii(b) Textiles, paper, rubber, etc.

1638 Industria cotoniera [The cotton industry].
Associazione Cotoniera Italiana, vai Dolomiti 34, 20127 Milano.
1948- monthly. L 45,650 yr (L 62,450 yr abroad). *It.
Includes a section 'Statistiche cotoniere' with data on machinery, productivity, foreign trade, prices, etc.
Note: there is a supplement to the June issues 'Rapporto sulla industria cotoniera italiana', which includes some statistics.

1639 L'industria della gomma [Rubber industry] (Associazione Nazionale fra le Industrie della Gomma, Cavi Elettrici ed Affini [National Association for the Rubber Industry, Electric Cables and Related Products]).
Assogomma, via S Vittore 36, 20123 Milano.
1957- monthly. Available only to interested persons who apply for membership to Assogomma at a special class at an annual subscription of L 500,000. *It.
Includes statistical tables on production, imports and exports of rubber products, as well as statistics in the text.

Δ B – iii(e) Engineering

1640 Notiziario statistico [Statistical newsletter] (Associazione Nazionale fra Industrie Automobilistiche [National Association for the Automobile Industry]).
Unione Italiana Costruttori Autoveicoli, Corso Galileo Ferraris 71, 10128 Torino.
1959- 11 a year. L 21,000 ($20 abroad) or L 210,000 yr ($180 yr abroad) for non-members. *It.
TF: each issue has the most recent information available, up to about three months prior to the date of publication.
Production, exports, imports, and new registrations by makes and models, provinces and regions. Some statistics for foreign countries.

1641 Automobile in cifre [Automobile industry in figures] (Associazione Nazionale fra Industrie Automobilistiche [National Association for the Automobile Industry]).
Unione Italiana Costruttori Autoveicoli, corso Galileo Ferraris 61, 10128 Torino.
1959- 1984 (published 1985). L 15,000 yr (L 23,000 or $25 yr abroad for non-members). *It.
Various tables and statistics concerning production, new registrations, current registrations, imports and exports of motor vehicles. Some statistics of roads, motorways, accidents, consumption and price of motor fuel, taxation, etc. Some data for foreign countries.

1642 L'auto estera in Italia [The foreign motor vehicle in Italy] (Unione Nazionale Rappresentanti Autoveicoli Esteri [National Union of Foreign Motor Vehicle Manufacturers]).
UNRAE, via Aureliana 2, 00187 Roma.
1965- 1983. not priced ('reserved for members of the association). 201p. *It.
TF: the 1983 edition, published early 1984, has data for 1982 and several earlier years. Some general data for 1982 and 1983.
Data on new registrations, imports, exports, production, etc. of passenger cars, buses, trucks and commercial vehicles.

Δ B - iii(e), continued

1643 Bollettino mensile [Monthly bulletin] (Unione Nazionale Rappresentanti Autoveicoli Esteri).
UNRAE, via Aureliana 2, 00187 Roma.
1965- monthly. not priced. *It.
TF: each issue has cumulated data for the year to the date of the issue, and is published three or four months later.
Sales of motor cars; foreign trade of various types of motor car, industrial vehicle, autobus, etc.

Δ B - iv Construction

1644 Annuario statistico dell'attività edilizia e delle opere pubbliche [Statistical yearbook of building and public works].
ISTAT, Roma.
1955- 1980-82. L 14,000. c 200p. ISSN 0075-1804. *It.
TF: the 1980-82 edition, published in 1984, has data for the years 1980 to 1982.
A general summary and detailed statistics on housing and building activity, production of buildings, public works, and indexes of cost, prices and profits. Retrospective data and international comparisons are also given.

Δ B - v Energy

1645 Reports of the Board of Directors, Board of Auditors, financial statements (ENEL).
Ente Nazionale per l'Energia Elettrica, via G. B. Martini 3, Roma.
(annual) 1981. not priced. *En & It eds.
TF: the 1981 report, published in 1982, has data for 1980 and 1981.
Data on power production, electricity sales and customer service, plant development, rural electrification, research and development, personnel, investment, etc.

Δ C External trade

1646 Statistica annuale del commercio con l'estero [Annual statistics of foreign trade].
ISTAT, Roma.
1939- 1982 (published 1984). Vol.1 L 13,000; vol.2 L 20,000. 2 vols. ISSN 0390-6558 (Vol.1) and ISSN 0390-6566 (Vol.2). *It.
Contents:
Vol 1: summary data; statistics of imports and exports arranged by countries of origin and destination subdivided by commodity groups; and transit trade.
Vol 2: detailed tables of statistics of imports and exports arranged by commodities subdivided by countries of origin and destination; and tables of re-imports and re-exports.

1647 Statistica mensile del commercio con l'estero [Monthly statistics of foreign trade].
ISTAT, Roma.
1935- L 15,000 or L 10,000 yr (L 110,000 yr abroad). ISSN 0535-9821. *It.
TF: each issue contains data for its data-month and is published about two months later.
Main tables of imports and exports arranged by commodities subdivided by countries of origin and destination. Other tables show imports and exports to the EEC.

1648 Analisi dell'interscambio commerciale con estero (1970-1982) [Analysis of foreign trade (1970-1982)].
Istituto Nazionale per lo Studio della Congiuntura, via Palermo 20, 00184 Roma.
1984. L 15,000. 189p. *It.
TF: data by months for the years 1970 to 1982.
Includes statistical tables & graphs of imports & exports, by value & by index numbers of quantity, etc.

Δ D Internal distribution and service trades

1649 Annuario statistico del commercio interno e del turismo [Annual internal trade and tourism statistics].
ISTAT, Roma.
1954- 1983 (published 1985). L 14,000. c 550p. ISSN 0075-1782. *It.
TF: has data for 1983 and also earlier years in some tables.
Detailed data on wholesale trade and retail trade, hotel and tourist trade.

Δ D - iv Tourism and travel

1650 Statistica del turismo [Statistics of tourism].
Ente Nazionale Italiano per il Turismo, via Marghera 2, 00185 Roma.
1950- 1979 (published 1982). not priced. 203p. *It.
TF: has data for 1979 and also some earlier years.
Numbers of visitors and motor vehicles entering the country; numbers of hotels, etc., and visitors staying in them; and movement of visitors by regions, nationalities, etc.

I

Δ E Population

< see also 1657

1651 Censimento generale della popolazione [General census of population].
ISTAT, Roma.
1861- 1981. *It.
TF: a census is taken every ten years. Results of the 1981 census are now being published.
Volumes published:
Provisional data (L 5,000)
Vol I: First provincial and community results of population and housing (L 6,500)
Vol II: Structural characteristics of the population and of housing
Part 1: Provincial fascicules (prices for each province vary)
Part 2: Regional fascicules (prices for each region vary)
Part 3: National data: Italy (L 25,000)
Vol III: Population by geographical district and locality.
Regional fascicules (Prices for each region vary).
Note: the 1971 census also has reports on families; sex, age & marital state; professions; education; etc.

1652 Popolazione residente e presente dei comuni: censimenti dal 1861 al 1981: circoscritizioni territoriali al 25 October 1981 [Population resident and present in the municipalities: censuses of 1861 to 1981: territorial limits at 25 October 1981].
ISTAT, Roma.
1985. L 14,000. 391p. *It.

1653 Popolazione e movimento anagrafico dei comuni [Population and migration by municipality].
ISTAT, Roma.
1957- 1981 (published 1982). L 7,500. 278p. ISSN 0075-1863. *It.

Δ E - i Vital statistics

1654 Annuario di statistiche demografiche [Yearbook of vital statistics].
ISTAT, Roma.
1951- 1985. Tomo I (1983) L 14,000; Tomo II (1981) L 25,000. 2 vols. ISSN 0075-1685. *It.

Δ E - ii Labour

< see also 1657

1655 Annuario di statistiche del lavoro [Yearbook of labour statistics].
ISTAT, Roma.
1959- 1984 (published 1984). L 9,000. c 250p. ISSN 0390-6450. *It.
TF: has data for 1983 and some earlier years.
The labour force, labour disputes, etc. Includes a section of retrospective statistics and the current data is given both nationally and regionally.

1656 Rassagna di statistiche del lavoro [Review of labour statistics] (Servicio Italiano Pubblicazioni Internationali S.r.l).
Editore S.I.P.I., viale dell'Astronomia 30, 00144 Roma.
1949- 6 a year. not priced. ISSN 0033-961X. *It.
TF: each issue has long runs of figures for years or quarters to about two months prior to the date of the issue.
The labour force, industrial occupations, return of work in industry, registrations for employment, hours of work, wages, cost of living and prices, social security, cost of labout in industry, labour conflicts, and some international data.

Δ F Social and political

1657 Statistiche sociali [Social statistics].
ISTAT, Roma.
Vol.I [1978]- Vol.II [1981]. L 7,000. c 200p. *It.
Data on population, health, education, labour, justice, incomes, family consumption, housing, recreation and culture, etc.

Δ F - i Standard of living

< see also 391

1658 Indici dei prezzi al consumo per le famiglie di operai e impiegati, 1961-82 [Consumer price indices in workers' families].
ISTAT, Roma.
1984. not priced. *It.

Δ F – ii Health and welfare

1659 Annuario di statistiche sanitarie [Yearbook of health statistics].
ISTAT, Roma.
1955/56- 1981 (published 1984). L 25,000. ISSN 0075-1758. *It.
Ages and causes of deaths, activities of the public and private hospitals and clinics, etc.

1660 Annuario statistico della previdenza e dell'assistenza sociale [Statistical yearbook of social insurance and social welfare].
ISTAT, Roma.
1951/52- 1979-82 (published 1984). L 25,000. ISSN 0075-1790. *It.
Public assistance, institutional and private assistance, insurance, etc.

Δ F – iii Education and leisure

1661 Annuario statistico dell'istruzione [Statistical yearbook of education].
ISTAT, Roma.
1949- 1984 (published 1985). Vol I: L 14,000; Vol II: L 11,000. 2 vols. *It.
Schools, teachers, students, etc. in elementary, secondary and other schools and courses, and also on university education. Retrospective data and international comparisons are included. Vol I: analytical data at national, regional and provincial levels; Vol II: data for towns.

1662 Annuario delle statistiche culturali [Yearbook of cultural statistics].
ISTAT, Roma.
1973- 1984 (published 1985). L 6,000. ISSN 0075-1677. *It.
Production of books, journal publishing, State publishing, and entertainment (theatre, cinema, sports, radio, and other cultural activities).

Δ F – iv Justice

1663 Annuario di statistiche giudiziarie [Yearbook of judicial statistics].
ISTAT, Roma.
1949- 1983 (published 1985). Vol I: L 9,000; Vol II: L 14,000. 2 vols. ISSN 0075-1715. *It.
TF: has data for 1982 and some preliminary figures for 1983.
Vol I: civil proceedings; Vol II: criminal proceedings.

Δ F – vi Elections

1664 Elezioni della Camera dei Deputati e del Senato della Repubblica [Elections to the Chamber of Deputies and the Senate of the Republic].
ISTAT, Roma.
1958- 1979. Vol 1: L 7,500 (1982); Vol 2: L 4,500 (1983). 2 vols. *It.
Vol 1: results by municipality; Vol 2: results confirmed by the Electoral College.

Δ G Finance

1665 Bollettino statistico [Statistical bulletin].
Banco d'Italia, via Nazionale 91, 00184 Roma.
1946- quarterly. not priced. ISSN 0392-467X. *It.
TF: contains data for each month of the quarter of the issue or the latest available, and is published about four months later. The bulletin is up-dated by a number of supplements, each on a particular subject, throughout the year.
Money, credit, the financial market, balance of payments, public finance, etc.

1666 Bollettino economico [Economic bulletin].
Banco d'Italia, via Nazionale 91, 00184 Roma.
1983- 2 a year. not priced. ISSN 0393-2400. *It.
TF: data for five or six years, and quarterly and/or monthly data for one or two years to about a month prior to the date of the issue.
Includes many statistical tables in the articles, and also a statistical appendix with 35 regular tables on finance, banking, money, credit, interest rates, etc. Mainly for Italy, but also includes data for some other countries for comparison.

1667 Il valore della lira dal 1861 al 1982 [The value of the lira from 1861 to 1982].
ISTAT, Roma.
1983. (irregular). L 5,000. 136p. *It.

Δ G – ii Public finance

1668 Annuario di contabilita nazionale [Yearbook of national accounts].
ISTAT, Roma.
(annual) 1983 (published 1984). Vol.I: L 10,000; Vol.II: L 9,000. 2 vols. *It.
Vol I: data on the national accounts of Italy on a national level; Vol II: on a regional level.

I

Δ G – ii, continued

1669 Quadri della contabilita nazionale italiana [Italian national accounts].
Istituto Nazionale per lo Studio della Congiuntura, via Palermo 20, 00184 Roma.
1983– 1983 (published late 1984). L 15,000. 89p. *It.
Three sections: 1. Historical data 1960–1983; 2. 1970–1983; 3. International comparisons.

1670 I conte degli italiani: compendio della vita economica nazionale [National accounts of Italy: survey of vital national economic factors].
ISTAT, Roma.
1967– 1984. L 6,500. 108p. ISSN 0390-6574. *It.
A compendium of the national economy, with statistical tables and graphs in the text, and also an appendix of retrospective data.

1671 Statistiche del bilanci delle amministrazioni regionali, provinciali e comunali [Administration statistics: regional, provincial and urban].
ISTAT, Roma.
1952/53– 1981 (published 1984). L 14,000. *It.
TF: has data for 1980 and 1981.

Δ G – iii Company finance

1672 Dati cumulativi di 1430 società italiane [Cumulated data on 1430 Italian companies].
Mediobanca, via Filodrammatici 10, Milano.
(annual) 1985. not priced. 312p. *It.
TF: has data for 1975 to 1984.
Detailed cumulated financial data of companies within each industry (not data on individual companies), including working and fixed capital, dividends, profit and loss account, etc.
Note: Mediobanca also issues annually 'Indice e dati relativi ad investimenti in titoli quotati nelle borse italiane' [Indices and data on investments in quoted Italian securities] and 'Le principali società italiane' [The principal Italian companies], both of which have financial data on individual companies.

Δ H Transport and communications

Δ H – i Ships and shipping

1673 Annuario statistico della navigazione marittima [Statistical yearbook of shipping].
ISTAT, Roma.
1946/51– 1983 (published 1984). L 8,500. 266p. ISSN 0075-1898. *It.
Voyages, cargoes, passengers, & oil tankers. Includes retrospective data & international comparisons.

Δ H – ii Roads and road transport

1674 Statistica degli incidenti stradali [Statistics of road accidents].
ISTAT, Roma.
1953– 1984 (published 1985). L 11,000. *It.

1675 Autoveicoli circolanti in Italia [Motor vehicles on the road in Italy].
Unione Italiana Costruttori Autoveicoli, corso Galileo Ferraris 61, 10128 Torino.
(annual) 1982 (published 1983). L 10,000 (L 20,000 or $15 abroad to non-members). *It.
Details of sales, models, supply, and technical characteristics.

Δ H – iv Aviation and air transport

1676 Civilavia statistica: nuova edizione [Air statistics: new edition].
Direzione Generale dell'Aviazione Civile, Ministero dei Trasporti, Piazzale degli Archivi, 00144 Roma.
1983. not priced. 414p. *It.
TF: with data for 1983 and some earlier years in some tables and graphs.
Part 1: Analysis of air transport at Italian airports; part 2: Air transport activity by Italian companies; part 3: Financial and economic statistics; part 4: Statistics relative to air transport (i.e., accidents, labour force, numbers of aircraft, aircraft registration).
Note: published in collaboration with ISTAT.

IRISH REPUBLIC
IRLANDE
IRLAND
EIRE

Central statistical office

1677 Central Statistics Office
Earlsfort Terrace, Dublin 2.
An Phríomh-oifig Staidrimh
Ardán Phort an Iarla, Baile Atha Cliath 2.
t 767531. tg Statistics, Dublin.
Set up in 1949 (when it took over the staff and the work of the Statistics Branch of the Department of Industry and Commerce) the Central Statistics Office is attached to the Department of the Taoiseach, directly responsible for the collection, compilation and publication of most government statistics, and it is also charged with the compilation of certain other statistical material which is produced as the by-product of administration. Special statistical compilations from unpublished material may be obtained for a fee. This office has been abbreviated to CSO, Dublin in entries between 1677-1756.

Libraries

The Central Statistics Office (see above) has an extensive library of statistical publications of the Irish Republic, of other countries and of international organisations. It is open to the public from Monday to Friday from 9.30 to 12.45 and from 14.30 to 16.45.
The libraries of Trinity College, Dublin and of University College, Dublin, also have collections of this type of material.

Libraries and information services abroad

The principal statistical publications of the Irish Republic are supplied to the Republic's embassies abroad: including:

United Kingdom	Irish Embassy, 17 Grosvenor Place, London SW1X 7HR. t 01-235 2171.
Australia	Irish Embassy, Arcana Street, Yarralumla, Canberra. t 73 3022.
Canada	Irish Embassy, 170 Metcalf Street, Ottawa K2P 1P3. t 233 6281.
USA	Irish Embassy, 2234 Massachusetts Avenue NW, Washington DC 20008. t (202) 462 3939.

Bibliographies

1678 Statistics of Ireland, by P.J. Meghan.
Published by the Institute of Public Administration, (57-61 Lansdowne Road, Dublin 4) in 1970, it describes the various statistics and statistical publications collected and issued by the Central Statistics Office.

1679 Irish economic statistics, by F. Kirwan & James McGilvray.
Published by the Institute of Public Administration, (see 1678) (2nd ed. 1983. £7.95), this is a guide to sources of collection, presentation and analysis of the main branches of economic statistics of Ireland.

1680 Social statistics in Ireland: a guide to their sources and uses, by James McGilvray.
Published by the Institute of Public Administration (see 1678) in 1977 (£3.50).

1681 A guide to regional statistics...by J.V. Curtin.
Published by An Foras Forbartha, St. Martin's House, Waterloo Road, Dublin 4 in 1972, the guide was compiled as an aid to planners and covers sources of regional statistics on population, employment and unemployment, agriculture, forestry, fisheries, industry, retail trade, inland transport, housing, education, health, tourism, recreation and amenities, income, investment, and public finance.

1682 Sources of economic information: Ireland, edited by Renuka Page.
Published by the Institute of Public Administration (see 1678) in 1985. Lists current documents in 21 subject sections, subdivided by Official publications, other Irish publications, other British publications, and publications of international organisations.

Publications compiled by the Central Statistics Office. 1980. Available free.

Statistical publications

Δ A General

1683 Statistical abstract of Ireland.
CSO, Dublin.
1932- 1981. £11.50. 380p. ISSN 0081-4660. *En.
TF: the 1981 edition, published in 1985, has data for several years to 1980.
Main headings:
Area & meteorology - Population & vital statistics - Agriculture, forestry, fisheries & land purchase - Industrial production (including census of building & construction data) - External trade - Internal trade - Social statistics - Education - Justice & defence - Finance - Transport & communications - Prices - Miscellaneous (wage rates, business organisations, co-operative societies, insurance, patents, etc) - Appendix: Northern Ireland.

Δ A, continued

1684 Irish statistical bulletin.
CSO, Dublin.
1965- quarterly. £1.25 or £5.00 yr. ISSN 0021-1370. *En.
TF: each issue is published about six to eight weeks after the end of the month to which it relates.
Quarterly features include industrial production reports, economic indicators, reviews of external trade, wage rates, employment and unemployment, transport, wholesale and retail price index numbers, agricultural prices and price indexes. Results of the annual census of industrial production are given as they become available and each issue has an index indicating earlier issues which contain the latest information regarding a particular industry or service. Included annually are the annual statement of the balance of international payments, the estimated quantity and value of the agricultural output, detailed statistics of livestock and crops, numbers and expenditures of visitors, index of wage rates, labour statistics, some transport statistics, business of advertising agencies, etc. The census of distribution results and statistics of hire-purchase business appear at intervals.

1685 Folder of Irish economic statistics.
Central Bank of Ireland, Economic Affairs Dept, Curran House, Fleet Street, Dublin 2.
1976- 7th, 1983 (published 1984). not priced. 218p. *En.
TF: has data for several years, quarters and months to 1983.
Demand - personal income expenditure, investment, government expenditure, external trade; prices - agricultural, consumer, trade, wholesale; production - agriculture, industry, services, building and construction; manpower - industry, building and construction, unemployment, banking and finance.
Note: supplemented by the quarterly bulletin of the bank.

1686 Economic series.
CSO, Dublin.
monthly. free. *En.
A printed release covering 75 individual monthly or quarterly series, designed to up-date the figures published each quarter in the 'Irish statistical bulletin' (1684).

1687 Faisnéis ráithiúil [Quarterly bulletin].
Banc Ceannais nah Éireann [Central Bank of Ireland], PO Box 559, Dame Street, Dublin 2.
1944- free (circulation limited/mailing list). *En.
TF: the latest data is included, usually two or three months prior to the date of the issue.
Includes a statistical appendix with data on main monetary indicators, interest rates and exchange rates, banking and other financial institutions, public finances, external trade and payments, economic indicators.
Note: the annual report, 'Tuarascáil bhliantúil', incorporates the Spring issue of the quarterly bulletin.

Δ B Production

Δ B - ii Agriculture, fisheries, forestry, etc

< see also 1683-6

Δ B - ii(a) Agriculture and horticulture

1688 Annual report of the Minister for Agriculture.
Government Publications Sales Office, Molesworth Street, Dublin 2.
1932- 1984. £3.60. 111p. ISSN 0332-1088. *En.
TF: the 1984 report, published in 1985, has data for 1984 and some earlier years.
Includes tables in the text on general economic survey, trade, cattle and beef, milk and dairy products, pigs and pigmeat, sheep and wool, poultry and eggs, horses, cereals and feedingstuffs, root crops, horticulture, grassland and fertilisers, farm improvement, education advise and training, animal health, etc.

1689 Annual review of the situation in agriculture.
Department of Agriculture, Economic Unit, Agriculture House, Dublin 2.
(annual) 1984. not priced. 18p. *En.
TF: the 1984 edition, published early 1985, has data for several years to 1984 (preliminary figures).
Examines developments in agricultural output, costs and incomes which have resulted from volume and price variations in the main commodities.
1. Commodity trends table; 2. Analysis by commodity; 3. Output, income and exports; 4. Appendix: summary of trends in the main agricultural economic indicators.

1690 Management data for farm planning (An Chomhairle Oiliúna Talmhaéichta [Council for Development in Agriculture]).
ACOT National Office, Frascati Road, Blackrock, Co Dublin.
(annual) 1984. not priced. 59p. ISSN 0332-4133. *En.
TF: the 1984 edition was published in December 1983.
Sets out budgets for use in farm planning. Summary data required for farm modernisation scheme; background budgets for main farming enterprises and for horticultural enterprises; poultry costings; etc.
Note: ACOT also issues an annual report which includes statistics of the Council's activities in agricultural education, training and advice.

Δ B – ii(a), continued

1691 Farm management survey (The Agricultural Institute).
An Foras Talúntais, 19 Sandymount Avenue, Dublin 4.
1966/67/68/69– 1983 (published 1984). not priced. 102p. *En.
The aim of the survey is to determine (a) the level of farm outputs, costs and incomes arising in agriculture; (b) the structure of farm outputs and expenditure; and (c) standards of farm performance for various farm types and sizes.

1692 Annual review...of the livestock and meat industry.
CBF – Irish Livestock and Meat Board, Clanwillian Court, Lower Mount Street, Dublin 2.
(annual) 1984. free. 77p. *En.
TF: the 1984 review, published early 1985, has data for 1981 to 1984 and averages for 1970/74 and 1975/79.
Title page reads 'Annual review 1984 and market outlook 1985'. Relates to cattle, beef, sheep and sheepmeat.
Note: also published is CBF weekly intelligence bulletin.

1693 World trade in sheep and sheepmeat...a statistical summary.
CBF – Irish Livestock and Meat Board, Clanwilliam Court, Lower Mount Street, Dublin 2.
(annual) 1984. free. 66p. *En.
TF: the 1984 edition, published in October 1984, has data for several years to 1983.
Irish sheep and sheepmeat statistics (numbers, artificial inseminations, output, prices, exports (by category); EEC numbers, trade, production, consumption; UK numbers, trade, prices; France numbers and trade etc.

1694 World trade in cattle and beef...a statistical summary.
CBF – Irish Livestock and Meat Board, Clanwilliam Court, Lower Mount Street, Dublin 2.
(annual) 1984. free. 85p. *En.
TF: the 1984 edition, published in January 1985, has data for several years to 1983.
Irish cattle and beef statistics (numbers, artificial inseminations, output, prices, and exports (by category); EEC numbers, trade, production, consumption; UK numbers, trade, prices; France numbers and trade; etc.

1695 Facts about the Irish dairy industry.
An Bord Bainne [Irish Dairy Board], Gratton House, Lower Mount Street, Dublin 2.
(irregular) 1985 update. free. 8p. *En.
TF: has data for 1983 and some earlier years.
Includes statistical tables on milk production, milk supply for manufacturing, and production and exports of Irish dairy products.

Printed releases issued by the Central Statistical Office (free) are:-

1696 Agricultural output (annual)

1697 Crops and livestock, June enumeration (annual)

1698 Livestock enumeration in December (annual)

1699 Pig enumeration – April, August (annual)

1700 Distribution of cattle and pigs by size of herd (biennial)

1701 Pigs slaughtered at bacon factories (weekly & monthly)

1702 Production of butter and separated milk powder (weekly)

1703 Agricultural output price index numbers (monthly)

1704 Agricultural input price index numbers (monthly).

Δ B – ii(b) Fisheries

1705 Fisheries annual report (Minister for Fisheries and Forestry).
Government Publications Sales Office, Sun Alliance House, Molesworth Street, Dublin 2.
1934– 1982 (published 1984). £2.20. 70p. *En.
Includes appendices on quantity and value of sea fish landed, comparisons of average price per tonne, imports and exports of fish and fish products, herring fishing, mackerel fishing, craft and personnel engaged in fishing, trawling and seining, finances, etc.

1706 Sea and inland fisheries statistical abstract.
(Information and Statistics Section, Sea Fisheries Division (11), Department of Fisheries and Forestry, Leeson Lane, Dublin 2.
(annual) 1982 (published 1983). free. 31 tables. *En.
Production, utilisation of catch, trade in fish and fishing products, miscellaneous (top ports, fishing power, employment, expenditure, etc).

Δ B – ii(c) Forestry

1707 Annual report of the Minister for Fisheries and Forestry on the Forest and Wild Life Service.
Forest and Wild Life Service, Sullivans Quay, Cork.
(annual) 1982. £1.57. *En.
Includes details of total area held by the Service, stocked area, lands acquired and afforested, expenditures, seed sown and sold, damage to forests caused by fire, timber marked and sold, area of private plantings, grants, etc.

1708 Inventory of woodlands of the Forest and Wild Life Service.
Forest and Wild Life Service, Sullivans Quay, Cork.
1973- free. *En.
Contains inventory forecasts of production from state forests by county, with tables illustrating forest type by area, volume and firewood at national and county level; weighted mean yield class, area and volume of main conifer species at national and county level; tables showing area, volume and firewood by age class of conifer and broadleaved species rated high forest at national level.

Δ B – iii Industry

< see also 1726

1709 Census of industrial production.
CSO, Dublin.
1979- 1981 (published October 1985). £2.50. 164p. ISSN 0790-6080. *En.
Contains full results of the annual census of industrial establishments and enterprises, including activities; numbers of establishments, by sector; production; turnover, etc. In 3 parts: 1: description; 2: results for organisatios with three or more persons engaged; 3: results for organisations with 20 or more persons engaged.

1710 Monthly industrial survey (Confederation of Irish Industry & The Economic and Social Research Institute).
Confederation of Irish Industry, Confederation House, Kildare Street, Dublin 2.
(monthly) not priced. *En.
Business forecasts by industry.

Printed releases issued by the Central Statistics Office (free) are:-

1711 Census of industrial production (annual)

1712 Quarterly industrial inquiry. Employment, earnings and hours of work (quarterly)

1713 Monthly industrial inquiry (monthly).

Δ B – iv Construction

1714 Construction industry statistics.
An Foras Forbartha [The National Institute for Physical Planning and Construction Research], St Martin's House, Waterloo Road, Dublin 4.
1980- 1984. £5.00. 54p. *En.
TF: has data for several years to 1983 or 1984.
Construction industry output, finance, structure of the industry, sectoral statistics (housing, commercial development, building materials, foreign trade), regional and international statistics.
Note: there are also press releases issued by the Central Statistics Office, 'Earnings and hours worked in building and construction' (monthly) and 'Index of employees in building and construction' (monthly).

Δ B – v Energy

1715 Annual report.
Electricity Supply Board, Lower Fitzwilliam Street, Dublin 2.
1927/28- 1982/83 (published mid-1983). not priced, 50p. *En.
Includes an appendix of generation statistics.

1716 Energy in Ireland (An Roinn Fuinnimh [Department of Energy]).
Department of Energy, 25 Clare Street, Dublin 2.
quarterly & annual. free. *En.
TF: each quarterly issue has data for five quarters to the quarter of the issue (provisional figures); the annual issue has data for the year and for several earlier years for comparison.
Includes official figures for sales and consumption of the primary energy sources in Ireland; statistical tables and diagrams of primary energy input, native and imported fuels, peat, peat briquettes, coal, oil, gas and electricity.

Δ C External trade

1717 Trade statistics of Ireland.
CSO, Dublin.
1930– monthly. £0.60 (December issue £1.00); or £7.70 yr. *En.
TF: each issue is published about four months after the end of the month covered and has data for the month, cumulated figures for the year to data, and for the corresponding period for the previous year.
The main detailed tables show imports and exports classified according to commodities. Other tables include trade with principal countries, by principal commodities and different areas, and export and import prices and volume index numbers.
Note: an annual 'External trade statistics' was published from 1923 to 1972.

1718 External trade – provisional figures.
CSO, Dublin.
monthly. free. *En.
TF: each issue is published about five or six weeks after the end of the period covered.
A printed release – a four-page bulletin of imports and exports by commodity section and division, by country for the month, cumulations for the year to date, and similar data for the previous year. Issued in advance of (1717).

1719 Animals exported by sea and air.
CSO, Dublin.
monthly. free. *En.
A printed release.

Δ D Internal distribution and service trades

1720 Census of distribution.
CSO, Dublin.
1951/74– 6th, 1977. 4 vols. *En.
TF: the results of the 1977 census are being published from 1982 onwards.
Coverage is extended to all permanent business premises exclusively or principally engaged in retail or wholesale trade.
Vol 1: Summary results for retailing and wholesale establishments (£1.35); vol 2: Detailed results for wholesale establishments (£2.25); vol 3: Detailed results for wholesale establishments (£1.12); vol 4: the final volume, will give detailed results at the enterprise level.

Δ D – i Wholesale and retail trade

1721 Index numbers of retail trade.
CSO, Dublin.
monthly. free. *En.
A printed release designed to measure short term trends in both the value and volume of retail trade.

1722 Wholesale price index.
CSO, Dublin.
monthly. free. *En.
A printed release which includes output price indices for manufacturing industries.

1723 Hire-purchase and credit sales.
CSO, Dublin.
(annually) free. *En.
A printed release giving the results of an annual enquiry.

Δ D – iii Advertising

1724 Advertising agencies.
CSO, Dublin.
(annual) free. *En.
A printed release giving the results of an annual enquiry into advertising agencies activities.

Δ D – iv Tourism and travel

1725 Estimated numbers and experditure of visitor to Ireland and Irish visitors abroad – summary results.
CSO, Dublin.
(annual) free. *En.
A printed release.

IRL

Δ E Population

1726 Census of population of Ireland.
CSO, Dublin.
1821- 1981. *En.
TF: a census is now taken every ten years, the results of the 1981 census being published from 1981 to 1985.
Contents of main volumes:
Vol I: Population of district electoral divisions, towns & larger units of area (£2.70)
Vol II: Ages and marital status: classified by areas (£4.95)
Vol III: House composition and family units (£2.20)
Vol IV: Principal economic status and industries (£3.45)
Vol V: Religion (£2.00)
Vol VI: Irish language (£2.00).

1727 Population and labour force projections, 1986-1991 (Central Statistical Office).
Government Publications Sales Office, Molesworth Street, Dublin 2.
1985. £1.25. 31p. *En.

Δ E - i Vital statistics

< see also 1683, 1742

1728 Tuarascáil ar staidreamh beatha [Report on vital statistics].
CSO, Dublin.
1953- 1982 (published 1985). £4.70. 215p. ISSN 0075-062X. *En.
The principal source of published information on vital statistics - births, infant mortality, marriages, marriages by religious denomination, deaths, deaths by causes, etc. Data for the whole country and by counties and provinces.

1729 Quarterly report on births, deaths and marriages (Central Statistics Office, from data supplied by the Registrar General).
CSO, Dublin.
£0.90 (£1.25 for December quarter). *En.
Summaries of births, deaths and marriages registered during the quarter in each county and county borough, and the number of deaths from each of the main causes. The December issue includes a summary for the year.

Δ E - ii Labour

< see also 1727

1730 The trend of employment and unemployment.
CSO, Dublin.
1935/36- 1977. £1.00. 75p. ISSN 0075-0638. *En.
An analysis of employment and unemployment, special sections being devoted to particular activities eg. agriculture, industry, transport, building, local authorities.
Note: temporarily suspended; an issue covering 1979-1983 was planned for publication in 1985.

1731 Labour force survey...first results (Central Statistics Office).
Government Publications Sales Office, Molesworth Street, Dublin 2.
1975- 1984 (published mid-1985). £1.50. 48p. ISSN 0790-5866. *En.
Includes data on economic status, occupation and industry in which working for all persons aged 15 years and over.

1732 Labour costs survey, 1981 in industry, distribution, credit and insurance.
CSO, Dublin.
1984. not priced. 31p. *En.
Results of a survey conducted in 1981 covering labour costs (ie. wages and salaries, employers contributions to social security, sick pay, holiday pay, training costs and payments in kind.

Printed releases issued by the Central Statistics Office (free) are:-

1733 Analysis of Live Register, distinguishing males, females, persons aged less than 25 years...(monthly)

1734 Industrial analysis of Live Register (monthly)

1735 Area of residence analysis of Live Register (quarterly)

1736 Age analysis of Live Register (quarterly)

1737 Occupational analysis of Live Register (quarterly)

1738 Particulars of industrial disputes (quarterly).

Δ F – i Standard of living

< see also 392

1739 Household budget survey.
CSO, Dublin.
1951/52– 1980 (published 1982). 4 vols. *En.
A large-scale national survey covering a representative sample of households in both urban and rural areas throughout the country. Vol 1: Summary results; vol 2: Detailed results for all households; vol 3: Results for urban areas and households; vol 4: Results for rural households.

1740 Monthly report (National Price Commission).
Government Publications Sales Office, Sun Alliance House, Molesworth Street, Dublin 2.
1972– £0.75 a copy. *En.
Each issue contains data on price control – analysis of price increases, world commodity prices and currency fluctuations, and the retail price of a particular commodity or commodities. There are usually some statistics in the text.

1741 Consumer price index.
CSO, Dublin.
quarterly. free. *En.

Δ F – ii Health and welfare

1742 Statistical information relevant to the health services (Planning Unit, Department of Health).
Government Publications Sales Office, Sun Alliance House, Molesworth Street, Dublin 2.
(annual) 1984. £2.90. 84p. *En.
TF: has data for 1982 or 1983 and earlier years for comparison.
Population and vital statistics, community protection programme, community health services, community welfare, psychiatric services, services for the handicapped, general hospital services, manpower statistics, expenditure statistics, and eligibility for health services.

1743 Hospital in-patient statistics.
Department of Health, Custom House, Dublin 1.
(annual) 1983 (published early 1985). free. unpaged. *En.
Survey data relating to acutre

Δ F – iii Education

1744 An Roinn Oideachais: tarascáil staitistiúil [Department of Education: statistical tables].
Government Publications Sales Office, Molesworth Street, Dublin 2.
(annual) 1981-82 (published 1984). £2.95. *En.
General education statistics and detailed data on primary, secondary (general), post primary, secondary and comprehensive and community, and vocational education; residential homes and special schools; student aid. Data includes numbers of students, schools, enrolments, teachers, and examinations.

1745 Accounts...and student statistics (An Údarás um Ard-Oideachas [The Higher Education Authority]).
Government Publications Sales Office, Molesworth Street, Dublin 2.
1972/73– 1982/83 (published mid-1984). £1.75. 66p. *En.
Accounts of the organisation for 1982 and statistics of students for the academic year 1982/83, including full-time and part-time undergraduate students and postgraduate students, subdivided by field of study and college; and degrees, diplomas and certificates gained.

1746 First destination of award recipients in higher education: a composite report (An t-Údarás um Ard-Oideachas [The Higher Education Authority].
Government Publications Sales Office, Molesworth Street, Dublin 2.
1982– 1983 (published early 1984). £1.50. 92p. *En.

Δ F – v Religion

< see 1726

Δ F – vi Elections

1747 Turthaí toghcháin agus aistriú na vótaí... Election results and transfer of votes (Central Statistics Office).
Government Publications Sales Office, Sun Alliance House, Molesworth Street, Dublin 2.
General election (November 1982) and (published 1983). £7. 64p. *En.
Bye-elections (March-November 1982).

Δ G - ii Public finance

1748 National income and expenditure.
CSO, Dublin.
1959- 1982 (published 1984). £2.50. 114p. ISSN 0075-0603. *En.
TF: has data for the years 1975 to 1982.
Official estimates of national income and expenditure, capital formation and savings, together with details of the transactions of the government sector classified in accordance with national income accounting definitions.

1749 Annual report of the Revenue Commissioners (Revenue Commissioners).
Government Publications Sales Office, Molesworth Street, Dublin 2.
1923- 1983 (published 1985). £3.20. 191p. *En.
Customs and Excise receipts (including beer, spirits, tobacco products, wine, oils, motor vehicles, betting, and other duties), death duties, stamp duties, wealth tax, capital acquisitions tax, income tax and corporation tax, capital gains tax, value added tax, etc.

1750 Balance of international payments.
CSO, Dublin.
Annual. free.
A printed release (free).

1751 Input-output tables...
CSO, Dublin.
1964- 1975. *En.
Statistical description of inputs and outputs of the different branches of the economic system and their relationships.

Δ G - iii Company finance

1752 Report of the Registrar of Building Societies (Registry of Friendly Societies).
Government Publications Sales Office, Molesworth Street, Dublin 2.
1977- 1983 (published 1985). £1. 25p. *En.
TF: has data for 1982 and 1983.
Data on number of societies; assets; share and deposit transactions and holdings, etc; net new investments; mortgages; investments; etc.

Δ H Transport and communications

Δ H - ii Roads and road transport

1753 Detailed return of motor vehicles registered and licensed for the first time.
CSO, Dublin.
monthly & annual. free. *En.
A printed release.

1754 Motor registration - provisional results.
CSO, Dublin.
monthly. free. *En.
A printed release.

1755 Statistics of omnibus road services.
CSO, Dublin.
monthly. free. *En.
A printed release.

1756 Road freight transport survey...
CSO, Dublin.
1979- 1982 (published late 1984). £1.75. 59p. *En.
A continuing sample survey of road transport freight activity, with data by type of owner and main use of vehicle, unladen weight, length of haul, seasonal analysis, commodity analysis by type of owner, age of fleet analysis, idle vehicles analysis.

ICELAND
ISLANDE
ISLAND
ÍSLAND

Central statistical office

1757 Hagstofa Íslands [Statistical Bureau of Iceland].
Hverfisgata 8-10, 101 Reykjavik.
t 26699.
The government institution in charge of general statistics (except national accounts, monetary statistics, balance of payments, and fisheries statistics). It is also in charge of civil registration in Iceland and operates a national registry which is used for both administrative and statistical purposes. Unpublished statistical data can often be supplied and a fee is generally charged unless the enquirer is a non-profiting-making institution. This bureau has been abbreviated to HI, Reykjavik for entries between 1757-1769.

Libraries

The Hagstofa Íslands (see above) has a small library where Icelandic publications may be consulted, as well as some publications of other countries and of international organisations. The staff speak Icelandic and English.

Libraries and information services abroad

Copies of statistical publications of Iceland are normally available for reference in Iceland's embassies, including:

United Kingdom	Icelandic Embassy, 1 Eaton Terrace, London SW1W 8EY. t 01-730 5131.
USA	Icelandic Embassy, 2022 Connecticut Avenue NW, Washington DC 20008. t (202) 265 6653.

Bibliographies

A duplicated list of publications is issued by the Statistical Bureau of Iceland (see above) at irregular intervals.

Statistical publications

Δ A General

< see also 076, 077, 078

1758 Tölfrædihandbók [Statistical abstract of Iceland].
HI, Reykjavik.
1967- 1984 (published 1984). not priced. 268p. *Is; table headings & contents list also in En.
TF: has data generally for 1983, sometimes only 1981 or 1982, and earlier figures in some tables.
Geography and climate - Population - Labour market - Agriculture - Fishing and fish processing - Manufacturing - Housing and construction - energy - Internal trade - External trade - Transport and communications - Credit and monetary conditions - National accounts - Public finance - Health and social affairs - Justice - Education and cultural activities - Elections.

1759 Hagtidindi [Statistical bulletin].
HI, Reykjavik.
1916- monthly. IKr 400 yr. ISSN 0019-1078. *Is.
TF: each issue has figures for the preceding month, and is published about two months later.
Data on fish catch, foreign trade by countries, imports of certain articles, imports by broad SITC groups, Reykjavik cost of living index, banking statistics, etc.
Note: an abridged version in English 'Statistical bulletin' is also available (1932- quarterly. free to subscribers of the Icelandic edition).

1760 Basic statistics of Iceland (National Economic Institute).
Ministry of Foreign Affairs, Reykjavik.
1983- 1984 (published 1984). not priced. 12 folded pages. *En.
TF: has data for 1982 and 1983.
Data on geography, climate, population, religion, indicators of living standards, elections, education, gross national product, employment, fisheries, farming, foreign trade, transport, energy, wages and prices.

Δ A, continued

1761 Economic statistics quarterly (Central Bank of Iceland).
Sedlabanki Islands, PO Box 160, 121 Reykjavik.
1980- quarterly. not priced. ISSN 0256-193X. *En & Is eds.
TF: each issue has data for several years and months to the latest available.
Short-term indicators, money and credit, non-bank financial institutions, financial institutions, balance of payments, foreign trade, exchange rates, Treasury finances, national accounts, production, employment, prices and incomes.
Note: the Bank also issues an annual report (1978- En & Is eds) which includes a statistical appendix with data on gross national product, price and wage indices, balance of payments, foreign trade, and finance generally.

Δ B Production

Δ B - ii(b) Fisheries

1762 Ægir [Sea].
Fiskifélag Islands [The Fisheries Association of Iceland], Höfn, Ingólfsstræti (PO Box 20), Reykjavik.
1908- semi-monthly. $8.50. *Is; summaries in En.
A magazine which includes running statistics on fisheries. One issue a year is usually dedicated to statistical information for the previous year; including catches and landings of fish, prices, utilisation and export, and fleet statistics.

Δ C External trade

1763 Verzlunarskýrslur [External trade].
HI, Reykjavik.
1912/35- 1984 (published 1985). not priced. 298p. *Is; table of contents & main headings also in En.
Main tables show detailed statistics of imports and exports arranged by CCCN commodity classification subdivided by countries of origin and destination. Other tables include the value of imports and exports arranged by SITC; by country of origin and destination subdivided by SITC groups; imports and exports by customs area; and consumption of coffee, sugar, tobacco and alcoholic beverages.

Δ E Population

1764 Mannfjöldaskýslur [Population and vital statistics].
HI, Reykjavik.
1911/15- 1961-70. Ikr 1000. *Is; table of contents & table headings also in En.
TF: published every ten years. The 1961-70 edition was issued in 1975.
Population, migration, citizenship, marriages, dissolution of marriages, births, adoptions, deaths, mortality and expectancy of life, and population projections, 1975-2000.

1765 Manntal [Population census].
HI, Reykjavik.
1703, 1920- 1960. Ikr 250. *Is.
The final report of the census.

Δ F Social and political

< see also 403, 407

Δ F - ii Health and welfare

< see also 403, 407

1766 Heilbrigdisskýeshur [Public health in Iceland] (Landlæknisembættid [Office of the Director General of Public Health]).
Landlæknisembættid, Langavegi 116, IS-105 Reykjavik.
1923- 1981-82 (published 1984). free. 224p. *Is; contents list & summary also in En.
Climate, population, births and deaths, causes of death, diseases, maternity, induced abortion, accidents, health personnel, hospitals, and immunisation.

Δ F - iv Justice

< see 414

Δ F - vi Elections

1767 Alþingiskosningar [Elections to the Althing].
HI, Reykjavik.
1908/14- *Is; contents list also in En.
Published after each election, with numbers of candidates and elected members, number of voters participating in the election, votes, void ballot papers, etc.

Δ G Finance

1768 Sveitarsjódareikningar [Communal finance].
HI, Reykjavik.
1953/62- 1971/76 (published 1978). Ikr 700. *Is.

1769 Fjármátidindi [Financial review] (Central Bank of Iceland).
Seolabanki Islands, PO Box 160, 121 Reykjavik.
1954- 3 a year. free. ISSN 0015-3346. *Is.
The journal of the Bank which includes some statistics.

L

LUXEMBOURG
LUXEMBURG

Central statistical office

1770 Service Central de la Statistique et des Études Économiques (STATEC) [Central Service of Statistics and Economic Research].
blvd Royal 19-21 (B.P. 304), 2013 Luxembourg.
t 4794-1.
STATEC is responsible for the collection, compilation and publication of statistics of population, agriculture, industry, tourism, retail trade, prices, finance, justice, etc. it is also responsible for censuses and enquiries, national accounts, etc. An annual report on the activities of STATEC is published in 'Bulletin du STATEC'. Unpublished statistical data will be supplied if available.
This service has been abbreviated to STATEC, Luxembourg for entries between 1770-1788.

Libraries

The library of STATEC (see above) is primarily for the personnel of STATEC, but it is available to the public for reference. Its collection includes statistical publications of international organisations, such as ILO, UN, OECD, and EEC, and official statistical publications of about 40 countries as well as those of Luxembourg. It is open to the public from 8.00 to 12.00 and 14.00 to 18.00. The staff speak French, German and English.

Libraries and information services abroad

Statistical publications of Luxembourg are supplied to Luxembourg embassies abroad for reference, including:
United Kingdom Luxembourg Embassy, 27 Wilton Crescent, London SW1X 85D. t 01-235 6961.
USA Luxembourg Embassy, 2200 Massachusetts Avenue NW, Washington DC 20008. t 265 4171.

Bibliographies

1771 Répertoire analytique des publications statistiques et économiques du 19e siècle à ce jour. 7th ed, 1984, issued by STATEC, as No.3 in the series 'Définitions et Méthodes' and up dated with annual supplements; the bibliography includes all publications of STATEC and the organisations it has superseded. STATEC also issues a sales list of its current publications from time to time, and this list is also published in 'Annuaire statistique' (1772).

Statistical publications

Δ A General

< see also 079, 080

1772 Annuaire statistique du Luxembourg [Statistical yearbook for Luxembourg].
STATEC, Luxembourg
1955- 1983/84 (published early 1984). FLux 980. 480p. ISSN 0076-1575. *Fr.
TF: has data for 1982 or 1983 and several earlier years.
Main sections:
Basic statistics - Geography and climate - Population - Economic statistics (national accounts, agriculture - silviculture, industry, crafts, services, money and credit, public finance, income and social security, consumer prices, research, and foreign economic relations (including foreign trade)) - Non-economic statistics (accidents, anthropometrics, education - culture, environment, justice, elections, religion, health, and sport) - International statistics.
Note: retrospective volumes were issued in 1962 and 1973 ('Annuaire statistique retrospective'. 2nd ed., 1973. FLux 800. 538p), and a volume for the war years ('Statistiques des années de guerre (1939-1945): complément à l'Annuaire statistique', 119p) was issued in 1980.

1773 Bulletin du STATEC (STATEC bulletin].
STATEC, Luxembourg
1963- 8-9 issues a year. FLux 100; FLux 680 yr. *Fr.
Results and commentaries on statistical enquiries, studies of economic problems of Luxembourg of general interest. Includes annual reports on the activities of STATEC, building activity, health, elections, motor vehicles, road accidents, agriculture (including the census), consumer price indices, demography, labour, investments, foreign trade, internal navigation, etc.

Δ A, continued

1774 Indicateurs rapides: statistiques [Quick indicators: statistics].
STATEC, Luxembourg.
Monthly (for each series). Series A to H1 FLux 480 yr (without D Special); Series A1 only FLux 240 yr; Series H only FLux 240 yr; Series J only FLux 240 yr; Series D Special FLux 2400 yr. *Fr.
TF: each issue is published less than one month after the end of the period covered.
The various series are:
A1 Consumer price index
A2 Construction price index (half-yearly)
A3 Industrial products price index
B1 Indexes of industrial activity
B2 Indexes of building activity
C Iron and steel - finance - transport - trade - employment and unemployment
D Registration of motor vehicles
D Special New registration of motor vehicles by trade mark
E Births, marriages, divorces, deaths
F Road accidents
G Building authorisations - buildings and houses
H1 Trade balance
H2 Trade with Belgium
J Results of business surveys (industry - building - transport).

1775 Notes trimestrielles de conjoncture [Quarterly notes...].
STATEC, Luxembourg.
1970- quarterly. FLux 100 or FLux 420 yr. *Fr.
Contains analytical commentaries based on the information given in the statistical series, 'Indicateurs rapides' (1774).

1776 Recueil de statistiques par commune [Abstract of statistics of municipalities].
STATEC, Luxembourg.
1967- 2nd, 1984 (published 1984). FLux 650. 157p. *Fr.
Main sections:
Geography and climate
Agriculture - silviculture
Services
Elections
Other statistics.
Population
Industry
Administration and finance
Education

1777 L'économie luxembourgeoise [The Luxembourg economy].
STATEC, Luxembourg.
1951- 1982 & 1983 (published 1985). FLux 480. 377p. ISSN 0070-881X. *Fr.
Includes statistics and statistical tables in the text on economic conditions generally, population and labour, production (agriculture - viticulture - forestry - industry - services), public finance and money market (including social security), prices - wages, investments and consumption.
Note: published as 'Cahiers économiques [Economic papers] no. 68, Series A'.

1778 L'année économique...et perspectives pour... [The economic year and perspectives for...].
STATEC, Luxembourg.
1972/73- 1983/84. FLux 175. 132p. *Fr.
TF: contains data for 1983 and perspectives for 1984.
Includes data on the economy (foreign trade, internal demand, labour, etc), agriculture & viticulture, iron and steel, other industries, energy, crafts and construction, services (transport, trade, tourism, financial services), active population and employment, wages and salaries, consumer prices, finance - money - credit, and balance of payments.
Note: published as No.1/1984 of 'Note trimestrielle de conjoncture'.

1779 Cahiers économiques [Economic papers].
STATEC, Luxembourg.
1951- FLux 300-400. *Fr.
Published in four series:
A - The Luxembourg economy (see 1777) issued annually
B - National accounts of Luxembourg (see 1787) issued annually
C - the results of industrial surveys, i.e., 'Liéconomie industrielle de Luxembourg, 1966-1981'
D - Various studies on agriculture, commerce, population, etc.

Δ B Production

Δ B - ii Agriculture, fisheries, forestry, etc

1780 Le recensement de l'agriculture [Census of agriculture].
STATEC, Luxembourg.
1950- 1983. *Fr.
The results of the 1983 census of agriculture, including data on crops, animals, machinery anc other agricultural installations, were published in 'Bulletin du STATEC' in 1984 and 1985.

L

Δ B – iii Industry

1781 Indices mensuels de l'activité: industrie et construction: années... [Monthly indices of activity: industry and construction: years...].
STATEC, Luxembourg.
1980/84– 1980/84 (published 1985). not priced. *Fr.

Δ B – iv Construction

< see 1781

Δ B – v Energy

1782 Exposé budgétaire de Monsieur le Ministre de l'Énergie... [Budgetary statement of the Minister...].
Ministère de l'Énergie, 19 blvd Royal, L-2449 Luxembourg.
(annual) 1984. not priced. various pagings. *Fr.
TF: has data for 1983 and also earlier years in some tables.
Includes statistical tables in the text on production, consumption, investment, stocks, sales, imports, etc. of coal, oil, natural gas and electric energy. Issued on the occasion of budgetary discussion for the 1985 budget.

Δ C External trade

1783 Statistiques du commerce extérieur de l'Union Belgo-Luxembourgeoise... [Statistics of foreign trade of the Belgo-Luxembourgeoise Economic Union].
INS, Bruxelles, Belgium
1948– monthly. FrB 275 (FrB 310 abroad); FrB 2800 yr (FrB 3250 yr abroad). ISSN 0072-6694. *Fr & Nl eds.
TF: each issue has data for the month and cumulations for the year to date, and is published two or three months later.
Includes principal results; trade by zones; and trade by country, subdivided by commodities, arranged both by the CCCN and the SITC.
Note: all information relates to BLEU, the figures for Belgian and Luxembourg foreign trade not being given separately.

Δ E Population

1784 Recensement de la population [Census of population].
STATEC, Luxembourg.
1900– 1981. FLux 250 each volume. 7 vols. ISSN 0076-1613. *Fr.
TF: a census is taken every ten years. The 1981 census reports were published in 1983-1985.
Contents:
1. Personal characteristics
2. Socio-economic characteristics
3. Internal migration and commuters
4. Households and families
5. Housing
6. Results by territorial subdivision
7. Technical report.

Δ E – i Vital statistics

1785 Statistiques du mouvement de la population [Demographic statistics].
STATEC, Luxembourg.
1904– 1966/82 (published mid-1984). FLux 500. 233p. *Fr.

Δ F Social and political

Δ F – v Religion

1786 Recueil de statistiques religieuses, 1870-1974 [Compendium of religious statistics, 1870-1974].
STATEC, Luxembourg.
1977. FLux 100. 152p. *Fr.

Δ G – ii Public finance

1787 Comptes nationaux [National accounts].
STATEC, Luxembourg.
1950- 1960/80 (published 1982). FLux 350. 185p. *Fr.
TF: the 1960/82 edition was to be published mid-1985.
Statistics and commentaries on the national accounts of Luxembourg.
Note: issued as 'Cahiers économiques, série B'.

Δ H Transport

1788 Les transports et les services annexes aux transports, 1970-1980 [Transport and services connected with transport, 1970-1980].
STATEC, Luxembourg.
1984. FLux 250. 120p. *Fr.
Results of enquiries, including the number of enterprises, employment, investment, VAT, etc.

M

MALTA
MALTE

Central statistical office

1789 Central Office of Statistics.
Auberge d'Italie, Merchants' Street, Valletta.
t 26380. tx 62099 Answerback MOD MLT.
The responsibilities of the Office include the collection, compilation, analysis and publication of statistics on the various demographic, social and economic aspects of Malta, as well as the compilation and publication of the revised electoral register and the conduct of general and municipal elections. Unpublished statistical information can often be supplied on request, and a fee is charged for the service. The office has been abbreviated to COS, Valletta in entries between 1789-1806.

Libraries

The library of the Central Office of Statistics (see above) is primarily intended for the use of employees, but publications of the Office may be consulted at the Royal Malta Library, Old Treasury Street, Valletta, which is a public library.

Libraries and information services abroad

Copies of Maltese statistical publications are available for reference in Maltese embassies and high commissions abroad, including:

United Kingdom High Commission for Malta, Malta House, 16 Kensington Square, London W8 5HH.
t 01-938 1712/6

Australia High Commission for Malta, 261 La Perouse, Red Hill, Canberra. t 95 0273

USA Maltese Embassy, 249 East 35th Street, New York, NY 10016. t (212) 725 2345/8.

Bibliographies

There is no comprehensive bibliography of Maltese statistics, but lists of official statistical publications available for sale are published at irregular intervals in the Maltese Government Gazette.

Statistical publications

Δ A General

1790 Annual abstract of statistics.
COS, Valletta.
1947- 1983 (published 1984). £2. 259p. ISSN 0081-4733. *En.
TF: most tables include statistics for several earlier years.
Main sections:
Area & climate - Population (including migration, nationality, vital statistics) - Justice & crime - Education & culture - Elections & referenda - Labour & prices (retail prices; also includes social security) - Industry - Agriculture & fisheries (including co-operative societies) - Transport & communications - Foreign trade - National accounts & balance of payments - Banking, insurance & public finance - Miscellaneous (government lottery).

1791 Quarterly digest of statistics.
COS, Valletta.
1960- 40c each issue. ISSN 0025-1437. *En.
TF: each issue contains data for several years and the last four or more quarters or months up to the date of the issue, it is published three or four months after the end of the period covered.
Climate, population and vital statistics, health, emigration, passenger movement, transport, external trade, retail prices, agricultural marketing, fisheries, public finance, banking, industry and labour.

1792 Economic trends.
COS, Valletta.
(bi-monthly) not priced. *En.

1793 Economic survey.
Economic Division, Ministry of Trade and Economic Planning, Valletta.
(annual) 1984. 50c. 41p. *En.
TF: the 1984 edition, published late 1984, has data for January-September 1983 and also two earlier years in some tables.
Overall economic performance, demand and output, labour market, incomes and prices, foreign trade and payments, monetary developments.

Δ A, continued

1794 Quarterly review.
Central Bank of Malta, Castille Place, Valletta.
1968- not priced. ISSN 0008-9273. *En.
TF: each issue has data for several complete years and about 24 months to one or two months prior to the date of the issue.
Includes statistics on the activities of the bank, Malta's external reserves, Maltese lire exchange rates, financial survey, money supply, loans and advances, interest rates, government revenue and expenditure, foreign trade, tourist trade, unemployment, and retail price index.
Note: the Annual report of the bank (1984. free. 55p) includes a section of text and diagrams on financial developments, but is mainly concerned with the activities of the bank and other Maltese banks. ISSN 0577-0653.

Δ B Production

Δ B - ii Agriculture, fisheries, forestry, etc

1795 Census of agriculture and fisheries.
COS, Valletta.
1955- 1982-83. 25c. 104p. *En.
TF: the 1982-83 report, published early 1984, has data for 1982/83 or 1983, and earlier years in some tables. The census is taken annually.
Whole-time and part-time farmers, hired labour, holdings and area, cultivation, area and yield of crops, value of crops, sales by organised markets, wholesale price and quantity index, inputs/outputs of the agricultural sector, livestock, milk production, farm machines implements, greenhouses, fishing population, fishing craft and implements, quantity and value of catch.

Δ B - iii Industry

1796 Census of industrial production.
COS, Valletta.
1955- 1982. Summary tables 40c; Report £1.50. 2 vols. ISSN 0076-3462. *En.
TF: the 1982 report was published in 1984, with data for 1980-1982. A census is taken annually.
For each industry, data are given on gross output; employment; wages; size of establishments; materials, fuel and other purchases; capital used; stocks and sales of finished products; etc.

1797 Industrial production statistics.
COS, Valletta.
(annual) 1984. £1.50. *En.

Δ C External trade

1798 Malta trade statistics.
COS, Valletta.
1876- quarterly. £2.00 each issue. *En.
TF: published about six months after the end of the period covered.
Detailed tables of imports and exports for the quarter under review as well as cumulations for the year to date, arranged by commodities subdivided by principal countries of origin and destination. Summary tables of imports, exports and re-exports by country.

Δ E Population

1799 Census of the Maltese Islands.
COS, Valletta.
1842- 1967. *En.
The following reports were published: A 74-page preliminary report. Report on housing characteristics. Report on economic activities (2 vols).

1800 Demographic review of the Maltese Islands (Central Office of Statistics).
Department of Information, Merchant Street, Valletta.
1961- 1983 (published 1984). 30c. 69p. ISSN 0076-3470. *En.

Δ E - i Vital statistics

1801 Vital statistics and statistical information on the incidence and mortality of disease in the Maltese Islands.
Department of Health, 15 Merchant Street, Valletta.
(annual) 1984 (published 1985). not priced. c 100p. *En.

Δ F – ii Health and welfare

< see also 1801

1802 Census of handicapped persons, 1972.
COS, Valletta.
1973. not priced. 38p. *En.

Δ F – iii Education and leisure

1803 Education statistics.
COS, Valletta.
1962/63- 1982/83 (published 1984). 90c. 162p. ISSN 0076-3489. *En.
Government primary schools, government secondary schools, technical education, private schools, and university. Data include numbers of pupils/students, classes, new pupils, school leavers, absences, schools, health services, teaching staffs, premises, etc.

Δ G Finance

Δ G – ii Public finance

1804 Malta financial report.
The Treasury, Floriana, Malta.
1960/61- 1983 (published 1984). £1.25. 200p. *En.
TF: has data for the financial year 1982/83.

1805 National accounts of the Maltese Islands.
COS, Valletta.
1955- 1983 (published early 1984). 75c. 55p. ISSN 0077-295X. *En.
TF: has detailed data for 1983 and summary tables for 1974 to 1983.
Industrial input and output, personal sector, government sector, capital formation, and balance of payments.

Δ H Transport and communications

1806 Shipping and aviation statistics.
COS, Valletta.
1956/57- 1983 (published 1984). 40c. 123p. ISSN 0080-9268. *En.
Number and net tonnage of vessels entering and clearing harbour, seamen engaged and discharged, and cargo loaded and unloaded; data for aviation, including number of aircraft, tonnage of cargo arriving and departing, and post office airmail; data on passengers and emigrants, all subdivided by nationality, etc; and data for tourism, including arrivals and departures by sea and air, average length of stay, subdivided by sex and age groups, nationality, etc.

MONACO
MONAKO

Central statistical office

1807 Service des Statistiques [Statistical service].
4 rue des Iris, Monte Carlo.
t 30 19 21.
The Service, which is under the authority of the Minister of State, collects information on various aspects of the economic life of the Principality and of the population. Information is supplied on request when available.

Statistical publications

Δ A General

< see also 1038a

1808 Statistiques annuelles [Annual statistics].
Service des Statistiques, 4 rue des Iris, Monte Carlo.
1967- 1973. not priced. 103p. *Fr.
TF: the 1973 edition, published in 1974, has data for 1971, 1972 and 1973.
Main sections:
Climate - Population - Health - Education - Employment - Internal trade - Foreign trade - Transport - Energy and water - Communication - Motor vehicles (registration, traffic, etc) - Tourism (including gaming & numbers of visitors to museums & gardens) - Miscellaneous (including numbers of ships & boats, sales of newspapers & journals, sales of tobacco, visitors to cinemas, social welfare, etc).

Δ C External trade

Note: foreign trade returns for the Principality are included in the statistics of France and are not published separately in detail. Statistics of imports and exports of Monaco can only be obtained from the Direction Géneral des Douanes et Droits Indirect, 8 rue de la Tour-des-Dames, 75436 Paris Cedex 09, France.

Δ E Population

1809 Recensement général de la population, 1982 [Census of population].
Mairie de Monaco, Service des Statistiques et des Etudes Economiques, Monte Carlo, Monaco.
1982. not priced. 114p. *Fr.

N

NORWAY
NORVEGE
NORWEGEN
NORGE

Central statistical office

1810 Statistisk Sentralbyrå [Central Bureau of Statistics].
0033 Skijyurgaha 15, (P.B. 8131 DEP), Oslo 1.
t (472) 41 38 20 tg
The Bureau is divided into three departments. The Statistical Department collects and processes statistics in the various subject fields, and also has an Interview Survey Division with almost 400 local agents; the Research Department does econometric analysis and deals with national accounts statistics; and the Production Department has a Central Register Division, and also deals with system development and programming, machine operations and printing, etc. Unpublished information can be supplied and a charge is made when a certain amount of work has to be done; if special machining is needed, the economic rate is charged. The bureau has been abbreviated to SS, Oslo for entries between 1810-1905.

Libraries

The library of Statistisk Sentralbyrå (see above) has a comprehensive collection of national, regional and international statistical publications. It is open from 8.00 to 15.30 September to 14 May, and from 8.00 to 15.00 from 15 May to 14 September. The staff speak Norwegian and English.

Libraries and information services abroad

Statistical publications of Norway are available for reference in the Norwegian embassies in the main countries, including:

United Kingdom Royal Norwegian Embassy, 25 Belgrave Square, London SW1X 8DQ. t 01-235 7151.
Canada Royal Norwegian Embassy, Royal Baule Centre, 90 Sparles Street, Suite 932, Ottawa, ONT KIP 5B4. t 237 5030.
USA Royal Norwegian Embassy, 2720 34th Street NW, Washington DC 20008. t 333 6000.

Bibliographies

1811 Veiviser i norsk statistikk [Guide to Norwegian statistics] (Statistisk Sentralbyrå).
A bibliography of Norwegian official statistics classified by subject, and covering all statistics prepared by the statistical office and other government agencies. Editions have been published at intervals since 1963 (latest 1985), and it is available free from the statistical office or Norwegian booksellers. *No, En.

1812 Fortegnelse over Norges offisielle statistikk og andre publikasjoner utgitt av Statistisk Sentralbyrå 1828-1976 [Catalogue of Norwegian official statistics and other publications published by the Central Bureau of Statistics] (Statistisk Sentralbyrå).
Contains chronological and subject listings with author and title indexes. The 3rd edition was published in 1978 and costs NKr 13 from the Central Bureau of Statistics. *No, En.

1813 Bibliografi over Norges offentlige publikasjoner [Bibliography of Norway's official publications] (Universitetsbibliotek, Oslo).
An annual publication issued by the University of Oslo, which includes official statistical publications.

1814 Publikasjoner fra Statistisk Sentralbyrå [Publications from the Central Bureau of Statistics].
An annual sales list. *No, En.

Statistical publications

Δ A General

< see also 076, 077, 078

1815 Statistisk årbok [Statistical yearbook].
SS, Oslo.
1880- 1985. NKr 40. 517p. ISSN 0078-1932. *No, En.
TF: has data for 1984 or 1983 and various earlier years.
Main sections:
Geography & climate - Population - Health - Labour market - National accounts & balance of payments - Agriculture, forestry & hunting - Fishing, sealing & whaling - Oil extraction, mining & quarrying, manufacturing - Electricity & gas supply, energy - Construction - External trade - Internal trade, community & private services - Water transport - Other transport & communication - Public finance - Money & credit - Prices - Wages & salaries - Income & property - Consumption - Dwellings & housing conditions - Social conditions - Justice & crime - Education & research - Culture - Holidays & out-door life - Elections - Miscellaneous (climate & population; coal mining; post, telegraph & telephone services) - International survey.

Δ A, continued

1816 Historisk statistikk [Historical statistics].
SS, Oslo.
1914- 1978. NKr 30. 325p. *No, En.
TF: issued at ten-yearly intervals, the 1978 edition, has data from the earliest figures available tc 1975.
A retrospective volume with the same subject coverage as the 'Statistisk årbok' (1815).

1817 Statistisk månedshefte [Monthly bulletin of statistics].
SS, Oslo.
1882- NKr 15 or NKr 150 yr. ISSN 0029-3636. *No; contents list also in En, De.
TF: each issue has data for several years and at least 24 months up to about two months prior to month of issue.
The labour market, national accounts, balance of payments, agricultural production, fishing, industrial production, orders, investments, building, external trade, internal trade, stocks, transport & communications, public finance, money & credit, prices, wages, social conditions, justice & crime, and some international statistics. Also tables published quarterly or semi-annually on population, hours of work, stocks, shipping and prices.

1818 Statistisk ukehefte [Weekly bulletin of statistics].
SS, Oslo.
(weekly) NKr 96 yr. ISSN 0550-0567. *No.
The main results from currently produced statistics, including periodic as well as occasioral surveys.

1819 Nye distriktstall [New district figures].
SS, Oslo.
(monthly) NKr 8 or NKr 70 yr. *No.
Presents results from currently produced regional statistics. There is one publication each month for each county, except Oslo and Akershus which are presented together. Includes some data on a municipal level.

1820 Økonomisk utsyn... [Economic survey] (Statistisk Sentralbyrå).
Universitetsforlaget, Oslo.
1946- 1984. NKr 30. 104p. ISSN 0078-1924. *No; summary in En.
TF: the 1984 edition, published mid-1985, has data for several years to 1984.
International economic situation, economic policy, production, labour market, investments, consumption, prices and wages, incomes, balance of payments & competitiveness, prospects, and national accounts.

1821 Economic bulletin.
Norges Bank, PO Box 336, Oslo 1.
1930- quarterly. free. ISSN 0029-1676. *En.
TF: each issue has long runs of annual and quarterly (or monthly) figures up to two or three months prior to the date of the issue.
Includes a statistical annex on banking, insurance, money and credit, foreign trade, national accounts, selected economic indicators, etc.

1822 Økonomiske analyser [Economic analysis].
SS, Oslo.
c 10 a year. not priced. *No.
Quarterly and yearly survey results and analysis of developments in the Norwegian and international economy; preliminary national accounts figures on a quarterly and annual basis; and also short articles on research being carried out by the Central Bureau of Statistics.

Δ B Production

1823 Industristatistikk [Manufacturing statistics].
SS, Oslo.
1885- 1983 (published 1985). NKr 35 each volume. 2 vols. Vol I: ISSN 0800-580X; Vol II: ISSN 0800-5818. *No; contents list & table headings also in En.
Vol I: data on establishments, persons engaged & compensation of employees; gross value of production, cost of goods & services consumed, and value added; capital formation, fire insurance & stocks; principal figures by county/municipality. Vol II: data on consumption of fuel & electricity in large establishments, by industry major group; production of selected commodities in large establishments; commodities produced in large establishments; consumption of principal raw materials in large establishments; and oil extraction.

Δ B - ii Agriculture, fisheries, forestry, etc

Δ B - ii(a) Agriculture and horticulture

1824 Jordbruksstatistikk [Agricultural statistics].
SS, Oslo.
1937- 1983 (published 1984). NKr 18. 120p. ISSN 0078-1894. *No, En.
TF: has data for 1983 and several earlier years.
Area, number of holdings and number of properties; yield; livestock, livestock production, etc; dairying; food consumption; means of production; personal holders (age, income combinations, etc), labour input); prices and working results.

Δ B – ii(a), continued

1825 Landbruksteljing [Census of agriculture and forestry].
SS, Oslo.
1907– 1979. NKr 20 each volume. 8 vols. *No, En.
TF: a census is taken every ten years. The results of the 1979 census were published between 1982 and 1985.
Contents:
Vol 1: Type of ownership, area resources.
Vol 2: Occupation – age – vocational training
Vol 3: Investments – machines – buildings
Vol 4: Agriculture – area utilisation
Vol 5: Livestock and poultry
Vol 6: Horticulture
Vol 7: Forestry
Vol 8: General survey (NKr 35).

1826 Arealbruksstatistikk for tettsteder [Land-use statistics for urban settlements].
SS, Oslo.
1982. NKr 15. 161p. *No, En.

1827 Veterinærstatistikk [Veterinary statistics].
SS, Oslo.
1960/66– 1983 (published 1985). NKr 25. 92p. ISSN 0303-6561. *No; table of contents also in En.
Data on veterinary treatments of animal diseases, public meat inspection, etc.

Δ B – ii(b) Fisheries

1828 Fiskeristatistikk [Fishery statistics].
SS, Oslo.
1868– 1983 (published 1984). NKr 35. 179p. ISSN 0333-3728. *No, En.
Data on fishermen and fishing boats, survey of stocks, the catch, processing, exports and imports, economic results, aggregate account, subsidies, etc.

1829 Fiskeritelling [Fishery census].
SS, Oslo.
1948– 1971. NKr 9 each vol. 4 vols. *No; contents list & table headings also in En.
TF: a census is taken every ten years.
Content:
Vol 1: number of fishermen and participation in fishing and other work.
Vol 2: fishing boats and the use of the boats for fishing and other trades.
Vol 3: fishing geat and sheds, ownership of the gear and fishing boats, economic data on the fishing boats, etc.
Vol 4: general summary.
Note: 'Fiskerstatistikk' [Survey of fishermen], last issued 1975, was a sample survey.

1830 Lakse- og sjøaurefiske [Salmon and sea trout fisheries].
SS, Oslo.
1963– 1983 (published 1984). NKr 18. 97p. ISSN 0550-0419. *No, En.
Data on caught salmon and sea trout, classified according to sea fishing and river fishing; special tables for drift net fishing; data on fishing rights and fishing licences; exports and imports of salmon and sea trout.

Δ B – ii(c) Forestry

1831 Skogstatistikk [Forestry statistics].
SS, Oslo.
1952– 1983 (published 1985). NKr 30. 108p. ISSN 0468-8155. *No, En.
TF: has data for 1983 and also some earlier years in some tables.
Forest areas and forest properties; growing stock and annual increment; production; forest regeneration; forest roads and technical equipment; labour force in forestry; prices and economy; forest and outfield fires; sample survey of forestry; hunting.

1832 Skogavvirkning til salg og industriell produksjon [Roundwood cut for sale and industrial production].
SS, Oslo.
1965/66– 1983/84 (published 1985). NKr 25. 52p. ISSN 0800-3637. *No, En.
Detailed figures by municipality on assortment, species of tree, and buyer group.

Δ B – ii(d) Hunting

1833 Jakstatistikk [Hunting statistics].
SS, Oslo.
1964– 1983 (published 1984). NKr 25. 62p. *No, En.
Game Fund, shooters, royal game hunting, small game shooting, bounties paid for predators killed, and other shooting and trapping.
Note: a historical volume 'Jakstatistikk, 1846-1988' was also issued.

Δ B - iii Industry

1834 Alkohol og andre rusmiddel [Alcohol and drugs].
SS, Oslo.
1913- 1983 (published 1984). NKr 12. 43p. ISSN 0332-7965. *No, En.
Licences for sale of alcoholic beverages; consumption; prices of alcohol; public care of alcoholics. Also data in connection with use of alcohol and drug drawn from the criminal and social statistics.

1835 Annual review.
Papirindustriens Sentralforbund [Norwegian Pulp and Paper Association], Drammensveien 30 (Postboks 2446 Solli), 0202 Oslo 2.
(annual) 1983. not priced. 19p. *En & No eds.
TF: has data for 1978 to 1982.
Chapters on markets, production, electricity prices & wood supply, include statistical tables & charts.

Δ B - iv Construction

1836 Bygge- og anleggsstatistikk [Construction statistics].
SS, Oslo.
1966- 1983 (published 1985). NKr 25. 76p. *No; table headings also in En.
General data; gross value of production; input; investment; persons engaged, salaries, wages, social expenses; ownership; figures by county; machinery stock; and one-man establishments.

1837 Byggearealstatistikk [Building statistics].
SS, Oslo.
1967- 1982 (published 1984). NKr 25. 94p. ISSN 0550-7162. *No; table headings also in En.
Building completed and started during the year, buildings under construction at the end of the year, by municipality, industry, type of dwelling, etc.

Δ B - v Energy

1838 Energistatistikk [Energy statistics].
SS, Oslo.
1970/77- 1983 (published 1984). NKr 18. 87p. *No, En.
A collection of statistics, mostly already available in other publications, including total energy consumption, electricity, crude oil, natural gas, petroleum products, coal and coke, prices and change in prices in different forms of energy.

1839 Oljevirksomhet [Oil activity].
SS, Oslo.
1977- 1984 (published 1985). NKr 25. 87p. ISSN 0333-2101. *No, En.
TF: has data for earlier years in some tables.
Comprehensive, detailed survey of the oil activities on the Norwegian part of the continental shelf. Principal figures for the group's crude petroleum, natural gas production and oil-well drilling; balance sheet for crude oil and natural gas; surveys, explorations and finds.

1840 Elektrizitetsstatistikk [Electricity statistics].
SS, Oslo.
1957- 1983 (published 1985). NKr 30. 87p. ISSN 0333-3799. *No, En.
Data on the number of establishments; capacity of installed machinery; transmission system and distribution network; production and consumption of electricity; value added; fixed capital formation; and also information on gas supply.

Δ C External trade

1841 Utenrikshandel [External trade].
SS, Oslo.
1884- 1984 (published 1985). NKr 50 each vol. 2 vols. ISSN 0078-1940. *No; table headings also in En.
Vol I: detailed tables of imports and exports arranged by the CCCN classification subdivided by countries of origin and destination; and by countries subdivided by commodities. Vol II: trade by commodities (SITC Rev.2), countries and customs districts, mode of transport, etc.

1842 Månedsstatistikk over utenrikshandelen [Monthly bulletin of external trade].
SS, Oslo.
1913- monthly. NKr 15 or NKr 120 yr. *No, En.
TF: each issue, containing data for that month and cumulated figures for the year to data, is published about six weeks after the end of the month.
Main tables show detailed statistics of imports and exports arranged by CCCN commodity classification. Other tables include foreign trade of ships, oil platforms and exports of crude oil and natural gas, quarterly index numbers of external trade, etc.

N

Δ D Internal distribution and service trades

1843 Bedriftsstelling... [Census of establishments].
SS, Oslo.
1935- 1974. 3 vols. *No, En
Contents:
Vol 1: Varehandel [Wholesale and retail trade] (NKr 13).
Vol 2: Tjeneskeyting m.v. [Service trade, etc] (NKr 11)
Vol 3: Oversikt [Summary] (NKr 13).
Size of establishments and trades, business done, investments, persons engaged, salaries and wages, etc.

Δ D – i Wholesale and retail trade

1844 Varehandelsstatistikk [Wholesale and retail trade statistics].
SS, Oslo.
1966- 1982. NKr 18. 150p. ISSN 0078-1959. *No, En.
TF: the 1982 edition, published in 1984, has data for 1982.
Establishments, employment and sales by major industry group by size; by trade district, municipality, county, etc; persons engaged and wages; statistics of accounts; and some current economic indicators (retail sales, retail price index, consumer price index).

Δ D – ii Service trades

1845 Tjenesteyting...forretningsmessig tjenesteyting, utleie av maskiner og utstyr, renovasjon og reinjøring, vaskeri- og renserivirksomhet [Services...business services, machinery and equipment rental and leasing, sanitary and similar services, laundries, laundry service and cleaning and dyeing plants].
SS, Oslo.
1979- 1982 (published 1984). NKr 18. 54p. ISSN 0800-4056. *No, En.

1846 Bilverkstader m.v...reparasjon kjørety hushaldningsapparat m.v. [Car repair shops, etc...repair vehicles, household apparatus, etc].
SS, Oslo.
1978- 1982 (published 1984). NKr 12. 39p. *No, En.
Information on establishments, persons engaged, wages, value of production, gross fixed capital formation, etc for the whole main industry group.

Δ D – iv Tourism and travel

1847 Reiselivsstatistikk [Statistics on travel].
SS, Oslo.
1977- 1983 (published 1984). NKr 18. 130p. ISSN 0333-208X. *No; contents list & table headings also in En.
A survey of available statistics, including hotel operations; camping site operations; other lodging places; hotels and boarding houses - total; arrivals and travel currency; holiday surveys; passengers carried on regular services by ships; passengers carried by air; and travel agencies.

1848 Ferieundersøkelsen [Holiday survey].
SS, Oslo.
1968- 5th, 1982 (published 1983). NKr 30. 102p. *No; contents list also in En.

Δ E Population

1849 Folke- og boligtelling [Population and housing census].
SS, Oslo.
1769- 1980. from NKr 20 to NKr 50 each vol. *No, En.
TF: a census is taken every ten years. 1980 census results being issueed from 1982-.
Contents:
Vol I: Housing; Vol II: Emloyment statistics; Vol III: Families and households.
Separate volumes for each municipality and each county, and a summary volume for the country of these volumes.
Note: a volume on education is to be published.

1850 Folkemengen etter alder og ekteskapelig status 31 Desember... [Population by age and marital status at 31 December...].
SS, Oslo.
1970- 1982 (published 1985). NKr 30. 141p. ISSN 0550-7170. *No, En.

1851 Framskriving av folkemengden...regionale tall [Population projections...regional figures].
SS, Oslo.
...to 1990- 1982-2025 (published 1982). NKr 35. 198p. *No, En.
Projected population figures by age, sex and regions, for the whole country to 2025 and for counties and municipalities to 2000.
Note: tables for trade districts are not published but are available from Statistisk Sentralbyrå.

N

Δ E, continued

1852 Familiestatistikk [Family statistics].
SS, Oslo.
1974- 4th, 1982 (published 1983). NKr 18. 99p. ISSN 0332-7957. *No; contents list & table headings also in En.
TF: issued at irregular intervals.
Families by type, numbers of children, one-parent families, single persons, etc., by county, region and for the country as a whole.

1853 Historiske tabeller over folkemengde, giftermål, 1911-1976 [Historical tables on population, marriages and deaths, 1911-1976].
SS, Oslo.
1978. NKr 13. 135p. *No, En.

1854 Folketallet i kommunane [Population in municipalities].
SS, Oslo.
1965/67- 1983-1985. NKr 25. 54p. ISSN 0550-0338. *No, En.
TF: the 1983-1985 edition, published in 1985, has data as at 1st January 1983, 1984 and 1985.
Note: a retrospective volume 1951 to 1980 is also available.

1855 Flyttestatistikk [Migration statistics].
SS, Oslo.
1967- 1984 (published 1985). NKr 25. 86p. ISSN 0550-8592. *No, En.
Data on registered internal migration and on immigration and emigration.

Δ E - i Vital statistics

1856 Folkemengdens bevegelse [Vital statistics and migration statistics].
SS, Oslo.
1880- 1983 (published 1984). NKr 25. 101p. *No, En.
Marriages, births, deaths and migration.

1857 Dodsårsaker [Causes of death].
SS, Oslo.
1964- 1982 (published 1984). NKr 25. 97p. *No, En.
Detailed tables on causes of death.

1858 Regionaldødelighet [Regional mortality].
SS, Oslo.
1969/72- 1976-1980 (published 1983). NKr 15. 100p. *No, En.

Δ E - ii Labour

1859 Arbeidsmarkedstatistikk [Labour market statistics].
SS, Oslo.
1967- 1984 (published 1985). NKr 35. 178p. ISSN 0078-1878. *No, En.
TF: has data for 1984 and 1983.
Results from the quarterly labour force sample surveys; employee statistics; employment statistics for central government employees and employees in publicly maintained schools; statistics on unemployment, vacancies, applicants for work, placements, curtail of operations, labour conflicts and various government measures to promote employment.

Δ E - iii Housing

< see also 1849

1860 Boforholdsundersøkelsen [Survey of housing conditions].
SS, Oslo.
1971- 2nd, 1981 (published 1983). NKr 45. 153p. *No, En.
Data on the dwelling (type of house, year of construction, size, space, etc), tenure status and means of acquiring dwelling, housing expenditure by owner or tenant, local environment, communications and service institutions.

Δ F Social and political

1861 Sosialt utsyn [Social survey].
SS, Oslo.
1974- 4th, 1983. NKr 24. 361p. ISSN 0333-0621. *No; contents list, table headings & summary also in En.
TF: survey is taken every third year. The results of the 1983 survey were published in 1984.
A review of the most existing statistical information on individuals and social conditions in Norway. Main emphasis is on time series, and subjects covered include population, health, education, housing, employment, income, social services, crimes, personal contacts and social relations, private consumption, leisure and vocations, and cultural participation.

Δ F, continued

1862 Sosialstatistikk [Social statistics].
SS, Oslo.
1977- 1983 (published 1985). NKr 30. 93p. ISSN 0333-2055. *No, En.
Data on kindergartens, child welfare, adoptions, social care, home-help services and old age care.

Δ F - i Standard of living

< see also 396

1863 Forbruksundersøkelse [Survey of consumer expenditure].
SS, Oslo.
1958- 1980-1982 (published 1984). NKr 24. 242p. *No, En.
Average consumer expenditure in private households, calculated in 1982 prices.

1864 Inntektsstatistikk [Income statistics].
SS, Oslo.
1967- 1979. NKr 15. 190p. *No, En.
TF: published at irregular intervals, the 1979 edition was published in 1982 and has data for 1979.
Distribution of personal income earners, households and corporations, by size of income and composition of income. Compiled from tax assessments.

1865 Lønnsstatistikk [Wage earners].
SS, Oslo.
1875- 1983 (published 1984). NKr 30. 108p. *No, En.
Note: this title is supplemented by special publications for various groups of wage-earners - agriculture and horticulture, mining and manufacturing, wholesale and retail trade, bank employees, insurance activity, publicly maintained schools, ocean transport, coasting trade, local government employees, hotels and restaurants, central government employees, business services & business, professional & labour associations.

1866 Lønnstelling for arbeidere i bergverksdrift og industri... [Wage census for workers in mining and manufacturing].
SS, Oslo.
1960- 4th, 3rd quarter of 1984 (published 1985). NKr 40. 172p. *No; summary, table of contents & table headings also in En.

1867 Levekårsundersøkelsen [Survey of level of living].
SS, Oslo.
1973- 1983 (published 1985). NKr 35. 230p. ISSN 0800-7233. *No, En.
Findings from the survey on changes in level of living, income and property, wages & material goods, employment, physical working environment, organisational working conditions, unpaid work, health, housing conditions, leisure activities, social relations, violence and security, and access to service.

1868 Lønninger og inntekter [Wages, salaries and income].
SS, Oslo.
(annual) 1982 (published 1985). not priced. 101p. *No, En.

1869 Formuesstatistikk [Property statistics].
SS, Oslo.
1962- 1979 (published 1982). NKr 30. 108p. *No, En.
TF: has data for 1979 and some earlier years.
Distribution of personal income earners, households and corporations by the size of the property.

Δ F - ii Health and welfare

< see also 403, 407

1870 Helsestatistikk [Health statistics].
SS, Oslo.
1962- 1983 (published 1985). NKr 30. 133p. ISSN 0332-7906. *No, En.
Health personnel and health institutions; operating expenditure and receipts in somatic hospitals and nursing homes; home-nursing; health condition; legal abortions, births and perinatal mortality; general mortality and causes of death.

1871 Helseinstitusjoner [Health institutions].
SS, Oslo.
(annual) 1983 (published 1984). NKr 30. 133p. ISSN 0332-7906. *No, En.
TF: has data for 1983 and for 1977 to 1983 in the section on health conditions.
Health personnel and health institutions; operating expenditures and receipts in somatic hospitals and nursing homes; home nursing; health conditions; legal abortions; births and perinatal mortality; general mortality and causes of death; and some main results (on the above subjects).

Δ F - iii Education

1872 Utdanningsstatistikk oversikt 1 oktober... [Education statistics survey 1 October...].
SS, Oslo.
1974- 1981 (published 1983). NKr 30. 115p. *No, En.
Pupils, schools, teachers in schools; expenditure for primary schools, upper secondary schools, universities and colleges.

1873 Utdanningsstatistikk: grunnskoler 1 oktober... [Education statistics: basic schools 1 October...].
SS, Oslo.
1888- 1984 (published 1985). NKr 25. 88p. ISSN 0332-804X. *No, En.
TF: has data as at 1st October 1984.
Pupils, classes and teachers in basic schools and special schools for the handicapped. Pupils in medical and social institutions, and municipal expenditure on primary schools.

1874 Utdanningsstatistikk: videregående skoler 1 oktober... [Education statitics: upper secondary schools...].
SS, Oslo.
1888- 1982 (published 1984). NKr 30. 147p. *No, En.
TF: has data as at 1st October 1982.
Pupils, classes, teachers, schools, etc.

1875 Utdanningsstatistikk: universiteter og hogskoler 1 oktober... [Educational statistics: universities and colleges 1 October...].
SS, Oslo.
1888- 1982 (published 1984). NKr 18. 132p. ISSN 0300-5631. *No, En.
TF: has data as at 1st October 1982.
Students by sex, type of school, residence, etc; schools by type and ownership/size; teachers full/part time, sex, age, etc.

1876 Utdanningsstatistikk: vaksenopplæring [Educational statistics: adult education].
SS, Oslo.
1888- 1983/84 (published 1985). NKr 25. 87p. ISSN 0332-8058. *No, En.
TF: has data for the 1983/84 academic year.
All adult education activities except correspondence schools and schooling within firms, including data on courses, participants, modes of education, etc.

1877 Kulturstatistikk [Cultural statistics].
SS, Oslo.
1975- 1982. NKr 15. 178p. *No, En.
TF: published every two years, the 1982 edition has data for earlier years in some tables.
Participation in different kinds of cultural activities, including religious communities, theatre and opera, libraries, film and cinema, radio and television, music, museums and art galleries, books, periodicals and newspapers, sports, artists, public records, education, private and public expenditure on cultural purposes, and purchase-systems.

1878 Tidsnyttingsundersøkelsen [Time budget survey].
SS, Oslo.
1971/72- 2nd, 1980/81 (published 1983). NKr 24. 188p. *No, En.
Includes the main findings of the survey - overview tables; individual groups of activity tables (income producing work, household work and family care, education, total work load, leisure, time spent with others, time spent with children, activity and persons present); and location.

Δ F - iv Justice

< see also 414

1879 Sivilrettstatistikk [Civil judicial statistics].
SS, Oslo.
1967- 1984 (published 1985). NKr 20. 42p. ISSN 0550-0532. *No, En.
Data on disputes, bankruptcy proceedings, compositions, and forced sales of real property.

1880 Kriminalstatistikk... [Criminal statistics...].
SS, Oslo.
1955- 1983 (published 1985). NKr 35. 179p. ISSN 0333-3914. *No, En.
Crimes investigated by the police; recidivism; sanctions by type of crime, age, sex, criminal record; imprisonments and discharges from penal institutions.

1881 Kriminalstatistikk: oversikt [Criminal statistics: survey].
SS, Oslo.
1960/72- 2nd, 1970-1982 (published 1984). NKr 18. 66p. *No; contents list & table headings also in En.
Survey on the development of criminality.
Note: issued in the series 'Statistiske analyser'.

Δ F – vi Elections

1882 Stortingsvalget [Storting elections].
SS, Oslo.
1906– 1981 (published 1982). NKr 25. 91p. *No, En.
Detailed statistics on the poll and distribution of valid votes.

1883 Fylkestingsvalget [County council elections].
SS, Oslo.
1975– 1982 (published 1984). NKr 30. 135p. *No, En.
Persons entitled to vote, valid votes, representatives by geographical divisions and party/electoral list, age and occupation.

1884 Kommunestyrevalget [Municipal council elections].
SS, Oslo.
1907– 1983 (published 1984). NKr 35. 162p. *No, En.
Poll and distribution of votes, representatives and nominees by party.

Δ G Finance

Δ G – i Banking

1885 Kredittmarkedsstatistisk: private og offentlige banker [Credit market statistics: private and public banks].
SS, Oslo.
1912– 1982 (published 1984). NKr 50. 312p. *No, En.
The results of a survey of all official statistics in the field of private and public banking.

Δ G – ii Public finance

1886 Nasjonalregnskap [National accounts].
SS, Oslo.
1949– 1975–1984 (published 1985). NKr 40. 233p. *No, En.
National accounts, domestic product by category of expenditure, gross and net domestic product by industry, private consumption, capital formation, factor income. Wages and salaries, entrepreneurial income and employment in industry, disposable income, public income and expenditure, etc.
Note: volumes of national accounts by county, 'Fylkesfordelt nasjonalregnskap' were issued for 1973; 1980 (published 1984).

1887 Kvartalsvis naskonalregnskap [Quarterly national accounts].
SS, Oslo.
1966/77– 1979–1984 (published 1984). NKr 30. 113p. ISSN 0800-9783. *No, En.
Includes similar data to 1885 above.

1888 Strukturall for kommunenes økonomi [Structural data from the municipal accounts].
SS, Oslo.
1974– 1982 (published 1984). NKr 30. 150p. *No.

1889 Skattestatistikk: inntektsåret [Tax statistics: income year...].
SS, Oslo.
1937/38– 1982 (published 1984). NKr 24. 151p. ISSN 0800-2940. *No, En.
Includes a survey of tax assessments (municipal and personal); of personal taxpayers by income, group, age, sex, occupational status, etc); of the self-employed; central government tax assessments of corporations, etc.

Δ G – iii Company finance

1890 Regnskapsstatistikk: oljeutvinning, bergverksdrift og industrie [Statistics of accounts: oil extraction, mining and manufacturing].
SS, Oslo.
1900– 1983 (published 1985). NKr 35. 168p. ISSN 0333-3795. *No; table headings also in En.
Data on profit and loss accounts and balance sheets for enterprises with 50 or more employees in the oil extraction, mining and manufacturing industries.

1891 Regnskapsstatistikk: engrosshandel [Statistics of accounts: wholesale trade].
SS, Oslo.
1971– 1983 (published 1985). NKr 30. 108p. ISSN 0333-3817. *No; table headings also in En.
TF: has data for some earlier years in some tables.
Profit and loss accounts and balance sheets for enterprises with the wholesale trade as the principal activity and with 50 or more employees.

1892 Regnskapsstatistikk: detaljhandel [Statistics of accounts: retail trade].
SS, Oslo.
1981– 1982–1983 (published 1985). NKr 25. 97p. ISSN 0800-5141. *No, En.
Data on profit & loss accounts, balance sheets & different ratios for enterprises in retail trade, including large joint-stock companies & co-operative societies in selected industry groups.

Δ G – v Insurance

1893 Kredittmarkedsstatistisk: livs- og skadeforsikringsselskaper m.v. [Credit market statistics: life and non-life insurance companies, etc].
SS, Oslo.
1912- 1974-1976 (published 1978). NKr 9. 69p. *No, En.
The results of a survey of all official statistics in the field of life & non-life insurance companies.

Δ G – vi Credit market

1894 Kredittmarkedsstatistisk: private kredittforefale og finansieringsselskaper [Credit market statistics: private credit institutions and private financial companies].
SS, Oslo.
1912- 1977 (published 1978). NKr 11. 65p. *No, En.
The results of a survey of all official statistics in the field.

1895 Kredittmarkedsstatistisk: fordringer og gjeld overfor utlandet [Credit market statistics: foreign assets and liabilities].
SS, Oslo.
1912- 1975-1976 (published 1978). NKr 11. 87p. *No, En.
The results of a survey of all official statistics on foreign assets and liabilities.

Δ H Transport and communications

1896 Samferdselsstatistikk [Transport and communication statistics].
SS, Oslo.
1958- 1983 (published 1984). NKr 24. 191p. *No; table headings also in En.
TF: has data for earlier years in some tables.
General data on water transport, railway transport, road transport, aviation, post, telecommunications and broadcasting. Also includes principal statistics of scheduled road transport, marine casualties, and road traffic accidents (for all of which there are more detailed separate publications).

Δ H – i Ships and shipping

1897 Sjøjaft [Maritime statistics].
SS, Oslo.
1983- 1984 (published 1985). NKr 30. 133p. ISSN 0468-8147. *No, En.
TF: has data for 1975 to 1983 or 1984.
Data on shipping and the national economy, the merchant fleet, etc. (size and structure, increase and decrease, vessels laid up, and merchant fleets of the world), crew, foreign-going trade, coastal trade, main results and developing trends.

1898 Godstransport på kysten: rutefart [Coastwise transport of goods: scheduled services].
SS, Oslo.
1964/65- 1979. not priced. c 80p. *No, En.
TF: the survey is taken every 10 years, and the results of the 1979 survey were published in 1982.
Findings of a survey on goods transported by Norwegian vessels in regular coastal service. Includes data on long-distance, local, and rural district services, on transport performance, and on distribution of goods by area and commodity group.

1899 Godstransport på kysten...leie og egentransport [Coastwise transport of goods...transport for hire or reward and on own account].
SS, Oslo.
1964- 1980 (published 1982). NKr 15. 147p. *No, En.
The results of a survey, including data on quantities of goods carried between countries, between trade regions and from/to trade districts and principal municipalities.

Δ H – ii Roads and road transport

1900 Rutebilstatistikk [Scheduled road transport].
SS, Oslo.
1967- 1983 (published 1985). NKr 25. 93p. ISSN 0550-0524. *No; table headings also in En.
TF: has data for some earlier years in some tables.
Establishments, vehicles, employees, transport performance and economy.

1901 Lastebiltransport: utvalgsundersøkelse [Road goods transport: sample survey].
SS, Oslo.
1963- 4th, 1978 (published 1980). NKr 15. 199p. *No, En.
TF: a survey is taken every five years.
Data on type of owner, type of vehicle, motive power of vehicle, registrations, mileage, long-distance transport, etc.

Δ H – ii, continued

1902 Eie og bruk av personbil: utvalgsundersøkelse [Private motoring: sample survey].
SS, Oslo.
1962- 4th, 1980 (published 1983). NKr 18. 161p. *No; contents list & table headings also in En.
Regional results, seasonal data, age and sex of drivers, age of cars, length of journeys, consumption of fuel, cars and vans owned by firms.

1903 Veitrafikkulykker [Road traffic accidents].
SS, Oslo.
1941/47- 1984 (published 1985). NKr 30. 125p. ISSN 0468-9198. *No, En.

Δ H – v Telecommunications and postal services

1904 Statistikk [Statistics] (Teledirektoratet [Telecommunications Administration]).
Teledirektoratet, Universitetsgate 2, (Postboks 6701, St Olav's pl, Oslo 1).
1857- 1983 (published 1984). not priced. 185p. ISSN 0800-2177 (English summary ISSN 0800-3653).
*No; separate summary available in En.
Administration, staff, lines and circuits, service locations for the public, internal exchange plant and subscriber equipment, subscriptions, traffic, tariffs, finances, service statistics.

Δ I Environment

1905 Miljøstatistikk...naturressurser og forurensinger [Environment statistics...natural resources and pollution].
SS, Oslo.
1976- 3rd, 1983. NKr 24. 306p. ISSN 0333-0621. *No; contents list & summary also in En.
TF: has data to 1981 or 1982.
A review of the most important statistical information on natural resources and pollution, including background (population, development and distribution, living conditions, health and mortality), natural resources and their use (area, water, air, plants, animals, energy), emissions and wastes.

NETHERLANDS
PAYS BAS
NIEDERLANDE
NEDERLAND

Central statistical office

1906 Centraal Bureau voor de Statistiek [Central Bureau of Statistics].
Prinses Beatrixlaan 428, Voorburg (Postbus 959, 2270 AZ Voorburg).
t 070-69 43 41. tx 32692 CBS NL. cables: Statistiek Voorburg.
The bureau is the only agency within the Dutch government which collects, compiles and publishes statistical information pertaining to all social, eonomic and cultural activities of the country, including population, judicial and criminal, socio-economic, educational, health, socio-cultural, manufacturing and construction, trade, traffic and transport, agricultural, and financial and national accounts statistics. The Statistical Analysis Department deals with econometric analysis and practical problems of a mathematical and statistical nature, advising all departments inside the Bureau and also institutes and individuals outside. Unpublished information can be supplied, and no charge is made for information not requiring considerable labour; where there must be a charge, a quotation is made to the enquirer before work commences. Enquiries concerning foreign trade statistics should be addressed to the Bureau at Kloosterweg 1, Heerlen (Postbus 4481 6401 CZ Heerlen) (t 045 736666. tx 56724 CBS NL).
Publications of this bureau are published by the Staatsuitgeverij, Christoffel Plantijnstraat, Den Haag.
The abbreviation CBS, Den Haag, has been used for entries between 1906-2061.

Libraries

The library of the Centraal Bureau voor de Statistiek (see above) has a large collection of statistical publications of the Netherlands, foreign countries, and international organisations. The reading room is open to the public from 9.00 to 16.00, Mondays to Fridays, and the library also handles enquiries by telephone and letter. The staff speak German, English, French and Spanish as well as Dutch.
Official publications of the Netherlands can also be consulted in the libraries of Dutch universities and colleges.

Libraries and information services abroad

The more general statistical publications of the Netherlands are available at most Netherlands embassies and legations abroad, including:

United Kingdom	Royal Netherlands Embassy, 38 Hyde Park Gate, London SW7. t 01-584 5040.
Australia	Royal Netherlands Embassy, 120 Empire Circuit, Yarralumla, Canberra ACT 2600. t 73 3111.
Canada	Royal Netherlands Embassy, 275 Slater Street, 3rd floor, Ottawa K1P 5H9. t 237 5030.
New Zealand	Royal Netherlands Embassy, Investment Centre, Featherston & Ballance Streets, Wellington C1. t 738 652.
USA	Royal Netherlands Embassy, 4200 Linnean Avenue NW, Washington DC 20008. t (202) 244 5300. Netherlands Information Service Library, 711 Third Avenue, New York, NY 10017. t Oxford 7 5544.

Bibliographies

1907 Systematisch overzicht van de CBS publikaties... [Systematic list of CBS publications...].
The Centraal Bureau voor de Statistiek published each year this comprehensive bibliography of CBS publications. It is kept up to date by a monthly list of publications issued during the month.
The 'Statistical yearbook (1908) and 'Statistisch zakboek' (1909) both contain a complete survey of publications issued since 1945. The 1943-46 edition of 'Jaarcijfers voor Nederland' included a survey of earlier publications.

Statistical publications

Δ A General

< see also 079, 080

1908 Statistical yearbook of the Netherlands.
CBS, Den Haag.
1881- 1984 (published 1985). Fl 84. 428p. ISSN 0077-6858. *En.
TF: has data for 1983 and some earlier years.
Main sections:
Area, climate & environment - Population - Public health - Housing - Religion & politics - Education & science - Culture & recreation - Labour - Establishments & enterprises - Agriculture & fisheries - Manufacturing industry - Distribution and service trade - Foreign trade - Traffic & transport - Money & banking - National accounts - Balance of payments - Public finances - Income & wealth - Consumption - Prices - Social affairs - Justice & security.

Δ A, continued

1909 Statistisch zakboek [Statistical pocketbook].
CBS, Den Haag.
1924- 1984. Fl 20.50. ISSN 0077-7463. *Nl.
TF: has data for 1983 and some earlier years.
Similar subject coverage to (1908) but in less detail.

1910 Maandschrift van het CBS [Monthly bulletin of the CBS].
CBS, Den Haag.
1944- Fl 7 or Fl 81.40 yr. ISSN 0028-2898. *Nl; table of contents also in En. An annual appendix in English contains descriptions & explanatory notes to the series.
TF: each issue has data for the last six years and the last 24 months to about two months prior to the date of the issue.
Contains about 600 series concerning population, public health, housing, labour, activity units, enterprises, agriculture & fisheries, manufacturing industry, distribution, foreign trade, traffic and transport, money and banking, public finance, consumption, prices, social affairs, justice and prisons, and miscellaneous subjects. Data illustrated by a number of graphs.

1911 85 jahr statistiek in tijdreeksen 1899-1984 [85 years of statistics...].
CBS, Den Haag.
1984. Fl 39.50. various pagings. *Nl; contents list also in En, De.
A historical volume with similar subject content to (1908).

1912 Regionaal statistisch zakboek [Regional statistical pocketbook].
CBS, Den Haag.
every two years. 1984 (published 1985). Fl 40. *Nl.
Data similar to (1908) but on a regional basis.

1913 Statistisch bulletin van het CBS [Statistical bulletin of the CBS].
CBS, Den Haag.
c 50a year. Fl 51.50 yr. ISSN 0077-6947. *Nl.
A news sheet used by CBS for quick reporting of the most important results of surveys or calculations as they become available. Examples includes the consumer price index, wholesale prices, labour reserve, and newly constructed dwellings.

1914 40 jahr statistiek in reeks en grafiek [40 years of statistics in series and graphs].
CBS, Den Haag.
1985. not priced. 16p. *Nl.

1915 Sociaal-cultureel kwartaalbericht [Socio-cultural quarterly report].
CBS, Den Haag.
1979- quarterly. Fl 18.90 or Fl 55.90 yr. *Nl; contents list also in En.
TF: each issue has data for several years and quarters to about six months prior to the date of the issue.
Articles of an analytical nature and surveys of key figures relating to socio-cultural phenomena. Information, including statistics, on social services, culture, tourism, leisure, cost and financing of socio-cultural facilities, and indicators for the experience of welfare by the Netherlands population.

1916 Sociaal-economische maandstatistiek [Monthly bulletin of socio-economic statistics].
CBS, Den Haag.
1953- monthly. Fl 11.90 or Fl 92.50 yr. *Nl; contents list & table headings also in En.
TF: published in the month of issue, and containing data for the previous month and some earlier months.
Employment, hours of work, and unemployment; wages and other labour conditions; social insurance and other social benefits; consumption, etc. (including consumer price indices). In each issue tables are preceded by brief interviews and articles.

1917 Algemene bedrijfstelling [General economic census] (CBS - Hoofdafdeling Economische Basistellingen, Voorburg).
CBS, Den Haag.
4th, 1978 (published 1985). 8 vols. *Nl.
Volumes issued are:
Vol 1. Methodological introduction (Fl 33.60)
Vol 2. General results by kind of activity (Fl 39)
Vol 2A. Mining and quarrying, manufacturing, public utilities, construction and installation on construction projects (Fl 26.75)
Vol 2B. Trade and repair of consumer goods (Fl 37.60)
Vol 2C. Hotels, restaurants, cafés, etc (Fl 20.25)
Vol 2D. Transport and storage (Fl 22.75)
Vol 2E. Banking, insurance and services (Fl 31.40)
Vol 3. General results by region (Fl 39).

1918 Statistiek van het ondernemingen- en vestigingenbestand: aantal ondernemingen en vestigingen naar aktiviteit, grootte, rechtsvorm en regio, 1 januari 1985 [Statistics of establishments and enterprises: number of enterprises by activity, size, legal form and region, 1st January 1985] (CBS, Voorburg).
CBS, Den Haag.
Fl 13.75. 35p. *Nl, En.
TF: published in 1985.

Δ B Production

Δ B – ii Agriculture, fisheries, forestry, etc

Δ B – ii(a) Agriculture and horticulture

1919 Landbouwtelling [Census of agriculture] (CBS, Voorburg).
CBS, Den Haag.
1960– 1983. 2 vols. *Nl.
Vol 1: General data.
Vol 2: Manpower in agriculture and horticulture (Fl 22.65).
Note: a census is taken annually and different aspects and subjects are dealt with each year.

1920 Landbouwcijfers [Agricultural data].
Landbouw-economisch Instituut, Conradkade 175, Den Haag.
1950– 1984 (published mid-1984). Fl 24.25. c 300p. *Nl, En – see note below.
TF: has data for several years to 1983.
Contains more detailed agricultural statistics than with a considerable amount of textual matter.
Note: a separate English translation of the table of contents and table headings has been published since 1981 with the title 'Statistical data on agriculture in the Netherlands'.

1921 Bodemstatistiek [land use statistics] (CBS, Voorburg).
CBS, Den Haag.
1948/49– 1983 (published 1985). Fl 23.40. ISSN 0169-0647. *Nl, En.
Note: earlier issues were titled 'Statistiek van de pacht- en koopprijzen van landbouwgronden'.

1922 Maandstatistiek van de landbouw [Monthly bulletin of agricultural statistics].
CBS, Den Haag.
1953– Fl 11.90 or Fl 95.40 yr. ISSN 0024-8754. *Nl; contents list & table headings also in En.
Up-to-date data on temperature, milk delivered to dairy-works & its products, quantities of milk & cream consumed, numbers of sows served and prognoses on the supply of pigs for slaughter, prices of agricultural & horticultural products, exports of agricultural products, employment on agrarian holdings, imports of farm tractors, etc.

1923 Statistiek van land- en tuinbouw [Statistics of agriculture and horticulture].
CBS, Den Haag.
1949– 1983 (published 1985). Fl 32.60. 113p. ISSN 0168-3918. *Nl, En.
TF: has data for 1980/81-1982/83 crop years or 1982 & 1983.
Land use, general data on holdings, arable crops, grass, horticultural crops, livestock, labour, prices, production & consumption, foreign trade, etc.

1924 Tuinbouwcijfers [Horticultural statistics] (Landbouw-economish Instituut & CBS).
CBS, Den Haag.
1968– 1984. Fl 19.50. c 150p. *Nl.
TF: has data for several years to 1983.
Contains more detailed horticultural statistics than (1923).

1925 Boomkwekerij in cijfers [Nurseries in figures].
Landbouw-economisch Instituut, Conradkade 175, Den Haag.
1981. not priced. 122p. *Nl.

1926 PVS...jaarverslag/statistiek [PVS...annual report/statistics].
Produktschap voor Siergewessen (PVS), Bezuidenhoutseweg 152, (Postbus 361), 2501 BE, Den Haag.
(annual) 1984 (published 1985). not priced. 120p. *Nl.
TF: has data for 1984 and earlier years in some tables.
Production, sales, etc. of flower bulbs, flowers and plants, etc.

Δ B – ii(b) Fisheries

1927 Statistiek van de visserij [Fishery statistics] (CBS, Voorburg).
Staatsuitgeverij, Den Haag.
1950– 1980 (published 1983). Fl 9.30. c 25p. ISSN 0077-7242. *Nl; list of tables & table headings also in En.
Landings & yield of fishery products, imports & exports of fish, purchase of materials by the fish-preserving factories, and sales of preserved fish.

1928 Maandcijfers van de visserij [Monthly bulletin of fishery statistics].
CBS, Den Haag.
1953– Fl 2.20 or Fl 22.50 yr. *Nl; list of tables & table headings also in En.
Up-dates the information given in (1927).

Δ B – ii(c) Forestry

1929 De Nederlandse bosstatistiek [Census of forest in the Netherlands] (CBS – Hoofdafdeling Landbouwstatistieken).
CBS, Den Haag.
1952/63– 1980–1983. *Nl, En.
TF: the 1980–1983 results are being published from 1985.
Contents:
Vol 1: the forested area, 1980–1983 (Fl 25.75).

1930 Statistisch bulletin: groothandel in hout en plaatmaterial [Statistical bulletin: wholesale trade in timber].
Nederlandse Houtbond [Netherlands Timber Trade Association], Keizergracht 298, 1016 E.W., Amsterdam.
1981/82– quarterly. not priced. *Nl.

Δ B – iii Industry

< see also 1988

1931 Produktiestatistieken [Production statistics].
CBS, Den Haag.
1951– 1983. prices vary. *Nl, En.
TF: varies with each title but publication is usually about a year after the end of the year covered.
Published in separate annual volumes for each industry, and including data on sales, production, consumption of raw materials and semi-fitted products, consumption of fuel, stocks, and unit value of selected goods sold. Titles are:
Slachterijen en vleeswarenindustrie [Slaughterhouses and meat-processing industry]
Uitgeverijen [Publishing]
Aardewerk-, baksteen- en dakpannenindustrie [Ceramic goods and clay products for construction]
Papier- en karton industrie [Paper- and board-mills]
Kunststofverwerkende industrie [Synthetic materials processing industry]
Tricot- en kousenindustrie [Knitting and hosiery mills]
Cacao-, chocolade- en suikerwerkindustrie [Cocoa, chocolate and confectionery industry]
Kledingindustrie [Manufacture of ready-made clothing]
Hout-en meubelindustrie [Wood and furniture industry]
Lederindustrie [Tanneries and leather finishing]
Schoenindustrie [Boot and shoe factories]
Tabakverwerkende [Tobacco products industry]
Tapijt- en vloermattenindustrie [Manufacture of carpets, rugs and mats]
Textielveredelingsindustrie [Finishing textiles]
Band- en overige textielindustrie [Narrow fabrics]
Rubberverwerkende industrie [Manufacture of rubber products]
Fabrieken van metalen meubelen [Manufacture of metal furniture]
Meelfabrieken, gort- enorijstpellerijen [Flour manufacturing, grain milling and husking]
Groente- en fruitverwerkende industrie [Vegetable and fruit processing industry]
Kalzandsteenindustrie [Manufacture of sand-lime bricks]
Scheepsbouw en scheepsreparatiebedrijven [Shipbuilding and repairing]
Lederwaren industrie [Leathergoods factories]
Grafische industrie [Printing]
Papierwaren industrie [Paper converting]
Elektrotechnische industrie [Electrical engineering]
Zuivelindustrie [Dairy industry]
Chemische industrie [Chemical industry]
Katoen- en wolindustrie [Cotton industry and wool industry]
Natuursteenbewerkingsbedrijven [Stone masons]
Binderijen [Binderies]
Suikerindustrie [Sugar factories]
Margarine- en oliefabrieken [Manufacture of margarine, edible oil and cooking fats]
Alcoholfabrieken en distilleerderijen, bierbrouwerijen en mouterijen, frisdrankenindustrie [Distilling factories, breweries and malt-houses, non-alcoholic carbonated drinks industry]
Brood-, banket-, beschuit-, koek- en biscuitfabrieken [Bread, cake, biscuit and rusk baking industry]
Veevoederindustrie [Animal feed industry]
Diverse branches van de voedingsmiddelenindustrie [Miscellaneous branches of the foodstuffs industry]
Rijwiel- en motorrijwielindustrie [Bicycle and motorcycle industry]
Fabrieken van niet-elektrische verwarmings- en kookapparaten [Manufacture of non-electrical heating and cooking appliances]
Gieterijen [Foundries]
Basis-metaalindustrie [Basic metal industry]
Smederijen, las- en slijpinrichtingen en oppervlaktebehandelingsbedrijven [Blacksmiths shops, industries engaged in welding, grinding and surface treatment of metals]
Grofsmederijen, stamp- en persbedrijven [Manufacture of forgings and metal stampings]
Schroeven, bouten en moeren, massadraaiwerkveren e.d. industrie [Manufacture of screw machine products, bolts, nuts and technical springs]
Tank-, reservoir- en pijpleidingbouw [Manufacture of tanks, reservoirs and industrial piping]
Constructiewerkplaatsen [Structural engineering]
Metalen emballage industrie en fabrieken van handgereedschappen, messen, bestekken, hang- en sluitwerk [Manufacture of cans, boxes, and other metal containers and manufacture of hand tools, cutlery, lock and key-sets, furniture, domestic and general purposes hardware]

Δ B - iii, continued

1931, continued

Landbouwmachine-industrie [Manufacture of agricultural machinery and equipment]
Metaalbewerkingsmachine-industrie en machinegereedschappenfabrieken [Manufacture of metal working machinery and interchangeable machine tools]
Fabrieken van machines en apparaten voor de voedingsmiddelen-, de chemische- en aanverwante industrieën [Manufacture of machinery and equipment for the food, the chemical and allied industries]
Hef-, e.a. transportwerktuigenindustrie, fabrieken van machines voor de mijnbouw, de bouwnijverheid, de bouwmaterialen en metalurgische industrie [Manufacture of hoisting machines and other mechanical handling equipment, machinery and equipment used by the mining industry, construction and basic metal industries]
Tandwielen, lagers en drijfwerkelementenindustrie [Manufacture of gears, bearings and other power transmission equipment]
Fabrieken van machines en apparaten voor de houten meubelindustrie, de textiel- en kledingindustrie, de wasserijen en chemische reiniging, de leder- en lederverwerkende ind. en grafische ind. [Manufacture of wood working machinery, textile machinery, commercial laundry machines, dry cleaning and pressing machines, leather working machinery, paper industry and printing trade machinery]
Stoomketel en krachtwerktuigenindustrie [Manufacture of steamboilers engines and turbines]
Kantoormachine-industrie [Manufacture of office machinery]
Fabrieken van pompen, compressoren, hydraulische pneumatische elementen, luchttechnische- en koelapparaten; weegwerktuigen, winkelmachines; appendages en machine-onderdelen, algemene machinebouw en machinereparatie inrichtingen [Manufacture of pumps, compressors, hydraulic and pneumatic equipment; airconditioning and ventilating machinery, refrigerators and equipment, weighing machines, vending machines; valves, machine-parts; industries engaged in manufacturing or repairing various kinds of machinery and equipments]
Auto-industrie en assemblagebedrijven, auto-onderdelenindustrie, vliegtuigbouw- en vliegtuigreparatiebedrijven [Manufacture and assembly of motor vehicles, manufacture of parts and accessories for motor vehicles, manufacture and repair of aircraft]
Carrosserie-, aanhangwagen-, en opleggerindustrie [Manufacture of bodies for motor vehicles of trailers and semi-trailers]
Metaalproduktenindustrie [Metal production]
Fabrieken van wagens voor intern transport en wagens zonder eigen beweegkracht [Manufacture of work trucks and not mechanically propelled vehicles]
Beton- en cementwarenindustrie [Manufacture of articles of concrete and cement]
Golfkarton en kartonnageindustrie [Corrugated board and folding carton converting]
Machine-industrie [Mechanical engineering]
Samenvattend overzicht van de industrie [Summary of manufacturing]
Kunstharsen e.d. industrie [Industry of synthetic resins and similar materials]
Industrie van chemische bestrijdingsmiddelen [Industry of chemical pesticides and similar products]
Kunstmeststoffen industrie [Manufacture of synthetic fertilisers]
Verfstoffen en kleurstoffen industrie [Manufacture of pigments and dyes]
Verf-, lak-, vernis en drukinktindustrie [Industry of paints, lacquers, varnishes and printers' ink]
Zeep-, was- en reinigungsmiddelen-parfumerie en kosmetica-industrie [Manufacture of soap and cleaning preparations, perfumes, cosmetics and other toilet preparations]
Industrie van diverse chemische grondstoffen [Manufacture of miscellaneous basic industrial chemicals]
Genees- en verbandmiddelenindustrie [Manufacture of drugs, medicines and dressings]
Industrie van diverse chemische produkten [Manufacture of miscellaneous final chemical products]
Chemische industrie [Chemical industry]
Textielwarenindustrie [Manufacture of made-up textile goods]
Cement-, kalk- en overige minerale produkten industrie; glasindustrie en -bewerkingsinrichtingen [Manufacture of cement, lime, plaster and non-metallic mineral products; manufacture of glass and glass products]
Medische instrumenten- en orthopedische artikelen industrie; tandtechnische werkplaatsen [Medical instruments and orthopedic articles industry; dental technical workshops]
Optische- en fototechnischeindustrie. Klokken en uurwerkenindustrie [Manufacture of optical and photo-technical products. Manufacture of clocks and clockworks]
Meet- en regelapparaten en overige instrumentenindustrie [Manufacture of measuring and controlling units]
Speelgoed- en sportartikelen industrie [Toys and sports articles industry].

1932 Maandstatistiek van de prijzen [Monthly bulletin of price statistics]
CBS, Den Haag.
1976- Fl 77.23 yr (Fl 138 yr with annex). *Nl.
TF: each issue has long runs of monthly figures to about two months prior to the date of the issue.
Price indices relating to consumption, production, imports & exports, and property items; data on international price trends; volume index numbers of production & consumption; and index numbers on the development of wages. The annex contains a specified list of price indices per group of goods and per commodity.

1933 Conjunctuurtest [Industry test] (CBS, Voorburg).
CBS, Den Haag.
1963- monthly. Fl 6.85 or Fl 54.60 yr. *Nl.
Up-to-date information on the latest development of manufacturing and construction industries, on the judgement of entrepreneurs regarding the situation in their enterprises and their expectations for the next month. Includes information on activity, stocks of unsold products, orders received and order position for consumer goods, capital goods and other goods. The building industry is limited to residential and non-residential buildings.
Note: this publication is devoted exclusively to tendencies and opinions, and has no absolute figures.

Δ B – iii, continued

1934 Samenvattend overzicht van de industrie [Summary of manufacturing] (CBS, Voorburg).
CBS, Den Haag.
1976/78– 1981–1983 (published 1985). Fl 14.50. 50p. ISSN 0168-5546. *Nl; contents list & table headings also in En.
Employment, development of employment and production, etc. Results are given by class of manufacturing and activity units; by group and subgroup of manufacturing.

1935 Maandstatistiek van de industrie [Monthly statistical bulletin of manufacturing].
CBS, Den Haag.
1953– Fl 12.75 or Fl 102 yr. ISSN 0470-6684. *Nl; contents list & table headings also in En.
Includes a survey of the main key figures on the economic situation; monthly information on production; sales for the most important divisions of industry with specifications by product (index numbers and absolute figures); quarterly data on turnover, orders on hand and received, persons employed; capital investments; shipbuilding; etc.

Δ B – iii(b) Textiles, paper, rubber, etc

1936 Jaaroverzicht [Annual survey].
Centraal Bureau der Nederlandse Katoen- Rayon- en Linnenindustrie, Schutterij 16, Veenendaal (Postbus 518, 3900 AM Veenendaal).
(annual) 1982–1983. not priced. 28p. *Nl.
TF: the 1982–1983 report, published late 1983, has data for 1980, 1981 and 1982.
Includes statistical tables on the industru, investment, capacity, machinery, production, foreign trade, and raw materials. Also some international data.

Δ B – iii(d) Metals, etc

1937 De metaal- en elektrotechnische industrie... [The metal and electrical industries] (De Groep Economisch Onderzoek en Statistiek van de Federatie Metaal- en Elektrotechnische Industrie).
Vereniging voor de Metaal- en de Elektrotechnische Industrie, Postbus 190, 2700 AD Zoetermeer.
(annual) 1982 & 1983 (published 1984). not priced. 29p. *Nl.
Includes data on production, trade, foreign trade, etc.

Δ B – iii(f) Other industries

1938 Automatiseringsstatistieken. Partikuliere sektor... [Automation statistics. Private enterprise sector] (CBS – Hoofdafdeling Statistieken van Industrie en Bouwnigverheid).
CBS, Den Haag.
1983– 1983 (published 1985). not priced. *Nl; table of contents & summary also in En.

Δ B – iv Construction

1939 Maandstatistiek van de bouwnijverheid [Monthly bulletin of construction statistics].
CBS, Den Haag.
1959– Fl 9.95 or Fl 79.50 yr. *Nl; contents list also in En.
TF: each issue has data for several complete years and several months up to about three months prior to the date of the issue.
Monthly data on building permits issued for dwellings and other constructions (industrial buildings, schools, hospitals, etc); civil engineering works; dwellings started and completed by mode of financing; etc; dwelling stock; average prices and volume of dwellings, building material.

1940 Verbruik bouwmaterialen...Nieuwbouw woningen [Consumption of building materials].
CBS, Den Haag.
1979/81– 1980–1982 (published 1984). Fl 13.70. *Nl.

Δ B – v Energy

1941 De Nederlandse energiehuishouding [Energy supply in the Netherlands].
CBS, Den Haag.
1961– quarterly. Fl 12.45 or Fl 36.50 yr. *Nl, En.
Quarterly figures on the quantitative and qualitative development of energy consumption; detailed quarterly data on manufacturing in industry and monthly figures for mutation enterprises – oil refineries, cokes, gas and electricity works (input, output per sources of energy); consumption for mutation; monthly production data on primary and secondary sources of energy; monthly figures on petroleum derivitives; etc.

1942 Statistiek van de elektriciteitsvoorziening in Nederland [Statistics of electricity supply in the Netherlands].
CBS, Den Haag.
1962– 1980–1981 (published 1984). Fl 12.45. c 35p. *Nl, En.
Production and consumption of electricity.

Δ B – v, continued

1943 Statistiek van de gasvoorziening in Nederland [Statistics of gas supply in the Netherlands].
CBS, Den Haag.
1949/53- 1980-1981 (published 1984). Fl 10.85. 32p. *Nl, En.
Production, distribution, demand and supply of gas.

Δ B – vi Research and development

1944 Speur- en ontwikkelingswerk in Nederland [Research and development in the Netherlands].
CBS, Den Haag.
1959- 1981 (published 1984). Fl 24.75. c 45p. *Nl; contents list & table headings also in En.
The results of an annual survey covering business enterprises, research institutes and universities.

Δ C External trade

< see also 2042

1945 Maandstatistiek ven de buitenlandse handel per goederensoort [Monthly statistical bulletin of foreign trade by commodities].
CBS, Den Haag.
1946- Fl 19.70 or Fl 157.50 yr. ISSN 0024-8738. *Nl; contents list & table headings also in En.
TF: each issue has data for that month and cumulations for the year to date, and is published from four to six weeks after the end of that month. The December issue contains data for the year as well as for December.
Detailed figures of imports and exports arranged by commodities subdivided by countries of origin and destination; entrepôt trade with the Belgo- Luxembourgeoise Economic Union; imports and exports from and to the BLEU; index numbers of foreign trade.

1946 Maandstatistiek van de buitenlandse handel per land [Monthly statistical bulletin of foreign trade by countries].
CBS, Den Haag.
1946- Fl 11.45 or Fl 91.20 yr. ISSN 0024-8746. *Nl; contents list & table headings also in En.
TF: each issue has statistics for that month and cumulations for the year to date, and is published about two months after the end of the period covered. The December issue has data for the year as well as for December.
Main tables show imports and exports arranged by countries of origin and destination subdivided by SITC groups. There are also summary tables by SITC sections and divisions, trade with important countries subdivided by SITC sections and divisions, warehousing under bond, etc.

Δ D Internal distribution and service trades

1947 Maandstatistiek van de binnenlandse handel en dienstverlening [Monthly bulletin of distribution and service trade statistics].
CBS, Den Haag.
1953- Fl 11.90 or Fl 95.40 yr. *Nl; contents list & table headings also in En.
TF: each issue has data for several complete years and several months up to about four months prior to the date of the issue.
Includes detailed data on turnover and/or stocks for a large number of wholesale and retail branches, as well as for a number of service sectors, mainly in the form of monthly or quarterly index numbers. Also data about employment and labour reserve, retaining pay and unemployment insurance and the development of wages and salaries in distribution and service trades.

Δ D – i Wholesale and retail trades

1948 Produktiestatistieken binnenlandse handel [Home trade statistics].
CBS, Den Haag.
(annual) 1983. 8 vols. *Nl, En.
Contents:
Detailhandel. Samenvattend overicht [Retail trade. Summary] (Fl 14.75)
Detailhandel in bloemen en planten, tuinbenodigdheden, dieren en dierbenodigdheden [Retail trade in flowers, plants and gardening requirements: pets and requisites for the care thereof] (Fl 11.50)
Detailhandel in textielgoederen [Retail trade in textiles]
Groothandel in huishoudelijke artikelen, ijzer- en metaalwaren, verf, behangselpapier [Wholesale trade in household goods, iron and metalware, wall-paper]
Groothandel in textielwaren, schoeisel en lederwaren [Wholesale trade in textiles, footwear and leather goods]
Groothandel in voedings- en genotmiddelen [Wholesale trade in food, beverages and tobacco]
Groothandel in hout, vlakglas, sanitair en boumaterialen [Wholesale trade in building & related materials].

1949 Economische basistellingen: groothandel en handelsbemiddeling in machines, technische benodigdheden en voertuigen, 1983 [Economic censuses: wholesale trade in machinery, technical requirements and transportation equipment].
CBS, Den Haag.
1985. Fl 17.50. 50p. *Nl, En.

Δ D – i, continued

1950 Produktiestatistieken dienstverlening [Production statistics in commercial service trades] (CBS, Voorburg).
Staatsuitgeverij, Den Haag.
(annual) 1983 (published 1985). 3 vols. *Nl, En.
Contents:
Handel in personenauto's en auto-accessoires, autoreparatiebedrijven [Trade in motorcars and car accessories repair shops] (Fl 20).
Detailhandel in en reparatiebedrijven van rijwielen, bromfietsen en motorrijwielen [Retail trade in bicycles, mopeds and motorcycles and repair shops] (Fl 12).
Hotels, restaurants, cafés, e.d.

Δ D – ii Service trades

1951 Horeca in cijfers [Horeca in figures].
Bedrijfschap Horeca.
1983. not priced. 93p. *Nl.
Data on hotels, restaurants, cafés, etc.

Δ D – iv Tourism and travel

1952 Statistiek vreemdelingenverkehr [Tourism statistics].
CBS, Den Haag.
1952- 1982. Fl 23.75. 78p. ISSN 0077-7447. *Nl.
TF: the 1982 edition, published in 1985, has data for 1982.
Foreign tourists in hotels, regionally and by town.

1953 Inkomend tourisme [Survey of incoming tourism].
CBS, Den Haag.
1984- 1984 (published 1985). 55p. *Nl, En.

1954 Vakantie onderzoek [Holiday survey] (CBS, Voorburg).
Staatsuitgeverij, Den Haag.
(annual) 1982 (published 1984). Fl 29.50. *Nl.

Δ E Population

1955 Algemene volkstelling, annex woningtelling [Population census of housing].
CBS, Den Haag.
1830- 14th, 1971. *Nl; an En translation of text is available separately.
Contents:
Vol 1A: Population by sex, age and marital status (Fl 24.50)
Vol 1B: Alien nationalities (Fl 15.50)
Vol 2: Existing marriages and fertility of married & formerly married women (Fl 36.60)
Vol 3: Religion (Fl 23.30)
Vol 5A: Attainment and attendance in education (Fl 15.50)
Vol 5B: Education and socio-economic category (Fl 17.05)
Vol 5C: Attainment in education at the third level (Fl 18.30)
Vol 6A: Households, families and dwellings (Fl 22)
Vol 1A: Population of the municipalities & of the territorial subdivisions of the municipalities (Fl 36.90)
Vol 1B: Number of inhabitants of localities & agglomerations (Fl 23.70)
Vol 2: Fertility. Principal data for each municipality (Fl 16.50)
Vol 3: Religion. Principal data for each municipality (Fl 21.50)
Vol 4A: General characteristics of the economically active population. Principal data for each municipality (Fl 15.60)
Vol 4B: Economic activity and occupation. Principal data for each municipality (Fl 17.65)
Vol 4C: Socio-economic characteristics of the economically active population. Principal data for each municipality (Fl 11.50)
Vol 5: Level of education and enrollment in education; principal data for each municipality (Fl 11.10)
Vol 6: Households families and dwellings. Principal data for each municipality (Fl 18.70)
Vol 7A: Economically active population working outside the municipality of residence. Principal data for each municipality (Fl 18.95)
Vol 7B: Commuting. Principal data for each municipality (Fl 17.65)
Vol 8: Population living in institutions. Principal data for each municipality (Fl 21.20)
Census monographs 1971
Housing situation in the Netherlands (Fl 22.50)
Rate of fertility (Fl 20.50)
Divorced and widowed persons (Fl 23.50)
Mutual characteristics of married persons (Fl 17.55)
Households with low incomes (Fl 27.50)
Nuptiality in the Netherlands (Fl 39.00)
Economic activity of women in the Netherlands (Fl 27.80)
Aging in the Netherlands (Fl 22.50)
Family life-cycle (Fl 23.50)
Preadults in relation to their families (Fl 18.65)
Various compositions of households (Fl 22.50)

Δ E, continued

1955, continued

Education in the Netherlands (Fl 22.50)
Religious denomination (Fl 26.40)
Growing and declining villages in the Netherlands (Fl 20.25)
Typologies of municipalities based on growth of population (Fl 40.60)
Typologies of municipalities by degrees of urbanization (Fl 27.00)
Regional labour markets (22.50)
Households, marriages and families (Fl 20.65).

1956 Jaarstatistiek van de bevolking [Annual bulletin of population statistics]
CBS, Den Haag.
1981- 1982 (published 1984). Fl 30.50. 151p. *Nl; summary, contents list & table headings also in En.
TF: has data for 1982 and key figures from 1965 to 1982.
Population size, natality, mortality, nuptiality, dissolution of marriages, external migration, and internal migration.
Note: previously the annual supplement to the monthly bulletin of population and health statistics, since split into two separate titles.

1957 Bevolking der gemeenten van Nederland [Population of the municipalities of the Netherlands].
CBS, Den Haag.
1944/46- (Jan) 1984 (published Oct 1984). Fl 12. *Nl.

1958 Maandstatistiek van bevolking [Monthly bulletin of population statistics].
CBS, Den Haag.
1953- Fl 8.50 or Fl 67.80 yr. ISSN 0024-8711. *Nl; contents list also in En.
TF: each issue has data for several complete years and several months to about three months prior to the date of the issue.
Population statistics, population forecasts and socio-demographic surveys. Includes monthly data on number of inhabitants, births, deaths, migration and marriages for the Netherlands, the provinces and municipalities with 25,000 or more inhabitants.

1959 Prognose van de bevolking van Nederland na 1980 [Forecast of the population of the Netherlands after 1980].
CBS, Den Haag.
Pt 1: 1982, Fl 24.50. Pt 2: 1984, Fl 21.45. *Nl.
Part 1: Results and some backgrounds; part 2: Model building and formulation of assumptions.

1960 Overlevingstafels naar burgerlijke staat, 1976-1980 [Life tables by marital status].
CBS, Den Haag.
1984. Fl 21.65. 103p. *Nl, En.

1961 Sterftetafels voor Nederland naar belangrijke doodsoorzaken, 1976-1980 [Life tables for the Netherlands by main causes of death].
CBS, Den Haag.
1984. Fl 15. 51p. *Nl; contents list & table headings also in En.

1962 Statistiek van de binnenlandse migratie [Internal migration statistics].
CBS, Den Haag.
1948/52- 1981 (published 1984). Fl 17. 59p. *Nl.
Data by groups of municipalities, by family heads and individually migrated persons, and by sex and occupation.

1963 Statistiek van de buitenlandse migratie [External migration statistics].
CBS, Den Haag.
1948/49- 1981 (published 1983). Fl 18.35. 63p. *Nl; contents list also in En.
Tables and graphs on immigration and emigration to and from the Netherlands, subdivided by nationals, aliens, etc.

Δ E - ii Labour

1964 Statistiek werkzame personen... [Statistics of employed persons].
CBS, Den Haag.
(annual) 1982 (published 1984). Fl 15. c 60p. *Nl.
Data by industry, by industrial group, and by province.

1965 Raming regionale beroepsbevolking, 1971-1980 [Labour force by region].
CBS, Den Haag.
1983. Fl 23.25. *Nl.

1966 Arbeidskrachtentelling [Labour force sample survey].
CBS, Den Haag.
(irregular) 1981 (published from 1985). *Nl.
Content:
Part 1: Method, population and labour force, employment and unemployment (Fl 55.10).

Δ E - ii, continued

1967 Buitenlandse werknemers in Nederland, 1979-1984 [Foreign workers in the Netherlands, 1979-1984] (CBS - Hoofdafdeling Statistieken van Arbeid en Lonen).
CBS, Den Haag.
1985. not priced. 14p. *Nl.

1968 Statistiek van de vakbeweging [Statistics of trade unions].
CBS, Den Haag.
1946- 1983 (published 1984). Fl 8.65. c 30p. *Nl.
TF: has data for 1983 and also earlier years in some tables.

Δ E - iii Housing

1969 Woningbehoeftenonderzoek...huisvesting, woonlasten en verhuizingen. Regionale kerncijfers [Housing demand survey...housing situation, costs of housing and moves. Regional key figures].
CBS, Den Haag.
1981. Fl 15.20. *Nl.

1970 Statistiek van de bejaardenoorden [Homes for the aged].
CBS, Den Haag.
1950- 1982 (published mid-1985). Fl 23.75. *Nl, En.

Δ F Social and political

1971 De Nederlandse jeugd: een inventarisatie van statistische gegevens [Youth in the Netherlands: a compilation of statistical data].
CBS, Den Haag.
1977. A continuing series. *Nl; contents list also in En.
Contents:
Part 1: Demographic data and state of health (Fl 17)
Part 2: Education and employment (Fl 23)
Part 3: Leisure, adult education and participation in social life (Fl 22)
Part 4: Juvenile delinquency and judicial child care and protection, special youth care in residential institutions, social services (Fl 27.30)
Part 5: Mobility and transport, housing...of young people (Fl 31.50).

Δ F - i Standard of living

< see also 392

1972 Loonstructuuronderzoek [Survey into the structure of earnings].
CBS, Den Haag.
1972- 3rd, 1979 (published 1983). Fl 30. c 65p. *Nl.
Survey of earnings of employees (manual and non-manual) in the wholesale and retail trade, banking and insurance.

1973 Onderzoek huishoudens met éénmalige uitkering [Survey of households receiving non-recurrent benefit].
CBS, Den Haag.
(annual) 1983 (published 1984). Fl 12.45. *Nl.

1974 Huishoudens: sociaal-demografische cijfers [Households: social-demographic figures].
CBS, Den Haag.
1981- 1981 (published 1984). Fl 13.70. 42p. *Nl.

1975 De personele inkomensverdeling [Distribution of personal income].
CBS, Den Haag.
(annual) 1982 (published 1985). Fl 16.75. 47p. *Nl.

1976 Personele inkomensverdeling...individuen [Distribution of personal income...individuals.
CBS, Den Haag.
1981- 1981 (published 1985). Fl 50. *Nl.
TF: issued every two years.
Note: 'Personele inkomensverdeling...Individuen. Kerncijfers' [...key figures] is available from CBS (1981. Fl 15).

1977 Personale inkomensverdeling...regionale gegevens [Distribution of personal income...regional data].
CBS, Den Haag.
(annual) 1981 (published 1985). Fl 27. *Nl.

1978 Personale inkomensverdeling...huishoudens, kerncijfers [Distribution of personal income...households, key figures].
CBS, Den Haag.
(annual) 1981 (published 1985). Fl 15. 40p. *Nl.

Δ F - i, continued

1979 Consumenten-conjunctuuronderzoek 1972-1983: een inventaristie van 35 conjunctuurenquêtes onder consumenten [Consumer survey 1972-1983: an inventory].
CBS, Den Haag.
1984. Dl.12.45. 36p. *Nl.
Includes some statistical tables.

Δ F - ii Health and welfare

< see also 2035, 2036

1980 Vademecum gezondheidsstatistiek Nederland [Vademecum of health statistics of the Netherlands].
CBS, Den Haag.
1977- 1984. Fl 27.50. 214p. *Nl; contents list also in En.
TF: has data for 1982, 1983 or the latest available, and some earlier years in some tables.
Data on population, social structure, way of living, environment, birth, aspects of health and disease in the population, diagnoses and treatment in curative health care, mortality, institutions, manpower and training, and financial data.

1981 Maandbericht gezondheidsstatistiek [Monthly bulletin of health statistics].
CBS, Den Haag.
1984. Fl 8.50 or Fl 64 yr. ISSN 0168-2962. *Nl; contains list & main headings also in En.
TF: each issue has monthly data for the last one or two years to the latest month available or five months prior to publication.
Includes monthly figures on perinatal and infant mortality, causes of death by age and province, fatal accidents, infectious diseases, sickness absenteeism. Quarterly figures (based on continuous health survey) on consultation of general practitioners and specialists, medicine consumption, and confinement to bed. Quarterly figures (number of beds, flow of patients, number of hospital days) of general hospitals, mental hospitals, institutions for mentally deficients, and nursing homes.

1982 Intramurale gezondheidszorg [Intramural health care].
CBS, Den Haag.
(annual) 1983 (published 1985). Fl 22.50. 70p. *Nl; contents list & table headings also in En.
National and provincial results on occupancy rate in hospitals, numbers of beds, running costs, labour, finances, etc.

1983 Diagnosestatistiek ziekenhuizen [Hospital morbidity statistics].
CBS, Den Haag.
1964/65- 1981-1982 (published 1985). Fl 50.20. 201p. ISSN 0548-1899. *Nl; contents list also in En.

1984 Kosten en financiering van de gezondheidszorg [Cost of health care].
CBS, Den Haag.
1953- 1982 (published 1984). Fl 14.40. 44p. *Nl; summary & contents list also in En.
TF: has data for several years to 1982.
The results of an investigation, with data by categories of institution, for hospitals (general, university, special, mental); nursing homes; maternity care centres; nurseries for toddlers; health services, etc.

1985 De leefsituatie van de Nederlandse bevolking van 55 jaar en ouder... [Well-being of the elderly population of the Netherlands. A survey on people aged 55 years and over...].
CBS, Den Haag.
1977- 1982. 5 vols. *Nl, En.
TF: the survey is taken occasionally. The 1982 results were published in 1984 and 1985.
Contents:
Part 1A: Key figures: house-keeping in family households, dwellings, mobility, health, care and assistance (Fl 27)
Part 1B: Key figures: leisure time activities (Fl 25.90)
Part 2: Extramural assistance to independent housing people (Fl 10.85)
Part 3: People living in homes for the elderly (Fl 18.90)
Part 4: Results of terminating gainful occupations... 1976-1982 (Fl 18.75).

1986 De leefsituatie van de Nederlandse bevolking...Kerncijfers [Well-being of the population in the Netherlands...Key figures].
CBS, Den Haag.
(annual) 1983 (published 1985). Fl 24.75. 155p. *Nl, En.
Note: a fuller report is issued in some years (i.e., 1977 in 4 vols).

1987 Beddenkwartaaltelling zwakzinnigenzorg: algemene gegevens [Census of beds in mental hospitals: general data].
Geneeskundige Hoofinspectie voor de Geestelijke Volksgezondheid, Leidschendam.
1983- 2 a year. not priced. *Nl.
Note: they also issue a similar publication relating to psychiatric hospitals.

1988 Statistiek der bedrijfsongevallen [Industrial accident statistics].
CBS, Den Haag.
(annual) 1982 (published 1984). Fl 10.85. *Nl, En.

Δ F - ii, continued

1989 Statistiek van de algemene bijstand [Statistics of public assistance].
CBS, Den Haag.
1965- 1977. Fl 9.60. *Nl, En.
TF: no later issue has been published.

Δ F - iii Education and leisure

1990 Statistiek van het basisonderwijs [Statistics of basic education].
CBS, Den Haag.
1949/53- 1983/84 (published 1984). Fl 14.65. c 30p. *Nl.
Numbers of pupils, classes, schools, teachers, etc. both for the country and regionally.

1991 Zakboek onderwojsstatistieken...Onderwijs cijfergewijs [Pocket book of educational statistics...Educational figuration].
CBS, Den Haag.
(annual) 1984. Fl 22.50. *Nl, En.
Wide selection of tables with current data on educational institutions, the receivers of education (including data on age and on flows of pupils in full-time education), the teaching staff and cost of education. Each issue has additional information on a number of specific subjects, which differ from year to year.

1992 Statistiek van de uitgeven der overheid voor onderwijs [Statistics of government expenditure on education].
CBS, Den Haag.
1946- 1982 (published 1985). Fl 14.50. c 40p. *Nl.

1993 Statistiek van het wetenschappelijk onderwijs [Statistics of university education].
CBS, Den Haag.
1937/38-1947/48- 1982/83 (published 1984). Fl 18.90. c 50p. *Nl.
Data on examinations and examination results, faculties, ages of students, etc.
Note: also issued is 'Statistiek van het wetenschappelijk onderwijs: de instroom in het studiejaar... regionaal bezien [Statistics on university education: regional differences in inflow in the study year...] (annual. 1982/83. Fl 23.50).

1994 Statistiek van het buitengewoon onderwijs [Statistics on special education].
CBS, Den Haag.
1939/47- 1983/84 (published 1984). Fl 9.50. c 30p. *Nl.
TF: has data for the school year 1983/84 and some earlier years.

1995 Het voortgezet onderwijs regionaal bezien [Regional aspects of secondary education].
CBS, Den Haag.
1948/49- 1982/83 (published 1984). Fl 21.65. c 50p. *Nl.
Data on schools, pupils, classes, teachers, etc.

1996 Statistiek van het lager beroepsonderwijs: eindexamens... [Statistics on junior vocational training: final examinations] (CBS - Hoofdafdeling Statistieken van Onderwijs en Wetenschappen, Voorburg).
CBS, Den Haag.
1983- 1983 (published 1985). *Nl.

1997 Statistiek van het lager beroepsonderwijs...: scholen en leerlingen [Statistics on junior vocational training...: schools and pupils] (CBS - Hoofdafdeling Statistieken van Onderwijs en Wetenschappen, Voorburg)
CBS, Den Haag.
1983/84- 1984/85 (published 1985). Fl 17.50. *Nl.

1998 Statistiek van het hoger beroepsonderwijs: agrarisch onderwijs [Statistics on vocational colleges: agricultural colleges].
CBS, Den Haag.
1983/84- 1983/84 (published 1984). Fl 8.65. *Nl.

1999 Statistiek van het beroepsonderwijs... [Statistics on vocational training].
CBS, Den Haag.
(annual) *Nl.
A series with various sub-titles:
Economisch en administratief onderwijs... [Economic and administrative education...] (1982/83. Fl 13.30)
Huishoud- en nijverheidsonderwijs [Domestic science training] (1984/85. Fl 13)
Technisch en nautisch onderwijs [Technical and nautical training] (1984/85. Fl 13)
Kunstonderwijs [Art colleges] (1982/83. Fl 9.50)
Agrarisch onderwijs [Agricultural training] (1983/84. Fl 10.50)
Sociaal-pedagogisch onderwijs [Socio-pedagogic training] (1984/85. Fl 10.50)
Opleidingsscholen voor kleuterleidsters., pedagogische academies [Nursery school teachers' training, primary school teachers' training] (1982/83. Fl 8.40)
Beroepsbegeleidend onderwijs. Leerlingwezen [Part-time training. Apprenticeship scheme] (1982/83. Fl 8.40)
Nieuwe lerarenopleiding [Secondary school teacher training] (1982/83. Fl 12.10).

Δ F – iii, continued

2000 Statistiek van het vwo, havo en mavo... [Statistics on pre-university education...] (CBS, Voorburg).
Staatsuitgeverij, Den Haag.
(annual) *Nl.
A series with various sub-titles:
In-, door- en uitstroom van de leerlingen [In, through and outflow and age of pupils] (1982/83. Fl 10.55)
Leraren en bevoegdheidssituatie [Teachers and lessons given, qualified and unqualified] (1982/83. Fl 10.55)
Eindexamens... [Final examinations] (1983. Fl 11.75)
Scholen en leerlingen [Schools and pupils] (1984/85. Fl 17.50).

2001 Lijst van scholen van het voortgezet onderwijs en statistische uitkomsten, 1 september...vwo, havo en mavo [List of secondary schools with statistical surveys, 1 September...pre-university education, senior and junior secondary education] (Ministerie van Onderwijs en Wetenschappen & CBS)
CBS, Den Haag.
1968- 1983 (published 1984). Fl 23.50. c 200p. *Nl.

2002 Lijst van scholen van het voortgezet onderwijs en statistische uitkomsten, 1 september...dag-/avondscholen voor vwo, havo [List of secondary schools with statistical surveys, 1 September...day schools for pre-university education, senior and junior secondary general education] (Ministerie van Onderwijs en Wetenschappen & CBS).
CBS, Den Haag.
1968- 1983 (published 1984). Fl 10.25. *Nl.

2003 Structuuronderzoek naar dag- en verblijfsrecreatie, 1982 [Structural survey of day and overnight recreation, 1982].
CBS, Den Haag.
1984. Vol 1: Fl 24.90; vol 2: Fl 19.80. 2 vols. *Nl, En.
Vol 1: day trips. Vol 2: overnight recreation.

2004 Statistiek van de openbare bibliotheken [Statistics of public libraries].
CBS, Den Haag.
1973- 1982 (published 1984). Fl 24. c 100p. *Nl.
Numbers of libraries, stock, personnel, finances, etc.
Note: also issued - 'Wetenschappelijke en speciale bibliotheken' [Libraries of institutions of higher education and special libraries] (annual. 1982 published 1985. Fl 18.70).

2005 Muziek en theater [Performing arts] (CBS, Voorburg).
CBS, Den Haag.
1975/76- 1979/80 & 1980/81 (both published 1984). Fl 23.95. *Nl.
The results of an annual survey, including data on concerts, opera/operetta, ballet, mime, youth theatre, etc.

2006 Sportaccommodatie [Sports facilities].
CBS, Den Haag.
1959- 3rd, 1980 (published 1981). Fl 21.25. *Nl.

Δ F – iv Justice

2007 Criminaliteit en strafrechtspleging... [Criminality and criminal justice] (CBS Hoofdafdeling Statistieken van Rechtsbescherming en Veiligheid, Voorburg).
CBS, Den Haag.
1982/83- 1982/83 (published 1985). Fl 32. c 70p. *Nl.
Data on criminal cases by region, activities of the courts of justice, juvenile delinquency, road traffic offences, etc.
Note: supercedes 'Criminale statistiek', 'Toepassing der wegenverkeerswet' and 'Statistiek jeugdcriminaliteit'.

2008 Maandstatistiek politie, justitie en brandweer [Monthly statistical bulletin of police, judiciary and fire service].
CBS, Den Haag.
1957- Fl 8.50 or Fl 67.85. ISSN 0548-1937. *Nl; contents table also in En.
Includes monthly data on criminality brought to the notice of the police, etc., on bankruptcies and on fires; quarterly data on cases dealt with by the civil and military courts, the detection and disposal of economic criminal cases and the sentences in regard to offences against the Road Traffic Act; half-yearly data on adoption and on the population of penal institutions and state asylums; yearly figures on criminal cases dealt with by district and cantonal courts, the transactions in the hands of the police and on the placing in custody of persons under age.

2009 Gevangenisstatistiek [Prison statistics].
CBS, Den Haag.
1950/51- 1981-1983 (published 1985). Fl 12.75. c 30p. ISSN 0077-6815. *Nl.

2010 Faillissementsstatistiek [Bankruptcies].
CBS, Den Haag.
1951- 1983 (published 1985). Fl 17.50. c 20p. ISSN 0077-6793. *Nl.

Δ F – iv, continued

2011 Burgerlijke en administrative rechtspraak [Civil and administrative jurisdication].
CBS, Den Haag.
1951– 1982 (published 1984). Fl 12.45. c 70p. *Nl.
Data on criminal cases, both civil and military, administrative activities, extraditions, personnel, etc.
Note: early title was 'Justitiele statistiek'.

Δ F – v Religion

2012 Financiële gegevens kerkgenootschappen [Financial data of religious denominations].
CBS, Den Haag.
(annual) 1982 (published 1985). Fl 10. *Nl.

Δ F – vi Elections

2013 Statistiek der verkiezingen: Tweede Kamer der Staten-Generaal [Election statistics: Second Chamber of the States-General].
CBS, Den Haag.
1931– 1982 (published 1984). Fl 18.50. c 150p. ISSN 703X. *Nl; contents list also in En.
Numbers of voters; numbers of voters by province; votes valid or blank, etc; costs for each political party, and membership of each chamber.

2014 Statistiek der verkiezingen: provinciale staten [Election statistics: provincial councils].
CBS, Den Haag.
1931– 1982 (published 1984). Fl 18.50. c 150p. ISSN 0077-7021. *Nl; contents list also in En.
Similar data to (2013).

2015 Statistiek der verkiezingen: gemeenteraden [Election statistics: municipal councils].
CBS, Den Haag.
1931– 1982 (published 1984). Fl 22.50. ISSN 0077-7013. *Nl; contents list also in En.
Similar data to (2013).

2016 Statistiek der verkiezingen (Europese parlement) [Election statistics (European Parliament)].
CBS, Den Haag.
(irregular) 1979. Fl 14. *Nl; contents list also in En.

Δ G Finance

2017 Quarterly statistics (The Netherlands Bank).
Martinus Nijhoff Publishers, c/o Kluwer Academic Publishers Group, PO Box 322, 3300 AH Dordrecht, for De Nederlandse Bank NV.
1970– not priced. *En & Nl eds.
TF: each issue has data for several years up to the date of the issue and is published three or four months later.
Includes a statistical annex with data on the Bank; other financial institutions; money supply and savings; monetary and financial developments; finance of domestic sectors; balance of payments; capital market; money market; interest rates, share prices and foreign currency rates; economic data; and international data.

2018 Maandstatistiek van het financiewezen [Monthly bulletin of financial statistics].
CBS, Den Haag.
1953– Fl 12.75 or Fl 103.10 yr. *Nl; contents list & table headings also in En.
Monthly and some quarterly data on banking, the capital market, the stock exchange, insurance and pension funds, public finance, balance of payments, and consumer credit. Annual statistics on some of these subjects and on inheritances, donations, concentrations of enterprises, private non-profit enterprises, etc.

2019 Statistiek der gemeentebegrotingen [Statistics of municipal budgets].
CBS, Den Haag.
1952/56– 1984 (published 1985). Fl 12.45. 39p. ISSN 0168-6879. *Nl.

2020 De nationale jaarrekeningen... [The production structure of the Netherlands economy].
CBS, Den Haag.
1948/56– Part XI. Fl 19.25. *Nl.
Input-output tables and input output coefficients, 1980. The share of the larger and smaller sized firms in the Dutch economy in 1979.

Δ G – ii Public finance

2021 Nationale rekeningen [National accounts].
CBS, Den Haag.
1948– 1984 (published 1985). Fl 55. ISSN 0168-3489. *Nl; from the 1983 ed. En translation of table headings, etc. is available separately.
TF: has data for some earlier years.
Note: also published in 1985 'Nationale rekeningen 1969–1981 met herziene reeksen voor de jaren 1969–1976' [National accounts, 1969–1981 with revised series for the years 1969–1976].

Δ G – ii, continued

2022 Regionale economische jaarcijfers [Economic annual figures by region].
CBS, Den Haag.
(annual) 1981–1982 (published 1985). Fl 17. *Nl.

2023 Statistiek van Rijksfinancien [Statistics of central government finance].
CBS, Den Haag.
1943/44– 1983–1984 (published 1985). Fl 32.50. *Nl.

2024 Statistiek der provinciale financiën. Rekeningen... [Statistics of provincial finances...].
CBS, Den Haag.
1948/49– 1982–1983 (published 1985). Fl 21. *Nl.

2025 Statistiek der waterschapsfinanciën. Rekeningen [Statistics of polder-board finances. Accounts].
CBS, Den Haag.
1964/66– 1982–1983 (published 1985). Fl 14.50. *Nl.

2026 Belastingdruk in Nederland [The burden of taxes in the Netherlands].
CBS, Den Haag.
1943– 1977–1978 (published 1984). Fl 18.65. c 100p. *Nl.
Data on local, provincial and national taxes, taxes relating to dikes, etc.

Δ G – iii Company finance

< see also 2010

2027 Statistiek van de investeringen in de nijverheid [Statistics of fixed capital formation in industry].
CBS, Den Haag.
1951/52– 1982 (published 1984). Fl 12.45. c 40p. *Nl; contents table & summary also in En.
Data on fixed capital formation in major industrial divisions.

2028 Statistiek van balans en resultatenrekeningen van Beurs' NV [Statistics of balances and profit and loss account of business corporations quoted on the Amsterdam Stock Exchange].
CBS, Den Haag.
1975– 1983 (published 1985). Fl 13.80. *Nl.

Δ G – iv Investment

2029 Institutionale beleggers...voorlopige uitkomsten... [Institutional investors...preliminary results].
CBS, Den Haag.
1966– 1982/1983 (published 1985). Fl 13.75. c 40p. ISSN 0077-6718. *Nl; contents list & summary also in En.
TF: final data for 1982 and preliminary results for 1983.
A survey of investments by institutional investors.

2030 Statistiek van de spaargelden [Statistics of savings].
CBS, Den Haag.
1965– 1983 (published 1984). Fl 8.65. c 35p. *Nl; contents list & summary also in En.
Summaries of data available on savings entrusted to credit-institutions & savings banks, agricultural credit institutions, and communal banks; deposits and withdrawals; velocity of circulation of the savings banks balances; number of savings accounts and specific ways of saving.

Δ G – vi Credit market

2031 Statistiek van het consumptief krediet [Statistics of consumer credit].
CBS, Den Haag.
1959– 1983 (published 1985). Fl 11. c 25p. *Nl; contents list also in En.
Data on credit granting, balance and profit and loss accounts, number of institutions covered by these tables, etc.

2032 Statistiek der hypotheken [Statistics of mortgages].
CBS, Den Haag.
1965– 1984 (published 1985). Fl 18.25. c 40p. *Nl; contents list & summary also in En.
Financial data on all mortgages on real estate and ships newly registered, both ordinary and credit mortgages.

Δ G – v Insurance

2033 Financiële gegevens levensverzekeringsmaatschappijen... [Financial data of life insurance companies]
(CBS – Hoofdafdeling Financiële Statistieken, Voorburg).
Staatsuitgeverij, Den Haag.
1981/83– 1981/83 (published 1985). ISSN 0169-4359. *Nl; contents list & summary also in En.

Δ G - v, continued

2034 Financiële gegevens schadeverzekeringsmaatschappijen [Financial data for non-life insurance companies] (CBS - Hoofdafdeling Financiële Statistieken, Voorburg).
Staatsuitgeverij, Den Haag.
1981/83- 1981-1983 (published 1985). Fl 15.75. *Nl; contents list & summary also in En.

2035 Diagnosestatistiek bedrijfsverenigingen [Social insurance sickness statistics].
CBS, Den Haag.
1958- 1982-1983 (published 1985). Fl 13.75. 46p. *Nl; summary & table headings also in En.

2036 Sociale verzekering, pensioenverzekering, levensverzekering [Social security, pension funds and life insurance].
CBS, Den Haag.
(annual) 1979-1983 (published 1984). Fl 26.70. *Nl, En.

Δ H Transport and communications

2037 Maandstatistiek van verkeer en vervoer [Monthly bulletin of transport and traffic statstics].
CBS, Den Haag.
1945- Fl 11.90 or Fl 95.40 yr. ISSN 0024-8770. *Nl; contents list also in En.
TF: each issue has data for several complete years and several months to about six months prior to the date of the issue.
Monthly series showing the development by branch of transport and detailed monthly or periodical figures on international goods traffic, transit, sea-going shipping, container traffic, Rhine shipping, inland navigation, lorry traffic, transport of passengers, use of motor-cars, traffic intensity, and traffic accidents.

2038 Zakboek verkeers- en vervoersstatistieken... [Pocket yearbook of traffic and transport statistics] (CBS - Hoofdafdeling Statistieken ven Verkeer en Vervoer, Voorburg).
CBS, Den Haag.
1984- 1984 (published 1985). Fl 16. *Nl; summary also in En.
Note: 'Transportstelling' [Transport census] was published in 8 parts in the 1970s and related to 1969 to 1972 or 1974.

2039 Veertig jaren verkeers- em vervoersstatistiek, 1938-1978 [Forty years of traffic and transport statistics, 1938-1978].
CBS, Den Haag.
1983. Fl 10. *Nl.
About 450 time series showing development of the fixed and mobile transport apparatus, the size of the transport of persons and goods by mode of traffic, the composition of the transported commodities, investments in means of transport, traffic density, traffic accidents, etc.

2040 Statistiek van het personenvervoer [Statistics of passenger transport].
CBS, Den Haag.
1943- 1983 (published 1984). Fl 17.50. 50p. ISSN 0077-7358. *Nl; contents list & main headings also in En.
Passenger transport by bus, tram, train; inter-urban passenger transport; municipal transport enterprises; local regular services; inter-urban regular services; inter-urban group transport; international transport by bus; national touring-bus trips; national touring-bus trips; railways; civil aviation; and sea transport.

2041 De mobiliteit van de Nederlandse bevolking... [Mobility of the Dutch population].
CBS, Den Haag.
(annual) 1984 (published 1985). Fl 19.75. *Nl, En.

2042 Statistisch van de aan-, af-, en doorvoer...Goederenvervoer van en naar Nederland [Statistics of the international goods traffic (imports, exports and transit trade). Good traffic from and to the Netherlands]
CBS, Den Haag.
1963- 1983 (published 1985). Fl 33.05. 193p. *Nl; contents list also in En.
Unloaded and loaded goods - total, sea-going shipping, inland shipping, rail transport, road transport, air transport, pipe-line transport, and transit trade with transhipment.

2043 Statistiek van het binnenlands goederenvervoer [Statistics of inland goods transport].
CBS, Den Haag.
1958- 1983 (published 1985). Part 1: Fl 19; part 2: Fl 20.50. 2 vols. ISSN 0077-7269. *Nl.
Pt 1: waterway transport and railways; Pt 2: road transport.

2044 Produktiestatistiek transport-, opslag- en communicatie [Production statistics: transport, storage and communication enterprises].
CBS, Den Haag.
1982- 1982 (published 1985). Fl 7.50 each volume. *Nl.
Volumes published:
Veem- en pakhuisbedrijven [Storage & warehousing]
Vervoer verwante bedrijven [Supporting services to transport]
Binnenvaartbedrijven [Inland shipping]
Expediteurs, cargadoors, bevrachters e.d. [Transporting companies, charters, etc]

[continued next page]

Δ H, continued

2044, continued

Reisbureaus [Travel agents]
Tram- en autobusbedrijven [Tramway and coach services]
Taxi-bedrijven [Taxi-services]
Goederenwegvervoerbedrijven [Goods transport by road for hire or reward]
Luchtvaartbedrijven [Air transport companies]
Kleine handelsvaart [Coastal shipping]
Grote vaart [Ocean going shipping]
Luchtvaart verwante bedrijven [Supporting services to air transport]
Binnenvaart verwante bedrijven [Supporting services to road transport]
Wegvervoer verwante bedrijven [Supporting services to inland navigation]
Zeevaart verwante bedrijven [Supporting services to marine transport]
Pijpleiding bedrijven [Pipeline transport].

Δ H - i Ships and shipping

2045 Statistiek van de aan-, af- en doorvoer...Goederenvervoer per land van de naar de zeehavens Rotterdam en Amsterdam [Statistics of the international goods traffic (imports, exports and transit-trace). Goods traffic by country from and to the ports of Rotterdam and Amsterdam].
CBS, Den Haag.
1950- 1983 (published 1985). Fl 48.25. *Nl; contents list in En.

2046 Statistiek van de zeevaart [Statistics of sea-borne shipping].
CBS, Den Haag.
1948- 1984. Fl 33.80. 119p. ISSN 0077-7250. *Nl; contents list also in En.
TF: has data for 1982.
Total port traffic at Dutch ports, and international trade shipping, including traffic and transport, container transport, roll on/roll off transport, and passenger transport.

2047 Statistiek van de binnenvloot [Statistics of the inland fleet].
CBS, Den Haag.
1947- 1 januari 1984 (published 1984). Fl 12.45. 40p., *Nl; contents list also in En.
Number of inland vessels, including tugs and pushercraft by size, province, propulsion, carrying capacity, and year of construction.

2048 Statistiek van de koopvaardijvloot [Statistics of the merchant marine].
CBS, Den Haag.
1949- 1983 (published 1984). Fl 9.50. c 30p. ISSN 0077-7129. *Nl.
The merchant marine under the Netherlands flag; merchant ships by type of ship, tonnage, class, size; Netherlands fleet of tugs, dredgers, etc. Also included are data on merchant ships of Netherlands overseas territories and world merchant marine fleet.

2049 Statistiek van de internationale binnenvaart [Statistics of international inland waterway transport].
CBS, Den Haag.
1948- 1984 (published 1985). Fl 31. c 100p. ISSN 0077-7102. *Nl; contents list also in En.
Amount of international shipping using Dutch ports and inland waterways, by nationality, tonnage and class, type of vessel, etc.

2050 Statistiek van de scheepvaartbeweging [Census of inland shipping at locks and bridges].
CBS, Den Haag.
(annual) 1983 (published 1985). Fl 16.50. *Nl.

Δ H - ii Roads and road transport

2051 Het bezit en gebruik van personenauto's [Ownership and use of passenger cars].
CBS, Den Haag.
1963- 1984 (published 1985). Fl 11.25. c 50p. *Nl; contents list also in En.
TF: has data for some earlier years.
Data by age of car, province and large cities; by age, sex, & occupation of principal user; average distances run annually.

2052 Statistiek van de motorvoertuigen [Statistics of motor vehicles].
CBS, Den Haag.
1946- 1984 (published 1985). Fl 12.45. c 50p. *Nl; contents list also in En.
TF: gives the situation as at 1st August 1984 and for ten earlier years in some tables.
Motor vehicles registered, by year of construction, by province and municipality, by economic-geographical area. Detailed statistics of passenger cars, delivery vans, lorries, tractors, special purpose vehicles and buses subdivided in the same way.

2053 Statistiek van de wegen [Statistics of roads].
CBS, Den Haag.
1966- 1 January 1983. Fl 10.85. c 30p & maps. *Nl; contents list also in En.
TF: published irregularly, the 1983 edition, published in 1985, relates to the situation at 1 January 1983.
Length, type of surface, width, class of roads, by province, region, district, etc. Data is related to the population, etc.

Δ H - ii, continued

2054 Statistiek van de verkeersongevallen op de openbare weg [Statistics of road traffic accidents].
CBS, Den Haag.
1947/48- 1984 (published 1985). Fl 27.75. c 100p. ISSN 0077-7234. *Nl; contents list also in En.
Road accidents and casualties, road accidents, casualties, drivers, vehicles; road accidents in which use of alcohol is verified; road accidents in which a driver or pedestrian was reported on account of the use of alcohol.

2055 Het bezit en gebruik van motorfietsen, 1984 [Ownership and use of motor-cycles, 1984].
CBS, Den Haag.
1985. Fl 11.50. 26p. *Nl; contents list also in En.

Δ H - iii Railways and rail transport

2056 Jaarverslag [Annual report] (N.V. Nederlandse Spoorwegen [Netherlands Railways]).
N.V. Nederlandse Spoorwegen, Moreelsepark, 3511 EP, Utrecht.
1938- 1983. not priced. 72p. *Nl; separate summary available in En, Fr & De.
TF: the 1983 report, published mid-1984, has data for several years to 1983.
Includes statistical data on finances (revenues, costs, investments), quantities (staff, rail-network, light rapid transit lines, passenger stations, rolling stock, passenger transport, goods transport, price index figures.

Δ H - iv Aviation and air transport

2057 Statistiek van de luchtvaart [Civil aviation statistics].
CBS, Den Haag.
1949- 1983 (published 1985). Fl 21.50. c 70p. ISSN 0077-7137. *Nl; contents list also in En.
World air transport and Dutch air transport, including the commercial fleet, aircraft by type, Royal Dutch Airlines/KLM/passenger transport inland, investments, profit and loss accounts of KLM and Schipol airport, aircraft movements, passengers transported, and goods transported.

Δ H - v Telecommunications and postal services

2058 PTT jaarverslag...staatsbedrijf der posterijen, telegrafie en telefonie [PTT annual report...Netherlands Postal and telecommunications services].
PTT, Den Haag.
1972- 1983 (published 1984). not priced. 99p. *Nl.
TF: has data for 1982 for comparison.
Includes statistical data on finances (operating results, investments, capital, income, etc) and traffic (mail, transactions at post office counters and postal giro services, deposits and withdrawals at National Savings Banks, telegrams, telex, telephone services, etc).

Δ I Environment

2059 Algemene milieustatistiek [General environment statistics].
CBS, Den Haag.
1973- 1979-1982 (published 1983). Fl 28.50. *Nl; complete En text available separately.
Data indicative of those activities that are a burden on the environment, including spatial demands, pressure of human activities on the environment such as population, production, energy consumption and traffic, streams of waste, consequences for the national environment and human health.

2060 Kwartaalbericht milieustatistieken [Environmental statistics quarterly].
CBS, Den Haag.
1984- quarterly. Fl 12.55 or Fl 37.10 yr. ISSN 0168-8065. *Nl; abstracts of articles also in En.
Articles on environmental subjects which include statistics.

2061 Fosfor in Nederland, 1970-1983 [Phosphorus in the Netherlands, 1970-1983].
CBS, Den Haag.
1985. not priced. 71p. *Nl; summary & contents list also in En.

PORTUGAL

Central statistical office

2062 Instituto Nacional de Estatística [National Statistical Institute].
Avenida António José de Almeida 5, 1078 Lisboa CODEX.
t 80 20 80 & 80 03 64. tx 43719 PC DINE.
The Institute has an information centre and four departments dealing with statistical studies, co-ordination and general administration, current statistics, and censuses and enquiries. A booklet 'O sistema nacional' / The national statistical system / describes the Portuguese statistical organisation. Unpublished statistical information can often be supplied and a fee is usually charged for this service. Statistical data is usually for continental Portugal the Azores and Madeira.
The Institute has been abbreviated to INE, Lisboa for entries between 2062-2113.

Libraries

The Library of the Instituto Nacional de Estatística (see above) has a large collection of Portuguese statistical publications, those of other countries, and of international organisations. The library is open to the public from 9.00 to 18.30, Monday to Friday, and the staff also speak French and English.

Libraries and information services abroad

Portuguese statistical publications are available for reference in Portuguese embassies abroad, including:

United Kingdom	Portuguese Embassy, 11 Belgrave Square, London SW1X 8PP. t 01-235 5331.
Australia	Portuguese Embassy, 8 Astrolobe Street, Red Hill, Canberra. t 95 9992.
Canada	Portuguese Embassy, 645 Island Park Drive, Ottawa K1Y 0B8. t 729 0883.
USA	Portuguese Embassy, 2125 Kalorame Road, NW, Washington DC 20008. t (202) 265 1643.

Bibliographies

2063 Inventário das estatísticas disponiveis no continente e ilhas adjacentes [Inventory of statistical information for Portugal and adjacent islands].
Published in 1970 by the Instituto Nacional de Estatística, the inventory is arranged by subject. *In, Pt.

A list of new statistical publications, both national and foreign received in the library of the Instituto Nacional de Estatística appears at the end of each issue of the 'Boletim mensal' (2065).

Statistical publications

Δ A General

2064 Anuário estatístico... [Statistical yearbook].
INE, Lisboa.
1875- 1983 (published 1985). Esc 1450. 294p. ISSN 0079-4112. *Pt, Fr.
TF: many tables also have data for three or four earlier years.
Main sections:
Geography & climate - Demography - Health - Employment & wages - Social security - Co-operative organisations - Education, cultural & recreational activities, sports - Justice - Agriculture, forestry & fisheries - Mining - Manufacturing - Energy & water supply - Construction - Housing - Transport & communications - Tourism - Foreign trade - Companies - Trade & prices - Money market & finance - Public finance - International comparisons.

2065 Boletim mensal de estatística... [Monthly bulletin of statistics].
INE, Lisboa.
1929- monthly. Esc 250, Esc 2500 yr (Esc 3000 yr abroad). ISSN 0032-5082. *Pt, Fr.
TF: each issue appears about six weeks after the end of the month and the latest figures may be for that month or for up to six months earlier, depending on the particular table. Some tables include retrospective data.
Climate; demography; health; employment; wages, and social security; agriculture, livestock & fisheries; industry, energy & water supply; construction; transport & communications; tourism; foreign trade; trade & prices; money market & finance; cultural & recreational activities.

2066 Banco de Portugal: report of the Board of Directors.
Banco de Portugal, avenida da República 65-10, 1094 Lisboa Códex.
(annual) 1983 (published 1984). free. 288p. ISSN 0870-0079. *En & Pt eds.
Includes a statistical appendix with data on demand, output & prices; balance of payments; monetary, exchange rates & budgetary policy; and financing economy, as well as an economic and financial survey and the balance sheets and accounts of the bank.

Δ A, continued

2067 Indicadores económicos: Portugal... [Economic indicators: Portugal].
Banco de Portugal, avenida da República 65-10, 1094 Lisboa Codex.
1973/78- 1978-1983 (published 1984). free. 21p. ISSN 0870-0087. *Pt, En.
Economic indices on employment and productivity, prices and wages, industrial production, national accounts, external accounts, exchange rates, Portuguese external debt, national accounts of the administrative public sector, monetary indicators, and interest rates.

2068 Boletim trimestral: estatística e estudos económicos [Quarterly bulletin: economic statistics and studies].
Banco de Portugal, avenida da República 65-10, 1094 Lisboa Codex.
1979- quarterly. free. ISSN 0870-0095. *Pt; summary of text also in En.
A section on the Portuguese economy (text and tables/diagrams) is trade, foreign trade and payments, production, employment - prices - wages, public finance).

2069 Portugal, 1935-1985.
INE, Lisboa.
1985. not priced. 73p. *Pt.
Data on population, education, health, and economic activity (production, agriculture, fisheries, forestry, extractive industries, manufacturing industries, energy, electricity, construction, retail trade, wholesale trade, foreign trade, transport and communications, tourism, wages, and prices).

Δ B Production

2070 Estatística industriais... [Industrial statistics].
INE, Lisboa.
1943- 2 vols (Vol 1: 1983 (published 1985) Esc 450, ISSN 0377-2314) & (Vol 2: 1981 (published 1985) Esc 2900, ISSN 0079-418X). *Pt, En.
Vol I: the mining industries, electricity, gas and water
Vol II: the manufacturing industries.
Both volumes include the number of establishments in each industry, and data on production, consumption of materials, machinery and equipment, power used, and personnel.
Note: 'Recenseamento industrial, 1972' [Industrial census, 1972] was published in 5 vols 1977-1978.

2071 Boletim mensal das estatísticas industriais [Monthly bulletin of industrial statistics].
INE, Lisboa.
1976- monthly. not priced. *Pt, Fr.
TF: each issue has data for the month or quarter and cumulations for the year to date, as well as comparative figures for the previous year, and is published three months later.
Data on industry (production, manpower, monthly index of industrial production, wages, hours of work, and indices); energy (production and consumption); water supply (consumption); construction (licenses, construction and repair, wages, average prices of construction materials, and indices of cost of civil construction).

Δ B - ii Agriculture, fisheries, forestry, etc

Δ B - ii(a) Agriculture and horticulture

2072 Estatísticas agrícolas [Agricultural statistics].
INE, Lisboa.
1942- 1983 (published 1985). Esc 900. 187p. ISSN 0079-4139. *Pt, Fr.
Climate & population; companies; property; structure of agricultural exploitation; fruit & olive groves; agricultural machinery; livestock; production; distribution; consumption & distribution; wages & prices; agricultural insurance; industries connected with agriculture; agricultural development; health & hygiene; education; economic accounts; food balances.

2073 Recenseamento agrícola: continente: total geral [Census of agriculture: Portugal: general totals].
INE, Lisboa.
1968- 1979 (published 1984). Esc 450. 290p. ISSN 0556-0918. *Pt.
Comprises 77 tables.
Note: there are also 18 district volumes and a volume of methods, questionnaire, etc.

2074 Estado das culturas e previsão de colheitos [State of cultivation and forecast of harvest].
INE, Lisboa.
(monthly) not priced. *Pt, Fr.

Δ B - ii(b) Fisheries

2075 Estatísticas da pesca [Fishery statistics].
INE, Lisboa.
1969- 1984 (published 1985). Esc 375. 61p. ISSN 0377-225X. *Pt, Fr.
The active fishing population, companies, fishing boats, personnel, production, trade, consumption, prices, etc.

Δ B - iii Industry

2076 Indices de produção industrial [Indexes of industrial production].
INE, Lisboa.
(monthly) not priced. *Pt, Fr.

2077 Inquérito trimestral de conjuntura à industria transformadora [Quarterly enquiry on the economics of manufacturing industry].
INE, Lisboa.
1977- Esc 1000 yr (Esc 1500 yr abroad). *Pt, Fr.
Data on the manufacture and consumption of consumer goods, investment in the industry, etc.
Note: preliminary data is issued in 'Inquérito trimestral de conjunctura à industria transformadora: anályse provisória de dados'.

Δ B - iii(a) Food products, beverages, tobacco

2078 Cadernos: mensais de estatística e informação [Monthly bulletin of statistics and information].
Instituto do Vinho do Porto, rua da Ferreira Borges, Porto.
1938- not priced. *Pt.
TF: each issue has data for that month compared with the same month of the previous year. Data is cumulated, the December issue carrying annual figures.
Data on the monthly movement of port wine, movement of certificates in existence, laboratory analysis, finances, taxes, etc.

Δ B - iii(d) Engineering

2079 Estatística máquinas-ferramentas [Statistics of machine tools].
Centro de Cooperação dos Industriais de Máquinas-Ferramentas, rue de Manuel Pinto de Azevedo 439, 4100 Porto.
(annual) 1981 (published 1983). free. 35p. *Pt.
Imports and exports of machine tools by type subdivided by country, by type, and by country. Also national production of types of machine tools.

2080 O comércio e a indústria automóvel em Portugal [Automobile trade and industry in Portugal].
Associação do Comércio Automóvel de Portugal (ACAP) and Associação dos Industriais de Montagem de Automóveis (AIMA), rua da Palmeira 6, 1200 Lisboa.
(annual) 1985. not priced. 117p. *Pt; contents table & summary also in Pt & En.
TF: has data for 1984 and some earlier years.
Production (assembly), registration, and circulation (on the road) of motor cars, motor cycles, commercial vehicles, and agricultural tractors, etc., by origin, type, etc. Also imports of parts and tyres.

Δ B - iv Construction

2081 Estatística da construção e da habitação... [Statistics of construction and housing].
INE, Lisboa.
1970- 1983 (published 1985). Esc 675. 139p. ISSN 0377-2225. *Pt, Fr.
Construction of public buildings, authorisations for construcion and repair of houses, construction and repair of houses, prices of materials for construction, etc.

Δ B - v Energy

2082 Estatísticas da energia [Statistics of energy].
INE, Lisboa.
1969- 1982 (published 1984). Esc 420. 110p. *Pt, Fr.
Production of primary and secondary power; production and distribution of energy; consumption of energy; and national energy balance.

Δ C External trade

2083 Estatísticas do comércio externo [Statistics of foreign trade].
INE, Lisboa.
1843- 1983 (published 1985). Esc 2600. 1042p. ISSN 0079-4147. *Pt; contents table also in Fr.
Detailed tables showing imports and exports and transit trade arranged by commodities, subdivided by countries of origin and destination; less detailed tables of imports and exports and transit trade arranged by countries subdivided by commodities; and summary tables.

2084 Boletim mensal das estatísticas do comércio externo [Monthly bulletin of foreign trade statistics].
INE, Lisboa.
1975- Esc 1500 yr (Esc 2000 yr abroad). ISSN 0377-2160. *Pt; contents list also in Fr.
TF: each issue has cumulated figures to the date of the issue, and is published about four months later.
Main tables show statistics of foreign trade arranged by commodities subdivided by countries of origin and destination; and other tables show direction of trade, and summary tables.

Δ C, continued

2085 Comércio externo português [Portugal's foreign trade].
Instituto do Comércio Externo (ICEP), avenido 5 de Outobro 101, 1016 Lisboa Codex.
(quarterly) free. *Pt.
TF: data is accumulated and the January-December issue is termed the annual. The 1983 annual was published in November 1984. Data for the current and corresponding period in the previous year is given in each issue.
Analysis of Portugal's foreign trade. Tables include exports and imports by area and country, and by commodities. The annual issue is more detailed than the quarterlies.

2086 Folha têxtil [Textile journal].
Instituto dos Têxteis, 4 Vale Pereiro, Lisboa.
1977- monthly. Esc 3000 yr. *Pt.
TF: each issue has cumulated data for the year to about three months prior to the date of the issue.
Data on imports and exports of various textiles, subdivided by countries of origin and destination.

Δ D Internal distribution and service trades

2087 Recenseamento a distribuição e serviços... [Census of distribution and service trades].
INE, Lisboa.
1969- 2nd, 1977 (published 1978). Esc 150. 292p. *Pt.
Numbers of establishments, employees, materials used, wages, sales, etc.
Note: there are also three volumes covering districts (Esc 150 each).

2088 Inquérito trimestral de conjuntura ao comércio [Quarterly enquiry into wholesale and retail trade].
INE, Lisboa.
1984- quarterly. Esc 500 yr. ISSN 0377-2373. *Pt.
TF: each issue has data for that quarter and some earlier figures, and is issued about six to eight weeks later.

Δ D - iv Tourism and travel

2089 Estatísticas do turismo... [Tourism statistics].
INE, Lisboa.
1969- 1982 (published 1983). Esc 650. 258p. *Pt, Fr.
General and detailed figures for hotel establishments - capacity, service personnel, receipts and expenditures, investment, movement of visitors, nights accommodated, length of stay of visitors, occupation taxes, and visitors by country of domicile. Also data for hostels, camping sites, and holiday villages.

2090 Inquérito...o turismo estrangeiro em Portugal [Enquiry concerning foreign tourists visiting Portugal].
Direcção-Geral do Turismo, Secretaria do Estado do Turismo, 86 avenue Ant° A Aguiar, 1099 Lisboa CODEX.
(annual) 1982 (published 1984). not priced. 161p. *Pt.
TF: has data for 1981 and 1982.
1: Global analysis of tourists (characteristics, motivation, organisation). 2: Analysis by countries of residence of tourists.

2091 Férias dos Portugueses, 1983 (análise de resultados) [Portuguese holidays, 1983 (analysis of results of survey)].
Direcção-Geral do Turismo, Secretaria do Estado do Turismo, 86 avenue Ant° A Aguiar, 1099 Lisboa CODEX.1984.
not priced. 51p. *Pt.
TF: data for five or more years to 1982/83 or 1983.
Tables and maps on number of days taken with holidays, locale, transport, via travel agencies, socio-economic groupings, etc.

2092 O turismo... [Tourism].
Direcção-Geral do Turismo, Secretaria do Estado do Turismo, 86 avenue Ant° A Aguiar, 1099 Lisboa CODEX.
1977- 1982 (published 1983). not priced. 287p. *Pt.
Incoming tourists by nationality, by frontier crossed; nights spent; hotels and hotel occupation; apartments and their occupation; camping, etc. and occupation; and investment in hotels.
Note: a 4-page advance publication, 'Tourism in...' has been published from 1983 onwards.

Δ E Population

2093 Recenseamento da população e da habitação [Census of population and housing].
INE, Lisboa.
1864- 1981. 19 vols. *Pt; contents list also in Fr.
TF: the results of the 1981 census were published in 1983 and 1984.
Contents are one national volume, 'Resultados definitivos: total do pais' (Esc 450) and 18 district volumes (Esc 200-300 each).

2094 Estimativas provisórias de população residente em Portugal 1980, 1981, 1982 e 1983 [Provisional estimates of population resident in Portugal].
INE, Lisboa.
1984. not priced. 14p. *Pt.

Δ E, continued

2095 Encuesta de migrações interiores... [Survey of internal migration].
INE, Lisboa.
1980/81- 1984 (published 1985). Esc 375. 32p. *Pt.

Δ E - i Vital statistics

2096 Estatísticas demográficas [Vital statistics].
INE, Lisboa.
1929/35- 1984 (published 1985). Esc 1000. 210p. *Pt; contents list also in Fr.

Δ E - ii Labour

2097 Estatístico do trabalho [Labour statistics].
Ministério do Trabalho e Segurança Social, Serviço do Estatística, Praça de Londres 2, 1091 Lisboa Codex.
1968- quarterly & annual. Esc 100 each issue. *Pt.
Within the series are issued a quarterly 'Inquérito emprego' [Employment survey] which covers a sample of about 8000 enterprises representing various sections of economic activity and geographical distribution. Annual issues within the series are 'Niveis de qualificação' [Survey on qualification levels] (1981 issue published early 1984. 84p) and 'Classes de remuneração' [Enquiry into wages and salaries] (1981 issue published 1983).

2098 Conflitos colectivos de trabalho [Collective labour disputes].
Ministério do Trabalho e Segurança Social, Serviço do Estatística, Praça de Londres 2, 1091 Lisboa Codex.
1980- 1982 (published 1985). Esc 300. 188p. *Pt.

2099 Inquérito do emprego... [Enquiry on employment].
INE, Lisboa.
1974/77- 1983/84 (published 1985). Esc 525. 178p. ISSN 0250-4251. *Pt.
TF: has quarterly data for 1983 and 1984.
Population, housing, households, type of work, hours of work, profession, branch of activity, etc.

Δ F Social and political

Δ F - i Standard of living

2100 Indices de preços no consumidor [Indexes of consumer prices].
INE, Lisboa.
(monthly) Esc 50 each issue. *Pt.

2101 Inquérito as despesas, 1973/74 [Family expenditure survey, 1973/74].
INE, Lisboa.
1977. Esc 120. 250p. *Pt.
Data for Portugal, Azores, Madeira and the four regions of Portugal.

Δ F - ii Health and welfare

2102 Estatística da saúde [Statistics of health].
INE, Lisboa.
1969- 1983 (published 1985). Esc 750. 233p. ISSN 0377-2268. *Pt, Fr.
Health establishments, movement of personnel in health establishments, vaccinations, morbidity and foetal mortality, mortality.

Δ F - iii Education and leisure

2103 Estatística do educação [Statistics of education].
INE, Lisboa.
1940/41- 1979 a 1982. Esc 600. 153p. ISSN 0079-4155. *Pt; contents list also in Fr.
TF: the 1979/1982 edition, published in 1985, has data for the academic years 1979/80, 1980/81, 1981/82.
General movement, infant education, basic education, secondary education, professional information courses, higher education, artistic education (music and dance).

2104 Estatística da cultura, recreio e desporto... [Statistics of culture, recreation and sport].
INE, Lisboa.
1979/82- 1979/82 (published 1984). *Pt, Fr.

Δ F - iv Justice

2105 Estatísticas da justiça [Judicial statistics].
INE, Lisboa.
1937- 1982 (published 1984). Esc 450. 145p. *Pt; contents list also in Fr.
TF: published every two years.
Contains data on civil justice, penal justice, prisons and special internment establishments, preventive organisations (police, customs, etc), personnel, etc.

P

Δ G Finance

2106 Estatísticas monetárias e financeiras [Monetary and financial statistics].
INE, Lisboa.
1947– 1983 (published 1985). Esc 750. 159p. *Pt, Fr.
Includes statistical data on monetary institutions, non-monetary institutions, loans, public funds, balance of payments and exchange market, etc.
Note: a quarterly bulletin was also issued between 1975 and 1983.

Δ G – ii Public finance

2107 Estatísticas das finanças públicas [Statistics of public finance].
INE, Lisboa.
1968– 1981 (published 1984). Esc 540. 128p. ISSN 0377-2276. *Pt; contents list also in Fr.
Development of receipts and expenses in the public sector, central administration, regional governments, and social security.

2108 Estatísticas das contribuições e impostes [Tax statistics].
INE, Lisboa.
1936– 1981 (published 1985). Esc 600. 200p. ISSN 0079-4120. *Pt, Fr.
Taxes from the land, industry, capital, stamps, donations, transfer of titles, haulage, vehicles, mines and minerals, added values, transactions, etc.

Δ G – iii Company finance

2109 Estatísticas das sociedades [Statistics of companies].
INE, Lisboa.
1939– 1978 (published 1980). Esc 200. c 450p. *Pt; contents list also in Fr.
Groups of companies by principal activity in Portugal and adjacent islands, companies in Portugal with activities overseas, and foreign companies with activities in Portugal. Data includes numbers of companies in each industry and in each category, and the financial state of the industries. Data on individual companies is not given.

Δ G – v Insurance

2110 Estatísticas de segurança social, associações sindicais e patronais [Statistics of social security co-operative and employers' associations].
INE, Lisboa.
1938/44– 1982 (published 1984). Esc 420. 102p. *Pt, Fr.
Numbers of enterprises and their activities.

Δ H Transport and communications

2111 Estatísticas dos transportes e comunicações [Statistics of transport and communications].
INE, Lisboa.
1970– 1981 (published 1984). Esc 600. 218p. ISSN 0377-2292. *Pt, Fr.
Data on all kinds of transport and communications – railways; roads, road accidents, vehicle registration, public transport, private transport, imports of vehicles, taxes; sea transport; inland navigation; international transport; air transport; and communications, post, telecommunications, and financial services.

Δ H – ii Roads and road transport

2112 Inquérito do transporte radioviário de mercadorias [Enquiry on road goods transport].
INE, Lisboa.
1975– 1983 (published 1985). Esc 1000. 248p. ISSN 0870-2586. *Pt.
Contains data on national transport in continental Portugal, Azores and Madeira; and on international transport, by commodities.

Δ H – iii Railways and rail transport

2113 Boletim estatístico [Statistical bulletin].
Companhia dos Caminhos de Ferro Portugueses SA, Campolide, Lisboa 1.
1950– monthly. not priced. *Pt.

POLAND
POLOGNE
POLEN
POLSKA

Central statistical office

2114 Glówny Urząd Statystyczny [Central Statistical Office].
al Niepodleglosci 208, 00-925 Warszawa.
t 25-48-86. tx 814581 Answerback GUS PL.
The Office is responsible for statistical investigations and studies in the field of economic, social and cultural activities; investigations and studies of technical progress; general censuses; coordination and supervision of the reporting activity for the whole national economy; co-operation with international organisations in the field of statistics; studies in statistical methods, etc. Unpublished statistical information is not made available. The Office's monthly 'Wiadomosci statystyczne' [Statistical news] is concerned with the theory and practice of statistics and informs about the results and methodological arrangements of statistical researches carried out by the Office and other organisations.
The office has been abbreviated to GUS, Warszawa for entries between 2114-2138.

Libraries

The library of Glówny Urząd Statystyczny (see above) has a large collection of statistical publications which may be consulted by the public.

Libraries and information services abroad

Copies of Polish statistical publications are available for reference in Polish embassies abroad, including:
United Kingdom Polish Embassy, 47 Portland Place, London W1. t 01-580 4224.
Canada Polish Embassy, 443 Daly Avenue, Ottawa K1N 6H3. t 236 0468.
USA Polish Embassy, 2040 16th Street NW, Washington DC 20009. t (202) 234 3800.

Bibliographies

2115 Bibliografia wydawnictw: Glówny Urzedu Statystcznego, 1918-1968.
This bibliography of the Central Statistical Office's publications, and later supplements, are available from the Office. They are in Polish.

Glówny Urząd Statystyczny also issues a sales list in Polish annually.

Statistical publications

Δ A General

2116 Rocznik statystyczny [Statistical yearbook].
GUS, Warszawa.
1941- 1984 (published 1984). Zl 240. 730p. ISSN 0079-2780. *Pl.
TF: has data for 1983 and several earlier years in many tables.
Main sections:
Geography - Environment - Parliament. People's council. Social organisations - Population - Employment, work conditions - National income - Finance - Incomes, earnings, cost of living - Company information - Investment & fixed assets - Industry - Construction - Agriculture - Forestry - Transport & communications - Foreign trade - Internal trade - Services, handicrafts - Prices - Community services - Housing economy - Science - Education & training - Culture & entertainment - Health - Tourism, recreation, sports - State administration & justice - International data.

2117 Mały rocznik statystyczny [Concise statistical abstract].
GUS, Warszawa.
1958- 1984. Zl 90. 458p. ISSN 0079-2608. *Pl
An abridged version of (2116).

2118 Concise statistical yearbook of Poland (abridged edition).
GUS, Warszawa.
1959- 1984 (published 1985). not priced. c 450p. *En; also available in Fr, De & Ru.
An abridged version, in English, of (2117).

2119 Biuletyn statystyczny [Statistical bulletin].
GUS, Warszawa.
1957- monthly. Zl 50 or Zl 300 yr. ISSN 0006-4025. *Pl; contents table in En & Ru at end of each issue.
TF: data is usually for the current year compared with the previous year, and the latest figures in each issue relates to two or more months prior to the date of the issue. Some tables have long runs of monthly and quarterly figures.
Monthly & quarterly selected data on the economic development of Poland: population; employment, wages & salaries; cost of living, household budgets; prices; finance; investment; industry; constructions; agriculture & forestry; transport; internal trade; services; external trade; international comparative statistics. Certain tables appear only twice a year, such as those on retail trade, entertairment & motor car registrations.

Δ A, continued

2120 Rocznik statystyczny powiatów [Statistical yearbook of counties].
GUS, Warszawa.
1966- 1974. Zl 40. 387p. *Pl.

2121 Poland: statistical data.
GUS, Warszawa.
1977- 1983. not priced. 88p. *En, Pl, De & Ru eds.
TF: published every two years this edition has data for 1970 to 1982.
Statistical data on structural changes and socio-economic development of the Polish People's Republic. Based on the principle in 'Mali rocznik' (2117).
Note: Polish title is 'Informator statystyczny'.

2122 Polska 1918-1978 [Poland 1918-1978].
GUS, Warszawa.
1978. Zl 10. 100p. *Pl.
Published to commemorate 60 years of independent Poland, and contains text and tables giving a picture of the society and administration of the country.

2123 Rocznik statystyczny gospodarki mieszkaniowe i komunalnej [Statistical yearbook of housing and local government].
GUS, Warszawa.
1965- 1973 (published 1974). Zl 30. c 150p. *Pl.
Data on housing, water, sewage, electricity, gas, central heating, roads and squares in towns, lighting, city communications, public transport, utilities, hotels, fires, finance, employment and wages in local government, etc.

Δ B Production

Δ B - ii Agriculture, fisheries, forestry etc

Δ B - ii(a) Agriculture and horticulture

2124 Rocznik statystyczny rolnictwa i gospodarki zywnosciowej [Statistical yearbook of agriculture].
GUS, Warszawa.
1965- 1978. Zl 115. 540p. *Pl.
TF: has data for 1976 and earlier years in some tables.
Development of agriculture in Poland, including agricultural population, agricultural production, crops, husbandry, private farms, state farms, co-operative farms, investments, employment, prices, mechanisation and electrification.

Δ B - iii Industry

2125 Rocznik statystyczny przemyslu [Yearbook of industry statistics].
GUS, Warszawa.
1956- 1983. Zl 330. 355p. *Pl.
TF: has data for 1982 and some earlier years.
Includes data on plants and enterprises, production, employment, wages, labour effectiveness in the basic branches of industry, techno-economic indices, fixed capital formation, investment outlays, handicrafts, etc.

Δ B - iv Construction

2126 Rocznik statystyczny budownictwa [Yearbook of construction statistics].
GUS, Warszawa.
1946/67- 1974. Zl 38. *Pl.
TF: published at irregular intervals, this edition, has data for 1972 or 1973 and earlier years.

Δ C External trade

2127 Rocznik statystyczny handlu zagranicznego [Yearbook of foreign trade statistics].
GUS, Warszawa.
1956- 1983. Zl 236. 314p. ISSN 0079-2691. *Pl; contents list also in En & Ru.
TF: has data for 1982 and some earlier years in some tables.
Main tables show imports and exports arranged by major industrial groups and commodities subdivided by countries of origin and destination, and imports and exports arranged by countries subdivided by major industrial groups and commodities.

2128 Polish foreign trade (Agpol-Polexportpress).
Sold abroad by the Foreign Trade Enterprise 'Ars Polona', Krakowskie Przedmieśchie 7/9, 00-068 Warszawa (PO Box 1001).
1949- monthly. $14.30 yr. ISSN 0032-2881. *En, Fr, De & Es eds.
A glossy magazine with general trade coverage. There are no regular tables but a few statistics are included in the text.

Δ E Population

2129 Narodowy spis powszechny [National population census].
GUS, Warszawa.
1960- 1970. not priced. *Pl.
Publications of the census include:
Wyniki wstępne [Preliminary results]
Dzietność kobiet [Birthrate] (Vol 1: all Poland; Vol 2: each province and large city)
Ludność zasoby mieszkaniowe indywidualne gospodarstwa rolne: Polska [Population and dwellings on farms: Poland].

2130 Rocznik demograficzny [Demographic yearbook].
GUS, Warszawa.
1945/66- 1985. Zl 300. 254p. ISSN 0079-2616. *Pl.
TF: has data for 1984 and earlier years.

Δ E - ii Labour

2131 Zatrudnienie w gospodarce narodowej [Employment and the national economy].
GUS, Warszawa.
(annual) 1979. Zl 30. 120p. *Pl.

Δ F Social and political

2132 Tendencje rozwoju spolecznego [Trends in social development].
GUS, Warszawa.
1979. Zl 150. 331p. *Pl; short summary in En & Ru.
Tables, included in the text, relate to various years in the 1970s.

Δ F - iii Education and leisure

2133 Rocznik statystyczny szkolnictwa [Statistical yearbook of education].
GUS, Warszawa.
1963/64- 1978/79 (published 1979). Zl 40. 251p. *Pl.
Data on educational development in Poland, including number of schools and colleges of various types in each region, numbers of pupils, graduates, teachers, etc.

Δ G Finance

2134 Rocznik statystyczny finansów [Yearbook of financial statistics].
GUS, Warszawa.
1973- 1978. Zl 60. c 300p. *Pl.
TF: has data for 1977 and some earlier years.
National income and expenditure, credit, money and savings, insurance of property and persons, business finance, and some social statistics.

Δ G - ii Public finance

2135 Rocznik statystyczny dochodu narodowego [Statistical yearbook of national income].
GUS, Warszawa.
1960/65- 1982. not priced. *Pl.

Δ G - iv Investment

2136 Rocznik statystyczny inwestycji i środków trwalych [Statistical yearbook of investment and fixed assets].
GUS, Warszawa.
1946/66- 1973. Zl 50. 541p. *Pl.

Δ H Transport and communications

2137 Rocznik statystyczny transportu [Yearbook of transport statistics].
GUS, Warszawa.
1965- 1973 (published 1974). Zl 60. *Pl.
Data on all types of socialised transport, including public roads, town transport, water routes, etc.

Δ H - i Ships and shipping

2138 Rocznik statystyczny gospodarki morskiej [Statistical yearbook of shipping].
GUS, Warszawa.
1945/68- 1978. Zl 50. c 230p. *Pl.
TF: has data for 1977 and some earlier years in some tables.
Data on ships and shipping, port trade, shipping enterprises, chandlery, foreign trade in goods, shipyard industry, the fishing industry and fishing boats, canning of fish, international trade in fish and fish products, education in seamanship, etc.

R

ROMANIA
ROUMANIE
RUMÄNIEN
ROMÂNIA

Central statistical office

2139 Direcţia Centrala de Statistica [Central Statistical Board].
Strada Stavropoleos no. 6, Bucureşti.
t 13 88 76. tx 11153, 4, 5 & 6, or 11450, 4, 8 & 9 Answerback DCSR.
The Board is charged with the task of organising, guiding and supervising the entire record-keeping and statistical work in the country. It collects, processes and analyses statistical material concerning the development of the national economy and socio-cultural life; carries out censuses, surveys, studies and other statistical enquiries, prepares reports on the fulfillment of statistical development plans, and issued statistical yearbooks, bulletins and other publications. Unpublished statistical information is supplied to researchers, specialists, the press, etc. on request. There are regional statistical boards in each administrative region and a town board in Bucharest. The organ of the Board is 'Revista de statistica', issued monthly (Lei 12.50 each issue).
This board has been abbreviated to DCS, Bucureşti for entries between 2139-2144.

Libraries

Romanian statistical publications may be consulted in the library of the Direcţia Centrala de Statistica (see above). They are also in Academia Republicii Populare Romine Biblioteca [Library of the Academy of the Socialist Republic of Romania], Calea Victoriei 125, Bucureşti; Biblioteca Centrala de Stat [State Central Library], Str. Jon Ghica 4, Bucureşti; the library of the Institutul de Documentare Tehnica [Institute for Technical Documentation], Str. V. Kuibisev 27-29, Bucureşti; and at the regional and district libraries of the higher economic educational institutes and the libraries of the regional statistical boards.

Libraries and information services abroad

Copies of the Romanian statistical yearbook and pocketbook are available for reference in Romanian embassies and legations abroad, including:
United Kingdom Romanian Embassy, 1 Belgrave Square, London SW1. t 01-235 0388.
USA Romanian Embassy, 1607 23rd Street NW, Washington DC 20008. t (202) 232 4747.

Statistical publications

Δ A General

2140 Anuarul statistic al Republicii Socialiste România [Statistical yearbook of the Socialist Republic of Romania].
DCS, Bucureşti.
1904- 1984. Lei 22. 376p. *Ro; translations of the text in En, Fr & Ru are available separately.
TF: has data for 1983 or 1983/84 and earlier years also in many tables.
Main sections:
General data - Population - Synthetic indicators - Labour force - Industry - Agriculture & forestry - Investments & construction - Transport & communications - Internal trade & service trades - Foreign trade - State budget - Education - Culture & arts - Public health & social assistance - Municipal services - International statistics.

2141 Buletin statistic trimestrial [Quarterly statistical bulletin].
DCS, Bucureşti.
1957- not priced. *Ro; separate translation of text is issued in Fr & Ru.
Data on population, industrial production, wages, agriculture, investments, transport, communications, trade, finance, etc.

2142 Romania economic data (Chamber of Commerce and Industry of the Socialist Republic of Romania).
The Chamber, 22 N. Balcescu blvd, Bucureşti.
(annual) 1983. free. 93p. *En.
TF: has data for 1982 and/or various earlier years.
General data, population, synthetic pointers [development of the national economy], labour force, industry, agriculture and forestry, investments, transport and telecommunications, foreign trade and the State budget.

Δ E Population

2143 Recensamîntul populaţiei şi locuinţelor [Census of population and housing].
DCS, Bucureşti.
1838- 1977 (published 1980). Lei 75 each vol. 2 vols. *Ro.
Vol 1: Demographic structure of the population. Vol 2: Socio-economic structure of the population.

2144 Anuarul demografic al Republicii Socialiste România [Demographic yearbook of the Socialist Republic of Romania].
DCS, Bucureşti.
1967- 2nd 1974. *Ro.

SAN MARINO

Central statistical office

2145 Ufficio Statale di Statistica [State Statistical Office].
via Carducci 145, Repubblica di San Marino.
t 99 27 58.
This office has been abbreviated to USS, Repubblica di San Marino, for entries between 2145-2154.

Statistical publications

Δ A General

2146 Annuario statistico [Statistical yearbook].
USS, Repubblica di San Marino.
1962- 1972-1980 (published 1981). vols 1, 2 & 4 L 4000 each; vol 3: L 5000 each. 4 vols. *It.
Contents:
Vol 1: Geography, climate, population
Vol 2: Health and social security
Vol 3: Education, culture, sport, elections, justice, agriculture, industry, construction & public works
Vol 4: Transport & communications, commerce & tourism, prices; labour & wages, public finance, & national accounts.
Note: earlier editions were titles 'Sintesi statistica socio-economica'.

2147 Bollettino di statistico [Statistical bulletin].
USS, Repubblica di San Marino.
1972- 5 a year. L 5000 yr (L 8000 yr abroad). *It.
Climate, health, population, justice, industry, services, commerce, tourism, construction, transport, prices, meat consumption, and employment.

Δ B Production

Δ B - ii Agriculture, fisheries, forestry, etc

2148 Censimento generale dell'agricoltura [General census of agriculture].
USS, Repubblica di San Marino.
3rd, 1975 (published 1977). L 3000. 213p. *It.
Cultivation and production of crops and animals, machinery, labour, land utilisation, vineyards, etc.

Δ B - iii Industry

2149 Censimento generale dell'industria e delle forze do lavoro nell'industria [General census of industry and the work force in industry].
USS, Repubblica di San Marino.
1979- 1979 (published 1980). L 5000. 357p. *It.
Includes detailed data on enterprises; structure of industry; machinery, transport, etc; organisation of production; investment; consumption; production; other aspects; and labour force.

Δ B - iv Construction

2150 Censimento generale edilizio [General census of building].
USS, Repubblica di San Marino.
1976. L 5000 for 2 vols. 2 vols. *It.
TF: the census was taken in November 1976.

Δ C External trade

No separate records are kept of imports into and exports from San Marino; when these are from or to countries outside Italy they are included in the figures for Italy. San Marinese exports consist mostly of handicraft products, particularly pottery.

Δ D Internal distribution and service trades

2151 Censimento generale del commercio [General census of commerce].
USS, Repubblica di San Marino.
1975. L 5000 for 2 vols. 2 vols. *It.

RSM

Δ E Population

2152 Censimento generale della popolazione [General census of population].
USS, Repubblica di San Marino.
1865- 5th, 1976 (published 1979). L 4000. 231p. *It.

2153 Dinamica demografica ed evoluzione sociale nella Repubblica di San Marino [Demographic and social development in San Marino].
USS, Repubblica di San Marino.
1975. L 1500. 137p. *It.
A monograph on the population of San Marino from medieval times to the end of 1974, with many tables and graphs. Covers total population; structure by gender, age, occupation, etc; migration; births, marriages and deaths.

Δ G Finance

2154 Reddito nazionale [National income].
USS, Repubblica di San Marino.
1959/70- 2nd, 1959/1980 (published 1981). L 1500. 48p. *It.
Detailed statistics of national income from the public and private sectors.

SWEDEN
SUEDE
SCHWEDEN
SVERIGE

Central statistical office

2155 Statistiska Centralbyrån [National Central Bureau of Statistics].
Karlavägen 100, 115 81 Stockholm.
t 08-7834000. tx 15261. tg Stabureau.
Founded in 1858, the Bureau is the central statistical authority for the production of official statistics, responsible for all statistics which are not associated with particular government offices for administrative reasons. Statistical information based on published or unpublished sources is supplied to a certain extent free of charge; for special processing and other extensive work a fee is charged. This bureau has been abbreviated to SC, Stockholm for entries between 2155-2218.

Libraries

The library of the Statistiska Centralbyrån (2155) has a large collection of Swedish official statistical publications, as well as the statistical publictions of international organisations and many individual foreign countries. The library is open to the public from Mondays to Fridays, from 9.00 to 15.00 from May to August and from 9.00 to 16.00 from September to April. It is closed on public holidays. English, German, French, Italian and Spanish are the languages, other than Swedish, spoken by the staff in the library.

Kungliga Biblioteket [The Royal Library] in Stockholm, university libraries, and many other libraries in Sweden have Swedish statistical publications available for reference.

Libraries and information services abroad

A great number of Swedish statistical publications are available for reference in the central statistical offices of many countries throughout the world and also in some Swedish embassies abroad, including:

United Kingdom	Swedish Embassy, 23 North Row, London W1R 2DN. t 01-499 9500
Australia	Swedish Embassy, Turrana Street, Yarralumla, Canberra ACT 2600. t 73 3033.
Canada	Swedish Embassy, 4411 MacLaren Street, 4th floor, Ottawa K2P 2H3. t 236 8553.
New Zealand	Swedish Embassy, 39 The Terrace, Wellington C1. t 720 909.
USA	Swedish Embassy, Watergate 600, 600 New Hampshire Avenue NW, Suite 1200, Washington DC 200037. t (202) 298-3500.

Bibliographies

2156 Årets tryck [Publications of the year].
Lists publications of the Statistiska Centralbyrån, is published by them and issued free of charge. *Sv, En.

2157 Meddelanden i samordningsfrágor [Reports on statistical co-ordination].
These reports, issued from time to time by Statistiska Centralbyrån, are intended to give information on co-operation within the province of statistics. They include various standards of classification and regional divisions and codes, and also annual bibliographical compilations such as 'Regional statistik vid SCB' [SCB regional statistics], 'Statlig statitik' [Government statistics], and 'Officiella statistiska publikationer utgivna i Sverige' [Official statistical publications issued in Sweden]. *Sv, En.

2158 Statistisk tidskrift [Statistical review].
Issued by Statistiska Centralbyrån 6 times a year, the review contains articles on the methods used in the production of statistics, and information on what is taking place in the field of statistics in Sweden and abroad. SKr 120 yr. *Sv; summaries & some articles in En.

A list of Swedish official statistical publications is also published each year in 'Statistisk årsbok för Sverige' (2159).

S

Statistical publications

Δ A General

< see also 076, 077, 078

2159 Statistisk årsbok för Sverige [Statistical yearbook of Sweden].
SC, Stockholm.
1914- 1986. SKr 215. 564p. ISSN 0081-5381. *Sv; contents table, preface & headings also in En.
TF: this edition, published late 1985, has data for five or six years up to 1983 or 1984.
Main sections:
Geographical data, weather & environment - Population - Agriculture, forestry & fishery - Mining & manufacturing - Energy - Housing & construction - Trade & services trades - Transport & communications - Labour market - Income & wealth - Prices & consumption - National accounts - Public finance - Enterprises - Credit market - Insurance - Social welfare - Public health & medical care - Justice - Education & research - Culture - Politics & religion - International statistics.
Note: 'Historisk statistik för Sverige'[Historical statistics of Sweden] (SKr 81 for 4 vols. SV, En) has data on population, 1720-1967; agriculture, etc. to 1955; foreign trade, 1732-1970; and a statistical summary.

2160 Allmän månadsstatistik [Monthly digest of statistics].
SC, Stockholm.
1963- SKr 40 or SKr 300 yr (supplement SKr 25). *Sv, En.
TF: most tables in each issue contain data for the last five years and the last 24 months up to one or two months prior to the month of the issue.
Includes short-term data on population; agriculture & fishing; mining, manufacturing & construction; energy; internal trade; foreign trade; transport & communications; labour market; prices; money & credit market; insurance; enterprises; investment & maintenance; public finance; justice; & a section of international data. The supplement is issued annually with information on sources, classification systems, etc.

2161 The Swedish economy (Ministry of Finance <u>and</u> National Institute of Economic Research).
Liber Tryck, 16289 Stockholm.
1960- 3 a year. not priced. *Sv & En eds.
TF: each issue has data for several years for up to 12 months prior to the date of the issue.
Articles and statistical tables, the latter including some international statistics and also national data on foreign trade, production, labour market, wholesale price index, household finance, investment, credit market, business tendancy serveys and national accounts, etc.
Note: the Swedish edition is titled 'Konjunkturläget'.

2162 Statistiska meddelanden [Statistical survey].
SC, Stockholm.
1963- SKr 3500 yr for complete series. *Sv; contents tables, summaries & table headings also in En.
The series mainly consists of preliminary reports, both those that are produced in their final form in books and reports and those that are not scheduled for any other form of publication. The series comprises the following sub-groups:
Am Labour market
Be Population
Bo Housing & construction
E Energy
F Enterprises
H Trade and service trades
HS Trade and service trades
IB Manufacturing, branch data
IV Manufacturing. Data on commodities
J Agriculture, forestry & fishery
K Credit market
Ku Culture
N National accounts
O Public finance
P Prices & consumption
R Legal statistics
S Social welfare
T Transport & communications
U Education & research.

2163 Information i prognosfrågor [Forecasting information].
SC, Stockholm.
1965- 10 a year. prices vary. ISSN 0082-0180. *Sv; contents table & summaries also in En.
Analyses and estimates of future population, manpower resources, supply and demand for selected professional and educational categories, etc. Each issue deals with a particular subject.

Δ B Production

Δ B - ii Agriculture, fisheries, forestry, etc

2164 Landbruksräkningen [Census of agriculture].
SC, Stockholm.
1927- 1981 (published 1983). not priced. 2 vols. *Sv; summary & main headings also in En.
TF: the census is taken every five years.
Data is for regional areas. Vol 1: statistics of holdings, holders, type of land, and arable land; vol 2: data on livestock, forestry, etc.

Δ B – ii(a) Agriculture and horticulture

2165 Jordbruksstatistisk årsbok [Statistical yearbook of agriculture].
SC, Stockholm.
1913– 1985. SKr 120. 251p. ISSN 0082-0199. *Sv; summary & main headings also in En.
TF: has data for 1984 and also earlier figures in some tables.
The structure of agricultural enterprises; labour force; land, real estate; buildings, machinery & plant; requisites; crop farming; horticultural cultivation; livestock; processing, trade & consumption; economics; insurances; agricultural training; farmers' co-operative associations; and international statistics.

2166 Jordbruksekonomiska meddelanden [The journal of agricultural economics]. (Statens Jordbruksnämnd [National Agricultural Marketing Board]).
Statens Jordbruksnämnd, 551 82 Jönköping.
1939– monthly. not priced. ISSN 0021-7441. *Sv, En.
TF: each issue contains long runs of figures for six or seven years up to about three months prior to the date of the issue.
Includes tables for the agricultural sector on production and trade in Sweden, foreign trade, prices (including consumer price index), levies and subsidies and food consumption. Also world production & trade, and international prices.

Δ B – ii(b) Fisheries

2167 Fiskestatistisk årsbok [Yearbook of fishery statistics].
SC, Stockholm.
1914– 1982. not priced. 93p. ISSN 0346-6973. *Sv; summary & main headings also in En.
TF: has data for 1981 and also earlier years in some tables.
Studies of fishing, enterprises: fishermen, fishing craft & fishing gear; catch regulations; catches in sea fisheries: fishing areas & fishing methods; the yield of sea fisheries: landings; consumption of fish; imports & exports of fish & fish products, etc; public administration & regulation of fish prices.

Δ B – ii(c) Forestry

2168 Skogsstatistisk årsbok [Yearbook of forestry statistics] (Skogsstyrelsen [National Board of Foresters]).
SC, Stockholm.
1942– 1984. not priced. 252p. ISSN 0491-7847. *Sv; summary & main headings also in En.
TF: has data for 1982 or 1983 and also earlier figures in some tables.
Includes ownership conditions, administration, forest and forest land, silviculture, logging operations & wood measurement, timber transports, inventories and consumption of forest products, forest industry production and economy, foreign trade and domestic consumption, prices, labour force in forestry, the economy of forestry, the forest sector in the national economy, and international statistics.

Δ B – iii Industry

2169 Industri [Manufacturing].
SC, Stockholm.
1911– 1983 (published 1985). not priced. 2 vols. ISSN 0082-0172. *Sv; summary & main heading also in En.
Contents: Vol.1 has data grouped according to the Swedish Standard Industrial Classification of Economic Activities, arranged by industry and including information on the number of establishments, value of output and value added, cost data, employment data, capacity of power equipment, capital and capital formation, etc. It also includes data on the quantity and cost of individually important raw materials consumed during the period. Vol.2 has data on production of commodities and of services grouped according to the CCCN and SITC Rev.2.

Δ B – iii(a) Food products, beverages, tobacco

2170 Alkoholstatistik [Alcohol statistics (Socialstyrelsen [National Board of Health and Welfare]).
SC, Stockholm.
1914– 1983 (published 1985). SKr 30. 51p. *Sv; summary & main headings also in En.
Data on sales of alcoholic beverages and light lager beer; average strength of alcohol in alcoholic beverages; retail sales outlets and restaurants; consumer expenditure, income of the State, rates of taxes and prices; cases of persons taken in charge for drunkenness; manufacture, import and export of alcoholic beverages and light lager beer; distilleries; industrial alcohol.

Δ B – v Energy

2171 Vattenfall: Statens Vattenfallsverk årsredovisining budgetaret [Power: State Power Board annual report].
Statens Vallenfallsverk, S-162 87 Vällingby.
1909– 1983/84 (published 1984). not priced. 36p. *Sv & En eds.
TF: has data for 1983/84 and 1982/83 for comparison.
A general review, followed by statement of income and balance sheet, and a financial analysis for the public utility, separate accounts being given for the Power and Canal sectors. Data includes finance, personnel, power supplies, forecasts, sales, deliveries, tariffs, production, etc.

S

Δ B – vi Research and development

2172 Forskningsstatistik [Research statistics].
SC, Stockholm.
1973/75– 1981–1983 (published 1984). SKr 50. *Sv; contents list also in En.
Research and development in technology and natural sciences in industry, public authorities, research institutions, organisations, etc.
Note: issued in the series 'Statistiska meddelanden'.

Δ C External trade

2173 Utrikeshandel [Foreign trade].
SC, Stockholm.
1911– 1984 (published 1985). SKr 90 each volume. 2 vols. ISSN 0082-0369. *Sv; summary & main headings also in En.
Vol 1: Utrikeshandel. Årsstatistik: import och export fördelning land/vara enligt SITC [Foreign trade. Annual statistics: imports & exports distributed by country/commodity according to SITC.
Vol 2: Utrikeshandel. Årsstatistik: import och export enligt CCCN med varutexter [Foreign trade. Annual statistics: imports & exports commodities according to the CCCN].

2174 Utrikeshandel, kvartalsstatistik [Foreign trade, quarterly statistics].
SC, Stockholm.
1961– Införsel [Imports] SKr 200 yr; Utförsel [Exports] SKr 200 yr. 2 vols for each quarterly issue.
ISSN 0039-727X. *Sv, En.
TF: each issue is published about three months after the end of the quarter covered.
Detailed statistics of imports and exports arranged by commodities and subdivided by countries of origin and destination.
Note: issued in the series 'Statistiska meddelanden', series H.

2175 Utrikeshandel månadsstatistik [Foreign trade, monthly statistics].
SC, Stockholm.
1913– SKr 250 yr. ISSN 0039-7288. *Sv, En.
TF: each issue is published about ten weeks after the month covered.
Includes detailed tables of imports and exports arranged by commodities, and various summary tables.
Note: published in the series 'Statistiska meddelanden', series H.

Δ D Internal distribution and service trades

Δ D – i Wholesale and retail trades

2176 Omsättning och butiksantal [Turnover and number of stores of the Swedish retail trade].
Handelns Utredningsinstitut, Eriksbergsgatan 10 B, Fack 100 41 Stockholm.
1970– 1983/84 (published 1985). SKr 375. *Sv; an En translation can be added to the main tables for a fee
TF: has data for several years to 1983.
Data on number of outlets, sales figures and market shares for various distribution channels in the food trade and in the specialised retail trades.

2177 Varuhusen [Department stores].
Handelns Utredningsinstitut, Eriksbergsgatan 10 B, Fack 100 41 Stockholm.
1970– 1983/84. SKr 350. *Sv; an En translation can be added for a fee.
Lists all the department stores in Sweden, and also includes statistics on department store development, total sales, size groups, etc.

2178 De störste detaljhandelsföretagen [The largest retail companies].
Handelns Utredningsinstitut, Eriksbergsgatan 10 B, Fack 100 41, Stockholm.
1970– 1983/84. SKr 450. *Sv.
Names and addresses of Sweden's 1000 largest retail companies ranked by turnover. Also includes numbers of stores and total turnover for each company.

Δ E Population

2179 Folk- och bostadsräkningen [Population and housing census].
SC, Stockholm.
1910– 1980 (published 1984 and 1985). 14 vols. *Sv; summaries & main headings also in En.
Part 1: Tabulation programme, charts & maps (published 1981)
Part 2:1: Developments between 1970, 1975 & 1980: type of activity
Part 2:2: Developments between 1970, 1975 & 1980: households & dwellings
Part 2:3: Area & population of localities: developments between 1975 & 1980.
Part 3: Population and cohabitation
Part 4: Dwellings
Part 5: Households
Part 6:1: Economically active resident population
Part 6:2: Economically active resident day-time population
Part 7: Commuting
Part 8:1: Population, employment, & last registered address
Part 8:2: Atlas
Part 9: Economically active population by occupations
Part 10: The planning & processing of the census.

Δ E, continued

2180 Befolkningsförändringar [Population changes].
SC, Stockholm.
1967- 1984 (published 1985 and 1986). *Sv; summary & main headings also in En.
Contents:
Part 1: parishes, communes, etc. (SKr 50. ISSN 0347-6715)
Part 2: migration between communes (SKr 90. ISSN 0347-6707)
Part 3: the whole country and the counties, etc. (SKr 90. ISSN 0347-6723).

2181 Folkmängd...enligt indelningen... [Population...according to the sub-divisions...].
SC, Stockholm.
1967- 1984 (published 1985). 2 vols. ISSN 0082-0164. *Sv; summary & main headings also in En.
TF: has data as at 31st December 1984.
Contents:
Part1-2: communes and parishes (SKr 40)
Part 3: distribution by sex, age, marital status, and citizenship, by communes, etc. (SKr 90).

Δ E - i Vital statistics

2182 Dödsirsaker [Causes of death].
SC, Stockholm.
1911- 1984 (published 1986). SKr 70. 251p. *Sv; summary & main headings also in En.

2183 Livslängdstabeller för artiondet... [Life tables for the decade...].
SC, Stockholm.
1841/1900- 5th, 1971-1980 (published 1984). not priced. 104p. *Sv; summary & main headings also in En.

Δ E - ii Labour

2184 Arbetsmarknadsstatistisk årsbok [Yearbook of labour statistics].
SC, Stockholm.
1973- 1982/83 (published 1983). SKr 100. 284p. ISSN 0347-6596. *Sv; summary & main headings also in En.
TF: has data for 1982 and some earlier years in many tables.
Includes summary statistics, and detailed data on employment and unemployment, labour costs, salaries and wages, etc.

2185 Arbetsmarknadsstatistik [Labour market statistics].
Arbetsmarknadsstyrelsen, Stockholm.
1953- quarterly. not priced. ISSN 0491-7456. *Sv.
Includes various supplements from time to time, such as 'Historiska tabeller' [Historical tables] (Vol 32, 1984, no.2); 'Platsstatistiken 1902-1982' [Vacancy statistics] (Vol 31, 1983, no.3B); and 'Arbetsmarknadsurbildningsstatistiken, 1959-1983' [Labour market training statistics] (Vol 32, 1984, no.4B).

2186 Kommunal personal... [Employees in municipalities].
SC, Stockholm.
1968- 1984 (published 1985). SKr 90. ISSN 0082-0202. *Sv; summary & main headings also in En.

Δ F Social and political

Δ F - i Standard of living

< see also 396

2187 Konsumentpriser och indexberäkninger [Consumer prices and price indices].
SC, Stockholm.
1931/39- 1984 (published 1985). SKr 40. 57p. ISSN 0562-875K. *Sv; summary & main headings also in En.
TF: has data for 1983 and 1984 and earlier years in some tables.

2188 Hushållsbudgetundersökningen [Family expenditure survey].
SC, Stockholm.
1958- 3rd, 1978. not priced. 3 vols. *Sv; summary & table headings also in En.
TF: parts 1 and 2 published 1980.
Contents:
Part 1: basic data about consumption of different goods & services by various types of households
Part 2: not yet published
Part 3: Expenditures on different goods & services by various types of households, 1958, 1969 & 1978.

2189 Löner [Wages].
SC, Stockholm.
1929- 1983 (published 1984). SKr 70 each vol. 2 vols. ISSN 0082-0210. *Sv; contents list & summary also in En.
Contents: Vol.1 has data on salaried employees in manufacturing, employees in wholesale and retail trade, etc; vol.2: has data on agricultural & industrial workers, salesmen, shop assistants & storemen in wholesale & retail trade, etc.

Δ F – i, continued

2190 Konsumptprisindex [Consumer price index].
SC, Stockholm.
(monthly) SKr 150 yr. *Sv; summary & main headings also in En.
Note: issued in the series 'Statistiska meddellanden'.

Δ F – ii Health and welfare

< see also 403, 407

2191 Allmän hälso- och sjukvård [Public health in Sweden].
Socialstyrelsen [National Board of Health and Welfare], Av H.B. Linnég 87, Vaxel, Stockholm.
1911- 1979 (published 1982). not priced. 147p. *Sv; summary & main headings also in En.
Data on health and sick care (including health services, and hospital care), health personnel, costs of health and medical care, diseases, deliveries, etc.

2192 Socialjänsten [Social welfare].
SC, Stockholm.
1961- 1982-1983 (published 1984). SKr 90. c 300p. *Sv; summary & main headings also in En.
Data on all types of social welfare and social assistance.

Δ F – iii Education and leisure

2193 Utbildningsstatistik årsbok [Statistical yearbook of education].
SC, Stockholm.
1978- 1984/85 (published 1985). SKr 80. c 500p. ISSN 0348-6397. *Sv; contents table also in En.
TF: has data for the academic year 1984/85 and also earlier figures in some tables.
Population by age, education; participation and educational attainment; children's day homes and family day homes; comprehensive schools; special schools for physical or mentally handicapped children and Swedish schools abroad; integrated upper secondary schools; higher education – undergraduate and postgraduate; folk high schools; municipal adult education; basic adult education; state schools for adult education; labour market training; adult education associations; teachers.

Δ F – iv Justice

< see also 414

2194 Rättsstatistisk årsbok [Yearbook of legal statistics].
SC, Stockholm.
1975- 1985. SKr 90. *Sv; summary, contents list & main headings also in En.
TF: contains the latest data available and also some earlier years.
Criminal statistics; and statistics concerning courts, the chief public prosecutor, the chancellor of justice, the ombudsman and others.

Δ F – vi Elections

2195 Allmänna valen [General elections].
SC, Stockholm.
1915- 1985. not priced. *Sv.
Sub-titled 'Huvudresultat' and contains the principal results.

Δ G Finance

2196 Sveriges Riksbank: statistisk årsbok [Swedish National Bank: statistical yearbook].
Sveriges Riksbank, Stockholm.
1978- 1984 (published 1985). not priced. 182p. ISSN 0348-7342. *Sv, En.
Data on the activities of the National Bank, commercial banks, other banks, finance houses, insurance institutions and pension funds, mortgage institutions and credit companies, central government, local governments, bonds, credit market, money supply, interest rates, balance of payments, and the foreign exchange market.

Δ G – i Banking

2197 Bankerna [Banking] (Bankinspektionen [Bank Inspection Day]).
SC, Stockholm.
1968- monthly. not priced. *Sv, En.
Rates of interest, and assets and liabilities of banks.

2198 Bankaktiebolagen, fondkommiddionårerna, fondbörsen [Banking and stock exchange statistics] (Bankinspektionen [Bank Inspection Boad]).
SC, Stockholm.
1967- 1984 (published 1985). SKr 70. *Sv; contents list, summary & list of terms also in En.
Summary tables of statistics of commercial banks, tables of statistics of individual commercial banks, data regarding stockbrokers & the stock exchange, & the Securities Register Service.

Δ G – i, continued

2199 Affärsbankerna [Commercial banks] (Bankinspektionen [Bank Inspection Board]).
SC, Stockholm.
1968- monthly. not priced. 15p. ISSN 0281-787X. *Sv; contents list also in En.
TF: each issue has data for that month.

2200 Sparbankerna [Savings banks].
SC, Stockholm.
1911- 1984 (published 1985). SKr 70. *Sv; summary & main headings also in En.

Δ G – ii Public finance

2201 Nationalräkenskaper...National accounts annual report.
SC, Stockholm.
1950/63- 1970-1984 (published 1986). not priced. 82p. *Sv; list of terms also in En.
Note: published in the series 'Statistiska meddelanden N'.

2202 Kommunernas finanser [Local government finance].
SC, Stockholm.
1918/21- 1984 (published 1985). SKr 70 (appendix SKr 25). *Sv; summary & main headings also in En.

2203 Taxeringsutfallet [Tax assessments].
SC, Stockholm.
1968- 1984 (published 1985). SKr 50. *Sv.
TF: has assessment statistics for 1984.
Note: issued in the series 'Statistiska meddelanden'.

2204 Inkomst och förmögenhetsfördelning [Distribution of income and assets].
SC, Stockholm.
1967- 1983 (published 1985). SKr 100. *Sv; summary & main headings also in En.
Contains data for the whole country, counties and municipalities.
Note: issued in the series 'Statistiska meddelanden'.

Δ G – iii Company finance

2205 Företagen: ekonomisk redovisning [Enterprises: financial statistics].
SC, Stockholm.
1950- 1983 (published 1985). SKr 70. 155p. ISSN 0387-1441. *Sv; contents list also in En.
Data on income, expenditure and profits of business enterprises.

Δ G – v Insurance

2206 Allmän försäkring... [National insurance] (Riksförsäkringsverket [National Social Insurance Board]).
SC, Stockholm.
1965- 1983 (published 1985). SKr 90. *Sv, En.
Data on sickness and parental insurance, pension insurance, family allowances, maintenance acvances, etc.

2207 Manadsstatistik för allmän försäkring och arbetsslade-försäkring [Monthly statistical data concerning the Swedish National Insurance Scheme work injury insurance] (Riksförsäkringsverket [National Social Insurance Board]).
SC, Stockholm.
available free of charge in Sweden. *Sv; contents list, etc. in En.
TF: each issue has data for one month about two months earlier than the date of the issue.

2208 Enskilda försäkringsanstalter [Private insurance companies] (Försäkringsinspektionen [Private Insurance Supervisory Service]).
SC, Stockholm.
1912- 1983 (published 1985). SKr 60. *Sv.

2209 Understodsföreningar [Friendly societies] (Försäkringsinspektionen [Private Insurance Supervisory Service]).
SC, Stockholm.
(annual) 1983 (published 1985). SKr 25. *Sv, En.

2210 Arbetsskador [Occupational injuries] (Arbetarskyddsstyrelsen [National Board of Occupational Safety] & SC).
SC, Stockholm.
1963- 1979. not priced. c 100p. *Sv.
Data on insurance, injuries, accidents, occupational diseases, etc.

Δ H Transport and communications

S

Δ H – i Ships and shipping

2211 Sjöfart [Shipping].
SC, Stockholm.
1911– 1983. SKr 70. 156p. ISSN 0562-877. *Sv; summary & main headings also in En.
Data on the merchant navy, special vessels, gross receipts of Swedish shipping, vessels entered and cleared in foreign and in home trade, goods unloaded and loaded in foreign and in home trade, general shipping dues, and harbour statistics.

Δ H – ii Roads and road transport

2212 Motor traffic in Sweden (A/B Bilstatistik [Automobile Statistics Inc., a part of the Association of Swedish Automobile Manufacturers and Wholesalers]).
A/B Bilstatistik, Box 5514, S-114 85 Stockholm.
1948– 1984. SKr 32. 40p. ISSN 0077-1619. *En & Sv eds.
TF: has data for 1983 and about ten earlier years for most tables.
Motor vehicles in use, new registrations, production, imports and exports, consumption of petroleum products, traffic accidents, road goods transport, driving license tests, control inspections, road network, motor vehicle taxes, etc.

2213 New registrations.
A/B Bilstatistik, Box 5514, S-114 85 Stockholm.
(monthly). SKr 580 yr. *En & Sv eds.
New registrations of cars, trucks, buses, caravans, motorcycles and snow-scooters, by make and model.
Note: also available is 'New car price-list' (6 a year. SKr 80 yr) with price-lists for new cars and trucks.

2214 Vägtrafikolyckor med personskada [Road traffic accidents with personal injury].
SC, Stockholm.
1935– 1984 (published 1985). SKr 40. *Sv; summary & main headings also in En.

Δ H – iii Railways and rail transport

2215 Sveriges järnväger [Railways of Sweden] (Statens Järnväger [State Railways]).
SC, Stockholm.
1911– 1983 (published 1985). SKr 40. *Sv; contents list & main headings also in En.
TF: has data for 1983 and some earlier years in some tables.
The annual report of Statens Järnväger, it includes statistical tables of private and State railways – length of lines, rolling stock, staff, passenger and goods traffic, ferry-boat traffic, railway accidents, etc.

Δ H – iv Aviation and air transport

2216 Flygplarsstatistik [Civil aviation statistics] (Luftfartsverket [Civil Aviation Board]).
SC, Stockholm.
(monthly) not priced. *Sv.

Δ H – v Telecommunications and postal services

2217 Televerket... [Telecommunications Administration...] (Televerket).
SC, Stockholm.
(annual) 1983/84 (published 1985). SKr 42. *Sv.
The annual report of the Telecommunications Administration.

2218 Postverket... [Post office] (Postverket).
SC, Stockholm.
(annual) 1983 (published 1985). SKr 30. *Sv.
The annual report of the Post Office.

FINLAND
FINLANDE
FINNLAND
SUOMI

Central statistical office

2219 Tilastokeskus [Central Statistical Office].
Annankatu 44, (PO Box 504), SF-00101 Helsinki.
t (9)0-17341. tx 122656 tikes sf.
A government institution producing statistical information and co-ordinating statistics produced by other government agencies. There are two groups: the Production Group and the Development and Administrative Group. The Production Group is further divided into departments: three for producing statistics and one for information technology. The Development and Administrative Group consists of the Administrative Division, the Planning and Co-ordination Division, Information and Marketing Division, the Interview Division and the Library. The Information and Marketing Division is responsible for public relations, marketing, publications and special surveys.
Publications of Tilastokeskus are issued by the state publishing house Valtion Painatuskeskus, Annankatu 44, 00100 Helsinki 10, abbreviated to VP Helsinki for entries between 2219-2302.

Libraries

The Library of Tilastokeskus (see above) has extensive sets of statistical publications of Finland, other countries and international organisations, serving as the central library of statistics. Besides the traditional library services it also offers information service. Information is provided free of charge unless extensive work or extra cost is involved; for special surveys and extensive work a fee is charged. It is open to the public during office hours throughout the year. The staff speaks Finnish, Swedish and English.
Eduskunnan Kirjasto [the Library of Parliament], Eduskuntakatu 1, Helsinki, also has extensive sets of statistical publications and is open to the public. Most other large Finnish libraries have available sets of Finnish statistical publications.

Library and information services abroad

The embassies of Finland in other countries do not usually have extensive sets of statistical publications of Finland. Libraries of national statistical offices receive extensive sets of statistical publications of Finland.

Bibliographies

2220 Guide to Finnish statistics.
Published in 1977 by Tilastokeskus [Central Statistical Office] in English, the guide gives summaries of the main Finnish official statistical publications.

2221 Valtion tilastojulkaisut...Government statistics (Tilastokirjasto [Statistics Library]).
A monthly catalogue of statistical publications issued by the Finnish government and its bodies. The catalogue is cumulated at the end of the year. Available from VP. *Fi, Sv, En.

2222 Tilastokirjasto 1856-1979 [Statistical publications, 1856-1979] (Tilastokirjasto).
A catalogue of publications in the 'Official statistics of Finland' and other series published by the Central Statistical Office. 352p. Published in 1980 by VP, price Fmk 50.

The latest Finnish official statistical publications are also listed in the statistical yearbook (2223) and on the back cover of the quarterly 'Bulletin of statistics' (2224).

Statistical publications

Δ A General

< see also 076, 077, 078

2223 Suomen tilastollinen vuosikirja [Statistical yearbook of Finland].
VP, Helsinki.
1879- 1983 (published 1984). Fmk 130. 529p. *Fr, Sv, En.
TF: has data for 1983 and some earlier years.
Main sections:
Area & climate - Population - Vital statistics - Agriculture - Fishing - Forestry - Industry - Building - Dwellings - External trade - Internal trade - Enterprises - Banking & credit - Insurance - Transport & communications - State finances - Communal finances - Income & property - National accounts - Consumption & prices - Labour market - Wages & salaries - Health & medical care - Social welfare - Education & culture - Justice & crime - Elections.

2224 Tilastokatsauksia [Bulletin of statistics].
VP, Helsinki.
1924- quarterly & monthly. quarterly Fmk 25, Fmk 85 yr; quarterly & monthly Fmk 135 yr. ISSN 0015-2390.
* quarterly Fi, Sv, En; monthly Fi; table headings also in Sv, En.
TF: quarterly issues have runs of several year's figures and at least 13 months prior to the date of the issue; monthly issues have data for three months prior to the date of the issue, which is usually issued three or four weeks later.
Quarterly issues include data on population, vital statistics, production, commerce, banking and credit, transport, national accounts, prices and wages, labour market, state finance, health, criminality, and other economic statistics. Monthly issues have the most important index series and data on employment and unemployment.

2225 Bank of Finland monthly bulletin.
Suomi Pankki, PO Box 160, SF-00101 Helsinki.
1921- free. ISSN 0005-5174. *En.
TF: the latest data included is about two months prior to the date of the issue, and earlier figures are also given.
In addition to the bank's statistics, this includes foreign exchange rates, money supply, foreign trade, balance of payments, price and indices, wages, production, labour and construction.

2226 Economic review.
Kansallis-Osake-Pankki, Aleksanterinkatu 44, SF-00101 Helsinki 10 (Box 10, SF-00101 Helsinki).
1948- twice a year. free. ISSN 0022-8419. *En & Fi eds.
TF: each issue (published in Spring and Autumn) contains the latest data available.
Includes a section on the economic situation in Finland (foreign trade and balance of payments; consumption and investment; production; employment; prices, incomes and costs; public finance; money and stock market) and a section of 'Facts about Finland', both of which include statistical tables.
Note: also available in microfilm from University Microfilms Ltd.

2227 Unitas: economic quarterly review.
Suomen Yhdyspankki Oy [Union Bank of Finland Ltd], Aleksanterinkatu 30, (PO Box 868) SF-00101 Helsinki.
1929- quarterly. free. *En, De, Fi & Sv eds.
TF: each issue has data for the last six years and 24 months up to between one and three months prior to publication.
Each issue has articles and a 4-page statistical appendix with regular tables on gross domestic product, production, foreign trade, prices, international price development, labour market, state finance, financial markets, Unitas share index, and the bank's finances.
Note: the bank also issues an annual booklet 'Facts about Finland' (1984 ed. 13p) with graphs, diagrams and statistical tables giving an overall view, and an annual report on the bank's activities.

2228 Economic survey...Finland (Valtiovarainministeriö: Kansantalousosasto [Economic Department of the Ministry of Finance]).
VP, Helsinki.
1949- 1984. Fmk 31. 139p. ISSN 0071-5271. *En, Fi & Sv eds.
TF: has data for four or five years to 1983 or 1984.
A supplement to the budget proposals with data on the national balance of supply and demand, foreign trade, agriculture, forestry, industrial production, construction, transport, internal trade, consumption, employment, prices, public finance, etc.

2229 Tilastotiedotus [Statistical reports] (Tilastokeskus).
VP, Helsinki.
1968- monthly, quarterly & annual. prices vary for series from Fmk 30-85; Fmk 600 for complete series.
*Fi, Sv; some with texts in En.
TF: issued monthly, quarterly & annually; in some cases also preliminary data. Also special surveys.
One subject is dealt with in each issue and the sub-groups are:
HI Hinnat [Price statistics]
JT Julkisyhteisöt [General government statistics]
KA Kauppa [Trade statistics]
KO Koulutus ja tutkimus [Education and research statistics]
KT Kansantalouden tilinpito [National accounting]
LI Liikenne [Transport statistics]
OI Oikeus ja vaalit [Judicial and election statistics]
PA Palkat [Wage statistics]
RA Talonrakennustoiminta [Construction statistics]
RT Rahoitus [Financial statistics]
TE Teollisuus [Industrial statistics]
TU Tulot [Income statistics]
TY Työvoima [Labour force statistics]
VL Väestö- ja asuntolaskennat [Population and housing censuses]
VÄ Väestö [Population statistics]
YM Ympäristö [Environment statistics]
YR Yritykset [Enterprise statistics].

Δ A, continued

2230 Indexsitiedotus... [Index reports...] (Tilastokeskus).
VP, Helsinki.
1968- monthly. Fmk 40 per series; Fmk 120 for complete series. *Fi, Sv.
There are five series:
Series TH Wholesale and production price index
Series KH Consumer price index and cost of living index
Series RK Building cost index
Series TR Cost index of road construction
Series AT Wage and salary index.

2231 Finland in figures (Central Statistical Office).
VP, Helsinki.
(annual) 1985 (published 1984). Fmk 3. 32p. *Fi, Sv, En & De eds. Ru ed. appears less frequently.
A mini data bank the size of a pocket calendar, giving up to date information on a broad range of subjects. Aimed at foreigners.

Δ B Production

Δ B - ii Agriculture, fisheries, forestry, etc

2232 Maatilarekisteri [Farm register] (Maatilahallituksen Tilastotoimisto [Statistics Bureau of the National Board of Agriculture]).
VP, Helsinki.
1980- 1981 (published 1984). Fmk 30. 118p. ISSN 0781-075X. *Fi, Sv, En.
Number of farms by size, ownership of farms, prevalence of land disposition.
Note: a census of agriculture was taken about every ten years from 1910 to 1969.

2233 Maa- ja metsätalous: maa- ja metsätalouden taloustilasto [Agriculture and forestry: economic statistics...] (Tilastokeskus).
VP, Helsinki.
1964/78- 1975-1982 (published 1984). Fmk 21. 81p. ISSN 0357-5527. *Fi, Sv; graphs & table headings also in En.

Δ B - ii(a) Agriculture and horticulture

2234 Maatalous: maatalouden vuositilasto [Agriculture: annual statistics of agriculture] (Maataloushallituksen Tilastotoimisto).
VP, Helsinki.
1941- 1982 (published 1983). Fmk 30. 76p. *Fi, Sv; summary, contents list & table headings also in En.
Area and crops of cultivation plants and the use of crops, pasture survey, numbers of domestic animals, production of animals, dairying, consumption of energy, etc.

2235 Maatilatalous: maatilatalouden yritys- ja tulotilasto [Farm economy: enterprise and income statistics of the farm economy] (Tilastokeskus).
VP, Helsinki.
1973- 1982 (published 1984). Fmk 50. 200p. *Fi; table of contents & table headings also in Sv & En.

2236 Maataloustilastollinen kuukausikatsaus [Monthly review of agricultural statistics] (Maataloushallituksen Tilastotoimisto).
Maatilahallitus [Board of Agriculture], Mariankatu 23, 00170 Helsinki 17.
1963- not priced. ISSN 0430-5329. *Fi, Sv; summary, contents list & table headings also in En.
Up-dates the annual volume (2234).

2237 Eläinlääkintölaitos...kertomus [Veterinary service...report] (Maa- ja Metsätalousministeriö: Eläinlääkintöosasto [Ministry of Agriculture: Veterinary Department]).
VP, Helsinki.
1930- 1981-82 (published 1984). Fmk 12. 32p. *Fi, Sv, En.

2238 Maanmittaus: Maanmittaushallituksen vuositilastoja [Land surveying: Statistical yearbook of the National Board of Survey].
Maanmittaushallititus, Opastinsilta 12, SF-00520 Helsinki.
1926- 1984 (published 1985). not priced. 34p. ISSN 0047-5319. *Fi, Sv, En.

2239 Tilastoa Suomen karjantarkkailutoiminnasta tarkkailuvuonna [Statistics of the activity of milk recording societies in Finland] (Maatilahallitus [Board of Agriculture]).
VP, Helsinki.
(annual) 1983 (published 1984). not priced. 57p. ISSN 0355-0885. *Fi, En.

Δ B – ii(c) Forestry

< see also 2233

2240 Metsätilastollinen vuosikirja [Yearbook of forest statistics] Metsänfuthimuslaitos [Finnish Forest Research Institute]).
VP, Helsinki.
1968- 1983 (published 1984). Fmk 28. 224p. *Fi, En; introduction & list of tables also in Sv.
TF: has data for 1982, 1983 and some earlier years.
Forest resources (seed and seedling production, silviculture and forest improvement work, costs, forest fires), labour force, forestry production (including wages, prices), long-distance transport, world consumption and forest balance, production of forest industries, foreign trade, & international statistics.

2241 Huttunen, terho, Suomen puunkäyttö, poistuma ja metsätase [Wood consumption, total drain and forest balance in Finland] (Terho Huttunen: Metsäntutkimuslaitos [Finnish Forest Research Institute]).
Metsäntutkimuslaitos, Unioninkatu 40A, SF-00170 Helsinki.
1981-1983 (published 1983). not priced. 46p. *Fi.

Δ B – iii Industry

2242 Teollisuustilasto [Industrial statistics] (Tilastokeskus).
VP, Helsinki.
1884- 1982 (published 1984). Vol 1: Fmk 72; Vol 2: Fmk 114.30. 2 vols. ISSN 0071-5344. *Fi, Sv; contents lists & table headings also in En.
Vol 1: Data by branch. Industrial activity by provinces, municipalities and groups of industries, types of ownership, value added, personnel, social security, power installed, etc.
Vol 2: Product data. Production, consumption of raw materials, consumption of containers and other packaging materials.
Note: What was vol.3 is now separately titled 'Energy statistics'.

2243 Työtapaturmat [Industrial accidents] (Työsuojeluhallitus [National Board of Labour Protection]).
VP, Helsinki.
1899/1900- 1983 (published 1984). Fmk 35. 154p. *Fi, Sv.

Δ B – iii(a) Food products, beverages, tobacco

2244 Alcohol statistics.
Alko Oy Ab, PO Box 35, SF-00101 Helsinki.
1973- 1984 (published 1985). not priced. 183p. ISSN 0356-6730. *En.
Production, sales, imports, prices, consumption, etc, of the various alcoholic beverages and of ethyl alcohol. State revenue from sales of alcohol, number of arrests for drunkenness, deaths from alcohol, etc.
Note: the English version is an abstract from the statistical yearbook of the State Alcohol Monopoly of Finland, which is published in Finnish and Swedish.

2245 Finnish food industry in figures.
Elintarviketeollisuusliitto [Finnish Food Industries' Federation], Unioninkatu 14, SF-00130 Helsinki 13.-
1981- 1984. not priced. ISSN 0781-3589. *En.
TF: has data for 1979 to 1983.
Production, labour, sales, exports and imports, consumption.

Δ B – iii(b) Textiles, paper, rubber, etc

2246 Statistical report (Suomen Sellulosayhdistys Finncell).
Finncell, Etaläesplanadi 2, 00130 Helsinki 13 (P.) Box SF-00101 Helsinki).
(annual) 1983. not priced. 24p. *En/De & Fi eds.
Output of wood pulp (sulphite, sulphate and mechanical) from the various mills in Finland. Includes detailed statistics of production and deliveries.

2247 Tekstiiliteollisuuden vuosikirja... [The textile industry yearbook] (Tekstiilivaltuuskunta [Association of Finnish Textile Industries] and Tekstiiliteollisuuden Työnantajaliitto [Employers' Association of Textile Industries]).
Tekstiilivaltuuskunta, Eteläranta 10, SF-00130 Helsinki.
(annual) 1984. free. 39p. *Fi; summary & table headings also in En & Sv.
TF: has data for several years to 1983 (production data for 1983 is preliminary).
Includes graphs on textile production, imports, exports, markets, wages, labour costs, etc.

Δ B – iii(d) Metals, etc. and (e) Engineering

2248 Finnish metal and engineering industry... (Federation of Finnish Metal and Engineering Industries and Employers' Association of the Finnish Metal Industries).
Suomen Metalliteollisuuden Keskusliitto, Eteläranta 10, SF-00130 Helsinki.
1968- 1984. free. 32p. *En, De & Fi, Sv eds.
TF: has data for 1978 to 1982 or 1983.
Diagrams on international trends & trends in Finland. Diagrams & statistical tables on industrial structure in Finland, output, investment, profitability, labour, labour costs, prices, foreign trade and international comparisons.

Δ B – iv Construction

2249 Talonrakennustilasto [Building statistics] (Tilastokeskus).
VP, Helsinki.
1960– 1983 (published 1985). Fmk 47. 188p. ISSN 0430-5604. *Fi, Sv, En.
TF: has data for 1983 and some tables for 1975 to 1983.
House construction, buildings completed, buildings started, buildings unfinished, building permits granted.

2250 Asuntotuotanto [Production of dwellings] (Tilastokeskus).
VP, Helsinki.
1960– 1983 (published 1985). 68p. ISSN 0355-2152. *Fi, Sv, En.
Quantity of dwelling construction, mainly in terms of physical units.

Δ B – v Energy

2251 Energiatilasto [Energy statistics] (Kauppa- ja Teollisuusministeriö: Energoaosasto [Ministry of Trade and Industry: Energy Department]).
VP, Helsinki.
1981– 1983 (published 1984). Fmk 30. 120p. ISSN 0358-2019. *Fi, Sv, En.
Energy consumption, imports and exports of energy, prices and taxes, public financing for energy investments and research.
Note: 'Energioversikt...' [Energy review] is a quarterly journal which includes some statistics (not priced. ISSN 0356-9276. Fi; summaries in En).

Δ B – vi Research and development

2252 Tutkimustoiminta [Research activity] (Tilastokeskus).
VP, Helsinki.
1971– 1981 (published 1983). Fmk 12. 49p. ISSN 0355-2233. *Fi, Sv, En.
Size of research and development staff, man-years completed, expenditure and financing of R & D.

Δ C External trade

2253 Ulkomaankauppa [Foreign trade] (Tullihallituksen Tilastotoimisto [Statistics Bureau of the Board of Customs]).
VP, Helsinki.
1917– 1983 (published 1984). Vol 1: Fmk 160; vol 2: Fmk 52; vol 3: Fmk 75. 3 vols. ISSN 0355-0249. *Fi, Sv; tables of contents & table headings also in En.
Vol 1: Basic statistics of foreign trade in terms of CCC Nomenclature.
Vol 2: Special statistics relating to foreign trade and Customs administration
Vol 3: Statistics on the development of foreign trade by countries and categories of goods as well as annual statistics on total trade and trade by countries in terms of the SITC classification.

2254 Ulkomaankauppa: kuukausijulkaisu [Foreign trade: monthly bulletin] (Tullihallitujsen Tilastotoimisto [Statistics Bureau of the Board of Customs]).
VP, Helsinki.
1918– Fmk 125 yr. *Fi, Sv; table of contents & table headings also in En.
TF: each issue has data for that month and cumulative figure for the year to date, and is published about six weeks after the end of the period covered.
Imports and exports arranged by SITC, trade with countries, imports and exports by area, trade with selected countries and selected divisions of SITC, imports and exports by CCCN, transit trade, imports and exports of the main classes of goods.

Δ D Internal distribution and service trades

Δ D – iv Tourism and travel

2255 Matkailun kehitys: matkailualan tilastojulkaisu [Tourism statistics].
Matkailun Edistämiskeskus [Finnish Tourist Board], Asemapäällikönkatu 12B, (PO Box 53, 00521 Helsinki) SF-00520 Helsinki.
1975– 1984. free. 44p. *Fi, Sv, En.
TF: has data for 1983 and some earlier years in some tables.
Trends in tourism, tourism in Finland, tourism abroad from Finland, tourism receipts and expenditure, accommodation capacity, utilisation of accommodation capacity.
Note: monthly and quarterly statistics are also published in 'Matkailon kehitys', a monthly review published by the Board.

Δ E Population

2256 Väestö- ja asuntolaskenta [Population and housing census] (Tilastokeskus).
VP, Helsinki.
1865- 1980. price per vol varies, Fmk 21-86. 19 vols. ISSN 0355-2136. *Fi, Sv, En.
TF: a census of population is taken every ten years, with a lesser census taken in 1985.
Contents:
1A: Occupation & industry: total population
1B: Occupation & industry: economically active population
1C: Occupation & industry: place of work
2 : Population & employment
3A: Income: economically active population
3B: Income: household-dwelling units & families
4 : Recipients of pensions
5 : Health disorders
6A: Education: total population
6B: Education: economically active population
7 : Household-dwelling units & families
8: Housing conditions
9: Dwelling stock
10: Building stock, business premises
11: Summer cottages
12: Regional data
13: Localities
14: Swedish-speaking population
15: Farmers
16: Foreign citizens
17: Population & housing, 1950-1980
18: Index
19: Labour force survey
Note: Väestö- ja asuntolaskenta Helsinki 1980 [Population and housing census Helsinki 1980] published 1982 by Helsingin Kaupunki: Tilastokeskus [City of Helsinki: Statistical Office].

2257 Väestö [Population] (Tilastokeskus).
VP, Helsinki.
1977- 1983 (published 1984 & 1985). Vol 1: Fmk 28; vol 2: Fmk 21; vol 3: Fmk 42. 3 vols. *Fi, Sv, En.
Contents:
Vol 1: Structure of population and vital statistics: whole country and provinces
Vol 2: Structure of population by municipality
Vol 3: Vital statistics by municipality.

2258 Väestöennusteet 1981-2020: koko maan väestöennusteet 1981-2020 [Population projections...population projections for the whole country, 1981-2020] (Tilastokeskus).
VP, Helsinki.
1983. not priced. 63p. ISSN 0355-208X. *Fi, Sv, En.
Note: in the series 'Tilastollisia tiedonantoja'.

2259 Väestön elinkeino: väestö elinkeinon mukaan kunnitain vuosina, 1880-1975 [Population by industry: population by industry and commune in 1880-1975] (Tilastokeskus).
VP, Helsinki.
1979. Fmk 50. 370p. *Fi, Sv, En.
TF: published in the series 'Statistiska meddelanden' no. 63.

Δ E - i Vital statistics

2260 Kuolemansyyt [Causes of death] (Tilastokeskus).
VP, Helsinki.
1936- 1981 (published 1984). Fmk 60. 341p. ISSN 0355-2144. *Fi, Sv, En.

2261 Kuolleisuus- ja eloonjäämistauluja [Life tables] (Tilastokeskus).
VP, Helsinki.
1924- 1976-80 (published 1984). 69p. ISSN 0355-2128. *Fi, Sv, En.

Δ E - ii Labour

2262 Työvoimatutkimus [Labour force survey] (Tilastokeskus).
VP, Helsinki.
1959/75- 1983 (published 1984). Fmk 23. 91p. *Fi; contents list & industry classification also in Sv & En.
Population of working age, unemployed persons, performed working days and hours, and results from flow statistics of labour force survey.

Δ F Social and political

2263 Tutkimustiivistelmiä vuonna, 1982 [Summaries of surveys] (Sosiaali- ja Terveysministeriö [Ministry of Social Affairs and Health]).
VP, Helsinki.
1983. not priced. 229p. *Fi.
Note: issued in the series 'Suomen virallinen tilasto, 32, Sosiaalisia erikoistutkimuksia' (ISSN 0071-5336).

Δ F - i Standard of living

< see also 396

2264 Kotitaloustiedustelu [Household survey] (Tilastokeskus).
VP, Helsinki.
1966- 4th, 1981 (published 1984). 2 vols. not priced. ISSN 0355-208X. * Fi; contents list also in En.

Δ F – i, continued

2265 Tulonjakotilasto [Income distribution statistics] (Tilastokeskus).
VP, Helsinki.
(annual) 1980 (published 1984). Fmk 27. 106p. *Fi.

2266 Suomalaisten elinolot [Living conditions in Finland] (Tilastokeskus).
VP, Helsinki.
1950/1975- 2nd, 1984. Fmk 89, 284p. *Fi, Sv, En.
TF: the 1st ed (1977) has data for 1950 to 1975; this 2nd ed has data for some 20 years up to 1980 or 1981.
Main sections: economic resources, population, families, health, education, labour force and working conditions, housing, environment, physical safety, criminality and judicial conditions, use of time and free time.
Note: No. 74 in the series 'Tilastollisia tiedonantoja' [Statistical surveys].

2267 Naisten aserma [Position of women] (Tilastokeskus).
VP, Helsinki.
(occasional) 1984. Fmk 60. 253p. *Fi, Sv, En.
TF: has data for 1982 and 1981 and some earlier years.
Main sections: family & children, education, economic activity, health and health hazards, unemployment, working conditions, income and earnings, use of time and leisure, social activity.
Note: No. 72 in the series 'Tilastollisia tiedonantoja' [Statistical surveys].

Δ F – ii Health and welfare

< see also 403, 407

2268 Terveydenhuolto...Lääkintöhallituksen vuosikirja... [Health services... yearbook of National Board of Health].
VP, Helsinki.
1884- 1981/82 (published 1984). Fmk 70. 280p. *Fi, Sv, En.
General information and detailed data on public health and community care, diseases, accidents, mental care, hospital care, pharmacies, drug factories and wholesale dealers in pharmaceutical products, legal medicine, health personnel, costs of public health and medical care, etc.

2269 Sociaalihuolto...sociaalihuoltotilaston vuosikirja... [Social welfare...yearbook of social welfare statistics] (Sociaalihallitus [National Board of Social Welfare]).
VP, Helsinki.
1957- 1982 (published 1985). Fmk 34. 134p. ISSN 0071-5328. *Fi; Sv & En summaries.

2270 Huoltoapu [Social assistance] (Sociaalihallitus [National Board of Social Welfare]).
VP, Helsinki.
1969- 1982 (published 1985). Fmk 21. 83p. *Fi, Sv.

2271 Kansaneläkelaitoksen tilastollinen vuosikirja [Statistical yearbook of the Social Insurance Institution].
Kansaneläkelaitos [Social Insurance Institution of Finland], Olavinkato 1A, SF-00100 Helsinki 10.
1969- 1983 (published 1984). not priced. 214p. ISSN 0071-5247. *Fi, Sv, En summaries.

Δ F – iii Education and leisure

2272 Yleissivistävät appilaitokset, lukuvuosi... [General education, school year...] (Tilastokeskus).
VP, Helsinki.
1883- 1981/82 (published 1983). Fmk 11. 53p. ISSN 0355-2446. *Fi, Sv, En.
Numbers of schools, pupils, teachers, and finances, etc.

2273 Korkeakoulut [Higher education] (Tilastokeskus).
VP, Helsinki.
1966/67- 1980/82 (published 1984). Fmk 19. 75p. ISSN 0355-2225. *Fi, Sv, En.
TF: has data for the 1980/81 and 1981/82 academic years.
Data on universities and colleges, students, teachers, finances, etc.

2274 Ammatilliset oppilaitokset [Vocational education] (Tilastokeskus).
VP, Helsinki.
1977- 1982 (published 1984). Fmk 18. 86p. *Fi, Sv, En.

2275 Kulttuuritilasto [Cultural statistics] (Tilastokeskus).
VP, Helsinki.
1977- 1981 (published 1984). Fmk 180. 683p. *Fi, Sv; summary & main headings also in En.
Statistical information on arts, communications, leisure, sports and youth activities.
Note: issued in the series 'Statistical surveys' no. 73.

Δ F – iv Justice

< see also 414

2276 Tuomioistuinten toiminta... tuomioistuimissa käsitellyt rikos-, siviili- ja hallinto-oikeudelliset asiat [Functioning of courts...criminal, civil and administrative cases concluded in courts] (Tilastokeskus).
VP, Helsinki.
1945- 1982 (published 1984). Fmk 34. 136p. ISSN 0355-2187. *Fi, Sv, En.

Δ F – iv, continued

2277 Rikollisuus. Tuomioistuinten tutkimat rikokset [Criminality. Criminal cases tried by the courts] (Tilastokeskus).
VP, Helsinki.
1951– 1982 (published 1984). Fmk 37. 150p. *Fi, Sv, En.

2278 Rikollisuus: poliisin tietoon tullut rikollisuus [Criminality known to the police] (Tilastokeskus).
VP, Helsinki.
1951– 1983 (published 1984). Fmk 45. 180p. *Fi, Sv, En.

Δ F – vi Elections

2279 Valtiolliset vaalit...Kansadedustajain vaalit... [National elections...Parliamentary elections] (Tilastokeskus).
VP, Helsinki.
1909– 1983. Fmk 32. ISSN 0355-2209. *Fi, Sv; summary & headings also in En.

2280 Valtiolliset vaalit...Tasavallan presidentin valitsijamiesten vaalit... [National elections...Elections of presidential electors] (Tilastokeskus).
VP, Helsinki.
1909– 1982. Fmk 20. *Fi, Sv; summary & headings also in En.

2281 Valtiolliset vaalit...Kunnallisvaalit... [National elections...Municipal elections] (Tilastokeskus).
VP, Helsinki.
1931– 1980. Fmk 20. ISSN 0355-2217. *Fi, Sv; summary & headings also in En.

Δ G Finance

2282 Bank of Finland year book.
Suomen Pankki, PO Box 160, SF-00100 Helsinki 10.
1921– 1983 (published 1984). not priced. 68p. ISSN 0081-9468. *En, Fi, & Sv eds.
Brief data on economic development, monetary policy and foreign exchange policy, as well as financial data on the central bank.

Δ G – i Banking

2283 Pankit...liikepankit, osuuspankit, säästöpankit ja kiinnitysluottopankit [The banks...commercial banks, co-operative banks, savings banks, and mortgage banks] (Tilastokeskus).
VP, Helsinki.
1910– 1982 (published 1984). Fmk 25. 54p. ISSN 0355-2454. *Fi, Sv, En.

Δ G – ii Public finance

2284 Kansantalouden tilinpito, 1981: aikasarjat vuosilta 1960–1981 [National accounts 1981: time series for 1960–1981] (Tilastokeskus).
VP, Helsinki.
1984. Fmk 55. 217p. *Fi, Sv, En.
Note: published as 'Statistical survey' no. 75.

2285 Aluetilinpito [Regional accounting] (Tilastokeskus).
VP, Helsinki.
1960/70– 1980 (published 1984). Fmk 30. 120p. *Fi, Sv; contents list also in En.
Production, employment and gross domestic fixed capital formation by provinces.

2286 Kuntien talous [Municipal finances] (Tilastokeskus).
VP, Helsinki.
1973– 1982 (published 1984). Fmk 15. 51p. *Fi, Sv, En.

2287 Tulo- ja varallisuustilasto [Statistics of income and property] (Tilastokeskus).
VP, Helsinki.
1929– 1982 (published 1984). Fmk 26. 101p. ISSN 0355-211X. *Fi, Sv, En.

2288 Panos-tuotostutkimus 1970 [Input-output structure of the Finnish economy, 1970] (Tilastokeskus).
VP, Helsinki.
1978. Fmk 38. *Fi, Sv; summary & table headings also in En.

Δ G – iii Company finance

2289 State owned companies (Ministry of Trade and Industry: State Owned Companies Advisory Board).
Kauppa- ja Teollisuusministeriö: Valtionyhtiöiden Neuvottelukunta, Aleksanterinkatu 10, SF-00170.
1974– 1983 (published 1984). not priced. 73p. *En.
Data in the text on the activities of individual state owned companies.

Δ G – v Insurance

< see also 2271

2290 Vakuutusyhtiöt... [Insurance companies...] (Sosiaali- ja Terveysministeriö [Ministry of Social Affairs and Health]).
VP, Helsinki.
1892- 1982 (published 1984). Fmk 105. 279p. *Fi, Sv, En.
Life insurance and pension assurance provided by law; life insurance; pension insurance; non-life insurance; and business of foreign insurance companies.

Δ H Transport and communications

2291 Liikennetilastollinen vuosikirja... [Yearbook of transport statistics] (Tilastokeskus).
VP, Helsinki.
1956- 1984. Fmk 38. 151p. ISSN 0430-5272. *Fi, Sv, En.
TF: has data for 1983 and various earlier years.
Data on railway traffic (lines, rolling stock, staff, passengers and goods traffic, etc), tramways (lines, traffic, investments), road traffic (registration of vehicles; construction of roads, bridges, etc; finance, accidents, imports), water transport (fleet, personnel, passenger and freight traffic, including sea and waterways), air traffic (runways, airports, liners, personnel traffic), and communications (telegraph and telex, telephones, radio stations, post).

2292 Tie- ja vesirakennukset [Roads and waterway construction] (Tie- ja Vesirakennuslaitos [Roads and Waterways Administration]).
VP, Helsinki.
1943- 1982 (published 1983). Fmk 42. 100p. *Fi, Sv.

Δ H – i Ships and shipping

2293 Merenkulku: kauppalaivasto... [Navigation: merchant fleet...] (Merenkulkuhallitus [National Board of Navigation]).
VP, Helsinki.
1938- 1982 (published 1983). Fmk 35. 55p. *Fi, Sv; table headings & summary also in En.
Contains data on the merchant fleet and its development, operations, value, freight income, etc, including data on the number of vessels of 19 net tons and over, by tonnage and by home port and by tonnage, age and value; value and gross freight revenue; laid-up time; and the manning of vessels.

2294 Merenkulku: meriliikenne Suomen ja ulkomaiden välillä... [Navigation: shipping between Finland and foreign countries] (Merenkulkuhallitus [National Board of Navigation]).
VP, Helsinki.
1917- 1983 (published 1984). Fmk 35. 91p. *Fi, Sv; table headings & summary also in En.
Data on shipping in Finnish ports, shipping between Finnish and foreign countries (including the nationality of vessels), arrivals and departures of vessels, passenger traffic, cargo carried by vessels arriving and departing, navigation and port dues, transport of motor vehicles, passenger traffic of ports, and sea-borne trade.

2295 Merenkulkutilastoa [Navigation statistics] (Merenkulkuhallitus [National Board of Navigation].
VP, Helsinki.
monthly. not priced. *Fi, Sv.
Up-dates some of the information included in (2293) and (2294).

2296 Suomen Satamaliiton tilastot...statistics [Finnish Port Association statistics].
Suomen Satamaliiton, Toinen linga 14, SF-00530 Helsinki.
(annual) 1983 (published 1984). free. 13p. *Fi, Sv, En.
Includes statistical data on revenues from port traffic in cities belonging to the Finnish Port Association, arrivals of ships and goods traffic, overseas traffic in the Association's ports by shipping method, technical data referring to ports (depth of channel, length of quays, number of cranes, storage area in warehouses, rails, etc), expenditure and value of port property, number of employees in the service of the Association's ports. All data given for individual ports.

Δ H – ii Roads and road transport

2297 Auto ja tie: tilastoa [Automobiles and highways in Finland: statistics].
Suomen Tieyhdistys [Finnish Road Association], Vironkatu 6, SF-00170 Helsinki.
1960- 1984. Fmk 100. 124p. *Fi, En.
TF: has data for 1983 and up to ten earlier years.
Articles and statistics on motor vehicle stock (registrations), sales of motor fuel, transport service of motor vehicle traffic, buses and bus traffic, imports of motor vehicles, motor vehicle traffic taxation, road expenditure (on construction, etc), road network, road construction, road traffic accidents, and international statistics.

Δ H – iii Railways and railway transport

2298 Rautatietilasto... [Railway statistics] (Rautatishallitus [Finnish State Railways: Board of Administration]) VP, Helsinki.
1913- 1983 (published 1984). not priced. 145p. *Fi; summaries in Sv & En.

Δ H – iv Aviation and air transport

2299 Tilastoja Suomen siviili-ilmailusta [Statistics of civil aviation].
Ilmailuhallitus [National Board of Aviation], PO Box 50, SF-00531 Helsinki.
(annual) 1974-1984 (published 1985). not priced. 32p. *Fi, En.
Aircraft, passenger traffic, freight traffic, landings, scheduled traffic, daily traffic flow, expenditure and revenue of civil aviation.

Δ H – v Telecommunications and postal services

2300 Posti- ja telelaitos [Posts and telecommunications] (Posti- ja Telelaitos [Posts and Telecommunications: General Directorate]).
VP, Helsinki.
1885- 1983 (published 1984). not priced. 232p. *Fi, Sv; summary & table headings also in En.

2301 Posti- ja telelaitoksen taloudellinen kahitys vuosina 1963-1983: graafinen esitys [The economic development of the Posts and Telecommunications of Finland during the years 1963-1983: graphical presentation].
Posti- ja Telehallitus, PO Box 529, SF-00101 Helsinki.
1984. not priced. 73p. *Fi.

Δ I Environment

2302 Ympäristötilasto, 1980 [Environmental statistics, 1980] (Tilastokeskus).
VP, Helsinki.
1981. Fmk 40. *Fi, Sv; summary & table headings also in En.
TF: data for 1960-1980, the main emphasis being on the most recent data.
Note: issued as 'Statistical survey no. 67'.

U S S R
SOVIET UNION
U R S S
SOWJET-UNION
C C C P

Central statistical office

2303 Центральное Статистическое Управление при Совете Министров СССР [Central Statistical Board of the Council of Ministers of the Soviet Union].
Kalinina 3, Moscow G-19.
t 103450.
The Board is responsible for the collection, compilation and publication of most official statistics of the Union, except foreign trade statistics. There is also a statistical office in the capital cities of each Republic of the Union.
The office has been abbreviated to ЦСУ, Москва in entries between 2303-2326.

Libraries

Научная Библиотека Центрального Статистического Управления [the Scientific Library of the Central Statistical Directorate] has a collection of statistical publications and its stock is available to the public.

Bibliographies

2304 Soviet economic statistics, ed. by Vladimir G. Treml and John P Hart published by Duke University Press, Durham, North Carolina, USA in 1972 this publication is about the statistics, including only a very few tables as examples. Covers national income, industry, agriculture, real income and consumption, prices and money statistics.

New books and official publications on statistics and calculations are described in the monthly journal Вестник статистики (see 2308). There is also an annual list of Russian statistical abstracts compiled by M C Kaser, in the periodical 'Soviet Studies' from 1967 onwards. A consolidated list of the first 431 of these abstracts was also published in 'St Anthony's Papers', no. 19 (Oxford 1966), p 134-155.

Statistical publications

Δ A General

2305 Народное хозяйство СССР: статистический ежегодник [National economy of the Soviet Union: statistical yearbook].
ЦСУ, Москва.
1956- 1984 (published 1985). 2r 70k. 573p. *Ru.
TF: many tables also have earlier figures.
Main sections:
Area & population - Summary data (basic indicators of the national economy of the USSR, development of the economy and culture of the USSR and other socialist countries in comparison with the economy and culture of capitalist countries) - Science & technical progress - Industry - Electric energy - Fuel industries - Ferrous metal industry - Chemical & petro-chemical industries - Machine construction & metal working - Timber, wood-working & the paper & pulp industries - Building materials industry - Light industry - Food industry - Agriculture - Arable farming - Animal husbandry - Collective farms - Co-operatives - Productivity of agricultural labour - Agricultural labour force - Transport & communications (rail, sea, river, main pipe-lines, motor transport, urban electric passenger transport, air transport, communications) - Capital construction - Labour - Trade (including retail prices) - Repairs and other services - Education and culture - Public health services.
In addition to All-Union data, there is data for autonomous republics, autonomous regions and national areas.
Note: similar statistical yearbooks are published in each of the republics and smaller communities by the local statistical offices.

2306 Народное хозяйство СССР 1922-1982 [National economy of the USSR, 1922-1982].
ЦСУ, Москва.
2r 30k. 624p. *Ru.
Contains similar subject data to 2305 above.
Note: similar volumes have been issued for many of the autonomous republics.

2307 СССР в цифрах: краткий статистический сборник [USSR in figures: concise statistical pocketbook].
ЦСУ, Москва.
1956- 1984 (published 1985). 60k. 270p. *Ru.
An abridged version of 2305.

Δ A, continued

2308 Вестник статистики [Statistical courier].
Международная Книга, Москва.
1919- monthly. 50k. *Ru.
Contains articles, information, and details of newly published books. At the end of each issue is a statistical appendix of several pages, containing recent statistics on various subjects, but they are not regular tables.

2309 Ekonomicheskaya gazeta [Economic gazette].
Izdatel´stvo Pravda, Ul. Pravdy 24, Moscow 125047.
1918- weekly. $9 yr. ISSN 0013-3132. *Ru.
Includes some production statistics.
Note: also available on microform from MIM.

2310 USSR facts and figures annual (J.L. Sherer).
Academic International Press, Box 111, Gulf Breeze, Fl. 32561, USA.
1977- vol.9, 1985. $45. 424p. *En.
Contains data on government, foreign affairs, the Communist Party, demography, armed forces, economy, energy, industrial development, agriculture, foreign trade and aid, health, education and welfare, culture and communications, transportation, religion, science and technology, and special topics.

2311 Soviet economic facts, 1917-1981 (Roger A. Clarke & Dubravko J.L. Matko).
Macmillan, 4 Little Essex Street, London WC2 & Free Press, New York.
(2nd edition 1983). £25. 242p. *En.
TF: the 1st edition was in published in 1972.
A useful collection of official statistics of a retrospective nature, with long runs of years to 1980 or 1981, covering general statistics, industrial production, agriculture, and unofficial recalculations and estimates. The sources used are listed.

2312 The Soviet Union: figures, facts, data (B. Lewytzkvj).
K.G. Saur, New York, London, etc.
1979. £35.50 or $85. 650p. *En.
TF: data from the beginning of the 20th century to the 1970s.
Includes data on population, politics, economy, labour, social structure, science, education, printing and publishing, living standards, public organisations, religion, etc.

2313 USSR: measures of economic growth and development, 1950-80. Studies prepared for the use of the Joint Economic Committee, Congress of the United States.
Superintendent of Documents, US Government Printing Office, Washington DC 20402.
1983. not priced. 411p. *En.
Includes gross national product of the USSR, 1950-80, index of industrial production in the USSR, index of agricultural production in the USSR, and index of consumption in the USSR.

2314 The USSR: a statistical and marketing review (Jennifer Carr).
Warwick Statistics Service, University of Warwick Library, Coventry CV4 7AL, England.
£30. 140p. *En.
Includes a little background data on the Republics, mainly as a whole (country and people, standard of living), and data on economics, industry, agriculture, natural resources, finance and trade.
Note: issued as Warwick Statistics Service Occasional review No. 3.

2315 Ecotass: the economic and commercial bulletin of the Soviet News Agency, TASS (Tass, Moscow, USSR).
Pergamon Press Ltd, Headington Hill Hall, Oxford OX3 0BW.
(weekly) $295 yr. ISSN 0013-0702. *En, Fr, It & De eds.
Includes some statistics in each issue but no regular tables.

2316 Handbook of Soviet social science data (Ellen Propper Mickiewicz, ed).
Free Press, New York.
1973. $14.95. 251p. *En.
TF: data included is for selected years between 1913 and 1968.
Includes statistical data on demography, agriculture, production, health, housing, education, elite recruitment and mobilisation, communications, and international relations.

Δ B Production

Δ B - ii Agriculture, fisheries, forestry, etc

2317 Soviet agricultural commodity trade, 1960-1976: a statistical survey CIA, National Foreign Assessment Center).
Document Expediting (DOCEX) Project, Exchange & Gift Division, Library of Congress, Washington DC 20540, USA
1978. not priced. not paged. *En.

2318 Prospects for Soviet agricultural production and trade.
OECD, Paris; or from sales agents.
1983. £6 or $12 or Fr 60. 118p. *En & Fr eds.

Δ B – ii(b) Fisheries

2319 Statistical yearbook (International North Pacific Fisheries Commission).
International North Pacific Fisheries Commission, 6640 Northwest Marine Drive, Vancouver, B.C., Canada V6T 1X2.
1970- 1981 (published 1985). not priced: limited distribution. 124p. ISSN 0535-1588. *En.
TF: has monthly and quarterly data for 1981.
Includes catch and effort statistics for the salmon fisheries of the USSR.

Δ B – v Energy

2320 Soviet oil, gas and energy databook (PetroStudies Co).
Noroil Publishing House Ltd., PO Box 480, N-4001 Stavanger, Norway.
1978. not priced. 239p. *En.
TF: has long runs of figures to 1976 or 1977.
Includes statistical tables on petroleum geology; oil reserves and production; natural gas resources and production; exploration and drilling offshore; petroleum machinery and tubular goods; coal resources and production; oil shale and peat resources and production; hydroelectric power resources and production; commercial nuclear power; resources and production of primary energy; oil refining and gas manufacturing; petrochemical industry; electricity production, transport and storage; tanker fleet; external trade in oil and in natural gas, coal and electricity; total energy exports, consumption, energy balances, investments, costs and rentability.

Δ C External trade

2321 Внешняя торговля СССР: статистический обзор [Foreign trade of the USSR: statistical survey].
Министерство Внешней Торговли, Москва.
1956- 1984 (published 1985). 2r 10k. 280p. *Ru.
TF: data for both 1983 and 1984.
Includes detailed tables showing USSR trade with each country, subdivided by commodities. There are also general tables of foreign trade by countries and of foreign trade by commodities.

2322 Foreign trade (Ministry of Foreign Trade).
Ministry of Foreign Trade, 4 Pudovkin Street, Moscow 119285 and Collet's Holdings Ltd., Denington Estate, Wellingborough, Northants NN8 2QT.
1931- monthly. £21 yr. ISSN 0134-8469. *En, Ru, Fr, Es & De eds.
Mainly text, but includes some statistics in the articles. No regular tables.

2323 Information bulletin.
British-Soviet Chamber of Commerce, 2 Lowndes Street, London SW1X 9ET.
(monthly) not priced. *En.
TF: each issue has cumulative data to about one or two months prior to the date of the issue.
Includes an appendix of statistical data on UK-Soviet trade by commodity, values only.

Δ E Population

2324 Переписи населения [Census of population].
ЦСУ, Москва.
1913- 1970. 7 vols. *Ru.
TF: censuses were taken in 1913, 1939, 1959, and 1970. The results of the 1970 census were published between 1972 and 1974.
Vol 1: has data on the numbers of inhabitants in the USSR, all-union and autonomous republics, administrative divisions and oblasts (83k)
Vol 2: is concerned with the data by sex, age group and marital condition (1r 17k)
Vol 3: is devoted to educational levels and attainments (2r 31k)
Vol 4: is concerned with the nationalities of the population (2r 68k)
Vol 5: with the distribution of the population, means of livelihood, etc (1r 25k)
Vol 6: is also concerned with the distribution of the population and with occupations (8r 29k)
Vol 7: is concerned with migration and the composition of the family (1r 83k).

Δ G Finance

2325 Soviet statistics on capital formation: a reference aid.
CIA, National Foreign Assessment Center, 5285 Port Royal Road, Springfield, Va 22161, USA.
1982. not priced. 16p. *En.
TF: data for several years to 1980.

2326 Soviet gross national product at current prices, 1960-1980: a research paper (CIA, National Foreign Assessment Center)
Document Expediting (DOCEX) project, Exchange & Gift Division, Library of Congress, Washington DC 20540, USA
1983. not priced. 30p. *En.

TR

TURKEY
TURQUIE
TURKEI
TURKIYE

Central statistical office

2327 Devlet Istatistik Enstitüsü [State Institute of Statistics].
Necati Bey Caddesi, 114 Ankara.
t 236330.
The Institute is the main data collecting agency of the country and is responsible for the collection and compilation of statistical data on all economic and social matters. It also provides statistical standards, conducts statistical surveys and analyses, publishes statistical data, assists in conducting and evaluating public opinion polls, and collects, compiles and publishes the results of censuses. Unpublished statistical information is supplied, free of charge, when available.
The Institute has been abbreviated to DIE, Ankara for entries between 2327-2403.

Libraries

The Research Library of Devlet Istatistik Enstitüsü (see above) has a collection of statistical publications of Turkey, other countries, and international organisations. It is open to the public from 8.30 to 12.00 and from 13.00 to 17.50, and the staff also speak English.

Libraries and information services abroad

Copies of Turkish statistical publications are available for reference in Turkish embassies abroad, including:

United Kingdom	Turkish Embassy, 43 Belgrave Square, London SW1X 8PA. t 01-235 4233.
Canada	Turkish Embassy, 197 Wurtenburg Street, Ottawa K1N 8L9. t 232 1577.
USA	Turkish Embassy, 1606 23rd Street NW, Washington DC 20008. t (202) 667 6400.

Bibliographies

2328 Yayin Katalogu, 1927-83 [Publications catalogue].
The catalogue of the publications of Devlet Istatistik Enstitüsü is available free on request. A revised edition is issued from time to time.

Statistical publications

Δ A General

2329 Türkiye istatistik yilligi [Statistical yearbook of Turkey].
DIE, Ankara.
1928- 1985. not priced. 435p. ISSN 0082-691X. *Tr, En.
TF: has data for several years to 1984.
Main sections:
Area & geography - Climate - Population - Demographic statistics - Health - Education & culture - Justice - Elections - Social security & social aid - Labour force & employment - Agriculture - Mining - Power - Manufacturing industry - Building construction - Transportation & communications - Tourism - Domestic trade & services - Foreign trade - Prices & indexes - Money, banking & insurance - Finance - National accounts - International statistics.

2330 Türkiye istatistik cep yilligi [Statistical pocketbook of Turkey].
DIE, Ankara.
1969- 1984. not priced. 328p. *Tr, En.
TF: has data for 1979 to 983.
Based on the data in the statistical yearbook (2329) and covering the same subjects.

2331 Aylik istatistik bülteni [Monthly bulletin of statistics].
DIE, Ankara.
1952- monthly. not priced. ISSN 0041-4263. *Tr, En.
TF: each issue includes data for about ten years and 12 or more months to the date of the issue.
Includes data on labour and social security; manufacturing industry, mining and electric energy; building construction; transport; foreign trade; prices and indices; finance, money and banking; companies; and international statistics.

2332 Aylik ekonomik gostergeler [Monthly economic indicators].
DIE, Ankara.
(monthly) not priced. *Tr, En.
TF: each issue has monthly figures for the last two or three years to the date of the issue, and is published three or four months later.
Contains major economic indicators and index numbers of Turkish national income, industrial production, domestic sales, stocks, employment, construction, prices, public finance, money and banking, balance of payments, receipts and expenditures of foreign travel, workers' remittances, gold and foreign exchange reserves, and foreign trade.

Δ A, continued

2333 Turkish economy.
Akbank T.A.S., Ankara.
1977- monthly. free. *En & Tr eds.
TF: each issue has runs of figures to about three months prior to the date of the issue.
Includes statistical data on banking, foreign trade, workers' remittances, wholesale price index, cost of living index (Istanbul and Ankara), exchange rates, and economic indicators on construction, price indices and foreign economic relations.

2334 Economic indicators of Turkey.
Türkiye Iş Bankasi A.S., Atatürk Bulvari 191, Ankara.
(annual) 1979-1983 (published 1984). free. 16p. *En & Tr eds.
Indicators of area, land use, population, GNP, agriculture, industry, foreign trade, balance of payments, public finance, investments, employment, communications, transportation, foreign tourism, money - deposits - loans, prices, net gold and foreign exchange reserves, and interest rates.

2335 Review of economic conditions.
Türkiye Iş Bankasi A.S., Atatürk Bulvari 191, Ankara.
1978- quarterly. free. ISSN 0034-6500. *En & Tr eds.
TF: each issue has the latest data available and is published about two months after the date of the issue.
Covers the general state of the Turkish economy, GNP, industry, foreign trade, balance of paumemts, public finance, banknotes in circulation, money supply, deposits - loans, Central Bank loans, credit stock, capital market, prices, industrial products markets, markets for agricultural export products, main economic decisions. Includes statistics and statistical tables in the text and there is a section of economic indicators.

2336 Economic report.
Türkiye Iş Bankasi A.S., Atatürk Bulvari 191, Ankara.
(annual) 1983 (published 1984). 68p. *Tr & En eds.
TF: has data for several years to 1983.
Economic conditions in the Western world, general economic conditions general outlook, GNP, investments, employment, foreign economic relations, public finance, money - deposits - loans, capital market, prices), sectoral developments (agriculture, industry, construction, services), developments in markets, conclusion and expectations.

2337 The Turkish economy.
Turkish Industrialists and Businessmen's Association, Cumhuriyet Caddesi, Ferah Apt., 233 9-10 Harbiye, Istanbul.
1976- 1983. not priced. 192p. *En.
TF: has data for 1982 and some earlier years.
Statistical tables are included in the text, which covers the Turkish economy, business climate, planned economy, growth performance, stabilisation programmes, foreign economic relations, foreign investments, foreign debt structure, prices, banking and credit, budget, energy, etc.

2338 Konjunktur [Economic trends].
Ticaret Bakanligi, Ankara.
1941- monthly. not priced. *Fr, Tr.
Includes statistical data on national income, indices of production, transport and communications, prices and prices indexes, foreign trade, insurance societies, and banks.

2339 Istanbul Ticaret Odasi mecmuasi [Journal of the Istanbul Chamber of Commerce].
Istanbul Ticaret Odasi, Gumuspala Caddesi, Eminonü, Istanbul.
1844- quarterly. not priced. *Tr; title & headings also in En.
TF: each issue has long runs of annual and monthly figures to about a month prior to the data of the issue.
Includes a section of statistical tables on production of minerals, crude petroleum and its derivatives, energy by type, industrial goods, foreign trade, Port of Istanbul imports and exports, cost of living index, and wholesale price indices.

2340 Economic report (Istanbul Chamber of Commerce).
Türkiye Ticaret Odasi, Gumuspala Caddesi, Eminonü, Istanbul.
(2 a year) not priced. *En & Tr eds.
Covers the important aspects of the socio-economic growth of Turkey in both public and private sectors. Tables are included in the text.

2341 The quarterly statistical survey (Central bank of the Republic of Turkey).
Türkiye Cumhuriyet Merkez Bankasi, Ankara.
1982- quarterly. free. *En.
TF: each issue has data for several years and quarters to about three months prior to the date of the issue.
Economic base (GNP, production), price indices, money and credit, balance of payments and foreign trade, exchange rates and international reserves.

2342 Türkiye de toplumsal ve ekonomik gelişmenin 50 yili 1973 [50 years in the social and economic development of Turkey, 1973].
DIE, Ankara.
1973- not priced. 506p. *Tr.
Includes statistical tables in the text.

Δ A, continued

2343 Yillik rapor [Annual report] (Central Bank of the Republic of Turkey).
Türkiye Cumhuriyet Merkez Bankasi, Ankara.
1932- 1984 (published 1985). free. 137p. *Tr & En eds.
TF: has data for five years to 1984.
Includes a section of statistical tables on fixed capital formation, gross national product, construction, transportation, communications, employment (including workers sent abroad), strikes and lockouts, balance of payments, foreign trade, money and banking, price indices, gold prices, etc.

2344 Para-kredi istatistikleri ozetleri [Summary of money and credit statistics] (Central Bank of the Republic of Turkey).
Türkiye Cumhuriyet Merkez Bankasi, Ankara.
(monthly) free. *En, Tr.
TF: each issue has data for the month of the issue and earlier monthly figures, and is published some months later.
Includes statistical data on main indicators, wholesale price index, cost of living indexes for Ankara and Istanbul, bank credits, bank deposits, gold and foreign exchange, foreign trade, etc.

2345 Turkish economy...statistical abstract (Istanbul Chamber of Commerce).
Istanbul Ticaret Odasi, Gumuspala Caddesi, Eminonu, Istanbul.
1970- 1983 (published 1984). not priced. 32p. *En & Tr eds.
TF: has long runs of figures to 1983.
Data on area and population, national income, agriculture, mining and industry, money - credit, prices, foreign trade, transportation, and finance.

2346 Turkey almanac.
Turkish Daily News, c/o Mr Ilnor Cevik, General Director, Tunus Caddesi, Kavaklidere, Ankara.
5th, 1981. TL 1000. 463p. *En.
Includes a few statistical tables on elections, defence, economy, labour, prices, banking, foreign trade, etc.

2347 The Arab world, Turkey, and the Balkans, 1878-1914: a handbook of historical statistics (Justin McCarthy).
G.K. Hall & Co., 70 Lincoln Street, Boston, Mass., 02111 USA.
1982. £52.70. c 300p. *En.
A collection of statistics on the late Ottoman Empire (includes modern-day Turkey).

2348 Genel sanayi ve işyerleri sayim [Ikmci aşama sonuçlari) [Census of industry and business establishments (second state results).
DIE, Ankara.
1927- 1980 (published from 1984). not priced. 4 vols. *Tr, En.
Contents:
Vol II: Small scale manufacturing industries. National total and selected 10 provinces
Vol III: Trade. Network total
Vol IV: Service, hotels, restaurants, pastry houses, cafés. National totals.

Δ B Production

Δ B - i Mines and mining

2349 Maden istatistikleri [Mining statistics].
DIE, Ankara.
1958/65- 1983 (published 1985). not priced. 51p. *Tr, En.
Data on establishments, employees, hours worked, wages and salaries, stocks, production and sales of minerals, materials and fixed assets, materials purchased, exports by countries, number of establishments with exploring licences by kinds of minerals. the minerals concerned are coal, lignite, asbestos, antimony, copper, barite, boron minerals, zinc, mercury, iron, chrome, lead, lead-zinc, sulphur, manganese, pyrites, sodium sulphate, emery, etc.

B - ii Agriculture, fisheries, forestry, etc

Δ B - ii(a) Agriculture and horticulture

2350 Tarimsal yapi ve üretim [Agricultural structure and production].
DIE, Ankara.
1951- 1982 (published 1984). free. 246p. *Tr, En.
Data on agricultural structure, production farm equipment, crops, livestock, fruit, poultry, and bees, for the whole country and for each province.

2351 Tarim sayimi sonuclari [Census of agriculture].
DIE, Ankara.
1927- 1970 (published 1972). not priced. *Tr.
1970 cari istatistikler ve tarim sayimi sonuclari [Current agricultural statistics and the 1970 census of agriculture] contains some preliminary statistical information. Earlier censuses were held in 1927, 1950 and 1963.

Δ B – ii(a), continued

2352 Tarim istatistikleri özeti [Summary of agricultural statistics].
DIE, Ankara.
1936/56- 1983 (published 1984). not priced. c 30p. ISSN 0082-6928. *Tr, En.
Summary data on land use, area cultivated, crops sown, production and yield, farm machinery and equipment.

2253 Ciftcinin eline gecen fiyatlar [Prices received by farmers].
DIE, Ankara.
1972- 1982. not priced. c 30p. *Tr, En.
TF: has data for 1979 and 1980.

Δ B – ii(b) Fisheries

2354 Su ürünleri anket sonuçlari [Fishery statistics].
DIE, Ankara.
1968- 1982 (published 1984). not priced. c 35p. *Tr, En.

Δ B – iii Industry

2355 Dönemler itibariyle imalat sanayii, istihdam – üretim – egilim (geçici sonuçlar... [Manufacturing industry (quarterly): employment – production – expectation (provisional results).
DIE, Ankara.
1972/74- quarterly. not priced. *Tr, En.

2356 Yillik imalat sanayii anket sonuclari [Annual survey of the manufacturing industry].
DIE, Ankara.
1972- 1981-82 (published 1986). not priced. 202p. *En, Tr.
Data on national totals of establishments, persons engaged, wages, goods and services purchased, value of stock, input-output and value added by industry.
Note: also published a few months earlier are preliminary results, '...(geçici sonuçlar).

2357 Imalat sanayii üretim indeksi, dönemler itibariyle [Manufacturing industry production indexes (quarterly).
DIE, Ankara.
1982- quarterly. not priced. *Tr, En.

2358 Şeker sanayii istatistikleri [Statistics of sugar industry].
Türkiye Şeker Fabrikaleri A.Ş., (Turkish Sugar Factories Corporation), Ankara.
1926/73- 1926-1978 (published 1980). 110p. *Tr, En.
World sugar structure (production, consumption of cane and beet sugar, prices, sugar balance), sugar industry in Turkey (history, agricultural activities, technological activities, activities of machine factories, personnel, commercial activities, and investments).

Δ B – iv Construction

2359 1970 binalar sayimi (belediye teskilati olan yerlerde)[1970 census of buildings (for places with municipalities)].
DIE, Ankara.
not priced. *En, Tr.
Note: an earlier census was taken in 1965.

2360 Inşaat istatistikleri: inşaat ruhsatnameleri ve yapi kullanma izin kagitlari [Construction statistics: construction permits and occupancy permits].
DIE, Ankara.
1971- 1983 (published 1985). not priced. 163p. *Tr, En.

Δ B – v Energy

2361 Türkiye elektrik istatistikleri yilligi [Annual bulletin of electrical statistics of Turkey].
Türkiye Elektrik Kurumu, Necati Bey Caddesi 36, Ankara.
(annual) 1981-1982 (published 1984). not priced. 116p. *En, Tr.
Data on installed capacity, production, peak load, consumption, energy transmission lines and transformers, personnel, investments and electrified villages.
Note: the annual report of the Turkish Electricity Board, published in Turkish and English editions, also includes statistical data on investments, operations, village electrification, etc.

Δ C External trade

2362 Diş ticaret istatistikleri [Foreign trade statistics].
DIE, Ankara.
(annual) 1983 (published 1984). not priced. 208p. *Tr, En.
Foreign trade statistics arranged by commodity chapter headings subdivided by countries of origin and destination; by countries subdivided by commodity chapter headings; and by customs offices subdivided by commodity chapter headings.
Note: more detailed statistics were published from 1926 to 1980, and unpublished disaggregated statistics are available by post on request.

Δ C, continued

2363 Aylik dis ticaret ozeti [Summary of monthly foreign trade].
DIE, Ankara.
(monthly) not priced. *Tr, En.
TF: each issue has data for that month and is published about two months later.
Provisional figures of foreign trade (4 pages each issue).

2364 Foreign trade of Turkey (Ministry of Commerce: General Secretariat of Foreign Trade: General Directorate of Assessment).
Ticaret Bakanligi, Ankara.
(quarterly) not priced. *En & Tr eds.
TF: each issue has cumulated figures for the year to date and is published about six months after the end of the period covered.
In four sections: the general outlook on Turkey's foreign trade; the general situation of Turkey's exports; the general situation of Turkey's imports, imports by commodity group, imports by financing resources; and foreign trade by country groups.

Δ D Internal distribution and service trades

Δ D – i Wholesale and retail trades

2365 Ic ticaret istatistikleri, ticaret sirketleri, firmalar ve tuketim kooperatifleri [Internal trade statistics, commercial companies, firms and consumers' co-operatives].
DIE, Ankara.
1965/66– 1980 (published 1981). not priced. 49p. *Tr, En.
Data on the numbers and capital of commercial companies by major provinces and by economic activity, and the numbers and sales of consumers' co-operatives by major provinces.

2366 Toptan fiyat istatistikleri: ticaret borsalatinda işlem gören maddeler [Wholesale price statistics: registered commodities in commodity exchanges.
DIE, Ankar.
1935– 1983 (published 1985). not priced. 68p. *Tr, En.

2367 Toptan eşya ve Tüketici fiyatlari aylik indeks bülten [Wholesale and consumer price indexes monthly bulletin].
DIE, Ankara.
1972– monthly. not priced. *Tr, En.
TF: each issue has runs of figures for two or three years, four quarters and months for the current year.

2368 Perakende fiat istatistikleri (seçilmis şehirlere ve maddelere göre yillik ortalama fiatlar) [Retail price statistics (annual average prices by selected cities and items)].
DIE, Ankara.
1948/70– 1984 (published 1985). not priced. 29p. *Tr, En.

Δ D – iv Tourism and travel

2369 Turizm istatistikleri... (vatandaş – yabanci, giriş – fikis) [Tourism statistics... (Turkish citizens and foreigners entry and exit)].
DIE, Ankara.
1965– 1983 (published 1985). not priced. 39p. *Tr, En.
Data on foreigners arriving, means of transport, province of entry, occupation, nationality, and object of travel; foreign visitors departing; and Turkish citizens entering and leaving the country.

Δ E Population

2370 Genel nufus sayimi [Census of population].
DIE, Ankara.
1927– 1980 (1981–). not priced. *Tr, En.
Volumes include:
Nüfsen sosyal ve ekonomik nitelikleri, %1 örnekleme sonuçlari [Social and economic characteristics of the population, 1% sample results]
Idari bölünüs [By administrative division]
Telegrafla al nan geçici sonuçlar [Preliminary cable results] (Tr only)
Daimi ikametgaha göre iç göçler [Domestic migration by permanent residence]
Sosyal ve ekonomik niteliker [Social and economic characteristics].
Note: a census was taken in 1985 and preliminary cable results were published in 1985.

Δ E – i Vital statistics

2371 Sosyalizasyon bolgelerinden derlenen dogum istatiskleri [Birth statistics in socialisation regions].
DIE, Ankara.
1968– 1975-76 (published 1979). not priced. *Tr, En.

Δ E - i, continued

2372 Evlenme istatistikleri [Marriage statistics].
DIE, Ankara.
1968- 1983 (published 1985). not priced. 26p. *Tr, En.

2373 Intihar istatistikleri [Suicide statistics].
DIE, Ankara.
1968- 1984 (published 1986). not priced. 13p. *Tr, En.

2374 Olüm istatistikleri (il ve ilçe merkezlerinde) [Death statistics (in province and district centres)].
DIE, Ankara.
1950- 1983 (published 1985). not priced. 75p. *Tr, En.

2375 Hayati istatiskler, il ve lice merkezlerinda olumler [Vital statistics, deaths in administrative centres of provinces and districts].
DIE, Ankara.
1950- 1979 (published 1981). not priced. c 150p. *Tr, En.

2376 Boşanma istatistikleri [Divorce statistics].
DIE, Ankara.
1968- 1983 (published 1984). not priced. c 30p. *Tr, En.

Δ E - ii Labour

2377 Istatistik yilligi [Statistical yearbook].
Is ve Isci Bulma Kurumu, Genel Müdürlügü, Cemal Cursal Caddesi no. 10, Ankara.
(annual) 1983 (published 1984). free. 77p. *Tr.
Contains statistical data on job seekers, job openings, placements and unemployed workers.

2378 Kirsal yerler handhalki işgücü anketi sonuclari [Household labour force survey results in rural areas].
DIE, Ankara.
1977. not priced. 108p. *Tr.
TF: data for 1973-1977.
Data on household numbers by duration of residence and age groups, labour force statistics, educational levels, marital statistics, etc.

2379 Kentsel yerler hanehalki işgücü anket sonuçlari [Urban places: household labour force survey].
DIE, Ankara.
1982- 1984 (published 1986). not priced. 217p. *Tr, En.
Distribution of employed, unemployed, retired members, by education, sex, age groups, etc., of a sample of 54 settlements with a population of more than 10,000.

Δ F Social and political

Δ F - i Standard of living

2380 Eskisehir tuketici harcamalari anket sonuclari [Results of the survey of consumer expenditure in Eskisehir].
DIE, Ankara.
1981. not priced. *Tr, En.
One of a series of separate booklets, each on a city, containing data on households, employment status of heads of households, consumption expenditures, distribution of income, etc. Others in the series are on Erzurum, Bursa, Samsun, Antalya, Diyarbakir, Ordu, Istanbul, Ankara, Izmir and Adana.

2381 Aylik fiyat indeksleri bülteni [Monthly bulletin of price indexes].
DIE, Ankara.
1972- monthly. not priced. *Tr, En.
TF: each issue has data for two years and 26 months to the date of the publication and is issued the following month.
Includes consumer price indices for various cities, cost of living index, and wholesale price index.

Δ F - ii Health and welfare

2382 Türkiye saglik istatistik yilligi [Health statistics yearbook of Turkey].
Saglik ve Sosyal Yardim Bakanligi [Ministry of Health and Social Assistance], Ankara.
1945- 1979-1981 (published 1983). not priced. 403p. *Tr, En.
Data on general population, health, manpower, hospitals, infectious diseases, mortality, preventive medicine, and statistics of socialised areas.

Δ F - iii Education

2383 Milli egitim istatistikleri, ilkögretim [National education statistics, primary education].
DIE, Ankara.
1923/32- 1982-83 (published 1984). not priced. 49p. *Tr, En.
Data on primary education, including pupils, schools, teachers, etc.

Δ F – iii, continued

2384 Milli egitim istatistikleri, ortaögretim [National education statistics, secondary education].
DIE, Ankara.
1923/32– 1982-83 (published 1985). not priced. 194p. *Tr, En.
Data on secondary education, including pupils, schools, teachers, etc.

2385 Milli egitim istatistikleri; mesleki ve teknikögretim... [National education statistics: vocational and technical secondary education].
DIE, Ankara.
1943/44– 1983-1984 (published 1986). not priced. 207p. *Tr, En.

2386 Milli egitim istatistikleri: yüksekögretim [National education statistics: higher education].
DIE, Ankara.
1943/44– 1982-83 (published 1984). not priced. c 65p. *Tr, En.

2387 Milli egitim istatistikleri, yaygin egitim [National education statistics, adult education].
DIE, Ankara.
1967/74– 1982-83 (published 1985). not priced. 74p. *Tr, En.

2388 Milli egitim istatistikleri: milli, halk, cocuk kutuphoneleri [National education statistics: national, public and children's libraries].
DIE, Ankara.
1959/68– 1969-1973 (published 1977). not priced. 180p. *Tr.

2389 Kültür istatistikleri [Cultural statistics].
DIE, Ankara.
1934/35– 1981-1982-1983 (published 1985). not priced. 252p. *Tr, En.
Data on printing houses and printing works; libraries (national, public, children's); museums; theatre, opera and ballets; cinemas.
Note: early edition also included sports.

Δ F – iv Justice

2390 Adalet istatistikleri [Judicial statistics].
DIE, Ankara.
1938– 1984 (published 1986). not priced. 101p. *Tr, En.

Δ F – vi Elections

2391 Milletvekili segimi sonuçlari; il ve ilçeler itibariyle [Results of the general elections for members of the House of Representatives...by province and district].
DIE, Ankara.
1961– 1982 (published 1984). not priced. unpaged. *Tr, En.

2392 Mahalli idareler seçimi sonuçlari... [Results of elections of local administrations...].
DIE, Ankara.
1963– 1984. not priced. 161p. *Tr, En.
Results of elections of local administrations, the elections of members of general province assembly, mayor, members of municipal assembly, muhtar (head of village and head of quarter), and council of eldermen.

Δ G Finance

Δ G – i Banking

2393 Balance sheets, profit and loss accounts, organisations, deposits and credits of banks in Turkey...
Banks Association of Turkey, Mithatpaşa Caddesi no. 12, Yenişehir, Ankara.
1975– 1980 (published 1981). not priced. 131p. *En & Tr eds.

2394 Üç aylik bülten [Quarterly bulletin] (Türkiye Cumhuriyet Merkez Bank [Central Bank of the Republic of Turkey]).
T.C.M.B., Ankara.
(quarterly) free. ISSN 0041-4336. *Tr, En.
TF: each issue has long runs of annual and monthly figures to the end of the quarter of the issue, and is published some 2-3 months later.
Data on the Central Bank, money banks and other financial institutions, finance, money, interest rates, exchange rates, etc.

Δ G – ii Public finance

2395 Bütçe ve kesin hesaplar, il özel idareleri ve köyler, 1977-80 [Budget and final accounts of special provinciap administrations and villages, 1977-80].
DIE, Ankara.
1984. not priced. *Tr, En.

Δ G - v Insurance

2396 Istatistik yilligi [Annual statistics].
Sosyal Sigortalar Kurumu [Social Insurance Institution], Ankara.
1977- 1978 (published 1979). not priced. 110p. *Tr, En.
TF: has data for 1974 to 1978.
Data on the numbers of work places and insured persons, days of contributions and wages; contingencies submitted to the institution (work injury, occupational disease, maternity, sickness, disability, old age and death); and medical treatments - activities.

Δ H Transport and communications

2397 Ulaştirma istatistikleri [Transport statistics].
DIE, Ankara.
1966- 1973/74 (published 1981). not priced. 179p. *Tr, En.
Data on land motor vehicles (cars, minibuses, buses, trucks, motorcycles, etc. by use, make, province, horse-power, etc); vessels (18 gross tonnage and over, by type, etc); coastwise and international sea traffic and transportation; air lines; maritime bank activities; and general post office activities.

2398 Ulaştirma istatistikleri: ozet tablolari...geçiçi sonuclar [Transport statistics: summary data...preliminary results].
DIE, Ankara.
1970/73- 1975-1978 (published 1979). not priced. 25p. *Tr, En.
Similar subject coverage to (2397).

2399 Ulaştirma ve trafik kazalari istatistikeri (geçici sonuclar [Transportation and road traffic accidents statistics (provisional results)].
DIE, Ankara.
(annual) 1982 (published 1984). not priced. 30p. *Tr, En.

Δ H - i Ships and shipping

2400 Deniz taşitlari, kabotaj ve uluslararasi deniz taşimaciligi [Statistics of vessels coastwise and international sea transportation].
DIE, Ankara.
1975/80- 1984 (published 1985). not priced. 35p. *Tr, En.
Data on ships of 18 gross tons and over and their characteristics, passengers and goods loaded and unloaded by Turkish and foreign ships in Turkish ports.

Δ H - ii Roads and road transport

2401 Türkiye karayollari istatistik yilligi [Annual statistics of Turkish highways] (General Directorate of Highways).
Karayollari Genel Müdürlügü, Sosyal Işler Müdürlügü, Tücetepe, Ankara.
1962/63- 1981. not priced. 120p. *Tr, En.
TF: has data to 1980.
Data about highways, highway activities, highway investments, motor vehicles and highway transport and traffic for Turkey. Also an international section with comparative figures.

2402 Trafik kazalari [Road traffic accidents].
DIE, Ankara.
1971/73- 1981 (published 1984). *Tr, En.
Note: a preliminary version is published earlier. 'Ulaştima ve trafik kazalari istatistikeri (geçici sonuçlar)'.

2403 Motorlu kara taşitlari istatistikleri [Road motor vehicle statistics].
DIE, Ankara.
1934/46- 1976-1980 (published 1984). not priced. *Tr, En.

VATICAN CITY
VATICAN
VATIKAN
CITTA DEL VATICANO

No statistics are published.

YUGOSLAVIA
YOUGOSLAVIE
JUGOSLAWIEN
JUGOSLAVIJA

Central statistical office

2404 Savezni Zavod za Statistiku [Federal Institute of Statistics].
Kneza Milosa 20, (PO Box 203), 11011 Beograd.
t 011 681-999. tx 11317 SAVTAT YU. tg Savstatistika Beograd.
The Institute is responsible for the statistical services throughout Yugoslavia, collaborating with the statistical institutes of the republics and districts. Unpublished statistical information can often be supplied for a fee. Apart from the publications described in the following pages the institute issues a quarterly review of international statistics, 'Tromesecni pregled medunarodne statistike'. This office has been abbreviated to SZS, Beograd for entries between 2404-2427.

Libraries

The library of Savezni Zavod za Statistiku (see above) has a large collection of statistical publications which may be consulted by the public. there are also smaller collections in the libraries of the statistical offices of the republic of Bosnia-Herzegovina, Croatia, Macedonia, Montenegro, Serbia and Slovenia.

Libraries and information services abroad

Yugoslavian statistical publications are available for reference in some Yugoslav embassies abroad, including:
United Kingdom Yugoslav Embassy, 5 Lexham Gardens, London W8. t 01-370 6105.
Canada Yugoslav Embassy, 17 Blackburn Avenue, Ottawa K1N 8A2. t 233 6289.
USA Yugoslav Embassy, 2410 California Street NW, Washington DC 20008. t (202) 462 6566.

Bibliographies

2405 Catalogue of publications, 1950-1978.
A 160-page booklet issued by Savezni Zavod za Statistiku, listing all publications of the institute in subject order and free on request.
En & Serbo-Croat editions.

Publications of Savezni Zavod Statistiku are also listed at the end of the statistical yearbook (2406).

Statistical publications

Δ A General

2406 Statistički godisnjak SFRJ [Statistical yearbook of the Federal People's Republic of Yugoslavia].
SZS, Beograd.
1954- 1984. ISSN 0585-1920. *Serbo-Croat; En translations of the text and tables and Fr & Ru translations of the contents are available free of charge.
TF: has data for 1983 and some earlier years.
Main sections:
Topography & climate - Summary of social & economic development - Socio-political system - Population - Employment & personal incomes - Economic balance - Social product - Human consumption - Collective & public consumption - Investment - Currency in circulation, savings & credit - Prices - General review of enomic activities - Agriculture - Forestry - Operation of irrigation systems, waterworks & supply - Manufacturing, mining & quarrying - Arts & crafts - Construction - Transport & communications - External trade - Domestic trade - Catering trades - Tourism - Education - Science - Culture & art - Physical culture - Public health - Social security - Social welfare - Administration of justice - Data for each of the republics, communes and towns - International statistics.

2407 Statistical pocketbook of Yugoslavia.
SZS, Beograd.
1955- 1983. Din 60. 255p. *En & Ru eds.
TF: has data for 1981 or 1982 and earlier years.
An abridged edition of 2406.

2408 Indeks: mesecni pregled privredne statistike [Index: monthly review of economic statistics].
SZS, Beograd.
1952- monthly. not priced. ISSN 0019-3585. *Serbo-Croat; En & Fr translation of text is available.
TF: issued about the 10th of each month, most tables contain figures for about the last six years and 24 months, up to one or two months prior to the date of the issue.
Monthly indices of manufacturing, production, construction, transport, retail trade, foreign trade, tourism, prices, cost of living, employment, nominal and real earnings, personal income, credit, investment, currency circulation, and savings.

Δ A, continued

2409 National Bank of Yugoslavia: quarterly bulletin.
Narodna Banka Jugoslavije, Bulevar Revolucije 15, Beograd.
1973- not priced. *En & Serbo-Croat eds.
TF: each issue has long runs of annual and monthly figures to about two months prior to the date of the issue.
Statistics and tables are included in the text, and a statistical appendix has data on social product, production (excluding agriculture), employment and personal incomes, revenues and domestic demand, price movements and cost of living, savings, balance sheets of banks, financing of housing and community development money supply, foreign trade, etc.

2410 Statistički bilten [Statistical bulletins].
SZS, Beograd.
1950- irregular. Din 600 or $66.67 yr. *Serbo-Croat.
Bulletins issued on a wide variety of economic and social subjects, some being ad hoc and some serial publications. From issue 1363 onwards the bulletins are available only on microfiche. Subjects include preliminary reports of censuses; stock breeding and fisheries; crop farming, fruit growing and viticulture; turnover of agricultural products; forestry; manufacturing, mining and quarrying; manufacturing organisations of associated labour; manufactured goods; scientific research and development organisations; foreign trade; domestic trade; domestic sales: sales facilities; catering; catering: accommodation facilities; tourism; family budgets of workers' households; survey on rural households; personal incomes; prices; primary and secondary schools; diplomas obtained; assets and funds of communes; transport and communication; registered motor vehicles and trailers.

2411 Yugoslav survey: a record of facts and information (Yugoslav Survey).
Jugoslovenska Stvarnost, Mose Pijade 8/1, Beograd.
1960- monthly. Din 600 or $20 yr. *En.
Includes a section of basic statistics on the economy, industry, etc., and there are also statistics and statistical tables in the articles.

Δ B Production

Δ B - i Mines and mining

2412 Statistical bulletin (CIPEC - Intergovernmental Council of Copper Exporting Countries).
CIPEC, 177 avenue de Roule, 92200 Neuilly-sur-Seine, France.
1975- 1983 (published 1984). not priced. 31p. *En, Es, Fr.
TF: has data for ten years to 1983.
Contains data relating to copper (production, consumption, foreign trade, stocks, average prices and turnover) in a concise form for the copper exporting countries, including Yugoslavia.

Δ B - iii Industry

Δ B - iii(e) Engineering

2413 Motorna industrija Jugoslavije [Yugoslav motor industry].
Poslovna Zajednica Proizvodjaca Motornih vozila [The Motor Vehicle Manufacturers' Association], Bulevar vojvode Misica 14, Beograd.
(annual) 1985. not priced. 98p. *Serbo-Croat, En.
TF: has data for 1984 and earlier years.
Production, registration, export, fuels and roads.

Δ B - iv Construction

2414 Gradevinarstvo [Construction].
SZS, Beograd.
1952/53- 1976 (published 1977). Din 10. 48p. *Serbo-Croat: En translation of text available.
A general review of development; structure of persons employed and personal incomes in construction; work done in the construction industry by the Federal Republic; the republics and towns; sales prices of dwellings built for the market; material consumed; building machinery; design services and construction work abroad.

Δ C External trade

2415 Statistika spoljne trgovine SFR Jugoslavije [Statistics of the foreign trade of Yugoslavia].
SZS, Beograd.
1946- 1981 (published 1982). Din 500. 646p. *Serbo-Croat; En (but commodity index only in Serbo-Croat).
TF: has data for 1981 and also for earlier years in minor tables. Later years are being published only in microfiche.
Imports and exports by commodities subdivided by countries of origin and destination. Also detailed tables showing imports and exports by countries subdivided by commodities. Other tables include imports and exports by sections and subdivisions of SITC, and transit trade.

Δ E Population

2416 Popis stanovnistva i stanova [Census of population and housing].
SZS, Beograd.
1921- 1981. *Serbo-Croat.
TF: a census is taken every ten years. Preliminary reports of the 1981 census are being published in the series 'Statisticki bilten' on microfiche (see 2410). So far, only six methodological volumes have been published in hard copy.

2417 Projekcije stanovnistva Jugoslavije, 1970-2000 god [Population projections for Yugoslavia, 1970-2000].
SZS, Beograd.
Din 150. 944p. *Serbo-Croat.

Δ E - i Vital statistics

2418 Demografska statistika [Vital statistics].
SZS, Beograd.
1950- 1979 (published 1982). Din 100. 275p. *Serbo-Croat; Fr translation of text available.
Population, evolution of the demographic situation, births, deaths, marriages, divorces. Statistics are given for the country as a whole, the republics, provinces, and certain data also for the communes.

2419 Nasilne smrti kao osnovni uzrok smrti u mortalitetu SFR Jugoslavije, 1976-1980 [Deaths by violence as a principal cause of death in mortality of the SFR Yugoslavia, 1976-1980].
SZS, Beograd.
1983. not priced. 85p. *Serbo-Croat; summary in En.
TF: published in the series 'Studije, analize i prikazi'.

Δ E - ii Labour

2420 Zaposlenost [Employment].
SZS, Beograd.
1956- quarterly. not priced. *Serbo-Croat.
TF: each issue has data to about six months prior to the date of the issue.

Δ F Social and political

Δ F - i Standard of living

2421 Lična potrosnja stanovnistva Jugoslavije, 1952-1981 [Personal consumption of the population of Yugoslavia, 1951-1981].
SZS, Beograd.
1983. not priced. 67p. *Serbo-Croat; summary in En.
TF: published in the series 'Studije, analize i prikazi'.

Δ F - iii Education and culture

2422 Visoke skole [Higher schools].
SZS, Beograd.
1951/52- 1974-75 (published 1976). Din 5. 40p. *Serbo-Croat; Fr translation available.
Data on number of establishments, students, staff, etc.

Δ F - iv Justice

2423 Punoletni ucinioci krivicnih dela protiv osnova socijaiistickog samoupravnog drustvenog uredenja i bezbednosti SFR Jugoslavije, 1973-1981: analiticki prikaz statistike kriminaliteta [Adult perpetrators of the criminal offences against the foundations of the socialistic self-management, social establishment and security of the SFR Yugoslavia, 1973-1981].
SZS, Beograd.
1984. not priced. 95p. *Serbo-Croat; summary in En.
TF: published in the series 'Studije, analize i prikazi'.

Δ G Finance

Δ G - i Banking

2424 Annual report (National Bank of Yugoslavia).
Narodna Banka Jugoslavije, Bulevar Revolucije 15, Beograd.
1927- 1984 (published 1985). not priced. c 80p. *En & Serbo-Croat eds.
TF: has data for 1984 and earlier years.
Data on the activities of the bank, all banks, money supply, etc. There is a statistical appendix and also tables in the text of the report.

Δ G – ii Public finance

2425 Društveni proizvod i narodni dohodak [Social product and national income].
SZS, Beograd.
1969/70- 1976 (published 1977). Din 15. 78p. *Serbo-Croat; Fr translation of text available.
National and national product of Yugoslavia and of the individual republics.

Δ G – iv Investment

2426 Investicije [Investment].
SZS, Beograd.
1966- 1977 (published 1978). Din 50. 196p. *Serbo-Croat; En translation available.
Investment in fixed assets; in Yugoslavia by investor's activity; of the Federal Republic by end use of investment; by the individual republics and by the autonomous provinces.

2427 Investicije u osnovna sredstva SFR Jugoslavije socijalistickih republika i socijalistickih autonomnih pokrajina, 1952-1981, u cenama 1972 [Fixed capital formation of the Yugoslavia socialist republics and socialist autonomous provinces, 1952-1981, at 1971 prices].
SZS, Beograd.
1983. not priced. 89p. *Serbo-Croat; summary in En & Ru.
TF: published in the series 'Studije, analize i prikazi'.

INDEX OF TITLES - INDEX DES TITRES - TITELREGISTER

References are to the serial numbers used in the text

SUBJECT INDEX

Whilst this index refers to the main subjects covered by publications listed in this guide, it does not refer to all the detailed headings included in those publications. The user is advised always to look at entries in Δ A.